ANNUAL EDITIONS

Educational Psychology 11/12
Twenty-Sixth Edition

EDITORS

Kathleen M. Cauley
Virginia Commonwealth University

Kathleen M. Cauley received her PhD in Educational Studies/Human Development from the University of Delaware in 1985. Her current research interests are student transitions to a new school, and the influence of assessment practices on motivation.

Gina M. Pannozzo
Center for Excellence in Urban and Rural Education, Buffalo State College

Gina M. Pannozzo received her PhD in Educational Psychology from the University of Buffalo in 2005. Her current research examines the relationships among student engagement patterns in school and dropping out.

Mc Graw Hill

Connect
Learn
Succeed™

The McGraw-Hill Companies

ANNUAL EDITIONS: EDUCATIONAL PSYCHOLOGY, TWENTY-SIXTH EDITION

Annual Editions is published by the **Contemporary Learning Series** group within the McGraw-Hill Higher Education division.

1 2 3 4 5 6 7 8 9 0 QDB/QDB 1 0 9 8 7 6 5 4 3 2 1

ISBN 978-0-07-805095-4
MHID 0-07-805095-2
ISSN 0731-1141 (print)
ISSN 2159-1091 (online)

Managing Editor: *Larry Loeppke*
Developmental Editor: *Dave Welsh*
Permissions Coordinator: *DeAnna Dausener*
Marketing Communications Specialist: *Mary Klein*
Marketing Coordinator: *Alice Link*
Senior Project Manager: *Joyce Watters*
Design Coordinator: *Margarite Reynolds*
Production Supervisor: *Sue Culbertson*
Cover Designer: *Kristine Jubeck*

Compositor: Laserwords Private Limited
Cover Images Credits: © Lars Niki (inset); © Photodisc/PunchStock (background)

Editors/Academic Advisory Board

Members of the Academic Advisory Board are instrumental in the final selection of articles for each edition of ANNUAL EDITIONS. Their review of articles for content, level, and appropriateness provides critical direction to the editors and staff. We think that you will find their careful consideration well reflected in this volume.

ANNUAL EDITIONS: Educational Psychology 11/12
26th Edition

EDITORS

Kathleen M. Cauley
Virginia Commonwealth University

Gina M. Pannozzo
Center for Excellence in Urban and Rural Education, Buffalo State College

ACADEMIC ADVISORY BOARD MEMBERS

Preface

Educational psychology is an interdisciplinary subject that includes human development, learning, intelligence, motivation, assessment, instructional strategies, and classroom management. The articles in this volume give special attention to the application of this knowledge to teaching.

Annual Editions: Educational Psychology 11/12 is divided into six units. An overview precedes each unit, which explains how the unit articles are related to the broader issues within educational psychology.

The first unit, *Perspectives on Teaching,* presents issues that are central to the role of teaching. The articles' authors provide perspectives on being an effective teacher and the issues facing teachers in the twenty-first century.

The second unit, entitled *Development,* is concerned with child and adolescent development. It covers the biological, cognitive, social, and emotional processes of development. The essays in this unit examine the ways in which developmental factors prepare students to do well in school, as well as the impact of school on child and adolescent development.

The third unit, *Individual Differences among Learners,* considers the individual differences among learners and how to meet those needs. It focuses on inclusive teaching, serving students who are gifted, gender issues, and multicultural education. Diverse students require an individualized approach to education. The articles in this unit review the characteristics of these children and suggest programs and strategies to meet their needs.

In the fourth unit, *Learning and Instruction,* articles about theories of learning and instructional strategies are presented. The selections on learning and cognition provide a broad view of different aspects of learning, covering areas such as brain-based education, memory and cognitive structures, mastery learning, backward design, and learning styles. The range of articles is designed to provide a breadth of topics that explore different approaches to how students learn, but

have in common a focus on increasing opportunities for students to build knowledge. The "Instructional Strategies" section includes articles on a range of research-based practices that are instructionally effective across a range of settings and age/grade levels and promote better learning. In the final subsection, this year's edition focused on the increasing role of technology in education. These articles address topics reviewing the "technology education" curriculum, Internet safety, plagiarism, and social networking.

The topic of motivation is perhaps one of the most important aspects of school learning. Effective teachers need to motivate their students both to learn and to behave responsibly. How to manage children and what forms of discipline to use are issues that concern parents as well as teachers and administrators. In addition, the climate or environment of the classroom greatly impacts their motivation, influencing how and in what ways students engage in learning activities. The articles in the fifth unit, *Motivation and Classroom Management,* present a variety of perspectives on motivating and engaging students, as well as present approaches to both general classroom management and more specific behavior problems routinely encountered by teachers.

In today's social and political climate, it is impossible to discuss education without devoting a piece of that discussion to issues related to accountability and assessing student learning. The articles in the sixth unit are broken into two subsections—a section on Standards, Accountability, and Standardized Testing and another on Classroom Assessment. The articles in the first section examine issues related to both the effectiveness of No Child Left Behind and high-stakes testing and the impact of accountability measures on students. The second section focuses on effective models of classroom assessment and covers topics such as reliability and validity, formative assessment, and peer and self-assessment. The theme of this section is integrating assessment with instruction to enhance student learning.

Finally, this edition includes a stronger emphasis on empirical studies, providing examples across a variety of research methods and topics. It continues to be increasingly important that educators at all levels possess the knowledge and skills to critically read, evaluate, and conduct well-designed investigations, whether the aim is to improve their personal instructional practice or advocate change to education policy at the school, local, or broader levels. We hope readers will find the articles

Other new and improved features for this edition include Learning Outcomes and Critical Thinking questions to help students better understand what they have read; an expanded selection of *World Wide Web* sites, which can be used to further explore the articles' topics; specific learning outcomes and a combination of both content understanding and reflective questions to enhance students' mastery of core concepts; and suggestions for additional reading that examine selected topics in greater depth and/or complexity.

This twenty-sixth *Annual Editions: Educational Psychology* has been revised in order to present articles that are current and useful. Your responses to the selection and organization of materials are appreciated. Please complete and return the postage-paid *article rating form* on the last page of the book.

Kathleen M. Cauley
Editor

Gina M. Pannozzo
Editor

Contents

UNIT 1
Perspectives on Teaching

UNIT 2
Development

The concepts in bold italics are developed in the article. For further expansion, please refer to the Topic Guide.

UNIT 3
Individual Differences among Learners

The concepts in bold italics are developed in the article. For further expansion, please refer to the Topic Guide.

The concepts in bold italics are developed in the article. For further expansion, please refer to the Topic Guide.

UNIT 4
Learning and Instruction

Unit Overview **110**

The concepts in bold italics are developed in the article. For further expansion, please refer to the Topic Guide.

The concepts in bold italics are developed in the article. For further expansion, please refer to the Topic Guide.

UNIT 5
Motivation, Engagement, and Classroom Management

The concepts in bold italics are developed in the article. For further expansion, please refer to the Topic Guide.

UNIT 6
Assessment

The concepts in bold italics are developed in the article. For further expansion, please refer to the Topic Guide.

The concepts in bold italics are developed in the article. For further expansion, please refer to the Topic Guide.

Correlation Guide

The *Annual Editions* series provides students with convenient, inexpensive access to current, carefully selected articles from the public press. **Annual Editions: Educational Psychology 11/12** is an easy-to-use reader that presents articles on important topics such as *teaching perspectives, individual differences, motivation,* and many more. For more information on *Annual Editions* and other *McGraw-Hill Contemporary Learning Series* titles, visit www.mhhe.com/cls.

This convenient guide matches the units in **Annual Editions: Educational Psychology 11/12** with the corresponding chapters in one of our best-selling McGraw-Hill Educational Psychology textbooks by Santrock.

Annual Editions: Educational Psychology 11/12	Educational Psychology, 5/e by Santrock
Unit 1: Perspectives on Teaching	**Chapter 1:** Educational Psychology: A Tool for Effective Teaching
Unit 2: Development	**Chapter 2:** Cognitive and Language Development **Chapter 3:** Social Contexts and Socioemotional Development
Unit 3: Individual Differences among Learners	**Chapter 3:** Social Contexts and Socioemotional Development **Chapter 4:** Individual Variations **Chapter 5:** Sociocultural Diversity
Unit 4: Learning and Instruction	**Chapter 6:** Learners Who Are Exceptional **Chapter 7:** Behavioral and Social Cognitive Approaches **Chapter 11:** Learning and Cognition in the Content Areas **Chapter 12:** Planning, Instruction, and Technology **Chapter 13:** Motivation, Teaching, and Learning
Unit 5: Motivation, Engagement and Classroom Management	**Chapter 14:** Managing the Classroom
Unit 6: Assessment	**Chapter 15:** Standardized Tests and Teaching **Chapter 16:** Classroom Assessment and Grading

Topic Guide

This topic guide suggests how the selections in this book relate to the subjects covered in your course. You may want to use the topics listed on these pages to search the Web more easily.

On the following pages a number of websites have been gathered specifically for this book. They are arranged to reflect the units of this Annual Editions reader. You can link to these sites by going to www.mhhe.com/cls

All the articles that relate to each topic are listed below the bold-faced term.

Academic achievement
45. Measuring the Achievement Elephant

Accountability
44. Grading Education

Action research
3. Embarking on Action Research
31. What Happens When Eighth Graders Become the Teachers?

Adolescent development
5. Supporting Adolescents Exposed to Disasters
9. Adolescent Decision Making: An Overview
10. Safe at School: An Interview with Ken Jennings
11. What Educators Need to Know about Bullying Behaviors
12. The Bridge to Character
13. Academic Instructors or Moral Guides? Moral Education in America and the Teacher's Dilemma

At-risk students
28. Learning-Style Responsiveness Approaches for Teaching Typically Performing and At-Risk Adolescents

Backward design
27. Backward Design: Targeting Depth of Understanding for All Learners

Behavior management
43. From Ringmaster to Conductor: 10 Simple Techniques that Can Turn an Unruly Class into a Productive One

Brain-based education
24. A Fresh Look at Brain-Based Education

Bullying
10. Safe at School: An Interview with Kevin Jennings
11. What Educators Need to Know about Bullying Behaviors

Cyberbullying
36. Assessing Middle School Students' Knowledge of Conduct and Consequences and Their Behaviors Regarding the Use of Social Networking Sites

Child development
6. Play and Social Interaction in Middle Childhood
7. Childhood Obesity in the Testing Era: What Teachers and Schools Can Do!
8. Why We Should Not Cut P. E.

Classroom assessment
26. Classroom Assessment and Grading to Assure Mastery
47. Using Self-Assessment to Chart Students' Paths
48. Peer Assessment
49. Assessment-Driven Improvements in Middle School Students' Writing

Classroom management
41. Middle School Students Talk about Social Forces in the Classroom
42. Classroom Management Strategies for Difficult Students: Promoting Change through Relationships
43. From Ringmaster to Conductor: 10 Simple Techniques That Can Turn an Unruly Class into a Productive One

Cognitive learning
24. A Fresh Look at Brain-Based Education
25. What Will Improve a Student's Memory?

Constructivism
32. Designing Learning through Learning to Design

Cultural diversity
20. Understanding Unconscious Bias and Unintentional Racism
21. Improving Schooling for Cultural Minorities: The Right Teaching Styles Can Make a Big Difference
22. Becoming Adept at Code-Switching

Effective teaching
1. What Makes a Great Teacher? PDK Summit Offers Many Ideas
21. Improving Schooling for Cultural Minorities: The Right Teaching Styles Can Make a Big Difference
27. Backward Design: Targeting Depth of Understanding for All Learners
29. "To Find Yourself, Think for Yourself": Using Socratic Discussions in Inclusive Classrooms
30. Setting the Record Straight on "High-Yield" Strategies

Elementary students
6. Play and Social Interaction in Middle Childhood
7. Childhood Obesity in the Testing Era: What Teachers and Schools Can Do!
8. Why We Should Not Cut P. E.

Engagement
39. Beyond Content: How Teachers Manage Classrooms to Facilitate Intellectual Engagement for Disengaged Students

Expertise
26. Classroom Assessment and Grading to Assure Mastery
40. "The Strive of It"

Gender
23. Gender Matters in Elementary Education: Research-Based Strategies to Meet the Distinctive Learning Needs of Boys and Girls

Gifted students
17. How Can Such a Smart Kid Not Get It?: Finding the Right Fit for Twice-Exceptional Students in Our Schools
18. The Relationship of Perfectionism to Affective Variables in Gifted and Highly Able Children
19. Social and Emotional Development of Gifted Children: Straight Talk

Internet References

The following Internet sites have been selected to support the articles found in this reader. These sites were available at the time of publication. However, because websites often change their structure and content, the information listed may no longer be available. We invite you to visit www.mhhe.com/cls for easy access to these sites.

Annual Editions: Educational Psychology 11/12

General Sources

American Educational Research Association
www.aera.net

The AERA homepage provides links to a variety of resources and publications commonly used by educational psychologists and educators, covering a broad spectrum of educational issues.

American Psychological Association
www.apa.org/topics/homepage.html

By exploring the APA's "PsycNET," you will be able to find links to an abundance of articles and other resources that are useful in the field of educational psychology.

Annenberg Media
www.learner.org

As an entity of the Annenberg Foundation, the focus of Annenberg Media is to advance excellent teaching in K-12 schools in the United States through multimedia and telecommunications formats. The Foundation is dedicated to providing teachers with resources that allow them to increase their expertise and help them improve their teaching methods. Of particular interest are four series of videos on demand titled: *Discovering Psychology: Updated Edition* (www.learner.org/resources/series138.html); *The Learning Classroom: Theory into Practice* (www.learner.org/resources/series172.html; and *Looking at Learning Again, Part I* (www.learner.org/resources/series106.html); and *Looking at Learning Again, Part II* www.learner.org/resources/series114.html).

ASCD
www.ascd.org

Formerly known as the Association for Supervision and Curriculum Development, ASCD.org is a professional organization for school leaders across the world. The website includes links to numerous online resources, curriculum materials and research dedicated to advancing best practices and policies for all learners.

Educational Resources Information Center
www.eric.ed.gov

This invaluable site provides links to all ERIC sites: clearinghouses, support components, and publishers of ERIC materials. Search the ERIC database for what is new.

National Center for Education Statistics
www.nces.ed.gov

The National Center for Education Statistics (NCES) represents the primary research arm of the U. S. Department of Education and is housed under the Institute of Education Sciences (IES). NCES conducts nationally representative studies on educational issues from broad perspectives. They provide information to Congress, national, state, and local level officials, organizations and agencies, and the general public. They also provide access to a vast array of data that are of interest to education professionals.

National Education Association
www.nea.org

Something—and often quite a lot—about virtually every education-related topic can be accessed at or through this site of the 2.3-million-strong National Education Association.

National Parent Information Network/ERIC
www.npin.org

This is a clearinghouse of information on elementary and early childhood education as well as urban education. Browse through its links for information for parents.

TeacherTube
www.TeacherTube.com

TeacherTube.com is a free site providing access to a wide range of resources and videos for educators at all levels.

U.S. Department of Education
www.ed.gov/pubs/TeachersGuide

Government goals, projects, and grants are listed here, plus many links to teacher services and resources.

UNIT 1: Perspectives on Teaching

American Academy of Pediatrics
www.aap.org/disasters

The American Academy of Pediatrics site on Children and Disasters has resources for schools, childcare, and families regarding disaster preparedness.

The Center for Innovation in Education
www.center.edu

The Center for Innovation in Education, self-described as a "not-for-profit, non-partisan research organization," focuses on KP12 education reform strategies. Click on its links about school privatization.

Classroom Connect
www.classroom.net

This is a major website for KP-12 teachers and students, with links to schools, teachers, and resources online. It includes discussion of the use of technology in the classroom.

Education World
www.education-world.com

Education World provides a database of literally thousands of sites that can be searched by grade level, plus education news, lesson plans, and professional-development resources.

The Federal Emergency Management Association
www.fema.gov/kids/teacher.htm

The Federal Emergency Management Association provides resources for teachers and parents regarding disaster preparedness, terrorism, school safety and fire safety at this site.

Internet References

Goals 2000: A Progress Report
www.ed.gov/pubs/goals/progrpt/index.html

Open this site to survey a progress report by the U.S. Department of Education on the Goals 2000 reform initiative. It provides a sense of the goals that educators are reaching for as they look toward the future.

Teacher Talk Forum
www.education.indiana.edu/cas/tt/tthmpg.html

Visit this site for access to a variety of articles discussing life in the classroom. Clicking on the various links will lead you to electronic lesson plans, covering a variety of topic areas, from Indiana University's Center for Adolescent Studies.

UNIT 2: Development

Association for Moral Education
www.amenetwork.org

AME is dedicated to fostering communication, cooperation, training, curriculum development, and research that link moral theory with educational practices. From here it is possible to connect to several sites on moral development.

Center for Adolescent and Families Studies
www.indiana.edu/~cafs

This site provides information on research practices of instruction. Also included is a link to other resources.

Child Welfare League of America
www.cwla.org

The CWLA is the United States' oldest and largest organization devoted entirely to the well-being of vulnerable children and their families. This site provides links to information about issues related to morality and values in education.

Kids Health
www.kidshealth.org

Resources for parents, kids and teens about a variety of health concerns are available here.

The National Association for Child Development
www.nacd.org

This international organization is dedicated to helping children and adults reach their full potential. Its home page presents links to various programs, research, and resources into such topics as ADD/ADHD.

National Association of School Psychologists (NASP)
www.nasponline.org

The NASP offers advice to teachers about how to help children cope with the many issues they face in today's world. The site includes tips for school personnel as well as parents.

Scholastic News Zone
www.scholasticnews.com

At this site, Scholastic classroom magazines provide up-to-date information to children, teachers, and parents online to help explain timely issues.

UNIT 3: Individual Differences among Learners

Autism Society
www.autism-society.org

The Council for Exceptional Children
www.cec.sped.org/index.html

This page will give you access to information on identifying and teaching gifted children, attention-deficit disorders, and other topics in gifted education.

Global SchoolNet Foundation
www.gsn.org

Access this site for multicultural education information. The site includes news for teachers, students, and parents, as well as chat rooms, links to educational resources, programs, and contests and competitions.

International Project: Multicultural Pavilion
www.curry.edschool.virginia.edu/curry/centers/multicultural/papers.html

Here is a forum, sponsored by the Curry School of Education at the University of Virginia, for sharing stories and resources and for learning from the stories and resources of others. These articles on the Internet cover every possible racial, gender, and multicultural issue that could arise in the field of multicultural education.

LD Online
www.ldonline.org

For teachers and parents, LD Online is the leading website for information about learning disabilities, learning disorders and differences.

Let 100 Flowers Bloom/Kristen Nicholson-Nelson
www.teacher.scholastic.com/professional/assessment/100flowers.htm

Open this page for Kristen Nicholson-Nelson's discussion of ways in which teachers can help to nurture children's multiple intelligences. She provides a useful bibliography and resources.

National Association for Multicultural Education
www.nameorg.org

NAME is a major organization in the field of multicultural education. The website provides conference information and resources including lesson plans, advice for handling touchy issues, and grant information.

National Attention Deficit Disorder Association
www.add.org

This site, some of which is under construction, will lead you to information about ADD/ADHD. It has links to self-help and support groups, outlines behaviors and diagnostics, answers FAQs, and suggests books and other resources.

National MultiCultural Institute (NMCI)
www.nmci.org

NMCI is one of the major organizations in the field of diversity training. At this website, NMCI offers conference data, resource materials, diversity training and consulting service information, and links to other related sites.

Internet References

Tolerance.org
www.tolerance.org

This site promotes and supports anti-bias activism in every venue of life. The site contains resources, a collection of print materials, and downloadable public service announcements.

UNIT 4: Learning and Instruction

Brain Based Education: Fad or Breakthrough? by Daniel Willingham
www.teachertube.com/members/viewVideo.php?video_id=74863&title=Brain_Based_Education__Fad_or_Breakthrough

This brief video by University of Virginia Professor Daniel Willingham identifies some of the primary criticisms and concerns about the field of brain-based education. mind-set by teaching them about how the brain works and to think about their brain as a "muscle."

Cyberbullying Research Center
Cyberbullying.us

This online resource is managed by two faculty members from Florida Atlantic University and the University of Wisconsin-Eau Claire. The website provides links and resources devoted to issues of cyberbullying in adolescents for teachers, parents, and students.

The Critical Thinking Community
www.criticalthinking.org

This site promotes educational reform through fair-minded critical thinking. The site also provides information and resources on critical thinking.

Education Week on the Web
www.edweek.org

At this page you can open archives, read special reports, keep up on current events, and access a variety of articles in educational psychology. A great deal of this material is helpful in learning and instruction.

Learning Styles Debunked
www.sciencedaily.com/releases/2009/12/091216162356.htm

An article from December 2009 summarizing an in-depth review of the literature and prior research on learning styles.

Learning Styles Don't Exist by Daniel Willingham
www.teachertube.com/members/viewVideo.php?video_id=119351&title=Learning_Styles_Don_t_Exist

Another video by well-respected psychologist Daniel Willingham, critiquing learning styles theories and research.

National Crime Prevention Council
www.ncpc.org/newsroom/current-campaigns/cyberbullying

The National Crime Prevention Council (McGruff the Crime Dog) provides information and resources devoted to cyberbullying.

Online Internet Institute
www.oii.org

A collaborative project among Internet-using educators, proponents of systemic reform, content-area experts, and teachers who desire professional growth, this site provides a learning environment for integrating the Internet into educators' individual teaching styles.

Teachers Helping Teachers
www.pacificnet.net/~mandel

This site provides basic teaching tips, new teaching-methodology ideas, and forums for teachers to share their experiences. It features educational resources on the Web, with new ones added each week.

The Teachers' Network
www.teachers.net

Bulletin boards, classroom projects, online forums, and Web mentors are featured on this site, as well as the book *Teachers' Guide to Cyberspace* and an online, four-week course on how to use the Internet.

Think U Know
www.thinkuknow.co.uk

This website is sponsored by the Child Exploitation and Online Protection Centre (CEOP) in the United Kingdom. It includes sites for students of different ages designed to help educate them about online safety and resources for parents and teachers. It has sponsored a number public service announcements on the topic that can be viewed on YouTube.

Wired Kids.org
www.wiredkids.org

Links to a number of websites sponsored by the organization with a variety of resources relating to Internet use for children of all age/grade levels.

World Intellectual Property Organization—What Is Intellectual Property?
www.wipo.int/about-ip/en

The World Intellectual Property Organization, an agency of the United Nations, provides a legal definition of intellectual property that might be of interest to students.

UNIT 5: Motivation, Engagement, and Classroom Management

Brainology
Brainology.us

This website provides information about the program developed by Carol S. Dweck and Lisa Sorich Blackwell designed to foster a growth mind-set.

Consistency Management and Cooperative Discipline
www2.ed.gov/pubs/ToolsforSchools/cmcd.html

A link to information about a classroom management program based on person-centered principles and the work of Dr. Jerome Freiberg.

Curriculum Based Measurement (CBM)
www.studentprogress.org/families.asp

This site provides an in-depth discussion of what curriculum based measurement is, frequently asked questions, and suggestions for implementation provided by the National Center on Student Progress Monitoring, which is federally funded by the Office of Special Education Programs.

Internet References

Effect Sizes Explained
www.psychology.wikia.com/wiki/Effect_size

Basic information defining effect size measures and how they are used for students who are unfamiliar with statistics.

I Love Teaching
www.iloveteaching.com

This site is a resource for new and veteran teachers as well as preservice teachers and student teachers. Information is broken out into various links such as "Encouraging Words," and "Classroom Management."

The Jigsaw Classroom
www.jigsaw.org

The jigsaw classroom is a cooperative learning technique that reduces racial conflict among school children, promotes better learning, improves student motivation, and increases enjoyment of the learning experience. The site includes history, implementation tips, and more.

Mihaly Csikszentmihalyi on Flow
www.ted.com/speakers/mihaly_csikszentmihalyi.html

A brief video by Mihaly Csikszentmihalyi discussing his seminal work on creativity and motivation, presented by TED.org, a nonprofit organization, devoted to bringing people together to talk about important ideas from technology, education, and design across the world.

North Central Educational Regional Laboratory
www.ncrel.org/sdrs

This site provides research, policy, and best practices on issues critical to educators engaged in school improvement. A number of critical issues are covered.

Teaching Helping Teachers
www.pacificnet.net/~mandel

This site is a resource tool for all teachers. It includes links to "Classroom Management," "Special Education," and more.

What Kids Can Do
www.whatkidscando.org

What Kids Can Do is a national nonprofit organization dedicated to promoting and sharing stories of young people who have made commitments to work with their schools and communities to address real-world issues/problems.

FairTest
www.fairtest.org

This site is the homepage for the National Center for Fair and Open Testing. The main objective of this group is to end the misuses and flaws of standardized testing and to ensure that evaluation of students, teachers, and schools is fair, open, valid, and educationally beneficial.

Kathy Schrock's Guide for Educators: Assessment
www.school.discovery.com/schrockguide/assess.html

Sponsored by Discovery School.com, this webpage has a comprehensive compilation of sites about classroom assessment and rubics.

National Assessment of Educational Progress (NAEP)
www.nces.ed.gov/nationsreportcard

The National Assessment of Educational Progress (NAEP) is a federally mandated ongoing nationally representtative assessment program of K-12 students in a variety of subjects.

National Council on Measurement in Education
www.ncme.org

This is one of the nation's key organizations for professionals involved in assessment, evaluation, testing, and other aspects of educational measurement. Click on the "Resources" tab for links to essential resources about testing in schools, and fair test practices for educators.

Phi Delta Kappa International
www.pdkintl.org

This important organization publishes articles about all facets of education. You can check out the online archive of the journal, *Phi Delta Kappan,* which has resources such as articles having to do with assessment.

Washington (State) Center for the Improvement of Student Learning
www.k12.wa.us

This Washington State site is designed to provide access to information about the state's new academic standards, assessments, and accountability system. Many resources and Web links are included.

UNIT 6: Assessment

Awesome Library for Teachers
www.neat-schoolhouse.org/teacher.html

Open this page for links and access to teacher information on everything from assessments to child development topics.

UNIT 1

Perspectives on Teaching

Unit Selections

Learning Outcomes

After reading this unit, you will be able to:

- Describe characteristics of effective teachers.

- Discuss how educational reform can help develop effective teachers.

- Explain the process of conducting an action research project.

- Explain how traumatic events can affect student learning.

- List ways in which teachers can help students deal with traumatic events during and immediately after the event, long-term, and on the anniversary of the event.

Student Website

www.mhhe.com/cls

Internet References

The American Academy of Pediatrics
www.aap.org/disasters

The Center for Innovation in Education
www.center.edu

Classroom Connect
www.classroom.net

Education World
www.education-world.com

Federal Emergency Management Association
www.fema.gov/kids/teachers.htm

Goals 2000: A Progress Report
www.ed.gov/pubs/goals/progrpt/index.html

Teacher Talk Forum
www.education.indiana.edu/cas/tt/tthmpg.html

Disaster Mental Health Institute
www.usd.edu/dmhi/publications.cfm

The teaching-learning process in school is enormously complex. Many factors influence pupil learning—such as family background, developmental level, prior knowledge, motivation, and, of course, effective teachers. Educational psychology investigates these factors to better understand and explain student learning. We begin our exploration of the teaching–learning process by considering the characteristics of effective teaching.

The first article offers an interesting perspective on what makes an effective teacher. The second article considers the role of educational reform efforts in developing effective teachers.

In the third paper, Ms. Brighton outlines steps for teachers to gather their own data so they can solve problems they encounter in their classroom thoughtfully and reflectively.

Finally, the last two articles address the effects of traumatic events on students and ways in which teachers can respond.

Educational psychology is a teacher resource that emphasizes disciplined inquiry, a systematic and objective analysis of information, and a scientific attitude toward decision making. The field provides information for decisions that are based on quantitative and qualitative studies of learning and teaching rather than on intuition, tradition, authority, or subjective feelings. It is our hope that this aspect of educational psychology is communicated throughout these readings, and that, as a student, you will adopt the analytic, probing attitude that is part of the discipline.

While educational psychologists have helped to establish a knowledge base about teaching and learning, the unpredictable, spontaneous, evolving nature of teaching suggests that the best they will ever do is to provide concepts and skills that teachers can adapt for use in their classrooms. The issues raised in these articles about effective teaching help us understand the teaching role and its demands. As you read articles in other chapters, consider the demands they place on the teaching role as well.

© BananaStock/PunchStock

What Makes a Great Teacher?
PDK Summit Offers Many Ideas

**Great teachers do more than just advance student learning.
They also spread their own expertise to other teachers.**

ERIN YOUNG

In his office, Thomas Guskey has a poster of a photo from 1989. In the photo, one student is standing in front of four tanks in Tiananmen Square in Beijing. To Guskey, the photo symbolizes courage—the same courage that educators need to call upon.

Guskey, the keynote speaker at the 2008 Phi Delta Kappa Summit on High-Performing Educators, urged attendees to become good leaders so they can lead the changes in education. But he warned that forging this path would take courage, similar to the courage displayed by the student in the photo as he stood before the tanks.

"Can you imagine the courage it took to do that?" Guskey asked. "That's the kind of stand you have to take. When you do that, it will instill courage in others."

Although educators may feel isolated when they try to create change in their organizations, they should remember that they have the knowledge base of the profession behind them, and they know what works and what doesn't, he said.

"We can't be satisfied with managing change; we have to lead change in our classrooms, schools, and districts," said Guskey, Distinguished Service Professor at Georgetown College in Georgetown, Kentucky. "We should use our knowledge base in good and positive ways to help kids learn in new and positive ways."

The keynote address was part of last November's PDK summit in San Antonio, Texas, and began with a panel discussion about what makes a great teacher. Panelist Barnett Berry, president of the Center for Teaching Quality, argued that great teachers do more than just advance student learning—to be great, they must also spread their own expertise.

"It's not one, it's not the other," he said. "It's both."

Mary Clement, a panelist and associate professor of teacher education at Berry College in Georgia, said her list of what makes a great teacher has five elements: education, teacher preparation, hiring, quality induction, and ongoing support in a quality workplace.

Participants at the 2008 Summit Said, a Great Teacher:

- Has the ability to be flexible, optimistic, self-reflective, progressive, and innovative;
- Must possess the ability to build relationships with students and teachers and have a passion for teaching;
- Excites a passion for learning in his or her students through skillful facilitation, using 21st-century tools;
- Goes beyond the classroom as a collaborator with colleagues;
- Wants to improve himself or herself by learning good instructional skills;
- Is someone who knows the curriculum and works well as part of a team;
- Builds relationships and facilitates lifelong learning;
- Collaborates with families, peers, and the community;
- Shows appreciation and enthusiasm for cultural differences;
- Inspires others to achieve their potential;
- Understands the complexity of the teaching and learning environment;
- Has consistently high expectations for all students;
- Recognizes and adapts when he or she isn't getting through to students;
- Addresses the needs of the whole child;
- Uses assessment to inform instructional decision making; and
- Gives back through mentoring.

"Who makes these things happen?" she asked. "We do. The people in this room. As one of my former professors always said, 'If not you, who? If not now, when?' We are professional educators. It's through our work, through our writing, our professionalism, and even our activism. This is how we can help to create and support the steps on my list that will make great teachers."

For panelist Sherie Williams, an assistant professor at Grand Valley State University in Grand Rapids, Michigan, the definition of a great teacher is a teacher who creates a balance between curricular knowledge and the ability to build relationships with students. Research shows that students learn better when they have a relationship with the teacher.

"To make a wonderful, exemplary teacher, we have to help people learn skills to build relationships in the classroom," she said.

But great teachers are not all alike, Guskey said. He asked audience members to think of a great teacher in their lives. About half of the audience selected a teacher who was harsh, demanding, and authoritative, while the other half selected a teacher who was nurturing, warm, and endearing.

"In all of our research on effective teachers, it's been very difficult for us to come up with any set of personality characteristics that defines a highly effective teacher," he said.

To further complicate the issue, Guskey said, research in Tennessee has shown that a great teacher in one setting may be a poor teacher in another setting. Tennessee has a value-added accountability program that can show on average, for each teacher, how much the teacher's students have learned throughout the year.

"You would think we should be able to identify those teachers who are getting remarkable results, go and look at what they do, and just have everybody do the same," Guskey said. "But what they've discovered is it's not that easy."

Instead, he said, teachers who are effective in rural schools fail when they're put into urban schools, even though they're doing the same things they did in the rural schools, and vice versa.

"They've really called into question this notion of best practices," Guskey said. "Maybe best practices depend on where you are, the kind of students you're teaching, the kinds of communities in which they live, the cultural background they bring to school. Those things really need to be built in, because if what's effective depends on the kind of students who are in front of you, then we have to prepare our teacher candidates to really be familiar with those kids, what they're facing, and how they can be effective with them."

He also reminded the audience that what students learn from great teachers often goes beyond what's in the lesson plan.

"We learn so much from teachers besides the things they set out to teach us," he said. "We carry forward those things for years and years afterward. How does that contribute to the effectiveness of teachers?" More pressingly, how do we help young people entering teaching improve that and gather that so that when they become teachers, that can be a part of the quality they bring to their students?

"You really need to go home and become good leaders," Guskey said. "We have the knowledge base, but finding ways to put it into practice will take real courage at all levels."

Critical Thinking

1. Given the characteristics discussed in the article, which are your strengths? Your weaknesses?
2. Consider effective teachers you have known, which of the listed characteristics apply? Are there others you might add?

ERIN YOUNG is managing editor of web and publications for Phi Delta Kappa.

From *Phi Delta Kappan*, by Erin Young, February 2009, pp. 438–439. Reprinted with permission of Phi Delta Kappa International, www.pdkintl.org, 2009. All rights reserved.

Reform: To What End?

We need a different orientation to school reform—one that embodies a richer understanding of teaching and learning.

MIKE ROSE

This is an exciting time for education as the federal government, state houses, and private philanthropies are all focusing on school reform. A lot of good ideas are in the air—thoughtful proposals for ways to change things, to imagine a new kind of schooling in the United States.

The history of school reform has taught us, however, that good ideas can become one-dimensionalized as they move from conception through policy formation to implementation. Also, in the heat of reform, politics and polemics can become an end in themselves, a runaway train of reform for reform's sake. In addition, reforms can have unintended consequences. As a reform plays out in the complex, on-the-ground world of districts, school boards, and classrooms, it can lead to counter productive practices. In the case of No Child Left Behind, for example, we saw the narrowing of the curriculum to prepare for high-stakes tests in math and language arts.

At this moment, when we're focusing so much attention on school reform and so much is possible, it would be good to step back and remind ourselves what we're ultimately trying to achieve. What is the goal of school reform? Most would agree it's to create rich learning environments, ones with greater scope and more equitable distribution than those we currently have.

As we reimagine school, some basic questions should serve as our touchstone for reform: What is the purpose of education in a democracy? What kind of people do we want to see emerge from U.S. schools? What is the experience of education when we do it well?

Happy as a Crab

One example of good teaching I saw comes from my book *Possible Lives: The Promise of Public Education in America* (Penguin, 1995/2006), an account of my travels across the United States to document effective public education. This 1st grade classroom in inner-city Baltimore has 30 students, all from modest to low-income households—the kinds of kids at the center of many school reforms.

As we enter the classroom, teacher Stephanie Terry is reading a book to her students, Eric Carle's *A House for Hermit Crab* (Simon and Schuster, 1991). Hermit crabs inhabit empty mollusk shells; as they grow, they leave their old shells to find bigger ones. In this story, a cheery hermit crab is searching for a more spacious home.

There's a glass case in the classroom with five hermit crabs—which Stephanie supplied—and 13 shells of various sizes. More than once during the year, students have noticed that a shell had been abandoned and that a larger one had suddenly become animated. As Stephanie reads the book, she pauses and raises broader questions about where the creatures live. This leads to an eager query from Kenneth about where in nature you'd find hermit crabs. "Well," says Stephanie, "let's see if we can figure that out."

She gets up and brings the case with the hermit crabs to the center of the room, takes the crabs out, and places them on the rug. One scuttles away from the group; another moves in a brief half circle; three stay put. While this is going on, Stephanie takes two plastic tubs from the cupboard above the sink and fills one with cold water from the tap and the other with warm water. Then she places both tubs side by side and asks five students, one by one, to put each of the crabs in the cold water. "What happens?" she asks. "They don't move," says Kenneth. "They stay inside their shells," adds Miko.

Stephanie then asks five other students to transfer the crabs to the tub of warm water. They do, and within seconds the crabs start to stir. Before long, the crabs are moving like crazy. "OK," says Stephanie. "What happens in the warmer water?" An excited chorus of students replies, "They're moving! They're walking all over! They like it! They're happy like the crab in the book!" "So what does this suggest about where they like to live?" asks Stephanie.

That night, the students write about the experiment. Many are just learning to write, but Stephanie told them to write down their observations as best as they could, and that she would help them develop what they write. The next day, the students take turns standing in front of the class reading their reports.

Miko goes first: "I saw the hermit crab walking when it was in the warm water, but when it was in the cold water, it was not walking. It likes to live in warm water."

Then Romarise takes the floor, holding his paper way out in his right hand, his left hand in the pocket of his overalls: "(1) I observed two legs in the back of the shell; (2) I observed that some of the crabs change [their] shell; (3) When the hermit crabs went into the cold water, they walked slow; (4) When the hermit crabs went into the warm water, they walked faster."

One by one, the rest of the students state their observations, halting at times as they try to figure out what they wrote, sometimes losing track and repeating themselves. But in a soft or loud voice, with a quiet sense of assurance or an unsteady eagerness, these 1st graders report on the behavior of the classroom's hermit crabs, which have now become the focus of their attention.

There's a lot to say about Stephanie's modest but richly stocked classroom and the skillful way she interacts with the children in it. But I'll focus on two important points: what Stephanie demonstrates about the craft and art of teaching and the experience of learning that she generates for her class.

Growing Good Teachers

Everyone in the current reform environment acknowledges the importance of good teaching. But most characterizations of teaching miss the richness and complexity of the work. The teacher often becomes a knowledge-delivery mechanism preparing students for high-stakes tests.

Everyone in the current reform environment acknowledges the importance of good teaching. But most characterizations of teaching miss the richness of the work.

Moreover, reform initiatives lack depth on how to develop more good teachers. There is encouragement of alternative pathways to qualification (and, often, animosity toward schools of education and traditional teacher training). There are calls for merit pay, with pay typically linked to test-score evidence of student achievement. There are general calls for additional professional development. And, of course, there is the widespread negative incentive: By holding teachers' "feet to the fire" of test scores, we will supposedly get more effort from teachers, although proponents of this point of view never articulate the social-psychological mechanisms by which the use of test scores will affect effort, motivation, and pedagogical skill.

But when you watch Stephanie, a very different image of the teacher emerges. She is knowledgeable and resourceful across multiple subject areas and is skillful at integrating them. She is spontaneous, alert for the teachable moment, and able to play out the fruits of that spontaneity and plan next steps incrementally as the activity unfolds. She believes that her students can handle a sophisticated assignment, and she asks questions and gives direction to guide them. Her students seem comfortable taking up the intellectual challenge.

What is interesting is that none of the current high-profile reform ideas would explain or significantly enhance Stephanie's expertise. Merit pay doesn't inspire her inventiveness; it doesn't exist in her district (although she would be happy to have the extra money, given that she furnished some classroom resources from her own pocket). Standardized test scores don't motivate her either. In fact, the typical test would be unable to capture some of the intellectual display I witnessed in her classroom. What motivates her is a complex mix of personal values and a drive for competence. These lead her to treat her students in certain ways and to continue to improve her skill.

A Human Capital Model

Some professional development programs are particularly good at capitalizing on such motivators. Several years earlier, Stephanie participated in a National Science Foundation workshop aimed at integrating science into the elementary school classroom. Teachers met for several weeks during the summer at the Baltimore campus of the University of Maryland, one of several regional training sites around the United States.

The teachers were, in Stephanie's words, "immersed in science"; they were reading, writing, observing presentations, and doing science themselves—all with an eye toward integrating science into their elementary school curriculums. The summer workshop extended through the year, as participating teachers observed one another's classrooms and came together on selected weekends to report on how they were incorporating science into teaching and give presentations themselves. "It gave us a different way," said Stephanie, "to think about science, teaching, and kids."

Because we are in the reimagining mode here, let me offer this: What if we could channel the financial and human resources spent on the vast machinery of high-stakes testing into a robust, widely distributed program of professional development? I don't mean the quick-hit, half-day events that so often pass for professional development, but serious, extended engagement of the kind that the National Science Foundation and the National Writing Project might offer—the sort of program that helped Stephanie conjure her rich lesson with the hermit crabs.

These programs typically take place in the summer (the National Writing Project runs for four weeks), although there are other options, including ones that extend through part of the school year. Teachers work with subject-matter experts; read, write, and think together; learn new material; hear from others who have successfully integrated the material into their classrooms; and try it out themselves.

Electronic media can be hugely helpful here, creating innovative ways for teachers to participate, bringing in people from remote areas, and further enabling all participants to regularly check in as they try new things. Such ongoing participation would be crucial in building on the intellectual community created during this kind of teacher enrichment program. All of this already exists, but we could expand it significantly if policymakers and reformers took into account this richer understanding of the teaching profession.

Although pragmatic lifestyle issues certainly come into play in choosing any profession, the majority of people who enter teaching do so for fairly altruistic reasons. They like working with kids. They like science, literature, or history and want to spark that appreciation in others. They see inequality and want to make a difference in young peoples lives.

The kind of professional development I'm describing would appeal to those motives, revitalize them, and further realize them as a teacher's career progresses. Enriched, widely available professional development would substitute a human capital model of school reform for the current test-based technocratic one. And because such professional development would positively affect what teachers teach and how they teach it, it would have a more direct effect on student achievement.

Enriched, widely available professional development would substitute a human capital model of school reform for the current test-based technocratic one.

Learning-Friendly Environments

For me, the bottom-line question is whether a particular reform will enable or restrict the kind of thing we see happening in Stephanie Terry's classroom. The hermit crab episode is, of course, drawn from a few days spent in just one classroom, but it represents some qualities I've seen again and again in good schools—K–12, urban or rural, affluent or poor. Let me delineate these qualities, and as you read them, ask yourself to what degree the reforms currently being proposed—from national standards to increased data collection to plans to turn around failing schools—would advance or impede their realization. Just as the representation of teaching is diminished in current education policy, so is the representation of learning. I have yet to see in policy initiatives a depiction of classroom life anywhere close to the one I just shared.

- *Safety.* The classrooms I visited created a sense of safety. There was physical safety which for children in some locations is a serious consideration. But there was also safety from insult and diminishment. And there was safety to take risks, to push beyond what you can comfortably do at present—"coaxing our thinking along," as one student put it.
- *Respect.* Intimately related to safety is respect, a word I heard frequently during my travels. It means many things and operates on many levels: fair treatment, decency, an absence of intimidation, and beyond the realm of individual civility, a respect for the history, language, and culture of the people represented in the classroom. Respect also has an intellectual dimension. As one principal put it, "It's not just about being polite—even the curriculum has to convey respect. [It] has to be challenging enough that it's respectful."
- *Student responsibility for learning.* Even in classrooms that were run in a relatively traditional manner, students contributed to the flow of events, shaped the direction of discussion, and became authorities on their own

experience and on the work they were doing. Think of Stephanie's students observing closely, recording what they saw, forming hypotheses, and reporting publicly on their thinking. These classrooms were places of expectation and responsibility.
- *Intellectual rigor.* Teachers took students seriously as intellectual and social beings. Young people had to work hard, think things through, come to terms with one another—and there were times when such effort took students to their limits. "They looked at us in disbelief," said one New York principal, "when we told them they were intellectuals."
- *Ongoing support.* It is important to note that teachers realized such assumptions through a range of supports, guides, and structures: from the way they organized curriculum and invited and answered questions, to the means of assistance they and their aides provided (tutoring, conferences, written and oral feedback), to the various ways they encouraged peer support and assistance, to the atmosphere they created in the classroom—which takes us back to considerations of safety and respect.
- *Concern for students' welfare.* The students I talked to, from primary-grade children to graduating seniors, had the sense that these classrooms were salutary places— places that felt good to be in and that honored their best interests. They experienced this concern in various ways—as nurturance, social cohesion, the fostering of competence, recognition of growth, and a feeling of opportunity.

The foregoing characteristics made the rooms I visited feel alive. People were learning things, both cognitive and social; they were doing things, individually and collectively—making contributions, connecting ideas, and generating knowledge. To be sure, not everyone was engaged. And everyone, students and teachers, had bad days. But overall, these classrooms were exciting places to be—places of reflection and challenge, of deliberation and expression, of quiet work and public presentation. People were encouraged to be smart.

How directly do current reforms contribute to promoting such qualities?

The Most Important Question

In an important 18th-century essay on education, journalist Samuel Harrison Smith wrote that the free play of intelligence was central to a democracy and that individual intellectual growth was intimately connected to broad-scale intellectual development, to the "general diffusion of knowledge" across the republic.

As we consider what an altered school structure might achieve, we should also ask the question, What is the purpose of education in a democracy?

As we consider what an altered school structure, increased technology, national standards, or other new reform initiatives might achieve, we should also ask the old, defining question, What is the purpose of education in a democracy? The formation of intellectually safe and respectful spaces, the distribution of authority and responsibility, the maintenance of high expectations and the means to attain them—all this is fundamentally democratic and prepares one for civic life. Teachers should regard students as capable and participatory beings, rich in both individual and social potential. The realization of that vision of the student is what finally should drive school reform in the United States.

Teachers should regard students as capable and participatory beings, rich in both individual and social potential.

Critical Thinking

1. If excellent teachers are more important to student achievement than excellent schools, how can educational reform put more effective teachers in the classroom?

2. Do you think that the effective teachers identified in either Article 1 or Article 2 create the learning-friendly classrooms identified by Mr. Rose? Explain your thinking.

3. Engage a teacher in conversation about the idea of school reform. Write a summary of your conversation to share with your peers in class.

MIKE ROSE is Professor of Social Research Methodology at the UCLA Graduate School of Education and Information Studies, Los Angeles, California. He is author of *Why School? Reclaiming Education for All of Us (New Press, 2009).*

Embarking on Action Research

You know what's amiss in your students' learning, but not how to make it right. You're not stuck; you're ready for action research.

CATHERINE M. BRIGHTON

Janice Templeton, a 6th grade math teacher at Marshall Middle School,[1] is worried about her students. Marshall's students come from a wide range of ethnic and economic backgrounds and present highly varied academic needs. Some of Janice's learners readily engage with math content, but others are singularly uninterested in studying math and aren't mastering basic concepts. These disengaged students are predominantly female, black, or English language learners.

Janice worries that this pattern of disengagement fits in with the underrepresentation of females and minority groups in high-level math at the high school and college levels. She's been reflecting on reasons for this problem and the steps she, as a middle-grade teacher, could take to stem the attrition of underrepresented students from math classes. But she feels unclear on what steps or changes will be most productive.

It might seem that this teacher is in an unenviable position because she's unsure what to do next. In fact, as a teacher who has identified a specific area of classroom practice that warrants additional inquiry, Janice is in an excellent position to embark on an action research study. Action research is a reflective, systematic inquiry that focuses on a relevant problem in teaching or learning for the purpose of enacting meaningful change to address that problem.

Action research is distinct from other research designs in that it emerges from stakeholders themselves. Like other types of empirical research, action research has clear procedures that practitioners must follow, albeit more fluidly, to arrive at sound conclusions. Let's look at how Janice's action research project exploring how to better serve her underachieving students used tools common to action research and progressed through the seven basic steps of the action research process.

Step 1: Identify a Focus

Action research can be done by one practitioner or in collaboration with others. Kurt Lewin, often called "the father of action research"[2] identified three models:

- *First-person action research* usually involves one teacher studying his or her own classroom to better understand his or her own behaviors, attitudes, practices, or context. The goal is often personal change.
- *Second-person action research* is collaborative and aims to better understand the issues or phenomena of a group. The goal of second-person action research is often to improve the dynamics of a group of interrelated individuals, such as a teacher team.
- *Third-person action research* studies a phenomenon or issue more globally to develop a generalization about the issue's causes or the effect of solutions across varied settings.

With any of these models, the first step is simple: Identify an area of teaching or learning that you are concerned about. You should then become more familiar with this topic, focus on a specific issue that is causing problems with your practice, and specify the research question that will guide the study.

Janice's focus emerged over several months as she watched specific groups of students disengage. She noticed many girls hesitating to answer questions aloud during discussions and avoiding exploration and risk taking in independent assignments. She noticed that many students who had attended Eastside Elementary—many of whom were black, Hispanic, or from low-income families—seemed to completely tune out each day's lesson. She watched the pattern of decreasing homework completion, increasing apathy toward class activities, and escalating off-task behaviors spread in segments of her classes.

To gain more insight into the concept of math disengagement, Janice read articles from education journals, spoke with other middle school math teachers, and joined online discussion groups. She attended an institute on differentiating instruction in mixed-ability classrooms, which gave her practical ideas for how to set up a classroom more focused on authentic tasks.

Through this information gathering, Janice gained a wider view of the issue and formulated two questions: Why do students from underrepresented groups frequently disengage from studying math? and What specific strategies increase students' willingness to study math?

She enlisted the help of other math teachers within her district. Because she noticed that students who had come from Eastside Elementary were particularly disengaged, Janice contacted 5th grade teachers there for their insights. She invited teachers from the high school to join the discussion. Most colleagues she contacted were eager to participate, and a core group agreed to meet every two weeks to investigate the issue of math disengagement and demographics, which gave Janice's inquiry elements of second-person action research.

Step 2: Develop a Plan of Action

The teacher formulates a plan, laying out what actions and measurements to take and what data to gather at various points—and who will do which tasks. Because the lineup of specific tasks may change as any project gains traction, this plan should include both tasks tied to specific classroom practices and goals connected to examining the issue in general.

Janice created a time line detailing when—over the course of a five-week unit on probability and statistics—she planned to collect information about students' perceptions of math and mastery of math concepts and when she anticipated that students with differing readiness levels would need to have guidance and support embedded in lessons. She knew that some students easily transferred data from numerical to graphical representations, for example, whereas others struggled mightily. So she planned lessons for both groups.

To create differentiated lessons tied to the same overarching learning goals, Janice looked over the 13 skills and objectives for this unit listed in the state standards and extracted four generalizations to guide the unit:

- Data can be represented in multiple forms.
- The functions of fractions, decimals, and percents are interrelated.
- Specific sampling strategies increase how well any findings can be generalized to a population from a smaller sample.
- Researchers can make effective predictions by following systematic procedures of probability and sampling.

Janice used these foundational principles to develop lessons that she hoped would increase student engagement and understanding of math.

The research team discussed how to begin the unit in an authentic manner, pointing out situations in which students might need to understand probability and statistics, such as in reporting sports players' achievements. Participants identified skills within the unit for which students' readiness levels varied widely, so that some would need more support and others would need opportunities to extend their learning. Together they designed a preassessment that enabled Janice to gather data on her students' attitudes, experiences, and familiarity with the skills she was about to teach.

To make this assessment non-threatening, they designed it as a puzzle and gave it to students to complete well in advance of beginning the unit. Students matched puzzle pieces containing key vocabulary with pieces containing appropriate definitions and matched word problems with their corresponding solutions. Students also identified their favorite hobbies and interests.

The first differentiated lesson Janice developed focused on understanding, creating, and using tree diagrams to determine probability in a given situation. The lesson involved group work and offered students a choice of participating in one of three groups connected to their reported interests. One activity situated the question within the context of race cars. This group designed a tree diagram for all the possibilities (and therefore the probability) of race cars with various body styles, colors, and accessories. Another posed a scenario from the fashion industry ("Calculate the probability of two models wearing the same combination of fashion accessories when each is provided the same limited options for headwear, shirts, and shoes"). A third tapped into students' interests in pets.

Members of the research team were committed to observing Janice teach this lesson and other newly designed lessons within the unit, and they helped her determine how to assess what students had learned through these lessons.

Step 3: Collect Data

At key points in the project, the teacher gathers the data identified in the action plan. As with other types of research, the findings will be stronger if the researcher examines multiple types of data.

Janice collected student artifacts from all her learners, including preassessments of students' math skills, interest inventories, and work samples. Other artifacts included exit cards (containing each student's answer to an ungraded question used to check for understanding) and student products created as part of an end-of-unit performance assessment. As the unit progressed, she discussed these artifacts with her research team. Her colleagues helped her use insights she gained from examining student work to shape how she embedded students' interests within subsequent lessons.

Janice also used her personal reflections as data. While she planned and taught the new lessons, she kept a reflective journal noting which students showed increasing engagement and skill (and which strategies fed such improvement) and which learners still languished. After the tree diagram lesson, she wrote,

> It was invigorating to have students work actively in teams of their choosing. The noise in the room was productive but lively, and students seemed much more invested in the study of math than they have been in recent days! The topics seemed to align well with their interests, and they all got involved. However, I have the nagging sense that some students aren't as challenged as they could be, so I need to go back to the team and get new ideas to extend the learning for those who are ready to go.

Janice noticed patterns in content and activities that students preferred. She found herself brainstorming additional ways she could tap into these preferences throughout the year.

Peer observations and student interviews rounded out the data gathering. Janice's team members visited her classroom, observed her guiding the newly developed lessons, noted students' responses, and shared their observations, which Janice recorded. These alternative perspectives to her recollections of how lessons transpired strengthened the validity of her findings.

Through informal focus group sessions, she also collected and acted on student feedback about the new instructional approaches. Feedback revealed that although many students liked working in groups (and she noted which ones those were), others yearned for the opportunity to work on tasks by themselves.

Step 4: Organize the Data

Only a highly systemized method of organizing the volume of data gathered during an action research project will reap the project's full benefits. This organizational system must be efficient, practical, and protective of sensitive or confidential information about specific students. Janice used only the students' initials and school identification number when she shared test scores during her team's sessions. She created a spreadsheet with cells such as pre-test score, interest areas, proficiency level, exit card score, and post-test score to reveal patterns across students and class sections. She calculated average scores for classroom tasks and plotted them on a chart, noting where clusters of students formed to inform her flexible grouping configurations.

Step 5: Analyze the Data and Draw Conclusions

This step of the process is ongoing as the teacher researcher continues to collect data. Use whatever analytic methods are appropriate to the research question(s)—both qualitative and quantitative—to interpret data. This step may require additional collaboration with guidance counselors, assessment specialists, or others within the school district who have expertise.

Janice and her team put their heads together to analyze the individual data components and discern a pattern across data sources. They laid out student work samples and discussed what these artifacts brought to light in combination with Janice's self-reflections and peer observers' notes. This closer look at the data indicated that tapping into students' interests increased their willingness to engage in math activities and consequently their achievement on the probability and statistics unit's post-test.

Engaging students was the first step: Once a tie-in to their interests got learners actually attending to what Janice was teaching, they followed a series of steps that led to the end result of more solid learning. Students who were more actively involved in lessons during the unit were more willing to ask questions of one another and the teacher when they encountered difficulty, and those who asked such questions and posed alternative answers or ways to solve whole-group questions subsequently showed greater understanding of content as measured by exit cards, performance assessments, and pencil-and-paper tests. Also, students who had the chance to work in small groups on a shared task were more willing to discuss their mathematical thinking.

The team concluded that designing new lessons and strategies to tap into students' interests increased all students' understanding of the math topics under investigation, including formerly resistant or struggling learners. They believed the project supported the hypothesis that students must first be engaged before they are willing to persist and achieve.

Step 6: Disseminate Findings

Janice and her team first shared their preliminary findings with the administrators at Marshall Middle School. They discussed the overarching principles of tapping into students' interests to boost their zeal for math and punctuated these insights with anecdotes from Janice's journal and her peers' observations of these principles in action.

To put a human face on how the project threaded math skills into students' life pursuits in a way that ignited learning passion, they described José, a quiet young man, largely uninterested in math in September. When Janice created probability lessons formulated around his passion for race cars, José opened up and shared with his classmates in math. For one marketing project, students collected survey data on classmates' perceptions and displayed their findings in an appropriate format. José selected the topic of students' interest in competitive racing. When faced with the challenge of skewed results, he successfully tackled the sophisticated technique of purposeful sampling.

School leaders were intrigued and suggested that the team share its findings at a professional learning community meeting that was investigating curriculum reform within the district.

Step 7: Develop a New Plan of Action

Ideally, the action research process results in the discovery of new information about improving learning conditions. Once this new information is acquired, the action researcher makes decisions about how to change practices to include this new learning—or whether to launch additional investigation. Janice and her team elected to revise additional math units to incorporate more avenues for students' interests.

Action Research and Teacher Growth

The action research process facilitates meaningful teacher change. The first two steps Janice Templeton took—identifying a problem and developing a plan of action to investigate it—were necessary precursors to deep changes in her approach and effectiveness with learners like José.

The action research process facilitates meaningful teacher change.

Janice moved beyond harboring an intuition that *something* needed to shift to capture tuned-out learners to reaching data-supported conclusions that ultimately changed her conceptual frameworks about teaching. She not only helped students in one school district cultivate a taste for math but also grew in her understanding of how to confront achievement gaps.

Notes

1. All names in this article are pseudonyms.
2. Lewin, K. (1958). *Group decision and social change.* New York: Holt, Rinehart, Winston.

Critical Thinking

1. Outline a plan for an action research project you can conduct in your first year of teaching.
2. Find an action research report in professional literature and write a review of how it fits the procedure identified in the article.

CATHERINE M. BRIGHTON is Associate Professor at the University of Virginia and Director of the University of Virginia Institutes on Academic Diversity; 434-924-1022; brighton@virginia.edu.

Teaching with Awareness: The Hidden Effects of Trauma on Learning

HELEN COLLINS SITLER

Few educators would disagree with this statement: "Trauma has always been part of learning and teaching" (Borrowman and White 2006, 182). Yet most teachers, K–college, know little about how to manage the classroom effects of trauma. In this essay, readers meet two students, Laurie and Will. Their experiences teach educators much about the intersections between trauma and learning. Laurie and Will speak to the need for a pedagogy that can be called teaching with awareness. Throughout the years, some more successful than others, I have learned that teaching with awareness benefits not only students like Laurie and Will, but also all learners.

Laurie is a fifth grader who almost never has her homework done, although her teacher has talked with her about it. She is also having trouble with reading. Will, a first-year college student, wears a hooded sweat-shirt pulled down shading his eyes and spends class time in a sleep-like posture—head sunk on his arm, which is flung across the surface of his desk.

One's first impressions of these students are revealing. The teacher who told me about Laurie said, "I've thought she was lazy, careless. I've thought she just wasn't trying very hard." As I began to work with Will, a student in my classroom, my first descriptors of him included resistant to authority, not ready to be in college, and weak student.

On the surface, both students appeared unmotivated and disengaged. Yet, although their behaviors suggested one thing, the reality of their lives revealed another. Each of these students is living with or recovering from psychological trauma. Laurie and Will are learners whose concerns outside the classroom overwhelmed them.

We have all taught students like Laurie and Will. We may well have tagged them with the same kinds of negative descriptors. Developing a pedagogy of awareness can help a teacher to reframe perceptions and consequently, help disengaged or difficult students reinvest in their learning.

What Is Trauma and How Does It Manifest Itself in a Classroom?

Clinical literature defines trauma as "an affliction of the power-less" in which the victim "is rendered helpless by overwhelming force[s]. . . . Traumatic events overwhelm the ordinary systems

of care that give people a sense of control, connection, and meaning" (Herman 1997, 33). Throughout the clinical literature, trauma is marked by violence. This encompasses instances of physical violence, like serious injury in a car accident and, of course, living in a household in which physical violence occurs with regularity.

The term *violence* also encompasses chronic, persistent conditions that cause long-term experiences of helplessness and lack of control (Bryant-Davis 2005; Herman 1997; Naparstek 2004). Life in poverty can be one such instance of violence. Children and adolescents still displaced by Hurricane Katrina can be another, as well as the experience of a child who has a parent or other significant adult serving in Iraq or Afghanistan. Trauma masks itself in classroom behaviors that can easily be interpreted erroneously. According to Naparstek, passivity with no interest in looking at the long-term or even at tomorrow, inability to concentrate, and lashing out verbally or physically are common behavioral effects of trauma. Horsman (2000) identifies still other behaviors as indicative. They include frequent absences, spacing out, and living in a constant state of turmoil.

Has every student who exhibits one or more of these behaviors been traumatized? No. However, some have experienced trauma. The point is, as teachers, we may be unaware that a student has experienced psychological trauma. Therefore, we need to teach in supportive ways. As Horsman (2000) noted, "The task is not to encourage educators to believe that they must learn to diagnose who has been traumatized and then treat them differently from other learners" (23). The task is to teach with a pedagogy of awareness that provides ongoing support for the needs of all learners.

Laurie and Will: What Do Their Stories Teach Us?

Laurie: Interference with Concentration and the Protective Role of Passivity

From Laurie, educators can learn how trauma interferes with concentration and creates passivity. Although Laurie's teacher initially described her as lazy and careless, she realized, "Now

I'm not so sure. Maybe she isn't lazy. Maybe she's just so overwhelmed with her parents' craziness that she's doing all she can." With her parents divorcing, Laurie bounced between two homes. Her teacher explained, "Sometimes she doesn't know which bus to take home. She doesn't know which house she's supposed to sleep in on any given night." Worse still, her mother told her that she was not sure she wanted Laurie with her at all. Teachers and administrators tried to intervene. Laurie's parents refused to come in for meetings. Laurie, at least, met with the guidance counselor.

Maslow's (1987) discussion of human needs sheds light on Laurie's situation and closely mirrors the clinical literature on trauma. According to Maslow, an individual's most basic needs are first physiological, followed by a sense of security, and then emotional, such as feeling love and a sense of belonging. Likewise, for a victim of trauma, a great necessity is safety, both physical and emotional (Herman 1997). Considering these criteria, Laurie was compromised at the most basic levels. Food, security, and love hung in question for her daily.

Trauma can also cause an individual to constrict his or her scope of activity (Herman 1997). Energy might be focused simply on getting through the day: What am I going to eat for lunch? Which bus will I take home? Will I be able to stay there tonight? Coping with concerns like these diverts energy away from other cognitive activity—doing word problems in math, remembering which homework is due, learning new vocabulary in a poem. Thinking about the future is diminished, if it is even possible; getting through each day might be all the student can cope with (Horsman 2000; Naparstek 2004).

The ultimate constriction is *freezing,* a protective mechanism through which an individual becomes passive and exerts no energy at all (Naparstek 2004). Horsman (2000) explains, "those who grew up in . . . chaotic homes have little experience of seeing regular effort lead to results" (81). Laurie's success, or lack of it, in school does nothing to resolve the chaos in which she lives. She might reason that the best strategy is to do nothing; perhaps then the turmoil will pass. The results spill over into the classroom. Homework is not done. Lessons in reading seem unimportant.

Faced with this, what can Laurie's teacher do? First, she can (and did) reframe her judgment of Laurie as lazy and careless. That reframing opens new ways to think about the pedagogy. A teacher who no longer perceives the student negatively can consider physical and emotional needs that are not being met. If a teacher can even partially address those needs, the student can focus more energy on learning. What physical needs does Laurie have that can be met in school? Does a teacher need to make sure she gets a lunch? That she gets a snack during her after-school tutoring? Does she need a new binder to keep track of her homework?

What emotional needs can be met in school? How can work in the classroom invite Laurie into welcome contact with caring others? Does her teacher greet her when she arrives? Does she encourage her when her work shows promise? Which students might Laurie connect with in reading and writing groups? If she needs to break away from the group to be alone when she feels too stressed, does space in the classroom allow that? Is there space in the library? What steps can her teacher take to show Laurie that small daily efforts like finishing her reading assignment will lead to predictable, visible progress? Should Laurie be invited to participate in lunchtime literature-circle discussions? Should she be helped to revise her poem so that it is included in the fifth-grade anthology?

Herman (1997) wrote, "Traumatized people feel utterly abandoned, utterly alone" (52). Laurie needs to feel a connection with a caring adult. Alone, she is in free fall. A teacher's small, caring actions can establish the classroom as a safe learning environment and convey that academic expectations for Laurie remain high.

Will: Aggressive Invisibility and Exemplar of Unrevealed Trauma

Will, a student in my class, teaches a double lesson. Perhaps most important, he exemplifies why it is always important to teach with caring attention. His behaviors displayed a pattern different from Laurie's distraction and passivity. Will was aggressively passive. I encountered him as a first-semester college freshman, only twelve weeks removed from high school. These same behaviors must have occurred during his high school classes. I wonder how many times he had challenged his high school teachers, how often he had been sent to the office for those challenges, and how frequently he had not completed assignments or done poorly on tests.

Will shrouded himself in his hooded sweatshirt. When he sat upright, he leaned his head back against the wall, eyes closed. He always looked asleep. In his first essay, about his high school football coach, anger exploded off the page. During his senior year, instead of battling opponents on the field, Will had spent his season battling his coach. He was benched. I wondered whether that first essay signaled Will's search for a new adversary. I waited, thankful later that if he had identified a new adversary in the college setting, it was neither I nor any other students in my class.

When he turned in his fourth and final paper, I finally understood the rage in his first essay and the challenging, aggressive stance that surfaced during the semester. In his senior year, Will had become responsible for his household, including his mother, too ill from chemotherapy to work, his aging grandmother, and his nephew. He attended school, and then football practice, although he did not play, then went to his job. Three of the four papers he wrote in my course represented his lived experience of trauma. I did not know this until the final week of the semester.

Clinical literature on trauma describes passivity (or freezing) as one possible response to overwhelming danger. Fight or flight is another (Naparstek 2004). Faced with circumstances he was helpless to prevent or change, Will chose to fight. In some cases of trauma, Herman (1997) wrote, "aggressive impulses become . . . unrelated to the situation in hand" (35). During high school, when he suddenly found himself responsible for his family, Will had no concrete entity to fight. Instead, he exerted his aggression against the football coach; he brought it to the college classroom in a milder but still challenging form.

How did Will and I manage to get through a semester successfully, especially when I had no knowledge of his high school history? I quickly discovered that his shrouded, slumped invisibility was a pretense. He was always able to answer when I called on him; thus, I did not challenge his clothing or his posture.

I also refused to confirm his belief that he was a poor writer. This was not false praise; he was a strong thinker and a strong reader. Notes I wrote on drafts and our conversations about writing pointed that out and pushed him for more. Horsman (2004b) suggests, "Helping students to feel they have worth may be the most crucial factor in supporting learning" (23). Will responded to the encouragement and the nudging. Horsman (2000) also recommends, "curriculum that helps make . . . small improvements visible and includes more exploration of what leads to successful learning" (84). Current pedagogy for teaching writing relies on explicit and ongoing reflective writing. Through those reflections, Will and all of his classmates could notice their progress, as well as the areas in which they needed to do more.

These first-year college writers also benefited from other elements in place in my classroom. Students who have experienced trauma may have difficulty staying present. Spacing out during class or actual absence is common (Horsman 2000). In light of this, I allow every student three chances to turn in late assignments with no excuses necessary. For students dealing with severe trauma, this is hardly adequate, but for others like Will, an occasional respite from due dates can make a difference. It affords some control over otherwise uncontrollable situations.

For Will, this meant he could go home to attend to a family matter if necessary. Or if his mind wandered during class and he missed hearing some crucial instruction for an assignment, he could make it up. For other students, the three chances meant that a psychology test could take precedence over an English paper. With a day's grace period for the paper, a student could do better work in both classes.

Establishing a climate of supportive cooperation is another key element in my classroom. Olson (2003) believed "effective teachers take at least two weeks [in the secondary setting] at the beginning of school to build a climate for learning and cultivate a spirit of community" (70). Students enter their first college writing class as strangers. They cannot remain so and effectively respond to one another's writing. We spend several class days learning one another's names and working in various group configurations before the first peer response to writing. This serves my purposes as a teacher of writing. But it serves students like Will, too, by inviting them into an emerging community, rather than allowing them to remain isolated and unknown to others in the same class.

Lessons about Trauma, Learning, and a Pedagogy of Awareness

According to Noddings (1992), "the need for care in our present culture is acute" (xi), not only for students who have experienced trauma, but also for all students. Our judgments of

students, too often erroneous, as with Laurie and Will, frame our interactions with them. I argue that our approaches to our students must include two key elements: (*a*) greater understanding of how trauma manifests itself in learners and (*b*) greater attention to learners as whole persons with physical and emotional, as well as cognitive needs.

Attention to physical and safety needs, the first two levels of Maslow's (1987) hierarchy and the first stage of recovery from trauma, is not enough. Students want teachers to engage them at Maslow's third level of caring. Horsman (2004a) offered this revealing excerpt from an interview with a young woman attending an after-school learning program:

> If you [a teacher] see a kid in that kind of situation . . . missing school and that stuff—if the child doesn't answer you, then you should at least ask them "Do you need food? Do you need any bus tickets?" . . . When I was going through grade school, I just had them buy me stuff . . . clothes and stuff, but no one specifically asked me "Natalie, what's wrong at your house?" Which they should have . . . . You could ask them specifically straight up, "okay do you have a problem at home?" If they say no, you ask them why are they missing school. If they still say nothing, then ask them what they need. . . . Believe me . . . if somebody else pays attention to them, they'll learn better. (5)

In her study of rural middle school girls, Seaton (2007), although not writing about trauma, reported similarly that students want their teachers to notice them and to engage them as people: "What these girls hoped for most was to know that their teachers care about them" (11). To explain what caring looks like, Seaton details a scene in which a middle school English teacher spends thirty minutes helping an eighth grader dig through a dumpster to find her lost retainer. The teacher did not teach his planned lesson that day, yet his dumpster diving was an educationally sound decision. First, a student who is not spending time worrying about how her parents will pay for a second two hundred dollar retainer can concentrate on learning. Second, he taught his students something more valuable and lasting than one day's lesson. Caring for the human needs of a person is paramount.

Increased demands on teachers make teaching with awareness a challenge. Expectations for student performance can overshadow other aspects of classroom life. Such teaching, as Varlas (2007) argued, can be as simple as asking how a student is feeling: "Ask me how I am. I may not always answer you, but it will make a difference" (1). In individual classrooms, teachers can ask directly about problems at home; work to fill a student's physical needs; help a student to stay focused on tasks; create opportunities for students to connect with caring adults and peers; offer outlets like art, music, physical activity, and reading or writing in which students might better express the issue troubling them (Bryant-Davis 2005; Horsman 2000). Every attempt will not succeed and neither will every student, but teachers need to make the attempt.

Individual teachers cannot do all of this work alone. Schools must develop systems to assist them. Laurie and Will, only by chance, found themselves in ideal situations. They were in classes small enough that teachers could get to know them. Prescriptive programs bound neither Laurie's teacher, nor me. Curriculum goals in teaching situations can be met in creative ways. Schools need to look closely at teacher loads and curriculum that allows skilled teachers to tap creative aspects of their competence. Art, music, and opportunities for physical movement and expression appear repeatedly in the clinical literature as important mechanisms through which those who experience trauma can begin to infuse those experiences with meaning and understanding (Bryant-Davis 2005; Naparstek 2004). The current testing culture, with an emphasis on test-taking practice at the expense of richer, more physically and emotionally involving experiences, works in opposition to the conditions and mechanisms that allow students like Laurie and Will to succeed in school.

Teachers also need time and space to talk with their colleagues about manifestations of trauma and mechanisms for helping students learn. Silence too often surrounds experiences of trauma, leaving teachers isolated from productive problem solving with colleagues (Horsman 2000). Guidance counselors need time and space to do what they have been trained for: counseling. Schools need to determine what is the best use of a guidance counselor's time. Rather than working primarily to prepare test materials, as happens in many schools, counselors need to be able to dedicate their time to individual and small-group counseling with students like Laurie and Will.

Trauma fractures one's sense of control, connection, and meaning (Herman 1997). Laurie and Will could not control their circumstances at home. Such students need opportunities to exert control over another aspect of their lives. Likewise, they need opportunities to find meaning in events in which they participate and to connect with other people. Students cannot always find productive pathways to accomplish these goals. Teachers who teach with awareness can provide some of those pathways. This is not so different from what every student needs from teachers—attention in individual, caring ways so that learning can proceed.

References

Borrowman, S., and E. M. White. 2006. Are you now, or have you ever been, an academic? In *Trauma and the teaching of writing,* ed. S. Borrowman, 181–99. Albany, NY: SUNY Press.

Bryant-Davis, T. 2005. *Thriving in the wake of trauma: A multicultural guide.* Westport, CT: Praeger.

Herman, J. 1997. *Trauma and recovery.* New York: Basic Books.

Horsman, J. 2000. *Too scared to learn: Women, violence, and education.* Mahwah, NJ: Erlbaum.

———. 2004a. *The challenge to create a safer learning environment for youth.* Toronto, Canada: Parkdale Project Read and Spiral Community Resource Group.

———. 2004b. *The impact of violence on learning for youth: What can we do?* Toronto, Canada: Parkdale Project Read and Spiral Community Resource Group.

Maslow, A. H. 1987. *Motivation and personality.* 3rd ed. New York: Longman.

Naparstek, B. 2004. *Invisible heroes: Survivors of trauma and how they heal.* New York: Bantam Books.

Noddings, N. 1992. *The challenge to care in schools: An alternative approach to education.* New York: Teachers College Press.

Olson, C. B. 2003. *The reading/writing connection: Strategies for teaching and learning in the secondary classroom.* Boston: Allyn and Bacon.

Seaton, E. E. 2007. If teachers are good to you: Caring for rural girls in the classroom. *Journal of Research in Rural Education* 22 (6), www.umaine.edu/jrre/22-6.pdf (accessed June 23, 2007).

Varlas, L. 2007. A whole child embrace. *Education Update* 49 (6): 1.

HELEN COLLINS SITLER, PhD, teaches composition and supervises preservice English education students in the English Department at Indiana University of Pennsylvania, Indiana, PA.

Supporting Adolescents Exposed to Disasters

ANNE K. JACOBS, ERIC VERNBERG, AND STEPHANIE J. LEE

The emerging physical, cognitive, and emotional capabilities of adolescents present a double-edged sword when it comes to facing disasters. On the one hand, adolescents' growing maturity and capabilities may offer some protection from intense fear or helplessness during the disaster and allow them to be more involved in constructive activities post-disaster to help regain a sense of control and efficacy. On the other hand, adults (or adolescents themselves) may overestimate adolescents' abilities and place greater burdens and responsibilities on their shoulders than they can bear. Similarly, autonomy-related desires to be independent and appear strong may interfere with adolescents' reaching out to parents and professionals when they need additional support in dealing with the crisis (Tatar & Amram, 2007). The purpose of the present article is to provide an overview of ways to prepare and support adolescents during different phases of a major disaster.

Before the Disaster

Taking action to support adolescents in the event of a disaster begins long before the onset of crisis. A risk factor for longer-lasting problems after a disaster is having greater trauma exposure during the disaster (Vernberg et al., 1996). Creating a family safety plan that includes input from the adolescent potentially reduces exposure and promotes a sense of safety. There are several resources available online to help in this process (Table 1). Safety plans should incorporate developmentally appropriate actions for adolescents, such as gathering supplies, monitoring the news for weather alerts, or keeping younger siblings calm. It remains important for parents to shield adolescents and minimize their exposure to traumatic sights, sounds, and smells. Investing time in staying connected as a family and creating nurturing, not restricting, relationships is important in prevention as well. Positive parent-child relationships characterized by less conflict are related to better adolescent coping after disasters (Gil-Rivas, Holman, & Silver, 2004).

School safety plans are worthy of review with a careful eye towards minimizing trauma exposure during disasters and building capacity for an appropriate post-disaster psychological response. Adolescents often look to their teachers and other school staff for support during and following disasters, making it important to prepare a well-informed and achievable plan (Dean et al., 2008). This often includes building relationships with community organizations involved in disaster mental health response before crises emerge to create an effective and efficient use of resources.

Although adolescents look to school personnel for post-disaster support, they are also typically reticent to utilize more specialized disaster mental health services (Tatar & Amram, 2007). Establishing plans that include evidence-based psychoeducation on posttraumatic stress reactions and coping may help normalize support-seeking and promote resilience after a disaster.

Impact and Short Term Adaptation Phases of Disasters
Reactions during and after the Event

It is believed that children are more vulnerable than adults to feeling helpless or overwhelmed during traumatic events (Silverman & La Greca, 2002), although investigation of the relative vulnerability of adolescents in the midst of crises is still in an early stage. In the days and weeks following the crisis phase of the disaster, adolescents' reactions vary. Feelings of hyperarousal and excess energy along with nightmares and intrusive thoughts about the disaster may cause sleep disturbances, difficulties concentrating in classes, and problems following-through with parents' expectations at home. Adolescents may find themselves consumed with fears that the disaster will happen again. For example, rainfall can trigger fears that another hurricane will occur. Some adolescents may struggle with feelings of guilt or shame over actions that they took, or failed to take, during the disaster. This can lead to depressed mood and feeling disconnected from others. At the other extreme, some teens focus on feelings of anger or revenge in response to others who are perceived to have contributed directly or indirectly to the disaster or difficulties getting resources post-disaster. Increased risk-taking and alcohol or drug use may also occur in response to feelings of hopelessness or pessimism for the future.

How to Help

There are several things that adults can do to support adolescent coping following a disaster. These guidelines are described in greater detail in the evidence-informed field operations guide, *Psychological First Aid*, 2nd Edition (PFA; National Child Traumatic Stress Network & National Center for Posttraumatic Stress, 2006). The goal of PFA is to reduce initial distress and foster adaptive functioning and coping among survivors. PFA comprises eight

Table 1 Online Resources Related to Supporting Adolescents Following Disasters

Organization and Web Address	Information Available
American Academy of Pediatrics www.aap.org/disasters/	• Family resource kit and action plans
American Medical Association www.ama-assn.org/ama/pub/category/16389.htm	• Resources for physicians and health professionals working with teens after natural disasters
American Red Cross www.redcross.org/services/prepare/0,1082,0_77_,00.htm	• Disaster preparedness plans
Disaster Mental Health Institute www.usd.edu/dmhi/publications.cfm	• Helping with issues of grief; includes books for youth dealing with death
Federal Emergency Management Agency www.fema.gov/kids/teacher.htm	• Curriculum, terrorism-related resources, and disaster resources for parents and teachers
International Society for Traumatic Stress Studies www.istss.org/resources/index.cfm	• Traumatic stress resources for clinicians, professionals, and the public
National Association of School Psychologists www.nasponline.org/resources/crisis_safety/ naturaldisaster_teams_ho.aspx	• Information for school crisis teams, predominately post-disaster responses and how to help
National Child Traumatic Stress Network www.nctsn.org/ www.nctsn.org/nccts/nav.do?pid= typ_nd_hurr_resource	• Preparedness, response, and recovery information • Family preparedness guide and preparedness wallet card
National Institute of Mental Health www.nimh.nih.gov/health/topics/child-and -adolescent-mental-health/children-and-violence.shtml	• Facts sheets for parents helping adolescents cope with violence and disasters
National Mental Health Information Center http://mentalhealth.samhsa.gov/cmhs/EmergencyServices/ after.asp	• Tips for talking about disasters for teachers, adults, and families

core actions which are described in more detail below. Contact and engagement refers to the need to check in with adolescents following a disaster. Adults should not assume that just because a teen is not asking for help, help is not needed. By introducing oneself, the PFA provider begins the process of helping adolescents re-engage with a calm, respectful, social support system that may have been disrupted during the disaster. In working with minors, it is important to try to obtain parental consent before interacting with the adolescent. When this is not possible, the provider is encouraged to make contact with the parent or guardian at the earliest opportunity and inform them of the basic content of the discussion with the adolescent.

Next, a sense of safety and comfort needs to be established. This pertains to promoting the physical safety of adolescents in an environment that may contain hazards and monitoring impulsive behaviors that may turn risky (e.g., going out to search for someone). A psychological sense of safety can be promoted by shielding adolescents from further trauma exposure such as grotesque scenes or disturbing sounds. Greater exposure to media coverage of the disaster has been linked to greater distress in younger children (Pfefferbaum et al., 2003). While it is recommended for parents to restrict children's viewing of such images, it is not feasible to cut adolescents off from the media in a similar way. Instead, parents or other adults should discuss media coverage with teens, and encourage breaks from media coverage to engage in positive activities.

Maintaining a sense of self-efficacy has been linked to better adjustment following traumatic events (Benight et al., 2000), so adults should look for ways to enlist adolescents in helpful activities such as keeping younger children calm and entertained.

Stabilization techniques are only used when adolescents are emotionally overwhelmed. They include actions such as: refocusing the adolescent's attention on the present by asking him or her to listen and look at you, to describe non-distressing features of the current surroundings, and to engage in "grounding" activities (e.g., naming non-distressing sounds or objects in the room, breathe in and out slowly). Information gathering allows adults to ascertain the adolescent's most pressing needs and concerns to identify the next step to take while avoiding detailed discussions of the traumatic event. The information gathered can help the PFA provider identify concerns that need immediate attention, become aware of adolescents who may be at a higher level of risk based on prior history or degree of trauma exposure, and tailor the PFA modules based on the adolescent's resilience and risk factors.

The fifth PFA core action is providing practical assistance through helping adolescents articulate their immediate needs, develop a realistic plan to meet these, and take action. Adult support may be needed to follow through on plans, so caregivers should be involved when appropriate. The PFA guide also gives guidance on how to prioritize when creating action plans. Connection with social supports is paramount following a disaster. As compared to younger children and many adults, adolescents tend to have diverse means of communicating with loved ones including texting, instant messaging, and chat rooms. Helping adolescents stay connected to others may include finding ways to get them access to the electronic means to do so. In a disaster situation where family and friends are not immediately available, adults can help isolated teens find a time and space separate from young children where they can connect with each other.

Information on coping includes offering basic information about stress reactions and adaptive and maladaptive coping. The focus of this section is to assist adolescents in coping by promoting positive functioning and increasing a sense of self efficacy. It is often helpful to talk with adolescents about common reactions to the type of trauma they experienced, thus normalizing their reactions and addressing concerns that they might be "going crazy." In the short-term, adults can support adolescents by relaxing some of their expectations at home and school with a plan to gradually return to typical routines. Despite the fact that adolescents are at a developmental stage typified by increased independence, they will benefit from emotional support of family members and friends. Instituting either formal family nights to engage in fun activities or allowing extra informal time to talk while running errands or working on a project together can help adolescents stay connected to their families during this difficult time. Temporarily increasing supervision may be necessary in order to monitor difficulties such as risk-taking, drug or alcohol use, or unsafe sexual activity. It is important to remember that these restrictions should gradually taper off as the need for a higher level of supervision decreases.

Adolescents often look to their teachers and other school staff for support during and following disasters, making it important to prepare a well-informed and achievable plan.

The *Information on Coping* module illustrates other types of behaviors that are likely to benefit adolescents following a disaster. Working together with other teens on constructive projects related to rebuilding life after a disaster, such as fundraising or cleaning up a neighborhood park can build upon adolescents' strengths in a healthy way. It is often important to have frank talks with adolescents about the need to wait longer before making major life decisions. Active coping strategies such as problem-solving, seeking social and/or spiritual support, and exercise are linked to better functioning after disasters (Carver, 1999; Smith, Pargament, Brant & Oliver, 2000). Non-productive coping strategies, including isolating oneself, trying to ignore the issue, and using drugs/alcohol, lead to more problematic functioning. It is important to help adolescents evaluate their coping strategies and find ones that are more likely to be successful. This is particularly warranted in the case of boys who tend to rely on nonproductive coping strategies more than girls do (Tatar & Amram, 2007).

Linkages with collaborate services includes steps to connect adolescents with helpful services within their community to support their physical and emotional health. Some signs that immediate professional help is warranted include: acting in ways that are potentially harmful to oneself or others, feelings of hopelessness, and severe difficulty coping with loss (such as refusing to believe that a loved one who died in the disaster is actually dead). Parents should be involved in this process because adolescents are unlikely to seek out or follow-through on services without adult support.

Long-Term Adaptation
Reactions
In the early stages after disasters, difficulties are not talked about in terms of "symptoms" or "disorders," instead, the view is one of normal individuals reacting to an abnormal event. For adolescents with high exposure to life threat, loss, or grotesque scenes, the presence of Posttraumatic Stress Disorder (PTSD) may need to be considered if difficulties in adjustment are severe and last longer than a month (Silverman & La Greca, 2002). PTSD is characterized by three clusters of symptoms:

- Re-experiencing the traumatic event (e.g., intrusive thoughts, recurring nightmares);
- Avoidance of traumatic reminders and numbness (e.g., avoiding activities, feeling detached, sense of a foreshortened future); and
- Increased arousal (e.g., problems falling asleep, angry outbursts, problems concentrating).

Careful assessment of adolescents who continue to experience difficulties is necessary as some of the symptoms of PTSD may mimic other disorders such as Attention Deficit Hyperactivity Disorder. Additionally, other disorders such as Separation Anxiety Disorder or depressive disorders may emerge with or without the occurrence of PTSD. In other cases, teens struggling with trauma-related symptoms in school have erroneously been labeled by adults as "lazy" (Stallard & Law, 1993).

It can be difficult for adults and even teens themselves to recognize that some of the difficult behaviors displayed several months out may indeed be related to the disaster that otherwise appears to be "over." Prevalence rates of PTSD vary between studies and types of traumatic events (Copeland, Keeler, Angold, & Costello, 2007), but returning to a healthy level of functioning without formal mental health intervention is the rule rather than the exception. Some adolescents may find that the disaster allowed them to demonstrate strengths and resilience they did not realize they possessed. Community responses following the disaster may increase adolescents' positive view of the society around them. Traumatic experiences may even result in adolescents pursuing a different area of study or possible vocation that they find meaningful.

How to Help
Adolescents are at risk for being overlooked in the aftermath of a disaster for several reasons, including the adults in the family being overwhelmed themselves and teens trying to protect their caregivers by not reporting their own emotional difficulties (Silverman & La Greca, 2002). Generally if adolescents are still struggling significantly to function at home, school, and/or with friends a month or two post-disaster, more formal mental health services may be warranted. There are a number of time-limited therapies that have shown promise in helping youth cope with PTSD symptoms including: Trauma-Focused Cognitive Behavioral Therapy (Cohen, Mannarino, & Knudsen, 2005; online training for professionals available at: http://tfcbt.musc.edu/), Cognitive Behavioral Intervention for Trauma in Schools (CBITS; Jaycox, 2003; Dean et al., 2008), and brief trauma/grief-focused psychotherapy (Goenjian et al., 1997). These therapies can be provided individually, within groups, in schools, or with families.

The therapies with empirical support so far are largely cognitive behavioral and tend to share some common strategies: providing information on coping and anger management skills, teaching techniques to deal with intrusive thoughts, relaxation techniques to counter hyperarousal, and gradual exposure to traumatic reminders while reprocessing the event in a constructive way. Adults can support adolescents by getting them connected to these services, participating in the therapy, and providing a supportive environment during this time.

It is important to note that there are some popular therapies (e.g., Thought Field Therapy, Traumatic Incident Reduction, and "energy" therapies) that have not been empirically supported, yet are widely advertised and utilized. Often these therapies lack grounding in a solid psychological theory and rely on personal testimonies as opposed to data to support their "successes" (Lilienfeld, 2007). Disasters can deplete families' emotional and financial resources. During a stage when money, time, and hope may be in short supply, it is important to ensure that adolescents get connected with the types of interventions that have the greatest likelihood of positive results.

Maintaining a sense of self-efficacy has been linked to better adjustment following traumatic events, so adults should look for ways to enlist adolescents in helpful activities.

Anniversaries

Reactions to anniversaries of major traumatic events are highly variable, ranging from a denial of negative feelings and desire to focus on the future to a recurrence of highly distressing emotions (Jordan, 2003). Reactions may also vary according to how widespread the disaster was. Adolescents who experienced a private traumatic event may have difficulties eliciting the support and understanding from others that they may need as the anniversary of the event approaches. In contrast, disasters with extensive impacts such as Hurricane Katrina tend to have anniversaries marked by increased media coverage and outreach efforts by mental health professionals and other organizations. These actions are intended to increase a sense of community support, but they may also result in unwanted and unproductive media exposure to frightening scenes from the disaster. Concerns specific to adolescents include spreading rumors or sharing "prophesies" of impending danger throughout their peer group (National Center for Child Traumatic Stress & Federation of Families for Children's Mental Health, nd).

The research regarding anniversary reactions in adolescents is limited, but a few suggestions for providing support have been offered. Adults are encouraged to allow time for adolescents to talk about their feelings related to the disaster, monitor their exposure to the media, and help them find constructive ways to deal with difficult feelings (National Center for Child Traumatic Stress & Federation of Families for Children's Mental Health, nd). While anniversaries may cause difficult feelings to reemerge, they are also valuable opportunities for adults to touch base with adolescents again to help them talk about their feelings now that they have some distance from the event.

Concluding Comments

The evidence base to guide prevention efforts for adolescents exposed to disasters continues to grow. This has allowed the development of evidence-informed guidelines and manualized materials that can be used in prevention efforts tailored for adolescents in schools, homes, and communities. Important steps can be taken to prevent traumatic exposure during and after disasters, foster conditions that promote resilience in post-disaster settings, and provide appropriate disaster mental health services for adolescents who need them.

References

Benight, C.C., Freyaldenhoven, R.W., Hughes, J., Ruiz, J.M., & Zoschke, T.A. (2000). Coping self-efficacy and psychological distress following the Oklahoma City bombing. *Journal of Applied Social Psychology, 30,* 1,331–1,344.

Carver, C.S. (1999). Resilience and thriving: Issues, models and linkages. *Journal of Social Issues, 54,* 245–266.

Cohen, J.A., Mannarino, A.P., & Knudsen, K. (2005). Treating sexually abused children: 1 year follow-up of a randomized controlled trial. *Child Abuse & Neglect, 29,* 135–145.

Copeland, W.E., Keeler, G., Angold, A., & Costello, E.J. (2007). Traumatic events and posttraumatic stress in childhood. *Archives of General Psychiatry, 64,* 577–584.

Dean, K.L., Langley, A.K, Kataoka, S.H., Jaycox, L.H., Wong, M., & Stein, B.D. (2008). School-based disaster mental health services: Clinical, policy, and community challenges. *Professional Psychology: Research and Practice, 39,* 52–57.

Gil-Rivas, V., Holman, E.A., & Silver, R.C. (2004). Adolescent vulnerability following the September 11th terrorist attacks: A study of parents and their children. *Applied Developmental Science, 8,* 130–142.

Goenjian, A.K., Karayan, I., Pynoos, R S., Minassian, D., Najarian, L.M., Steinberg, A.S., & Fairbanks, L.A. (1997). Outcome of psychotherapy among early adolescents after trauma. *American Journal of Psychiatry, 154,* 536–542.

Jaycox, L. (2003). Cognitive Behavioral Intervention for Trauma in Schools (CBITS). Longmont, CO: Sopris West Educational Services.

Jordan, K. (2003). What we learned from the 9/11 first anniversary. *The Family Journal: Counseling and Therapy for Couples and Families, 11,* 110–116.

Lilienfeld, S.O. (2007). Psychological treatments that cause harm. *Perspectives on Psychological Science, 2,* 53–70.

National Center for Child Traumatic Stress, & Federation of Families for Children's Mental Health (nd). *Tips for families on anticipating anniversary reactions to traumatic events.* Retrieved March 13, 2008 from www.nctsnet.org/nctsn_assets/pdfs/edu_materials/tips_families.pdf.

National Child Traumatic Stress Network and National Center for Posttraumatic Stress (2006). *Psychological first aid: Field operations guide* (2nd Edition). [Authors in alphabetical order: Melissa Brymer, Anne Jacobs, Chris Layne, Robert Pynoos, Josef Ruzek, Alan Steinberg, Eric Vernberg, & Patricia Watson]. Available at www.NCTSNt.org and www.NCPTSD.org. Los Angeles, CA: Author.

Pfefferbaum, B., Seale, T.W., Brandt, E.N., Pfefferbaum, R.L., Doughty, D.E., Rainwater, S.M. (2003). Media exposure in children one hundred miles from a terrorist bombing. *Annals of Clinical Psychiatry, 15,* 1–8.

Silverman, W.K., & La Greca, A.M. (2002). Children experiencing disasters: Definitions, reactions, and predictors of outcomes. In A.M. La Greca, W.K. Silverman, E.M. Vernberg, & M.C. Roberts (Eds.), *Helping children cope with disasters and terrorism* (pp. 11–33). Washington, DC: American Psychological Association.

Smith, B.W., Pargament, K.I., Brant, C., & Oliver, J.M. (2000). Noah revisited: Religious coping by church members and the impact of the 1993 Midwest flood. *Journal of Community Psychology. Special Issue: Spirituality, religion, and community psychology, 28,* 169–186.

Stallard, P., & Law, F. (1993). Screening and psychological debriefing of adolescent survivors of life-threatening events. *British Journal of Psychiatry, 163,* 660–665.

Tatar, M., & Amram, S. (2007). Israeli adolescents' coping strategies in relation to terrorist attacks. *British Journal of Guidance and Counselling, 35*, 163–173.

Vernberg, E.M., La Greca, A.M., Silverman, W.K., Prinstein, M. J. (1996). Prediction of posttraumatic stress symptoms in children after Hurricane Andrew. *Journal of Abnormal Psychology, 105*, 237–248.

Critical Thinking

1. Choose one of the online resources mentioned in Table 1. Prepare a report on the recommendations.

2. List suggestions mentioned in the article to help students during and after the traumatic event, for the long term, and on the anniversary of the event.

ANNE K. JACOBS received her PhD in Clinical Child Psychology from the University of Kansas in 2001. She is a Project Coordinator with the Terrorism and Disaster Center where she served as a primary author of the *Psychological First Aid Field Operations Guide* and is participating in the development of *Skills for Psychological Recovery*. ERIC M. VERNBERG earned a PhD in Clinical Psychology from the University of Virginia in 1988 and is now Professor of Psychology and Applied Behavior Science at the University of Kansas. He is Board Certified in Clinical Child and Adolescent Psychology. He has been actively involved in disaster mental health research and service for more than 16 years. His scholarly work includes an influential series of studies on children's recovery from Hurricane Andrew and the book *Helping Children Cope with Disasters and Terrorism* (American Psychological Association, 2002). Additional information on Dr. Vernberg's work is available online at www2.ku.edu/~clchild/faculty. STEPHANIE J. LEE is an undergraduate psychology student at Southern Nazarene University.

From *The Prevention Researcher*, September 2008, pp. 7–10. Copyright © 2008 by Integrated Research Services, Inc. Reprinted by permission.

UNIT 2
Development

Unit Selections

Learning Outcomes

After reading this unit, you should be able to:

- Explain the value of play in middle childhood.

- Prepare a plan to help reduce childhood obesity.

- Summarize arguments for requiring physical education.

- Explain how school safety and bullying are related.

- Summarize steps teachers can take to reduce bullying.

- Paraphrase the four natural moral tendencies.

- Present pros and cons for addressing moral issues in the schools.

Student Website

www.mhhe.com/cls

Internet References

Association for Moral Education
    www.amenetwork.org
Center for Adolescent and Families Studies
    www.indiana.edu/~cafs
Child Welfare League of America
    www.cwla.org
Kids Health
    www.kidshealth.org
The National Association for Child Development
    www.nacd.org
National Association of School Psychologists (NASP)
    www.nasponline.org
Scholastic News Zone
    www.scholasticnews.com

The study of human development provides us with knowledge of how children and adolescents mature and learn within the family, community, and school environments. Educational psychology focuses on the description and explanation of the developmental processes that make it possible for children to become intelligent and socially competent adults. Psychologists and educators are presently studying the idea that biology as well as the environment influence cognitive, personal, social, and emotional development and involve predictable patterns of behavior.

The perceptions and thoughts that young children have about the world are often quite different when compared to those of adolescents and adults. That is, children may think about moral and social issues in a unique way. Children need to acquire cognitive, moral, and social skills in order to interact effectively with parents, teachers, and peers. Human development encompasses all of the above skills and reflects the child's intelligent adaptation to the environment.

Today the cognitive, moral, social, and emotional development of children takes place in a rapidly changing society. The article "Play and Social Interaction in Middle Childhood" discusses the importance of play for supporting all areas of the development of children. The next two articles titled "Child Obesity in the Testing Era: What Teachers and Schools Can Do!" and "Why We Should Not Cut P. E." address the importance of physical development and health to children's learning and development.

Adolescence brings with it the ability to think abstractly and hypothetically and to see the world from many perspectives. Adolescents strive to achieve a sense of identity by questioning their beliefs and tentatively committing to self-chosen goals. Their ideas about the kind of adults they want to become and the ideals they want to believe in sometimes lead to conflicts with parents and teachers. Adolescents are also sensitive about

© SW Productions/Getty Images

espoused adult values versus adult behavior. Ideally, middle and secondary school teachers will teach the whole child and help children develop socially as well as cognitively. The first article in this section addresses role teachers can take in helping teens make better decisions. The next two articles discuss bullying from two perspectives. First, we hear from Kevin Jennings about his experiences with bullying as a child and his plans to promote safe schools nationally in his role as Assistant Deputy Secretary in the Office of Safe and Drug-Free schools in the U. S. Department of Education. The next author dispels myths about bullying and provides resources to help educators eliminate bullying behaviors in schools. The last two articles consider the role that teachers can play in developing character and students' moral growth.

Play and Social Interaction in Middle Childhood

Play is vital for a child's emotional and cognitive development. But social and technological forces threaten the kinds of play kids need most.

DORIS BERGEN AND DORIS PRONIN FROMBERG

Play is important to the optimum development of children during their middle childhood years. Unfortunately, though there is abundant research evidence showing that play supports young children's social, emotional, physical, and cognitive development, it has often been ignored or addressed only minimally (Fromberg and Bergen 2006). However, when young adults are asked to recall their most salient play experiences, they typically give elaborate and joyous accounts of their play during the ages of eight to 12 (Bergen and Williams 2008). Much of the play they report involves elaborate, pretense scripts conducted for a long duration at home, in their neighborhood, or in the school yard. The respondents report that they either personally played the roles or used small objects (action figures, cars, dolls) as the protagonists. They also report games with child-generated rules that they adapted during play. For example, they might have had bike-riding contests or played a baseball-like game that uses fence posts for bases and gives five-out turns to the youngest players. These young adults believed that their middle childhood play helped them learn "social skills," "hobbies," and often "career decisions" that influenced their later, adult experiences.

For many children, the opportunities for such freely chosen play are narrowing. Much of their play time at home has been lost to music, dance, or other lessons; participation on sport teams (using adult-defined rules); and after-school homework or test preparation sessions. At the same time, many schools, especially those considered to be poor performers, have reduced or eliminated recess (Pellegrini 2005). Often, the only outdoor time in the school day is the 10 to 15 minutes left from a lunch period, with rules such as "no running allowed." Thus, the importance of play during middle childhood must be reemphasized by educators who understand why it facilitates skilled social interaction, emotional regulation, higher cognitive processing, and creativity.

Many schools, especially those considered to be poor performers, have reduced or eliminated recess.

Defining Middle Childhood Play

At any age, for an activity to count as play, it must be voluntary and self-organized. Children identify an activity as play when they choose it, but they define the same activity as work when an adult chooses it for them (King 1992). Play differs from exploring an object because such exploration answers the question: "What can it do?" In contrast, play answers the question: "What can I do with it?" (Hutt 1976).

Play in middle childhood continues to include practice play (repeating and elaborating on the same activities, often in the service of increasing skill levels), pretense (using symbolic means to envision characters and scenarios, using literary and other media experiences, as well as real-life experience sources), games with rules (revising existing games or making up elaborate games that have negotiated rules), and construction play (building and designing structures or artistic works). All of these types of play show increasing abilities to deal with cognitive, social, and emotional issues, as well as increases in physical skills.

The rules of play become apparent as children oscillate between negotiating the play scenarios and seamlessly entering into the activities, whether in selecting teams and rules for game play or borrowing media characters to "become" the pretend characters. Script theory, a kind of grammar of play (Fromberg 2002), outlines this oscillating collaborative process. The play process develops throughout the middle childhood years with 1) props becoming more miniaturized, 2) play episodes more extended, 3) language more complex, 4) themes more coherent, and 5) physical prowess more refined.

The Value of Middle Childhood Play

As the memories of young adults testify, play continues to be very valuable during the middle childhood years. Social and emotional competence, imagination, and cognitive development are fostered by many types of play.

Social and emotional competence. Although adults may provide the space and objects with which their children play, during play children practice their power to self-direct, self-organize, exert self-control, and negotiate with others. Even when engaged in rough-and-tumble play, if it was a mutual decision, the children involved demonstrate self-control (Reed and Brown 2000). Such experiences build confidence in deferring immediate gratification, persevering, and collaborating. Even when the play deals with hurtful themes, the children's intrinsic motivation ensures that the play serves a pleasurable, meaningful purpose for the players. For example, role playing threat, aggression, or death can help children deal with the reality of such issues.

Affiliation. Children who negotiate their play together fulfill their need for affiliation. How to enter into play successfully is a negotiation skill, and it requires practice and the opportunity to be with peers. The loner child who stands on the outside of a group and observes may not have these skills; these children may meet their needs for affiliation by joining a gang or by resorting to bullying and violence.

Cognitive development. Middle childhood play fosters cognitive development. Children exercise their executive skills when planning pretense scripts, using symbols in games, designing constructions, and organizing games with rules. For example, in construction play with blocks, exploratory manipulation precedes the capacity to create new forms. These three-dimensional constructions help older children develop the visual-spatial imagery that supports learning in mathematics, chemistry, and physics. Outdoor seasonal games that require eye-hand coordination and aiming—such as hopscotch, jump rope, tag, and baseball—also build the imagery that supports such concepts. Fantasy play can involve scripts that go on for days and become extremely elaborate. Sociodramatic play is a form of collaborative oral playwriting and editing, which contributes to the writer's sense of audience (Fromberg 2002). Thus, scripts often are written to guide the play.

Humor is very evident in middle childhood play, and although some is "nonsense" humor, most involves cognitive incongruity, which demonstrates what children know. That is, by using puns, jokes, exaggerations, and other word play, they show their knowledge of the world and gain power and delight in transforming that knowledge in incongruous ways. Much of this joking is designed to shock adults, but it also demonstrates children's increasing knowledge of the world. Playful use of language also shows up in "Pig Latin" and other code languages, which both include the play group and exclude others. Learning and performing "magic" tricks is also a delight and requires understanding the laws of objects and thus how to appear to bypass those laws.

Most humor involves cognitive incongruity, which demonstrates what children know.

Imagination and creativity. Children dramatize roles and scenarios with miniature animals, toy soldiers, and media action figures, using themes from their experiences, including "playing school." Some urban children might dramatize cops and gangs. Children in both urban and rural areas engage in such pretense, trying on a sense of power and independence, by imagining "what if" there were no adult society. As they try roles and pretend possible careers, they seek privacy from adults during much of this play, preferring tree houses, vacant lots, basements, or other "private" spaces. Symbolic games, such as Monopoly (using a board or online forms), as well as other computer or board games, add to the development of social learning

and competence as children increasingly become precise about following the rules of the game.

When children have had opportunities to practice pretense and use their imaginations, researchers have found that they're more able to be patient and perseverant, as well as to imagine the future (Singer and Singer 2006). Being able to imagine and role play a particular career, rent and furnish an apartment, and negotiate other aspects of daily living makes those actions seem less daunting later on.

Contemporary Middle Childhood Play

Play for children in this age group has changed. Today, there are virtual, technology-enhanced play materials, a constriction of play space from the neighborhood to one's own home and yard, and the actual loss of free time and school time to devote to active play.

Technology. For children in the middle childhood years, virtual reality technology now provides three-dimensional interactive games, such as Nintendo's Wii, which uses hand-held devices that can detect motion. These interactive games may be so engaging that children, mainly boys, abandon other activities that build negotiation skills and social competence with other children. Children also increasingly "instant message," creating abbreviation codes—a form of power—and demonstrate their deepening digital literacy. In addition, they listen to music on iPods, play virtual musical instruments, and make virtual friends with whom they interact. This period of childhood affords different opportunities for children in less affluent families, however, resulting in a widening gap in types of technology-enhanced play materials and experiences among children from different socioeconomic levels. For example, though children can initially access some websites without cost, devices and software require purchases that are seductive, with consoles and accessories rising in cost.

Gender roles also are affected by technology. Virtual reality computer games for girls, such as Mattel's Barbie Girls, reinforce stereotypes. Boys are especially interested in virtual action games.

Spaces for play. Many parents are reluctant to allow their children to range far in their neighborhoods for the kinds of social experiences that were common for earlier generations. This could be caused by frequent media reports of potential dangers (Louv 2008). Parents may see city environments as too dangerous, and suburban parents may believe that homes are too far apart to allow children to walk to friends' houses or gather in neighborhood outdoor areas.

Suburban parents may believe that homes are too far apart to allow children to walk to friends' houses.

Time for freely chosen play. Administrators and teachers pressured to increase academic performance often reduce recess to a short period or omit it altogether because they believe this time is "wasted" or that it just will be a time for children to engage in bullying or other unacceptable behaviors. They also may fear lawsuits because of perceived dangers in freely chosen play, as indicated by prohibitions against running. In spite of research indicating that attention to school tasks may be greater if periods of recess are interspersed (Opie and Opie 1976), some adults don't seem to realize the potential of play as a means of supporting academic learning. Thus, time for play has been reduced both in the home and school environments.

Adult Facilitation of Play

Because middle childhood play is so valuable for social, emotional, cognitive, and physical development and because some trends seem to prevent play's full elaboration and development during these years, adults must become advocates for play and facilitators of play in middle childhood. There are a number of ways they can do this.

Providing play resources. When adults provide indoor and outdoor space and materials, children can adapt and use them creatively. The best kinds of materials have more than a single use but can be modified by interaction with others and elaborated with imagination.

Engaging in play interaction. When adults provide real choices, children can build the trust they need to cope with solving physical problems and negotiating emerging interpersonal play. Adults should appreciate process and effort without judging outcomes. They might assist less play-competent children's interactions by offering relevant materials to help their children be invited into pretense games that other children have started.

Assessing play competence. Educators, in particular, often find that most children comply with their suggestions about play activities, but there may be one or two who do not appear to be participating or, on closer observation, appear to comply, but in their own ways. Teachers, in particular, need to appreciate the multiple ways in which children may represent experiences and display a sense of playfulness. In addition, teachers' assessments should also include observations of children's play competence, especially as it relates to development of imaginative and creative idea generation.

Supporting gender equity. Gender equity and children's aspirations are affected by sanctions and warrants. For example, boys have traditionally dominated play involving 3-D constructions, though some girls are now participating in Lego Robotics teams. To make girls more likely to participate, teachers should place themselves near 3-D construction areas or planned "borderwork" (Thorne 1993). Teachers should be sure to provide materials and equipment that do not have gender-suggestive advertising (Goldstein 1994). In this way, all children can be encouraged to have greater expectations for themselves.

Summary

Play has always been important in middle childhood, but its forms have changed with society and, in some cases, its very existence has been threatened. Parents and educators can facilitate aspects of play that support emotional, social, cognitive, and creative growth. To understand the importance of play for these children, they only have to recall the salience of their own play during this age period.

References

Bergen, Doris, and Elizabeth Williams. "Differing Childhood Play Experiences of Young Adults Compared to Earlier Young Adult Cohorts Have Implications for Physical, Social, and Academic Development." Poster presentation at the annual meeting of the Association for Psychological Science, Chicago, 2008.

Fromberg, Doris P. *Play and Meaning in Early Childhood Education.* Boston: Allyn & Bacon, 2002.

Fromberg, Doris P., and Doris Bergen. *Play from Birth to 12.* New York: Routledge, 2006.

Goldstein, Jeffrey H., ed. *Toys, Play, and Child Development.* New York: Cambridge University Press, 1994.

Hutt, Corinne. "Exploration and Play in Children." In *Play: Its Role in Development and Evolution,* ed. Jerome S. Bruner, Alison Jolly, and Kathy Sylva, 202–215. New York: Basic Books, 1976.

King, Nancy. "The Impact of Context on the Play of Young Children." In *Reconceptualizing the Early Childhood Curriculum,* ed. Shirley A. Kessler and Beth Blue Swadener, 42–81. New York: Teachers College Press, 1992.

Louv, Richard. *Last Child in the Woods: Saving Our Children from Nature-Deficit Disorder.* Chapel Hill, N.C.: Algonquin Books, 2008.

Opie, Iona A., and Peter M. Opie. "Street Games: Counting-Out and Chasing." In *Play: Its Role in Development and Evolution,* ed. Jerome S. Bruner, Alison Jolly, and Kathy Sylva, 394–412. New York: Basic Books, 1976.

Pellegrini, Anthony D. *Recess: Its Role in Education and Development.* Mahwah, N.J.: Lawrence Erlbaum Associates, 2005.

Reed, Tom, and Mac Brown. "The Expression of Care in Rough and Tumble Play of Boys." *Journal of Research in Childhood Education* 15 (Fall-Winter 2000): 104–116.

Singer, Dorothy G., and Jerome L. Singer. "Fantasy and Imagination." In *Play from Birth to 12: Contexts, Perspectives, and Meanings,* ed. Doris P. Fromberg and Doris Bergen, 371–378. New York: Routledge, 2006.

Thorne, Barrie. *Gender Play: Girls and Boys in School.* New Brunswick, N.J.: Rutgers University Press, 1993.

Critical Thinking

1. Describe characteristics of play in middle childhood.
2. Why should play be a significant part of an elementary school day? What forms should it take?
3. Summarize ways in which teachers or parents can facilitate play in middle childhood.

DORIS BERGEN is distinguished professor of educational psychology at Miami University, Oxford, Ohio, and co-director of the Center for Human Development, Learning, and Technology. With Doris Pronin Fromberg, she co-edited the book, *Play from Birth to Twelve,* 2nd ed. (Routledge, 2006). **DORIS PRONIN FROMBERG** is a professor of education and past chairperson of the Department of Curriculum and Teaching at Hofstra University, Hempstead, New York.

From *Phi Delta Kappan,* by Doris Bergen and Doris Pronin Fromberg, February 2009, pp. 426–430. Reprinted with permission of Phi Delta Kappa International, www.pdkintl.org, 2009. All rights reserved.

Childhood Obesity in the Testing Era: What Teachers and Schools Can Do!

Suzanne M. Winter

In this era of increasing accountability and high-stakes testing in schools, a serious paradox has surfaced. Children are becoming overweight at an alarming rate, and mounting evidence points to a relationship between obesity and poor school performance. Ironically, pressure to improve children's academic achievement has led many schools to adopt certain policies, such as eliminating recess or reducing the number of physical education (PE) classes, that put children at greater risk of obesity (Cook, 2005). Critics have characterized schools as "obesogenic" environments that promote obesity through sedentary academic work, limited physical activity, and cafeteria fare of low nutritional value (Davidson, 2007). Furthermore, obesity is thought to be particularly of concern for children of minorities and those in poverty, who are already at high risk for underachievement (Centers for Disease Control and Prevention [CDC], 2008b; Mirza et al., 2004).

Teachers and schools can provide powerful leadership to help reverse the worldwide epidemic of childhood obesity while they endeavor to improve children's academic success. This article describes five strategies to guide teachers and schools in the fight against childhood obesity.

Strategy 1
Get in the Know! Stay Informed

Scope of the problem. Childhood obesity is epidemic in the United States and represents an increasing public health problem worldwide (CDC, 2008b). According to the U.S. National Health and Nutrition Examination Survey (NHANES), obesity rates for U.S. children have risen sharply in a single generation, with rates doubling for preschoolers and quadrupling for school-age children! Although rates have plateaued, one third of children in the United States are currently overweight or obese—health experts caution that these numbers are dangerously high (CDC, 2008b; Ogden, Carroll, & Piegai, 2008).

Multiple influences lead to childhood obesity, including genetic, cultural, and environmental factors. Associated conditions, such as cardiovascular disease, insulin resistance and Type 2 diabetes, orthopedic problems, sleep apnea, psychosocial dysfunction, and other serious problems, can result and threaten a child's health for a lifetime (CDC, 2008a).

Obesity threatens to widen the achievement gap.

Increasing obesity rates threaten to widen the achievement gap that already exists among children. Those who are at highest risk of school failure, children in poverty and minorities, are also at the highest risk of obesity. The rate of increase in obesity for black, Native American, and Hispanic children is double that for white children (Crawford, Story, Wang, Ritchie, & Sabry, 2001; Mirza et al., 2004). Racial disparities in child and maternal health account for nearly one quarter of the school readiness gap between black and white preschoolers, and poor nutrition contributes to this persistent gap. In the United States, poor children become obese from eating too much food that is deficient in iron, B vitamins, and other critical nutrients essential for neural and cognitive development (Currie, 2005).

When schools know the scope of childhood obesity in their area, school leadership is likely to make informed decisions, improve policies, and implement more effective programs to address this crisis. While few states require schools to collect body mass index and fitness data, local health agencies may have statistics that will reveal the extent of the problem. With local data, schools can inform parents and mobilize community obesity prevention efforts.

All school personnel need information and training about this issue. When children are overweight and performing poorly in school, teachers who are well-informed can serve as a resource for children and parents. Providing all teachers with high-quality training on health, nutrition, and physical activity can improve children's chances to beat the odds. One way teachers can stay informed is by reading professional journals and visiting credible websites, regularly.

Strategy 2
Design a School Action Plan

Teachers and schools can create an action plan by:

- Starting early with prevention.
- Providing extra support in the early grades.
- Self-evaluating and examining school policies and practices.
- Collaborating with parents.
- Building a school-community partnership.

The role of schools. The obesity epidemic is extremely serious and experts worldwide have issued calls to action (Expert Committee on the Assessment, Prevention and Treatment of Child and Adolescent Overweight and Obesity, 2007; World Health Organization, 2004). Schools have a unique opportunity to lead the fight on obesity. As hubs in the community, schools have tremendous potential to reach large numbers of children and families. Schools already influence children's eating patterns by providing one or more meals daily. Physical education opportunities provided at school influence children's patterns of physical activity. School personnel, such as teachers and nurses, can deliver programs designed to improve children's health-related knowledge and behaviors (Cole, Waldrop, D'Auria, & Garner, 2006; Davis, Davis, Northington, Moll, & Kolar, 2002).

The CDC has developed an instrument called the School Health Index (SHI), which is designed to aid schools in conducting a comprehensive self-assessment. The SHI can be found at http://apps.nccd .cdc.gov/shi/defaultaspx and will help teachers, administrators, and advisory committees create an action plan for their schools. The self-assessment helps schools become aware of strengths and weaknesses in their policies and programs related to students' health.

Start early—with prevention. We cannot afford to wait—increasingly, obesity is striking younger children. NHANES data reveal that 9.5% of children under the age of 2 are already overweight (National Center for Health Statistics, 2007). Research underscores the need for prevention-focused programs that are implemented early in a child's life (Parsons, Power, Logan, & Summerbell, 1999; Rolland-Cachera, Deheeger, Maillot, & Bellisle, 2006). Prevention strategies can complement existing school readiness programs, such as Head Start and community child care centers. With the trend toward serving younger children in elementary schools and with child care programs being located more commonly on high school campuses, these settings can also be targeted for early prevention programs involving families.

An analysis of the Early Childhood Longitudinal Study (ECLS-K) revealed that children who become overweight between kindergarten and 3rd grade have poorer school outcomes than those who did not become overweight during the early grades. Girls suffered greater consequences than boys, with girls scoring lower on math and reading achievement tests. Teachers reported that overweight girls had less self-control and more social and behavioral problems (Datar & Sturm, 2006). Teachers who notice a weight gain pattern in girls during the early grades can seek collaboration with school health personnel and, together, involve parents. School nurses can give priority to screening young children in the early grades, checking motor development, and paying special attention to the weight status of girls.

Build a school–community partnership. When schools can involve not only parents but also agencies and stakeholders in the community, a strong partnership can evolve. As part of the Healthy Youth for a Healthy Future program, the U.S. Department of Health and Human Services has published checklists of steps for parents, caregivers, schools, teachers, and the community to use to prevent obesity in children. These checklists, located at www.surgeongeneral .gov/obesityprevention/pledges/index.html, are useful in drawing all key stakeholders into the school planning process. Besides offering tangible goals, the program asks parents and teachers to make a firm commitment toward improving their own health, thus becoming good role models for children.

School-community partnerships can be the best use of limited community resources, and they offer a wealth of opportunities for teachers and schools to reach children early. Such partnerships mobilize a variety of health agencies to make services more accessible to families. The concept of a "community school" implies a partnership between the school and the community's health agencies and social services (Blank, Berg, & Melaville, 2006). The American Council for Fitness and Nutrition (ACFN) studied successful grassroots community programs, identifying characteristics of effective obesity prevention programs. ACFN found that programs were most successful when healthful eating and activity topics were taught together in culturally

sensitive ways, using positive approaches that emphasized fun and enjoyment. Programs were goal-oriented and used role models who were supportive and never punitive (ACFN, 2006).

Strategy 3
Promote Positive Psychosocial Development of Children

Teachers and schools can promote children's psychosocial development by:

- Fostering a positive and supportive school context.
- Helping children develop self-regulation.
- Using an authoritative interaction style.
- Providing good modeling and social learning opportunities.

Psychosocial health and school success. Children who are overweight have lower self-esteem, feel less athletically competent, and are more concerned about their appearance and body image (Franklin, Denyer, Steinbeck, Caterson, & Hill, 2006). They are at higher risk for developing psychological problems, such as depression and eating disorders (Allen, Byrne, Blair, & Davis, 2006). Combining overweight and socioeconomic factors, such as low income, appears to increase the risk of mental health problems in young children (Sawyer et al., 2006). Girls who are overweight appear at greater risk of psychosocial problems, including poor self-control, more conduct problems, and difficulty with social acceptance (Datar & Sturm, 2006; Judge & Jahns, 2007).

The relationship between overweight and low achievement is fairly consistent from early childhood through high school. Psychosocial problems associated with childhood obesity add to the complexity of this relationship. Evidence suggests that school culture—the values and norms of students and teachers—also may influence childhood obesity and its psychosocial effects (Crosnoe & Müller, 2004). Fostering a positive and supportive school context can help children avoid psychosocial problems associated with overweight. Support at school is especially important for overweight girls, who are at high risk of psychosocial problems.

Use an authoritative interaction style. Research has identified four interaction styles of parents and teachers: authoritarian, authoritative, indulgent, and uninvolved. Each style varies on two dimensions: sensitivity toward the child and demands for child self-control. Authoritarian teachers are insensitive and coercive, indulgent or permissive teachers make few demands to help children learn acceptable behavior, and uninvolved teachers provide no support or structure for children. The ideal interaction style is authoritative.

Authoritative teachers respond to children and place developmentally appropriate demands on their behavior (Baumrind, 1991). Authoritative interaction helps children develop self-regulation and thereby builds their competence and self-esteem. Authoritative teachers seldom reward children with food and instead offer choices, which may involve more time for physical activities. Children's eating environments are critical social contexts for the development of eating behaviors. When teachers use an authoritative interaction style during supervision of meals and snacks, they encourage children to try new foods or establish good eating patterns through facilitation. In contrast, authoritarian teachers use coercion, such as the admonition to "Clean your plates!," which interferes with children's self-control and responses to their own natural cues (Patrick, Nicklas, Hughes, & Morales, 2005; Rhee, Lumeng, Appugliese, Kaciroti, & Bradley, 2006).

Provide good modeling and social learning opportunities.

Social Cognitive Theory (SCT) demonstrates that children can learn by observing and modeling the behaviors of others. Teachers can be powerful role models who promote healthful eating and physical activity. When teachers eat only healthful meal and snack options in view of children, they provide strong modeling that may influence children to choose more healthful snacks. School settings provide many opportunities for social learning. For example, teachers can apply SCT techniques to increase children's physical activity by encouraging non-competitive physical activities, such as dancing, that emphasize participation and social interaction with peers. SCT techniques are highly effective and commonly used in schools. Teachers, in collaboration with school nurses, dieticians, and health personnel, can help use these techniques to promote children's health (Cole et al., 2006).

Strategy 4
Promote Healthy Diet and Nutrition

Teachers and schools can promote better nutrition by:

- Helping promote healthful eating habits and good nutrition.
- Creating a positive eating environment.
- Increasing food security of families in poverty.
- Respecting cultural preferences of families.

Diet quality and school performance.

Fast food has become a dominant dietary staple of many U.S. children, and fast food consumption results in lower quality diets. Americans have become a fast food culture, with consumption of fat-dense, sugary meals and snacks accepted as the norm in all socioeconomic strata (Bowman, Gortmaker, Ebbeling, Pereira, & Ludwig, 2004; Nestle, 2002; Schlosser, 2001). Among American children who are poor and at high risk of becoming obese, insufficient food is not typically the problem. Rather, poor children in the United States are likely to consume more calories than they need, but the foods they consume are high in fat and sugar and low in nutritional quality. Ironically, food-insecure children who miss meals due to their family's lack of resources are more likely to be obese (Currie, 2005). When a school serves children who have food insecurity, it is important to ensure that families have access to community resources that will improve the diet quality of their children.

The link between diet quality and school performance is consistent and has been reported to hold true across all socioeconomic levels. Children who consume a poor diet that fails to meet recommended guidelines for key nutrients experience difficulty in school. Conversely, children who regularly eat a variety of nutritious foods are more likely to experience success in school (Florence, Asbridge, & Veugelers, 2008; Taras & Potts-Datema, 2005). Teaching children about nutrition and good dietary choices is an important responsibility shared by parents and schools.

Help children acquire healthful eating and lifestyle habits.

Children acquire their preferences for foods very early in life, and changing these preferences becomes progressively more difficult (Nicklas & Fisher, 2003). The mother's food preferences may limit the variety of foods offered to children (Skinner, Carruth, Wendy, & Ziegler, 2002). Family patterns of feeding children and the kinds of foods that parents offer are influenced by cultural heritage (Briefel, Ziegler, Novak, & Ponza, 2006; Kaiser et al., 2003). Unfortunately, children from minority groups are at higher risk for diets that fail to meet recommended guidelines (Mier et al., 2007).

Teachers can successfully deliver curricular lessons aimed at helping children to develop healthful lifestyle habits, such as eating more fruits and vegetables, increasing physical activity, and watching less television (Cole et al., 2006). By preschool, some children have already adopted eating patterns with inadequate nutritional intake of key nutrients, such as iron, zinc, and Vitamin D. It is critical for teachers and parents to encourage children to eat nutrient-rich foods essential for optimal growth and development (Zive, Taras, Broyles, Frank-Spohrer, & Nader, 1995).

Strategy 5
Encourage Physical Activity

Teachers and schools can increase physical activity by:

- Scheduling recommended amounts of physical activity.
- Integrating physical activity into a balanced "whole child" curriculum.
- Reducing sedentary behavior with enriched school environments.

Increase physical activity in the school day.

During this era of emphasis on high-stakes testing and academic accountability, many schools have adopted policies that reduce or eliminate opportunities for PE in favor of increased time for academic subjects. However, no credible evidence exists to support the belief that increasing time in PE during school will have a negative effect on children's academic achievement. To the contrary, evidence shows that increasing time for physical education results in cognitive benefits that may improve children's academic performance (Carlson et al., 2008; Coe, Pivarnik, Womack, Reeves, & Malina, 2006). There appears to be no legitimate justification for reducing physical activity and PE programs in schools. In fact, increasing time for physical activity during the school day is associated with increased academic advantages, especially for girls (Carlson et al., 2008; Datar & Sturm, 2004).

Experts recommend 60 minutes of moderate to vigorous physical activity daily to prevent obesity in children. Elementary schools should provide at least 150 minutes of physical education a week and daily unstructured recess breaks of at least 20 minutes (Expert Committee on the Assessment, Prevention and Treatment of Child and Adolescent Overweight and Obesity, June 8, 2007; National Association for Sport and Physical Education, 2008). For younger children, providing many options for fun, gross motor activities within well-equipped free play environments is essential (Bower et al., 2008; Council on Sports Medicine and Fitness and Council on Health, 2006; Timmons, Naylor, & Pfeiffer, 2007). Environment appears to make a difference in the activity levels of young children. Access to well-equipped playgrounds with diverse features and occasional bouts of more structured activity result in increased physical activity, improved confidence, and better motor skills for young children (Bower et al., 2008; Reilly & McDowell, 2003; Reilly et al., 2006).

Reduce children's sedentary behavior through enriched school environments.

Children's engagement in such sedentary activities as watching television, playing video games, and using computers increases throughout childhood while the time they spend in physical activity drops. It has been reported that by the age of 23 months, 48% of toddlers are viewing two hours of television per day, and the amount of television viewing rises with age (Certain & Kahn, 2002). Not surprisingly, engagement in sedentary options predicts the amount of time spent engaged in physical activity

(Timmons et al., 2007). Consequently, it is critical for teachers to use active instruction integrated into a "whole child" balanced curriculum. Music and movement integrated into academic lessons are attention-grabbing and add extra minutes of physical activity to a child's day. A "move to learn" curriculum approach can significantly increase physical activity of children (Connor-Kuntz & Drummer, 1996; Silence, 2006; Trost, Fees, & Dzewaltowski, 2008).

Conclusion

The sad irony of the testing era is that our zeal to improve children's academic performance has led to a decline in children's health, and childhood obesity rates have risen to dangerously high rates. Paradoxically, some of the school policies adopted to help improve test scores may reduce children's chances of performing well by contributing to their ill health. Clearly, children in poverty, racial and ethnic minorities, and girls in general, have an increased risk of obesity, which might negatively affect their academic achievement. The intent of this article is to raise the consciousness of teachers about this risk and to equip them with strategies for examining school policies and changing practices toward promoting more healthful schools, homes, and community contexts for children. With schools and teachers as key leaders, communities can begin to reverse obesity trends and improve the chances for all children to be successful in school. While much remains to be discovered, mounting research strongly suggests that attention to children's health is critical to improving the school performance and academic outcomes for all children.

References

Allen, K. L., Byrne, S. M., Blair, E. M., & Davis, E.A. (2006). Why do some overweight children experience psychological problems? The role of weight and shape concern. *International Journal of Pediatric Obesity, 1*(4), 239–247.

American Council for Fitness and Nutrition. (2006). *Successful grassroots health and wellness programs: Exploring common traits*. Washington, DC: Author.

Baumrind, D. (1991). The influence of parenting style on adolescent competence and substance use. *Journal of Early Adolescence, 11*(1), 56–95.

Blank, M. J., Berg, A. C., & Melaville, A. (2006). *Growing community schools: The role of cross-boundary leadership*. Washington, DC: Coalition for Community Schools.

Bower, J. K., Hales, D. P., Tate, D. F., Rubin, D. A., Benjamin, S. E., & Ward, D. S. (2008). The childcare environment and children's physical activity. *American Journal of Preventive Medicine, 34*(1), 23–29.

Bowman, S. A., Gortmaker, S. L., Ebbeling, C. B., Pereira, M., & Ludwig, D. S. (2004). Effects of fast-food consumption on energy intake and diet quality among children in a national household survey. *Pediatrics, 113*(1), 112–118.

Briefel, R., Ziegler, P., Novak, T., & Ponza, M. (2006). Feeding infants and toddlers study: Characteristics and usual nutrient intake of Hispanic and non-Hispanic infants and toddlers. *Journal of the American Dietetic Association, 106*(1, Supplement 1), 84.e81–84.e14.

Carlson, S. A., Fulton, J. E., Lee, S. M., Maynard, M., Brown, D. R., Kohl, H. W., et al. (2008). Physical education and academic achievement in elementary school: Data from the Early Childhood Longitudinal Study. *American Journal of Public Health, 98*(4), 721–727.

> # Important Websites to Check Often!
>
> U.S. Department of Agriculture
> www.usda.gov
> American Dietetic Association
> www.eatright.org
> Centers for Disease Control and Prevention
> www.cdc.gov
> Robert Wood Johnson Foundation
> www.rwjf.org
> Kids Health
> www.kidshealth.org
> American Medical Association
> www.ama-assn.org

Centers for Disease Control and Prevention. (2008a). *Contributing factors [electronic version]. Overweight and obesity*. Retrieved July 16, 2008, from www.cdc.gov/nccdphp/dnpa/obesity/contributing_factors.htm

Centers for Disease Control and Prevention. (2008b, May 22, 2007). *Overweight prevalence. Overweight and obesity*. Retrieved July 16, 2008, from www.cdc.gov/nccdphp/dnpa/obesity/childhood/prevalence.htm

Certain, L. K., & Kahn, R. S. (2002). Prevalence, correlates, and trajectory of television viewing among infants and toddlers. *Pediatrics, 109*, 634–642.

Coe, D. P., Pivarnik, J. M., Womack, C. J., Reeves, M. J., & Malina, R. M. (2006). Effect of physical education and activity levels on academic achievement in children. *Medicine and Science in Sports and Exercise, 38*, 1515–1519.

Cole, K., Waldrop, J., D'Auria, J., & Garner, H. (2006). An integrative research review: Effective school-based childhood overweight interventions. *Journal for Specialists in Pediatric Nursing, 11*(3), 166–177.

Connor-Kuntz, F., & Drummer, G. (1996). Teaching across the curriculum: Language-enriched physical education for preschool children. *Adapted Physical Activity Quarterly, 13*, 302–315.

Cook, G. (2005). Killing PE is killing our kids the slow way. *Education Digest: Essential Readings Condensed for Quick Review, 71*(2), 25–32.

Council on Sports Medicine and Fitness and Council on Health. (2006). Active healthy living: Prevention of childhood obesity through increased physical activity. *Pediatrics, 119*, 1834–1842.

Crawford, P. B., Story, M., Wang, M. C., Ritchie, L. D., & Sabry, Z.I. (2001). Ethnic issues in the epidemiology of childhood obesity. *Pediatric Clinicians of North America, 48*(4), 855–878.

Crosnoe, R., & Müller, C. (2004). Body mass index, academic achievement, and school context: Examining the educational experiences of adolescents at risk of obesity. *Journal of Health and Social Behavior, 45*(4), 393–407.

Currie, J. (2005). Health disparities and gaps in school readiness. *The Future of Children, 15*(1), 117–138.

Datar, A., & Sturm, R. (2004). Physical education in elementary school and body mass index: Evidence from the early childhood longitudinal study. *American Journal of Public Health, 24*(9), 1501–1506.

Datar, A., & Sturm, R. (2006). Childhood overweight and elementary school outcomes. *International Journal of Obesity, 30*(9), 1449–1460.

Davidson, F. (2007). Childhood obesity prevention and physical activity in schools. *Health Education, 107*(4), 377.

Davis, S. P., Davis, M., Northington, L., Moll, G., & Kolar, K. (2002). Childhood obesity reduction by school based programs. *The ABNF Journal, 6*, 145–149.

Expert Committee on the Assessment, Prevention and Treatment of Child and Adolescent Overweight and Obesity. (2007, June 8). *Expert committee releases recommendations to fight childhood and adolescent obesity* [Electronic Version]. Retrieved July 30, 2008, from www.aap.org/advocacy/releases/june07obesity.htm

Florence, M. D., Asbridge, M., & Veugelers, P.J. (2008). Diet quality and academic performance. *Journal of School Health, 78*(4), 209–215.

Franklin, J., Denyer, G., Steinbeck, K. S., Caterson, I. D., & Hill, A.J. (2006). Obesity and risk of low self-esteem: A statewide survey of Australian children. *Pediatrics*, 118(6), 2481–2487.

Judge, S., & Jahns, L. (2007). Association of overweight with academic performance and social and behavioral problems: An update from the early childhood longitudinal study. *The Journal of School Health*, 77(10), 672–678.

Kaiser, L. L., Melgar-Quinonez, H., Townsend, M. S., Nicholson, Y., Fujii, M. U., Martin, A. C., et al. (2003). Food insecurity and food supplies in Latino households with young children. *Journal of Nutrition Education and Behavior*, 35(3), 148–153.

Mier, N., Piziak, V., Kjar, D., Castillo-Ruiz, O., Velazquez, G., Alfaro, M. E., et al. (2007). Nutrition provided to Mexican-American preschool children on the Texas-Mexico border. *Journal of the American Dietetic Association, 107*(2), 311–315.

Mirza, N. M., Kadow, K., Palmer, M., Solano, H., Rosche, C., & Yanovski, J. A. (2004). Prevalence of overweight among inner city Hispanic-American children and adolescents. *Obesity Research, 12*, 1298–1310.

National Association for Sport and Physical Education. (2008). *Comprehensive school physical activity programs* [position statement]. Reston, VA: Author.

National Center for Health Statistics. (2007, July 17, 2008). *Prevalence of overweight, infants and children less than 2 years of age: United States, 2003–2004*. Retrieved July 18, 2008, from www.cdc.gov/nchs/products/pubs/pubd/hestats/overweight/overwght_child_under02.htm

Nestle, M. (2002). *How the food industry influences nutrition and health*. Berkeley, CA: University of California Press.

Nicklas, T. A., & Fisher, J. O. (2003). To each his own: Family influences of children's food preferences. *The Journal of Pediatric Nutrition and Development, 102*, 13–20.

Ogden, C. L., Carroll, M. D., & Flegal, K.M. (2008). High body mass index for age among US children and adolescents, 2003–2006. *Journal of the American Medical Association, 299*(20), 2401–2405.

Parsons, T. J., Power, C., Logan, S., & Summerbell, C. D. (1999). Childhood predictors of adult obesity: A systematic review. *International Journal of Obesity, 23*(Suppl 8), S1–S107.

Patrick, H., Nicklas, T. A., Hughes, S. O., & Morales, M. (2005). The benefits of authoritative feeding style: Caregiver feeding styles and children's food consumption patterns. *Appetite, 44*, 243–249.

Reilly, J. J., Kelly, L., Montgomery, C., Williamson, A., Fisher, A., McColl, J. H., Lo Conte, R., Patón, J. Y., & Grant, S. (2006). Physical activity to prevent obesity in young children: Cluster randomised controlled trial. *British Medical Journal, 333*, 1041–1043.

Reilly, J. J., & McDowell, Z. C. (2003). Physical activity interventions in the prevention and treatment of paediatric obesity: Systematic review and critical appraisal. *Proceedings of the Nutrition Society, 62*, 611–619.

Rhee, K. E., Lumeng, J. C., Appugliese, D. P., Kaciroti, N., & Bradley, R. H. (2006). Parenting styles and overweight status in first grade. *Pediatrics, 117*(6), 2047–2054.

Rolland-Cachera, M., Deheeger, M., Maillot, M., & Bellisle, F. (2006). Early adiposity rebound: Causes and consequences for obesity in children and adults. *International Journal of Obesity, 30*(Suppl 4), S11–S17.

Sawyer, M. G., Miller-Lewis, L., Guy, S., Wake, M., Canterford, L., & Carlin, J. B. (2006). Is there a relationship between overweight and obesity and mental health problems in 4- to 5-year-old Australian children? *Ambulatory Pediatrics, 6*(6), 306–311.

Schlosser, E. (2001). *Fast food nation: The dark side of the all-American meal*. Boston: Houghton Mifflin.

Silence, M. (2006). 10 myths about preschool fitness debunked. *American Fitness*, 53–55.

Skinner, J. D., Carruth, B. R., Wendy, B., & Ziegler, P.J. (2002). Children's food preferences: A longitudinal analysis. *Journal for the American Dietetic Association, 102*(11), 1638–1647.

Taras, H., & Potts-Datema, W. (2005). Obesity and student performance at school. *Journal of School Health, 75*(8), 291–295.

Timmons, B. W., Naylor, R-J., & Pfeiffer, K. A. (2007). Physical activity for preschool children—how much and how? *Canadian Journal of Public Health*. Revue Canathenne de Santé Publique, 98 (Suppl 2), S122–134.

Trost, S. G., Fees, B., & Dzewaltowski, D. (2008). Feasibility and efficacy of a "move and learn" physical activity curriculum in preschool children. *Journal of Physical Activity & Health, 5*(1), 88–103.

World Health Organization. (2004). *Obesity: Preventing and managing the global epidemic. Report of a WHO consultation on obesity 1999*. Geneva, Switzerland: Author.

Zive, M. M., Taras, H. L., Broyles, S. L., Frank-Spohrer, G. C., & Nader, P. R. (1995). Vitamin and mineral intakes of Anglo-American and Mexican-American preschoolers. *Journal of the American Dietetic Association, 95*(3), 329–335.

Critical Thinking

1. Choose one of the five strategies for reducing childhood obesity identified in the article. Outline a plan for implementing it in your first year of teaching.

2. Visit one of the websites listed in the article and prepare a report on the recommendations.

SUZANNE M. WINTER is Associate Professor of Early Childhood and Elementary Education, Child and Adolescent Policy Research Institute, The University of Texas at San Antonio.

Why We Should Not Cut P.E.

Eliminate physical education to increase time for reading and math, the theory goes, and achievement will rise. But the evidence says otherwise.

STEWART G. TROST AND HANS VAN DER MARS

Thinking of cutting physical education? Think again. Even as we bemoan children's sedentary lifestyles, we often sacrifice school-based physical education in the name of providing more time for academics. In 2006, only 3.8 percent of elementary schools, 7.9 percent of middle schools, and 2.1 percent of high schools offered students daily physical education or its equivalent for the entire school year (Lee, Burgeson, Fulton, & Spain, 2007).

We believe this marked reduction in school-based physical activity risks students' health and can't be justified on educational or ethical grounds. We'll get to the educational grounds in a moment. As to the ethical reasons for keeping physical activity part of our young people's school days, consider the fact that childhood obesity is now one of the most serious health issues facing U.S. children (Ogden et al., 2006).

School-based physical education programs engage students in regular physical activity and help them acquire skills and habits necessary to pursue an active lifestyle. Such programs are directly relevant to preventing obesity. Yet they are increasingly on the chopping block.

The Assumption: Time in the Gym Lowers Test Scores

No Child Left Behind (NCLB) has contributed to this trend. By linking federal funding to schools' adequate yearly progress in reading and mathematics, NCLB has created an environment in which such classes as physical education, music, and art are viewed as nonessential and secondary to the academic mission of the school.

According to a national study conducted by the Center on Education Policy in 2007, since the passing of NCLB in 2002, 62 percent of elementary schools and 20 percent of middle schools have significantly increased the instructional time they allocate to reading/language arts and math. To accommodate such increases, 44 percent of school districts reported cutting time in such areas as social studies, art, music, physical education, and recess. On average, schools reduced the time allotted to these subjects by more than 30 minutes per day.

But is the assumption that eliminating physical education improves academic performance sound? Not according to the evidence. A comprehensive review of the research shows that academic performance remains unaffected by variations in time allocated to physical education. In fact, in studies that did show physical activity had an effect, increasing instructional time for physical education resulted in *improvements* in academic performance.

> **Is the assumption that eliminating physical education improves academic performance sound? Not according to the evidence.**

The Evidence: P. E. Does Not Hurt—and May Help

In study after study, researchers have concluded that devoting more instructional time to physical education or another in-school physical activity program does not harm academics. Five prominent studies show that students' achievement levels remained unchanged when schools increased or reduced instructional time for physical education.

- Researchers in Australia studied 350 5th graders in seven schools throughout the country. They increased instructional time for physical education for some students by 210 minutes per week.

After 14 weeks, there were no significant differences in math or reading skills between students who received additional physical education instruction and those who completed the standard three 30-minute periods of physical education per week (Dwyer, Coonan, Leitch, Hetzel, & Baghurst, 1983).

- A study in California investigated the effect on academic achievement of an intensive two-year program in seven schools that more than doubled the amount of time elementary students spent in physical education. Neither overall academic achievement nor achievement in language arts and reading were adversely affected (Sallis et al., 1999).

- A study of 214 6th graders in Michigan found that students enrolled in physical education had grades and standardized test scores similar to those of students who were not taking physical education, despite receiving nearly an hour less of daily instruction in core academic subjects (Coe, Pivarnik, Womack, Reeves, & Malina, 2006).

- A study involving 287 4th and 5th graders in British Columbia evaluated the effects of daily classroom physical activity sessions on academic performance. Ten elementary schools participated. Although students who attended schools implementing this program spent approximately 50 more minutes per week in physical activity, their standardized test scores in mathematics, reading, and language arts were equivalent to those of students in control schools (Ahamed et al., 2007).

- A study involving more than 500 Virginia elementary schools examined the effect of *decreasing* time for physical education, music, and art on academic performance. Reducing or eliminating the time students spent in these content areas did not increase academic achievement (Wilkins et al., 2003).

In addition, three major studies indicate that when students participate in physical education, achievement is positively affected for some groups.

- A Canadian study examined the effects on 546 elementary students' academic performance of one additional hour per day of physical education. Students in grades 2 through 6 who received additional physical education earned better grades in French, mathematics, English, and science than did students who received the standard one period per week (Shephard, 1996).

- Studying 311 4th grade students in two schools, Tremarche, Robinson, and Graham (2007) found that students who received 56 or more hours of physical education per school year scored significantly higher on Massachusetts' standardized tests in English and language arts than did comparable students who received 28 hours of physical education per year. There were no significant differences on mathematics scores.

- A longitudinal study by the Centers for Disease Control and Prevention followed two national samples involving 5,316 students from kindergarten to 5th grade. Girls who participated in physical education for 70 or more minutes per week had significantly higher achievement scores in mathematics and reading than did girls who were enrolled in physical education for 35 or fewer minutes per week. Among boys, greater exposure to physical education was neither positively nor negatively associated with academic achievement (Carlson et al., 2008).

The evidence is clear. Decreasing time for physical education does not significantly improve academic performance. Consequently, in an education climate that demands evidence-based instructional practices, the policy of reducing or eliminating school-based physical activity programs cannot be justified.

The Link between Physical Fitness and Academic Performance

The case for sacrificing physical education is further eroded by studies reporting a significant positive relationship between physical fitness and academic performance. In a nutshell, physically active, fit youth are more likely to have better grades and test scores than their inactive counterparts.

Physically active, fit youth are more likely to have better grades and test scores than their inactive counterparts.

National health surveys involving large representative samples of children and teens from the United States, Australia, Iceland, Hong Kong, and the United Kingdom have reported statistically significant positive correlations between physical activity and academic performance (Trost, 2007). One study analyzed data from nearly

12,000 U.S. high school students. Students who reported participating in school-based physical activities or playing sports with their parents were 20 percent more likely than their sedentary peers to earn an *A* in math or English (Nelson & Gordon-Larsen, 2006).

An analysis of fitness testing results from more than 800,000 students in California revealed a significant positive correlation between physical fitness achievement and performance on state achievement tests in reading and mathematics (Grissom, 2005). And in a study conducted in Illinois, children who performed well on two measures of physical fitness tended to score higher on state reading and math exams than low physical performers, regardless of gender or socioeconomic status (Castelli, Hillman, Buck, & Erwin, 2007).

Although the relationship between physical activity and academic performance requires more research, available evidence suggests that the academic mission of schools may be better served by providing *more* opportunities for physical activity. In fact, controlled studies strongly suggest that engaging in physical activity throughout the school day makes students more focused and ready to learn.

The academic mission of schools may be better served by providing *more* opportunities for physical activity.

Research has shown that aerobic exercise can improve memory and executive functioning in school-age youth, especially those who are overweight (Buck, Hillman, & Castelli, 2008; Davis et al., 2007). Drawing on a meta-analysis of more than 40 studies that looked at how engaging in regular physical training affects cognition, Sibley and Etnier (2003) concluded that regular physical activity significantly improves multiple categories of cognitive function in children and adolescents. Researchers found improvements in perceptual skills, IQ, scores on verbal and mathematics tests, concentration, memory, achievement (as measured by a combination of standardized test scores and grades), and academic readiness.

Giving students breaks for physical activity throughout the school day can significantly increase on-task behavior. A study conducted in North Carolina evaluated the effects of a classroom-based program that, for 12 weeks, gave students daily 10-minute breaks for organized physical activity. Researchers observed students in grades K through 5 for 30 minutes before and after each break. On average, the activity breaks increased on-task behavior by 8 percent. Among students who tended to be least

focused in class, the breaks improved on-task behavior by 20 percent (Mahar et al., 2006).

Researchers don't understand well the physiological mechanisms responsible for enhancements in cognition related to physical activity. However, emerging evidence from neuroscience suggests that regular physical activity promotes the growth of new brain cells, stimulates formation of blood vessels in the brain, and enhances synaptic activity or communication among brain cells (Hillman, Erickson, & Kramer, 2008).

What We Can Safely Conclude

The research on the relationship between physical education and academic performance does have limitations. For one, the majority of studies have been conducted at the elementary school level; we need additional studies in middle and high schools. In addition, most studies use the *amount* of time spent in physical education as the key independent variable, without considering the *quality* of instruction. Studies of the effects of in-school physical activity on cognitive functioning also often lack what researchers call ecological validity (transferability of findings). For example, research findings may not transfer to school physical education settings if a study was conducted in a lab or if the type, amount, or intensity of physical activity in the study differed greatly from a typical session in a school gymnasium.

Perhaps most important, we know too little about the effect of in-school physical education on academic performance among students at the highest risk for obesity, including low-income children and those from black, Latino, American Indian, and Pacific Islander backgrounds.

Notwithstanding these limitations, we believe the evidence is sufficiently robust to enable us to draw the following conclusions:

- Decreasing (or eliminating) the time allotted for physical education in favor of traditional academic subjects does not lead to improved academic performance.
- Increasing the number of minutes students spend per week in physical education will not impede their academic achievement.
- Increasing the amount of time students spend in physical education may make small positive contributions to academic achievement, particularly for girls.
- Regular physical activity and physical fitness are associated with higher levels of academic performance.
- Physical activity is beneficial to general cognitive functioning.

Implications for Policymakers

Keeping in mind that overweight and obesity are compromising the health of one-third of U.S. students, we see three clear implications of these conclusions.

Conclusion 1: Policymakers must stop trying to justify cuts to physical education on the grounds that such cuts will strengthen school achievement or, ultimately, the economy.
To be sure, a strong academic education contributes to the future economic health of our society. However, the nation's economic and public health are linked in a delicate balance. It is indefensible to support an education system based primarily on promoting economic productivity in people who will likely be too unhealthy to enjoy whatever benefits come their way.

Conclusion 2: Policymakers, school administrators, and teachers should stop arguing over whether physical education is essential.
Physical education is now crucial for promoting and increasing physical activity for children and youth. Considering the amount of time students spend in school and the generally accepted mandate of schools to model wholesome life choices, the negative effect of keeping students sedentary all day seems obvious. Although school physical education programs cannot single-handedly reverse the trend of weight gain in youth, they can create conditions that help students learn the importance of leading physically active lives—and encourage them to lead such lives.

Conclusion 3: School administrators must aggressively make room for physical education.
Administrators may feel hamstrung because of the current climate, but they can promote healthier schools by recognizing the barriers to out-of-school physical activity that exist for many students, working with physical education staff to maximize opportunities for physical activity for all students, and monitoring what goes on in physical education classes.

Those who help shape the education of children can no longer ignore the evidence about physical activity and academics, as well as the serious negative health consequences of further reducing physical education. Physical activity is crucial to shaping future generations of healthy people. It has a legitimate claim to part of the school day.

References

Ahamed, Y., Macdonald, H., Reed, K., Naylor, P. J., Liu-Ambrose, T, & McKay, H. (2007). School-based physical activity does not compromise children's academic performance. *Medicine and Science in Sports and Exercise, 39*(2), 371–376.

Buck, S. M., Hillman, C. H., & Castelli, D. M. (2008). The relation of aerobic fitness to stroop task performance in preadolescent children. *Medicine and Science in Sports and Exercise, 40*(1), 166–172.

Carlson, S. A., Fulton, J. E., Lee, S. M., Maynard, M., Brown, D. R., Kohl, III, H. W., & Dietz, W. H. (2008). Physical education and academic achievement in elementary school: Data from the early childhood longitudinal study. *American Journal of Public Health, 98*(4), 721–727.

Castelli, D. M., Hillman, C. H., Buck, S. M., & Erwin, H. E. (2007). Physical fitness and academic achievement in third- and fifth-grade students. *Journal of Sport and Exercise Psychology, 29*(2), 239–252.

Center on Education Policy (2007). *Choices, changes, and challenges: Curriculum and instruction in the NCLB era.* Washington, DC: Author.

Coe, D. P., Pivarnik, J. M., Womack, C. J., Reeves, M. J., & Malina, R. M. (2006). Effect of physical education and activity levels on academic achievement in children. *Medicine and Science in Sports and Exercise, 38*(8), 1515–1519.

Davis, C. L., Tomporowski, P. D., Boyle, C. A., Waller, J. L., Miller, P. H., Naglieri, J. A., & Gregoski, M. (2007). Effects of aerobic exercise on overweight children's cognitive functioning: A randomized controlled trial. *Research Quarterly for Exercise and Sport, 78*(5), 510–519.

Dwyer, T., Coonan, W. E., Leitch, D. R., Hetzel, B. S., & Baghurst, R. A. (1983). An investigation of the effects of daily physical activity on the health of primary school students in South Australia. *International Journal of Epidemiology, 12*(3), 308–313.

Grissom, J. B. (2005). Physical fitness and academic achievement. *Journal of Exercise Physiology Online, 8*(1), 11–25.

Hillman, C. H., Erickson, K. I., & Kramer, A. F. (2008). Be smart, exercise your heart: Exercise effects on brain and cognition. *National Review of Neuroscience, 9*(1), 58–65.

Lee, S. M., Burgeson, C. R., Fulton, J. E., & Spain, C. G. (2007). Physical education and physical activity: Results from the School Health Policies and Programs Study 2006. *Journal of School Health, 77*(8), 435–463.

Mahar, M. T., Murphy, S. K., Rowe, D. A., Golden, J., Shields, A. T., & Raedeke, T. D. (2006). Effects of a classroom-based program on physical activity and on-task behavior. *Medicine and Science in Sports and Exercise, 38,* 2086–2094.

Nelson, M. C., & Gordon-Larsen, P. (2006). Physical activity and sedentary behavior patterns are associated with selected adolescent health risk behaviors. *Pediatrics, 117,* 1281–1290.

Ogden, C. L., Carroll, M. D., Curtin, L. R., McDowell, M. A., Tabak, C. J., & Flegal, K. M. (2006). Prevalence of overweight and obesity in the United States, 1999–2004. *Journal of the American Medical Association, 295*(13), 1549–1555.

Sallis, J. F., McKenzie, T. L., Kolody, B., Lewis, M., Marshall, S., & Rosengard, P. (1999). Effects of health-related physical education on academic achievement: Project SPARK. *Research Quarterly for Exercise and Sport, 70*(2), 127–134.

Shephard, R. J. (1996). Habitual physical activity and academic performance. *Nutrition Reviews, 54*(4), S32–S36.

Sibley, B. A., & Etnier, J. L. (2003). The relationship between physical activity and cognition in children: A meta-analysis. *Pediatric Exercise Science, 15,* 243–256.

Tremarche, P., Robinson, E., & Graham, L. (2007). Physical education and its effects on elementary testing results. *Physical Educator, 64*(2), 58–64.

Trost, S. G. (2007). *Active education: Physical education, physical activity and academic performance* (Research Brief). San Diego, CA: Robert Wood Johnson Foundation Active Living Research. Available: www.activelivingresearch.com/alr/alr/files/Active_Ed.pdf

Wilkins, J. L., Graham, G., Parker, S., West-fall, S., Fraser, R. G., & Tembo, M. (2003). Time in the arts and physical education and school achievement. *Journal of Curriculum Studies, 35,* 721–734.

Critical Thinking

1. Write a letter to the principal at the school your first-grade child attends opposing the principal's decision to cut physical education down to once a month so more time can be devoted to academics. Make sure you incorporate the data included in the article in your letter.

2. Develop a list of five key points you can share with parents who are concerned about the lack of physical education in the school their children attend.

Stewart G. Trost is Associate Professor in the Department of Nutrition and Exercise Sciences at Oregon State University in Corvallis; stewart.trost@oregonstate.edu. **Hans van der Mars** is Professor in the College of Teacher Education and Leadership at Arizona State University in Mesa; hans.vandermars@asu.edu.

Adolescent Decision Making

An Overview

Adolescence is a time of great changes that result in desire for autonomy in decision making, and by mid to late adolescence, most individuals have the cognitive abilities to understand and judge risks. Nevertheless, adolescents may lack the psychosocial traits required to consistently make and act upon mature decisions.

BONNIE HALPERN-FELSHER

Adolescence is a time of great and rapid cognitive, psychological, social, emotional, and physical changes. These changes result in a more adult-like appearance, an increased ability to think abstractly, greater need for autonomy and independence, increased social and peer comparison, and greater peer affiliation. These changes typically translate into adolescents' desire to participate in, and eventually lead, their decision making. Learning to make decisions, experiencing related positive and negative consequences, and learning from these outcomes is an important developmental task.

In general, with some cultural variation, adolescents are afforded opportunities to make decisions in a wide range of areas such as friendship, academics, extracurricular involvement, and consumer choices. Simultaneously, their ability to make competent decisions is sometimes called into question because adolescence is also often a time of engagement in risky behaviors, such as using alcohol, tobacco and other drugs, or engaging in risky sexual activity. Often these behaviors represent simple adolescent experimentation, while for a few adolescents these early behaviors represent the first in a line of more harmful behaviors.

This article will provide an overview of adolescent decision making, including definitions of competent decision making, descriptions of decision-making models, and the physical, cognitive, social and emotional influences on adolescent decision making. This article will also discuss implications of adolescent decision making that are relevant to health educators, healthcare providers, policy makers, and adolescent researchers.

Definitions of Competent Decision Making

Definitions of what constitutes a competent decision vary widely. It is important to note that competent decision making refers to the *process* of *how* the decision was made. Competent decision making is *not* determined by the actual behavior or outcome. For example, while adults might disagree with an adolescent's decision to have sex, an adolescent can still demonstrate decision-making competence by showing that he or she has considered and weighed all of the options (e.g., have sex, not have sex, just kiss), risks (e.g., getting pregnant, feeling guilty), benefits (e.g., pleasure), and other key components involved in the decision-making process, as described next.

Since adults are generally considered competent in the eyes of the law, many have used adults as the gold standard against which to compare adolescents. Other definitions of decision-making competence employ a model against which to compare individuals. For example, the legal standards of informed consent stipulate that decisions must be made knowingly; that one must understand all procedures, related risks, and alternative courses of action; and that a person's choice must be made without substantial input or control from others (e.g., Gittler, Quigley-Rick, & Saks, 1990; Poythress, Lexcen, Grisso, & Steinberg, 2006).

Models of Decision Making

Normative models of decision making are commonly used in theory, empirical investigation, and policy to describe competent decision making. These models describe the most common steps that one should take in order to make the most rational decision for the individual. As noted above, competent decision making is defined as the process, not the ultimate decision. Normative models encompass elements similar to the legal definition, with the components articulated in terms of five general processes: 1) identifying all possible decision options; 2) identifying the possible consequences of each option, including all possible related risks and benefits; 3) evaluating the desirability of each consequence; 4) assessing the probability or likelihood that each particular consequence will actually occur, should that course of action be adopted; and 5) combining all information using a decision rule, resulting in the identification of the best option or action. It is important to note that in this decision-making process, it is expected that one not only consider engaging in a particular action, but that one also considers the consequences associated with *not* choosing an event or behavior. This is especially important for adolescents, for whom often the choice is between engaging or not engaging in a risky behavior, both of which have positive and negative outcomes for youth (Beyth-Marom, Austin, et al., 1993; Beyth-Marom & Fischhoff, 1997).

These models of decision making have been typically used to explain engagement in health-compromising or health-promoting behavior, such as tobacco use, alcohol use, sexual behavior, seatbelt use, and so on. Many theories of health behavior have incorporated elements of these normative decision-making models, including the Theory of Reasoned Action (Ajzen, 1985), Theory of Planned Behavior (e.g., Fishbein & Ajzen, 1975), and the Health Belief Model (e.g., Rosenstock, 1974). While specific model components vary across theories, in general these theories assume that adoption of health promoting and health compromising behaviors are the result of a deliberative, rational, and analytical process, with the outcome of this process leading to increased or decreased likelihood of performing the behavior. Specifically, as shown in Figure 1, intentions to engage and actual engagement in health-related behavior is determined by an individual's:

1. assessment concerning both the potential positive and negative consequences of their actions or inactions, such as feeling more relaxed after smoking a cigarette or getting into an accident if driving drunk;
2. perceptions of their vulnerability to those consequences, such as the perceived percent chance that one would get pregnant after having unprotected sex;
3. desire to engage in the behavior despite potential consequences (e.g., I know that I can get an STD from having sex, but it is more important to me to keep my relationship); and
4. perceptions of the extent to which similar others are engaging in the behavior (e.g., most of my friends are using marijuana, so why can't I?).

While these decision-making models have been extremely useful in predicting a number of behaviors, the application of these models is limited when used to explain behaviors involving more irrational, impulsive, or socially undesirable behavior, such as tobacco use. Importantly, when placed within a developmental framework, decision making must be defined as much more than a series of complex cognitive, analytic, and rational processes. Instead, for an adolescent, the process of decision making must be immersed within the set of psychosocial, contextual, emotional, and experiential changes that define adolescence (e.g., Cauffman & Steinberg, 2000). These rational decision-making models are also less applicable to adolescents and some young adults for whom the ability to analytically process information is not yet fully formed (Gibbons et al., in press; Michels, Kropp, Eyre, & Halpern-Felsher, 2005; Reyna & Farley, 2006).

Dual-Process Models

To address the less deliberate and more social, emotional, and reactive process often employed by adolescents, it is useful to consider dual-process models that reflect multiple paths to decision making. One important path reflects the more analytic, rational processing discussed above. In this path, decision making includes deliberate, cognitive processing such as consideration of consequences and perceptions of risks and benefits; attitudes about the behaviors and related outcomes; and injunctive social norms such as what one believes others expect them to do and not do. These factors are expected to predict intentions to behave, with intentions being the most immediate predictor of actual behavior. This path also includes additional decision-making criteria (e.g., Gibbons et al., in press; Reyna & Farley, 2006), such as:

- the willingness to make a decision;
- the capacity to make autonomous decisions;
- searching for, recognizing, and incorporating new information relevant to the decision;
- the ability to judge the value of advice from other sources;
- the willingness to change one's decisions;
- the ability to implement and carry out one's decisions;
- the ability to evaluate and learn from one's decisions;
- the ability to reach decisions one is satisfied with; and
- the ability to make decisions that are consistent with one's goals.

Their ability to make competent decisions is sometimes called into question because adolescence is also often a time of engagement in risky behaviors.

The second path represents the less planned and more experience-based, reactive, and affective path often employed by adolescents. This path includes descriptive social norms such as personal perceptions and misperceptions about the extent to which peers and other important groups are engaging in a behavior as well as images or perceptions regarding others who have engaged or are engaging in a behavior. For example, adolescents are less likely to smoke if they hold negative images that smokers are dirty, wrinkled, and have yellow teeth.

This path also includes variation in adolescents' psychosocial maturity to make decisions (Cauffman & Steinberg, 2000), including the following:

- acknowledgement that adolescents' decisions are often impulsive rather than planned;
- ability to recognize and acknowledge when advice is needed;
- social perspective taking, or the ability to recognize that other people may have a different point of view or set of knowledge from one's own;
- future perspective taking, including the ability to project into the future, to consider possible outcomes associated with various choices, and to plan for the future.

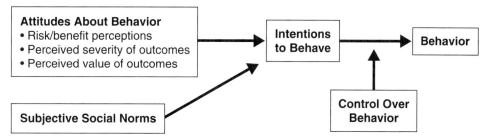

Figure 1 General model of health-related decision making.

These variables are expected to predict willingness to consider a behavior. Willingness to engage is differentiated from the planful notion of intentions. While one may not have an active plan in mind to smoke or have unprotected sex, it is often the case that adolescents find themselves in situations in which they would consider engaging in the behavior even though they were originally committed to avoiding it. Figure 2 depicts these processes.

Adolescents' decisions are often impulsive rather than planned.

A particular focus within all of these models of decision making, especially as they pertain to adolescents, has been the notion of risk perceptions or risk judgments. Individuals' beliefs about the degree to which they are vulnerable to specific negative outcomes are viewed as crucial factors in individuals' decisions concerning health-damaging and health-promoting behaviors. More specifically, theory and research indicates that individuals take risks in part because they believe they are invulnerable to harm, or less likely to experience harm compared to others (e.g., Song et al., in press). More recently, research suggests that in addition to health risks (e.g., lung cancer, pregnancy), adolescents view perceptions of and knowledge about social risks as critical in their decision making. This makes sense when one realizes that adolescence is a time when peers and other social factors play a large role in adolescent development, and therefore their decisions. It has also been recognized that an emphasis on perceived risk alone may be inadequate to predict or change behavior because risk is only part of the behavioral decision-making equation. Adolescents' perceptions of benefits have also been shown to factor into their decision-making equations, and may explain why adolescents engage in particular behaviors despite known risks (e.g., Goldberg, Halpern-Felsher, & Millstein, 2002; Millstein & Halpern-Felsher, 2002; Song et al., in press).

Factors Influencing Adolescent Decision Making
Gender Differences in Decision Making

Adolescent boys and girls do differ in their perceptions of and concerns over health-related risks and benefits. For example, girls are more likely to believe that they can get pregnant from

having unprotected sex, get lung cancer from smoking, and have an accident while driving drunk. In contrast, boys perceive that they are more likely to experience positive outcomes, such as experiencing pleasure from sex. Despite these differences in perceptions, studies have not determined whether the actual decision-making process differs between adolescent boys and girls. The few studies that have examined gender differences in decision making have generally found that the process is remarkably similar (e.g., Michels et al., 2005).

Age Differences in Decision Making

Given the importance of understanding age differences in competent decision making, there are surprisingly few studies that have compared adolescents' and adults' decision making, or examined age differences in decision-making competence within the adolescent years. A review of the small literature base paints a mixed picture regarding adolescent decision-making competency, with some studies suggesting no or few age differences between adolescents and adults, and others showing significant age differences, with younger adolescents demonstrating less competence than older adolescents and/or adults. The age differences reported by these studies suggest that competence continues to increase throughout adolescence and into young adulthood. Furthermore, many of the attributes that are thought to be essential for competent decision making, such as resistance to peer pressure, self-reliance, perspective taking, future time perspective, and impulse control, also increase with age and over time (see, for example, Halpern-Felsher & Cauffman, 2001; Steinberg & Monahan, 2007).

Cultural Variation in Decision Making

Unfortunately, few studies have examined cultural variation in adolescent decision-making competence or decision-making processing.[1] However, there is racial, ethnic, and cultural variation in certain areas of psychosocial development known to influence decision-making capacities, such as autonomy, orientation to the future, and values for academic achievement. Research has also documented that approaches to decision making itself vary. For example, in some cultures (such as some Native American or Asian cultures), decision making is a group dynamic, with much input and directive from the family or other adults. In these decisions, not only is the individual considered, but the impact that the decision and potential outcomes have on family members and others is put into the decision-making equation. In contrast, in other cultures such as in Northern Europe, decision making is more of an individual

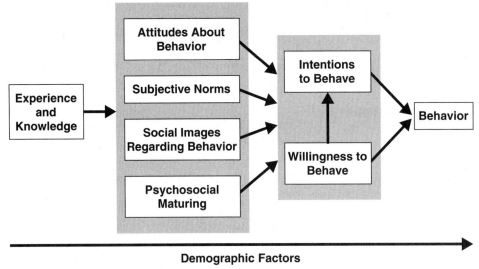

Figure 2 Dual-process model of adolescent decision making: cognitive, psychosocial, and experiential factors.

process, and the impact of the decision on the family is less likely to enter into the decision process. Clearly, in order to successfully understand and encourage competent adolescent decision making, one must have sufficient understanding of the relevant cultural systems that underlie decision making.

The Role of Experience and Knowledge

Adolescents simply have less experience with and knowledge about making decisions than do adults. Thus, adolescents have fewer opportunities to receive feedback, whether positive or negative, for the choices they have made. Experience with and knowledge about choices and obtaining feedback from decisions is especially important when one considers that perceptions of risks and benefits play a critical role in decision making. To the extent that adolescents have less experience with and less knowledge about making decisions, as well as less experience with decision outcomes, they might believe that they are less likely to experience harm and therefore discount harm in the future. Adolescents are also less aware of the cumulative nature of their behaviors as they have received so little feedback (Jacobs, 2004).

The Role of Social/Peer Affiliation

In addition to the vast number of individual-level physical, social, and emotional transformations occurring, adolescence is also defined as a time in which the social environment is also greatly changing. Compared to children, adolescents are less likely to be in structured and supervised settings, and they are more likely to affiliate with similar-aged peers rather than adults. Such environmental and social changes certainly lead to increased opportunities to make decisions and receive feedback. These decisions are also influenced by the normative behavior of adolescents' peers as well as by their perceived norms—that is, the extent to which they believe their peers are engaging in certain behaviors or making decisions. Simultaneous to adolescents' greater peer affiliation, they are also struggling with learning to make more

autonomous decisions, which requires the ability to resist undue influence from others (e.g., Gibbons et al., in press).

> **In order to successfully understand and encourage competent adolescent decision making, one must have sufficient understanding of the relevant cultural systems that underlie decision making.**

Brain Development

There are four lobes in the brain: parietal lobe, occipital lobe, temporal lobe, and the frontal lobe. The frontal lobe is the largest part of the brain, and contains the prefrontal cortex, which is located in front of the brain, behind the forehead. The prefrontal cortex is responsible for executive functions, including cognition, thought, imagination, abstract thinking, planning, and impulse control. In short, the prefrontal cortex oversees critical abilities for decision making. Research has shown that gray matter, or the tissue in the frontal lobe responsible for our ability to think, is reduced or "shed" during the adolescent and young adult years. Simultaneously, a process of myelination occurs, where the white matter in the brain matures to work more efficiently. These processes have been shown to continue through age 25. As such, the aspects of the brain responsible for decision making and impulse control are not fully developed until young adulthood, with males developing even slower than females (see for example, Giedd, 2008).

> **Adolescents' perceptions of benefits have also been shown to factor into their decision-making equations, and may explain why adolescents engage in particular behaviors despite known risks.**

Implications and Importance of Adolescent Decision Making

The questions of how adolescents make decisions and the extent to which adolescents can and do make informed choices have been of great interest to researchers and practitioners in diverse areas including the behavioral sciences, medicine, social work, law, and social policy. A number of compelling forces have motivated this interest. The primary motivator has been the desire to understand and prevent adolescents' engagement in risky behavior. Adolescents' decisions to engage in risky behaviors have led many to conclude that adolescents take risks because they perceive low likelihood of experiencing negative consequences, perceive themselves to be invulnerable to harm, and have poorly developed decision-making skills. Others have interpreted adolescents' risky behavior as evidence of their impulsive nature and that they are easily persuaded by others. As such, intervention and prevention programs focus on enhancing decision-making competence through various knowledge and skill-building efforts. For example, extensive efforts have been made to provide adolescents with information about risks, particularly health risks, to reduce their engagement in risky behavior. Program curricula have also focused on developing adolescents' skills, such as skills to resist peer pressure.

More recently, it has been recognized that rather than solely focusing efforts on disseminating information about the health implications of risky behavior, we need to broaden our discussions to include aspects of decision making most relevant and immediate to youth. For example, we need to acknowledge potential benefits of various risky behaviors, and provide youth with safer ways of obtaining similar benefits or learning how to delay the need or acknowledge and defer the desire for such benefits. We also need to include in the discussion social consequences that adolescents highly value in their decision-making process. For example, studies have shown that adolescents care greatly about whether they are popular or look more grown up, and such desires to gain positive social feedback and avoid negative social consequences influences their decisions (e.g., Ott, Millstein, Ofner, & Halpern-Felsher, 2006). Finally, we need to encourage youth to make conscious decisions and help them set meaningful boundaries for themselves that encompass their goals, relationship desires, and other developmental needs.

Concern over adolescents' decision-making competence is also relevant to adolescents' rights to make certain decisions, such as whether to participate in research studies, obtain medical treatment, or refuse medical treatment. Given results demonstrating adolescents' relative lack of maturity, many of these rights have been greatly restricted by federal, state, and local laws. Such presumptions about the inherent immaturity of adolescents are pervasive within the law. For example, the age of majority is 18 years in all but three states (Alaska, Nebraska, and Wyoming, where the age is 19). Individuals below age 18 are neither expected nor permitted to be responsible for their own welfare. Similarly, research showing that adolescents' decision making is less competent compared to adults or compared to standards set forth in normative decision-making models has led to justifying raising the age at which adolescents accused of violent crimes may be tried as adults (Gittler et al., 1990; Grisso et al., 2003; Poythress et al., 2006).

Summary

In summary, there is great interest and importance in understanding the extent to which adolescents are able to make competent decisions. Adolescence is a time of great changes that result in desire for autonomy in decision making, and by mid to late adolescence, most individuals have the cognitive abilities to understand and judge risks. Nevertheless, adolescents may lack the psychosocial traits required to consistently make and act upon mature decisions. It is thus imperative that we protect adolescents from serious harm while simultaneously providing them with appropriately risky opportunities to practice and grow their decision-making skills.

Note

1. Culture in this case encompasses a broad definition, including race, ethnicity, country of origin, acculturation, language use, economic status, and social status.

References

Ajzen, I. (1985). From intentions to actions. In J. Kuhl & J. Beckman (Eds.), *Action Control from Cognition to Behavior.* New York: Springer-Verlag.

Beyth-Marom, R., Austin, L., Fischhoff, B., Palmgren, C., & Jacobs-Quadrel, M. (1993). Perceived consequences of risky behaviors: Adults and adolescents. *Developmental Psychology, 29,* 549–563.

Beyth-Marom, R., & Fischhoff, B. (1997). Adolescents' decisions about risks: A cognitive perspective. In J. Schulenberg, J.L. Maggs, & K. Hurrelmann (Eds.) *Health risks and developmental transition during adolescence* (pp. 110–135). Cambridge, UK: Cambridge University Press.

Cauffman, E., & Steinberg, L. (2000). (Im)maturity of Judgment in Adolescence: Why adolescents may be less culpable than adults. *Behavioral Sciences & the Law, 18,* 741–764.

Fishbein. M., & Ajzen, I. (1975). *Beliefs, attitudes, intention, and behavior: An introduction to theory and research.* Reading, MA: Addison-Wesley.

Gibbons, F.X., Houlihan A.E., & Gerrard, M. (In Press). Reason and reaction: The utility of a dual-focus, dual-processing perspective on promotion and prevention of adolescent health risk behavior. *British Journal of Health Psychology.*

Giedd, J.N. (2008). The teen brain: Insights from neuroimaging. *Journal of Adolescent Health, 42,* 335–343.

Gittler, J., Quigley-Rick, M., & Saks, M.J. (1990). *Adolescent health care decision making: The law and public policy.* Washington, DC: Carnegie Council on Adolescent Development.

Goldberg, J.H., Halpern-Felsher, B.L., & Millstein, S.G. (2002). Beyond invulnerability: The importance of benefits in adolescents' decision to drink alcohol. *Health Psychology, 21,* 477–484.

Grisso, T., Steinberg, L., Woolard, J., Cauffman, E., Scott, E., Graham, S., et al. (2003). Juveniles' competence to stand trial: A comparison of adolescents' and adults' capacities as trial defendants. *Law and Human Behavior, 27,* 333–63.

Halpern-Felsher, B.L., & Cauffman, E. (2001). Costs and benefits of a decision: Decision-making competence in adolescents and adults. *Journal of Applied Developmental Psychology, 22,* 257–273.

Jacobs, J. (2004). Perceptions of risk and social judgments: Biases and motivational factors. In R.J. Bonnie & M.E. O'Connell (Eds.), *Reducing underage drinking: A collective responsibility* (pp.417–436). Washington, DC: The National Academies Press.

Michels, T.M., Kropp, R.Y., Eyre, S.L., & Halpern-Felsher, B.L. (2005). Initiating sexual experiences: How do young adolescents make decisions regarding early sexual activity? *Journal of Research on Adolescence, 15,* 583–607.

Millstein, S.G., & Halpern-Felsher, B.L. (2002) Perceptions of risk and vulnerability. *Journal of Adolescent Health, 315,* 10–27.

Ott, M.A, Millstein, S.G., Ofner, S., Halpern-Felsher, B.L. (2006). Greater expectations: Adolescents' positive motivations for sex. *Perspectives on Sexual and Reproductive Health. 38,* 84–89.

Poythress, N., Lexcen, F.J., Grisso, T., & Steinberg, L. (2006). The competence-related abilities of adolescent defendants in criminal court. *Law and Human Behavior, 30,* 75–92.

Reyna, V.F., (2006) & Farley, F. Risk and rationality in adolescent decision making. Implications for theory, practice, and public policy. *Psychological Science in the Public Interest 7,* 1–44.

Rosenstock, I.M. (1974). Historical origins of the health belief model. In M.H. Becker (Ed.)1, *The health belief model and personal health behavior* (pp. 1–8). Thorofare, NJ: Charles B. Sclack.

Song, A.V., Morrell, H., Cornell, J.L., Ramos, M.E., Biehl, M., Kropp, R.Y., & Halpern-Felsher, B.L. (in press). Perceptions of tobacco-related high risk and low benefit predict adolescent tobacco initiation. *American Journal of Public Health.*

Steinberg L., & Monahan, K.C. (2007). Age differences in resistance to peer influence. *Developmental Psychology, 43,* 1,531–1,543.

Critical Thinking

1. What does competent decision making look like?

2. Summarize the factors that influence adolescent decision making.

3. Discuss whether it is appropriate to teach adolescents how to make better decisions in a secondary school classroom.

DR. BONNIE HALPERN-FELSHER (HalpernFelsherB@peds.ucsf.edu) is an Associate Professor in the Division of Adolescent Medicine, Department of Pediatrics, University of California, San Francisco. She is also the Associate Director of the General Pediatrics Fellowships, and is a faculty member at UCSF's Psychology and Medicine Postdoctoral Program, The Center for Health and Community, the Center for Tobacco Control Research and Education, the Comprehensive Cancer Center, and the Robert Wood Johnson Scholars Program. **DR. HALPERN-FELSHER** is a developmental psychologist whose research has focused on cognitive and psychosocial factors involved in health-related decision making, perceptions of risk and vulnerability, health communication, and risk behavior; and she has published in each of these areas.

Safe at School

An Interview with Kevin Jennings

Bullied in school, Kevin Jennings now devotes his life to making schools safe for all children.

JOAN RICHARDSON

Kappan: I've had the chance to read your memoir (*Mama's Boy, Preacher's Son*, 2007) but I'm assuming most of my readers haven't done so. I think it's important for them to know a bit about your family and where you came from in order to understand some of your ideas about school safety.

Jennings: I grew up in a very poor family in the rural South. I'm the youngest of five children. I was much younger than my siblings. My dad died when I was eight, leaving my mom with me to raise. My mother was a brilliant woman, one of the smartest people I ever knew. Unfortunately, she grew up a woman in Appalachia in the 1920s, which means that she really never had a chance. She had to drop out of school in 6th grade to pick cotton and tobacco to keep her brothers and sisters alive during the Depression.

She was completely self-educated. She read voraciously. She had a dream that one of her kids would go to college. That was her only big dream in life. As her youngest, kind of her last chance, I became the focus of that dream. So I really can't remember a time when education wasn't held up to me as the most important thing. My doing well in school was *the* most important thing. I don't know quite how she did it. She made it seem completely logical. She made it seem inevitable that, of course, I would go to college and I would go to the best college I could get into. Even though no one in our family had ever done it and we had no money to pay for it. After my father died, my mother cleaned houses, she worked at McDonald's. She got whatever kind of job she could get with a 6th-grade education.

Like a lot of poor people, our lives were very unstable, and we moved pretty frequently. When things were doing a little better, we'd get a more expensive trailer. Then we couldn't afford it and we'd have to give it up and move again. So I ended up attending 11 different schools in four states in the course of my childhood. Yet, somehow, my mother maintained this kind of stability.

When I look back now, knowing what I know about the risk factors for a kid dropping out of school and not getting into

college, I had every single one. But from that experience, I learned that a really strong parent can compensate for a lot of deficiencies. I could very easily have been a dropout instead of a Harvard graduate. I am very aware that there is a very thin line for a lot of kids.

Early Years in School

Kappan: So, what was school like for you when you were young?

Jennings: School was a place that I both loved and hated. I loved it because I loved learning. I hated it because I was targeted at a pretty young age for bullying and harassment. That really started because, in the kind of communities where I grew

---

Mama's Boy, Preacher's Son

One boy in the trailer park, John, took special delight in humiliating me at the bus stop every day. His favorite thing to do was to wait until we got off the bus in the afternoon and, with all the kids on the bus still watching and all the other kids from the trailer park gathered around, order me to sit down on the pavement and not move until he was out of sight. Faced with the seemingly impossible odds against successfully fighting off John and his posse, I would sit down. This brought howls of laughter from the other kids, laughter that echoed as the bus pulled away. Once the bus pulled away, John and his buddies would saunter off, but this didn't mean my ordeal was over. Sometimes, they would hide so that, when I turned the corner, John would scream at me for having gotten up without his permission and would order me to sit a second time. . . . On some days, they would do this repeatedly, so that the half-mile walk to our trailer could take me an hour or more.

up, boys didn't do homework and didn't pay attention in class. Boys watched NASCAR and football. So I really started getting picked on in elementary school, and it was awful.

On Sunday nights, I would get what my mother called that "Sunday funny feeling." We used to always watch the "Wonderful World of Disney" on Sunday nights. When the theme music played at the end of the show, I would start to get very nauseous because I knew the weekend was over and that I had to get up and go to school the next morning.

The worst years for me were 7th, 8th, and 9th grades. In 9th grade, I finally got up the nerve to go and tell the counselor. I said, this is what's happening to me. It's happening every single day. Could you please do something about it?

I'll never forget him saying, well, "which kids is it?" I named some of the kids. They were some of the most popular kids in the school. He replied, "I know those kids. I don't believe they'd do that." It was just clear that nobody was going to be there for me.

Ironically, the only math class I ever did well in was my 9th-grade geometry class. Mr. Cobb was the only teacher who consistently intervened when I was bullied in the class and in the hallways. A lot of my philosophy of education came from Mr. Cobb. I wasn't then and never have been good at math. But because Mr. Cobb made me feel like he cared about me, I would do anything to do well in geometry. It was the first and last A I ever got in a math class.

I think that so much of student achievement comes back to whether young people feel like we care about them, that we value them, that we notice them. We know that when young people are in schools where they have that sense of belonging, they come to school, they do better in school, they graduate from school.

Gender Harassment

Kappan: Was there a point where the harassment turned the corner and became more because of your sexual orientation?

Jennings: I don't think kids actually make that distinction. I think what happens is that they know that terms like the "f" word are just acceptable language in a lot of places. It's the word you can say. Kids say that about anyone they don't like. It's just that, for me, it struck a special terror in my heart because I was struggling with my sexual identity during those years. Like a lot of LGBT (lesbian, gay, bisexual, and transgender) people, I felt "different" from an early age, and the fact that my classmates seemed to be able to sniff it out terrified me.

But I don't think only gay kids get called [uses an anti-gay slur]. Most kids who get called that are actually not gay. Kids are smart. They figure out pretty quickly what behaviors will be tolerated and what behaviors will not be tolerated.

When I was at GLSEN (Gay, Lesbian, and Straight Education Network), our 2005 study found that the three main causes for harassment were appearance, real or perceived gender orientation, and gender identity.

When I started getting called the "f" word in middle school, it wasn't because kids thought I was gay. It's because it's the most damaging word you could use and no one would stop you. For me, it hit home in a particularly frightening manner.

Kappan: Your descriptions of the harassment you experienced are really chilling. It's very disturbing to read them. I find it so interesting that, in spite of a lot of discomfort at school, to put it mildly, you decided to become a teacher and more or less put yourself back into the same situation.

Jennings: I look back at that with a sense of amazement myself. It's ironic that I chose to go back and spend my time in the source of my greatest nightmares. I think there was an unconscious desire to go back and fix it, to make sure that kids didn't go through what I went through.

And there were other reasons. I was raised in a very religious family, and I was taught that to whom much is given, much is expected. The year I was graduating from Harvard in 1985, it felt immoral to me to just take my degree and go out and try to earn a lot of money. I was the first person in my family to ever have this opportunity. To have that opportunity because of incredible sacrifices from people like my mother, I felt like I had a responsibility to give back. The second reason is that a disproportionate number of first-generation college graduates go into education. Partly, that's because it's the only field they know. I didn't know any lawyers, any businessmen, any doctors growing up. I had no conception of what people in those jobs did. I knew what a teacher did, and I could see myself doing it.

Changing Attitudes

Kappan: You hear a lot these days about kids, at least teenagers, being more comfortable with diversity in schools, with students of different races, different ethnicities, different sexual orientations. Do you think that's true, or is there just as much harassment, bullying of students these days as there was during your teenage years?

Jennings: We can't really answer the question of whether there's more or less because there were no scientific studies 30 years ago. It's all based on conjecture.

But when I was at GLSEN, we did find that, if you're an LGBT student, being harassed will be the rule, not the exception for you. There are obviously some advantages and supports for LGBT students today that I didn't have. Teenagers may be more comfortable coming out these days, but being more visible also makes you a bigger target. I felt very alone. I don't think that LGBT kids today feel alone in the same way that I did 30 years ago. But that varies a lot on where they're living and where they're going to school.

Republican Opposition

Kappan: Let's switch focus and talk about the 53 House Republicans who would like to have you fired from your job. (A letter organized by Rep. Steve King (R-Iowa) signed by 52 other House Republicans was sent to President Obama on Oct. 15 demanding that he fire Jennings for "pushing a pro-homosexual agenda" and because he "lacks the appropriate qualifications and ethical standards to serve in this capacity.")

Kevin Jennings

Position: Assistant deputy secretary, Office of Safe and Drug-Free Schools, U.S. Department of Education.

Age: 46.

Education: Bachelor's degree in history, Harvard University, 1985. Joseph Klingenstein Fellow, Teachers College Columbia University, 1993. Master's degree in interdisciplinary studies, Columbia University, 1994. Master's degree in business administration, New York University, 1999.

Professional History: High school history teacher, Moses Brown School, Providence, Rhode Island, 1985–87 and Concord Academy, Concord, Massachusetts, 1987–95. Became faculty advisor to the nation's first Gay-Straight Alliance. Founded the Gay, Lesbian, and Straight Education Network (GLSEN) as a local volunteer group in the Boston area, 1990. Appointed by Gov. William Weld to co-chair the education committee of the Governor's Commission on Gay and Lesbian Youth and was principal author of its report, *Making Schools Safer for Gay and Lesbian Youth: Breaking the Silence in Schools and in Families.* The commission led the fight that made Massachusetts the first state to outlaw discrimination against public school students on the basis of sexual orientation. Executive director, GLSEN, 1990–2008.

Civic Service: Member, board of directors, Harvard Alumni Association. Member, board of trustees, Union Theological Seminary, New York City. President, board, Tectonic Theatre Project. National fundraising chair, Appalachian Community Fund.

Books: Author, *Mama's Boy, Preacher's Son* (Beacon, 2007) and *Always My Child* (Simon & Schuster, 2003); editor, *One Teacher in 10* (Alyson Publications, 2004), *Becoming Visible: A Reader in Gay and Lesbian History for High School and College Students* (Alyson Publications, 1994), and *Telling Tales Out of School: Gays, Lesbians, and Bisexuals Revisit Their School Days* (Alyson Publications, 1998).

Web Site: kevinjennings.com

Jennings: I'm not going to talk about that. I came here to do a job. People can say what they want. I am here to do my job the best that I can.

Kappan: I assume that before Arne Duncan hired you that he was aware that you were gay, aware of where you worked.

Jennings: I think he had read my résumé.

Kappan: So I assume there must have been some anticipation, even expectation that this would happen. I'm curious about the conversations that took place before you joined the Department of Education.

Jennings: The week I was offered the job, I heard the story of Carl Joseph Walker-Hoover, an 11-year-old boy in Springfield, Mass.

Mama's Boy, Preacher's Son

The hardest part was feeling like there was nowhere to turn. Teachers like Mr. Cultrou joined in the harassment; others stood by and let it happen. No one spoke up . . . the relentless daily mocking of the "faggot" was the alpha and the omega of my school day.

He had been repeatedly harassed and bullied by students. I don't know if the school did something that didn't work or if they did nothing at all. But in April, he hung himself with an electrical cord. When I heard that story, I decided that if I was offered the job of making sure that things like that never happened again, it would be profoundly immoral of me to say no. That's why I accepted the offer.

Kappan: Since the letter was sent to President Obama, have there been any other activities since then?

Jennings: Quite honestly, that is not my focus. I'm focused on the work I'm doing. I have not broken stride for one second because of this. I have a very clear set of goals. Everybody knew when I was hired that I had an "agenda." I've been very clear about that from the start.

Kappan: So, what is that agenda?

Jennings: We know that students learn best in a school where they feel truly safe. I am here to make that happen for more kids. What do we mean by safe? Well, to me, a truly safe school goes way beyond just nobody carrying a gun to school. Although that's a given, or at least it should be, although it is not in far too many places. In a truly safe school, you're physically safe, you're emotionally safe. You're not sitting in Mr. Jennings' history class wondering whether you're going to find something written on your locker or if you're going to be called names in the hallway or whether someone is going to try to sell you drugs in the bathroom and therefore you have to "hold it" until you get home. Because if that's what you're thinking about, you're not going to learn history.

Those things are the floor of what we need. Then we also need to make sure that all kids feel like they belong, that all kids feel like they're valued. That is the new, much more comprehensive definition of safe schools under the leadership of Secretary Duncan.

Just as we have standards around academic goals, we need standards around school climate because what gets measured is what gets done. We're only going to put school climate at the priority level it deserves—which to me is at the top—if we have standards around it and start measuring it. And we need a data system so parents know what kind of environment a kid will encounter in a school.

Kappan: So, you want to include this in the Common Core standards?

Jennings: Yes. If we don't get this one right, the other ones don't matter. Right now, they're really focused on the academic standards. This one is much newer. We have to build understanding of the concept first.

At one of the groups where I talked about this, one gentleman said, "I think we have a good climate in our schools. They're all air conditioned now." So we're even using language that some people don't understand.

We're not first up to bat, and I'm not troubled by that. The Common Core movement is right to start on the things where there's already widespread agreement. We're way down the road. That's fine. This is a new field in many ways. We're still fighting over the definition of school climate. But I can promise you it does not include air conditioning.

Once we have standards and a scientific way of measuring school climate, state and local authorities will be able to pinpoint which schools need improvement and implement policies and programs to drive that process.

Kappan: My perception is that there's been a lot of change because of grassroots efforts. Local kids are pushing for change through Gay-Straight Alliances, and parents in groups like PFLAG (Parents, Families, and Friends of Lesbians and Gays) are pushing for that change. Your work at GLSEN helped empower them. Now, you're proposing a very top-down approach. That's very different and presents its own set of problems with school districts. Why make that shift? Why not continue with the grassroots strategy that you've already proven can be successful?

Jennings: You need both. Part of the goal of standards is to empower people at the grassroots. Every parent ought to be able to go on the web to find a building-level safety rating.

Kappan: How's that going to influence change?

Jennings: If you went on the web and saw that your child's school was rated unsafe, my prediction is that you're going to be in somebody's face pretty fast. Right now, parents have no reliable way of knowing how safe their school is for their kids. The truth is that kids don't come home and tell their parents how unsafe their schools are or how unsafe they feel in schools. They're not telling parents, particularly as they get older, that drugs are being sold in the bathroom or that they're being bullied. My mother was the last person to find out that I was being bullied.

Kappan: I have to question your belief that that will work. Plenty of districts and local schools publish report cards with test scores and other indicators about how well kids are learning. But there are still many, many places where parents don't push back and demand academic excellence. What makes you think they'll push back if you tell them schools are unsafe?

Jennings: Safety is very visceral to parents. I said to the Secretary on my first day here that when parents put their kids on the bus in the morning, they ask themselves two questions. Is my child going to be safe? Is my child going to learn? And they ask them in that order.

You're more likely to get an upset parent in your office if the parent perceives that their child is not safe than if they believe their child isn't learning geometry.

Mama's Boy, Preacher's Son

In 7th grade, studying was even more uncool and sports moved from semi-friendly games of kickball at recess to cutthroat games like "smear the queer" in gym class. For the uninitiated, smear the queer is a game where one boy gets the football and all the others try to hit him hard enough to make him fumble, after which another boy picks up the ball and the cycle begins all over. What "physical education" this imparted was unclear to me, unless it was intended as an object lesson in Darwinian survival. . . . On the rare occasions when the ball inexplicably ended up in my hands, my classmates seemed to turn on me with a special relish, screaming "queer" especially loudly as they belted me.

Our school climate system will be based on four pillars. First, of course, we need incident-based data. We need to know about disciplinary suspensions and expulsions. Second, we'll do surveys of students, surveys of families, and surveys of staff. For example, do the families feel like they can go to school and get the information they need about their children? We know that parental engagement is critical to school success.

If parents don't feel engaged with the school, then children won't feel engaged with the school. Finally, there are surveys of the staff. If the staff doesn't feel safe at school, if the staff doesn't feel respected, if the staff doesn't feel supported, how can they support the kids?

This helps empower people at the grassroots because it gives them information that they need and don't have. It actually asks them what they need and what they think and gives them a voice.

If they have a problem, we're going to help them get better. No one in this department believes in unfunded mandates. If we're going to go out the door with new expectations about school climate, it's got to be matched with new resources. The beginning of that is a new grant program coming out of this department where we'll be providing possibly as much as $70 million for investments in school climate projects.

Bullying vs. Guns & Drugs

Kappan: By targeting climate issues and bullying issues, some will suggest that you're really targeting issues that apply most to suburban and rural and small-city districts and not the hard issues of physical violence and drugs in urban districts.

Jennings: School climate to us has several issues. It is not just bullying and harassment. That's one small component of school climate. We want to look at engagement with school. Do kids feel academically challenged? Do they feel like they're wanted at school? Do they have positive relationships with the adults in the schools? Do they have positive relationships with their peers? Second, we want to know from parents whether they have positive relationships with teachers and the principal. Do they feel welcome in the school? Number three is physical safety, which is bullying, harassment, weapons, and substance use. Fourth is the environmental health of the school, by which we mean what's the actual shape of the school. Do they have the books they need, do they have tech support, is there toilet paper in the bathrooms?

All of those components are critical to a healthy school climate. We also propose to develop follow-up surveys. Then we want to drill down into the areas where they have challenges so that we can more closely identify the problem.

What we're trying to develop is a standard that every school should have, whether it's urban, rural, or suburban. There can be one standard, but the solution cannot be one size fits all. Not only do we have to provide funding if we're going to have this new system, we also have to provide solutions. Fortunately, the Office of Safe and Drug-Free Schools has been funding cutting-edge work on solutions at local districts around the country. The solutions are not here in Washington, but we do know where some of the solutions are. We need to do a better job of connecting people to those who have already found the solutions.

This is a commitment to every district in the country and a commitment to helping them address the most salient issue in their community.

Kappan: Why do you think this is the right time for this issue?

Jennings: We have the perfect storm. We have an unprecedented flow of money and an unprecedented feeling of alarm about education. I am not naïve. I don't believe if we have safety standards that schools are going to change overnight. But I do know that what gets measured is what gets done. Over time, it will force this issue onto the agenda. There will always be a role for grassroots activism. What the government can do is to push those ideas along a little faster.

I'm hearing loud and clear from people at the grassroots that they need help with this issue. We can't just crank out standardized tests and expect that will make our schools better. We have to look at everything that a child needs to succeed.

If they're sitting in the classroom and they're hungry, they're not going to learn. If they're sitting in that classroom and they're terrified about what will happen when they try to walk home that afternoon, they're not going to learn.

Kappan: How will you measure your success?

Jennings: If, when I leave office, parents have access to a system that tells them if their children are attending a safe school, I will have succeeded.

The process of change is like a relay race. I have the baton for a few years. My job is to ensure that we're little further ahead in the race and, like a good relay team member, be ready to pass that baton to the next person with a lead toward the end goal of a safe school for every child.

My job is to ensure that the next generation has something to build on. That's how you say "thank you" to those who made sacrifices that allowed you to be where you are. Andy Warhol said, "They always say time changes things, but you actually have to change them yourself." I'm here to help change things.

Critical Thinking

1. What would you include in an assessment of school climate?
2. How should schools address the needs of LGBT youth?

JOAN RICHARDSON is editor-in-chief of *Phi Delta Kappan* magazine.

What Educators Need to Know about Bullying Behaviors

SANDRA GRAHAM

Peer victimization—also commonly labeled *harassment* or *bullying*—is not a new problem in American schools, though it appears to have taken on more epic proportions in recent years. Survey data indicate that anywhere from 30% to 80% of school-age youth report that they have personally experienced victimization from peers, and 10% to 15% may be chronic victims (e.g., Card and Hodges 2008). A generation ago, if we had asked children what they worry most about at school, they probably would have said, "Passing exams and being promoted to the next grade." Today, students' school concerns often revolve around safety as much as achievement, as the perpetrators of peer harassment are perceived as more aggressive and the victims of their abuse report feeling more vulnerable.

In the past 10 years—perhaps in response to students' growing concerns—there has been a proliferation of new studies on school bullying. For example, a search of the psychology (PsycINFO) and Educational Resources Information Center (ERIC) databases using the key words *peer victimization, peer harassment,* and *school bullying* uncovered 10 times more studies from 2000 to 2010 than during the previous decade (about 800 versus 80).

Even though the empirical base has increased dramatically during these past 10 years, many widespread beliefs about school bullying are more myth than fact. I label these beliefs as myths because researchers who study bullies and victims of many different ages and in many different contexts have not found them to be true.

I define peer victimization as physical, verbal, or psychological abuse that occurs in and around school, especially where adult supervision is minimal. The critical features that distinguish victimization from simple conflict between peers are the intent to cause harm and an imbalance of power between perpetrator and victim. This intended harm can be either direct, entailing face-to-face confrontation; indirect, involving a third party and some form of social ostracism; or even "cyber-bullying." Taunting, name-calling, racial slurs, hitting, spreading rumors, and social exclusion by powerful others are all examples of behaviors that constitute peer victimization. My definition doesn't include the more lethal types of peer hostility, such as those seen in the widely publicized school shootings; although some of those shootings may have been precipitated by a history of peer abuse, they remain rare events. My definition emphasizes more prevalent forms of harassment that affect the lives of many youth and that the American Medical Association has labeled a public health concern.

Myth #1: Bullies have low self-esteem and are rejected by their peers.

A portion of this myth has its roots in the widely and uncritically accepted view that people who bully others act that way because they think poorly of themselves. Recall the self-esteem movement of the 1980s whose advocates proposed that raising self-esteem was the key to improving the outcomes of children with academic and social problems. Yet there is little evidence in peer research to support the notion that bullies suffer from low self-esteem. To the contrary, many studies report that bullies perceive themselves in a positive light, often displaying inflated self-views (Baumeister et al. 2003).

Many people also believe that everybody dislikes the class bully. In truth, research shows that many bullies have high status in the classroom and have many friends. Some bullies are quite popular among classmates, which may in part account for their relatively high self-esteem. In our research with middle school students, we have found that others perceive bullies as especially "cool," where coolness implies both popularity and possession of desired traits (Juvonen, Graham, and Schuster 2003). As young teens test their need to be more independent, bullies sometimes enjoy a new kind of notoriety among classmates who admire their toughness and may even try to imitate them.

> Six myths cloud our understanding of bullying behavior in schools and prevent us from addressing the issue effectively.

Myth #2: Getting bullied is a natural part of growing up.

One misconception about victims is that bullying is a normal part of childhood and that the experience builds character. In contrast, research quite clearly shows that bullying experiences increase the vulnerabilities of children, rather than making them more resilient. Victims are often disliked or rejected by their peers and feel depressed, anxious, and lonely (Card and Hodges 2008). Part of this psychological distress may revolve around how victims think about the reasons for their plight. For example, repeated encounters with peer hostility, or even an isolated yet especially painful experience, might lead that victim to ask, "Why me?" Such an individual might come to blame the predicament on personal shortcomings, concluding, "I'm someone who deserves to be picked on," which can increase depressive affect (Graham, Bellmore, and Mize 2006). Some victimized youth also have elevated levels of physical symptoms, leading to frequent visits to the nurse as well as school absenteeism. It is not difficult to imagine the chronic victim who becomes so anxious about going to school that she or he tries to avoid it at all costs. Nothing is character building about such experiences.

Myth #3: Once a victim, always a victim.

Although there is good reason to be concerned about the long-term consequences of bullying, research remains inconclusive about the stability of victim status. In fact, there is much more discontinuity than continuity in victim trajectories. In our research, only about a third of students who had reputations as victims in the fall of 6th grade maintained that reputation at the end of the school year and, by the end of 8th grade, the number of victims had dropped to less than 10% (Nylund, Nishina, Bellmore, and Graham 2007). Although certain personality characteristics, such as shyness, place children at higher risk for being bullied, there are also a host of changing situational factors, such as transitioning to a new school or delayed pubertal development, that affect the likelihood of a child continuing to get bullied. These situational factors explain why there are more temporary than chronic victims of bullying.

Myth #4: Boys are physical and girls are relational victims and bullies.

The gender myth emerges in discussions that distinguish between physical and psychological victimization. The psychological type, often called "relational bullying," usually involves social ostracism or attempts to damage the reputation of the victim. Some research has suggested that girls are more likely to be both perpetrator and target of the relational type (for example, Crick and Grotpeter 1996). Because a whole popular culture has emerged around relationally aggressive girls

Resources

Teaching Tolerance, a project of the Southern Poverty Law Center

Dedicated to reducing prejudice, improving intergroup relations, and supporting equitable school experiences for children. Teaching Tolerance provides free educational materials to teachers. The organization's magazine, *Teaching Tolerance,* is also available free to educators. www.tolerance.org

Office of Safe and Drug-Free Schools

Provides in-depth, online workshops focused on bullying prevention: "Exploring the Nature and Prevention of Bullying." Materials from that workshop are available online. www2.ed.gov/admins/lead/safety/training/bullying/index.html

In addition, clicking on the link for "Resources and Links" will connect you with a lengthy list of relevant organizations, books, web sites, and videos.

Gay, Lesbian and Straight Education Network (GLSEN)

Provides resources and support for schools to implement effective and age-appropriate antibullying programs to improve school climate for all students. www.glsen.org

---

Zero tolerance policies often don't work as intended and can sometimes backfire, leading to increases in antisocial behavior.

(so-called *queen bees* or *alpha girls*) and their victims, putting these gender findings in proper perspective is important. In many studies, physical and relational victimization tend to be correlated, suggesting that the victim of relational harassment is also the victim of physical harassment. Moreover, if relational victimization is more prevalent in girls than boys (and the results are mixed), this gender difference is most likely confined to middle childhood and early adolescence (Archer and Coyne 2005). By middle adolescence, relational victimization becomes the norm for both genders as it becomes less socially accepted for individuals to be physically aggressive against peers. Relational victimization is a particularly insidious type of peer abuse because it inflicts psychological pain and is often difficult for others to detect. However, it's probably a less gendered subtype than previously thought.

Myth #5: Zero tolerance policies reduce bullying.

Zero tolerance approaches, which advocate suspending or expelling bullies, are sometimes preferred because they presumably

> ### How can schools and teachers respond to bullying?
> Adults should intervene whenever they witness a bullying incident. Use bullying incidents as teachable moments to stimulate conversations, not merely as opportunities to punish the perpetrator. Teach tolerance for differences and an appreciation of diversity.

> Bullying experiences make children more vulnerable, not more resilient.

send a message to the student body that bullying won't be tolerated. However, research suggests that these policies often don't work as intended and can sometimes backfire, leading to increases in antisocial behavior (APA Zero Tolerance Task Force 2008). Moreover, black youth are disproportionately the targets of suspension and expulsion, resulting in a racial discipline gap that mirrors the well-documented racial achievement gap (Gregory, Skiba, and Noguera 2010). Before deciding on a discipline strategy, school administrators must consider the scope of the problem, who will be affected, the fairness of the strategy, and what messages are communicated to students.

Myth #6: Bullying involves only a perpetrator and a victim.

Many parents, teachers, and students view bullying as a problem that's limited to bullies and victims. Yet, much research shows that bullying involves more than the bully-victim dyad (Salmivalli 2001). For example, bullying incidents are typically public events that have witnesses. Studies based on playground observations have found that in most bullying incidents, at least four other peers were present as either bystanders, assistants to bullies, reinforcers, or defenders of victims. Assistants take part in ridiculing or intimidating a schoolmate, and reinforcers encourage the bully by showing their approval. However, those who come to aid the victim are rare. Unfortunately, many bystanders believe victims of harassment are responsible for their plight and bring problems on themselves.

Thoughts on Interventions

Educators who want to better understand the dynamics of school bullying will need to learn that the problems of victims and bullies aren't the same. Interventions for bullies don't need to focus on self-esteem; rather, bullies need to learn strategies to control their anger and their tendency to blame others for their problems. Victims, on the other hand, need interventions that help them develop more positive self-views, and that teach them not to blame themselves for the harassment. And peers need to learn that as witnesses to bullying, their responses aren't neutral and either support or oppose bullying behaviors.

Most bullying interventions are schoolwide approaches that target all students, parents, and adults in the school. They operate under the belief that bullying is a systemic problem and that finding a solution is the collective responsibility of everyone in the school. Two recent meta-analyses of research

on antibullying programs suggest that the effects are modest at best (Merrell et al. 2008; Smith et al. 2004). Only about a third of the school-based interventions included in the analyses showed any positive effects as measured by fewer reported incidents of bullying; a few even revealed increased bullying, suggesting interventions may have backfired. These findings don't mean schools should abandon whole-school interventions that have a research base. Instead, the modest results remind us that schools are complex systems and what works in one context may not be easily portable to other contexts with very different organizational structures, student demographics, and staff buy-in. Research on decision making about program adoption reveals that many teachers are reluctant to wholly embrace bullying interventions because they either believe the curriculum doesn't provide enough time and space to integrate such policies or that parents are responsible for developing antibullying attitudes (Cunningham et al. 2009).

Although obvious gains from systemwide interventions may be modest, teachers can take steps on an individual and daily basis to address bullying. First, teachers should never ignore a bullying incident. Because most bullying occurs in "un-owned spaces" like hallways and restrooms where adult supervision is minimal, teachers should respond to all bullying incidents that they witness. A response by a teacher communicates to perpetrators that their actions are not acceptable and helps victims feel less powerless about their predicament. This is especially important because students often perceive school staff as unresponsive to students' experiences of bullying.

Second, when possible, adults can use witnessed bullying incidents as "teachable moments," situations that open the door for conversations with students about difficult topics. For example, teachers may intervene to confront students directly about why many youth play bystander roles and are unwilling to come to the aid of victims, or how social ostracism can be a particularly painful form of peer abuse. At times, engaging in such difficult dialogues may be a more useful teacher response than quick and harsh punishment of perpetrators.

Finally, one meaningful factor that consistently predicts victimization is an individual's differences from the larger peer group. Thus, having a physical or mental handicap or being highly gifted in a regular school setting, being a member of an ethnic or linguistic minority group, suffering from obesity, or being gay or lesbian are all risk factors for bullying because individuals who have these characteristics are often perceived to deviate from the normative standards of the larger peer group. Students also tend to favor the in-group (those who are similar to them) and to derogate the out-group (those who are different). A strong antidote to this tendency is to teach tolerance for differences, an appreciation of diversity, and the value of multiple social norms and social identities co-habiting the same school environment. The effects of teaching tolerance may last a lifetime.

References

American Psychological Association Zero Tolerance Task Force. "Are Zero Tolerance Policies Effective in the Schools? Evidentiary Review and Recommendations." *American Psychologist* 63 (December 2008): 852–862.

Archer, John, and Sarah Coyne. "An Integrated Review of Indirect, Relational, and Social Aggression." *Personality and Social Psychology Review* 9, no. 3 (2005): 212–230.

Baumeister, Roy F., Jennifer D. Campbell, Joachim I. Krueger, and Kathleen D. Vohs. "Does High Self-Esteem Cause Better Performance, Interpersonal Success, Happiness, or Healthier Lifestyles?" *Psychological Science in the Public Interest* 4 (May 2003): 1–44.

Card, Noel, and Ernest V. Hodges. "Peer Victimization Among Schoolchildren: Correlates, Causes, Consequences, and Considerations in Assessment and Intervention." *School Psychology Quarterly* 23, no. 4 (December 2008): 451–461.

Crick, Nicki, and Jennifer Grotpeter. "Children's Treatment by Peers: Victims of Relational and Overt Aggression." *Development and Psychopathology* 8, no. 2 (1996): 367–380.

Cunningham, Charles E., Tracy Vaillancourt, Heather Rimas, Ken Deal, Lesley Cunningham, Kathy Short, and Yvonne Chen. "Modeling the Bullying Prevention Program Preferences of Educators: A Discrete Choice Conjoint Experiment." *Journal of Abnormal Child Psychology* 37, no. 7 (October 2009): 929–943.

Graham, Sandra, Amy Bellmore, and J. Mize. "Aggression, Victimization, and Their Co-Occurrence in Middle School." *Journal of Abnormal Child Psychology* 34 (2006): 363–378.

Gregory, Anne, Russell Skiba, and Pedro Noguera. "The Achievement Gap and the Discipline Gap: Two Sides of the Same Coin?" *Educational Researcher* 39, no. 1 (January 2010): 59–68.

Juvonen, Jaana, Sandra Graham, and Mark A. Schuster. "Bullying Among Young Adolescents: The Strong, the Weak, and the Troubled." *Pediatrics* 112 (December 2003): 1231–237.

Merrell, Kenneth W., Barbara Gueldner, Scott Ross, and Duane Isava. "How Effective Are School Bullying Intervention Programs? A Meta-Analysis of Intervention Research." *School Psychology Quarterly* 23, no. 1 (March 2008): 26–42.

Nylund, Karen, Adrienne Nishina, Amy Bellmore, and Sandra Graham. "Subtypes, Severity, and Structural Stability of Peer Victimization: What Does Latent Class Analysis Say?" *Child Development* 78, no. 6 (2007): 1706–1722.

Salmivalli, Christina. "Group View on Victimization: Empirical Findings and Their Implications." In *Peer Harassment in School: The Plight of the Vulnerable and Victimized,* ed. Jaana Juvonen and Sandra Graham: 39–420. New York: Guilford, 2001.

Smith, J. David, Barry Schneider, Peter Smith, and Katerina Ananiadou. "The Effectiveness of Whole-School Anti-Bullying Programs: A Synthesis of Evaluation Research." *School Psychology Review* 33, no. 4 (2004): 547–560.

Critical Thinking

1. Visit one of the web resource sites noted in the article and write a review of the site for your peers.

2. Which of the myths do you think is most pervasive? What can you do to address it?

3. Should anti-bullying be part of the school curriculum?

4. Summarize steps that teachers can take to address bullying in school.

SANDRA GRAHAM is a professor of education in the Graduate School of Education and Information Studies, University of California Los Angeles.

The Bridge to Character

To help students become ethical, responsible citizens, schools need to cultivate students' natural moral sense.

WILLIAM DAMON

Once when I was a guest on a radio talk show, a parent phoned in to tell us about a school incident that frustrated and disturbed her. A few weeks earlier, the parent had received a curt note from her son's 5th grade teacher informing her that her son had been caught taking lunch money out of his classmates' backpacks. Students in the class had been reporting missing lunch money for some time, and the school finally identified this woman's son as the culprit.

The woman requested a meeting at the school, and the next day she found herself in a room with the 5th grade teacher and an assistant principal who was there in the role of guidance counselor. The woman expressed her dismay at her son's behavior and said that she was determined to see that it never happened again. She then asked how they could work together to give him the message that stealing is wrong.

The teacher and counselor greeted this question with a moment of awkward silence. Then the counselor said something along the lines of, "Well, it's important for you to know that we are speaking with your son about this incident, and we are not referring to it as 'stealing.' We don't want to give your child a self-image as a thief, which could only stigmatize him. Instead, we are calling it 'uncooperative behavior,' and we have explained to him that he will never be popular if he continues to act this way. This approach reflects our professional judgment, and we recommend that you take the same approach and support our efforts."

The mother said that when she tried to discuss the matter with her son, he "just blew it off" by saying, "Don't worry, Mom, the school is handling this." She had no confidence that the boy had learned any kind of indelible lesson from his misconduct.

Now the school, in its well-intended but clumsy way, certainly tried to meet this student where he was, playing on his desire for popularity and social acceptance.

But by consciously avoiding terms like *right, wrong,* and *stealing* (the literal description of the student's deed), the school rejected moral language that could guide the student throughout his life. The message the school offered the boy was instrumental and amoral: You should avoid actions that will make you unpopular. This is hardly a charter for a life of ethical integrity.

The Building Blocks

Morality is a natural part of the human system. Every child begins life with the rudimentary building blocks of character. Four such blocks identified in recent scientific studies are empathy, fairness, self-control, and obligation (Damon, 1992, 1999; Kochanska, Murray, & Harlan, 2000; Thompson, 1998; Wilson, 1993).

Every child begins life with the rudimentary building blocks of character.

Empathy, the capacity to experience another's pleasure or pain, provides the foundation for caring and compassion. Even newborns cry when they hear sounds of crying and show signs of pleasure at happy sounds; by the second year of life, it is common for children to comfort a peer or a parent in distress.

A concern for fairness emerges as soon as children begin playing with friends. When a playmate grabs all the cookies or refuses to relinquish a spot on a swing set, the protest "That's not fair!" is a predictable response, because even very young children understand that they have an obligation to share with others. The child's desire for self-control can be seen in an infant's eagerness to regularize behavior through repetition, rituals, and rules. Obligation expresses itself in children's wishes to follow the directives and expectations of their caregivers.

Yet despite these robust early beginnings, the child's natural moral sense requires nurturing if it is to develop into a mature and reliable commitment to act in a caring and ethical manner. For one thing, the child's initial moral inclinations rely entirely on transient mood states. A flash of anger in a 3-year-old quickly extinguishes any empathy for the playmate who provoked the anger. In addition, the child's early leanings do not come with any program for moral action. We would not want to count on children to create a just social world, as *The Lord of the Flies* by William Golding (Coward-McGann, 1954) illustrated in a chilling way.

The Need for Guidance

In order for children's natural moral capacities to become fully formed character dispositions, their natural empathy must develop into a sustained concern for others, their sense of fairness must grow into a commitment to justice, their desire for self-control must grow into a sense of personal responsibility, and their feeling of obligation must become a determination to contribute to noble purposes beyond the self. Without this kind of growth, the child's early capacities may atrophy or take on grotesque forms.

For example, a counselor working with delinquent youth recalled one homicidal 14-year-old saying that he felt broken-hearted whenever he thought about people cutting down trees for Christmas (Samenow, 1984). This boy had wreaked violence on numerous people without regret, yet he felt sadness for fallen pine trees. The annals of criminal justice are full of such cases, psychopaths who have feelings for a pet or a younger sister but who treat nearly everyone else with absolute callousness.

Adult guidance is an essential ingredient in transforming children's natural moral inclinations into dependable and effective character traits. Education provides the bridge from the natural virtues to lives of ethical integrity and compassion.

All students enter school with a rich and lively morality, stemming from the moral inclinations they were born with and enhanced by their experiences since birth. They care about their family and friends and want to do the right thing. At the same time, they don't always know what the right thing is, and they (like all of us) are capable of selfish, destructive, and dishonorable behavior.

It is the vital responsibility of every school to work with the vigorous moral sense that students bring with them in a way that turns these inclinations into solutions for the ethical challenges students will confront. In a world where parents are not always on the scene and many communities have disintegrated, the bridge from a student's natural moral sense to the student's established moral character runs through the school.

The bridge from a student's natural moral sense to the student's established moral character runs through the school.

Making the Most of Opportunities

The boy who stole lunch money no doubt had a moral sense. He very likely cared about other people in his life, including at least some of his classmates, and he almost certainly understood that losing valued property is painful. When he stole the money, he probably did not think about how his actions caused pain for others. Nor did he take seriously the social laws against stealing. These are insights that any school should be prepared to teach. The boy's behavior provided the school with an opportunity for education about the moral implications of stealing and other antisocial behavior, as well as about the purpose of societal laws. On this chance to score valuable points toward its moral education aims, the school dropped the ball.

In my travels to schools, I have witnessed many similar missed opportunities. The most common of these revolve around cheating and other breaches of academic integrity. Cheating and plagiarism on homework assignments occur with astonishing frequency—I have heard rates as high as 80 percent of students who have done this at least once during high school—yet relatively few schools use such incidents to teach moral awareness.

How can schools teach such awareness? I suggest that they emphasize the following four messages:

1. Cheating is unfair because it gives the cheater an unfair advantage over students who do not cheat.
2. Cheating breaks the trust between student and teacher.
3. Cheating violates the school rules, and rules are necessary for preserving social order and individual rights.
4. Cheating is dishonest behavior, and no one wants to become a person who is known (by self and others) as dishonest.

These four points all connect with students' natural moral capacities: fairness, empathy, social regulation, and self-control. But they also show students how their natural inclinations apply to real-world challenges, such as living up to the code of academic integrity, despite temptations to do otherwise.

In the stealing example that I presented at the outset of this article, the school could have emphasized the *moral*— not just instrumental—reasons why people shouldn't steal. Such moral reasons include respecting the rights of others in the same way that you expect them to respect your rights (the Golden Rule); refraining from disreputable behavior so you will be known as a person of integrity; upholding rules that are necessary for social harmony and justice; and having compassion for peers who need the goods you might steal from them. When a teacher conveys such principles to a student, the teacher conveys both an understanding of how decent societies work and a program for a life of good character.

Considering Student Concerns

The example of the lunch-money thief was a case of a school's stooping to a student's level rather than attempting to elevate it. Rather than show the student how his deed violated important moral norms, the school did little more than validate the idea—already familiar enough in early adolescence—that popularity is desirable.

But at least as common as such mistakes are examples of the opposite sort—that is, schools that pay too little attention to what students know or care about. These schools try to reach students with language that is too removed from their own motives and experiences. In such cases, no bridges at all are built, and the students ignore or misunderstand the schools' messages.

Recently a friend who works with a major state education department showed me the standards that the state currently uses to guide instruction in 8th grade civics. As we read through the document, we both felt abashed at our ignorance of many of the concepts that the standards required. Students were expected to be able to "describe the nation's blend of civic republicanism, classical liberal principles, and English parliamentary traditions" and to "analyze the principles and concepts codified in state constitutions between 1777 and 1781 that created the context out of which American political institutions and ideas developed." We looked at each other in amazement: This is meant for 8th graders, not political science doctoral students!

In all the nuanced treatments of political process and constitutional democracy, it was hard to see what any 13-year-old could connect with. Missing entirely were insights about the kinds of issues that children have experienced: governing play and games through social rules; establishing just solutions when peers disagree; respecting authority (including determining whether authority is legitimate); and obtaining redress for legitimate grievances.

When civics is taught through the lens of a student's own concerns and experiences, it comes to life. For example, the civil rights movement of the 1960s taught thousands of young people—many of whom had experienced discrimination in their own lives—valuable lessons about constructive civic participation and democracy that have lasted them a lifetime (see MacAdam, 1988).

Moral and character education must consist of more than skin-deep efforts that ask students to merely recite virtuous words such as honesty, tolerance, respect, courage, and so on. Moral and character education need to engage students in activities that help them acquire regular habits of virtuous behavior. Such active engagement nurtures students' capacity to make moral choices freely.

Toward an Enduring Moral Sense

Teachers should make the effort to present admirable examples to the young, and they should regularly discuss with students the deep questions of meaning, purpose, and what really matters in life. Our research shows that youngsters learn moral truths by seeing them enacted in the lives of real people and by reflecting on how this informs their own search for direction (Damon, 2009). At the same time, it is essential that teachers help build bridges from students' own lived experiences to their development of a mature moral character.

To accomplish this, teachers must be careful not to lose their students in a barrage of negativity. Character education, in addition to teaching children what not to do (don't lie, don't cheat, don't act disrespectfully, and so on) also must have a positive side, inspiring young people to dedicate themselves to higher purposes. In the long run, it is a sense of positive inspiration that captures students' imaginations.

Charitable work is one way to introduce students to a larger purpose. Research has found that community service programs, especially when combined with reflection about the significance of serving others, are powerful supports for character development (Hart, Atkins, & Donnelly, 2006; Youniss & Yates, 1997).

Another source of inspiration that students are eager to speak about is vocation, which goes beyond working to earn a living (as important as that is). The idea that work can be a calling—a means of using one's skills and talents to contribute to the betterment of the world—is a powerful source of purpose for any student. As a discussion topic, the meaning of work fits naturally into many parts of the school day. Teachers, guidance counselors, and coaches can all take part in helping students develop a sense of vocation.

To fulfill their character education missions, schools should make special efforts to provide students with these sources of inspiration, enabling young people to discover their own admirable purposes. Once young people are committed to truly noble aims, they won't need external injunctions to walk the straight and narrow path.

References

Damon, W. (1992). *The moral child.* New York: The Free Press.
Damon, W. (1999). The moral development of children. *Scientific American, 281,* 72–88.

Damon, W. (2009). *The path to purpose: How young people find their calling in life.* New York: Free Press.

Hart, D., Atkins, R., & Donnelly, T. M. (2006). Community service and moral development. In M. Killen & J. Smetana (Eds.), *Handbook of moral development* (pp. 633–656). Mahwah, NJ: Erlbaum.

Kochanska, G., Murray, K. T., & Harlan, E. T. (2000). Effortful control in early childhood: Continuity and change, antecedents, and implications for social development. *Developmental Psychology, 36,* 220–232.

MacAdam, D. (1988). *Freedom summer.* New York: Oxford University Press.

Samenow, S. E. (1984). *Inside the criminal mind.* New York: Random House.

Thompson, R. A. (1998). Empathy and its origins in early development. In S. Braten (Ed.), *Intersubjective communication and emotion in early ontogeny* (pp. 144–157). Cambridge, UK, and New York: Cambridge University Press.

Wilson, J. Q. (1993). *The moral sense.* New York: Free Press.

Youniss, J., & Yates, M. (1997). *Community service and social responsibility in youth.* Chicago: University of Chicago Press.

Critical Thinking

1. Explain the four natural moral capacities mentioned by Damon.

2. What would you advise the teacher to say to the student taking money from another's backpack? What's problematic with the way she handled it?

3. Using Damon's four points about students' natural moral capacities, how would you address students who are fighting in the halls?

WILLIAM DAMON is Professor of Education at Stanford University and Director of the Stanford Center on Adolescence, Stanford, California; wdamon@stanford.edu.

Academic Instructors or Moral Guides? Moral Education in America and the Teacher's Dilemma

HUNTER BRIMI

Occasionally, a student asks me to write a letter of recommendation or fill out a recommendation form for college. When complying with these requests, I often find that the application requires me to address the issue of the applicant's character or integrity. Most of the time, I know the student well enough, I think, to at least make an educated guess regarding this aspect of him or her. Yet, because I work with approximately one hundred students each term, I rarely feel that I know the candidate that well. Furthermore, although I can attest to a student's academic performance ("She's a dedicated student, a pleasure to teach!") and abilities ("His writing sparkles!"), I generally do not feel as well prepared to make similar judgments about his or her moral character. After all, I teach English; the students' grades depend largely on their acumen as readers, writers, thinkers, and test takers. Unless I have witnessed a memorable act of student dishonesty or cruelty, I have no basis to assume that any of my students possess less than admirable moral character. My assessments involve literature and rhetoric more than they do morals and ethics.

Of course, as an English teacher, I often delve into the topic of moral and ethical behavior as the class explores characters and conflicts in their reading. We talk about the dilemmas that John Proctor faces in *The Crucible* and the actions of *The Return of the Native's* Eustacia Vye. We debate societal issues such as euthanasia and, When I am feeling brave, abortion or gay marriage. I have taught some classes in which I felt that a brief overview of ethical philosophies was prudent. I generally start these discussions with a series of hypothetical situations such as the following:

Your friend, Suzy, comes from a disadvantaged family. Her father died a couple of years ago, and her mother is a verbally abusive alcoholic. Money is scarce. Between classes one day, you see Suzy at her locker, crying. On investigation, you find that she has lost ten dollars that her mother gave

her to buy a coupon book (a school fundraising item) for the family. After talking to her, you walk toward your next class. Along the way, you see Eddie, the school bully, walking toward his next class. You slow down, hoping he will not see you, but he does and he "accidentally" bumps into you. "Excuse me!" he chuckles as you struggle to maintain your balance. As he walks into his classroom, you notice a twenty-dollar bill fall out of his book bag. He has not noticed and neither has anyone else. The bill lies on the floor in front of you. What do you do?

After the kids think about their responses individually, I place them into groups that I have strategically chosen, hoping to generate maximum disagreement. After the groups share their thoughts with the class, I use their feedback to initiate my exposition of ethical and moral theories. I am careful not to espouse one student's viewpoint over another's, preferring to play devil's advocate with every viewpoint.

Over the years, I have heard many students express views that show little regard for ethical behavior. Obviously, a dilemma such as the previous one challenges the students who seek to do the right thing. However, those students do not usually compose the majority of the class. Considering the number of students in my school who belong to churches and youth groups, this surprises me. In fact, during one discussion of chivalry in conjunction with medieval British literature, I asked about whether honor still mattered in today's society. One student summed up the general feeling in the class when he claimed that people negotiate what is right or wrong to get what they need or want. Earlier in the term, the students in this class had discussed heroes in small groups. When one student challenged another's choice of hero because he had an extramarital affair, the other student retorted, "So? Everyone cheats on their wife."

Granted, the views of these students do not speak universally for every student in every classroom in America. But the existence of these attitudes leads me to ponder another hypothetical:

You are a high school English teacher. The quality of your work is measured by your students' performance on county and state standardized tests. Do you spend time on character or moral education? Or do you, in the words of a colleague, "imagine that your students all go home after school, read the Bible, drink milk, and go to bed before ten o'clock"?

According to curricular guidelines, the answer appears to be, "No, you do not teach morality." After all, how does a teacher measure morality? And in a culturally pluralistic society, why would a teacher want to take the chance of forcing his or her views on a captive audience?

Yet, all schools (and societies, for that matter) must have rules for behavior. Freedom cannot be absolute; no one wants chaos. So, even if we do not teach morals, we expect moral behavior. Historically, the key question has been, "How?" How do we generate moral behavior? Perhaps in fear of spewing unwanted religious or philosophical dogma, public schools in America eschew a cognitive approach. Instead, schools take a behaviorist approach, and students learn to act in fear of punishment while hoping for reward.

This reality is the result of an education system that serves a changing population with ever-evolving needs. To best appreciate this phenomenon, we need to consider significant developments in the history of education in America in light of moral education. Then, we must look at the current state of moral education in America.

A History of Moral Education in America
Pre-1800: Religious Morality

The relative emphasis on morals has varied throughout the history of American education, shifting in importance with changes in our perception of what schools should do. In colonial America, educators primarily trained children to act morally and in the confines of religious expectations. Although the goals of schooling gradually evolved from acculturation to producing economically viable students and to training students who could compete in a global economic market, the amount of attention paid to moral education has lessened. The only real constant, in terms of moral education, has been an insistence on a behaviorist approach. Simply put, when it comes to moral values, American policymakers primarily want students to act appropriately, whether they have internalized a real sense of moral virtue or not.

The early history of American education repeatedly tells the story of schools attempting to instill (or force, in some populations) in students a set of values. For example, colonial schools primarily taught the Christian values that the larger adult population promoted (Lickona 1993; Mulkey 1997). One need look no further than the formation of *town schools* in seventeenth century Massachusetts under the "Old Deluder Satan Act" to discover the early reasoning behind schooling (Urban and Wagoner 2004). Religious-based education in the New World so strongly marked the preferences of the time that it survived schools inspired by Enlightenment thinkers (most notably, Benjamin Franklin) who advocated a curriculum aimed at producing practical thinkers (Urban and Wagoner).

The Nineteenth Century: American Protestant Values

In the infancy of the American nation, with Constitutional emphasis on separate church and state, educators departed from a strictly religious view of morality. Instead, the focus shifted to secular notions of virtue that acculturated newcomers to the country. By the 1830s, a steadily growing immigrant population flooded America. Educational policy responded with a curriculum heavy in American values, especially those needed for factory workers (e.g., promptness, respect, and dependability). Aiding this cause were the McGuffey Readers, which focused on the values of the country's earliest patriots, especially George Washington (Ingall 2002). In these stories, we see what Mosier (ctd. in Ingall) deemed a merge between "Christian and middle class ideas" (123).

This idea progressed during Horace Mann's lifetime. Mann, of course, was instrumental in the formation of the *common schools* that passed along broad, Protestant values to a new generation of Americans, including the children of increasingly larger numbers of immigrants. Although teaching religious doctrine was not the main goal of these schools, religion was clearly the basis for the values they sought to instill. This continued into the 1870s, when taxation began to completely support schools and new laws took the Bible out of the classroom (Urban and Wagoner 2004).

We see in this early history of American education the power of the schools to teach students values not solely for the betterment of the individual, but more important, for the stability of the society. Just as willing immigrants were taught the values of their new homeland, so too did Native Americans and black slaves experience indoctrination. Even before *Plessy v. Ferguson* (1896) and *Brown v. Board of Education of Topeka* (1954), the education of blacks in this country had been a muddied subject. Although slaveholders in the early nineteenth century allowed their slaves to attend Sunday school (after all, the promise of freedom in heaven could make the harshness of captivity more endurable), allowing these men and women too much education risked creating a population full of dangerous ideas concerning freedom and natural rights. The worst fears of the masters came to fruition with the Turner Rebellion of 1831 and, subsequently, Sunday schools were off-limits to the slave population (Urban and Wagoner 2004).

The slave population did, however, provide an opportunity for a renaissance of religious-based education. During the Civil War, Union supporters established schools to Christianize newly freed slaves on the islands off of the South Carolina coast (Urban and Wagoner 2004). At the end of the Civil War, the New England Freedman's Aid Society initiated a movement to bring the word of God to the former population. In this movement, New Englanders again journeyed south to instill an ignorant population with their Christian values (Urban and Wagoner).

Those individuals hoping to spread a national code of conduct also targeted Native Americans. By the 1860s, long after early settlers attempted to Christianize the "heathens" in colonial America, reservation day schools were established to bring Native Americans into mainstream culture. By the 1880s, men such as Richard Henry Pratt (founder of the Carlisle Indian School) were establishing boarding schools in which such acculturation could occur more effectively away from the traditions still upheld on reservations (Urban and Wagoner 2004).

1900–60: Bureaucracy and Education for the Economic Good

Although much of the nineteenth century included educational philosophies that worked to stabilize society by instilling certain beliefs into students, educators in the next century were more overtly concerned with producing specific behaviors. The Common School of Mann began to give way to David Tyack's "One Best System," a bureaucratic juggernaut that began grouping students according to age and grade level (Urban and Wagoner 2004). With this new type of school, different values became emphasized. According to Urban and Wagoner, "Punctuality, regularity, obedience, and silence were expected and rewarded" (174). But this is not to say that moral education was completely absent from schools during the early twentieth century. In his Children's Morality Code of 1916, William Hutchins articulated values such as honesty, duty, teamwork, and self-control (Mulkey 1997). Of course, these moral traits did little more than create compliant pupils at school. In a study conducted at the end of the 1920s, Hartshorne and May (ctd. in Beachum and McCray 2005) concluded that the current practices in teaching morality had no positive effect on the moral behavior of students. One of the chief criticisms these researchers made involved the use of direct instruction in the matter (Leming, ctd. in Beachum and McCray).

By the middle of the twentieth century, the country had witnessed a second world war and had begun to shift its educational goals. Although the schools based on the organization of Tyack and the curriculum of *The Cardinal Principles of Secondary Education* report of 1918 addressed issues such as ethical behavior and citizenship, schools after World War II attempted to focus on producing graduates who possessed economic viability. Vocational educator Charles Prosser (ctd. in Urban and Wagoner 2004) proposed a curriculum aimed at giving students the technical skills they would need to survive in the modern world.

By the end of the 1950s, this emphasis on job and life training (coupled with the child-centered philosophies of the Progressives of the 1930s) came under scrutiny. The decade in which the Soviet Union attained nuclear weaponry and sent a satellite into space marked a drastic shift in American education. In 1959, the National Defense Education Act placed the federal government in a policymaking role in the nation's education. Specifically, schools increased efforts in teaching math and science so that American students could compete with their Soviet counterparts (Urban and Wagoner 2004). Character education was not completely abandoned, but it certainly held no real curricular value in comparison with the needs the Soviet threat mandated. In short, modern schools attempted to adapt to modern times. As we can see, as instruments and creations of society, schools emulate their societies.

1960–2000: Attempts at a Revival

The 1960s saw the advent of the values clarification movement. This idea, which researchers Louis Raths, Merrill Harmon, and Sidney Simon (ctd. in Beachum and McCray 2005) spawned, espoused educating students about moral decisions without imposing the teachers' or communities' preferred values. Basically, values clarification required teachers to present hypothetical situations (much like my aforementioned situation) and allow students to discuss possible actions in these situations. The hope was to let students talk their way into a cognitive respect for appropriate moral action.

Values clarification reportedly works well, as exemplified by Lawrence Kohlberg's "Six Stages of Moral Development" (Mulkey 1997). According to this theory, people develop their moral judgment in sequenced stages that range from acting to attain rewards or avoid punishment at the lowest level to acting out of respect for human life at the highest level (Mulkey). Kohlberg believed that students could advance through these ordered steps through discussions such as those proposed by values clarification.

The key to Kohlberg's theory and values clarification lies in students developing through cognitive contemplation of behavior. A student could vicariously experience situations that life might not present him with until several years later. Hypothetically, the student would benefit by having their future behavior meet the standards that the community at large would prefer. Of course, this means that teachers would have to patiently allow all students to express their opinions and work through a thought process that earlier attempts at moral indoctrination circumvented. In other words, instead of telling kids how to act (as was the case in American educational history), teachers would have to rely on the students to discover how to act.

Unfortunately, teachers and researchers discovered that students did not always follow the desired path and move toward desired behaviors. The lack of appropriate guidance and the leeway granted to individual perceptions of acceptable behavior permitted students to justify whatever behavior they felt was desirable. Mulkey (1997) cites William Kilpatrick, who wrote that students learned, "A value is essentially what you like or love to do" (91). Students might stall at or revert to a level of thinking aligned with the second stage of Kohlberg's theory: believing that what is right simply corresponds to what meets their individual needs or desires. Recall my student who accepted infidelity because "everyone cheats on their wives."

So, if allowing students to develop at their own risk does not produce tangible results, what then? The 1980s answer to this question came in the form of a behaviorist approach that William Bennett's renewed emphasis on biblical morality spearheaded, especially through encouraging school prayer (Urban and Wagoner 2004). Although mandatory school prayer represents a gross breach of the Constitutional guarantee of separation of church and state, many state officials in this decade passed laws allowing for moments of silence, tacitly permitting students to pray (Urban and Wagoner). If schools cannot tell kids how to act, officials reasoned, religion certainly could. Hence, encouraging prayer in schools could rejuvenate moral education in youth.

Further evidence of a return to behaviorism lies in the many social programs of the 1980s. The most memorable involved the war on drugs and the "Just Say No" campaign. In the campaign, we see behavior depicted as simply right or wrong. Rather than allowing students to engage in the moral reasoning Kohlberg advocated, they were expected to do what they were told: resist drugs, abstain from sex, or adhere to whatever behavior was deemed correct and appropriate.

Despite these efforts in the 1980s, reform in moral education continued to be a hot topic in the 1990s. In "The Return of Character Education," Thomas Lickona (1993) gave three reasons America should take a renewed interest in the topic. First, he cited a disintegration of the family. He argued, "schools have to teach the values kids aren't learning at home" (8). Next, he detailed startling statistics that indicated depraved teenage behavior. For example, he cited a study from Kikuchi that revealed, in a survey of two thousand sixth through ninth graders, two thirds of the boys and half of the girls felt it was "acceptable for a man to force sex on a woman" when involved in a dating relationship for half a year or more (9). Finally, Lickona called for an increased effort in character education so, as a nation, America could recognize that

> we do share a basic morality, essential for our survival; that adults must promote this morality by teaching the young, directly and indirectly, such values as respect, responsibility, trustworthiness, fairness, caring, and civic virtues; and that these values are not merely

subjective preferences but that they have objective worth and a claim on our collective conscience. (9)

In other words, Lickona advocated a return to a philosophical approach—specifically, an approach that focuses on our Western heritage and Aristotle's virtue ethics.

Lickona (1998) elaborated on this approach in "Character Education: Seven Crucial Issues." He insisted that character consists of virtues, which he defined as "objectively good human qualities such as wisdom, honesty, kindness, and self-discipline" (77). He also wrote that due to their "intrinsic goodness," these "virtues don't change" (77). According to this logic, religious and cultural beliefs should be irrelevant to good behavior. However, good behavior is not a result of simply memorizing the difference between right and wrong.

Lickona (1998) equated virtues with habits; in other words, they are instilled cognitively. He listed three psychological aspects of character. He wrote, "Character must be broadly conceived to encompass the cognitive, affective, and behavioral aspects of morality: moral knowing, moral feeling, and moral action" (78). This means that a student must do more than act according to what is right; he must first know and feel what is right internally. As such, this calls for a much more cognitive approach to moral and character education than what American education has sought in the past two hundred years.

Where Are We Now?

By the end of the 1990s, however, the need for character education appeared at an apex in the wake of the Columbine shootings. Programs such as "Character Counts" and its "Six Pillars of Character" (trustworthiness, respect, responsibility, fairness, caring, and citizenship) came into vogue (Josephson Institute Center for Youth Ethics 2008). The effectiveness of these programs is in doubt, however, halfway through the first decade of the twenty-first century. For one thing, they are not emphasized as viable (i.e., measurable) parts of the curriculum.

This does not mean that curricular and accreditation standards completely ignore moral behavior. For example, the Council on Accreditation and School Improvement, Southern Association of Colleges and Schools (2005) addresses this in its accreditation rubric under "Standard 9: Citizenship" (12). This standard states, "The school helps students develop civic, social, and personal responsibility," and in 9:1, "[the school] fosters and maintains a safe and orderly environment that promotes honesty, integrity, trustworthiness, responsibility, citizenship, self-discipline, and respect" (12). Notice that these standards do not define a curriculum for this matter.

Tennessee, where I currently reside, also does not define a real curriculum for character or moral education, although it does legally provide for its inclusion in Tennessee schools. According to Tennessee Code Annotated 49-6-1007 (a), "The course of instruction in all public schools shall include character education to help each student develop positive values and improve student conduct as students learn to act in harmony with their positive values and learn to become good citizens in their school, community, and society" (Tennessee Department of Education 2005).

Measurement is a key factor. In the new millennium, a discussion of American education cannot take place outside the realm of the No Child Left Behind Act. Measurement lies at the core of this legislation. After all, how do we know students are learning if we cannot measure their learning? So, we have standardized tests that we hope prove what children have and have not learned in their core curricular courses. Morality, however, is not as easy to quantify. Certainly, a school can keep track of its office referrals, suspensions, detentions, and expulsions, but this only documents the worst behaviors of what should be a fraction of the total school population. A student might never step into the principal's office or sit for detention, but he or she may not experience moral growth, either, Staying out of trouble does not equate to becoming a mature moral actor.

Therefore, although we do create curricular standards for moral behavior, assessment may still be difficult. We could look to Britain for an example of a nation that has provisions for religious education and citizenship in its National Curriculum (Department for Education and Skills, and Quality and Curriculum Authority 2005). The Department for Education and Skills and the Quality and Curriculum Authority author a national curriculum that has placed a greater emphasis on moral development since a social crisis of the mid-1990s (McCulloch and Mathieson 1995). The British system divides school children into four key stages that correspond to students' ages. (For example, key stage four includes students age 11–19.) This curriculum includes a section called *personal, social, and health education* in each key stage. In key stage four, students should, among other things, learn "to challenge offending behaviour, prejudice, bullying, racism and discrimination assertively and take the initiative in giving and receiving support" and learn "about the role and responsibilities of a parent, and the qualities of good parenting and its value to family life" (Department for Education and Skills, and Quality and Curriculum Authority 2005, 217). The Office for Standards in Education (2008) enforces these standards through comprehensive inspections and published reports. Narrative reports from this organization summarize the progress of entire schools on these and other standards.

Meanwhile, although American schools do have programs, classes, and assemblies to address issues such as sex education, drug education, personal health, and family living, the amount of accountability is at a much lower standard. One problem is that students do not take these programs seriously. Romanowski (2003) reported that students do not seriously consider such efforts because they are treated like small children during the presentation. He wrote of a test program, "Because of what the students perceived as a simplistic presentation of character traits, they were quick to dismiss the program" (33). He also suggested that some teachers are reluctant to participate or require student participation in this particular program.

Teacher nonparticipation is understandable in an era when we are careful to not impose unwanted beliefs on others. In the early years of the modern education system, neighborhood and common schools could espouse local community standards to students. Yet, with the centralization that occurred after the National Defense Education Act in 1959, decisions about class content lie not in the hands of mainly homogenous communities but instead with bureaucracies that make decisions affecting wide constituencies. Furthermore, cultural pluralism has become widespread, resulting in a paucity of homogenous communities. Under these circumstances, teachers may be wise in choosing not to address moral issues.

Conclusion

Let us return to the original dilemma: What is my role as a teacher in the moral development of students? Perhaps we can learn from the British model. This does not mean that we should promote a set of standards for moral education, and we certainly do not want to devise a rubric to measure such standards. Yet, the British have recognized the plurality that exists in their society. In fact, although the country has a state church, the *Non-Statuary National Framework for Religious Education* of Britain has been drafted with support from a wide range of religious organizations, including Muslims, Hindus, Jews, members of Greek and Russian Orthodox churches, Catholics, and Buddhists. In terms of moral education, then, the country has emphasized universal virtues that allow the schools to teach values in such a way as to avoid conflicts in religious doctrine. Although our American accreditation bodies and curricular documents seek to advocate a similar approach, the general public seems more reluctant to abandon religious ideology for a secular, philosophical approach.

Currently, however, American teachers have little official incentive to engage in much discussion of morality with students. Yet, when we read about crime in our communities, watch a high-speed police chase, or hear the details of a school shooting, we cannot so easily shirk responsibility for assisting students' moral growth. Parents and the wider family should hold the highest degree of responsibility in this matter. However, if they fail, we are perhaps the only barrier left between the students and potentially life-devastating decisions.

References

Beachum, F., and C. McCray. 2005. Changes and transformations in the philosophy of character education in the 20th century. http://www.usca.edu/essays/vol142005/beachum.pdf (accessed November 8, 2005).

Brown v. Board of Education of Topeka, 347 U.S. 483 (1954).

Council on Accreditation and School Improvement, Southern Association of Colleges and Schools. 2005. *Accreditation standards 2005.* http://www.sacscasi.org/region/standards/ SACS_CASI_K-12_Standards_InternetVer.pdf (accessed December 3, 2005).

Department for Education and Skills, and Quality and Curriculum Authority. 2005. *National curriculum handbook,* http://www .dfes.gov.uk/14-19/documents/National%20Curriculum% 20Handbook.pdf (accessed December 3, 2005).

Ingall, C. 2002. Pendulum politics: The changing contexts of Jewish moral education. *Journal of Jewish Education 68* (1): 13–20.

Josephson Institute Center for Youth Ethics. 2008. Character counts! The biggest character education program in the nation. http:// charactercounts.org (accessed October 20, 2008).

Lickona, T. 1993. The return of character education. *Educational Leadership 51* (3): 6–11.

———. 1998. Character education: Seven crucial issues. *Action in Teacher Education* 20:77–84.

McCulloch, R., and M. Mathieson. 1995. *Moral education through English 11–16.* London: David Fulton.

Mulkey, Y. J. 1997. The history of character education. (Character in sport and physical education). *The Journal of Physical Education, Recreation and Dance 68* (9): 35–37.

Office for Standards in Education. 2008. About us. http://www./liu.edu/ cwis/cwp/library/workshop/citapa.htm (accessed April 27, 2008).

Plessy v. Ferguson, 163 U.S. 537 (1896).

Romanowski, M. 2003. Lessons for life. *American School Board Journal 190* (11): 32–35.

Tennessee Department of Education. 2005. *Tennessee character education definition.* http://tennessee.gov/education/sp/ spcharactered/sptca4961007a.htm (accessed December 3, 2005).

Urban, W., and J. Wagoner. 2004. *American education: A history.* 3rd ed. Boston: McGraw-Hill.

Critical Thinking

1. Discuss whether it is appropriate to address adolescent moral judgment in a secondary school classroom.
2. Describe how moral education has evolved throughout history.

HUNTER BRIMI, PhD, teaches high school English in Knoxville, TN.

UNIT 3

Individual Differences among Learners

Unit Selections

Learning Outcomes

After reading this unit, you should be able to:

- Construct a plan to work with students who have emotional or behavioral disorders.
- Discuss strategies to help students with autism be successful in school.
- Share a rationale for implementing universal design in your future classroom.
- Describe the needs of a "twice-exceptional" student.
- Explain perfectionism and how it can be helpful to learning.
- Summarize the challenges gifted students can face.
- Explain how unconscious biases can influence interactions with students.
- State reasons why findings about cultural minorities can be misused.
- Describe a plan to address gender differences for the grade level at which you plan to teach.

Student Website

www.mhhe.com/cls

Internet References

Autism Society
www.autism-society.org

The Council for Exceptional Children
www.cec.sped.org/index.html

Global SchoolNet Foundation
www.gsn.org

International Project: Multicultural Pavilion
www.curry.edschool.virginia.edu/curry/centers/multicultural/papers.html

LD Online
www.ldonline.org

Let 100 Flowers Bloom/Kristen Nicholson-Nelson
www.teacher.scholastic.com/professional/assessment/100flowers.htm

National Association for Multicultural Education
www.nameorg.org

National Attention Deficit Disorder Association
www.add.org

National MultiCultural Institute (NMCI)
www.nmci.org

Tolerance.org
www.tolerance.org

The Individuals with Disabilities Education Improvement Act of 2004 (IDEIA) gives children with disabilities the right to an education in the least-restrictive environment, due process, and an individualized educational program that is specifically designed to meet their needs. Professionals and parents of children with special needs are responsible for developing and implementing an appropriate educational program for each child. The application of these ideas to classrooms across the nation caused great concern among educators and parents when first enacted in 1975. Classroom teachers whose training did not prepare them for working with children who have special needs expressed negative attitudes about mainstreaming. Special resource teachers also expressed concern that mainstreaming would mitigate the effectiveness of special programs for the disabled and would force cuts in services. Parents feared that their children would not receive the special services they required because of governmental red tape and delays in proper diagnosis and placement.

As the laws evolved, the term "inclusion" was introduced in 1991. Inclusion tries to assure that children with disabilities will be fully integrated within the classroom. Many of the above concerns have been studied by psychologists and educators, and their findings have often influenced policy. For example, research has indicated that inclusion is more effective when regular classroom teachers and special resource teacher scollaborate and work cooperatively.

The articles concerning students with exceptional learning needs confront some of these issues. The first two articles address strategies that teachers can use to include students with emotional and/or behavioral learning needs or students with autism in the typical classroom. The article by Margaret Flores addresses issues of universal design and how curriculum and instruction can be designed to benefit all struggling learners.

Other exceptional children are the gifted and talented. These children are rapid learners who can absorb, organize, and apply concepts more effectively than the average child. They often have IQs of 140 or more and are convergent thinkers (i.e., they give the correct answer to teacher or test questions). Convergent thinkers are usually models of good behavior and academic performance, and they respond to instruction easily; teachers generally value such children and often nominate them for gifted programs. There are other children, however, who do not score well on standardized tests of intelligence because their thinking is more divergent (i.e., they can imagine more than one answer to teacher or test questions). These gifted divergent thinkers may not respond to traditional instruction. They may become bored, respond to questions in unique and disturbing ways, and appear uncooperative and disruptive. Many teachers do not understand these unconventional thinkers and fail to identify them as gifted. In fact, such children are sometimes labeled as emotionally disturbed

© Comstock/PictureQuest

or mentally retarded because of the negative impressions they make on their teachers. In addition, some gifted students may have a disability that makes it difficult for them to learn. The first article helps us understand the needs of the "twice-exceptional" student who is both gifted and has a disability. Because of the range of abilities and talents of students identified as gifted, a great deal of controversy surrounds programs for the gifted. Such programs should enhance the self-esteem of all gifted and talented children, motivate and challenge them, and help them realize their creative potential. The articles by Mary Christopher and Jennifer Shewmaker and by Tracy Cross address ways in which the social and emotional needs of gifted students can be met.

The third subsection of this unit concerns student diversity. Just as labeling may adversely affect the disabled child, it may also affect the child who comes from a minority ethnic background where the language and values are quite different from those of the mainstream culture. The term "disadvantaged" is often used to describe these children, but it is negative, stereotypical, and apt to result in a self-fulfilling prophecy whereby teachers perceive such children as incapable of learning. Teachers should provide academically and culturally diverse children with experiences that they might have missed in the restricted environment of their homes and neighborhoods. This section starts off with an article about "blink of an eye" racism and how well-intentioned people, including teachers, can show subtle biases as they interact with minority individuals. The remainder of the articles in this section suggest ways to create culturally compatible classrooms. The first article helps the reader uncover his or her biases, and the others address ways to effectively teach children from different cultures and meet the needs of dialectically diverse students. The last article concerns gender differences in the classroom.

Improving the Way We Think about Students with Emotional and/or Behavioral Disorders

K<small>ELLEY</small> S. R<small>EGAN</small>

Creating a positive classroom setting is exciting for teachers. At the beginning of the school year, before even meeting the students, anticipation mounts and teachers begin to consider every possible detail. The event is much like that of arranging a party. First, the host must consider the environment. She selects the colors, the place settings, and images to post, the seating arrangements, and the visual effects to enhance the setting for all those attending. She also thinks about who will be seated next to each other and considers the structure or flow of the party—when will the band begin to play? And when will the guest of honor make a toast?

Second, unless everyone is aware of her role, a party can be uncomfortable for both the host and the attendees. The primary objective of the party is for everyone to learn more about one another. The host must consider her own role in arranging the party. Will she take the lead and facilitate mingling among those attending while remaining on the periphery of the small groups? Will a best friend or family member be on hand to share in the lofty burden of maintaining a successful event? Or will she want to be the center of the party? And what role should the members of the party take on? Clear, specific details could be described on the invitation—what to bring, what to wear, and the timeframe for the party. Expectations lead to minimal surprises—communicating clearly will govern a successful evening.

Finally, the host considers the food to serve the guests. These choices are endless, and a considerable amount of time is required to learn all the various selections in addition to the essential items that everyone will need to access. Once the host understands the comprehensive list of vendors, she makes a selection after considering each individual's needs. Some may prefer seafood, others may prefer spicy selections or light finger foods. So, the host differentiates according to the preferred eating "style." A stand-up or sit-down event? Plastic dinnerware? Fine china?

And the most obvious preplanning component for a party is to make a list of everyone to invite. How are they selected? The host presumably has a positive relationship with everyone attending her engaging party. However, when those attending are given the option to bring one selected "guest," the host's ability to be proactive in achieving an ideal guest list is affected. The unexpected may drift in, and if so the host may have a nagging concern about the possibility of an unfamiliar guest challenging her harmonious environment. The dynamic will certainly be altered, and some of those attending may be unable to meet the objective of the party. What does the host do? What does a teacher do to maintain a positive learning environment while still supporting a student with an emotional and/or behavioral concern?

We can never fully prepare for the unexpected—be it a party event or a classroom event. Teacher preparation programs provide preservice teachers with evidence-based teaching strategies, skills of behavior management, and various field experiences. The greatest learning however, is acquired the very first year of instruction in the teacher's own classroom. Teaching students with emotional and/or behavioral disorders (EBD) may prove to be the most challenging for preservice teachers. However, when teachers begin to take a proactive role in shaping their perceptions and subsequent behaviors toward a student with EBD, looking closely for the student hiding underneath these behaviors, a positive learning environment and a positive student-teacher relationship ensues. One cannot exist without the other.

The supervision of novice teachers in the field illuminates four considerations that may improve the way we think about students with EBD as members of our positive learning environment: *reflection, relationships, roles,* and *resources.*

1. Before managing the behaviors of others, adults must be able to manage their own. Foremost, a teacher of a student(s) with EBD should be a *reflective* practitioner, that is, she should consider her mindsets, biases, and perceptions of students with EBD.
2. The teacher should develop a *relationship* with every student in order to establish trust and a commitment to the established ground rules.

Party	Classroom
• Decorations, seating, tables, colors, place settings	• Posters, bulletin boards, seating, tables, space, designated areas
• Date, time, space, activities	• Routines, schedule, roles
• Atmosphere, flow, dress code	• Teaching style, groupings, philosophy
• Food	• Curriculum, methods, strategies
• Invitation list	• Grade level, ALL students
• ??Unexpected guests	• Students with EBD

1. Participate thoughtfully
2. Follow directions
3. Use materials appropriately
4. Raise your hand

3. The teacher should strengthen the teacher-student relationship by empowering students with a sense of belonging and clarity in an environment that has clearly defined *roles* for learning, playing, and participating.
4. The teacher should provide and use creative *resources* to support the learning and behavior of the individual with EBD.

Guiding Consideration 1: Reflection

Well-qualified teachers enter the classroom believing that all students should be valued, can learn, and have an innate need to belong. These ideals of the first-year teacher can be diminished when atypical student behaviors surface. Teachers initially trust the practical tools they acquire from preparation programs detailing how to create a positive behavior management system in the classroom. When these tools fail to demonstrate any success with a particular student, teachers may feel inadequate, incompetent, and helpless, often resorting to traditional means of behavior management (i.e., punishment; Sugai & Horner, 2002). They may claim that they have exhausted all tools and therefore find insult to their futile attempts to engage a learner. In fact, high stress and a lack of preparation in the area of behavior management may be a leading contributor to attrition in the field of special education (Billingsley, 2004). When struggling to manage the behaviors of a particular student or class, reflecting on our own perceptions and skills is necessary. A lack of self-awareness may actually lead to problematic student behaviors and negatively affect classroom management and learning (Richardson & Shupe, 2003; Sutherland & Wehby, 2001).

A mindset often preventing the progress of novice teachers is that of "control" versus "manage." Beliefs about behavior will certainly affect how we respond to behavior. Consider that everything a teacher and a student does is behavior—behavior is both purposeful and motivated. For new and experienced teachers, behavior management may be misconstrued as control—a need for fulfilling their own ego. Ego, unfortunately, is often a culprit hindering a positive classroom environment. Reflecting and considering our own ego is a task central in life but is particularly salient in the classroom, where power can sometimes

validate our self-efficacy beliefs. No one can *control* another individual's behavior. However, we as teachers can attempt to *manage* student behaviors.

When a teacher is struggling with a particular student behavior or an emotional concern, she should look critically at the behavior a student displays—assess the pattern of the situation and determine the function of the behavior, collect objective data, and consider replacement behaviors. Practical and reputable solutions have been developed by the Center on Positive Behavioral Interventions and Supports. Positive behavioral interventions and supports (PBIS) feature evidence-based interventions and supports across varying levels of intensity and settings (e.g., districtwide, statewide, schoolwide, classroomwide, and individually) to prevent the development and intensification of problem behaviors and subsequently maximize academic success for all students (National Technical Assistance Center on Positive Behavior Interventions and Supports, 2008). For students with EBD or students with characteristics similar to those of a child with EBD, the behavioral management systems may need to be individualized. See boxes, "What Are Positive Behavioral Interventions and Supports (PBIS)?" and "What Is a Functional Behavioral Assessment (FBA) and What Is a Behavioral Intervention Plan (BIP)?"

Thoughtful reflection and productive collaborations with individuals in the school building (e.g., counselors, behavioral specialists, special educators) allow teachers to become engaged in this diagnostic process rather than reluctant to work with a particular child and/or resistant to the possibility of change.

Another response would be to start reflecting within—closely examine the established mindsets and perceptions one may have about a child who appears unmotivated with a low self-concept, a negative attitude, or a reluctance to participate. The teacher's preconceptions and ego should be removed from the equation—the child's reaction is not necessarily about the teacher. Children with EBD often display their hurt outwardly to others without discretion as to the recipient of their anxiety or aggression. Focusing on our own reaction is manageable and productive in effecting change in others. The psychoeducator Nicholas Long embraces the notion of adjusting teacher behavior with the Conflict Cycle paradigm. (The conflict cycle is a component of one theoretical model to explain challenging behaviors. Multiple approaches should be considered when working with students with EBD).

The Conflict Cycle model (Figure 1) asserts that students with EBD tend to come to the school environment with irrational beliefs—beliefs that are grounded in their personal experiences and poor self-concept (Long & Morse, 1996). These beliefs persist, causing the stress to affect their thoughts and feelings. Their irrational thoughts foster their feelings, yet the teacher tends to enter their world only when the child's thoughts and feelings enfold into an exhibited behavior. Students with EBD

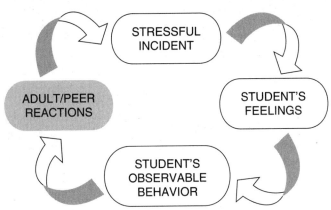

Figure 1 Conflict cycle.

are characterized by internalizing (e.g., anxiety, fear, depression, social withdrawal) and externalizing behaviors (e.g., aggression, overactivity, noncompliance, and delinquency; Coleman & Webber, 2002). During the child's time of crisis, teachers have the ability to feed into the student's irrational beliefs (e.g., ALL teachers are against me) or choose to manage their behaviors and proceed in a different direction. With the goal of maintaining a positive learning environment, a teacher can alter her response to a student with EBD and choose to not perpetuate the cycle of irrational beliefs of the child. Depending on the individual situation, such responses may include providing clear choices for the child, planned ignoring, providing the child with a direction and then moving away, and/or reminding the child of his goals. Our responses are most effective when there is an established relationship with a child and when we free ourselves from our own ego. Looking beyond the child's veil of surface behaviors, we may proceed with an empathic way of thinking.

Guiding Consideration 2: Relationships

A frequent adult reaction to conflict in classrooms is to redirect a child and to deliver expectations. Choosing words with care is essential because one comment can create or destroy a positive student relationship. A student's self-control, social competence, and even academic performance can often indicate the depth of the interpersonal relationship between the child and the teacher(s) in the school (Murray & Greenberg, 2006). Students with EBD are characterized by their inability to develop and maintain positive interpersonal relationships with others. Peers may reject them, and their reputations may precede them from one grade to the next. No one can argue that positive energy can empower others. For example, increasing the rate of a teacher's behavior-specific praise to a child with EBD can increase the ontask behavior of that child (Sutherland, Wehby, & Copeland, 2001).

The teacher of a child with EBD has the task of building trust with that student. Trust can be fostered by the teacher's sincerely demonstrating that she/he values the child, provides for their needs, and sets them up for success. The child should know that despite all misgivings on a particular day, the next day is anew and the routine and the trust will persist.

What Are Positive Behavioral Interventions and Supports (PBIS)?

Elementary and high schools in more than 30 states and the District of Columbia have employed features of PBIS in order to reduce problem behaviors and enhance learning environments. The Office of Special Education Programs (OSEP) funded Technical Assistance Center on Positive Behavioral Interventions and Supports (PBIS) provides methods to teach staff and all students how to establish behavioral expectations (school-wide and/or individually), acknowledge appropriate behavior, use ongoing data to make decisions, and establish a continuum of consequences for violating behavioral expectations. PBIS has been positively associated with a decrease in discipline referrals, an increase in instructional time, and an increase in perceived school safety (Sugai & Horner, 2006). The state of Maryland reports that 467 schools trained to use features of PBIS attribute their successful implementation to the investment in technical assistance, staff development activities, and behavior support coaches (Barrett, Bradshaw, & Lewis-Palmer, 2008).

Although elements of PBIS suggest a positive impact for students in both general and special education, the federal government has mandated that those students with individualized educational programs (IEPs) receive a functional assessment of behavior. Problematic behaviors of students tend to be progressive throughout schooling and given the significance of discipline problems and aggression in schools, the federal government has mandated that student IEPs should include a functional behavioral assessment (FBA) with a proactive positive behavioral intervention plan (BIP; Individuals With Disabilities Education Act, 2004).

The teacher of a child with an emotional and/or behavioral concern has the task of building trust with that student.

Students with EBD have a low self-concept, and despite attempts of teachers to overflow their insatiable buckets with positive reinforcement, they often continue to seek more. This need can be exhausting for teachers considering class size and schedules—and the reality that one individual cannot be a solid figure for every student. Just like teachers, children are only human; relating to just one adult may be all they are able to do initially. Consider finding at least one other adult who can connect with that student—someone who will provide his time, energy, and care.

Teachers and facilitators of the classroom environment should also arrange opportunities for students with EBD to develop positive relationships with their peers. Identifying these students'

What Is a Functional Behavioral Assessment (FBA) and What Is a Behavioral Intervention Plan (BIP)?

An FBA is a process in which a team of individuals (a) identifies a problematic behavior to target and (b) observes the environmental events that precede and follow the behavior in order to develop a hypothesis statement as to why the problematic behavior is occurring (Scott, Anderson, & Spaulding, 2008). An example of a hypothesis statement may resemble the following cloze example from Scott et al.: "In [description of a specific routine], when [antecedent] occurs, the student will [explicit behavior observed]. When this happens, [consequences] occurs. Thus, the function of the behavior is [specific function of behavior is described]."

When an effective hypothesis is formed, the team may then act on the design and execution of a BIP, sometimes referred to as a behavioral support plan. The design of the BIP, very much contingent on the effectiveness of the FBA, is fluid in its development, with the ultimate goal being to teach an alternative skill or replacement behavior to the targeted problem behavior (Maag & Katsiyannis, 2006). Maag and Katsiyannis emphasize that the BIP include a summary of the findings from the generated hypothesis, a clear description of the operationalized behavior (include the type of data used to evaluate the behavior), a summary of all modifications to the plan, instructional strategies, positive and differential consequences, and future replacement behaviors.

teacher. This reluctance is a reflection of limited academic achievement across all areas of instruction and again, a reflection of such students' irrational beliefs—for example, "I will not succeed at this math test because I am horrible at math." Accurate assessment of a student's ability enables a teacher to plan for and design the optimal role for him that can contribute to a positive experience.

In addition, clarity of expectations for everyone's role supports the success of student learning. Cooperative learning methods (i.e., peer tutoring, peer-assisted learning strategies) of instruction have been conducive to positive social and academic outcomes for participants with disabilities, as in this role, they overcome many obstacles to learning when provided structured student roles and an opportunity to learn with others (Ginsburg-Block, Rohrbeck, & Fantuzzo, 2006). When using cooperative learning methods, teachers should support students with EBD by verbally rehearsing the routines of all individuals involved. Posting a visual reminder of the sequenced tasks to be followed supports students' clear understanding of the expectations. All students can use such a posted listing not only for self-regulation but for assisting peers as well.

Communicated expectations, both verbalized and displayed visually, support students with EBD. A teacher can support all students when she provides a visual schedule for each school day, refers to it, and uses it to share what is expected in the environment. Task-analyzing this support system means to also provide an agenda for each lesson within that school day (Figure 2). Students with EBD may need even further supports by hearing the expectations of each activity within an individual lesson. Frequent reminders and a system of referring back to these posted and verbalized expectations can act as anchors for classroom teachers to minimize behavioral disruptions that can lead instruction and focus astray. Communicated expectations limit surprises and reinforce everyone's learning.

Academic and behavioral self-regulatory techniques are specific tools used to support and empower students who respond to structure and routine. These techniques include self-monitoring checklists with a written guide that cues the student to complete sequenced steps of a specific task (Reid, Trout, & Schartz, 2005). Students can take a role in planning for their day, recording the events of the day, and even making self-evaluations of their performance. Frequent and consistent feedback encourages desired behaviors and empowers students as they gain skills of independence.

strengths can give them unique roles in the classroom so that they are perceived positively by others in their community of learners. Every arrangement made should be carefully thought out with the intent of optimal success. If a child has difficulty understanding integers, teach them. If a child has difficulty with spelling, provide him with tools to support this area. If a child has difficulty with social skills, teach them social skills, model them, and provide opportunities for the child to generalize these skills. Educating is about making connections and teaching others how to do so.

Guiding Consideration 3: Roles

The roles of the teacher and the student in a classroom need clarity. From one lesson to the next, the roles vary; For example, a cooperative group exercise establishes very different roles for the teacher and the students in comparison with a direct instruction lesson. Likewise, roles vary during an interactive writing lesson versus an independent writing exercise. An accurate assessment of a student's ability is necessary when establishing the roles of both teacher and student. Often, students with EBD are reluctant to perform independently of the

Guiding Consideration 4: Resources

Just as food selection is a crucial component of a party's success, the resources teachers use can be a crucial component of a harmonious classroom setting—of rich learning. Selected resources can enhance or alter student learning. A "resource" is a broad term that certainly varies from one county to the next and sometimes from one school to the next. However, one consistency is that any student identified with EBD will have an IEP, and this documentation is the first step when identifying resources for the student to be successful in the classroom. The

(Check off items as they occur.)

Objective: To measure and draw right, acute, and obtuse triangles using the appropriate tools.

1) Find an angle in 2 minutes and TAG IT! ☐

2) Motivate: Geo Riddle mania ☐

3) Group Roles – Share Job Tasks ☐

4) SMART BOARD class review ☐

5) Group TRY It! ☐

6) Respond in Math Journals ☐

7) Wrap-up ☐

Figure 2 A visual self-monitoring checklist for a lesson's agenda.

modifications and accommodations provided on the student's IEP support his access to the general curriculum. Such modifications may include adapting the length or type of paper-pencil tasks, using assistive technology, and/or permitting intermittent breaks while a student is working on a particular task.

The IEP will also indicate other individuals who will be working with this student—individuals who are rich resources for the teacher to use to best meet the needs of the student. For example, the student may be receiving services from a school counselor or services from a speech and language therapist. Although consultation and collaboration among personnel within special education is routine, the notion can be somewhat challenging to translate into practice. Often, individuals may be underutilized. Any individual who interacts with a student is a resource. When defeat feels just around the corner and the teacher has tried everything to engage the child, communicating with a parent, a counselor, another teacher, or the art/music/physical education teacher may bring new insight into the situation.

Resources commonly used by teachers include consumable materials, basal readers, textbooks, and/or programmatic materials (e.g., SRA/Corrective Reading, Englemann et al., 1999; Read Naturally®, 2001; Step Up to Writing®, 2007). Many research-based commercialized programs are adopted by the county, so teachers may or may not have options about using all or components of the specified program. However, teachers generally have autonomy when selecting methods of instruction. Varying the methods of instruction and employing differentiated curriculum enhancements (i.e., mnemonics, text-structure analysis, peer tutoring, sample practice; Scruggs & Mastropieri, 2007) can ensure that the teacher is meeting the needs of diverse learners in the classroom. Creative materials that support the vast methods of instruction are one way to accommodate student preference for perceptual input. The four modalities of perceptual input include visual, auditory, and the often underutilized kinesthetic and tactile modalities. Children with EBD are often resistant to paper-pencil tasks and respond favorably to hands-on

activities that involve active participation and experiential learning. Integrating a variety of methods tends to foster the internalization of new material for students with disabilities in contrast with more traditional modes of instruction (e.g., science content, Scruggs & Mastropieri; social studies content, Spencer, Scruggs, & Mastropieri, 2003).

A third resource to consider is yourself! Self-evaluation is often used to promote teacher introspection and to identify the crucial aspects of teaching. Teacher behavior, such as asking high-quality questions and providing positive praise, affects student behavior and can result in increased on-task behavior and lower levels of inappropriate behavior (Good & Brophy, 1994; Kauchak & Eggen, 2007; Sutherland & Wehby, 2001). Self-evaluation seems pertinent if we have the student's interest in mind. For example, teachers can record frequency data on the occurrences of positive reinforcement in the classroom, occurrences of opportunities to respond, and additional teacher behaviors that may encourage or suppress productive learning environments. Feedback is central to the process of learning any skill, and because teaching is often conducted in isolation, teachers may need to generate this feedback in creative ways.

Just as we would consider how to collect data regarding the function of a student's behavior, the same tools can be used for self-evaluation. For example, teachers may audiorecord 20 to 30 minutes of a classroom session, videotape a 50-minute lesson, and/or ask another teacher to observe her classroom. An audiorecording could monitor the use of language—perhaps the teacher's most powerful tool in the classroom (e.g., How often am I praising Jamal? Do I ask Mary multiple questions back to back? Do I frequently elicit student responses?).

Whether you are the host of a party or the lead teacher of a lesson, the desired outcome should be a positive experience for everyone. When teachers consider reflection, relationships, roles, and resources, not only are students with EBD supported, but all students are given the opportunity for high achievement. All participants enjoy the party.

References

Barrett, S. B., Bradshaw, C. P., & Lewis-Palmer, T. (2008). Maryland state-wide PBIS initiative systems, evaluations, and next steps. *Journal of Positive Behavior Interventions, 10,* 105–114.

Billingsley, B. (2004). Special education teacher retention and attrition: Critical analysis of the research literature. *Journal of Special Education, 38,* 39–55.

Coleman, M. C, & Webber, J. (2002). *Emotional and behavioral disorders: Theory and practice* (4th ed.). Boston: Allyn & Bacon.

Englemann, S., Becker, W., Camine, L., Eisele, J., Haddox, P., Hanner, S., Johnson, G., Meyer, L., Osborn, J., & Osborn, S. (1999). *Corrective Reading Series.* Columbus, OH: McGraw-Hill.

Ginsburg-Block, M. D., Rohrbeck, C. A., & Fantuzzo, J. W. (2006). A meta-analytic review of social, self-concept, and behavioral outcomes of peer-assisted learning. *Journal of Educational Psychology, 98(4),* 732–749.

Good, T. L., & Brophy, J. E. (1994). *Looking in classrooms* (6th ed.). New York: HarperCollins.

Individuals With Disabilities Education Act of 2004, 20 U.S.C. 1401–82 (2004).

Kauchak, D. P., & Eggen, P. D. (2007). *Learning and teaching: Research based methods* (5th ed.). Boston: Pearson.

Long, N. J., & Morse, W. C. (1996). *Conflict in the classroom.* (5th ed.) Austin, TX: Pro-Ed.

Maag, J. W, & Katsiyannis, A. (2006). Behavioral intervention plans: Legal and practical considerations for students with emotional and behavioral disorders. *Behavioral Disorders, 31,* 348–363.

Murray, C., & Greenberg, M. T. (2006). Examining the importance of social relationships and social contexts in the lives of children with high-incidence disabilities. *Journal of Special Education, 39(4),* 220–233.

National Technical Assistance Center on Positive Behavior Interventions and Supports. (2007). Retrieved June 1, 2008, from www.PBIS.org/main.htm

Read Naturally® Repeated Reading Program. (2001). St. Paul, MN: Read Naturally, Inc.

Reid, R., Trout, A. L., & Schartz, M. (2005). Self-regulation interventions for children with attention-deficit hyperactivity disorder. *Exceptional Children, 71,* 361–378.

Richardson, B. G., & Shupe, M. J. (2003). The importance of teacher self-awareness in working with students with emotional and behavioral disorders. *TEACHING Exceptional Children, 36,* 8–13.

Scott, T. M., Anderson, C. M., & Spaulding, S. A. (2008). Strategies for developing and carrying out functional assessment and behavior intervention planning. *Preventing School Failure, 52,* 39–49.

Scruggs, T. E., & Mastropieri, M. (2007). Science learning in special education: A case for constructed versus instructed learning. *Exceptionality, 15,* 57–74.

Spencer, V., Scruggs, T. E., & Mastropieri, M. A. (2003). Content area learning in middle school social studies classrooms and students with emotional and behavioral disorders: A comparison of strategies. *Behavioral Disorders, 28,* 77–93.

Step Up to Writing®. (2007). Longmont, CO: Sopris West Educational Services.

Sugai, G., & Horner, R. H. (2002). Introduction to the special series on positive behavior support in schools. *Journal of Emotional and Behavioral Disorders, 10,* 130–135.

Sugai, G., & Horner, R. H. (2006). A promising approach for expanding and sustaining school-wide positive behavior support. *School Psychology Review, 35,* 245–259.

Sutherland, K. S., & Wehby, J. H. (2001). The effect of self-evaluation on teaching behavior in classrooms for students with emotional and behavioral disorders. *Journal of Special Education, 35,* 161–171.

Sutherland, K. S., Wehby, J. H., & Copeland, S. R. (2001). Exploring the relationship between increased opportunities to respond to academic requests and the academic and behavioral outcomes of students with emotional and behavioral disorders. *Journal of Emotional and Behavioral Disorders, 22(2),* 113–121.

Critical Thinking

1. Summarize the four guiding considerations for providing a positive learning environment for students with emotional and/or behavioral disorders.
2. Using the conflict cycle model, how can you intervene in a student's irrational aggressive outburst against another student?
3. Explain what is meant by positive behavioral interventions and supports and how they can enhance learning environments.

KELLEY S. REGAN (CEC VA Federation), Assistant Professor of Special Education, College of Education and Human Development, George Mason University, 4400 University Drive MS IF2. Office: Krug Hall IIIA. Fairfax, VA 22020 (e-mail: kregan@gmu.edu).

Sam Comes to School: Including Students with Autism in Your Classroom

DIANA FRIEDLANDER

Sam's first day of school was different from everyone else's. He walked into the brightly lit, cheerful classroom and quickly became engrossed in the faint whirring of an overhead fan. Chewing on his shirtsleeve, he began rocking and humming. His eyes darted from the welcome message the teacher had printed on the board to posters of color words and days of the week and names printed above each cubby, avidly reading each word and trying to make sense of this new world. Whereas most of the children were eager to meet their teacher and classmates, Sam did not notice them or the other adults in the classroom. Sam's autism created an invisible barrier around him, protecting him from the social world of the classroom and allowing him to find comfort in familiar sounds, symbols, and patterns. At times, however, the barrier was not enough and other stimuli sent him into a panicky terror.

Autism: A Social Disorder

Autism is one of a group of developmental disorders called Autism Spectrum Disorders (ASDs). ASDs include a wide continuum: Autism, Pervasive Development Disorder, Asperger's Syndrome, Fragile X Syndrome, and Obsessive Compulsive Disorder (Cohen and Volkmar 1997). Researchers are beginning to understand the genetic components of autism, which affects about 1 in 166 children born in the United States (Frombonne 2007). This frequency is put in perspective by the statistical knowledge that only 1 in 800 babies is born with Down Syndrome (Centers for Disease Control and Prevention 2006).

Most children diagnosed with an ASD have difficulty in social areas, such as picking up cues from their environment and the ability to form typical relationships. Language is another area of difficulty. Although children with an ASD may have adequate expressive language, sometimes beyond their years, receptive language may be compromised. Sensory integration is another troublesome spot. Students with an ASD can have difficulty regulating input into their central nervous system, resulting in sensitivity to touch, sound, taste, or smell. Sam once told a story of how he caught a snake after hearing it slither.

When a child is diagnosed with autism, a lack of social or emotional reciprocity in his or her classroom experience causes the most impact. The social aspects of childhood and school come easily to most children, but not to children with autism. Children learn to thrive and grow in their environment by watching and copying others; however, those who have autism often fail to make these social connections. Their isolation causes them to remain inexperienced in a world of comparably savvy children and can make adolescence an unnavigable maze.

Help with Getting It

Teachers slowly come to know their students. In the first few days of class they find out who is an avid reader or a social butterfly, who has the book out and is on the correct page, and who needs their hand held on the way to and from the lunchroom. Find out all you can about your student with autism before he or she arrives in your classroom; this will ease the transition for the student, for you, and for the class. Parents are the most important resource because they know their child best. As with all children, those who have autism are unique. Although they may share some common strengths and weaknesses, each child's individual needs must be evaluated.

Teachers should consider that children with autism are generally rigid in their thinking and behaviors. Typically, once they gain an understanding of a specific concept, they tend to access related information in the confines of that concept. For example, one child learned that a specific pet was called a *dog;* therefore, all pets became known to that child as dogs. This concrete analysis of the world helps them to maintain an orderly and comfortable life with few surprises. Routinization and rituals are common behaviors among some students with autism, as the familiar bears less uncertainty. Often behaviors that are troublesome in school are actually manifestations of uncertainty and lack of order or ritual, which can be frightening to children with autism. Sometimes a child's controlled world may not blend well with the organization you had planned to make your classroom work. A meeting with parents and their child before school begins will give you and the family time to plan for and avoid pitfalls. Parents have a good sense of how their child will react in a given setting. They have developed strategies to make life at home and school work for their child. Brainstorming with them on how to make this transition easy will pay off.

In some cases, easing the transition can be as simple as allowing the child to visit his or her classroom a few times in late summer or setting up a buddy system with a familiar child. Often, you will need to take further steps. For example, a clearly delineated visual schedule, often written out or using drawings or photographs, can help ease the uncertainty of time and transitions by providing advance notice and giving the child with autism a visual cue as to what comes next, thereby increasing his or her comfort level and allowing him or her to internalize the change and respond better. Seeing the chart change or participating in changing the icons helps the child understand and accept change (Quill 1995). Students who have relied on this type of system to help structure their early school years can progress to the more sophisticated support of a highly organized day planner or an electronic personal organizer. Parents can provide assistance by predetermining where their child might encounter difficulty throughout the school day and sharing various techniques for addressing these difficulties. Together, you can formulate an environmental support plan to help the child meet daily expectations.

Implementation of this plan must be consistent or it will add to the child's anxiety level. It must be appropriately designed to meet each child's unique needs; if Sam needs to adapt to a busy cafeteria, he should be taught supportive strategies. This may include bringing comfort foods from home, having a designated seat, being told exactly how much time he has to eat before he is expected to clean up his place, or being assigned a buddy who understands his discomfort and who will model appropriate lunchroom protocol for him until he understands it.

I Did Not Teach Him to Read

Parents often report to teachers that their child possesses precocious reading decoding ability with little to no instruction. Hyperlexia (precocious reading ability accompanied by difficulty acquiring language or social skills) is not a rare phenomenon in these children. Decoding symbols, a visual and spatial task, is a unique strength for some children with autism. Armed with advance awareness of these highly developed visual learning abilities, you can begin to think of ways to use this strength in your classroom.

Gray (1994) developed the Social Stories method to help children with autism capitalize on their visual learning abilities. In this method, an educator, parent, or individual close to the child creates a captioned picture book to improve the social understanding of people on both sides of a social equation. This technique can be extremely helpful in new settings in which expectations for your class may seem clear to you but may not be for your student with autism. Teachers can also use it to encourage or change behaviors by explaining with visual support just what it is you want your student to do and how. For example, a visit to the school library was a difficult time for Sam. The librarian told him he could borrow two books on each weekly visit. When Sam chose to borrow magazines, he was only allowed one because a different rule applied and he became loud and anxious. The teacher drew a Social Story to show him taking one magazine home. This visual explanation

helped Sam to understand the change in procedure and calm his behavior. Social Stories can be helpful to students with autism in all aspects of their lives because they teach social expectations to students who may otherwise have difficulty attaining them. They are tools that can be used to lessen the anxiety a student's misreading of social cues creates. Written on an individual basis, they address any situation that may arise, such as a simple procedure like using the library or a more complex dynamic like asking for a date.

The Squeezing Machine

A lack of understanding of one's social world along with an unregulated sensory integration system can be anxiety producing. As students grow and mature, they face uncharted territory. These challenges are often met with heightened anxiety and overt behaviors. Temple Grandin (1995), a professor who writes simply and honestly about her own autism, describes an anxiety reducing machine she built at age eighteen that consisted of two heavily padded boards that squeezed along the sides of her body. This machine produced the sensory input she craved and desensitized her overworked nervous system, thus reducing her anxiety.

Children with autism sometimes feel sensory overload in environments in which most people feel comfortable. Overhead lighting, especially fluorescent lights that buzz or flash; noise from fans or air conditioners; the clinking of dishes in the cafeteria down the hall; or a line tapping against a metal flagpole outside can send them into a tailspin. Sensory issues in which the central nervous system craves input may also appear. These children need constant sensory stimulation and may benefit from wearing a weighted vest, having a fidget toy, sitting on an inflated or rice-filled chair cushion, or using an exercise band strung between the front legs of their chair that they can push with their foot or leg. These sensitivities and the strategies for coping with them can influence learning, attention, behavior, and social interaction.

Support from parents and a knowledgeable occupational therapist are crucial in developing a sensory diet. Classroom teachers have the responsibility of observation and intervention and of providing reliable feedback to support staff. Creating opportunities for students to move about freely and to have some decision making in determining their sensory levels is essential.

What Teachers Need to Do

The inclusion of children with autism into the general education classroom affords teachers gifts and responsibilities; like all students, however, instruction and environmental considerations must be differentiated for them to reach their potential as learners. Here are some simple strategies teachers can use to help all students succeed:

- Order the classroom in almost every way. Maintain a posted schedule and encourage older students to use the strategies they have learned to organize their school lives. Always give students notice of expected due dates and upcoming tests. When possible, give advance reminders of half days, schedule and class changes, and fire drills.

- Use consistent visual cues and supports to navigate the school day and to complete academic tasks. This may include different-color desk folders for each subject, specific bins for turning in completed work, or a hands-on system for ordering lunch choices (i.e., one that uses visual supports such as picture cards of available food choices placed in appropriate baskets). Students who change classes may find it easier to leave materials behind in a designated place so they do not have the added responsibility of organizing them each class period.
- Be aware of sensory issues and consult professional staff and parents when developing strategies.
- Provide social supports and models to help students with autism learn socially appropriate behaviors from peers.
- Develop a behavioral plan that supports classroom expectations and promotes learning in a general education program.

Pay attention to your verbal directions. Fewer words are always better and a clearly defined message that is consistent works best. Students like Sam can and do learn and grow in the general education classroom. The daily opportunities for interaction with other students are vital to their social, communication, and academic progress. When a student with autism is given the opportunity to observe and interact, peers and others in the greater world of school teach targeted and nontargeted information by example. Providing all students with a rich, inclusive classroom environment that includes individual goals will foster mutual respect and understanding for all.

References

Centers for Disease Control and Prevention, National Center for Health Statistics. 2006. Health, United States, 2006. http://www .cdc.gov/nchs/hus.html (accessed December 18, 2006).

Cohen, D., and F. Volkmar. 1997. *Handbook of autism and pervasive developmental disorders.* New York: Wiley.

Frombonne, E. 2007. *Autism Spectrum Disorders; Rates, trends and links with immunizations.* Lecture presented at Advances

Appendix

Support Organizations for Families, Teachers, and Practitioners Working with Students Who Have Autism Spectrum Disorder

The Autism Society of America is a voice and resource in education, advocacy, services, research, and support for the autism community. http://www.autism-society.org/

Autism Collaboration raises millions of dollars each year for research in autism with an eye toward parent driven decisions. http://www.autism.org/

Autism Speaks provides autism information, resources, and news on research and treatments. http://www .cureautismnow.org

Centers for Disease Control and Prevention Autism Information Center is the official information site on autism and provides general information, screening procedures, treatments. and research updates. http://www.cdc.gov/ncbddd/dd/ddautism.htm

in Autism Conference: New Insights in the Diagnosis, Neurobiology, Genetics, and Treatment of Autism, New York.

Grandin, T. 1995. *Thinking in pictures.* New York: Doubleday.

Gray, C. 1994. *The new social story book.* Arlington, Texas: Future Horizons.

Quill, K. A., ed. 1995. *Teaching children with autism.* New York: Delmar.

Critical Thinking

1. Describe some of the characteristics of autism.
2. What are some strategies teachers can implement to help a student with autism be successful?

DIANA FRIEDLANDER is a special education inclusion teacher in elementary education in Ridgefield, CT, and a doctoral candidate at Western Connecticut State University.

Universal Design in Elementary and Middle School

Designing Classrooms and Instructional Practices to Ensure Access to Learning for All Students

MARGARET M. FLORES

The Association for Childhood Education International's (ACEI) mission includes helping educators meet the needs of students in a climate of societal change. One such change is the increasing diversity of learning needs within elementary and middle school classrooms. Increased numbers of students with disabilities served within the general education classroom have contributed to this diversity (U.S. Department of Education, 2005). Students with diverse needs present a challenge for elementary and middle school teachers because it may be difficult to ensure that all students meet expectations. Under current legislation, such as the No Child Left Behind Act (2002), all students, including those with disabilities, are expected to be proficient at grade level by 2013. Similarly, the Individuals With Disabilities Education Improvement Act (2004) states that students with disabilities should have increased access to the general education curriculum and that accommodations should be designed according to the students' needs.

In carrying out the mission of ACEI and complying with federal legislation, it is important that students with disabilities have accommodations written into their individualized educational programs (IEPs) and that these students receive accessible instruction. General education teachers play a critical role in both IEP development and implementation of accessible instruction. As members of the multidisciplinary IEP team, general education teachers have a unique understanding of curricular materials, texts, equipment, and technology within the general education setting that is critical in designing appropriate accommodations. These accommodations should support teachers' other role, that of implementing instruction that is assessible to all students. While this role may seem daunting, tools are available for designing classroom environments and instruction that are conducive to the learning of all students.

Universal Design for Instruction (UDI) is a set of principles helpful in guiding this process. UDI, designed by the Center for Applied Special Technology, is a framework that has been successful for all students, including those with disabilities in general education settings (Cawley, Foley, & Miller, 2003; McGuire, Scott, & Shaw, 2006; Pisha & Coyne, 2001; Pisha & Stahl, 2005). UDI ensures that all students have access to instruction through the following principles: 1) equitable use, 2) flexibility in use, 3) simple and intuitive, 4) perceptible information, 5) tolerance for error, 6) low physical effort, and 7) size and space for approach and use. The purpose of this article is to provide an overview of UDI, as well as practical classroom applications for elementary and middle school teachers.

Equitable Use

Equitable use means that all students can use materials, equipment, and technology in the classroom. The most common materials that can be inaccessible to students with disabilities are textbooks. As students advance in school, the emphasis on reading to learn increases and accessibility of textbooks becomes increasingly important in the content areas as students move through to middle school. Textbooks are inaccessible if students' reading levels are several levels below their grade placement, students cannot read the print due to its small size, and/or students have difficulty holding a book due to its size and weight. However, textbooks can be made accessible to students through the use of books on tape and through digital texts (Boyle et al., 2003; Twyman & Tindal, 2006). Books on tape are available through such nonprofit organizations as Readings for the Blind and Dyslexic, a free service for school districts and individuals with reading and visual disabilities. Digital texts allow for physical access, magnification of print, changes in contrast (i.e., increased color contrast between the print and page background), as well as audio output.

Technology, classroom equipment, and materials may not be accessible to all students, due to various student characteristics. Equipment and materials may be difficult to grasp or manipulate and/or visually perceive. Fortunately, equipment and materials used for instruction can be made accessible to all students through the use of grips, changes in size and dimension, and high-contrast materials. For lower and intermediate elementary students, these materials might include: special grips for pencils or other writing utensils; adaptive scissors; use of high contrast and/or large print, pictorial directions, and/or audio directions within learning centers; use of paper with raised lines; and manipulatives that are made easier to grip through size and texture (D'Angiulli, 2007; Judge, 2006; Russell et al., 2007). Although these materials will continue to be helpful for students at the late elementary and middle school level, additional items might include high-contrast print materials and graphic organizers or diagrams, and the use of graphic organizers and diagrams with raised lines (D'Angiulli, 2007; Russell et al., 2007).

Technology difficulties include becoming "lost" when searching the Internet for research, the computer font being too small or lacking color contrast, motor difficulties interfering with mouse manipulation, keyboard keys being too small, or the keyboard's lack of color contrast. As students progress through elementary and middle school, they will use technology more independently for research. Technology solutions for these students include the creation of web quests, in which the necessary websites are linked and/or the sites are contained within a single main site (Skylar, Higgins, & Boone, 2007). For all students, regardless of their grade level, computer equipment can be modified through the use of mouse balls that accommodate for fine motor difficulty, high contrast, and/or large-print stickers placed on top of keyboard keys. Keyboards are also available with large keys. Computer software is available to provide audio output so that print can be read to the student. The contrast of the screen and print can be adjusted to provide appropriate color contrast.

Flexibility in Use

Flexible use means that instruction and accompanying activities accommodate a wide range of individual preferences and abilities. Instruction can be designed in a variety of ways to accommodate a variety of learning strengths. It is helpful to design instruction using several different modes in order to make learning accessible for students with diverse learning needs.

Visual representation. Adding visual representations in the form of graphic organizers or schematic maps helps students organize concepts and information (Boulineau,

Fore, & Hagan-Burke, 2004; Ives, 2007; Lovitt, & Horton, 1994; McCoy & Ketterlin-Geller, 2004; Williams et al., 2007). These tools also help students recognize relationships between ideas and concepts. Students who have difficulties processing information, and students who lack background knowledge, may have difficulty connecting ideas and understanding how ideas come together to form overall concepts. Emphasis on pictures and symbols may be more appropriate when designing graphic organizers for elementary students. For middle school students, the use of graphic organizers or schematic maps may be helpful as instructional advance organizers and as instructional guides throughout units. The use of color, size, and shape also can be helpful in emphasizing relationships and hierarchies within graphic organizers. Other ways to appeal to visual learners at all grade levels is through pictures and videos. Visual depictions of information and relationships also may be helpful for memory or retention by providing students with an avenue for "picturing information in their mind."

Hands-on activities. Hands-on activities can be helpful for students, at all grade levels, who have difficulty acquiring information by more traditional means (Butler, Miller, Crehan, & Babbitt, 2003; Cass, Cares, Smith, & Jackson, 2003; Kerry–Moran, 2006; Kinniburgh & Shaw, 2007; Mastropieri et al., 2006; Witzel, Mercer, & Miller, 2003). Although these types of activities may be associated with science in the form of experiments and demonstrations, they provide opportunities throughout content areas. In mathematics, the use of manipulatives is a way to increase understanding of concepts and procedures, regardless of grade level. Although using and managing the use of manipulatives may be challenging, research has shown that students with learning disabilities need an average of three experiences with manipulatives in order to understand mathematical concepts (Mercer & Miller, 1992). In addition to building understanding, hands-on and participatory activities provide students who have difficulty expressing themselves through oral and written language with an opportunity to demonstrate their understanding.

Assignment completion. It is important to assess students' understanding of concepts and ideas; however, providing one avenue for expression of one's understanding may lead to inaccurate results. For example, students with learning disabilities in writing may not be able to fully express their ideas in writing, but they could discuss them in detail. Offering assignment or project menus could provide a variety of ways in which students can demonstrate their understanding. A menu allows all students to choose their preferred format without singling out particular students. For example, students might be given the option of writing a paragraph (for younger students) or an essay (for older students), an oral report to a group or through audio recording, or a multimedia presentation. The choices offered should each allow for appropriate assessment of students' understanding of the target objective or concept.

Another way to be flexible about assignment completion throughout elementary and middle levels is through cooperative grouping. Cooperative groups should be structured so that all members of the group have roles and responsibilities. These roles should be tailored to students' strengths and weaknesses and lead to active participation for all students. Each student should be accountable for his or her contribution to the group, as well as for the overall group's performance. The provision of individual roles ensures that all students actively learn and contribute, rather than only a few members of the group completing the work.

Simple and Intuitive

Simple and intuitive means that instruction is easily understood, regardless of students' experience, knowledge, or language skills. This includes priming students' background knowledge prior to beginning instruction. Priming background knowledge involves explaining how new information is connected to prior knowledge and experience. For example, an instructional unit about the American Civil War might include discussions about instances when students might have felt that another person or group did not attend to their point of view or needs. The experiences of students and how this discussion is moderated will differ depending on the grade level. Another way to make instruction simple and intuitive for elementary and middle school students is through analogies between new concepts and well-known concepts. It is important to be aware of students' diverse experiences while creating or designing these analogies, so that all students easily connect the two concepts.

Using consistent language is another way of making instruction simple and intuitive for elementary and middle school students. Students with language processing deficits and/or students who are second language learners have difficulty understanding instruction when each explanation involves different vocabulary and terminology. Therefore, using similar language each time an explanation is provided will lead to more efficient learning and understanding. In addition, language should be not only appropriate for a given skill, task, or concept, but also easily understood by students. Keep explanations as simple as possible, adding vocabulary instruction, if needed.

Perceptible Information

Perceptible information refers to that information that can be perceived regardless of skill and ability. This includes the use of instructional materials with appropriate color contrast for students with visual impairments. Black and yellow provide the highest color contrast, and computer screens, PowerPoint presentations, keys on computer keyboards, and handouts

can be adjusted to allow for increased visual perception. Seating within the classroom also can provide for increased perception. Placing students near the instructor and away from windows and hallways will increase students' ability to hear, see, and attend to instructional activities. Assignments and instructional materials also can be made more perceptible by changing their format. This begins with directions that are written clearly and at a level that students with various reading abilities can understand. Format also includes the amount of space between activities or problems, the use of lines for written responses, the layout, and the order of questions. Activities and assignments that involve written problems or scenarios can be adjusted for readability. Tests and quizzes that accompany textbooks may not be written at a level that all students understand. The wording of questions can be changed so that students are assessed based on their level of subject matter knowledge, rather than on their reading ability.

Tolerance for Error

Tolerance for error means that students have the opportunity to engage in ongoing assignments and projects. This allows for revision and editing over time, and students receive credit for correcting their errors. Students have the opportunity for feedback and ongoing learning. Over time, students learn from their mistakes and practice the appropriate skill, an opportunity that is lost with one-time assignments. These ongoing assignments and projects would be appropriate, regardless of students' grade placement.

Low Physical Effort

Low physical effort means that all students have access to materials and activities without great physical effort. The use of technology can decrease the amount of physical effort (Bahr & Nelson, 1996; Strassman & D'Amore, 2002; Tumlin & Heller, 2004). For example, if writing is physically taxing for students with fine motor difficulties, then the use of a keyboard can be of assistance. Hardware, software, and accessories are available to make computers accessible to students with more significant motor difficulties. Classroom materials, such as scissors, writing utensils, lab equipment, and desks, are all available in versions that are easily accessible for students with physical disabilities (Judge, 2006). These accommodations allow students to focus their attention and energy on learning rather than on manipulating materials.

Size and Space for Approach and Use

Size and space for approach and use means enough space is available so that all students can participate. The classroom is set up so that all students can maneuver throughout the room and participate in a variety of activities without

Mr. Jackson teaches 3rd grade at North Hills Elementary School and utilizes UDI in order to make his classroom accessible to a diverse group of learners. Mr. Jackson's room includes three types of learning centers (mathematics, writing, and reading), a classroom library (which includes audio books), an area for small-group instruction, and an area for whole-group instruction. Therefore, he has flexibility in his grouping, allowing him to individualize instruction for a small group while others are engaged in alternate learning activities. He places the learning centers along one side of the room, far enough apart so that students in one center will not be distracted by students in another, but still allowing easy movement from one to another. The large group area consists of grouped desks (conducive for cooperating group work) placed in a semicircle formation in front of the classroom's whiteboard. The classroom library (close to the reading center) and the small-group area are situated on each end of the room. Mr. Jackson has instituted a class book club in which students chose books based on the groups' interests. Mr. Jackson has acquired audio-books from the Association for the Blind and Dyslexic so that all students can participate fully in the experience. Each learning center includes written (large print, high contrast) directions, pictorial directions, and audio directions through headsets. Menus of activities also are included for each center in order to differentiate them based on students' strengths. The materials for the centers are modified according to students' needs. For example, the math center's manipulatives are large, with high-contrast coloring. The keyboards are portable and can be moved throughout learning areas. The students' written work can be saved on the classroom computer so it can be downloaded for editing and printing later.

Figure 1 Mr. Jackson's 3rd-grade classroom: UDI example for elementary level classroom.

Ms. Vargas is a member of a four-person team and teaches 7th-grade science at Green Oaks Middle School. She utilizes the principles of UDI to make her science class accessible to diverse groups of learners. Ms. Vargas' science textbook package includes audio versions of the text that she makes available to students with visual and learning disabilities. Ms. Vargas has acquired software and hardware that allows students to scan print materials into the classroom computer, which then converts the print into an audio format. Prior to beginning an instructional unit, Ms. Vargas provides all students with a schematic map for the unit. She refers to the map often and highlights important connections between concepts learned previously and those in the current lesson. When instruction involves lecture and note taking, Ms. Vargas provides all students with an outline that includes key words and a hierarchical structure to ensure that students have useful study notes. Students also may audio-record classroom instruction. During these lectures, Ms. Vargas uses PowerPoint presentations with a large, high-contrast font. During laboratory activities, students work in pairs, with each person responsible for specific duties. Plastic (rather than glass) containers and equipment are used and materials are kept on a series of lazy Susans so that they may be accessed easily. When needed, Ms. Vargas modifies the procedures so that larger weights and volumes can be used, allowing students with fine motor problems to grip and move containers and objects more easily. Laboratory reports can be produced either in writing (handwritten or word processed) or as an audio recording. More complicated lab reports and projects are ongoing assignments in which students complete the product in stages and receive feedback.

Figure 2 Ms. Vargas' 7th-grade classroom: UDI example for a middle level classroom.

excess physical effort. Students with physical disabilities have enough space to engage in the same types of activities as students without disabilities. Movement throughout the room and transition to activities is facilitated by its layout and design. Enough space is available between learning centers within elementary classrooms and middle school classrooms. Students should be able to move easily from small-group instruction to other areas within the room. As students begin to change classrooms, backpacks and other student materials can create clutter and hazards for students with visual impairments, physical disabilities, and/or students who use wheelchairs. Providing a special area within the room for these materials or using individual storage crates under chairs or tables can alleviate this problem.

Conclusion

The scenarios in Figures 1 and 2 are from elementary and middle level classrooms that exemplify different UDI principles in action. Figure 1 describes a 3rd-grade classroom

in which the following principles are emphasized: equitable use, flexibility in use, perceptible information, low physical effort, and size and space for approach. Figure 2 describes a 7th-grade classroom in which the following principles are emphasized: equitable use, flexibility in use, simple and intuitive, perceptible information, tolerance for error, and size and space for approach.

Students with disabilities have IEPs that are written each year by a multidisciplinary team, including, but not limited to, general education teachers, special education teachers, parents, and administrators. The general education teacher has the most experience and information about the curriculum, activities, and materials used within the general education setting. In order to ensure that instruction is accessible to all students, appropriate modifications and accommodations need to be planned and implemented. The general education teacher is a critical participant in this process because of his or her knowledge of the general education setting. Parents, special education teachers, and administrators might not be as knowledgeable about what might be needed within this setting. The general education teacher could add valuable

Table 1 Books That Provide Resources and Additional Information about Implementation of Universal Design for Instruction

Rose, D. H., Meyer, A., & Hichcock, C. (2005). *The universally designed classroom.* Cambridge, MA: Harvard University Press.

This book provides an introduction to Universal Design and is useful for teachers, administrators, and parents. It includes strategies and resources for creating a classroom that provides access to the general education curriculum for all students.

Rose, D. H., & Meyer, A. (2002). *Teaching every student in the digital age: Universal design for learning.* Alexandria, VA: Association for Supervision and Curriculum Development.

This book provides an overview of Universal Design for Learning, as well as real-world strategies for implementing Universal Design in the classroom. The authors explicitly connect ideas and concepts, using graphic organizers and examples throughout the book.

Council for Exceptional Children. (2005). *Universal design for learning.* Upper Saddle River, NJ: Prentice Hall.

This book serves as a practical guide to implementing Universal Design in the classroom. It includes a case-based scenario about teachers' experiences with Universal Design. Discussion questions throughout the book offer opportunities for application and reflection upon the content.

Table 2 Interactive Websites That Provide Tools for the Implementation of Universal Design for Instruction Principles

Websites

Lesson Builder: http://lessonbuilder.cast.org

This site provides models and tools to create and adapt lessons in order to increase accessibility for all students. Model lesson plans across content areas and grade levels are included.

Book Builder: http://bookbuilder.cast.org

This site provides information and the tools to create engaging digital books for students. Universally designed books will engage, and provide access for, diverse groups of students.

Creating Accessible WebQuests and Web-based Student Activities: www.4teachers.org

This site offers tools and resources to integrate technology into the classroom. These include Web lessons, quizzes, rubrics, classroom calendars, and other tools for student use.

suggestions about modifications and accommodations that might be otherwise overlooked. The principles of universal design should guide this planning process. The general education classroom should be thought of with regard to the students' accessibility, specifically in terms of equitable use, flexibility in use, simple and intuitive, perceptive in formation, perceptible in formation, tolerance for error, low physical effort, and size and space for approach and use.

The No Child Left Behind Act (2002) requires that students with disabilities perform proficiently on grade level in all areas by 2013. These are high expectations to meet. Therefore, it is critical that all students have access to instruction within the general education classroom. Students' IEPs provide for the necessary accommodations and modifications for access to instruction. The multidisciplinary team who creates a student's IEP is responsible for assessing the student's needs and designing the necessary modifications. The general education teacher has unique knowledge of the curricular standards, instructional activities, materials, and physical design of the classroom. The awareness of these factors, as well as the knowledge of the principles of universal design, provides teachers with the tools necessary to fully participate in this process of meeting students' needs and ensuring that all students have access to instruction.

References

Bahr, C. M., & Nelson, N. W. (1996). The effects of text-based and graphics-based software tools on planning and organizing of stories. *Journal of Learning Disabilities, 22,* 355–270.

Boulineau, T., Fore, C., & Hagan-Burke, S. (2004). Using story mapping to increase the story grammar of elementary students with learning disabilities. *Learning Disability Quarterly, 27*(2), 105–114.

Boyle, E. A., Rosenberg, M. S., Connelly, V. J., Gallin-Washburg, S., Brinckerhoff, L. C., & Banerjee, M. (2003). Effects of audio-texts on the acquisition of secondary level content by students with mild disabilities. *Learning, Disability Quarterly, 26,* 204–214.

Butler, F. M., Miller, S. P., Crehan, K., & Babbitt, B. P. (2003). Fraction instruction for students with mathematics disabilities: Comparing two teaching sequences. *Learning Disabilities Research and Practice, 18*(2), 99–111.

Cass, M., Cates, D., Smith, M., & Jackson, C. (2003). Effects of manipulative instruction on solving area and perimeter problems by students with learning disabilities. *Learning Disabilities Research and Practice, 18*(2), 112–120.

Cawley, J. F., Foley, T. E., & Miller, J. (2003). Science and students with mild disabilities. *Intervention in School and Clinic 38,* 160–171.

D'Angiulli, A. (2007). Raised-line pictures, blindness, and tactile beliefs: An observational case study. *Journal of Visual Impairment and Blindness, 101,* 172–178.

Individuals with Disabilities Education Improvement Acts of 2004, Pub. L. No. 108–446, 118 Stat. 2647 (2004) (amending 20 U.S.C.§§ 1440 et seq.).

Ives, B. (2007). Graphic organizers applied to secondary algebra instruction for students with learning disorders. *Learning Disabilities Research and Practice, 22*(2), 110–118.

Judge, S. (2006). Constructing an assistive technology toolkit for young children: Views from the field. *Journal of Special Education Technology, 21*(4), 17–24.

Kerry-Moran, K.J. (2006). Nurturing emergent readers through readers' theater. *Early Childhood Education Journal, 33,* 317–323.

Kinniburgh, L., & Shaw, E. (2007). Building reading fluency in elementary science through readers' theater. *Science Activities, 44*(1), 16–20.

Lovitt, T. C, & Horton, S. V. (1994). Strategies for adapting textbooks for youth with learning disabilities. *Remedial and Special Education, 15,* 105–116.

Mastropieri, M. A., Scruggs, T. E., Norland, J. J., Berkley, S., McDuffie, K., Tornquist, E. H., & Connors, N. (2006). Differentiated curriculum enhancement in inclusive middle school science: Effects on classroom and high stakes tests. *Journal of Special Education, 40*(3), 130–137.

McCoy, J. D., & Ketterlin-Geller, R. (2004). Rethinking instructional delivery for diverse student populations: Serving all learners with concept-based instruction. *Intervention in School and Clinic, 40*(2), 88–95.

McGuire, J. M., Scott, S. S., Shaw, S. F. (2006). Universal design and its application in educational environments. *Remedial and Special Education, 27,* 166–175.

Mercer, C. D., & Miller, S. P. (1992). Teaching students with learning problems in math to acquire, understand, and apply basic math facts. *Remedial and Special Education, 13*(3), 19–35.

Pisha, B., & Coyne, P. (2001). Smart from the start. *Remedial and Special Education, 22,* 197–203.

Pisha, B., & Stahl, S. (2005). The promise of new learning environments for students with disabilities. *Intervention in School and Clinic, 41,* 67–75.

Russell M. E., Jutai, J. W., Strong, J. G., Campbell, K. A., Gold, D., Pretty, L., & Wilmot, L. (2007). The legibility of typefaces for readers with low vision: A research review. *Journal of Visual Impairments and Blindness, 101,* 402–415.

Skylar, A. A., Higgins, K., & Boone, R. (2007). Strategies for adapting webquests for students with learning disabilities. *Intervention in School and Clinic, 43*(1), 20–28.

Strassman, B. K., & D'Amore, M. (2002). The write technology. *Teaching Exceptional Children, 34*(6), 28–31.

Tumlin, J., & Heller, K. W. (2004). Using word prediction software to increase fluency with students with physical disabilities. *Journal of Special Education Technology, 19*(3), 5–14.

Twyman, T., & Tindal, G. (2006). Using computer-adapted, conceptually based history text to increase comprehension and problem-solving skills of students with disabilities. *Journal of Special Education Technology, 21*(2), 5–16.

U.S. Department of Education. (2002). *No Child Left Behind: A desktop reference.* Washington, DC: Author.

U.S. Department of Education, National Center for Education Statistics. (2005). *The condition of education 2005* (NCES 2005–094).

Williams, J. P., Nubla-Kung, A. M., Pollini, S., Stafford, K. B., Garcia, A., & Snyder, A. E. (2007). Teaching cause and effect text structure through social studies content to at-risk second graders. *Journal of Learning Disabilities, 40*(2), 111–120.

Witzel, B. S., Mercer, C. D., & Miller, S. P. (2003). Teaching algebra to students with learning difficulties: An investigation of an explicit instruction approach. *Learning Disabilities Research and Practice, 18*(2), 121–131.

Critical Thinking

1. Explain universal design.
2. Identify five ways you can implement universal design for the grade level at which you plan to teach.

MARGARET M. FLORES is Assistant Professor, Special Education, Department of Interdisciplinary Learning and Teaching, University of Texas at San Antonio.

How Can Such A Smart Kid Not Get It?

Finding the Right Fit for Twice-Exceptional Students in Our Schools

NINA YSSEL, MIKE PRATER, AND DEB SMITH

In the past two decades, the educational and social-emotional needs of twice-exceptional children have been addressed in gifted and special education literature. An awareness of the challenges many of these students experience in the classroom resulted in some outstanding programs created exclusively for this population; but in schools generally, the unique needs of these students are for the most part not met (Weinfeld, Barnes-Robinson, Jeweler, & Shevitz, 2002). The situation of twice-exceptional students who receive only remediation with no enrichment is unfortunately not limited to isolated cases.

During the past 6 years, we have worked and interacted with twice-exceptional middle school students as well as with their parents at an annual residential summer camp. Through surveys and interviews with the parents and their children, the difficulties that twice-exceptional students encounter at school emerged. Furthermore, parents' perceptions of the impact of a successful learning experience during one week of camp have been noteworthy. When teachers focus on strengths rather than weaknesses, and when twice-exceptional students are provided with appropriate coping strategies and accommodations, social and academic success is indeed possible.

The purpose of this article is to present parents' perceptions of educational and social-emotional difficulties their twice-exceptional children experience. The snapshots of twice-exceptional middle school students are interspersed with views and research findings from existing literature. Finally, a few successful strategies are described, and recommendations for the classroom are included.

In this article we use both terms, "twice-exceptional" and "gifted with learning disabilities (G/LD)," to describe this population. The former includes all students with disabilities who are gifted (e.g., those with Asperger's syndrome, Attention Deficit Hyperactivity Disorder [ADHD], emotional disabilities); the latter refers only to gifted students with learning disabilities. At times it is necessary to use this narrower term to describe a student's specific exceptionalities.

Programming Issues Identified in Literature

When discussing appropriate and effective programming, typical characteristics of twice-exceptional students must be examined. Students who are identified as G/LD have characteristics of both exceptionalities. Some of the characteristics they share with their gifted peers include strength in problem solving (Silverman, 1989), a strong verbal vocabulary, creativity, a sophisticated sense of humor, and intense interests in specific areas (Nielsen & Higgins, 2005; Silverman, 1989). G/LD students also demonstrate characteristics typically associated with students with learning disabilities, including impulsive behaviors, distractibility, lack of organizational skills (Baum, Cooper, & Neu, 2001), processing difficulties, and low academic self-esteem (Nielsen, 2002).

In the case of the twice-exceptional student whose specific learning disability is not the primary exceptionality, the so-called "gifted characteristics" described above would still be present, but those associated with the other exceptionality (e.g., ADHD, Asperger's syndrome) might vary. We have found that regardless of the disability, problems with organizational skills, attention, and low academic self-esteem are very common, and most twice-exceptional students with whom we have interacted at camp need intervention in these areas.

This dichotomy, a pattern of strengths and weaknesses demonstrated by twice-exceptional children, is the issue that must be addressed to enable social and academic success (Weinfeld et al., 2002). Reis and Ruban (2005) referred to several studies that underscore the importance of concentrating on the gifts rather than the disability in order to foster creative and productive G/LD students. Nielsen (2002) and Weinfeld et al. (2002) concurred, arguing that these students should first and foremost be seen as gifted learners. However, the view that deficits should be remediated before enrichment can occur is fairly common in schools (Baum et al., 2001).

Through the years, different programming models and options for twice-exceptional students have been identified. Fox,

Brody, and Tobin (1983) considered four aspects to be included when programming for G/LD students: (a) gifted programming in the areas of strength, (b) developmental instruction in subjects of average growth, (c) remedial teaching in areas of disability, and (d) adaptive instruction in areas of disability. More recently, Nielsen (2002) envisioned a continuum of service options, for example, a more intensive level of service for twice-exceptional students whose disability is more severe. On the other hand, those with mild learning disabilities could receive all of their services within the general education classroom with support from gifted and special educators. Newman (as cited in Reis & Ruban, 2005) suggested three service delivery systems for G/LD students: intervention in the general education classroom, partial pull-out programs, and self-contained programs. Reis and Ruban (2005) advocated the success of alternative strategies for this population, including access to advanced technology in all classes, extracurricular opportunities (summer or after-school programs) to pursue interests, and counseling support and positive peer support programs. Researchers are, therefore, in agreement that twice-exceptional students' unique educational and emotional needs require an individualized approach. The question is, do schools offer any of these options based on individual needs or do they follow a one-size-fits-all approach?

Summer Camp

Six years ago, our first one-week, residential summer camp for twice-exceptional middle school students was held on the campus of a Midwestern university. This camp has become an annual event, with many campers returning year after year. The purpose of the camp is to provide enrichment in a supportive environment, thereby addressing two of the programming needs suggested by Fox et al. (1983): gifted programming and adaptive instruction. Enrichment is theme-based, focusing on art and science; our campers are engaged in critical thinking, creative problem solving, and reflection. A strong emphasis on the social and emotional well-being of the campers is another component that guides our approach and implementation. This is an opportunity for developing important social relationships among the campers and an enduring social support network.

In order to provide a supportive environment where these goals can be met, we admit a maximum of 20 campers. Attendance has varied between 15 to 20 campers per summer. Two instructors (art and science) coteach classes and are assisted by three teaching assistants and the director of the camp. Teaching assistants typically include special education majors in their senior year, graduate students, and teachers. Campers stay in a dormitory on campus during the week of camp, with three additional adults serving as camp counselors.

Participants

Although we have returning campers every year, recruitment is important. In early spring, campers are recruited through e-mails to special education directors and gifted and talented coordinators in the state. A description of our camp is also included in a list of summer camps on the state department of education website, and presentations at conferences and parent organizations as well as the news media have been effective forums for recruitment.

Our target group includes middle school students (grades 6–8) who are twice-exceptional. Documentation of both exceptionalities must be provided (e.g., an IEP and documentation of participation in gifted programming). On average, 90% of the campers are G/LD; exceptionalities of the remaining 10% have included Asperger's syndrome and emotional disabilities. The majority of campers are male, with the percentage of female campers varying between 10–25%.

Parent Questionnaires

During July 2007, parents of campers were asked to complete a questionnaire (see Appendix) about their children's educational experiences. Eighteen parents (mothers or fathers) completed the questionnaires during the last 30 minutes of an informational meeting on the first day of camp. The questionnaire consisted of 13 open-ended questions focusing on the child's identification, programming, interests, participation in extracurricular activities, study and organizational skills, social-emotional well-being, and the parents' perceptions of their child's educational experiences.

Enrichment vs. Remediation

Results of the parents' responses to the questionnaire indicated that 10 out of 18 students (56%) were identified/recognized as twice-exceptional at school. Identification or recognition of both exceptionalities did not necessarily translate into service: Only five of the 18 students (28%) received both enrichment and remediation.

Three parents described their children's experiences with regards to this issue:

> For the most part our school has been very cooperative when it comes to working with "A" and his learning difficulties, not so with his giftedness.

> ["B's"] giftedness is not addressed at all in his programming other than to note how much he is underachieving. It's frustrating for me, it must be utterly maddening for him!

> ["C"] was recognized as gifted (talking to him is like talking to a high school kid, according to his second-grade teacher) but not acknowledged as gifted and he received no enrichment whatsoever.

Parent responses reflected what has been reported in the literature on this issue: Twice-exceptional students usually receive services for one exceptionality, seldom for both, and, unfortunately, it is the strengths that are most often ignored (Baum et al., 2001).

Remediation, Compensatory Strategies, and Accommodations

Thirteen of the 18 campers (72%) reportedly had difficulties with language arts. These difficulties were mostly problems with handwriting, and especially written expression. In most cases, the reading problems that resulted in original diagnoses/eligibility for special education services were less of an issue in middle school; problems with written expression, however, continued to present much frustration.

Whereas the emphasis should be on these students' giftedness (Nielsen, 2002) rather than on remediation, remediation of their weaknesses cannot be ignored (Nielsen & Higgins, 2005). Teachers must consider the problems many twice-exceptional students have with basic skills, organizational skills, distractibility, and social-emotional issues when planning interventions. Weinfeld, Barnes-Robinson, Jeweler, and Shevitz (2006) underscored the need for instruction in writing, reading, math calculations, study skills, and learning strategies, as well as social skills.

Baum et al. (2001) provided the following excellent explanation of the struggle of students who have learning disabilities in reading and writing but are gifted in nonverbal areas: With the emphasis traditional elementary school settings place on basic skills in reading, writing, and math "much of the curriculum is a secret language arts lesson" (p. 480). These students have ideas and knowledge to share but have intense difficulties expressing what they know and can do through the traditional ways required in classrooms—poor spelling, handwriting, and difficulties with written expression lead to frustration and often, behavior problems. Teachers must also find alternate ways in which these students can access information and demonstrate their knowledge. By allowing them to express abstract ideas in a concrete way through visual and kinesthetic experiences, the barrier of verbal (and written) communication can be removed (Baum et al., 2001).

Teachers must also find alternate ways in which these students can access information and demonstrate their knowledge. By allowing them to express abstract ideas in a concrete way through visual and kinesthetic experiences, the barrier of verbal (and written) communication can be removed.

A parent described her son's difficulties in the classroom as follows: "He ["C"] loves learning but hates, hates writing." His mother also mentioned a successful learning experience; rather than writing a conventional paper, the assignment was "If you were a reporter and had to describe the bones in the human body, what would you say?" This illustrates the statement of Weinfeld et al. (2006) that bright students should be able to demonstrate their knowledge without being hindered by their areas of weakness. Baum et al. (2001) pointed out that G/LD students, specifically those experiencing difficulties with basic skills, should have options of gathering information that "do not insult their intelligence" (p. 482). Therefore, because "C's" problems with written expression could be bypassed, he was not only successful but still refers to the alternate assignment as one of his favorite learning experiences that year.

Organizational Skills

Sixteen out of 18 (89%) campers reportedly had problems with organizational skills and study skills/learning strategies. In two cases, the problems seemed less serious (e.g., "he needs to be reminded"), but in most cases the difficulties were significant:

> "B" loses materials accidentally and on purpose. He cannot find notes to study (the few he takes), doesn't fill out his agenda, has no clue how to study for a test or figure out salient facts to study, and has tremendous difficulty figuring out what the teacher wants as an answer.

Another camper's parent described the difficulties as follows:

> "E" loses things all the time and constantly needs redirection and reminders on where to put his stuff to stay organized. He always thinks he's studied enough but he hasn't. I have to tell him to do more. [He] doesn't seem to have strategies for remembering what he's studied.

For another camper, issues with organizational skills resulted in a change of placement:

> . . . ["D] was expected to get himself and the necessary belongings from place to place quickly with an extreme amount of stimulation to his senses. I felt his teachers would have liked to help but they repeatedly stated that they did not have the time. He needed to be taught the organizational and coping skills necessary for success in this new environment.

Appeals from the mother for support did not have the desired effect; suggestions from her might be implemented for a short period, but the teachers did not follow through. After "D" started developing anxiety attacks, his parents removed him from public school. He is now homeschooled.

Social-Emotional Needs

Social-emotional issues presented problems for 11 of the 18 campers (61%).

> ["B"] attempts to fit into larger groups but doesn't know how to do it. He'll be impulsive, loud, brash, and very active on the one hand. At other times, he chooses not to participate and will withdraw and not make the attempt.

Another parent described her son's problems as not serious, yet "C" "sometimes makes odd jokes that kids don't really get. . . . It still takes him a long time to call someone 'friend.'"

Social-emotional issues can be devastating for all children. In the case of twice-exceptional students, a poor academic self-concept and difficulties in the social realm present a particular problem. Baum et al. (2001) described the risk of these students becoming loners or demonstrating problem behaviors, a pattern of continuous failure that results in a loss of confidence in their own ability. In order to boost academic self-efficacy, twice-exceptional students must be empowered by opportunities to be successful; traditional self-esteem programs alone cannot accomplish this. A nurturing climate and emotional support are, therefore, crucial elements in effective learning experiences for this population (Coleman, 2005).

Twice-exceptional children often feel isolated, "as if they are one of a kind" (Nielsen & Higgins, 2005, p. 11) and simply not fitting in with their peers (King, 2005). They also might be rejected because they are interested in topics not shared by peers (Baum et al., 2001). This has become evident to us at every camp. The conversations are usually not your typical adolescent conversation; our campers enjoy talking to their peers about topics that interest them, ranging from physical science and astronomy, to animals and technology. It is imperative, therefore, that twice-exceptional students have the opportunity to spend time with peers who also are twice-exceptional; they do not always fit into the general or gifted population, nor with those students who have only learning disabilities (Nielsen, 2002). A parent's comment that his son loves coming to camp because "E" "thoroughly enjoys interacting with others who think like him," illustrates the enjoyment of social connections with like-minded peers. Weinfeld et al. (2006) pointed out that social and emotional issues are linked to a student's lack of achievement; a program that attends to all of the needs and strengths of the twice-exceptional student will have a positive effect on behaviors and attitudes. A comment from one of the parents explained this well:

This has been his only positive academic experience since kindergarten. Knowing that ["B"] is not the only one in the world who is smart, but also academically/socially limited has helped his overall self-esteem. He was very fired up at the beginning of his school year last year because his self-efficacy for academics improved.

A parent described the positive impact of the camp experience:

His self-esteem was raised incredibly by the independence he had and by participating in truly challenging and stimulating activities. In addition to his discovery, "S" is now embracing his differences and accepting them. He is better able to appreciate his uniqueness and not be ashamed of it.

Social networking within a supportive atmosphere is important and certainly one of our goals. It is, however, encouraging to hear from parents that positive experiences during one week could have a long-lasting effect, spilling over into improved learning: "'A' was very excited last year when his math teacher started to talk about the math pattern that was taught last year in camp. 'A' was the only one in the class who knew anything about the concept."

Observations and Recommendations for the Classroom

Throughout the past 6 years, we have been astounded at the powerful imaginative abilities of most of our campers, abilities that are not always recognized in the classroom, specifically because of the emphasis on traditional means of expression. Many times, we have observed students completely withdrawn and cautious on the first day. Then, once they begin producing art and taking pride in it, they stand up and begin explaining their work to anyone who will listen. It is important not to eliminate the written portion when documenting their work; however, it does not always have to be the only standard used to evaluate success or failure. By differentiating instruction and offering multiple approaches to content, process, and product (Tomlinson, 2001), twice-exceptional students will be able to demonstrate what they have learned through alternate projects.

At camp we allow short periods of time, creative moments, to allow ideas to flow. Twice-exceptional students are able to envision abstract forms and combinations of experienced phenomena but are often accused of daydreaming or being off task when they need time to focus on their thoughts and mental images. Projects are structured to allow students a chance to think, first on their own, next on paper, and then as part of a conversation with the teacher or their peers. When they begin acting on their ideas in learning tasks, they must be able to modify what they are doing based on new ideas that come to them.

Twice-exceptional students are often distractible and have difficulty paying attention in class. According to Baum et al. (2001), sustained attention is possible if they are engaged in areas of strength and interest. The school curriculum should be developed to engage the student; it is possible for these students to be "transformed from passive consumers of extant knowledge to active creators of new knowledge" (Baum et al., 2001, p. 484). Our experiences at camp corroborate this claim. "B," who is constantly in trouble at school due to behavioral problems, is extremely successful at camp where he is engaged and can focus on an activity that is geared toward his interest and learning style.

Our campers, especially those with ADHD, often "change the channel" during a long project. This could be an obstacle; however, as long as the student can remain engaged with the core idea that is being learned, shifting rapidly from task to task can actually lend itself to a more holistic learning experience. This shifting requires the teacher to prepare several smaller activities reflecting the multiple facets and points of view that would have been combined into a single, larger project—a strategy we have found to be very effective.

Twice-exceptional children are often frustrated by their own inability to focus on a single task, or because they can complete some tasks more quickly than their peers. With a group of related activities that can be done multiple times, learning becomes cumulative and individualized based on interest and ability, which meets the academic needs of the twice-exceptional child. An example from the camp provides multiple avenues to this end. If the class is learning about the growth of crystals (an actual example from one of our camps), the teacher establishes multiple stations in the room and groups the students with learning partners. Station 1 might require the creation of crystals based on a type of salt and Station 2, the creation of crystals using sugars. Station 3 could involve examining and identifying different types of crystals through a microscope, at Station 4 students might be drawing crystalline forms that correspond to photos of types of crystals, and Station 5 might involve dissolving crystalline structures using various liquids. This requires thorough preparation and should be organized within the instructional plan as a large block of time rather than as a single lesson with time for only one or two tasks in the group. There should be sufficient time for some learners to complete all of the tasks and some learners to focus and produce in-depth results in one or two tasks. The student compiles the results from the completed tasks in a notebook or portfolio that he or she may use in a presentation. The cumulative learning from this event sets the stage for the next lesson or task group.

We have found it essential to include planned secondary and tertiary activities in every lesson. Some students will simply not be able to work on a single task for the entire lesson; therefore, more time is allotted for a lesson in order to include these secondary and tertiary activities. Our campers are not allowed to engage in unrelated activities as a first choice. Secondary activities that relate to the lesson or to the larger unit are prepared and kept at specific stations in the room. If the primary activity is, for example, a project in which students must design and describe a biome, secondary activities may include a teacher-created board game about matching animals to biomes, a video about specific biomes and how they are affected by external influences, books, puzzles, and other games about various biomes and their characteristics.

As a third choice, tertiary activities that use the same learning or thinking skills but address a different topic are kept at a different station. These activities may include puzzles that involve combining elements to create a new form, articles and books about various animals and their species characteristics, and/or art projects about drawing landscapes and designing new animal species. It is important that the student be directed toward secondary activities first, then to tertiary activities. It is also very important that these activities are not seen as a reprieve from having to complete the primary learning activity or learning task group. Students must understand that they will have to return to the primary task and complete it. Finally, teachers should choose secondary and tertiary activities that are not simply "play time" activities; instead, the primary task should be exciting and engaging so that the student takes pride in completing it.

In order to be successful, these students need compensating strategies (Reis & Ruban, 2005), ranging from the use of technology to strategies that can easily be implemented in any classroom. Baum et al. (2001) suggested the use of visual organizers such as graphic organizers and webs to help students with difficulties in sequential organization and linear tasks. We also have found graphic organizers particularly effective in helping our campers stay focused and on task.

Conclusion

It is a challenge, but not impossible to provide appropriate programming/ intervention for twice-exceptional students. Many of the strategies discussed can be provided within the general education classroom; however, effective programming cannot be accomplished without collaboration among teachers (Kennedy, Higgins, & Pierce, 2002; Robinson, 1999). Providing the right fit in terms of programming is not the responsibility of only the special education teacher and teacher of the gifted, but of a team of experts. The teacher of the gifted must certainly provide the expertise in appropriate services to foster the students' strengths. The special educator is an expert in study skills, learning strategies, and compensatory strategies. General education teachers are the content experts, and school counselors must be aware of the concerns of twice-exceptional students who might be misunderstood, unidentified, and underserved (Assouline, Nicpon, & Huber, 2006).

Although the team approach is highly recommended, teacher training programs should nevertheless include in-depth training for both special education and gifted education teachers; they must know how to identify twice-exceptional students and provide programming (Nielsen, 2002). The following example, provided by a parent of one of our campers, underscores the need for training so that educators can understand the strengths and weaknesses of the twice-exceptional child:

> On a trip to a museum as a 4-year-old, "B" identified all nine planets. His interests are confined and intense, but I think teachers have trouble understanding how such a smart kid can so not get it. He constantly has to fight the

---

Appendix A: Camp Discoveries

Name of Camper _____

1. Please describe your child's strengths and weaknesses in all areas (academic, social, organization).
2. Has your child been identified as twice-exceptional?
3. How old was your child when you realized he or she is gifted? What were some of the strengths you noticed?
4. How did you learn that he or she has a disability?
5. Does your child receive enrichment as well as remediation and support?
6. Does your child like school?
7. Does your child participate in IEP meetings?
8. Can your child identify/discuss his or her strengths and learning problems?
9. Tell me about any successful, memorable experience that your child has experienced at school.
10. What are some of the difficulties your child is experiencing at school?
11. Does he or she participate in extracurricular activities (including sports)?
12. Tell me about your child's passions/interests.
13. Does your child have social difficulties? Please elaborate.
14. Does your child have problems with organizational and study skills? If so, please describe.
15. If your child is a returning camper, how has this camp been beneficial?

"lazy attitude, not trying" labels. Teachers don't understand that it is all very difficult for him all the time, that it's impossible for him to maintain a consistent effort all day, every day. They see kids with lesser innate ability being more successful because those kids are "trying" in their eyes.

Not only should we understand "how such a smart kid can so not get it," but also be prepared to provide an appropriate education that would enable twice-exceptional students to receive support in areas of need and validation for their strengths.

References

Assouline, S. G., Nicpon, M. F., & Huber, D. H. (2006). The impact of vulnerabilities and strengths on the academic experiences of twice-exceptional students: A message to school counselors. *Professional School Counseling, 10*(1), 14–24. Retrieved from Academic Search Premier.

Baum, S. M., Cooper, C. R., & Neu, T. W. (2001). Dual differentiation: An approach for meeting the curricular needs of gifted students with learning disabilities. *Psychology in the Schools, 38,* 477–490.

Coleman, M. R. (2005). Academic strategies that work for gifted students with learning disabilities. *Teaching Exceptional Children, 38*(1), 28–32.

Fox, L. H., Brody, L., & Tobin, D. (1983). *Learning disabled gifted children: Identification and programming.* Baltimore, MD: University Park Press.

Kennedy, K. Y., Higgins, K., & Pierce, T. (2002). Collaborative partnerships among teachers for students who are gifted and have learning disabilities. *Intervention in School and Clinic, 38*(1), 36–49.

King, E. W. (2005). Addressing the social and emotional needs of twice-exceptional students. *Teaching Exceptional Children, 38*(1), 16–20.

Nielsen, M. E. (2002). Gifted students with learning disabilities: Recommendations for identification and programming. *Exceptionality, 10,* 93–111.

Nielsen, M. E., & Higgins, L. D. (2005). The eye of the storm: Service and programs for twice-exceptional learners. *Teaching Exceptional Children, 38*(1), 8–15.

Reis, S. M., & Ruban, L. (2005). Services and programs for academically talented students with learning disabilities. *Theory Into Practice, 44,* 148–159.

Robinson, S. M. (1999). Meeting the needs of students who are gifted and have learning disabilities. *Intervention in School and Clinic, 34,* 195–204.

Silverman, L. K. (1989). Invisible gifts, invisible handicaps. *Roeper Review, 12,* 27–42.

Tomlinson, C. A. (2001). *How to differentiate instruction in mixed-ability classrooms.* Upper Saddle River, NJ: Pearson Education.

Weinfeld, R., Barnes-Robinson, L., Jeweler, S., & Shevitz, B. (2002). Academic programs for gifted and talented/learning disabled students. *Roeper Review, 24,* 226–233.

Weinfeld, R., Barnes-Robinson, L., Jeweler, S., & Shevitz, B. R. (2006). *Smart kids with learning difficulties: Overcoming obstacles and realizing potential.* Waco, TX: Prufrock Press.

Critical Thinking

1. What is a "twice-exceptional" student? Describe the need of these students.

2. Explain five supports that can help twice-exceptional students be successful.

3. What kind of research study is this?

The Relationship of Perfectionism to Affective Variables in Gifted and Highly Able Children

How does perfectionism relate to gifted and high-ability learners?

MARY M. CHRISTOPHER AND JENNIFER SHEWMAKER

Does the presence of perfectionist tendencies lead to more serious emotional issues or does it support enhanced achievement? Parents, educators, and gifted learners themselves often consider these issues as they deal with the ramifications of such perfectionist tendencies. This study focused on exploring perfectionism and its relationship to social, emotional, and academic issues for gifted and highly able learners.

Since the studies of Hollingworth (1926, 1942), researchers have discussed social-emotional characteristics along with the resulting issues and problems of gifted children. However, little research has been done on the aspects of perfectionism and its relationship to affective variables in gifted and highly able children.

Research presents conflicting views of social-emotional characteristics of gifted learners (Janos & Robinson, 1985; Moon & Hall, 1997; Moon, Kelly, & Feldhusen, 1997; Neihart, 1999; Silverman, 1993). "Some studies suggest that these children are highly motivated, well-adjusted, socially mature, open to new experiences, independent, and possess high self-concepts and a high tolerance for ambiguity" (Keiley, 2002, p. 43). In contrast, other studies support the idea that giftedness accompanies a tendency to develop social-emotional difficulties, such as social isolation and loneliness, which may lead to depression, anxiety, phobias, and interpersonal problems (Jackson, 1998; Kaiser & Berndt, 1986; Piechowski, 1997; Silverman, 1993).

Popular thought supports the idea that depression and suicide occur at higher rates in gifted individuals than the rest of the population, but research studies have not confirmed that belief (Neihart, Reis, Robinson, & Moon, 2002). Gifted students remain undistinguishable from average students in levels of depression or suicidal ideation (Baker, 1995; Cross, 1996;

Cross, Gust-Brey, & Ball, 2002; Neihart et al., 2002). Several writers have linked characteristics of gifted children to risk factors for depression, perfectionism, and anxiety (Greenspon, 2000; Orange, 1997; Parker & Adkins, 1995; Schuler, 2000). Based on such claims, Roeper (1995, 1996) advocated that educators should work on understanding the whole gifted person, including social-emotional issues, rather than merely academic concerns. The Teaching for Intellectual and Emotional Learning (TIEL) model espouses connecting cognitive and social-emotional components in educational programming for gifted children (Folsom, 2006). More research is needed to clarify the relationship between perfectionism and affective variables in the gifted population and to aid educators who work with gifted students struggling with these issues in developing effective responses to their perfectionist tendencies. Self-Oriented Perfectionism (SOP) is characterized by exacting standards set for one's self. This subtype exhibits a healthy component that may propel one toward higher levels of effort and achievement. Socially Prescribed Perfectionism (SPP) represents internalization of the perceived perfectionistic expectations of significant others in one's life.

The complex construct of sensitivity, intensity, and perfectionism produces common characteristics and counseling concerns for gifted children and adolescents (Webb, Meckstroth, & Tolan, 1982). Research relating the constructs of perfectionism to gifted individuals supports three conclusions: (a) perfectionism may result in pathological problems; (b) perfectionism in gifted individuals may contribute to high achievement; and (c) attributions of perfectionism fall along a range of continuums (Adderholdt-Elliott, 1991; Ford, 1989; Hollingworth, 1926; Karnes & Oehler-Stinnett, 1986; Lovecky, 1994; Roeper, 1982; Silverman, 1990). Research has suggested that perfectionism is best understood as a multidimensional concept (Enns & Cox, 2002).

Pathological Aspects of Perfectionism

Several studies focus on the pathological aspects of perfectionism; therefore, some researchers have viewed perfectionism in a negative perspective. Perfectionists "strain compulsively and unremittingly toward impossible goals and measure their own worth entirely in terms of productivity and accomplishment" (Burns, 1980). Pacht (1984) viewed perfectionism as inherently destructive, causing psychological problems. Adderholdt-Elliot (1991) considered perfectionistic tendencies of the gifted to be based in high standards, birth order, parents, teachers, and peer pressure. Some researchers suggest that unrealistic expectations, such as those centered in perfectionism, can lead to stress, anxiety, depression, and suicide (Callahan, 1993; Cross, 1996; Cross et al., 2002; Hewitt & Dyck, 1986; Hewitt, Flett, & Turnbull-Donovan, 1992; Huggins, Davis, Rooney, & Kane, 2008; Huprich, Porcerelli, Keaschuk, Binienda, & Engle, 2008; LaPointe & Crandell, 1980). Others suggest that expectations of perfection may lead gifted students to be more anxious and depressed (Thompson & Perkins, 2004) and that both SPP and SOP are associated with depression in both gifted and nongifted students (Hewitt et al., 2002).

In particular, perfectionism that involves excessive self-scrutiny and the tendency to be overly critical of oneself and focuses on others' perceptions of one's achievement has been associated with depressive symptoms (Dunkley & Blankstein, 2000). This type of perfectionism is also associated with a perceived lack of social support, in which individuals do not effectively seek social support even from their closest friends (Dunkley & Blankstein, 2000; Dunkley, Zuroff, & Blankstein, 2003). It has been proposed that this perceived lack of social support is a maladaptive aspect of perfectionism (Priel & Shahar, 2000). Some studies have suggested that perceived lack of social support is a critical factor in perfectionist individuals' adjustment (Dunkley & Blankstein, 2000; Dunkley et al., 2003) and that socially prescribed perfectionism, in particular, may lead to significant conflict in interpersonal relationships (Hewitt, Flett, & Mikail, 1995). In this same study, Hewitt et al. (1995) concluded that both Other-Oriented and Self-Oriented Perfectionism were associated with low relationship satisfaction. Socially Prescribed Perfectionism has been linked with maladaptive relationship behaviors, such as destructive problem-solving approaches (Flett, Hewitt, Shapiro, & Rayman, 2001). Generally, socially prescribed perfectionism has been linked with maladaptive behaviors (Stoeber, Feast, & Hayward, 2009). Hewitt and Flett (2004) have linked socially prescribed perfectionism with affective variables such as anxiety and depression. Huggins et al. (2008) found that socially prescribed perfectionism was a significant indicator of depression for preadolescents. Other researchers have found a tendency in some perfectionists toward neurotic coping strategies that lead to dysfunction, social anxiety, and poor health (Biran & Reese, 2007; Laurenti, Bruch, & Haase, 2008; Pritchard, Wilson, & Yamnitz, 2007; Stoltz & Ashby, 2007).

Perfectionism Resulting in Achievement

Some theorists suggest that gifted students may tend to have perfectionist strivings that result not necessarily in frustration, but in the healthy pursuit of achievement (Enns & Cox, 2002; LoCicero & Ashby, 2000; Parker, 2000). "In a positive form, perfectionism can provide the driving energy that leads to great achievement" (Roedell, 1984, p. 127). American children tend to express perfectionism through healthy achievement rather than academic and personal difficulties (Parker, 2000). The talented artists or musicians work intently to perfect their skills and abilities to produce the best work possible. Scientists work throughout their careers to find the cure for cancer or solutions to environmental problems. A common thread found in eminent scientists was an absorption in their work (Roe, 1970). The drive for excellence leads these gifted individuals to persevere and achieve their ultimate goal. "The most consistent characteristic of creative achievers is enthusiastic devotion to work" (Ochse, 1990, p. 130), which results in the high standards and a drive for excellence found in perfectionism. SOP, which is mainly an internal form of perfectionism, has been associated with conscientiousness, self-esteem, and academic motivation (Hewitt & Flett, 2004; Miquelon, Vallerand, Grouzet, & Cardinal, 2005; Molnar, Reker, Culp, Sadava, & DeCourville, 2006). Recent studies have shown that perfectionists had higher academic achievement, life satisfaction, and pride than their nonperfectionist peers (Must, 2008; Stoeber, Harris, & Moon, 2007; Witcher, Alexander, Onwuebuzie, Collins, & Witcher, 2007).

Range of Attributions of Perfectionism

Perfectionism in the literature has been theorized to be a construct that has multiple dimensions that may have either negative or positive effects on school-aged youth (Gilman, Ashby, Sverko, Florell, & Varjas, 2005). Hamachek (1978) viewed perfectionism as falling on a continuum from normal to neurotic. Normal perfectionists "derive a real sense of pleasure from the labors of painstaking effort" (Hamachek, 1978, p. 27). This healthy type focuses on perseverance, high achievement, and high standards. Neurotic perfectionists are "unable to feel satisfaction because in their own eyes they never seem to do things good enough to warrant that feeling" (Hamachek, 1978, p. 27). This unhealthy type results in frustrating behaviors that possibly lead to psychological and physiological disorders, such as depression (Hewitt & Dyck, 1986), eating disorders (Axtell & Newton, 1993), obsessive-compulsive personality disorders (Rasmussen & Eisen, 1992), suicide (Callahan, 1993; Cross, 1996; Cross et al., 2002), and alcoholism (Frost, Marten, Lahart, & Rosenblate, 1990)

This healthy type [of perfectionist] focuses on perseverance, high achievement, and high standards.

In a study using the Frost Multidimensional Perfectionism Scale (FMPS; Frost et al., 1990), Parker (1997) identified three types of academically talented adolescents: dysfunctional perfectionists, healthy perfectionists, and nonperfectionists. Dysfunctional perfectionists exhibited characteristics of anxiety, social detachment, hostility, and overcompetitiveness. Healthy perfectionists behaved agreeably and were socially well-adjusted, goal-oriented, and not neurotic. Nonperfectionists dealt with narcissistic tendencies and appeared distracted, disorganized, and undisciplined.

A study conducted by Schuler (2000) supports Hamachek's continuum of perfectionism. Schuler studied gifted adolescents in a rural community using the FMPS. Fifty-eight percent of the participants exhibited perfectionism in a healthy range resulting from a sense of order and organization that helped them achieve their personal best. They attributed their success to hard work, drive for perfection, and competition with friends. They considered doing their best as more important than what they produced. Twenty-eight and a half percent of the participants showed a fixation on making mistakes and a constant state of anxiety, which resulted in the neurotic form of perfectionism. Their focus rested in grades rather than doing their best and saw competition with friends in a negative light.

Hewitt and Flett (1991) described three dimensions of perfectionism: Self-Oriented, Other-Oriented, and Socially Prescribed. Results from their study, using their own Multidimensional Perfectionism Scale (MPS) indicated that SOP and SPP accompanied depression and maladjustment in both patients and non-patients. Self-Oriented Perfectionism focused on a desire to be perfect, unrealistic standards, and failures, flaws, and shortcomings. SPP emphasized a need to meet exaggerated expectations of the individual that one perceived to be held by others. Although negative psychological problems may correlate to these types of perfectionism, the push toward perfectionism may accompany positive adjustment and achievement (Hamachek, 1978; Hewitt & Flett, 1991). Speirs Neumeister (2004) investigated Hewitt and Flett's (1991) typology of self-oriented and socially prescribed perfectionism in relation to first-year college honor's students' responses to success and failure. Results from the study suggested that socially prescribed perfectionists minimized their successes and maximized their failures, giving external attributions for them. The researchers labeled this pattern as unhealthy, stating that it may correlate with perfectionism and depression. In contrast, self-oriented perfectionists took pride in their success and attributed that success to their own abilities and hard work. When failure occurred, they made realistic attributions that were situation specific. This healthy style of perfectionism fueled continued motivation and preserved self-concept.

Although social-emotional issues have commonly been linked to perfectionism in gifted individuals, empirical studies suggest that perfectionism exists in a population that includes a range of abilities (Parker, 2000). Gifted children or children with high academic ability are not at a greater risk for being perfectionists (Neihart, 1999; Nugent, 2000). "For a minority of gifted adolescents, perfectionism is a destructive force with detrimental consequences while for most it is a healthy aspect

of their lives resulting in positive growth" (Schuler, 2000, p. 190). Some empirical research suggests that gifted children who exhibit perfectionism may demonstrate healthy achievement rather than maladjustment (Ablard & Parker, 1997; Dweck, 1986; Dweck & Leggett, 1988; Heyman & Dweck, 1992; Parker, 1997).

Empirical knowledge about perfectionism and its connection to the gifted population is limited at best. Few studies have focused on perfectionism in gifted children and adolescents (Baker, 1995; Orange, 1997; Parker, 1997; Schuler & Siegle, 1994). Participants in one study of high school students that held high standards evidenced higher grade point averages and showed lower scores on measures of depression and self-esteem (Accordino, Accordino, & Slaney, 2000). Gilman and Ashby (2000) studied the effect of perfectionism on middle school students and found similar results to Accordino et al.'s (2000) study. A study by Dixon, Lapsley, and Hanchon (2004) examined the relationship of perfectionism to psychiatric symptoms, adjustment, self-esteem, and coping in a sample of gifted high school students. They found that some features of perfectionism, "such as organization and high personal standards (and parental expectations), could be cultivated to promote academic and personal adjustment in adolescents" (Dixon et al., 2004, p. 105). More recently, researchers who have examined perfectionism in students with a range of abilities have found that gifted students are no more likely to evidence signs of perfectionism than their nongifted or disabled peers (Greenspon, 2008; O'Brien, 2006). These conclusions lead to the suggestion that additional research with gifted children and adolescents could provide evidence demonstrating the effect of perfectionism on achievement and social-emotional well-being.

Purpose of Study

The purpose of this study was to explore the relationship between the perfectionism orientation of gifted and highly able children with the affective areas of depression, anxiety, and perfectionism. It was hypothesized that Socially Prescribed Perfectionism (SPP) would be positively correlated with depression levels in the gifted child and adolescent sample. It was also hypothesized that anxiety levels in the gifted child and adolescent sample would be positively correlated with SPP. Given the inconsistency in findings regarding anxiety and perfectionism, particularly in the gifted population, it was also hypothesized that Self-Oriented Perfectionism (SOP) would be negatively correlated with anxiety levels in the gifted child and adolescent sample.

Methodology

This study occurred during a 2-week summer enrichment program for gifted children. This program occurs each summer at a small, private university in a rural community in Texas. Teachers in this program hold graduate degrees in gifted education. The summer enrichment program serves as a culminating practicum experience for graduate students who are completing their master's degree in gifted education at the university in which the gifted program is housed. The program provides higher level thinking and creative problem solving experiences that are often not available to students in their local school programs. Directors of the program keep costs to a minimum and provide scholarship opportunities, allowing gifted children and adolescents from diverse socioeconomic status levels to participate in the camp.

Participants

The participants in this study consisted of 240 children between the ages of 7 and 14 years. Gender of participants included 58% male and 42% female. Self-identified ethnicity fell into seven categories: Caucasian (76%), Hispanic (9%), Asian American (4%), Indian/Pakistani (2.4%), Native American (1.2%), African American (1%), and Other (6.4%).

All participants were identified as gifted by one of two criteria: They had previously been identified and served through their school's program for gifted and talented children/youth or they were tested by the program staff using standardized group intelligence instruments and scored within the 90th percentile on the composite score of ability. Those students previously identified as gifted met the identification qualifications outlined by their local school district. According to the Texas Education Agency's (2000) *Texas State Plan for the Education of Gifted/ Talented Students,* local school districts must design their own identification system for students to enter their gifted program. The system must include multiple assessment criteria, including both objective and subjective measures, such as group administered ability (IQ) tests and achievement tests, teacher inventories, parent inventories, portfolios, and grades. If students had not been previously identified in their local school district, individual ability/ reasoning tests and an informal parent inventory were administered. The ability tests used for identification included the Wechsler Primary and Preschool Scale of Intelligence (Wechsler, 2002), and the Test of Nonverbal Intelligence, Third Edition (Brown, Sherbenou, & Johnsen, 2006).

Instruments

Researchers administered three assessments to participants in the study: Children's Depression Inventory (CDI; Kovacs, 1983), Revised Children's Manifest Anxiety Scale (RCMAS; Reynolds & Richmond, 1978), and Child and Adolescent Perfectionism Scale (CAPS; Hewitt, Flett, & Turnbull, 1994). Children took the assessment in a classroom group setting. All instruments were administered as required by the manual.

The CDI (Kovacs, 1983) measures symptoms of depression through a 27 item self-report instrument. Each item consists of three statements. For each item, the individual is asked to select the statement that best describes his or her feelings for the past 2 weeks. Subscales include Negative Mood, Interpersonal Problems, Ineffectiveness, Anhedonia, and Negative Self-Esteem. On the CDI, Negative Mood is defined as feeling sad, crying, worrying about "bad things," being bothered or upset by things, and being unable to make up one's mind. Interpersonal Problems are defined as problems/difficulty in interaction with people, trouble getting along, social avoidance, and social isolation. Ineffectiveness is defined as negative evaluation of

one's ability and school performance. Anhedonia is defined as "endogenous depression" including impaired ability to experience pleasure, loss of energy, sleep/ appetite problems, and sense of isolation. Negative Self-Esteem includes feelings of low self-esteem, self-dislike, lack of love, and suicidal thoughts. The intended age range for using the CDI is 7 to 17 years of age. Several studies have demonstrated good internal consistency for the CDI, ranging between 0.83 and 0.94 (Saylor, Finch, Spirito, & Bennett, 1984).

The RCMAS (Reynolds & Richmond, 1978) measures symptoms of anxiety through a 37 item self-report instrument that requires a yes or no answer to specific questions. Subscales include Physiological Anxiety, Worry/Oversensitivity, and Social Concerns/Concentration. On the RCMAS, Physiological Anxiety is defined as the index of a child's expression of physical manifestations of anxiety. Worry/Oversensitivity items contain the word "worry," and suggest the person is afraid, nervous, and in some manner oversensitive to environmental pressures. This scale measures the internalization of anxiety. Social Concerns/Concentration are defined as concern about self vis-à-vis other people or express some difficulty concentrating, and feel unable to live up to expectations of other significant individuals in their lives. The age range for the RCMAS is 6 to 19 years. Test-retest reliability coefficients range from .66 to .67 at 9 months, with an internal consistency coefficient of .85.

The CAPS (Hewitt et al., 1994) is a 22-item self-report instrument that has two subscales, Self-Oriented and Socially Prescribed Perfectionism. This is a downward extension of the Multidimensional Perfectionism Scale (MPS; Hewitt & Flett, 1991). Participants endorse items in relation to how they view them as true for themselves, such as, "I try to be perfect in everything that I do." On the CAPS, SOP is characterized by exacting standards set for one's self. This subtype exhibits a healthy component that may propel one toward higher levels of effort and achievement. SPP represents internalization of the perceived perfectionistic expectations of significant others in one's life. The age range for the CAPS is 6 to 16 years. Good internal consistency and adequate test-retest reliability have been reported (Castro, Gila, Gual, Lahortiga, Saura, & Toro, 2004).

Procedure

At the beginning of the study, researchers provided consent forms for parents to sign and return in order for their children to participate in the study. Ninety-six percent of the parents of all of the students participating in the camp granted permission for participation and all of these students participated. At the beginning of each day on the second, third, and fourth days of camp, children were administered the instruments by graduate students. Each administration took approximately 15 minutes to conduct. The instruments were administered in the following order: CAPS, CDI, and RCMAS.

Results

Descriptive statistics were gathered that indicated that, on the CAPS, more of the students in the current study rated themselves as exhibiting behaviors and feelings consistent with SOP than with SPP, with 43.5% of respondents rating themselves as exhibiting characteristics of SOP and 14.6% of respondents rating themselves as exhibiting characteristics of SPP.

A correlational analysis was conducted in order to evaluate the extent to which participants' ratings of their own perfectionism and their symptoms related to depression and anxiety were related. A traditional Bonferroni adjustment was made to reduce type I error, adjusting the p value from $p < .05$ to $p < .007$.

Researchers calculated a Pearson correlation coefficient between SPP and the CDI Depression scale ($M = 39.256$, $SD = 4.682$). The resulting correlation was $r = .206$, a modest positive relationship that was significant at the .007 level ($p = .003$) and accounted for 30% of the variance. A Pearson correlation coefficient was also calculated between SPP and the sub-scales of the CDI. The resulting correlation for the Anhedonia subscale ($M = 12.126$, $SD = 2.151$) was $r = .195$, a modest positive relationship that was significant at the .007 level ($p = .004$) but accounted for only 4% of variance. The results of this analysis are consistent with expectations in that SPP was positively correlated at a statistically significant level with depression. It is interesting to note that modest relationships that were statistically significant were also found between SPP and the Anhedonia subscale of the CDI. Researchers also calculated a Pearson correlation coefficient between SOP and the CDI Depression scale. The resulting correlation was $r = .097$, which was not statistically significant ($p = .169$). Correlations are shown in Table 1.

In addition, a Pearson correlation coefficient was calculated between SOP and the RCMAS Anxiety scale ($M = 16.807$, $SD = 6.414$). The resulting correlation was $r = -.334$, a modest negative relationship at the .007 level ($p = .000$) of significance that accounted for 12% of the variance. Correlations were also computed between SPP and the

RCMAS Anxiety scale and subscales. The resulting correlation for the Anxiety scale and SPP was $r = -.432$, a moderately negative relationship at the .007 level ($p = .000$) of significance accounting for 19% of the variance. Correlations are shown in Table 2.

No other statistically significant correlations were found between types of perfectionism and affective areas measured. These findings were consistent with our expectations in that SOP was negatively correlated in a statistically significant way with anxiety. However, the findings were not consistent with our expectations in that the statistically significant relationship that was found between SPP and Anxiety was in the negative direction. Although none of the correlations' coefficients were above .50 and were considered modest, they were powerful due to the size of the sample, showing significant trends.

Discussion

Three features of the results of this study are particularly important: (a) the positive correlation between depression and socially prescribed or externally derived perfectionism; (b) the positive correlation between specific aspects of depression, such as physiological symptomology and socially prescribed or externally derived perfectionism; and (c) the negative correlation between anxiety and both self-oriented/internally and socially prescribed/externally derived perfectionism.

The relationship between Depression and SPP was confirmed in the gifted population and has been found in other samples (Hewitt et al., 2002; Stoeber et al., 2009; Thompson & Perkins, 2004). This finding, while replicating others in some ways, is important in that this study used a relatively large rural sample of gifted students, which represents a different population than has been represented in previous studies. These results support the research that suggests that perfectionism exists in a population that includes a range of abilities (Parker, 2000) in that they are the same as those found in other populations (Hewitt et al., 2002; Thompson & Perkins, 2004). These findings are consistent with research that suggests that expectations of perfection may lead students to be more depressed (Callahan, 1993; Hewitt & Dyck, 1986; Hewitt et al., 1992; LaPointe & Crandell, 1980, Thompson & Perkins, 2004; Stoeber et al., 2009). It also confirms the research that suggests that particular types of perfectionism may lead to unhealthy emotional development (Biran & Reese, 2007; Hamachek, 1978; Laurenti et al., 2008; Pritchard et al., 2007; Schuler, 2000; Stoltz & Ashby, 2007).

In this sample of gifted students, those who rated themselves as having high levels of socially prescribed perfectionism also rated themselves as having high levels of depression, in particular those symptoms involving anhedonia. The fact that this specific aspect of depression, which involves physiological symptoms of depression, was linked in this sample with SPP is interesting. These findings suggest that not only general symptoms of depression but particular manifestations may be linked with perfectionist tendencies that arise from external expectations.

In contrast to findings in other studies (Thompson & Perkins, 2004), the positive relationship between Anxiety and SPP

Table 1 Correlations Among Types of Perfectionism and CDI Depression Scores

Type of perfectionism	Depression totals
Socially Prescribed Perfectionism (SPP)	.206*
Self-Oriented Perfectionism (SOP)	.097

* $p < .007$ for all analyses. CDI = Children Depression Inventory.

Table 2 Correlations Among Types of Perfectionism and RCMAS Anxiety Scores

Type of perfectionism	Anxiety totals
Socially Prescribed Perfectionism (SPP)	-.432*
Self-Oriented Perfectionism (SOP)	-.334*

* $p < .007$ for all analyses. RCMAS= Revised Children's Manifest Anxiety Scale.

was not confirmed in this study. It may be that this is due to the fact that the study was conducted during the summer months and while subjects were participating in an activity that they elected to attend. Subjects may have been less anxious than they would have been during the academic school year when required to participate in particular subject study and activities not of their own choosing.

Some limitations to this study were present. One limitation related to the fact that the population used in this study included students who scored in the 90th percentile and above on ability and achievement tests. Most school programs developed for gifted and talented students serve gifted students functioning in the 95th percentile or above on identification measures. Therefore, the population of the current study may not represent populations served in all gifted education programs. Another limitation resulted from the fact that the instruments used in this study were self-report instruments, which rely on the subject to report his or her own thoughts and feelings. The results of self-report instruments may not be reliable if the subjects involved do not report truthfully.

Conclusions

The findings from this study provide additional insights into the relationship between perfectionism, depression, and anxiety in gifted students. Because the study analyzed data correlationally, no assumptions of causality can be assumed. Therefore, researchers do not conclude that perfectionism causes depression or that perfectionism reduces incidence of anxiety. Participants who showed a tendency for socially prescribed perfectionism also showed characteristics of "endogenous depression" involving difficulty experiencing pleasure, loss of energy, sleep/appetite problems, and sense of isolation. Participants exhibiting high levels of both self-oriented and socially prescribed perfectionism expressed low levels of anxiety.

These results support Hewitt and Flett's (1991) thesis that perfectionism exists on a continuum and that while some types of perfectionism (SPP) tend to occur with depression, it may also be negatively correlated with levels of anxiety. These data regarding tendencies toward depression support previous studies suggesting that perfectionist tendencies are linked to depression in gifted students (Callahan, 1993; Hewitt & Dyck, 1986; Hewitt et al., 1992; Hewitt et al., 2002; LaPointe & Crandell, 1980). The results about feelings of anxiety do not support previous studies and literature reviews suggesting that perfection correlates to anxiety in gifted students (Greenspon, 2000; Neihart et al., 2002; Schuler, 2000; Thompson & Perkins, 2004).

Although results from this study cannot be generalized to the larger population of gifted individuals, they do suggest several implications for home and school. They suggest that parents and teachers focus on providing gifted students with realistic expectations while offering a consistent level of challenge in the early grade levels. This combination of challenge and realistic expectations allows students to experience intellectual challenge as a positive learning experience rather than something to be avoided.

> **[A] combination of challenge and realistic expectations allows students to experience intellectual challenge as a positive learning experience rather than something to be avoided.**

These findings indicate that perfectionism may not necessarily be anxiety provoking for gifted students. Students who evidence tendencies toward perfectionism should be encouraged to be aware of their own levels of anxiety and to understand when they may be putting too much pressure on themselves. This approach allows children the opportunity to use their perfectionist tendencies to excel while providing them with guidance regarding potential anxiety.

The results of this study suggest that perfectionist tendencies that focus on external expectations may accompany more depressive symptomology. Students who evidence this type of perfectionism (SPP) should be encouraged to be aware of their moods and to monitor their expectations. It is also important in these circumstances that there be frank communication between the parent, child, and school community regarding the messages that are being sent by others regarding expectations for perfection. Gifted learners who evidence SPP may need assistance in learning how to communicate their feelings effectively and seek social support when appropriate.

The TIEL model of teaching might be particularly useful in working with these issues. This model espouses observations of students to monitor both intellectual and social-emotional development (Folsom, 2006). Using this method provides teachers of gifted students with a framework from which to observe the child's emotional development in specific areas that may be useful in developing the ability to enjoy challenge rather than becoming overwhelmed by expectations of perfectionism. For example, the TIEL model emphasizes the need for empathy, including caring for oneself, as well as the divergent abilities of flexible thinking and being able to see options. Empathy and specifically learning to care for oneself is important in allowing a child to understand his or her own internal drive for perfection and discriminate this from pressure from others to achieve perfection. Flexibility of thinking and the ability to see options allows the child to develop skills that can benefit him or her in the problem-solving process when faced with the inability to achieve perfection. The teachers of gifted children who struggle with SPP and manifest symptoms of depression might benefit from using the TIEL model to observe the child's skills in these areas and then to design lessons or extensions of lessons that focus on the further development of these skills.

This study suggests several issues that may be examined in future research. The moderate correlations between the specific subscale of the CDI of Anhedonia with SPP suggests that research investigating the relationship between specific sets of depressive symptomology and socially prescribed perfectionism may be helpful in furthering the understanding of the extent of this relationship in gifted individuals in particular. It also suggests that future research studies focus on the usefulness of specific educational models, such as the TIEL model, in aiding in the development of social-emotional learning.

References

Ablard, K. E., & Parker, W. D. (1997). Parents' achievement goals and perfectionism in their academically talented children. *Journal of Youth and Adolescence, 26,* 651–667.

Accordino, D. B., Accordino, M. P., & Stanley, R. B. (2000). An investigation of perfectionism, mental health, achievement, and achievement motivation in adolescents. *Psychology in the Schools, 37,* 535–545.

Adderholdt-Elliott, M. (1991). Perfectionism and the gifted adolescent. In M. Birely & J. Greenshaft (Eds.), *Understanding the gifted adolescent: Educational, developmental, and multi-cultural issues* (pp. 65–75). New York, NY: Teachers College Press.

Axtell, A., & Newton, B. J. (1993). An analysis of Adlerian life themes of bulimic women. *Individual Psychology: Journal of Adlerian Theory, Research, & Practice, 49,* 58–67.

Baker, J. A. (1995). Depression and suicidal ideation among academically gifted adolescents. *Gifted Child Quarterly, 39,* 218–223.

Biran, M. W., & Reese, C. (2007). Parental influences on social anxiety: The sources of perfectionism. *Journal of the American Psychoanalytic Association, 55,* 282–285.

Brown, L., Sherbenou, R. J., & Johnsen, S. K. (2006). *Test of Nonverbal Intelligence, Third Edition.* Austin, TX: PRO-ED.

Burns, D. D. (1980). The perfectionist's script for defeat. *Psychology Today, 14*(11), 34–44.

Callahan, J. (1993). Blueprint for an adolescent suicidal crisis. *Psychiatric Annals, 23,* 263–270.

Castro, J., Gila, A., Gual, P., Lahortiga, F., Saura, B., & Toro, J. (2004). Perfectionism dimensions in children and adolescents with anorexia nervosa. *Journal of Adolescent Health, 35,* 392–398.

Cross, T. L. (1996). Examining claims about gifted children and suicide. *Gifted Child Today, 18*(3), 46–48.

Cross, T. L., Gust-Brey, K., & Ball, P. B. (2002). A psychological autopsy of the suicide of an academically gifted student: Researchers' and parents' perspectives. *Gifted Child Quarterly, 46,* 247–265.

Dixon, F. E., Lapsley, D. K., & Hanchon, T. A. (2004). An empirical typology of perfectionism in gifted adolescents. *Gifted Child Quarterly, 48,* 95–106.

Dunkley, D. M., & Blankstein, K. R. (2000). Self-critical perfectionism, coping, hassles, and current distress: A structural equation modeling approach. *Cognitive Therapy and Research, 24,* 713–730.

Dunkley, D. M., Zuroff, D. C., & Blankstein, K. R. (2003). Self-critical perfectionism and daily affect: Dispositional and situational influences on stress and coping. *Journal of Personality and Social Psychology, 84,* 234–252.

Dweck, C. S. (1986). Motivational processes affecting learning. *American Psychologist, 41,* 1040–1048.

Dweck, C. S., & Leggett, E. L. (1988). A social-cognitive approach to motivation and personality. *Psychological Review, 95,* 256–273.

Enns, M. W., & Cox, B. J. (2002). The nature and assessment of perfectionism: A critical analysis. In G. L. Flett & P. L. Hewitt (Eds.), *Perfectionism: Theory, research, and treatment* (pp. 33–62). Washington, DC: American Psychological Association.

Flett, G. L., Hewitt, P. L., Shapiro, B., & Rayman, J. (2001). Perfectionism, beliefs, and adjustment in dating relationships. *Current Psychology, 20,* 289–311.

Folsom, C. (2006). Making conceptual connections between gifted and general education: Teaching for intellectual and emotional learning (TIEL). *Roeper Review, 28,* 79–87.

Ford, M. A. (1989). Students' perceptions of affective issues impacting the social and emotional development and school performance of the gifted/talented youngsters. *Roeper Review, 11,* 131–134.

Frost, R. O., Marten, O., Lahart, C., & Rosenblate, R. (1990). The dimensions of perfectionism. *Cognitive Therapy and Research, 14,* 449–468.

Gilman, R., Ashby, J. S., Sverko, D., Florell, D., & Varjas, K. (2005). A study of perfectionism in American and Croatian youth. *Personality and Individual Differences, 39,* 155–166.

Gilman, R., & Ashby, J. S. (2000). Multidimensional perfectionism in a sample of middle school students: An exploratory investigation. *Psychology in the Schools, 40,* 677–689.

Greenspon, T. S. (2000). The self experience of the gifted person: Theory and definitions. *Roeper Review, 22,* 176–182.

Greenspon, T. S. (2008). Making sense of error: A view of the origins and treatment of perfectionism. *American Journal of Psychotherapy, 62,* 263–282.

Hamachek, D. E. (1978). Psychodynamics of normal and neurotic perfectionism. *Psychology, 15,* 27–33.

Hewitt, P. L., Caelian, C. F., Flett, G. L., Sherry, S. B., Collins, L., & Flynn, C. A. (2002). Perfectionism in children: associations with depression, anxiety, and anger. *Personality and Individual Differences 32,* 1049–1061.

Hewitt, P. L., & Dyck, D. G. (1986). Perfectionism, stress, and vulnerability to depression. *Cognitive Therapy and Research, 10,* 137–142.

Hewitt, P. L., & Flett, G. L. (1991). Perfection in the self and social contexts: Conceptualization, assessment, and association with psychopathology. *Journal of Personality and Social Psychology, 60,* 456–470.

Hewitt, P. L., & Flett, G. L. (2004). *Multidimensional Perfectionism Scale (MPS).* Toronto, Canada: Multi-Health Systems.

Hewitt, P. L., Flett, G. L., & Mikail, S. (1995). Perfectionism and family adjustment in pain patients and their spouses. *Journal of Family Psychology, 9,* 335–347.

Hewitt, P. L., Flett, G. L., & Turnbull, W. (1994). Borderline personality disorder: An investigation with the Multidimensional Perfectionism Scale. *European Journal of Personality Assessment, 10,* 28–33.

Hewitt, P. L., Flett, G. L., & Turnbull-Donovan, W. (1992). Perfectionism and suicide potential. *British Journal of Clinical Psychology, 31,* 181–190.

Heyman, G. D., & Dweck, C. S. (1992). Achievement goals and intrinsic motivation: Their relation and their role in adaptive motivation. *Motivation and Emotion, 16,* 231–247.

Hollingworth, L. S. (1926). *Gifted children: Their nature and nurture.* New York, NY: Macmillan.

Hollingworth, L. S. (1942) *Children above the 180 IQ Stanford-Binet: Origin and development.* Yonkers-on-Hudson, NY: World Book.

Huggins, L., Davis, M. C., Rooney, R., & Kane, R. (2008). Socially prescribed and self-oriented perfectionism as predictors of depressive diagnosis in preadolescents. *Australian Journal of Guidance and Counseling, 18,* 182–194.

Huprich, S. K., Porcerelli, J., Keaschuk, R., Binienda, J., & Engle, B. (2008). Depressive personality disorder, dysthymia, and their relationship to perfectionism. *Depression and Anxiety, 25,* 207–217.

Jackson, P. S. (1998). Bright star—Black sky: A phenomenological study of depression as a window into the psyche of the gifted adolescent. *Roeper Review, 20,* 215–221.

Janos, P. M., & Robinson, N. M. (1985). Psychosocial development in intellectually gifted children. In F. D. Horowitz & M. O'Brien (Eds.), *The gifted and talented: Developmental perspectives* (pp. 149–195). Washington, DC: American Psychological Association.

Kaiser, C. F., & Berndt, D. J. (1986). Predicators of loneliness in the gifted adolescent. *Gifted Child Quarterly, 29,* 74–77.

Karnes, F., & Oehler-Stinnett, J. (1986). Life events as stressors with gifted adolescents. *Psychology in the Schools, 23,* 406–414.

Keiley, M. K. (2002). Affect regulation and the gifted. In M. Neihart, S. M. Reis, N. M. Robinson, & S. M. Moon, (Eds.), *The social and emotional development of gifted children: What do we know?* (pp. 41–50). Waco, TX: Prufrock Press.

Kovacs, M. (1983). *The Children's Depression Inventory: A self-rated depression scale for school-aged youngsters.* Unpublished manuscript, University of Pittsburgh, Pittsburgh, PA.

LaPointe, K. A., & Crandell, C. J. (1980). Relationship of irrational beliefs to self-reported depression. *Cognitive Therapy and Research, 4,* 247–250.

Laurenti, H. J., Bruch, M. A., & Haase, R. F. (2008). Social anxiety and socially prescribed perfectionism: Unique and interactive relationships with maladaptive appraisal of interpersonal situations. *Personality and Individual Differences, 45,* 55–61.

LoCicero, K. A., & Ashby, J. S. (2000). Multidimensional perfectionism in middle school age gifted students: A comparison to peers from the general cohort. *Roeper Review, 20,* 39–42.

Lovecky, D. V. (1994). Exceptionally gifted children: Different minds. *Roeper Review, 17,* 116–120.

Miquelon, P., Vallerand, R. J., Grouzet, F. M. E., & Cardinal, G. (2005). Perfectionism, academic motivation, and psychological adjustment: An integrative model. *Personality and Social Psychology Bulletin, 31,* 913–924.

Molnar, D. S., Reker, D. L., Culp, N. A., Sadava, S. W., & DeCourville, N. H. (2006). A mediated model of perfectionism, affect, and physical health. *Journal of Research on Personality, 40,* 482–500.

Moon, S. M., & Hall, A. S. (1997). Family therapy with intellectually and creatively gifted children. *Journal of Martial and Family Therapy, 24,* 59–80.

Moon, S. M., Kelly, K. R., & Feldhusen, J. F. (1997). Specialized counseling services for gifted youth and their families: A needs assessment. *Gifted Child Quarterly, 41,* 16–25.

Must, S. (2008). The dual effects of parenting and perfectionism on maladjustment and academic performance of affluent suburban adolescents. *Dissertation Abstracts International, 68.* (UMI No. 0419–4217)

Neihart, M. (1999). The impact of giftedness on psychological well being. *Roeper Review, 22,* 1–4.

Neihart, M., Reis, S. M., Robinson, N. M., & Moon, S. M. (2002). *The social and emotional development of gifted children: What do we know?* Waco, TX: Prufrock Press.

Nugent, S. A. (2000). Perfectionism: Its manifestations and classroom-based interventions. *Journal of Secondary Gifted Education, 11,* 215–222.

O'Brien, D. R. (2006). Distinguishing between students with and without learning disabilities: A comparative analysis of cognition, achievement, perceptual skills, behavior, and executive functioning. *Dissertation Abstracts International, 67.* (UMI No. AA13209081)

Ochse, R. (1990). *Before the gates of excellence: Determinants of creative genius.* New York, NY: Cambridge University Press.

Orange, C. (1997). Gifted students and perfectionism. *Roeper Review, 20,* 39–41.

Pacht, A. R. (1984). Reflections on perfectionism. *American Psychologist, 39,* 286–390.

Parker, W. D. (1997). An empirical typology of perfectionism in academically talented children. *American Educational Research Journal, 34,* 545–562.

Parker, W. D. (2000). Healthy perfectionism in the gifted. *Journal of Secondary Gifted Education, 11,* 173–183.

Parker, W. D., & Adkins, K. K. (1995). Perfectionism and the gifted. *Roeper Review, 17,* 13–17.

Piechowski, M. M. (1997). Emotional giftedness: The measure of intrapersonal intelligence. In N. Colangelo & G. A. Davis (Eds.), *Handbook of gifted education* (2nd ed., pp. 398–381). Boston, MA: Allyn & Bacon.

Priel, B., & Shahar, G. (2000). Dependency, self-criticism, social context, and distress: Comparing moderating and mediating models. *Personality and Individual Differences, 28,* 515–525.

Pritchard, M. E., Wilson, G. S., & Yamnitz, G. B. (2007). What predicts adjustment among college students? A longitudinal panel study. *Journal of American College Health, 56,* 15–21.

Rasmussen, S. A., & Eisen, J. L. (1992). The epidemiology and clinical features of obsessive compulsive disorder. *Psychiatric Clinics of North America, 15,* 743–758.

Reynolds, C., & Richmond, B. (1978). "What I think and feel": A revised measure of children's manifest anxiety. *Journal of Abnormal Child Psychology, 6,* 271–280.

Roe, A. (1970). A psychologist examines sixty-four eminent scientists. In P. E. Vernon (Ed.), *Creativity: Selected readings* (pp. 23–51). Harmondsworth, UK: Penguin.

Roedell, W. C. (1984). Vulnerabilities of highly gifted children. *Roeper Review, 6,* 127–130.

Roeper, A. (1982). How the gifted cope with their emotions. *Roeper Review, 5,* 21–26.

Roeper, A. (1995). *Selected writing and speeches.* Minneapolis, MN: Free Spirit.

Roeper, A. (1996). A personal statement of philosophy of George and Annemarie Roeper. *Roeper Review, 19,* 18–19.

Saylor, C., Finch, A., Spirito, A., & Bennett, B. (1984). The Children's Depression Inventory: A systematic evaluation of psychometric properties. *Journal of Consulting and Clinical Psychology, 52,* 955–967.

Schuler, P. A. (2000). Perfectionism and gifted adolescents. *Journal of Secondary Gifted Education, 11,* 183–192.

Schuler, P. A., & Siegle, D. (1994). [Analysis of the Multidimensional Perfectionism Scale with middle school gifted students]. Unpublished raw data.

Silverman, L. K. (1990). The crucible of perfectionism. In B. Holyst (Ed.), *Mental health in a changing world* (pp. 39–49). Warsaw, Poland: The Polish Society of Mental Health.

Silverman, L. K. (1993). The gifted individual. In L. K. Silverman (Ed.), *Counseling the gifted and talented* (pp. 3–28). Denver, CO: Love.

Speirs Neumeister, K. L. (2004). Interpreting successes and failures: The influence of perfectionism on perspective. *Journal for the Education of the Gifted, 27,* 311–335.

Stoeber, J., Feast, A. R., & Hayward, J. A. (2009). Self-oriented and socially prescribed perfectionism: Differential relationships with intrinsic and extrinsic motivation and test anxiety. *Personality and Individual Differences, 47,* 423–428.

Stoeber, J., Harris, R. A., & Moon, P. S. (2007). Perfectionism and the experience of pride, shame, and guilt: Comparing healthy perfectionists, unhealthy perfectionists, and non-perfectionists. *Personality and Individual Differences, 43,* 131–141.

Stoltz, K., & Ashby, J. S. (2007). Perfectionism and lifestyle: Personality differences among adaptive perfectionists, maladaptive perfectionists, and nonperfectionists. *The Journal of Individual Psychology, 63,* 414–423.

Texas Education Agency. (2000). *Texas state plan for the education of gifted/talented students.* Austin: Texas Education Agency.

Thompson, K., & Perkins, T. S. (2004). *The relationship of socially prescribed perfectionism to concurrent measures of depression and anxiety in a nonclinical sample of adolescents* (Unpublished thesis). Abilene Christian University, Abilene, TX.

Webb, J., Meckstroth, E., & Tolan, S. S. (1982). *Guiding the gifted child: A practical source for parents and teachers.* Columbus: Ohio Psychology Press.

Wechsler, D. (2002). *Wechsler Primary and Preschool Scale of Intelligence* (3rd ed.). San Antonio, TX: Pearson Education.

Witcher, L. A., Alexander, E. S., Onwuebuzie, A. J., Collins, K. M. T., & Witcher, A. E. (2007). The relationship between psychology students' levels of perfectionism and achievement in a graduate-level research methodology course. *Personality and Individual Differences, 43,* 1396–1405.

Critical Thinking

1. Compare and contrast the two perspectives on perfectionism.
2. What kind of research study is this?
3. Summarize the findings of the study.
4. Summarize the implications of the study.

Social and Emotional Development of Gifted Children: Straight Talk

Tracy L. Cross, PhD

In the past year I have been asked during interviews on two different occasions what message I would like to convey directly to parents, teachers, and counselors of gifted children. Consequently, I have had a fair amount of time to think about this and have developed a list of eight topics I think are important enough to speak to quite directly.

1. The first topic that I would like to address is the question "Are all students gifted?" The answer to this question is no. As Jim Gallagher has said on many occasions, "gifted in what?" To be gifted one must ultimately be gifted in something. All children are wonderful. They are considered in many cultures as the most valuable beings in the world. Even so, they are not gifted by the profession's definitions. Giftedness is a scientific construct that has a relatively circumscribed definition. Therefore, only a small portion of children would actually be identified as gifted.

2. Students with gifts and talents are as equally mentally and physically healthy (if not more so) as the general population of students. Studies in the United States going back 80 or more years, along with multiple more recent studies, have illustrated this fact again and again. Even in very specific areas such as suicidal behavior, recent research has shown that suicide ideation among the gifted is at the same level or less than that of the general population. And, while we do not know for sure in terms of prevalence rates of completed suicide, significant differences between the general population and students with gifts and talents have not been shown.

3. This third issue is difficult to describe as it deals with how we come to know about gifted children. Who are the gifted, and how do we come to find them? We tend to define giftedness as children who require a special education. We tend to identify them on the basis of the potential or abilities for outstanding performance in the future. Then, over time, we anoint them gifted or talented on the basis of their achievement in a specific domain.

Although these three emphases of definition, identification, and recognition seem quite similar, in fact they are different. With young students who have verbal skills, we typically find them with some indication on a standardized test or a hint a teacher picks up on. This is really an effort to predict the future

by determining that a child has a need warranting a special education. Then we bring to bear what we can in terms of teaching, curriculum, and other opportunities to develop these potentialities into talent areas such as mathematics, language arts, and the like. The primary problem is that we know there are influences on each of these three areas, including social class. So, economic status tends to end up being a very important variable that prevents us from identifying and providing the services these children need to be successful. This is very important given the increasing diversity in our country. This is, in my opinion, the most important issue of our day—finding and servicing all of the children with gifts and talents.

4. Another very important issue is the fact that many of us have changed our views about what giftedness is, from that of an entity, meaning something that one is born with, to a phenomenon that is incremental in its development. Professionals including Carol Dweck have written about this way of thinking. The incremental model is much more representative of what actually takes place in a person's life from birth until death relative to developing specific skills. Across the lifespan, people receive instruction, struggle with some failure and develop knowledge and skills. This is a much healthier notion to guide the efforts of a parent, teacher, or counselor in terms of the work we do on behalf of our children. We should not think of them as fully formed because someone has anointed them as gifted (entity model). But, rather, we should think of them as requiring a special education now and over time. With our expertise being brought to bear, the child will hopefully reach his or her full potential.

5. The fifth topic is parenting and the development of students with gifts and talents. The research base here over the years has been rather meager but it is growing. We know from research on the development of children in general that there are predictable outcomes of parenting styles and approaches. As we continue to pursue the development of students with gifts and talents, we need to conduct considerable research in this area so we can better guide and prepare parents to work with children. Engaging children in dialogue that accentuates communication, while at the same time helping them individuate, can lead to high levels of agency and greater life successes. Until the

research base in this area expands, however, we would be wise to draw on the best practices of parenting research in general. We also can draw from research investigating the lived experiences of gifted students and how they cope with their lives in school. These two databases will shed light on parenting issues. With gifted studies research, we should carefully monitor the growing research bases on perfectionism and resiliency and gifted students. Insights about parenting students with gifts and talents, while in its early stages, are being revealed, holding great promise for guiding parenting practices in the future.

6. The next issue is diversity and giftedness. There is so much yet to know about diversity and gifted students that we are just scratching the surface. All groups of people have samples within them who have outstanding potential to develop into great talents within and outside of the traditional culture they represent. Moreover, as we become more diverse as a country, this fact has become increasingly obvious in some areas such as the visual arts, where there is a physical manifestation of emerging talent that most adults can recognize. It is easy to garner the resources to support these students while other talent domains such as early mathematic potential or logic takes awhile to reveal itself in a manner that the general population can understand. So much work needs to be done in the area of diversity and giftedness to maximize the potential of all the students.

An interesting corollary to the diversification of America intersecting with the technology evolution is playing out socially among our students. We have been living through fascinating changes in American culture over the past 20 years or so as an evolution of technologies in terms of laptop computers, desktop computers, and, more recently, gaming in the extent to which people from all walks of life participate in these activities. One of the manifestations of this evolution has been the change of the language associated historically with gifted children such as being called a *nerd,* a *geek,* a *brainiac,* or any number of other things. This evolution where gifted children often are top competitors in games, in fixing computers, or in setting up things has raised their status in the general population. Stores have Geek Squads and adults will use the term *geek* or *nerd* as an adjective rather than a noun. I think it is showing that as our country becomes more diverse, being an academically or intellectually gifted person gets defined in the broad context and over time is becoming less as a problem for gifted people as compared to what it was 50 or even 20 years ago.

7. True for the general population of adolescents, and especially true for some gifted adolescents, is the desire for authenticity among the adults they deal with. In my work at the Indiana Academy, I observed that many intellectually gifted adolescents desired interactions to be absolutely authentic and when they assess that an adult person is not being authentic—genuine—not only do they devalue that person but it causes them conflict in trying to make sense out of the importance they describe to adults and the authentic behavior. For some of these gifted young people, they conclude that most people are inauthentic most of the time and that the only true feeling is that of pain, and that every other feeling state is more manufactured than authentic. There are all sorts of negative ramifications to the belief that this feeling state of pain is the only genuine one. One of the results is students will find ways to feel pain so they feel themselves to be authentic, so they have feelings they can identify, and so they can gain a sense of relief. We know from our research that cutting behavior among our youth, adolescents, and young adults has increased quite a bit in the last 20 years and in my opinion is quite likely associated in some cases with this desire for authenticity.

8. The last important issue is that it is incumbent upon us as adults to act proactively on behalf of students with gifts and talents. The important point here is that we should all feel morally obligated to act on behalf of students with gifts and talents because not to do so is, in fact, choosing not to act. Inaction has all sorts of consequences for gifted students in terms of their not being challenged in school, feeling frustrated, feeling unvalued, feeling like there is something wrong with them, and so forth. We cannot be guilty of turning a blind eye to the social and emotional issues and needs of students with gifts and talents. If we do nothing, we become complicit in the decline of their psychological well-being.

One approach to engaging others is for us use language that does not pit us against our colleagues. For example, when we talk about students with gifts and talents, we should frame our conversation within the goal set that our schools should aspire to all students maximizing their potential, including gifted children. This will allow a different kind of conversation to be held than often occurs. This goal for students runs counter to minimum competency testing common to the U.S. Changing the conversation from minimum competency to maximizing the potential of all students will dramatically affect the opportunities for all students, including students with gifts and talents.

The social and emotional development of students with gifts and talents lasts a lifetime. We have learned many important lessons about how to help them develop during their school-age years and with this newfound knowledge have corresponding responsibility to act. The eight issues discussed in this column bring to light some of the current thinking that can be helpful to those of us (parents, teachers, counselors) who are in important positions to help them develop. Understanding what giftedness actually is and is not, how to identify it, moving from an entity model of giftedness to an incremental model, continuing to strive to be as effective a parent as one can be, and understanding the needs of authenticity enable adults to assist in the social and emotional development of students with gifts and talents.

Critical Thinking

1. What does it mean to be gifted?
2. What challenges do gifted students face?

Understanding Unconscious Bias and Unintentional Racism

Acknowledging our possible biases and working together openly is essential for developing community in our schools.

JEAN MOULE

In the blink of an eye, unconscious bias was visible to me, an African American. A man saw my face as I walked into the store and unconsciously checked his wallet. On the street, a woman catches my eye a half block away and moves her purse from the handle of her baby's stroller to her side as she arranges the baby's blanket. In the airport, a man signals to his wife to move her purse so it is not over the back of her chair, which is adjacent to the one I am moving toward. What is happening in these instances? Were these actions general safety precautions? If so, why did the sight only of my brown face, not the others who moved among these individuals, elicit these actions?

I believe these are examples of "blink of the eye" racism. Such unconscious biases lead to unintentional racism: racism that is usually invisible even *and especially* to those who perpetrate it. Yet, most people do not want to be considered racist or capable of racist acts because the spoken and unspoken norm is that "good people do not discriminate or in any way participate in racism" (Dovidio and Gaertner 2005, p. 2).

Such unconscious biases affect all of our relationships, whether they are fleeting relationships in airports or longer term relationships between teachers and students, teachers and parents, teachers and other educators. Understanding our own biases is a first step toward improving the interactions that we have with all people and is essential if we hope to build deep community within our schools.

Biases are rooted in stereotypes and prejudices. A stereotype is a simplistic image or distorted truth about a person or group based on a prejudgment of habits, traits, abilities, or expectations (Weinstein and Mellen 1997). Ethnic and racial stereotypes are learned as part of normal socialization and are consistent among many populations and across time. An excellent illustration of this phenomenon is a recent exchange that repeated Clark's classic 1954 doll study. In a video, completed by a 17-year-old film student and disseminated through the media, a young black child clearly reflects society's prejudice: The child describes the black doll as looking "bad" and the white doll as "nice" (Edney 2006). Children internalize our society's biases and prejudices, as have all of us; they are just a little less able to hide it. I am reminded of the story of a 4-year-old in an affluent suburb who remarked to her mother upon seeing a young Latina while in line at the grocery store, "Look, mommy, a baby maid."

And when we receive evidence that confronts our deeply held and usually unrecognized biases, the human brain usually finds ways to return to stereotypes. The human brain uses a mechanism called "re-fencing" when confronted with evidence contrary to the stereotype. Allport coined the term: "When a fact cannot fit into a mental field, the exception is acknowledged, but the field is hastily fenced in again and not allowed to remain dangerously open" (Allport 1954, p. 23). This is illustrated by such statements as "some of my best friends are black." That statement, while used to deny bias, has within it the seeds of a defense of negative feelings toward blacks. The context of the statement usually means that "my best friend" is an exception to stereotypes and, therefore, that other blacks would *not* be my friends. Thompson (2003) refers to this as *absolution* through a connected relationship (i.e., I am absolved from racism because my best friend is black). Dovidio and Gaertner describe this inability to connect stated beliefs and unconscious bias as *aversive racism,* "the inherent contradiction that exists when the denial of personal prejudice co-exists with underlying unconscious negative feelings and beliefs" (2005, p. 2).

In many situations, from either the dominant or the oppressed, simple unconscious associations may drastically change outcomes. An example is Steele and Aaronson's (1995) work on *stereotype threat,* in which the performance of African-American students in a testing situation was cut in half by asking them to identify their race at the start of the test. This simple act unconsciously reminded students of the stereotypes connected with their race. Moreover, when asked at the end of the test, the students who were primed to remember their race were unable to identify the reminder as a factor in their poorer test score (Steele 1997).

In ambiguous situations, people's minds may also *reconstruct* a situation in order to conform to their stereotypes. An example is a study of people who harbor negative attitudes about African Americans: In a quickly seen image in which a white man with a weapon chases a black man, some people reverse the race of the perpetrator of the violence in order to make it conform with their preconceived notions (Diller and Moule 2005). Such unconscious biases have a role in determining the length of jail sentences (Vedantam 2005) and the fact that, regardless of explicit racial prejudices, police officers are more likely to shoot an unarmed black target than an unarmed white target (Correll et al. 2002).

Regarding violence, it is important to remember that we are programmed to quickly discern who is enemy and who is friend, for in

Uncovering Biases

Because people are more likely to act out of unconscious or hidden bias, knowing that you have a bias for or against a group may cause you to compensate and more carefully consider your possible responses or actions. Acknowledging biases often opens doors for learning and allows people to consciously work for harmony in classrooms and communities (Polite and Saenger 2003). How do we find a key to unlock this door to the mind? The Implicit Association Test (IAT) has helped millions of people—those who accept the often startling results—reveal their unconscious biases to themselves (https://implicit.harvard.edu/implicit/).

Anthony Greenwald and Mahzarin Banaji developed the test in the mid-1990s because "it is well known that people don't always 'speak their minds,' and it is suspected that people don't always 'know their minds' " (Greenwald, McGhee, and Schwartz 1998). The IAT "presents a method that convincingly demonstrates the divergences of our conscious thoughts and our unconscious biases," according to the Harvard website on Project Implicit.

Strangely enough, the first evidence of this unconscious bias came from insects and flowers. Greenwald made a list of 25 insect names and 25 flower names and found that it was far easier to place the flowers in groups with pleasant words and insects in groups with unpleasant words than the reverse. It was just difficult to "hold a mental association of insects with words such as 'dream,' 'candy,' and 'heaven,' and flowers with words such as 'evil,' 'poison' and 'devil'" (Vedantam 2005, p. 3).

Greenwald then took the next step and used stereotypically white-sounding names, such as Adam and Emily, and black-sounding names, such as Jamal and Lakisha, and grouped them with pleasant and unpleasant words. According to Vedantam, Greenwald himself was surprised: "I had as much trouble pairing African-American names with pleasant words as I did insect names with pleasant words" (Vedantam 2005, p. 3). His collaborator, Banaji, was even more self-reflective, "'I was deeply embarrassed,' she recalls. 'I was humbled in a way that few experiences in my life have humbled me'" (p. 3).

This unconscious pairing has direct real-world consequences. Unconscious bias allows people who consciously said they wanted qualified minority employees to then unconsciously rate résumés with black-sounding names as less qualified. With other factors held constant, white-sounding names at the top of résumés triggered 50% more callbacks than African-American names. Human resources managers were stunned by the results. Explicit bias can occur not only without the intent to discriminate, but despite explicit desires to recruit minorities (Bertrand and Mullainathan 2004).

In *See No Bias,* Vedantam (2005) shares the disappointment and surprise that two recent test takers experienced when they found that their results on the Implicit Association Test did not mesh with their perceived views of themselves. To the dismay of these individuals, the test results were also in conflict with their life and career goals. Vedantam describes in detail a woman, an activist, taking a recent version of the test:

The woman brought up a test on her computer from a Harvard University website. It was really very simple: All it asked her to do was distinguish between a series of black and white faces. When she saw a black face, she was to hit a key on the left; when she saw a white face, she was to hit a key on the right. Next, she was asked to distinguish between a series of positive and negative words. Words such as "glorious" and "wonderful" required a left key, words such as "nasty" and "awful" required a right key. The test remained simple when two categories were combined: The activist hit the left key if she saw either a white face or a positive word, and hit the right key if she saw either a black face or a negative word.

Then the groupings were reversed. The woman's index fingers hovered over her keyboard. The test now required her to group black faces with positive words, and white faces with negative words. She leaned forward intently. She made no mistakes, but it took her longer to correctly sort the words and images.

Her result appeared on the screen, and the activist became very silent. The test found she had a bias for whites over blacks.

"It surprises me I have any preferences at all," she said. "By the work I do, by my education, my background. I'm progressive, and I think I have no bias. Being a minority myself, I don't feel I should or would have biases."

"I'm surprised," the woman said. She bit her lip. "And disappointed." (p. 2)

Such reactions should not really be a surprise according to the writings of many white anti-racist activists, including Tim Wise, who acknowledge residual racism still inside them. Wise notes how unconscious bias relegates the role of whiteness or race "to a nonfactor in the minds of whites" (2005, p. 18). When the role of whiteness or race becomes clear to a person, such as the activist described above, surprise and disappointment are likely results.

the past—and certainly in many places in the world today—the ability to quickly identify friend or foe may be a matter of life or death (Begley 2004).

While I started this piece with evidence of people who responded to their gut reactions to my brown skin in surprising nonverbal ways, many of the same people would be quite gracious if given another second or two. Recent research shows that while most

people have an instant activity in the "fight or flight" amygdala part of their brains upon encountering an *unexpected* person or situation, that first reaction is often consciously overridden in a nanosecond by many people in order to overcome built-in biases and respond as their better, undiscriminating selves. This ability to overcome embedded biases is particularly important when we consider that, "although many white Americans consider themselves unbiased, when unconscious stereotypes are measured, some 90% implicitly link blacks with negative traits (evil, failure)" (Begley 2004, p. 1).

I pick up subtle clues, either consciously or unconsciously, as to who is a good, open contact for me versus someone who may have difficulty engaging with me easily based on race.

Changing Attitudes

Do we have the ability to change our attitudes and behaviors? Gladwell explains the two levels of consciousness in a manner that gives us hope. He says that in many situations, we are able to direct our behavior using our conscious attitudes—what we choose to believe or our stated values—rather than our "racial attitude on an *unconscious* level—the immediate, automatic associations that tumble out before we've even had time to think" (2005, p. 84). He continues, "We don't deliberately choose our unconscious attitudes . . . we may not even be aware of them" (p. 85). Because our unconscious attitudes may be completely incompatible with our stated values, we must know just what those unconscious attitudes are, for they are, as Gladwell states, a powerful predictor of how we may act in some spontaneous situations.

Gladwell describes the type of circumstances where blacks and whites will both engage and disengage around climate and personal relation issues:

> If you have a strongly pro-white pattern of associations . . . there is evidence that that will affect the way you behave in the presence of a black person. . . . In all likelihood, you won't be aware that you are behaving any differently than you would around a white person. But chances are you'll lean forward a little less, turn away slightly from him or her, close your body a bit, be a bit less expressive, maintain less eye contact, stand a little farther away, smile a lot less, hesitate and stumble over your words a bit more, laugh at jokes a bit less. Does that matter? Of course it does. (pp. 85–86)

Gladwell goes on to describe the possible repercussions of these unconscious biases at a job interview. The same factors may affect behaviors in parent-teacher conferences or affect student outcomes in classrooms.

Another study describes matching whites with blacks for the completion of a task (Dovidio and Gaertner 2005). Whites were first divided into two groups: those who expressed egalitarian views and those who expressed their biases openly. These individuals were then observed to see if their actions, such as those described by Gladwell, showed unconscious biases. Each white person then engaged in a problem-solving task with a black person. The time it took to complete the joint task was recorded (see Table 1).

Two important points bear emphasis here. First, the African-American individuals, either consciously or unconsciously, were aware of the behavior that showed bias. In this study, "blacks' impressions of whites were related mainly to whites' unconscious attitudes . . . the uncomfortable and discriminatory behavior associated with aversive racism is very obvious to blacks, even while whites either don't recognize it or consider it hidden" (Dovidio and Gaertner 2005, pp. 3–4). I know that as an African American, when I enter

Table 1 Biased and Unbiased White Individuals' Time to Complete Paired Task

White Member of Pair	Time to Complete Task with a Black Person
Unbiased in word and behavior	4 minutes
Biased in word and behavior	5 minutes
Unbiased by self-report, behavior shows bias	6 minutes

a room of white people, I pick up subtle clues, either consciously or unconsciously, as to who is a good, open contact for me versus someone who may have difficulty engaging with me easily based on my race.

Second, white individuals who said they were unbiased, yet showed nonverbal biased behavior, reported their impressions of their behavior related to their *publicly expressed* attitudes and were likely to maintain their stated level of biases when questioned. Therefore, they are likely to blame *the victim,* the black individual, for their slowness in completing the task (and incidentally, possibly reinforce their stereotypes). Sleeter contends, "We cling to filters that screen out what people of color try to tell us because we fear losing material and psychological advantages that we enjoy" (1994, p. 6).

We are far better off to acknowledge our possible biases and to try to work together openly with that knowledge.

It is important to note that the *well-intentioned* are still racist:

> Because aversive racists may not be aware of their unconscious negative attitudes and only discriminate against blacks when they can justify their behavior on the basis of some factor other than race, they will commonly deny any intentional wrongdoing when confronted with evidence of their biases. Indeed, they do not discriminate intentionally. (Dovidio and Gaertner 2005, p. 5)

For example, if white individuals who are self-deceived about their own biases were sitting in a position to influence a promotion decision, they might not support the advancement of a "difficult" black individual and would select another factor as a reason for their action, rather than see or acknowledge their own conflicted perceptions.

This study on task completion strongly suggests that we are far better off to acknowledge our possible biases and to try to work together openly with that knowledge. If we mask our true attitudes, sometimes invisible to our own selves, we will continue to work slowly or unproductively. Consider the white individuals whose conflict over their true or hidden selves and their outward statements made a simple task both time-consuming and psychologically difficult for both the black individuals and themselves (Dovidio and Gaertner 2005).

Unintentional racism is not always determined by whether an individual possesses prejudiced beliefs or attitudes, and it can take many different forms. These forms include the unconscious gestures mentioned before or "the dominant norms and standards."

When Race Becomes an Issue

Dovidio and Gaertner Offer Some Suggestions for Action:

- When a person of color brings up race as an issue—listen deeply!
- If the person indicates that he or she is offended, don't be defensive.
- Do not begin talking quickly.
- Do not explain why they are misinterpreting the situation.
- Do not begin crying. (These are some of the most infuriating responses people of color encounter when they challenge a situation that feels wrong.)
- If you hear about something third-hand, don't get angry. Remember that it is almost never completely safe for a person of color to challenge a dominant perception.

Source: Dovidio, Jack F., and Sam L. Gaertner. "Color Blind or Just Plain Blind." *Nonprofit Quarterly* (Winter 2005): 5.

Finally, Teaching Tolerance, a group dedicated to reducing prejudice, improving intergroup relations, and supporting equitable school experiences for our nation's children, says, "We would like to believe that when a person has a conscious commitment to change, the very act of discovering one's hidden biases can propel one to act to correct for it. It may not be possible to avoid the automatic stereotype or prejudice, but it is certainly possible to consciously rectify it" (2001, p. 4). Otherwise, we are all at the mercy of a blink of the eye.

References

Allport, Gordon. *The Nature of Prejudice.* Cambridge, Mass.: Addison-Wesley, 1954.

Applebaum, Barbara. "Good, Liberal Intentions Are Not Enough: Racism, Intentions, and Moral Responsibility." *Journal of Moral Education* 26 (December 1997): 409–421.

Begley, Sharon. "Racism Studies Find Rational Part of Brain Can Override Prejudice." *Wall Street Journal,* November 19, 2004, p. B1.

Bertrand, Marianne, and Sendhil Mullainathan. "Are Emily and Greg More Employable Than Lakisha and Jamal?" *American Economic Review* 94 (2004): 991–1013.

Correll, Joshua, Bernadette Park, Charles. M. Judd, and Bernd Wittenbrink. "The Police Officer's Dilemma: Using Ethnicity to Disambiguate Potentially Threatening Individuals." *Journal of Personality and Social Psychology* 83 (December 2002): 1314–1329.

Delpit, Lisa. "The Silenced Dialogue: Power and Pedagogy in Educating Other People's Children." *Harvard Educational Review* 58 (August 1988): 280–298.

Diller, Jerry V., and Jean Moule. *Cultural Competence: A Primer for Educators.* Belmont, Calif.: Wadsworth, 2004

Dovidio, Jack F., and Sam L. Gaertner. "Color Blind or Just Plain Blind." *Nonprofit Quarterly* (Winter 2005).

Edney, Hazel Trice. "New 'Doll Test' Produces Ugly Results." *Portland Medium,* August 18, 2006, pp. 1, 7.

Gladwell, Malcolm. *Blink: The Power of Thinking Without Thinking.* New York: Little, Brown, 2005.

Greenwald, Anthony, Debbie E. McGhee, and Jordan L. K. Schwartz. "Measuring Individual Differences in Implicit Cognition: The Implicit Association Test." *Journal of Personality and Social Psychology* 74 (June 1998): 1464–1480.

Harvard University. "Project Implicit." 2007. https://implicit.harvard.edu/implicit.

Polite, Lillian, and Elizabeth B. Saenger. "A Pernicious Silence: Confronting Race in the Elementary Classroom." *Phi Delta Kappan* 85 (December 2003): 274–278.

Sleeter, Christine E. "White Racism." *Multicultural Education* 1 (Summer 1994): 1, 5–8.

Steele, Claude. "A Threat in the Air: How Stereotypes Shape Intellectual Identity and Performance." *American Psychologist* 52 (June 1997): 613–629.

Steele, Claude M., and Joshua Aaronson. "Stereotype Threat and Intellectual Test Performance of African Americans." *Journal of Personality and Social Psychology* 69 (November 1995): 797–811.

Because many people believe these norms and standards are culturally neutral and universally right, true, and good, they do not understand how these norms and standards oppress others. They are not even aware of this possibility—and, in this sense, such racism is unintentional. (Applebaum 1997, p. 409)

Hard Work of Honesty

Unpacking our levels of consciousness and intent requires hard work. First, there needs to be unswerving, unnerving, scrupulous honesty. Individuals need to become less focused on feeling very tolerant and good about themselves and more focused on examining their own biases. One must realize and accept that the foundation and continuation of a bias may have, at its root, personal and group gain.

I recall sharing with my graduate and undergraduate students that true equity will be reached when 40% of all service people . . . meaning hotel housekeepers, groundskeepers, etc., are white men. The loss from 80% of the managerial jobs in this country to 40%, their proportion of the population, would be an actual loss in the number of jobs currently *allotted* to them based on race and gender. That is, they would not have the jobs they may perceive as expected and modeled as their right in the workplace. Can we all embrace such a future? Delpit maintains, "Liberal educators believe themselves to be operating with good intentions, but these good intentions are only conscious delusions about their unconscious true motives" (Delpit 1988, p. 285). I am not quite that cynical. I believe in change, slow as it may be.

Individuals need to become less focused on feeling very tolerant and good about themselves and more focused on examining their own biases.

Teaching Tolerance. "Hidden Bias: A Primer." 2001. www.tolerance
.org/hidden_bias/tutorials/04.html.

Thompson, Audrey. "Tiffany, Friend of People of Color: White
Investments in Antiracism." *International Journal
of Qualitative Studies in Education* 16 (January 2003):
7–29.

Vedantam, Shankar. "See No Bias." *Washington Post,* January 23,
2005, p. 3. www.vedantam.com/bias01-2005.html.

Weinstein, Gerald, and Donna Mellen, "Anti-Semitism Curriculum
Design." In *Teaching for Diversity and Social Justice,* ed.
Maurine Adams, Lee Anne Bell, and Pat Griffin. New York:
Routledge, 1997.

Wise, Tim. *White Like Me: Reflections on Race from a Privileged
Son.* Brooklyn, N.Y.: Soft Skull, 2005.

Critical Thinking

1. Take the Implicit Association Test at www.implicit.harvard
.edu/implicit. What is your reaction?
2. How might unconscious biases influence your interactions
with students or their parents?
3. How might you respond if a student accuses you of
discriminating against him or her?

JEAN MOULE is an associate professor at Oregon State University,
Corvallis, Oregon, and president of the Oregon Chapter of the National
Association for Multicultural Education. She is co-author of the book,
Cultural Competence: A Primer for Educators (Wadsworth, 2004),
and writes the "Ask Nana" column for *Skipping Stones,* a multicultural
magazine for children.

From *Phi Delta Kappan,* by Jean Moule, January 2009, pp. 321–326. Reprinted with permission of Phi Delta Kappa International, www.pdkintl.org, 2009. All rights reserved.

Improving Schooling for Cultural Minorities: The Right Teaching Styles Can Make a Big Difference

Hani Morgan

Many minority groups in the United States tend to struggle in school. In 2004–2005, for example, the dropout rate for African American and Hispanic students exceeded that of white students (NCES 2007). Students from those groups are also less-frequently identified as gifted or talented (Elhoweris et al. 2005). Students from minority groups who tend to do well academically, such as Asian Pacific American children, can also experience difficulties in American schools. Pang (2008) discusses research indicating that the self-esteem of Asian Pacific American students is often lower than that of African American or Caucasian youth, in part because educators often misunderstand their needs.

One reason minority students are likely to encounter more problems in schools than mainstream students involve incomplete knowledge of minority students' learning and communication styles. Authors such as Banks (2006) and Pewewardy (2008) emphasize that minority students differ in the ways they learn and communicate. Those differences result partly from what a given culture considers appropriate or normal. In particular, child-rearing practices often differ from culture to culture. This paper will discuss how various cultures' communication styles and learning patterns can lead to conflicts and low academic achievement. The article also offers guidelines to avoid practices that can intensify the problems of educating students from cultural minority groups.

Minority students and even their parents may endure poor experiences if teachers fail to understand the ways people from different cultures communicate and learn. Students from a particular culture are likely to perform poorly academically, regard school negatively, and break classroom rules (Dunn and Dunn 1993) if teaching styles do not match the ways they communicate and learn.

Avoiding Conflicts

One day in a fourth-grade classroom, a teacher notices two children of apparent Hispanic descent fighting. Walking toward the children, she asks them why they are quarreling. The two students look at the floor and say nothing. The teacher then takes out a referral form and tells the children, "If you do not look me in the eye right now and tell me what the fighting is all about, I will have the two of you suspended." The students continue to look at the floor, and the teacher proceeds to take severe disciplinary action against them.

At another school, an Arab parent new to America visits a classroom to learn about her child's progress. The parent approaches the teacher and stands about twelve inches away as she introduces herself. The teacher immediately takes a step back because she is unaccustomed to such close quarters with a visitor. The parent, now uncomfortable herself, decides that the teacher is not a warm and caring person.

These hypothetical examples involve cultural differences between groups that could lead to conflict. Teachers who thoroughly understand the cultures and communication styles of the groups mentioned are more likely to prevent such misunderstandings from worsening. In the first example, the Hispanic students are undoubtedly showing the teacher respect, but the teacher probably perceives them as deceitful. The reason for this is that Hispanic parents, like those of many other minority groups, teach their children to respect adults by looking down and remaining quiet. By contrast, Caucasian students are often taught that such behavior is disrespectful (Norman and Keating 1997).

The second case involves cultural differences concerning conversational distance. Individuals from Arab, Latin American, and Southern European countries generally stand much closer during conversations than do Americans, who usually remain at least twenty inches apart in such situations (Gollnick and Chinn 2009). A teacher unaware of that fact can unknowingly send a negative message to a parent or student from one of those groups.

Simply patting a child's head can cause conflict between cultures. For many Americans such behavior expresses approval; however, such pats could offend various Southeast Asian parents and children, many of whom believe that a person's spirit resides in the head (Gollnick and Chinn 2009).

Those examples by no means exhaust the cultural conflicts teachers can encounter when teaching diverse groups of students. Ethnographers often study a given culture extensively to document the numerous different communication and learning styles among cultures. In addition, each group contains many subgroups. Arabic cultures, for example, can vary greatly from country to country as well as in socioeconomic class, geographic location, and religion. In addition, those Arabs who have decided to do things the American way will not be offended when educators speak to them at a distance greater than that used in Arab countries.

Differences in Learning Style

Various specialists in educating different cultural groups (e.g., Banks 2006; Gollnick and Chinn 2009) emphasize how students from different cultures learn differently. African American and Latino students, for example, tend to improve academically with cooperative learning methods of teaching (Aronson and Gonzales 1988). Such students tend to be *field-dependent:* they prefer working together. Research on Native American Indian and Alaska Native students suggests that they too prefer cooperative learning (Pewewardy 2008). In contrast, Anglo-American students, who tend to be *field-independent,* prefer to work alone (Banks 2006). Field-independent students are more likely to be detached, goal oriented, competitive, analytical, and logical (Irvine and York 1995; Pewewardy 2008). It is easier for such students to break down a whole subject or topic and understand that its parts added together can re-form the whole.

Differences in learning styles can often be explained by cultural norms and values. Native American cultures, for example, tend to value possessions much less than Anglo culture. As a result, Native Americans greatly respect people who share. Conversely, they are more likely to distrust someone with many possessions (Pewewardy 2008). That norm makes Native American students more likely to help other students and less likely to show that they know an answer if others do not. Judging Native American students as unmotivated or learning disabled because they do not raise their hands in response to a difficult question may unknowingly discriminate against them.

Although in many cases fear of showing off may also deter Asian Pacific American students from offering answers individually, their cultures' emphasis on humility and modesty makes them more likely to help one another (Pang 2008). Such cultures often view the teacher as an authority figure who transmits knowledge to students. Consequently, Asian Pacific American parents often expect their children to remain relatively quiet and to avoid discussion, which they regard as challenging the teacher's knowledge. Likewise, many Asian Pacific American students only reluctantly express their feelings in creative writing, speech, and English, because their parents teach them to conceal their feelings (Pang 2008).

In addition, other students frequently believe that Asian students' academic success raises standards and makes school more difficult for everyone else. Their academic, physical, and linguistic characteristics often lead other students to consider them "nerds" (Pang 2008). In addition, teachers may not realize that some Asian students have trouble academically.

Treating Students Identically

Teachers may believe that treating all students the same way avoids discriminating against any group, but that practice in itself is discriminatory (Banks 2006; Gollnick and Chinn 2009). Requiring all students to follow one style of teaching can inadvertently favor the students who are most comfortable with the teacher's style of teaching. America's tremendous cultural diversity presents another difficulty for the culturally responsive teacher. The sheer number of cultures represented in a particular classroom can make it difficult or even impossible to address each one adequately. Although no easy answers can be offered for such concerns, knowledge of cultural differences will certainly avert many conflicts.

The "insider's" perspective that students and teachers of the same culture share helps them understand one another's teaching and communicating. Nieto and Bode (2008) refer to Foster's (1997) research, which demonstrates how shared norms of language use can benefit African American children. Foster concluded that when one African American teacher interacted with African American students and used a preaching style of speaking to direct the students, the teacher created a positive classroom climate absent in other classrooms.

The U.S. Census Bureau (2006) indicates that more than 80 percent of U.S. teachers are Caucasian. It is therefore understandable that teachers unfamiliar with students' cultures or upbringings can misdiagnose ethnic minority students as learning disabled, and it is not always feasible to reduce conflicts by matching teachers' and students' cultural backgrounds. In addition, many members of a given culture may lack interest in working as teachers or developing the skills good teaching requires, even with students from similar backgrounds.

Misusing Research on Cultural Differences

As previously discussed, generalizations can weaken culturally responsive teaching and even foster discrimination. Nieto and Bode (2008) refer to research on teachers who believed that Hispanic students would feel uncomfortable in leadership roles and consequently prefer to share and work cooperatively. As a result, the teachers rarely allowed Hispanic students to work or make decisions on their own, although they allowed other students to do so. Teachers who lacked enough books for all students provided each non-Hispanic student with individual copies but made Hispanic children share.

That is a clear example of stereotyping and misusing research on how cultural differences relate to learning styles. Students' deficiencies in certain skills or their likelihood of failing at certain tasks does not mean such skills or tasks need not be taught. Culturally responsive teaching emphasizes gradually developing the skills and values a particular group lacks (Bennett 2007; Pewewardy 2008; Swisher 1991). Students benefit from exposure to the ways and values of different cultures (Pewewardy 2008), but their school experiences are likely to prove negative if they are constantly overwhelmed with values and teaching styles that differ from those of their cultures.

Some teachers may also hold low expectations of minority students because of statistics indicating that many will drop out or underachieve; that belief too is discriminatory, for much research shows that minority students seldom excel unless teachers hold high expectations (Gollnick and Chinn 2009; Nieto and Bode 2008).

Culturally Responsive Teaching

Although teachers in a culturally diverse society must reach students who learn and communicate in many different ways, the challenges should not overwhelm those who follow certain guidelines. Bennett (2007) notes that many teachers are gifted and capable of bridging cultural gaps. For students struggling with a particular skill such as performing a task individually rather than cooperatively, teachers can make the task easier or introduce the skill for a limited time (Bennett 2007; Pewewardy 2008; Swisher 1991).

To do that, teachers must examine their own teaching styles and understand the learning styles of their students without making generalizations. Teachers tend to teach the way they have learned unless deliberately challenged to teach otherwise (Bennett 2007). Rather than assume that a child from a given group has a particular learning style, they must use observation as well as consultation with parents to determine the child's best means of accomplishing a task.

One of the best teaching strategies in a culturally diverse society is to use as many modes as possible: logical-mathematical, linguistic, musical, spatial, bodily kinesthetic, interpersonal, naturalistic, and intrapersonal. Those categories of intelligences were first formulated by Howard Gardner (1993). Nieto and Bode (2008) emphasize the implications of multiple intelligences for culturally responsive teaching: due to social, political, or geographic circumstances, many members of a given culture may be more advanced in one intelligence than members of another culture. Including activities that emphasize as many intelligences as possible rather than just one or two will likely create a more-democratic setting for diverse students. Such a strategy will also benefit classes with little or no diversity because within any given cultural group, the various members themselves learn in different ways. However, teachers need to remember that such a practice alone is insufficient to improve schooling experiences for many minority students.

Conclusion

At the 2004 Democratic National Convention, Barack Obama won the hearts of many Americans when he said, "There is not a Black America and a White America and Latino America and Asian America—there is the United States of America." Nonetheless, the unity Mr. Obama celebrated in that speech may not materialize in U.S. Schools unless educators understand how different cultures communicate and learn. Current statistics on dropout rates and achievement indicate alarming trends among certain groups. By making school a more-satisfying experience for many cultural minority groups, culturally responsive teaching should provide a better chance for academic gains.

Although considering a student's background is important, educators must remember that cultural groups are ever-changing and diverse. Educators often forget or ignore that, and as a result, diversity programs can lead to disappointing results (Banks 2006). When members of a cultural group are viewed as similar to one another, a process termed *essentializing* occurs—a dangerous practice that can lead to discrimination (as in the example involving Hispanic students discussed earlier). Research that identifies certain groups' learning styles or behavioral patterns can help teachers analyze individual students' needs. For students weak in certain skills due to cultural norms, introducing the needed skills gradually allows students more time to learn new ways of accomplishing tasks. Introducing too many teaching or communicating methods unfamiliar to students of a particular culture increases the chances of frustrating them and sentencing them to poor school experiences.

References

Aronson, E., and A. Gonzalez. 1988. "Desegregation, Jigsaw, and the Mexican-American Experience." In *Eliminating Racism: Profiles in Controversy,* ed. P. A. Katz and D. A. Taylor, 301–314. New York: Plenum.

Banks, J. A. 2006. *Cultural Diversity and Education: Foundations, Curriculum, and Teaching.* New York: Pearson Education.

Bennett, C. I. 2007. *Comprehensive Multicultural Education: Theory and Practice.* New York: Pearson Education.

Dunn, R., and K. Dunn. 1993. *Teaching Secondary Students through Their Individual Learning Styles: Practical Approaches for Grades 7–12.* Boston: Allyn & Bacon.

Elhoweris, H., K. Muta, N. Alsheikh, and P. Holloway. 2005. "Effect of Ethnicity on Teachers' Referral and Recommendation Decisions in Gifted and Talented Programs." *Remedial and Special Education* 26: 25–31.

Foster, M. 1997. *Black Teachers on Teaching.* New York: The New Press.

Gardner, H. 1993. *Frames of Mind: The Theory of Multiple Intelligences.* New York: Basic Books.

Gollnick, D. M., and P. C. Chinn. 2009. *Multicultural Education in a Pluralistic Society.* Upper Saddle River, N.J.: Pearson Prentice Hall.

Irvine, J. J., and D. E. York. 1995. "Learning Styles and Culturally Diverse Students: A Literature Review." In *Handbook of Research on Multicultural Education,* ed. J. A. Banks and C. A. M. Banks, 484–497. New York: Macmillan.

National Center for Education Statistics (NCES). 2007. Compendium report. *Dropout rates in the United States: 2005.* Retrieved July 24, 2009, from <http://nces.ed.gov/pubs2007/2007059.pdf>.

Nieto, S., and P. Bode. 2008. *Affirming Diversity.* New York: Pearson Education.

Norman, K. I., and J. F. Keating. 1997. *Barriers for Hispanics and American Indians Entering Science and Mathematics: Cultural Dilemmas.* Retrieved July 24, 2009, from <www2.ed.psu.edu/CI/Journals/97pap22.htm>.

Pang, V. O. 2008. "Educating the Whole Child: Implications for Teachers." In *Classic Edition Sources: Multicultural Education,* ed. J. Noel, 127–131. New York: McGraw-Hill.

Pewewardy, C. 2008. "Learning Styles of American Indian/Alaska Native Students." In *Classic Edition Sources: Multicultural Education,* ed. J. Noel, 116–121. New York: McGraw-Hill.

Swisher, K. 1991. "American Indian/Alaskan Native Learning Styles: Research and Practice." Retrieved July 24, 2009, from www.ericdigests.org/ pre-9220/indian.htm.

U.S. Census Bureau. 2006. *Statistical Abstract of the United States: 2006.* Washington, D. C.: U.S. Government Printing Office.

Critical Thinking

1. Explain whether you agree or disagree with this statement: "It is important to teach all students in the same way to avoid discriminating against any student."

2. Identify two cultural groups that you might expect in the community in which you plan to teach and list some of the differences that you might see and how you'd accommodate for them.

3. How are findings about cultural differences misused?

HANI MORGAN, EdD, is an assistant professor of curriculum, instruction, and special education at the University of Southern Mississippi.

From *Educational Horizons,* Winter 2010, pp. 114–120. Copyright © 2010 by Hani Morgan. Reprinted by permission of the author.

Becoming Adept at Code-Switching

By putting away the red pen and providing structured instruction in code-switching, teachers can help urban African American students use language more effectively.

REBECCA S. WHEELER

It was September, and Joni was concerned. Her 2nd grade student Tamisha could neither read nor write; she was already a grade behind. What had happened? Joni sought out Melinda, Tamisha's 1st grade teacher. Melinda's answer stopped her in her tracks. "Tamisha? Why, you can't do *anything* with that child. Haven't you heard how she talks?" Joni pursued, "What *did* you do with her last year?" "Oh, I put her in the corner with a coloring book." Incredulous, Joni asked, "All year?" "Yes," the teacher replied.

Although extreme, Melinda's appraisal of Tamisha's performance and potential as a learner is not isolated. In standardized assessments of language acquisition, teachers routinely underrate the language knowledge and the reading and writing performance of African American students (Cazden, 2001; Ferguson, 1998; Godley, Sweetland, Wheeler, Minnici, & Carpenter, 2006; Scott & Smitherman, 1985). A typical reading readiness task asks the student to read five sentences (*The mouse runs. The cat runs. The dog runs. The man runs. Run, mouse, run!*). As Jamal reads, *Da mouse run. Da cat run. Da dog run. Da man run. Run, mouse, run,* his teacher notes 8/15 errors, placing him far below the frustration level of 3/15. She assesses Jamal as a struggling reader and puts him in a low reading group or refers him to special education.

Through a traditional language arts lens, Tamisha's 1st grade teacher saw "broken English" and a broken child. Through the same lens, Jamal's teacher heard mistakes in Standard English and diagnosed a reading deficit. These teachers' lack of linguistic background in the dialects their students speak helps explain why African American students perform below their white peers on every measure of academic achievement, from persistent over-representation in special education and remedial basic skills classes, to under-representation in honors classes, to lagging SAT scores, to low high school graduation rates (Ogbu, 2003).

Across the United States, teacher education and professional development programs fail to equip teachers to respond adequately to the needs of many African American learners. We know that today's world "demands a new way of looking at teaching that is grounded in an understanding of the role of culture and language in learning" (Villegas & Lucas, 2007, p. 29). Unfortunately, many teachers lack the linguistic training required to build on the language skills that African American students from dialectally diverse backgrounds bring to school. To fill this need, elementary educator Rachel Swords and I have developed a program for teaching Standard English to African American students in urban classrooms (Wheeler & Swords, 2006). One linguistic insight and three strategies provide a framework for responding to these students' grammar needs.

One Linguistic Insight

When African American students write *I have two sister and two brother, My Dad jeep is out of gas,* or *My mom deserve a good job,* teachers traditionally diagnose "poor English" and conclude that the students are making errors with plurality, possession, or verb agreement. In response, teachers correct the students' writing and show them the "right" grammar.

Research has amply demonstrated that such traditional correction methods fail to teach students the Standard English writing skills they need (Adger, Wolfram, & Christian, 2007). Further, research has found strong connections among teachers' negative attitudes about stigmatized dialects, lower teacher expectations for students who speak these dialects, and lower academic achievement (Godley et al., 2006; Nieto, 2000).

An insight from linguistics offers a way out of this labyrinth: Students using vernacular language are not making errors, but instead are speaking or writing correctly following the language patterns of their community (Adger el al., 2007; Green, 2002; Sweetland, 2006; Wheeler & Swords, 2006). With this insight, teachers can transform classroom practice and student learning in dialectally diverse schools.

Three Strategies

Equipped with the insight that students are following the grammar patterns of their communities, here is how a teacher can lead students through a critical-thinking process to help them understand and apply the rules of Standard English grammar.

Scientific Inquiry

As the teacher grades a set of papers, she may notice the same "error" cropping up repeatedly in her students' writing. My work in schools during the past decade has revealed more than 30 Informal English grammar patterns that appear in students' writing. Among these, the following patterns consistently emerge (see also Adger et al., 2007; Fogel & Ehri, 2000):

- Subject-verb agreement (*Mama walk the dog every day.*)
- Showing past time (*Mama walk the dog yesterday* or *I seen the movie.*)
- Possessive (*My sister friend came over.*)
- Showing plurality (*It take 24 hour to rotate.*)
- "A" versus "an" (*a elephant, an rabbit*)

A linguistically informed teacher understands that these usages are not errors, but rather grammar patterns from the community dialect transferred into student writing (Wheeler, 2005). Seeing these usages as data, the teacher assembles a set of sentences drawn from student writing, all showing the same grammar pattern, and builds a code-switching chart (see Fig. 1). She provides the Formal English equivalent of each sentence in the right-hand column. She then leads students through the following steps:

- *Examine sentences.* The teacher reads the Informal English sentences aloud.
- *Seek patterns.* Then she leads the students to discover the grammar pattern these sentences follow. She might say, "*Taylor cat is black.* Let's see how this sentence shows ownership. Who does the cat belong to?" When students answer that the cat belongs to Taylor, the teacher asks, "How do you know?" Students answer that it says *Taylor cat,* or that the word *Taylor* sits next to the word cat.
- *Define the pattern.* Now the teacher helps students define the pattern by repeating their response, putting it in context: "Oh, *Taylor* is next to *cat.* So you're saying that the owner, *Taylor,* is right next to what is owned, cat. Maybe this is the pattern for possessives in Informal English: *owner + what is owned?*" The class has thus formulated a hypothesis for how Informal English shows possession.
- *Test the hypothesis.* After the teacher reads the next sentence aloud, she asks the students to determine whether the pattern holds true. After reading *The boy coat is torn,* the teacher might ask, "Who is the owner?" The students respond that *the boy* is the owner. "What does he own?" The students say that he owns *the coat.* The teacher then summarizes what the students have discovered: "So *the boy* is the owner and *the coat* is what he owns. That follows our pattern of *owner + what is owned.*" It is important to test each sentence in this manner.
- *Write Informal English pattern.* Finally, the teacher writes the pattern, *owner + what is owned,* under the last informal sentence (Wheeler & Swords, 2006).

Possessive Patterns

Informal English	Formal English
Taylor cat is black.	Taylor's cat is black.
The boy coat is torn.	The boy's coat is torn.
A giraffe neck is long.	A giraffe's neck is long.
Did you see the teacher pen?	Did you see the teacher's pen?
The Patterns	**The Patterns**
owner + what is owned	owner + 's + what is owned
noun + noun	noun + 's + noun

Figure 1 Code-switching chart for possessive patterns.

Comparison and Contrast

Next, the teacher applies a teaching strategy that has been established as highly effective—comparison and contrast (Marzano, Pickering, & Pollock, 2001). Using *contrastive analysis,* the teacher builds on students' existing grammar knowledge. She leads students in contrasting the grammatical patterns of Informal English with the grammatical patterns of Formal English written on the right-hand side of the code-switching chart. This process builds an explicit, conscious understanding of the differences between the two language forms. The teacher leads students to explore what changed between the Informal English sentence *Taylor cat is black* and the Formal English sentence *Taylor's cat is black.* Through detailed comparison and contrast, students discover that the pattern for Formal English possessive is owner + 's + what is owned.

Code-Switching as Metacognition

After using scientific inquiry and contrastive analysis to identify the grammar patterns of Informal and Formal English, the teacher leads students in putting their knowledge to work. The class uses *metacognition,* which is knowledge about one's own thinking processes. Students learn to actively code-switch—to assess the needs of the setting (the time, place, audience, and communicative purpose) and intentionally choose the appropriate language style for that setting. When the teacher asks, "In your school writing, which one of these patterns do you think you need to use: *Owner + what is owned?* or *owner + 's + what is owned?*" students readily choose the Standard English pattern.

Because code-switching requires that students think about their own language in both formal and informal forms, it builds cognitive flexibility, a skill that plays a significant role in successful literacy learning (Cartwright, in press). Teaching students to consciously reflect on the different dialects they use and to choose the appropriate language form for a particular situation provides them with metacognitive strategies and the cognitive flexibility to apply those strategies in daily practice. With friends and family in the community, the child will choose the language of the community, which is often Informal English. In school discussions, on standardized tests, in analytic essays, and in the world of work, the student learns to choose the expected formal language. In this way, we add another linguistic code, Standard English, to the students language toolbox.

A Successful Literacy Tool

Research and test results have demonstrated that these techniques are highly successful in fostering the use of Standard English and boosting overall student writing performance among urban African American students at many different grade levels (Fogel & Ehri, 2000; Sweetland, 2006; Taylor, 1991). Using traditional techniques as a teacher at an urban elementary school on the Virginia peninsula, Rachel Swords saw the usual 30-point gap in test scores between her African American and white 3rd grade students. In 2002, her first year of implementing code-switching strategies, she closed the achievement gap in her classroom; on standardized state assessments, African American students did as well as white students in English and history and outperformed white students in math and science. These results have held constant in each subsequent year. In 2006, in a class that began below grade level, 100 percent of Sword's African American students passed Virginia's year-end state tests (Wheeler & Swords, 2006).

Transforming Student Learning

Fortunately, Joni knew that Tamisha was not making grammatical mistakes. Tamisha *did* know grammar—the grammar of her community. Now the task was to build on her existing knowledge to leverage new knowledge of Standard English. When Joni tutored her after school, Tamisha leapfrogged ahead in reading and writing. Despite having started a year behind, she was reading and writing on grade level by June. How did she achieve such progress? Her teacher possessed the insights and strategies to foster Standard English mastery among dialectally diverse students. Even more important, Joni knew that her student did not suffer a language deficit. She was able to see Tamisha for the bright, capable child she was.

Using *contrastive analysis*, the teacher builds on students' existing grammar knowledge.

Joni has laid down the red pen and adopted a far more effective approach, teaching students to reflect on their language using the skills of scientific inquiry, contrastive analysis, and code-switching. We have the tools to positively transform the teaching and learning of language arts in dialectally diverse classrooms. Isn't it time we did?

References

Adger, C. T., Wolfram, W., & Christian, D. (Eds.). (2007). *Dialects in schools and communities.* Mahwah, NJ: Erlbaum.

Cartwright, K. B. (in press). *Literacy processes: Cognitive flexibility in learning and teaching.* New York: Guilford Press.

Cazden, C. B. (2001). *Classroom discourse: The language of teaching and learning* (2nd ed.). Portsmouth, NH: Heinemann.

Ferguson, R. F. (1998). Teachers' perceptions and expectations and the black-white test score gap. In C. Jencks & M. Phillips (Eds.), *The black-white test score gap* (pp. 273–317). Washington, DC: Brookings Institution.

Fogel, H., & Ehri, L. (2000). Teaching elementary students who speak Black English vernacular to write in Standard English: Effects of dialect transformation practice. *Contemporary Educational Psychology, 25,* 212–35.

Godley, A., Sweetland, J., Wheeler, S., Minnici, A., & Carpenter, B. (2006). Preparing teachers for dialectally diverse classrooms. *Educational Researcher, 35*(8), 30–37.

Green, L. (2002). *African American English: A linguistic introduction.* Cambridge, UK: Cambridge University Press.

Marzano, R., Pickering, D., & Pollock, J. (2001). *Classroom instruction that works: Research-based strategies for increasing student achievement.* Alexandria, VA: ASCD.

Nieto, S. (2000). *Affirming diversity: The sociopolitical context of multicultural education* (3rd ed.). White Plains, NY: Longman.

Ogbu, J. (2003). *Black American students in an affluent suburb: A study of academic disengagement.* Mahwah, NJ: Erlbaum.

Scott, J. C., & Smitherman, G. (1985). Language attitudes and self-fulfilling prophecies in the elementary school. In S. Greenbaum (Ed.), *The English language today* (pp. 302–314). Oxford, UK: Pergamon.

Sweetland, J. (2006). *Teaching writing in the African American classroom: A sociolinguistic approach.* Unpublished doctoral dissertation, Stanford University.

Taylor, H. U. (1991). *Standard English, Black English, and bidialectalism: A controversy.* New York: Lang.

Villegas, A. M., & Lucas, T. (2007). The culturally responsive teacher. *Educational Leadership, 64*(6), 28–33.

Wheeler, R. (2005). Code-switch to teach Standard English. *English Journal, 94*(5), 108–112.

Wheeler, R., & Swords, R. (2006). *Code-switching. Teaching Standard English in urban classrooms.* Urbana, IL: National Council of Teachers of English.

Critical Thinking

1. Describe code-switching.
2. Explain the importance of code-switching for working with speakers of a dialect.
3. Create a code switching chart.

REBECCA S. WHEELER is Associate Professor of English Language and Literacy, Department of English, Christopher Newport University, Newport News, Virginia; rwheeler@cnu.edu.

Author's note—Kelly B. Cartwright, Associate Professor of Psychology, Christopher Newport University, crafted the section "Code-Switching as Metacognition."

From *Educational Leadership,* April 2008, pp. 54–58. Copyright © 2008 by ASCD. Reprinted by permission. The Association for Supervision and Curriculum Development is a worldwide community of educators advocating sound policies and sharing best practices to achieve the success of each learner. To learn more, visit ASCD at www.ascd.org

Gender Matters in Elementary Education
Research-based Strategies to Meet the Distinctive Learning Needs of Boys and Girls

VIRGINIA BONOMO

Research indicates that gender influences how children learn. Those findings do not necessarily mean that boys learn one way and girls another. Still, there are significant differences with respect to gender and how our brains develop. Researchers have found that no single area of development influences those gender differences: rather, a combination of developmental differences affects the brain, sensory motor, and physical development. In order to teach to gender differences, educators need to be aware of them and have knowledge of effective gender-based teaching strategies.

Brain-based Gender Differences

The research has established that the male brain is on average 10 to 15 percent larger and heavier than the female brain. However, in addition to size, differences in the autonomy of the brain are present across genders. Using brain mapping, research has established that men possess on average more than six times the amount of gray matter related to general intelligence than women, while women have nearly ten times the amount of white matter related to intelligence than do men. One study also indicates that differences in the brain areas correlate with IQ between the sexes (Kaufmann

Table 1   Gender-based Differences between Girls and Boys

Girls	Boys
Girls can multitask better than boys because the female corpus callosum is 26 percent larger than the male. The corpus callosum is the nervous tissue that sends signals between the two halves of the brain.	In the male brain, a larger area is devoted to spatial mechanical functioning and half as much to verbal emotive functioning.
Girls have the ability to transition between lessons more quickly and are less apt to have attention span issues.	Boys utilize the cerebral cortex less often than girls and they access the primitive areas of the brain more often while performing the same types of activities or tasks.
The neural connectors that create listening skills are more developed in the female brain and therefore enhance listening skills, memory storage, and tone of voice discrimination in girls.	For the male brain to renew or recharge it will go into rest states, while the female brain does so without rest states or sleep.
Girls make fewer impulsive decisions than boys due to a higher serotonin level.	Boys have less serotonin and less oxytocin, which makes them more impulsive and less likely to sit still to talk to someone.
The female brain has 15 percent more blood flow than the male brain, allowing for enhanced integrated learning.	Boys structure or compartmentalize learning due to the fact that they have less blood flow to the brain.
Because girls have more cortical areas devoted to verbal functioning, they are better at sensory memory, sitting still, listening, tonality, and the complexities of reading and writing (the skills and behaviors that tend to be rewarded in school).	Boys' brains are better suited to symbols, abstractions, and pictures. Boys in general learn higher math and physics better than girls. Boys prefer video games for the physical movement and destruction. Boys get into more trouble for not listening, moving around, sleeping in class, and incomplete assignments.

Adapted from Sax 2006, 192

and Elbel 2001). That study and an ongoing series of other studies make it evident that one part of males' brains, the inferior parietal lobe, is generally larger. That lobe is involved in spatial and mathematical reasoning, skills that boys tend to perform better than girls. The left side of the brain, which is responsible for the ability to use language and connected to verbal and written ability, develops sooner in girls, and girls therefore tend to perform better than boys in those areas (Gabriel and Schmitz 2007).

Although those differences are significant, it is important to examine how that information relates to developmental gender differences. More-recent research indicates that the significant difference between girls and boys is not the brain's structure but the size and sequence of development in the different regions of the brain. In 2007 a longitudinal study conducted by the National Institutes of Health demonstrated consistent sex differences in the speed of the brain's maturation (Lenroot et al. 2007). It also showed that boys' brains develop differently than girls' brains. Rather than develop along the same lines as girls' brains, only slower, boys' brains develop at a different order, time, and rate than girls' in the areas of the brain that affect language, spatial memory, and motor coordination. While the areas involved in language and fine motor skills mature about six years earlier in girls than in boys, the areas involved in targeting and spatial memory mature some four years earlier in boys than they do in girls (Hamlon, Thatcher, and Cline 1999).

Sensory-Perception-based Differences

Sex differences are prevalent not only in brain-based research but in sensory-perception research as well. Studies have found significant differences in the ways boys and girls hear, see, and smell. Only recently have researchers begun examining sensory perception and sex differences in education. In 2001, Dr. Edwin Lephart, the director of neuroscience at Brigham Young University, became the first to search for sex differences by examining dead animals' eyeballs. He found dramatic differences in how the eye is constructed in the male versus in the female: for instance, the visual cortices are fundamentally different.

In addition to such contrasts in construction, the male eye is drawn to cooler colors such as silver, black, blue, and gray, and boys tend to draw pictures of moving objects. In contrast, the female eye is drawn to textures and colors. It is also oriented toward warmer colors—reds, yellow, and oranges. Girls tend to draw more-detailed visuals with faces and people; boys draw more object-based pictures (Sax 2006). In addition, a comprehensive study of newborn infants demonstrated that female infants responded to faces and male infants responded favorably to moving objects, such as mobiles placed above the cribs (Killgore, Oki, and Yurgelun-Todd 2001).

Although consideration of sensory perception is relatively new, the first evaluation of hearing in girls versus boys was conducted in the 1960s. The study found that girls hear better than boys, especially in higher ranges—frequencies above 2 kHz (Corso 1963). A later study found that among 350 newborn babies, the girls' hearing was more sensitive than boys', especially in the 1000–400 Hz range, which is critical for speech discrimination (Cassidy and Ditty 2001). In addition, more-recent studies have confirmed girls' superior hearing at higher frequencies. That may be due to girls' shorter, stiffer cochleae, which provide a more-sensitive response to frequency (Corso 1963). The research also concludes that such differences increase as children get older. Girls interpret a loud speaking tone as yelling: thinking the speaker is angry, they may tune out. Girls' more-finely tuned aural structure makes them more sensitive to sounds than boys are (Kaufmann 2009).

In addition to hearing and sight, a female's sense of smell under certain conditions is at least one hundred thousand times more sensitive than a male's. Such differences can prove significant in determining interest and success in the classroom environment (Dalton 2006, cited in Sax 2006).

Physical Differences

The autonomic nervous system maintains blood pressure, body temperature, and internal homeostasis. It is divided into two parts: 1) the sympathetic nervous system, which is responsible for the "fight or flight" response (the adrenalin-mediated cascade of accelerated heart rate, vasoconstriction, dilated pupils,

Table 2 Autonomic Differences between Girls and Boys

	Girls	Boys
The response to a stressful situation is activated by different parts of the nervous system depending upon gender.	Girls' responses derive from the parasympathetic part of the autonomic nervous system.	Boys' responses derive from the sympathetic part of the autonomic nervous system.
What is the primary humoral difference between the two genders?	Acetylcholine	Adrenalin
What is the reaction when the system is activated?	The female will react by freezing or feel unable to move or react physically to the situation.	The male tends to feel a sense of excitement and the senses are enhanced.
How will the students feel?	The female tends to feel sick or nauseated and feel stress.	The male will enjoy the experience.

Adapted from Sax 2006, 190–200

etc., triggered by violence or confrontation, which prepares the organism to fight or to run away), and 2) the parasympathetic nervous system, responsible for "rest and digest," i.e., mediating digestion and underlying the slower heart rate, vasodilatation, and increased continuous blood flow (flushing) that in turn affect the response to higher ambient temperatures (Sax 2006).

Studies are demonstrating a gender-related difference in the organization of the two systems. Apparently, the female autonomic system is influenced more by the parasympathetic nervous system; in contrast, the male sympathetic nervous system has a greater influence on the control of autonomic responses. The greatest probable effect of those divisions pertaining to gender is that exposure to threats or confrontations sharpens males' senses and exhilarates them. Most females exposed to such stimuli feel dizzy and may have trouble expressing themselves or reacting.

Consider a situation in which a teacher calls upon a child and expects a quick answer: how differently will the boys and girls react? Knowledge of those differences can sway teaching strategies to enhance student success.

Biological Differences

Research conducted on ambient temperature in the classroom has reached some surprising conclusions. A professor was shocked to visit a prominent all-boys school and find it uncomfortably chilly. Appalled to find such conditions in an expensive school, she asked the headmaster about the temperature. He replied, "If you turn up the heat, the boys go to sleep. Not literally asleep, but they might as well be. If it's too warm in the classroom, the boys get sluggish and their eyelids get heavy. If you keep it just a little chilly, the boys learn better" (Sax 2006). Ergonomic specialists have found that the ideal ambient temperature is about 71 F for young men, as opposed to 77 for women. Because the study group wore bathing suits, the ideal temperature in school clothes would most likely be about 2 F lower, or 69 for boys and 75 for girls. Keep in mind that the researchers excluded students who might have been overweight or underweight, because the conditions would have skewed their ambient temperatures (Beshir and Ramsey 1981). Given that temperature is a factor in attentiveness, an educator should consider how that might impact late-spring or early-fall afternoon lessons.

How Is This Relevant to Education? Strategies for Teaching with Respect to Gender Differences

Although dozens of studies published in the past five years have demonstrated dramatic sex differences in brain-based, sensory-perception-based, and autonomic function, the educational literature has not emphasized the studies and their potential significance for education. Dr. Bruce Perry, a Houston neurologist, believes that our current educational system creates an environment that is biologically disrespectful, even if well intended (Gurian and Stevens 2005).

Table 3 Brain-based Genetic Differences in Girls and Boys

Girls Usually	Boys Usually
Hear better than boys.	Have 35 percent less hearing than girls due to the cochlea length in the ear.
Can discriminate between objects better than boys.	Locate objects better than girls.
Focus on faces and warm colors.	Focus on movement and cold colors.
Use the advanced portion of the brain.	Use more of the primitive parts of their brains.
Can explain and describe their feelings.	Find it difficult to talk about feelings.
Develop language and fine motor skills about six years earlier than boys.	Develop targeting and spatial memory about four years earlier than girls.
Multitask well and make easy transitions.	Focus on a task and transition more slowly.
Friendships are focused on other girls.	Friendships are focused on a shared activity.
Find conversation important.	Find conversation unnecessary.
Self-revelation and sharing are precious parts of a friendship.	Self-revelation is to be avoided if possible.
Enjoy a close relationship with a teacher.	May not ask for help to avoid being perceived as "sucking up" to a teacher.
Like to be faced, looked in the eye, and smiled at.	Avoid eye contact and prefer you sit beside them.
Retain sensory memory details well.	Don't retain sensory details.
Do not deal with moderate stress well.	Deal with moderate stress well.
Want to be with friends when under stress.	Want to be alone when under stress.
Feel sick or nauseated when faced with threat and confrontation.	Feel excited when faced with threat and confrontation.
Prefer to read fiction.	Prefer nonfiction.

Adapted from Gurian 2003

What, then, will encourage the educational system to respect gender differences? Educators should be educating themselves about gender differences in all areas of development and then building upon that knowledge with sound instructional design and implementation strategies for teaching with respect to gender differences. As they apply their knowledge of the brain, sensory perception, and physically based differences to an action classroom plan, they need to realize how those differences develop in children. The following table shares some actions educators could witness in girls and boys. Keep in mind that there can be many variations among the sexes as well: some boys may tend to have the usual girls' traits and vice versa.

Based on the research conducted and reviewed on gender differences, educators need to consider implementing strategies that will successfully engage both boys and girls in the classroom. Here are some suggested strategies:

BOYS

- Be brief and involve them actively in the lesson. Encourage them with quick praise, cut down on written tasks, and use models and rubrics they can follow. Challenge them—boys thrive on competition.

- Keep a close eye on boys, but let them play. Without a physical outlet, their aggressiveness will show up elsewhere inappropriately. Thus, provide large spaces for boys when possible.

- Lessons should be kinesthetic and experiential. Use a variety of manipulatives. Be aware of ambient temperature—try to keep the boys from warmer areas in the classroom. Males do not hear as well as girls, so move them closer to the instruction.

GIRLS

- Girls work well in groups when they are facing one another or the teacher. Find activities that allow them to help the teacher. Don't protect girls from activities that may cause them to get dirty or skin their knees a bit, which could promote "learned helplessness." Safe-risk activities provide opportunities for girls to take calculated risks.

- Girls do not respond well to loud, sharp, short tones. They prefer softer voices. Girls enjoy tying lessons into emotions. They respond to descriptive phrases. Loud, repetitive noise can be distracting and disturbing to girls.

- Make it bold: girls prefer a lot of colors. Use puzzles to promote perceptual and symbolic learning. Girls' attention will focus on overheads or writing on the chalkboard. (West 2002)

Conclusion

We can conclude from the research that there are significant differences in how boys and girls learn. The cognitive differences are brain based; behavioral differences can be brain based or a result of responses from brain-based differences. The very architecture of the brain and the resultant differences in sensory perception and physical skills differ markedly between the sexes in the classroom and in society. Understanding those differences will help educators provide a positive and encouraging environment for their students and promote teaching with respect to gender differences.

References

Beshir, M., and J. Ramsey. 1981. "Comparison between Male and Female Subjective Estimates of Thermal Effects and Sensations." *Applied Ergonomics* 12: 29–33.

Cassidy, J., and D. Ditty. 2001. "Gender Differences among Newborns on a Transient Otoacoustic Emissions Test for Hearing." *Journal of Music Therapy* 37: 28–35.

Corso, J. 1963. "Aging and Auditory Thresholds in Men and Women." *Archives of Environmental Health* 61: 350–356.

Gabriel, P., and S. Schmitz. 2007. "Gender Differences in Occupational Distributions among Workers." *Monthly Labor Review* (June).

Gurian, M. 2003. *The Boys and Girls Learn Differently Action Guide for Teachers.* San Francisco: Jossey-Bass.

Gurian, M., and K. Stevens. 2005. "With Boys in Mind." *Educational Leadership* (November).

Hamlon, H., R. Thatcher, and M. Cline. 1999. "Gender Differences in the Development of EEG Coherence in Normal Children." *Developmental Neuropsychology* 16 (3): 479–506.

Kaufmann, C. 2009. "How Boys and Girls Learn Differently." Retrieved May 21, 2010, from www.rd.com/content/printContent.do?contentID=103575.

Kaufmann, C., and G. Elbel. 2001. "Frequency Dependence and Gender Effects in Visual Cortical Regions Involved in Temporal Frequency Dependent Pattern Processing." *Human Brain Mapping* 14 (1): 28–38.

Killgore, W., M. Oki, and D. Yurgelun-Todd. 2001. "Sex-specific Developmental Changes in Amygdale Response to Affective Faces." *Neuroreport* 12: 427–433.

Lenroot, R., N. Gogtay, D. Greenstein, E. Wells, G. Wallace, L. Clasen, J. Blumental, J. Lerch, A. Zijdenbos, A. Evans, P. Thompson, and J. Geidd. 2007 "Sexual Dimorphism of Brain Developmental Trajectories during Childhood and Adolescence." *NeuroImage* 36: 1065–1073.

Sax, L. 2006. "Six Degrees of Separation: What Teachers Need to Know About the Emerging Science of Sex Differences." *Educational Horizons* 84 (Spring): 190–212.

West, P. 2002. *What Is the Matter with Boys?* Sydney: Choice Books.

Critical Thinking

1. Create a chart showing the sensory and physical differences between boys and girls.

2. Which gender differences do you think are most important to address in lesson plans? How would you do so?

3. Are the gender differences sufficient to argue for separate classes for boys and girls? Explain your position.

VIRGINIA BONOMO is an instructor in the Department of Early Childhood and Elementary Education at Bloomsburg University of Pennsylvania.

UNIT 4
Learning and Instruction

Unit Selections

Learning Outcomes

After reading this unit, you will be able to:

- Describe some of the key findings from cognitive research and their implications for classroom instruction.
- Identify common misconceptions about human memory and provide examples of common mnemonic devices that can be used to aid in memorization and recall of information.
- Define mastery learning and explain key components necessary to implementing an effective mastery learning program.
- Explain what backward design is what steps are involved in planning instruction. You should also be able to begin using the steps to plan instructional units/lessons.
- Identify the differences between tactual and kinesthetic learning styles, why they are reported to be especially important for at-risk adolescents, and some of the key criticisms of learning style approaches.
- Describe what Socratic seminars are and how you might incorporate them into your teaching.
- State common mistakes schools and districts make when attempting to implement "high-yield" strategies.
- Summarize the methods and key findings from an action research project and make connections between what the teacher found and effective practices highlighted in other articles in the book.
- Define reciprocal and nonreciprocal peer tutoring, summarize findings from an intervention with elementary students, and identify implications for your practice.
- Explain key components of the technology education standards, how it should be implemented, and student learning assessed.
- Examine the issue of plagiarism both in the K-12 classroom context, as well as your personal experiences as a student in higher education.
- Describe common forms of cyberabuse reported by young adolescents.
- Summarize the methods and key findings from a survey study that questioned middle school students about their social networking experiences, knowledge of appropriate Internet behaviors and risk of online predators, and their own behaviors.

Student Website
www.mhhe.com/cls

Internet References

Brain Based Education: Fad or Breakthrough? by Daniel Willingham
www.teachertube.com/members/viewVideo.php?video_id=74863&title=Brain_Based_Education__Fad_or_Breakthrough

Cyberbullying Research Center
www.Cyberbullying.us

The Critical Thinking Community
www.criticalthinking.org

Education Week on the Web
www.edweek.org

Learning Styles Debunked
www.sciencedaily.com/releases/2009/12/091216162356.htm

Learning Styles Don't Exist by Daniel Willingham
www.teachertube.com/members/viewVideo.php?video_id=119351&title=Learning_Styles_Don_t_Exist

National Crime Prevention Council
www.ncpc.org/newsroom/current-campaigns/cyberbullying

Online Internet Institute
www.oii.org

Purdue Online Writing Lab (OWL @ Purdue)—Avoiding Plagiarism
www.owl.english.purdue.edu/owl/resource/589/1

The Role of Socratic Questioning in Thinking, Teaching and Learning
www.criticalthinking.org/articles/the-role-socratic-questioning-ttl.cfm

Sir Ken Robinson on Schools and Creativity
www.ted.com/speakers/sir_ken_robinson.html

Teachers Helping Teachers
www.pacificnet.net/~mandel

The Teachers' Network
www.teachers.net

Think U Know
www.thinkuknow.co.uk

Wired Kids.org
www.wiredkids.org

World Intellectual Property Organization—What Is Intellectual Property?
www.wipo.int/about-ip/en

Although there are many theories of how people learn, learning can be broadly defined as a relatively permanent change in behavior or thinking due to experience. Learning is not a result of change due to maturation or temporary influences. Changes in behavior and thinking are the result of complex interactions between students' individual characteristics and their daily environments encountered both in and out of school. An ongoing challenge for educators involves understanding these interactions so that opportunities for learning are maximized for all students. This unit focuses on ways of viewing a variety of processes related to learning and instructional strategies that can be supportive to a broad range of learner needs. Each article emphasizes different personal and environmental factors that influence students, with the underlying theme that students construct meaning through an active process involving making sense of the world through interactions with their environment. The articles in this section reflect an emphasis on research-based strategies that have been applied in schools to improve learning.

Prior to the 1960s, behaviorism was the most well-known theory of learning and helped shaped our understanding of how students learn and the necessary elements of educational environments. Most practicing and prospective teachers are familiar with concepts such as classical conditioning, reinforcement, and punishment, and there is no question that behaviorism has made significant contributions to our understanding of human learning. Beginning in the late 1960s and early 1970s, educational psychologists have focused on cognitive, social psychological, and constructivist theories to examine and explain how we learn.

Cognitive psychologists and researchers are continually expanding our knowledge of how the brain works, as well as our understanding of complex cognitive processes. Both areas focus on important procedures related to how we receive, process, and store information, as well as access information essential for all learning for later use. This section begins with a trio of articles that focus on the cognitive theories and the importance of cognitive structures in the brain to learning. In the first article, Mr. Jensen re-examines recent research by neuropsychologists and cognitive scientists that has led to a growing focus on education that is "brain-based." Article 25 reviews the basics of how human memory works and focuses on how teachers can work with students to build their memory of information through the use of mnemonic devices. In Article 26, the authors discuss the effect of initial learning on forgetting and relearning. In highlighting this relationship, they suggest that one of the most important factors explaining the differences among learners is the amount of time required to initially learn content/develop knowledge to a high level, not ability differences. Therefore, they advocate the use of Mastery Learning as a method for ensuring all students reach a high level of mastery of essential content.

According to constructivists, it is important for students to actively create their own understanding and reorganize existing knowledge to incorporate this new knowledge. This emphasizes the importance of providing students with meaningful, authentic contexts so students develop understandings that allow them

© SW Productions/Brand X Pictures/Getty Images

to connect their learning to real-world applications and existing knowledge. Social psychology is the study of the nature of interpersonal relationships in social situations. Social psychological theories emphasize the affective, social, moral, and personal learning of students. Both constructivist and social psychological theories highlight the importance of social context of learning environments and the need for students to interact with others in order for learning to occur. Finally, both social-psychological and constructivist approaches emphasize the important roles of self-efficacy and self-regulation to student learning. The last two articles in this section emphasize instructional approaches geared toward creating learning opportunities that allow students to encounter content in dynamic ways.

Instructional strategies are teacher behaviors and methods of conveying information that affect learning. Teaching methods or techniques can vary greatly, depending on objectives, group size, types of students, and personality of the teacher. For example, discussion classes are generally more effective for enhancing critical thinking skills than are individualized sessions or lectures. In addition, constructivist approaches to instruction such as problem- or project-based learning have gained popularity, particularly in math and science. Regardless of the approach, the goal is to foster higher-level thinking by engaging students in complex cognitive activities.

Four articles help illustrate how teachers can apply principles of educational psychology to their classrooms. In "To Find Yourself, Think for Yourself", the authors propose the use of Socratic seminars to foster reading critically and facilitate the analysis of literature. A well-developed overview of how to implement Socratic discussions effectively is provided. In Article 30, Robert Marzano endeavors to set the record straight with regard to the way schools have chosen to implement the "high-yield" strategies outlined by he and his colleagues in a number of recent books. He cautions that no strategy comes with a guarantee and that educators should focus on developing a common language of instruction rather than a set of specific "must-use" strategies. The final two articles in this section provide examples of two different types of educational research. Ms. Stecz discusses an action research project she undertook with her eighth-grade students.

She examines the implications of having students work in small groups to learn and subsequently teach content to their peers in elementary grades. The final article in this section summarizes the collaborative efforts of a high school teacher and university researcher to implement a design-based learning unit in science.

With continual advances in technology, teachers find they have to compete with the latest "bells and whistles" to attract and maintain students' attention during instruction. They are continually challenged to enhance their instruction by integrating novel and innovative technologies. However, research examining the impact of technology on learning is, at present, inconclusive; while concerns about students' awareness and safety with respect to Internet use and social networking continue to grow. For the final subsection, four articles have been chosen that examine a number of issues related to technology education and technology integration in the classroom. These articles focus on topics ranging from the "technology education" curriculum, to plagiarism in the Internet age, to teaching children about Internet safety, to examine middle school students' knowledge of appropriate behaviors on social networking sites.

A Fresh Look at Brain-Based Education

Eric P. Jensen

Ten years ago John Bruer, executive administrator of the James S. McDonnell Foundation, began a series of articles critical of brain-based education. They included "Education and the Brain: A Bridge Too Far" (1997), "In Search of . . . Brain-Based Education" (1999), and, most recently, "On the Implications of Neuroscience Research for Science Teaching and Learning: Are There Any?" (2006). Bruer argued that educators should ignore neuroscience and focus on what psychologists and cognitive scientists have already discovered about teaching and learning. His message to educators was "hands off the brain research," and he predicted it would be 25 years before we would see practical classroom applications of the new brain research. Bruer linked brain-based education with tabloid mythology by announcing that, if brain-based education is true, then "the pyramids were built by aliens—to house Elvis."

Because of Bruer's and others' critiques, many educators decided that they were simply not capable of understanding how our brain works. Other educators may have decided that neuroscience has nothing to offer and that the prudent path would be simply to ignore the brain research for now and follow the yellow brick road to No Child Left Behind. Maybe some went so far as to say, "What's the brain got to do with learning?" But brain-based education has withstood the test of time, and an accumulating body of empirical and experiential evidence confirms the validity of the new model.

Many educationally significant, even profound, brain-based discoveries have occurred in recent years, such as that of neurogenesis, the production of new neurons in the human brain. It is highly likely that these discoveries would have been ignored if the education profession hadn't been primed, alerted, and actively monitoring cognitive neuroscience research and contemplating its implications and applications. Here, I wish to discuss how understanding the brain and the complementary research can have practical educational applications. I will make a case that narrowing the discussion to only neurobiology (and excluding other brain-related sciences) diminishes the opportunity for all of us to learn about how we learn and about better ways to teach. In addition, I will show how the synergy of biology, cognitive science, and education can support better education with direct application to schools.

In 1983 a new model was introduced that established connections between brain function and educational practice. In a groundbreaking book, *Human Brain, Human Learning,* Leslie Hart argued, among other things, that cognitive processes were significantly impaired by classroom threat. While not an earthshaking conclusion, the gauntlet was thrown down, as if to say, "If we ignore how the student brain works, we will risk student success." Many have tied brain function to new models either of thinking or of classroom pedagogy. A field has emerged known as "brain-based" education, and it has now been well over 20 years since this "connect the dots" approach began. In a nutshell, brain-based education says, "Everything we do uses our brain; let's learn more about it and apply that knowledge."

A discussion of this topic could fill books, but the focus here will be on two key issues. First, how can we define the terms, scope, and role of brain research in education? That is, what are the disciplines and relevant issues that should concern educators? These issues are multidisciplinary. Evidence will show that "brain-based" is not a loner's fantasy or narrow-field model; it's a significant educational paradigm of the 21st century. Second, what is the evidence, if any, that brain research can actually help educators do our job better? Is there now credibility to this burgeoning field? What issues have critics raised? Can the brain-based advocates respond to the critics in an empirical way?

Defining Brain-Based Education

Let's start this discussion with a simple but essential premise: the brain is intimately involved in and connected with everything educators and students do at school. Any disconnect is a recipe for frustration and potential disaster. Brain-based education is best understood in three words: engagement, strategies, and principles. Brain-based education is the "engagement of strategies based on principles derived from an understanding of the brain." Notice this definition does *not* say, "based on strategies given to us by neuroscientists." That's not appropriate. Notice it does not say, "based on strategies exclusively from neuroscience and no other discipline." The question is, Are the approaches and strategies based on solid research from brain-related disciplines, or are they based on myths, a well-meaning mentor teacher, or "junk science"? We would expect an educator to be able to support the use of a particular classroom strategy with scientific reasoning or studies.

Each educator ought to be professional enough to say, "Here's *why* I do what I do." I would ask: Is the person actually *engaged in using* what he or she knows, or does he or she simply have knowledge about it without actually using it? Are teachers using strategies based on the science of how our brain works? Brain-based education is about the professionalism of knowing why one strategy is used instead of another. The science is based on what we know about how our brain works. It's the professionalism to be research-based in one's practices. Keep in mind that if you don't know *why* you do what you do, it's less purposeful and less professional. It is probably your collected, refined wisdom. Nothing wrong with that, but some "collected, refined wisdom" has led to some bad teaching, too.

While I have, for years, advocated "brain-based" education, I never have promoted it as the "exclusive" discipline for schools to consider. That's narrow-minded. On the other hand, the brain is involved in everything we do at school. To ignore it would be irresponsible. Thus an appropriate question is, Where exactly is this research coming from?

The Broader Scope of Brain-Based Education

Brain-based education has evolved over the years. Initially it seemed focused on establishing a vocabulary with which to understand the new knowledge. As a result, many of us heard for the first time about axons, dendrites, serotonin, dopamine, the hippocampus, and the amygdala. That was the "first generation" of brain basics, the generation that introduced a working platform for today's generation. There was no harm in doing that, but knowing a few words from a neuroscience textbook certainly doesn't make anyone a better teacher. Times have changed. The brain-based movement has moved on from its infancy of new words and pretty brain scans.

Today's knowledge base comes from a rapidly emerging set of brain-related disciplines. It isn't published in just highly regarded journals such as *Nature, Science,* and the *Journal of Neuroscience.* Every people-related discipline takes account of the brain. As an example, psychiatry is now guided by the journal *Biological Psychiatry,* and nutrition is better understood by reading the journal *Nutritional Neuroscience.* Sociology is guided by the journal *Social Neuroscience.* Some critics assert that sociology, physical fitness, psychiatry, nutrition, psychology, and cognitive science are not "brain-based." That's absurd, because if you remove the brain's role from any of those disciplines, there would be no discipline. There is no separation of brain, mind, body, feelings, social contacts, or their respective environments. That assertion is old-school, "turf-based," and outdated. If the research involves the brain in any way, it is "brain-based." The brain is involved in everything we do.

The current model of brain-based education is highly interdisciplinary. Antonio Damasio, the Van Allen Distinguished Professor and head of the department of neurology at the University of Iowa Medical Center and an adjunct professor at the Salk Institute in La Jolla, California, says, "The relation between brain systems and complex cognition and behavior, can only be explained satisfactorily by *a comprehensive blend of theories* and facts related to *all the levels of organization* of the nervous system, from molecules, and cells and circuits, to large-scale systems and physical and social environments. . . . We must beware of explanations that rely on data from one single level, whatever the level may be." Any single discipline, even cognitive neuroscience, should be buttressed by other disciplines. While earlier writings did not reflect it, today we know that brain-based learning cannot be founded on neuroscience; we have learned that it requires a multidisciplinary approach.

The Brain Is Our Common Denominator

Today, many of the school- and learning-related disciplines are looking to the brain for answers. There's no separating the role of the brain and the influence of classroom groupings, lunchroom foods, school architecture, mandated curricula, and state assessments. Each of them affects the brain, and our brain affects each of them. Schools, assessment, environments, and instruction are not bound by one discipline, such as cognitive science, but by multiple disciplines. In short, schools work to the degree that the brains in the schools are working well. When there's a mismatch between the brain and the environment, something at a school will suffer.

Schools present countless opportunities to affect students' brains. Such issues as stress, exercise, nutrition, and social conditions are all relevant, brain-based issues that affect cognition, attention, classroom discipline, attendance, and memory. Our new understanding is that every school day changes the student's brain in some way. Once we make those connections, we can make choices in how we prioritize policies and strategies. Here are some of the powerful connections for educators to make.

1. The human brain can and does grow new neurons. Many survive and become functional. We now know that new neurons are highly correlated with memory, mood, and learning. Of interest to educators is that this process can be regulated by our everyday behaviors. Specifically, it can be enhanced by exercise, lower levels of stress, and good nutrition. Schools can and should influence these variables. This discovery came straight from neuroscientists Gerd Kempermann and Fred Gage.

2. Social conditions influence our brain in ways we didn't know before. The discovery of mirror neurons by Giacomo Rizzolatti and his colleagues at the University of Parma in Italy suggests a vehicle for an imitative reciprocity in our brain. This emerging discipline is explored in *Social Neuroscience,* a new academic journal exploring how social conditions affect the brain. School behaviors are highly social experiences, which become encoded through our sense of reward, acceptance, pain, pleasure, coherence, affinity, and stress. This understanding suggests that we be more active in managing the social environment of students, because students are more affected by it than we thought. It may unlock clues to those with autism, since their mirror neurons are inactive. This discovery suggests that schools should not rely on random social grouping and should work to strengthen prosocial conditions.

3. The ability of the brain to rewire and remap itself by means of neuroplasticity is profound. The new *Journal of Neuroplasticity* explores these and related issues. Schools can influence this process through skill-building, reading, meditation, the arts, career and technical education, and thinking skills that build student success. . . . Without understanding the "rules for how our brain changes," educators can waste time and money, and students will fall through the cracks.

4. Chronic stress is a very real issue at schools for both staff and students. Homeostasis is no longer a guaranteed "set point." The discovery championed by neuroscientist Bruce McEwen is that a revised metabolic state called "allostasis" is an adjusted new baseline for stress that is evident in the brains of those with anxiety and stress disorders. These pathogenic allostatic stress loads are becoming increasingly common and have serious health, learning, and behavior risks. This issue affects attendance, memory, social skills, and cognition. Acute and chronic stress is explored in *The International Journal of Stress Management, The Journal of Anxiety, The Journal of Traumatic Stress,* and *Stress.*

5. The old-school view was that either environment or genes decided the outcomes for a student. We now know that there's a third option: gene expression. This is the capacity of our genes to respond to chronic or acute environmental input. This new understanding highlights a new vehicle for change in our students. Neuroscientists Bruce Lipton and Ernest Rossi have written about how our everyday behaviors can influence gene expression. New journals called *Gene Expression, Gene Expression Patterns,* and *Nature Genetics* explore the mechanisms for epigenetic (outside of genes) changes. Evidence suggests that gene expression can be regulated by

what we do at schools and that this can enhance or harm long-term change prospects.

6. Good nutrition is about far more than avoiding obesity. The journals *Nutritional Neuroscience* and the *European Journal of Clinical Nutrition* explore the effects on our brain of what we eat. The effects on cognition, memory, attention, stress, and even intelligence are now emerging. Schools that pay attention to nutrition and cognition (not just obesity) will probably support better student achievement.

7. The role of the arts in schools continues to come under great scrutiny. Five neuroscience departments and universities (University of Oregon, Harvard University, University of Michigan, Dartmouth College, and Stanford University) currently have projects studying the impact of the arts on the brain. *Arts and Neuroscience* is a new journal that tracks the connections being made by researchers. This is a serious topic for neuroscience, and it should be for educators also. Issues being explored are whether the arts have transfer value and the possibility of developmentally sensitive periods for the arts.

8. The current high-stakes testing environment means some educators are eliminating recess, play, or physical education from the daily agendas. The value of exercise to the brain was highlighted in a recent cover story in *Newsweek.* More important, there are many studies examining this connection in *The Journal of Exercise, Pediatric Exercise Science,* and *The Journal of Exercise Physiology Online.* The weight of the evidence is that exercise is strongly correlated with increased brain mass, better cognition, mood regulation, and new cell production. This information was unknown a generation ago.

9. Stunning strides have been made in the rehabilitation of brain-based disorders, including fetal alcohol syndrome, autism, retardation, strokes, and spinal cord injury. It is now clear that aggressive behavioral therapies, new drugs, and stem cell implantation can be used to influence, regulate, and repair brain-based disorders. *The Journal of Rehabilitation* and *The International Journal of Rehabilitation Research* showcase innovations suggesting that special education students may be able to improve far more than we once thought.

10. The discovery that environments alter our brains is profound. This research goes back decades to the early work of the first trailblazing biological psychologists: Mark Rosenzweig at the University of California, Berkeley, and Bill Greenough at the University of Illinois, Urbana-Champaign. In fact, a new collaboration has emerged between neuroscientists and architects. "The mission of the Academy of Neuroscience for Architecture" according to the group's website, "is to promote and advance knowledge that links neuroscience research to a growing understanding of human responses to the built environment." This is highly relevant for administrators and policy makers who are responsible for school building designs.

Since our brain is involved in everything we do, the next question is, Is our brain fixed, or is it malleable? Is our brain shaped by experience? An overwhelming body of evidence shows our brain is altered by everyday experiences, such as learning to read, learning vocabulary, studying for tests, or learning to play a musical instrument. Studies confirm the success of software programs that use the rules of brain plasticity to retrain the visual and auditory systems to improve attention, hearing, and reading. Therefore, it stands to reason that altering our experiences will alter our brain. This is a simple but profound syllogism: our brain is involved in all we do, our brain changes from experience, therefore our experiences at school will change our brain

in some way. Instead of narrowing the discussion about brain research in education to dendrites and axons, a contemporary discussion would include a wider array of topics. Brain-based education says that we use evidence from all disciplines to enhance the brains of our students. The brain is involved with everything we do at school, and educators who understand take this fact into consideration in the decision-making process.

Brain-Based Education in Action

An essential understanding about brain-based education is that most neuroscientists don't teach and most teachers don't do research. It's unrealistic to expect neuroscientists to reveal which classroom strategies will work best. That's not appropriate for neuroscientists, and most don't do that. Many critics could cite this as a weakness, but it's not. Neuroscience and many related disciplines (e.g., genetics, chemistry, endocrinology) are what we refer to as basic science. The work is done in labs, and the science is more likely to provide general guidelines or to suggest future directions for research. Of all the neuroscience studies published each month, only a small fraction have potential relevance for education.

Clinical and cognitive research are mid-level research domains. In clinical and cognitive studies, humans are more likely (but not always) to be subjects in controlled conditions. Finally, applied research is typically done "in context," such as in a school. Each domain has different advantages and disadvantages. Critics of using neuroscience for educational decision making assert that the leap is too great from basic science to the classroom. I agree with that assertion; education must be multidisciplinary. I never have proposed, and never will, that schools be run solely based on neuroscience. But to ignore the research is equally irresponsible. Let's use a typical example that is "pushed" by the brain-based advocates, such as myself. . . .

Is There Evidence That Brain Research Can Help Educators?

This question is highly relevant for all educators. To repeat our definition, brain-based teaching is the active engagement of practical strategies based on principles derived from brain-related sciences. All teachers use strategies; the difference here is that you're using strategies based on real science, not rumor or mythology. But the strategies ought to be generated by verifiable, established principles. An example of a principle would be "Brains change based on experience." The science tells us how they change in response to experience. For example, we know that behaviorally relevant repetition is a smart strategy for learning skills. We know that intensity and duration matter. Did anyone 20 years ago know the optimal protocols for skill-building to maximize brain change? Yes, some knew them through trial and error. But at issue is not whether any educator has learned a revolutionary new strategy from the brain research. Teachers are highly resourceful and creative; literally thousands of strategies have been tried in the classrooms around the world.

The issue is, Can we make *better*-informed decisions about teaching based on what we have learned about the brain? Brain-based education suggests that we not wait 20 years until each of these correlations is proven beyond any possible doubt. Many theories might never be proven beyond reasonable doubt. It's possible that the sheer quantity of school, home, and genetic factors will render any generalizable principle impossible to prove as 100% accurate. As educators, we must live in the world of "likely" and "unlikely" as opposed to the world of "certainty." . . . The neuroscience merely supports other disciplines, but it's a discipline you can't see with your naked eyes, so it's worth reporting. Brain-based advocates should be pointing out how neuroscience parallels, supports, or leads the related sciences. But neuroscience is not a replacement science. Schools are too complex for that.

The Healthy Role of Critics

Almost 40 years ago, Thomas Kuhn's seminal work, *The Structure of Scientific Revolutions,* described how society responds when there is a significant shift in the prevailing paradigm. Kuhn argued that such a shift is typically met with vehement denial and opposition. Brain-based education has faced all of those reactions, and, a generation later, the paradigm continues to strengthen, not weaken. Over time, as more peer-reviewed research and real-world results accumulate, the novel paradigm gains credibility. The fact is, there will always be critics, regardless of overwhelming, highest-quality evidence. Having critics is a healthy part of society's checks and balances. All paradigm shifts attract critics.

As an example, Harvard's highly respected cognitive scientist Howard Gardner has endured his share of criticism from neuroscientists who were uncomfortable with his brain-based evidence for the theory of multiple intelligences. Yet, while subjected to two decades of criticism, Gardner's work has made and continues to make a profound and positive difference in education worldwide. His ideas are in thousands of schools, and teachers are asking, "How are my students smart?" Some critics were fearful of a new paradigm; others were more territorial, protecting their turf and crying foul at any change in the benchmarks for intelligence. And still others will attack and attack again, offering only negatives. What is unhealthy is when critics resort to sarcasm and sink to linking brain-based education to Elvis, pyramids, and aliens. That displays an embarrassing lack of scholarship and is disrespectful to those who work hard to improve education.

Critics often do have valid criticisms. For example, they mock policies (as they have every right to) that claim that a district is "brain-based" if every kid has a water bottle on his or her desk. No responsible advocate for brain-based education would argue that making water available is based on cutting-edge revelations about the brain. John Bruer argued that "we can only be thankful that members of the medical profession are more careful in applying biological research to their professional practice than some educators are in applying brain research to theirs." This would be humorous except for the fact that, according to a study published in the *Journal of the American Medical Association,* the third leading cause of death in the United States (over 100,000 deaths per year) is medical incompetence and malpractice. Is this the model of research and application that educators should be following? I think not. Give educators some credit. Much better to err on the side of enthusiasm and interdisciplinary research than to be part of the "head in the sand club."

Critics also commonly attempt to marginalize the discussion about brain-based education by using highly selective research (versus that from the prevailing majority of neuroscientists) to dispute scientific points. Examples of artificially "controversial" issues include whether "sensitive developmental periods," "gender differences," or "left-right brain differences" exist or can guide instructional practices. Turning these kinds of mainstream understandings into myths is akin to the current Administration's spin on global warming. For years, conservative Presidents have referred to global warming as the "Global Warming Debate," as if scientists are split 50–50 on the subject. The reality is that there is a nearly universal scientific consensus on both the effects of global warming and who is responsible for it.

The same can be said for the topics mentioned above. There is little controversy over whether sensitive periods, gender differences, or hemispheric specificity exist. There is no controversy over the value of developmentally appropriate instruction or removing gender biases from curriculum and instruction. There is no reputable debate over the significance of hemisphericity, either. Neuroscience giants like Michael Gazzaniga have invested careers exploring this field. Any critic who asserts that there is no significant difference between the instructional implications of our left and right hemispheres should answer the question, If each hemisphere has little functional difference, would you voluntarily undergo a hemispherectomy? That's a ridiculous question and, of course, everyone's answer would be no!

John Bruer says that he is "notorious" for his "skepticism about what neuroscience can currently offer to education." He argues that cognitive psychology, not neuroscience, is the strongest current candidate for a basic science of teaching. I happen to agree with that statement. I do believe that cognitive neuroscience has provided a great deal for educators and will continue to do so. The field has generated countless relevant insights. My own bias is toward psychology because I am currently a PhD student in psychology. But even the term "psychology" is morphing into "cognitive neuroscience" because "psychology" implies a behaviorist orientation and "cognitive neuroscience" suggests a biological underpinning. For me, it's all about the interdisciplinary nature of understanding the brain, the mind, and education.

Having said that, the critics do have one thing right: brain-based education must move from being a "field" to becoming more of a "domain." An academic field is merely an aggregate or collection of forces within that territory. Brain-based education is merely a "field" right now. It is composed of scholars, consultants, publishers, staff developers, neuroscientists, conferences, and school programs. That's far from concise and replicable, yet it is typical for the start of a new movement. For brain-based education to mature, it must become a "domain." Domains have all of the same "players" as "fields," but there's an important distinction. Domains have accumulated a clear set of values, qualities, and even criteria for acceptance and validity. As brain-based education matures, it will become a "domain." From that more credible perspective, it will be easier to say if an instructional or assessment principle is "brain-based" because, right now, we can't say that. Brain-based education has grown past the "terrible twos" and the tween years. The bottom line is that before it can become accepted as a mature adult, it must forge its way out of the tumultuous teens and emerge with an accepted body of core structures that define its identity with more than a pretty picture of a brain scan. That maturing process is well under way.

Validation of Brain-Based Education

Today, as a result of years of work by brain-based educators, educators are a far more informed profession. They are more professional, they look more at research, and they are increasingly more capable of understanding and incorporating new cognitive neuroscience discoveries than they were 10 years ago. More schools of education are incorporating knowledge from the brain sciences than would have done so if we had followed the critics' advice and crawled into an intellectual cave for 25 years. Many forward thinkers have stayed tuned to such sources as Bob Sylwester's monthly column in *Brain Connection,* Scientific Learning's Internet journal that's regularly read by thousands of educators and parents. Sylwester, formerly a professor at the University of Oregon and a widely published authority on brain-based education, has been "connecting the dots" for educators for a decade.

. . . They don't get it; it's all about being interdisciplinary. Another breakthrough is the new face-recognition software for learning social skills called "Let's Face It." It was developed by Jim Tanaka and his research team, who were interested in solutions for autism. It's likely critics will say that the product comes from a long history of human face recognition; ergo, it's not *really* a breakthrough. Other neuroscientists have recently penned "translational" books showing a "science to the classroom" connection. They include the luminary Michael Posner on attention, Sally Shaywitz on dyslexia, and Helen Nevills and Pat Wolfe on reading.

Two major conference organizations, PIRI and the Learning Brain EXPO (the author's company), have produced "science to the classroom" events for 10 years. These biannual events have engaged more than 100 highly reputable, often award-winning, neuroscientists to speak in translational terms to educators. The list of speakers has been a veritable "who's who" in cutting-edge, interdisciplinary neuroscience. This has come about only as a result of the collaboration of educators and scientists linking the research directly to those in the schools. Whether the presenter was a biological psychologist, neuroscientist, or cognitive scientist is irrelevant; they've all spoken on science to the classroom.

How reputable is brain-based education? Harvard University now has both master's and doctoral degrees in it. Every year, Harvard's Mind, Brain, and Education (MBE) program produces about 40 graduates with master's degrees and two to four doctors of education, who go on to interdisciplinary positions in research and practice. "Our mission is to build a movement in which cognitive science and neuroscience are integrated with education so that we train people to make that integration both in research and in practice," says Prof. Kurt Fischer, director of the program. This intersection of biology and cognitive science with pedagogy has become a new focus in education. Interest in the program is high in Canada, Japan, Australia, South Korea, England, South Africa, New Zealand, Argentina, and other countries. There's also a peer-reviewed scientific journal on brain-based education. The journal, which is published quarterly by the reputable Blackwell publishers and the International Mind, Brain, and Education Society (IMBES), features research, conceptual papers, reviews, debates, and dialogue.

Conclusion

Today, 10 years after the mudslinging criticism of brain-based education, it's appropriate to say, "We were right." In fact, because of the efforts of the brain-based community to inform educators, thousands are currently using this knowledge appropriately to enhance education policy and practice. There are degree programs in it, scientific journals, and conferences; and peer-reviewed brain-related research now supports the discipline. There are countless neuroscientists who support the movement, and they demonstrate their support by writing and speaking at educational conferences.

As an author in the brain-based movement, I have reminded educators that they should never say, "Brain research proves . . ." because it does not prove anything. It may, however, suggest or strengthen the value of a particular pathway. What educators should say is, "These studies suggest that XYZ may be true about the brain. Given that insight, it probably makes sense for us, under these conditions, to use the following strategies in schools." This approach, which is a cautionary one, sticks with the truth. When one is careful about making causal claims, the connections are there for those with an open mind.

The science may come from a wide range of disciplines. Brain-based education is not a panacea or magic bullet to solve all of education's problems. Anyone who claims that is misleading people. It is not yet a program, a model, or a package for schools to follow. The discussion of how to improve student learning must widen from axons and dendrites to the bigger picture. That bigger picture is that our brain is involved with everything we do at school. The brain is the most relevant feature to explore, because it affects every strategy, action, behavior, and policy at your school. New journals explore such essential topics as social conditions, exercise, neurogenesis, arts, stress, and nutrition. A school cannot remove arts, career education, and physical education and at the same time claim to be doing what's best for the brains of its students. These are the issues we must be exploring, not whether someone can prove whether a teacher's strategy was used before or after a neuroscience study provided peer-reviewed support for that strategy.

Today, there is still criticism, but the voices are no longer a chorus; they're a diminishing whine. For the critic, it's still "my way or the highway." That's an old, tired theme among critics; the tactic of dismissing another's research by narrowing the discussion to irrelevant issues, such as whether the research is cognitive science, neurobiology, or psychology. They're all about the mind and brain. The real issues that we should be talking about are what environmental, instructional, and social conditions can help us enrich students' lives. To answer that, it's obvious that everything that our brain does is relevant and that's what should now be on the table for discussion. Yes, we are in the infancy of brain research—there's so much more to learn. But dismissing it is not only shortsighted, it's also dead wrong. At this early stage, that would be like calling the Wright Brothers' first flight at Kitty Hawk a failure because it only went a few hundred yards. And let's remember, the Wright Brothers had no credibility either; they were actually bicycle mechanics, not aviators. The future belongs not to the turf protectors, but to those with vision who can grasp interdisciplinary trends as well as the big picture. Nothing is more relevant to educators than the brains of their students, parents, or staff. Brain-based education is here to stay.

Critical Thinking

1. What is meant by the term "brain-based" education?

2. Jensen provides a description of 10 different connections between current cognitive research and learning in school. Select two and describe how they might inform and influence your understanding of the learning process.

3. Based on what you learned in the article, explain how you might respond to a colleague who tells you he or she is planning his or her teaching for the year to rely solely on brain-based education strategies.

From *Phi Delta Kappan*, February 2008, pp. 409–413, 414–417. Copyright © 2008 by Eric P. Jensen. Reprinted by permission of Phi Delta Kappan and Eric P. Jensen.

What Will Improve a Student's Memory?

How does the mind work—and especially how does it learn? Teachers' instructional decisions are based on a mix of theories learned in teacher education, trial and error, craft knowledge, and gut instinct. Such gut knowledge often serves us well, but is there anything sturdier to rely on?

Cognitive science is an interdisciplinary field of researchers from psychology, neuroscience, linguistics, philosophy, computer science, and anthropology who seek to understand the mind. In this regular *American Educator* column, we consider findings from this field that are strong and clear enough to merit classroom application.

DANIEL T. WILLINGHAM

Question: I often have students tell me that they studied for a test, meaning that they reviewed their notes and the textbook, but they still did not do well. If they have reviewed the material, why don't they remember it? Is there anything I can do to help them study more effectively?

Answer: Many of my students also tell me that they reviewed their notes and were quite surprised when they did not do well on the test. I've found that these students typically know little about how their memories work and, as a result, do not know how to study effectively.

In this article, I'll discuss what to tell your students about how memory works: how to commit things to memory, to avoid forgetting, and to know when they've studied enough. I'll provide examples for classroom demonstrations to make the abstract ideas more vivid for your students, and I'll describe how they can apply those abstract ideas when they study.

From the time a child enters school until she earns a diploma, her principal task is to learn new facts and skills. It would seem natural, therefore, that somewhere along the way (perhaps around sixth grade or so, when schoolwork really becomes demanding) she would be told something about how her memory works—and something about how to make it work better. But that rarely happens. In fact, most college students report that they have improvised their own systems of study.[1] In this article, I will describe three principles of memory that are relevant to most of the learning that students do in elementary and secondary school (and, for that matter, most of the learning that adults need to do too). The three principles I'll describe apply equally to all sorts of learning—from memorizing new vocabulary words, to reading a novel so as to prepare for a class discussion the next day on its plot and style, to conducting a chemistry lab in the morning in order to compare the outcome with examples in a problem set to be handed out that afternoon.

Memory is a vast topic of study, and much is known about it. Let's take the broad question, what will improve a student's memory?, and break it into three more manageable parts: (1) How can I commit things to memory? (2) How can I avoid forgetting the things I have committed to memory? (3) How can I be certain that I have actually committed to memory the things I want to know? I will take up each of these questions in turn. Then, we'll apply what we've learned to the classroom.

How Can I Commit Things to Memory?

Some of what we experience day to day is stored away in our minds for future reference, but much of it is not. For example, you might describe in vivid detail the interior of a quaint ice cream parlor you visited last summer, but be unable to recall what flavor ice cream you had. Why would your memory system hold on to part of that experience—the parlor—and discard another—the flavor? The short answer is that you remember the part that you thought about.

One of the interesting features of your memory system is that you don't control what is stored. *Wanting* to remember something doesn't have much bearing on whether or not you will actually remember it.[2] Indeed, when you think about it, most of what you remember is not stuff that you consciously tried to store. Your knowledge of current events, of movie plots, of your friends' latest doings—you didn't try to commit any of that to memory. What you did do was think about those things. And here's how you should think about memory: it's the residue of thought, meaning that the more you think about something, the more likely it is that you'll remember it later.

But wait, before you think about that so much that you commit it to memory, let me clarify one point. It's only the most salient bit—the part you *really* think about—that turns into a memory. Back in that ice cream parlor, while you were selecting your ice cream and then eating it, you certainly devoted some thought to the flavor. But if it's the interior that you recall later on, then that's the part to which you devoted most of your attention and thought.

It can be hard to grasp just how specific, or narrow, your thoughts—and thus your memories—can be, so let's walk through one more example. Suppose you encounter a barking dog while on a walk. There are several aspects of the dog that you could think about. you could think about the *sound* of the dog's bark, what the dog *looked* like, or the *meaning* of the bark (why it's barking, whether it's barking at you, the likelihood that a barking dog will bite, and so on). Each of these thoughts will lead to different memories of the event the next day. If you think about the sound of the dog's bark, the next day you'll probably remember that quite well, but not its appearance.[3] Now, suppose that when you saw the barking dog, you thought mostly about what a nuisance the noise must be to the neighbors. If, the next day, I asked, "Did you see anything on your walk that could bite?" you might well say, "No, I don't think I did."[4] To put this example into broader terms, even simple concepts have multiple aspects of meaning; which one of these you think about will determine what you remember.

Thus, the first principle for students is that *memories are formed as the residue of thought.* You remember what you think about, but not every fleeting thought—only those matters to which you really devote some attention.

I'll discuss what this principle means for the classroom in more detail below, but it's worth pausing now to note an important implication. It is vital to know what you're going to want to remember later, because that dictates how you should think about the material. Most of the time, teachers want students to know what things mean. Thus, the advice offered to students should center on ways to help them think about meaning and avoid study methods that do not encourage them to think about meaning.

How Can I Avoid Forgetting the Things I Have Committed to Memory?

In my experience, people usually believe that forgetting happens over time; if you don't use a memory, you lose it. That may be a factor in forgetting, but it's probably not a major one. This may be hard to believe, but sometimes the memory isn't gone—it's just hard to get to. So, more important than the passage of time or disuse is the quality of the *cues* you have to get to the memory. Cues are bits of information that are the starting point for retrieving a memory. The good news is that the right cue can bring back a memory that you thought was lost. For example, you might believe that you remember very little of your childhood home, but when you visit as an adult, the sight of the house acts as a cue that brings memories flooding back. Or you may think that you have forgotten all of your high school Spanish, but a few days of constant exposure to Spanish when you visit Mexico leaves you understanding much more than you expected.

A poor cue, in contrast, will not get you access to a memory, even if you know that the memory is in the system. For example, suppose that I say to a friend, "Here's the $20 I owe you," whereupon he says, "You don't owe me $20." A better cue would offer more information, like this: "Remember, we were at Macy's and I wanted to buy that shirt but their computer wouldn't take my card so I had to borrow cash?" Your access to things that are stored in your memory will succeed or fail depending on the quality of the cues. One obvious source of forgetting, then, is poor cues. You haven't really forgotten—you just can't retrieve the memory at the moment because you don't have the right cues.

So far my examples have been cues that come from the environment (be it a house or a friend), but when you are trying to remember something, you generate your own cues. This process is sometimes obvious, as when you've lost something and you mentally try to retrace your steps. But sometimes it isn't: the process can be so rapid that it's not very noticeable. For example, even a student who is very well prepared for an exam on American history must prompt her memory when answering a broad essay question on a test, such as, "Analyze the eventual impact of the Louisiana Purchase on the events leading to the American Civil War." The environment (that is, the exam) provides very few cues to memory—the student must generate her own. A well-prepared student will do this rapidly, with each bit of information recalled serving as a cue for another.

As we've seen, sometimes a cue isn't good because it doesn't offer enough detail or the right detail. At other times, a cue isn't good because it leads to more than one memory. For example, suppose I give you a list of words to remember and the list includes several fruits. You, clever memorizer that you are, mentally categorize the list, thinking, "Some of the words were fruits." Doing so lets you generate a good cue at recall ("Let's see, I know some of the words were fruits . . ."). But what happens if I give you a second list, which again includes some fruits? Now your cue ("some of the words were fruits") will not be so effective because it leads to two memories: fruits from the first list and fruits from the second list. How to untangle them?

Students face this problem all the time. Some to-be-remembered material interferes with other to-be-remembered material, and the greater the similarity between them, the more likely that the cues will be the same, and therefore the more ambiguous they will be. Thus, studying French vocabulary and then working some geometry problems probably won't cause much interference. But studying French vocabulary and then studying Spanish vocabulary will: for example, the cue *red* calls up both *rouge* and *rojo*.

So, our second principle is that *memories are inaccessible mostly due to missing or ambiguous cues.* Thus, to minimize forgetting, we will focus on ways to ensure that we have cues and that they are distinctive.

How Can I Be Certain That I Have Actually Committed to Memory the Things I Want to Know?

Do you know who played Han Solo in the film *Star Wars?* Do you know the atomic number for Iron? Do you know the name of the professional football team that plays in Seattle? We are usually able to provide rapid answers to such questions (even if the answer is "no"), and the way we do so might seem obvious. You use the question as a cue, and either there is, or is not, a relevant entry in your memory. But that can't be the whole story, because sometimes you have a *feeling* that you know the answer, even if you can't call it up right now.

Researchers have found that people's feeling-of-knowing is meaningful—if you feel that you know something, it is more likely that you do know it than if you feel that you don't—but it is an imperfect guide. One way to test the accuracy of feeling-of-knowing is to give people a series of general information questions like those above. For each, the person must say whether he would know the answer if he saw it. Often, instead of a simple yes or no, the person is asked to make a probability judgment, such as, "I'm 75 percent sure I know the answer." After each judgment, the person sees four possible answers and must choose one. If the person's feeling-of-knowing is accurate, his probability judgments should match the proportion of questions he gets right. For example, taking all the questions for which he professed

Myths of Memory

Myth 1: Subliminal learning or sleep learning is possible. "Subliminal" means outside of awareness. For example, you might listen to a recording of music that has a simultaneous, almost inaudible track of someone reading an informative essay. If you listen to this recording enough times, will you come to know the content of the essay, even if the voice was always subliminal? No. Stimuli that are outside of awareness can have a subtle impact on some types of behavior,[1] but you won't be able to consciously access the memory the way you would access a regular memory. Sleep learning—in which the essay would be played as you slept with the hope that you would remember it upon waking—unfortunately works no better than subliminal learning.[2]

Myth 2: Memory is like a video recording. One sometimes reads that all of your experiences are recorded perfectly in your memory and you only forget things because you don't have the right cues. One also sometimes hears, as supporting evidence, that hypnosis can improve memory; it's as though the hypnotic state gives you direct access to the memory without the need for cues. This idea seems plausible, given what we've said in the main article about the importance of cues, and it is, of course, impossible to disprove—a supporter of the idea can always claim that every experience is stored away, just waiting for the right cue. But most memory researchers don't believe that this is true. It would be an odd and terribly inefficient way to design a memory system. The hypnosis claim is testable, and has been shown to be wrong. Hypnosis doesn't make memory any more accurate, although it does make people more confident that they are right.

Myth 3: There are herbal supplements or pharmaceuticals that can enhance memory or attenuate the cognitive decline associated with aging. There are a few—a very few—suggestive findings, and there are a lot of claims that go far beyond what the data support. Simply put, we are not there yet.[3]

Myth 4: memory depends on the input modality. You have probably seen some version of this: "We remember 10 percent of what we read, 20 percent of what we hear, 30 percent of what we see, 50 percent of what we see and hear, 70 percent of what we discuss with others, 80 percent of what we personally experience, and 95 percent of what we teach others." In the main article, I've argued that the most important factor determining whether or not a memory is long lasting is how much you think about it. The ordering of the activities may roughly correspond—you will definitely think about material carefully if you teach it to others— but the ordering could easily change. There are many things that I read (e.g., professional journal articles) that I remember much better than things I experience (e.g., my drive to work this morning).[4]

—D.T.W.

Endnotes

1. Laurie T. Butler and Dianne C. Berry, "Understanding the Relationship between Repetition Priming and Mere Exposure," *British Journal of Psychology* 95 (2004): 467–87.
2. Louis Aarons, "Sleep-Assisted Instruction," *Psychological Bulletin* 83 (1976): 1–40.
3. Peter H. Canter and Edward Ernst, "*Ginkgo biloba* is Not a Smart Drug: an Updated Systematic Review of Randomized Clinical Trials Testing the Nootropic effects of *G. biloba* extracts in Healthy People," *Human Psychopharmacology: Clinical and Experimental* 22 (2007): 265–78; and Mark A. McDaniel, Steven F. Maier, and Gilles O. Einstein, "'Brain-Specific' Nutrients: A memory Cure?" *Psychological Science in the Public Interest* 3 (2002): 12–38.
4. For interesting detective work on the origins of this memory myth, see Will Thalheimer, "People remember 10%, 20% . . . Oh Really?" May 1, 2006, www.willatworklearning.com/2006/05/people_remember.html (accessed August 5, 2008).

75 percent confidence, he should get 75 percent of those questions right (taking into account that he'll likely get 25 percent correct by guessing from among the four answers).

People usually believe that forgetting happens over time; if you don't use a memory, you lose it. This may be hard to believe, but sometimes the memory isn't gone—it's just hard to get to. So, more important than the passage of time or disuse is the quality of the *cues* you have to get to the memory.

Experiments like this[5] show that most adults think they know more than they actually do.* Somewhat surprisingly, school-age children† are about as good as adults in gauging their knowledge.[7]

Of course, given that adults are not so effective in judging what they know, it is no great compliment to children that they perform equally well.

This clearly poses a problem for a student trying to decide if he has studied enough. If students (like adults) tend to be more confident in their knowledge than is warranted, we would expect that they will, on average, not study enough. That prediction is borne out by experimental work. For example, in one study,[8] fourth- and fifth-grade students were given a passage of school-related material (either social studies or science) to be read and learned. All students were told that they should study so that they would know the material very well. After studying, they took a 10-item multiple choice test. The experimenters estimated how much studying each student needed to acquire such knowledge by using another passage and test of equal difficulty and seeing how much study time each student needed to get 100 percent on the test. Then they compared that required time with the amount of time students themselves allocated to the task. The key finding was that students allocated, on average, just 68 percent of the time needed to get the target score.[9]

---

*The exception is when people judge that there is no chance that they know something. On occasion, they actually do know, and so in these cases people are underconfident.

†There are other ways of testing the accuracy of feeling-of-knowing, and children are worse than adults on some of these,[6] but these paradigms bear little resemblance to schoolwork.

If students (like adults) tend to be more confident in their knowledge than is warranted, we would expect that they will, on average, not study enough. That prediction is borne out by experimental work. In one study, fourth- and fifth-grade students allocated, on average, just 68 percent of the time needed.

We can sum this up by saying the third principle is that *people tend to think their learning is more complete than it really is.* Thus, to help students study effectively, we need to find ways to get them to assess their knowledge more realistically.

Applying These Principles to Classroom Work

I've summarized three principles that are important to how your memory system operates. What concrete strategies can you suggest to your students to capitalize on these principles? I'll address these strategies in two broad categories: forming memories and retrieving memories.

Forming Memories

The first principle—memory is the residue of thought—describes how memories are formed. What remains in your memory from an experience depends mostly on what you thought about during the experience. Given that we typically want students to retain meaning, we will mostly want students to think about what things mean when they study. It would be nice if you could simply tell your class, "When you read your textbook, think about what it means." Naturally, you know that's not the case. The instruction to "think about meaning" is difficult to follow because it is not specific enough. A better strategy is for students to have a specific task that will force them to think about meaning.*

Through a series of studies, reading researcher Michael Pressley[11] figured out a way to do this that asked students to pose just one simple, specific question. He encouraged students to ask themselves "why?" at the end of each sentence as they read passages. In one study, fourth-through eighth-grade students read brief passages about animals.[12] For example, one began, "The Western Spotted Skunk lives in a hole in the ground. The skunk's hole is usually found on a sandy piece of farmland near crops." After reading each sentence, students were to ask themselves why that piece of information might be true. The researchers found that doing so produced a quite sizable benefit to memory, compared with students who were simply told to read the passage and remember it.

Although this strategy is effective for shorter passages, it's not clear that it would apply well to longer ones. I cannot imagine students asking themselves "why?" after each sentence of a textbook chapter—but I can imagine them asking why at the end of every few paragraphs or every section.

Another strategy that might achieve the same goal is to have students search for and write out the main ideas of a textbook chapter after they have read it. Next, they can identify how the author elaborates on these points. Students can draw a hierarchical diagram with the main chapter ideas at the top of the diagram, and branching down to subordinate ideas that support the main ideas. The point of this exercise is to get students thinking about what the main ideas of the chapter actually are, and to think about how the author supports those ideas. It is a broader-scale version of Pressley's strategy of getting students to ask "why?"

Still another technique is to ask students to write an outline of a textbook chapter or of their notes from a unit. Then ask students to try to write a *different* outline. Is there another way to organize the material? Students might also use a different format: if they used the standard outline format (alternating numbers and letters), they might use a flow diagram, or a hierarchy, or a cross-referenced document like a website. Again, the goal is to give students a concrete task that they cannot complete without considering which ideas have been covered and how they relate to one another.

Knowing that memory is the residue of thought also gives us some insight into what study strategies will *not* work. Unfortunately, these include the two that I most often encounter as a college instructor. When I ask a student how he studied for a test, the typical answer is that he copied his notes (or marked them with a highlighter) and read over the textbook. Neither strategy guarantees that the student will think about what the material means. Even worse, viewing the material several times leads to the illusion that one knows it because it seems increasingly familiar, but viewing the material does not give it much sticking power in memory. For example, how well do you know what a penny looks like? Is "Liberty" written on the front or the back? Is Lincoln wearing a tie? Most people don't know the details of a penny's appearance,[13] despite having seen thousands of pennies. Repetition (like copying notes or rereading a text) is helpful, but only when one repeats thinking about meaning. "Shallow" repetition (i.e., that does not focus on meaning) is not as helpful as it seems.

"Think about meaning" sounds like good advice, but there are things to be learned that are, essentially, meaningless. For example, what should students do when learning that *rojo* is the Spanish word for *red?* Meaningless material is difficult to learn because it is hard to find a good cue. As discussed above, remembering is prompted by cues, and it is hard to associate the cue (the Spanish word for *red*) with the target memory (*rojo*) when the cue and memory have no meaningful relation. Ironically, learning something by rote memorization is a great time to get creative. The memorization strategies (called mnemonics) listed in the table give students ways to make up meaningful relationships. And the more creative or distinctive, the better.

Mnemonics work largely (but not exclusively) by using the first two principles described earlier. Mnemonics make meaningless material more meaningful, giving you something to think about and a good cue. For example, the acrostic and acronym techniques give you the first letter of the to-be-remembered item, an excellent cue. Then too, many of the mnemonics encourage the use of visual imagery. Imagery is helpful because it makes cues more distinctive and less ambiguous. When you create a visual image of a duck, you must think of a *particular* duck. You must specify its size, proportions, coloring, posture, etc. All of these details make the duck more distinctive, and thus less likely to be confused with other ducks, and therefore a better cue to the target memory.

---

*This is, of course, the basic idea behind SQ3R and similar study strategies. The acronym stands for five things to do as you read: Survey what you will read, generate Questions as you survey, as you read try to answer the questions, Recite the important information as you progress, and Review when you have finished reading. There are many other similar strategies, each with its own acronym. There is some evidence that they are effective,[10] but much less than one might expect. These methods are widely taught; so if what I've said is right, wouldn't they be highly effective, and therefore frequently used? I think the problem with these methods is that they are difficult to do well. It's hard to know what questions to ask before you know what you're reading, and it's hard to remember to answer the questions as you're trying to understand the text. Students need a strategy that is more specific.

Mnemonic	How It Works	Example	Principle Used
Pegword	Useful for memorizing lists of unrelated items in order. You create a visual image of each item in the list with a "peg" word. You have already committed the pegs to memory, so they provide cues for the to-be-remembered items.	Pegs are usually easy to learn because they rhyme with numbers. "One is a bun, two is a shoe, three is a tree," and so on. If you wanted to remember the list *onion, duck, artist,* you would associate *onion* with a bun (e.g., a man making a face because his sandwich contains only onion), *duck* with shoes (e.g., a duck trying to paddle on a pond with big tennis shoes on), and *artist* with a tree (e.g., a man with a beret and a palette who made his artist's smock into a hammock between two maple trees).	The pegs provide cues to memory. Using bizarre imagery helps to ensure that the cues are distinctive and unlikely to be confused with other cues.
Method of Loci	Useful for memorizing lists of unrelated items in order. You commit a "mental walk" to memory—a familiar route with separate, identifiable locations—then create a visual image that associates each item on the list with a location on the mental walk.	Here's a mental walk from my front door to my driveway. The first location is my front porch, which has a bird's nest by the door, the second is the sidewalk, which has a large crack, the third is my asphalt driveway with a red paint stain. To memorize the list *onion, duck, artist,* I would associate *onion* with my front door, perhaps by putting onions in the nest instead of eggs. Then I'd associate *duck* with the sidewalk by imagining the duck with its beak stuck in the crack, and *artist* with an artist admiring the paint stain on the asphalt.	The stations on the walk provide cues to memory. As with the pegword strategy, using bizarre imagery helps to ensure that the cues are distinctive and unlikely to be confused with other cues.
Acronym	Create an acronym using the first letter of each of the to-be-remembered items; if you can remember the acronym, you have a good cue for each of the items.	The Great Lakes can be remembered with HOMES (Huron, Ontario, Michigan, Erie, Superior), the wavelength order of the visible spectrum of light with ROY G. BIV (red, orange, yellow, green, blue, indigo, violet).	The first letter of each item is a good cue to memory, and using a word (such as *homes*) is meaningful, and therefore easier to remember than a random set of letters would be.
Acrostic	Create an easy-to-remember sentence in which the first letter of each word provides a cue for the to-be-remembered material. A sentence is always easier to remember than disconnected words, and often one can create a vivid visual image of it, which makes it memorable.	To remember the order of the notes on the treble clef, countless children have memorized "Every Good Boy Does Fine." Likewise, the order for operations in arithmetic can be remembered with "Bless My Dear Aunt Sally" (brackets, multiplication, division, addition, subtraction).	Like the acronym method, acrostics provide a good cue for each item and are easy to remember because they are formed with meaningful material, in this case a sentence.
Music or Rhymes	The to-be-remembered material is set to a familiar tune, set to a rhythm, or made into a rhyme.	Music and rhymes are used a lot with young children, as in learning the alphabet with the ABC song and in learning how many days are in each month with the rhyme "30 days hath September. . . ."	If you forget the words, the melody can provide a cue to help you remember it. A rhyming cue ("another month must rhyme with September") is also useful.
Mnemonic Associations	Something in the to-be-remembered material is associated with an aspect of the material that is hard to remember.	These are often useful in spelling. To remember that the administrator of a school is spelled with a final *pal* (not *ple*), note that she is your *pal*. To remember how to spell *grammar* (not *grammer*), think "don't *mar* your work with bad gram*mar*." Here's one more: "stala**c**tites grow from the **c**eiling; stala**g**mites from the **g**round."	These associations inject meaning into meaningless associations. The last three letters of principal are meaningless when considered as separate letters, but the mnemonic makes them into the meaningful word *pal*.

(continued)

Keyword	Often used for foreign vocabulary words. Find an English word that is close in sound to the foreign vocabulary word. Then create a visual image that connects the English sound-alike word to the translation of the foreign word.	The Spanish word for *mushrooms* is *champiñones,* which sounds like the English word *champions.* Create a visual image of a boxing champion in the ring, arms aloft in victory, wearing big mushrooms on his hands instead of gloves.	This mnemonic uses a two-step process. The image creates an association between the cue word, *mushroom,* and another word, *champion,* which then is used as a sound cue for the to-be-remembered material *champiñones.*

Retrieving Memories

How can students ensure that what they learn is not forgotten? There are a few things students might do. one, which is explained in the table on mnemonics, is to select distinctive cues so as to decrease the likelihood that they will be ambiguous. Another way to make memories longer lasting is to distribute studying over time—in other words, don't cram. Students will sometimes (with perverse pride) brag that they studied immediately before a test, scored well, but soon forgot what they had learned. Research bears out their boasts. Studying at several different times means that you are used to cuing and retrieving the memory at lots of different points in time. But if learning is all crammed into the same time, you have always cued and retrieved the memory during the same time. When you cram, the memory becomes associated with the particular time you study, making the memory harder to retrieve later on (although this is not the only factor[14]). But if you distribute studying, the memory doesn't have that association because you keep studying it at different times. Naturally, this sound advice—study early and often—is difficult for students to follow. Small wonder that most books on study skills have a chapter on time management.

The final strategy to avoid forgetting is to overlearn. Students know that they forget, so if they study just to the point that they know the material, what will happen when they take a quiz the next day? Some forgetting will have occurred—they won't know the material as well as they did the night before. This should be obvious to students once it's pointed out to them—but just as students tend to overestimate how complete their learning is, they also tend to underestimate their own forgetting.[15] The solution is straightforward. Students should study until they know the material and then keep studying. How long they should continue studying depends on how long they hope to retain the material, how they will be tested, and other factors, but a good rule of thumb is to put in another 20 percent of the time it took to master the material.

This advice—to continue studying after you know the material—requires that you can accurately gauge how complete your knowledge is. What can be done to help students better know what it is they know? The most important advice for them is to test themselves the way they will be tested. Students tend to gauge their knowledge based on their feeling-of-knowing; as they "read over their notes," they get an increasing feeling of familiarity. But a feeling of familiarity is not the same thing as being able to reproduce the material on a test.[16] how many teachers have heard a student say, "I *know* it, I just can't explain it"? Most likely, the student understands it when *you* explain it, but doesn't understand it well enough to explain it herself. The best way to test oneself is to explain the material to another person, ideally one who can ask sensible follow-up questions. This method will provide a much better metric for the student as to what she really knows. As an added bonus, testing yourself in this manner helps the material stay in memory.

> **Mnemonics work largely (but not exclusively) by giving you something to think about and a good cue. Imagery is helpful because it makes cues less ambiguous. When you create a visual image of a duck, you must think of a *particular* duck. The details make the duck more distinctive, and therefore a better cue to the target memory.**

The box below summarizes the three principles of memory and the corresponding recommendations. Much more could be written about memory, but the topic can quickly become overwhelming. The three principles discussed here are the most important for students. Naturally, these principles will be more meaningful to your students if they see them in action, so see the following page for some classroom demonstration ideas.

---

1. Memories are formed as a residue of thought.

   - If you want to remember what things mean, you must select a mental task that will ensure that you think about their meaning.
   - If what you want to remember has little meaning, use a mnemonic.

2. Memories are lost mostly due to missing or ambiguous cues.

   - Make your memories distinctive.
   - Distribute your studying over time.
   - Plan for forgetting by continuing to study even after you know the material.

3. Individuals' assessments of their own knowledge are fallible.

   - Don't use an internal feeling to gauge whether you have studied enough. Test yourself, and do so using the same type of test you'll take in class.

Demonstrations of the Three Principles

If you'd like to teach your students about how memory works, it may be useful to illustrate the three principles from the main article in your class. here are some demonstrations you might use.

Demonstration 1

This exercise illustrates that (1) students do not need to try to remember in order for things to get in memory, and (2) thinking about meaning is much more effective for getting material into memory than thinking about other aspects of the content.

What to Tell Your Students:

Please get out a blank piece of paper and number the lines from 1 to 30, so that you have 30 places to put answers. [Wait until they have completed this task. To save time, you can distribute sheets with numbered lines.] *I'm going to read aloud 30 words and for each word you just have to perform one of three tasks. Each task is really simple.*

The first is called spoken to the left. *If I turn my head to the left like this* [demonstrate] *when I say the word, then you should write "y" on your paper for "yes." But if I keep my head looking straight at the class, then you should write "n" for "no." So for example, I might say, "Spoken to the left?* [Turn your head to the left as you say the next word.] *Shell."* *And you would write "y" on your paper. Okay?*

The second task is called A or U. *If I say "A or U?" you should write "y" for "yes" if the following word has either an A or a U in it. So if I say, "A or U? Doctor." You would write "n" for "no."*

The third task is called rate for pleasantness. *For that one, I want you to listen to the word I say, and think of whether it makes you think of pleasant things or unpleasant things. Then write a number from 1 to 7 showing how pleasant the word is. A 1 means it's really unpleasant—for example, the word "injury" might get a 1. Write a 7 if it's really pleasant—for example, "birthday." Use numbers between 1 and 7 for medium pleasantness.*

You have to listen carefully because there are three tasks, and I'm going to mix them up. I'll tell you right before each word which task you should do for that word. Let's try a couple of each for practice; you don't need to write your answers for these.

A or U? Save
Spoken to the left? [Keep your head straight.] *Worth*
Rate for pleasantness: Coin
Rate for pleasantness: Tiny
A or U? Moral
Spoken to the left? [Turn your head to the left.] *Upper*

Any questions?

What to Do:

Read each item and then pause for students to answer, which should only take a moment.

1. *Spoken to the left?* [Keep your head straight.] *Hundred*
2. *Rate for pleasantness: Corn*

3. *A or U? Cool*
4. *Spoken to the left?* [Keep your head straight.] *Rate*
5. *A or U? Jump*
6. *Spoken to the left?* [Turn your head to the left.] *Place*
7. *Rate for pleasantness: Urge*
8. *A or U? Country*
9. *Spoken to the left?* [Turn your head to the left.] *Entirely*
10. *A or U? About*
11. *Rate for pleasantness: Diamond*
12. *Spoken to the left?* [Keep your head straight.] *Into*
13. *Rate for pleasantness: Welcome*
14. *A or U? Window*
15. *Spoken to the left?* [Turn your head to the left.] *Hold*
16. *Rate for pleasantness: Airplane*
17. *Spoken to the left?* [Keep your head straight.] *Thread*
18. *A or U? Match*
19. *Spoken to the left?* [Turn your head to the left.] *Fleet*
20. *Rate for pleasantness: Fruit*
21. *A or U? Melt*
22. *Spoken to the left?* [Turn your head to the left.] *Training*
23. *Rate for pleasantness: Race*
24. *A or U? Only*
25. *Rate for pleasantness: Winter*
26. *A or U? Single*
27. *Rate for pleasantness: Disease*
28. *A or U? Yourself*
29. *Spoken to the left?* [Keep your head straight.] *Else*
30. *Rate for pleasantness: Camp*

Then Tell Your Students:

Now I'd like you to try to remember all of the words that you were asked to judge. You can omit the practice words, but see how many of the others you can remember. Turn over the paper you just used, and write down as many as you can.

How to Score the Data:

It is easiest to have the students score their own papers. Show them (for example, on an overhead projector) the 30 words, grouped by task—there are 10 of each. Ask them to count how many words out of 10 they got right for each of the three tasks. Then ask for a show of hands: how many people got the most right for the *rate for pleasantness* task, then the *A or U* task, and then the *spoken to the left* task? (You can let students raise their hands twice if there is a tie.)

How to Interpret What Happened:

It's a very good bet that students will remember the most from the pleasantness task. You can highlight two points to students. First, they remembered lots of words even though they were *not* trying to remember them. You might also point out how much of what is in their memory is not stuff that they tried to remember, as described in the main article. Second, you should point out that the pleasantness task was the "winner" because it forced students to think about what the words meant. Students could answer the *A or U* question

Demonstrations of the Three Principles   *(continued)*

by just thinking of the spelling. But on the *rate for pleasantness* task, they had to think of meaning, and that's what really helps memory.

Demonstration 2

This exercise demonstrates the interference that occurs when you continually use the same cue to try to remember more and more material. Thus, it shows that it is important to try to use different, distinctive cues.

What to Tell Your Students:

I'm going to read a list of words to you. All you need to do is listen to the words and then, when I say "go," write down as many as you can remember. We'll do several of these lists. For each one, you only need to remember the words from the list that I just read to you. [Students should have a piece of paper and a pencil or pen ready.]

What to Do:

Read each of the lists below at a rate of about one second per word. At the end of the list, say "go." There is a natural tendency to use a slightly different tone (usually higher pitch) for the last word of the list. Try to resist that tendency and to read the last word just as you read the others. After you say "go," give the students some time to try to recall the words, but it needn't be terribly long (perhaps 15 or 20 seconds). Given a longer time they probably will not remember much more. After each list, ask students to draw a line on their paper or indicate in some other way that they are remembering a new list.

> List 1: *Apple, Blueberry, Grape, Orange, Raspberry, Watermelon, Fig*
> List 2: *Lime, Pear, Cherry, Strawberry, Honeydew, Mango, Kiwi*
> List 3: *Apricot, Banana, Peach, Lemon, Grapefruit, Blackberry, Plum*
> List 4: *Firefighter, Teacher, Chef, Secretary, Police Officer, Tailor, Doctor*

How to Score the Data:

For this one you probably don't even need to have them score their answers as correct (although you certainly could). Just ask students to count how many words they remembered from each list. Then ask, "How many got more words right on the first list than on the third list?" Most should. Then ask, "How many got more words right on the third list than on the first list?" There should be very few of these. Finally ask, "How many got more words right on the fourth list than on the third list?" Again, most students should have done so.

How to Interpret What Happened:

Students will, of course, remember that the list consisted of fruits, so when they try to remember the words on the list, they try to think of fruits. But that cue becomes more ambiguous with each new list, because the cue "fruits that the teacher just read to me" gets crowded with words that are correct (the current list) and words that are incorrect (words from the

previous list). But students use a different, unambiguous cue for the final list (occupations) and so recall improves.

Demonstration 3

This demonstration shows that people are generally more likely to be overconfident about what they know than underconfident.

What to Tell Your Students:

I'm going to ask you to make some judgments about what you know. For each question, I want you to take just a second or two and then write down "yes" or "no," regarding whether you think you know that information. You won't have time to actually try to remember it, just make a quick judgment about whether you think you could, if you had enough time.

What to Do:

Obviously, this demonstration will not work if you pose questions that are too easy or too hard—students will confidently say that they can or cannot answer them, and they will be right! Here are some ideas for questions that might work, but if they look too easy or difficult to you, replace them with more suitable questions. Make sure that you don't pose questions with just one answer (e.g., "Who was the first actor to play James Bond?"), because such questions encourage students to consult their memory for the answer, and to make their judgment on that basis. Here are some ideas for questions.

1. *Can you name the seven dwarfs?* (Dopey, Grumpy, Doc, Happy, Bashful, Sneezy, Sleepy)
2. *Can you name the world's continents?* (North America, South America, Antarctica, Africa, Europe, Asia, Australia)
3. *Can you name five [or four, or seven] recent presidents?* (G. W. Bush, Clinton, G. H. W. Bush, Reagan, Carter, Ford, Nixon, etc.)
4. *Can you name the presidents on Mount Rushmore?* (Lincoln, Washington, Jefferson, Teddy Roosevelt)
5. *Can you name the members of the Beatles?* (John Lennon, Paul Mccartney, George Harrison, Ringo Starr)
6. *Can you name the states on the eastern seaboard?* (Maine, New Hampshire, Massachusetts, Rhode Island, Connecticut, New York, New Jersey, Delaware, Maryland, Virginia, North Carolina, South Carolina, Georgia, Florida)
7. *Can you name the first four elements of the periodic table?* (Hydrogen, Helium, Lithium, Beryllium)
8. *Can you name the titles of the seven Harry Potter books? (*Harry Potter and the Sorcerer's Stone, Harry Potter and the Chamber of Secrets, Harry Potter and the Prisoner of Azkaban, Harry Potter and the Goblet of Fire, Harry Potter and the Order of the Phoenix, Harry Potter and the Half-Blood Prince, Harry Potter and the Deathly Hallows)

After students make their judgments for two or three questions, ask them to go ahead and write down the answers. Even if they said that they couldn't remember, they should try their best and guess if necessary.

(continued)

Demonstrations of the Three Principles *(continued)*

How to Score the Data:

For this demonstration it is important that students know whether their memory was accurate, so you must give them the correct answers for scoring. Once they know whether their memory was accurate, ask for a show of hands: how many students, for any of the questions, judged that they *would* be able to answer the question but then were not able to? Next, ask for a show of hands for all those who thought they would *not* be able to answer the question correctly, but actually were able to do so. There ought to be more of the former than the latter, reflecting the general overconfidence of memory.

How to Interpret What Happened:

Tell your students that overconfidence about what we know is a pervasive feature of memory. The consequence is that we *think* we know things that we actually don't quite know. This means that you can't rely on your gut feeling when trying to judge whether or not you know something—for example, when trying to judge whether you are prepared for a test or need to study a little more. The only way to combat the problem is to test yourself, and see whether the material is actually in your memory.

—D.T.W.

For Further Readings

For more information about memory, I recommend these books:

Alan Baddeley, *Your Memory: A User's Guide* (Richmond Hill, Ontario: Firefly Books, 2004).

Kenneth L. Higbee, *Your Memory: How It Works and How to Improve It,* 2nd ed. (New York: Marlowe, 2001).

See also the following "Ask the Cognitive Scientist" columns:

"Practice Makes Perfect—But Only If You Practice Beyond the Point of Perfection," *American Educator,* Spring 2004, www.aft. org/pubs-reports/american_educator/spring2004/cogsci.html.

"Why Students Think They Understand—When They Don't," *American Educator,* Winter 2003–04, www.aft.org/pubs-reports/american_educator/winter03-04/cognitive.html.

"Students Remember . . . What They Think About," *American Educator,* Summer 2003, www.aft.org/pubs-reports/american_educator/summer2003/cogsci.html.

"Allocating Student Study Time: 'Massed' versus 'Distributed' Practice," *American Educator,* Summer 2002, www.aft.org/pubs-reports/american_educator/summer2002/askcognitivescientist.html.

Notes

1. Nate Kornell and Robert A. Bjork, "Optimizing Self-Regulated Study: The Benefits—and Costs—of Dropping Flashcards," *Memory* 16 (2008): 125–36.

2. See, for example, Thomas S. Hyde and James J. Jenkins, "Differential Effects of Incidental Tasks on the Organization of Recall of a List of Highly Associated Words," *Journal of Experimental Psychology* 82 (1969): 472–81; Michael E. J. Masson and Mark A. McDaniel, "The Role of Organizational Processes in Long-Term Retention," *Journal of Experimental Psychology: Human Learning and Memory* 7 (1981): 100–110; and Thomas O. Nelson and Susan K. Vining, "Effect of Semantic versus Structural Processing on Long-Term Retention," *Journal of Experimental Psychology: Human Learning and Memory* 4 (1978): 198–209.

3. C. Donald Morris, John D. Bransford, and Jeffery J. Franks, "Levels of Processing versus Transfer Appropriate Processing," *Journal of Verbal Learning and Verbal Behavior* 16 (1977): 519–33.

4. J. R. Barclay, John D. Bransford, Jeffery J. Franks, Nancy S. McCarrell, and Kathy Nitsch, "Comprehension and Semantic Flexibility," *Journal of Verbal Learning and Verbal Behavior* 13 (1974): 471–81.

5. See, for example, Baruch Fischhoff, Paul Slovic, and Sarah Lichtenstein, "Knowing with Certainty: The Appropriateness of Extreme Confidence," *Journal of Experimental Psychology: Human Perception and Performance* 3 (1977): 552–64.

6. Claudia M. Roebers, "Confidence Judgments in Children's and Adults' Event Recall and Suggestibility," *Developmental Psychology* 38 (2002): 1052–67.

7. Earl C. Butterfield, Thomas O. Nelson, and Virginia Peck, "Developmental Aspects of the Feeling of Knowing," *Developmental Psychology* 24 (1988): 654–63; and Kathrin Lockl and Wolfgang Schneider, "Developmental Trends in Children's Feeling-of-Knowing Judgements," *International Journal of Behavioral Development* 26 (2002): 327–33.

8. Maribeth Gettinger, "Time Allocated and Time Spent Relative to Time Needed for Learning as Determinants of Achievement," *Journal of Educational Psychology* 77 (1985): 3–11.

9. See also Linda Leal, Nancy Crays, and Barbara E. Moely, "Training Children to Use a Self-Monitoring Study Strategy in Preparation for Recall: Maintenance and Generalization Effects," *Child Development* 56 (1985): 643–53; and Nate Kornell and Robert A. Bjork, "The Promise and Perils of Self-Regulated Study," *Psychonomic Bulletin and Review* 14 (2007): 219–24.

10. See, for example, Michael Allen Martin, "Students' Applications of Self-Questioning Study Techniques: An Investigation of Their Efficacy," *Reading Psychology* 6 (1985): 69–83.

11. See, for example, Michael Pressley and Pamela Beard El-Dinary, "Memory Strategy Instruction That Promotes Good Information Processing," in *Memory Improvement: Implications for Memory Theory,* ed. Douglas J. Herrmann, Herbert Weingartner, Alan Searleman, and Cathy McEvoy (New York: Springer-Verlag, 1992), 79–100; and Michael Pressley, Sonya Symons, Mark A. McDaniel, Barbara L. Snyder, and James E. Turnure, "Elaborative Interrogation Facilitates Acquisition of Confusing Facts," *Journal of Educational Psychology* 80 (1988): 268–78.

12. Eileen Wood, Michael Pressley, and Philip H. Winne, "Elaborative Interrogation Effects on Children's Learning of Factual Content," *Journal of Educational Psychology* 82 (1990): 741–48.

13. Raymond S. Nickerson and Marilyn Jager Adams, "Long-Term Memory for a Common Object," *Cognitive Psychology* 11 (1979): 287–307.

14. For a review, see Nicholas J. Cepeda, Harold Pashler, Edward Vul, John T. Wixted, and Doug Rohrer, "Distributed Practice in Verbal Recall Tasks: A Review and Quantitative Synthesis," *Psychological Bulletin* 132 (2006): 354–80.

15. Asher Koriat, Robert A. Bjork, Limor Sheffer, and Sarah K. Bar, "Predicting One's Own Forgetting: The Role of Experience-Based and Theory-Based Processes," *Journal of Experimental Psychology: General* 133 (2004): 643–56.

16. Andrew P. Yonelinas, "The Nature of Recollection and Familiarity: A Review of 30 Years of Research," *Journal of Memory and Language* 46 (2002): 441–517.

Critical Thinking

1. Explain what Willingham meant by the statement, "memories are formed as the residue of thought."

2. Think of an important concept or information that is essential for students to have memorized and be able to easily/quickly recall because it is used frequently in your class. Develop a new mnemonic device to aid students' learning and explain how it reflects one of the types provided in the article.

3. Ask a group of five or six friends/peers to participate as "students" in one of the demonstrations described in the article. Score the data you collect as indicated and then discuss the results of what you found with the group. What the results the same or different from what you anticipated based on the reading? How did your "students" respond to the activity?

DANIEL T. WILLINGHAM is professor of cognitive psychology at the University of Virginia. His new book, *Why Don't Students Like School?,* will be available in spring 2009. For his articles on education, go to www.danielwillingham.com. Readers can pose specific questions to "Ask the Cognitive Scientist," *American Educator,* 555 New Jersey Ave. N.W., Washington, DC 20001, or to amered@aft.org. Future columns will try to address readers' questions.

Classroom Assessment and Grading to Assure Mastery

JAMES P. LALLEY AND J. RONALD GENTILE

Achieving learning standards is at the forefront of current educational philosophy, and is the goal of sound educational practice. That "all children can learn" and there will be "no child left behind" presume that teaching and assessment practices must benefit all children. Agreement in principle is nearly universal. Practical implementation, however, is another matter. One philosophy of learning and instruction that has a long history of targeting instruction and achievement for all students is mastery learning. This article examines (a) fundamental tenets that mastery learning is built upon, (b) the clear connection between learning standards and mastery learning, and (c) how mastery is often erroneously implemented. It then outlines the defining features of mastery and how to implement them. These defining features include developing clear objectives, setting a mastery standard, using criterion-referenced assessments, and grading incentives for students to learn beyond initial mastery.

Who among us, when frustrated by the blank looks on our students' faces, has not uttered the phrase, "You've *had* this before!"? Of course, they had encountered it before, perhaps even passed a test on it, but they forgot it. The evidence has been clear (since Ebbinghaus, 1885/1964) that even when material is initially mastered to a high standard, much will be forgotten in a few hours or days. The good news is that relearning is faster—that is there is a savings of time in relearning over initial learning and that memory will continue to improve with additional practice beyond mastery—technically called *overlearning*. Under optimal conditions, such as practice to the point of automaticity (Schneider & Shiffrin, 1977) or sufficient distributed practice, organization, and use of material (Bahrick, 1984a, 1984b), knowledge and skills can achieve relative permanence.

This, of course, is the kind of memory developed by experts in a field, which allows them to more quickly access their memories to solve problems or acquire new information (Chi, Glaser, & Rees, 1982; deGroot, 1965; Halpern & Bower, 1982; Rumelhart & Norman, 1981). Learners who do not achieve mastery in the initial phase of learning show none of these benefits. Instead, they show considerable forgetting within hours or days, little (if any) savings in relearning, and no overlearning (by definition), because practice makes perfect only if the practice is essentially correct.

Figure 1 illustrates the ups and downs of learning/forgetting for initially successful and unsuccessful learners (masters and nonmasters, respectively). For a positive example (the learners portrayed in Figure 1A), consider your own experience as a teacher. The first time teaching a unit, there is quite a bit to learn, despite the courses you took at college. With each successive preparation for that unit, however, it is gratifying that relearning is not only quicker, but you are organizing the material better, as well as inventing new examples and exercises. By the tenth iteration of this unit, you experience virtual total recall, with a vast repertoire of examples on which to draw. The material is becoming so natural to you that you find yourself agreeing with other teachers that "the students seem less prepared every year." You are losing empathy with the beginning student, as relative experts often do. But this is the difference between an expert and a teacher: "An expert can do it; a teacher can do it but also remembers what it takes to progress from novice to expert" (Gentile & Lalley, 2003, p. 5).

For a negative example (Figure 1B), consider students who have been unsuccessful in their original learning of addition and subtraction of fractions. Their forgetting will likely be close to complete, because they learned so little in the first place. They are even likely to complain, when subsequently confronted with this material, that they "never had this before." This may not be just an excuse: They may really not remember it. Worse, their next attempt will probably also be unsuccessful because, after all, most teachers spend less time reviewing material than they spend teaching it originally. Thus, by the third or fourth encounter with fractions, these students will recall having had it before but they will also recall that they were not good at fractions. They are well on their way to learned helplessness, with the attendant cognitive, behavioral, and emotional baggage that is often called *math anxiety* (Gentile & Monaco, 1986; Peterson, Maier, & Seligman, 1993).

There is also a problem regarding prerequisite knowledge. When students have mastered prerequisites, they are ready for the current lesson, and thus can begin the upward acceleration toward mastery of the new material. If required prior knowledge is missing—or worse, incorrect—then students are not ready to learn to multiply or divide fractions, to continue the above example, and it takes a long time before they begin to show progress in learning the current lesson.

A. When Original Learning is Adequate (Mastery)

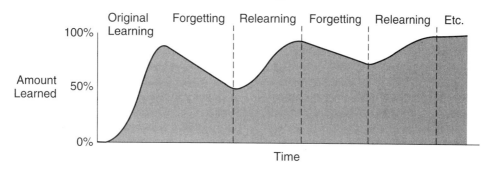

B. When Original Learning is Inadequate (Nonmastery)

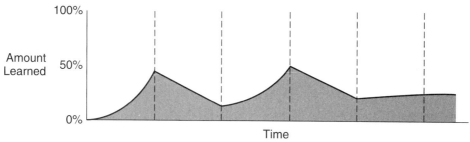

Figure 1 Hypothetical learning/forgetting curves, mastery versus nonmastery. Reprinted with permission of the publisher from Gentile, J. R. & Lalley, J. P. (2003). *Standards and Mastery Learning: Aligning Teaching and Assessment So All Children Can Learn.* Thousand Oaks, CA Corwin Press, p. 6.

In general, from cognitive theory, and especially from the research on experts versus novices discussed below, each cognitive and perceptual act is an interpretation or construction of new information in terms of what is already known. Indeed, how could it be otherwise? Consider reading. Those who are better informed can understand what they read, learn to read better, and then are more prepared to learn from reading. Those who lack prerequisite knowledge and/or have difficulty reading will be unprepared to use reading to increase their knowledge. The rich get richer, the poor get poorer, and the learning/memory curves diverge further.

Mastery Learning and Assessment

The above discussion distinguishes between mastery and expertise, with the former being a necessary first step—but only a first step—toward what eventually might develop into the latter with concentrated, in-depth, and extended study and practice. In typical classrooms, one of the major goals is to introduce relative novices to ideas, skills, or strategies that are fundamental to a discipline and, therefore, prerequisites for more advanced courses and continued development in that discipline. Whatever else is taught in each course, we need to assure that each student masters those fundamentals as a criterion for a passing grade (Gentile, 2004).

Mastery learning requires that each student achieve a preestablished standard of performance on a specified set of instructional objectives in a criterion-referenced manner—that is, without regard to how well others are doing. Well-implemented programs:

1. identify significant, mastery objectives in terms of their necessity as prerequisites for subsequent learning, requiring students to learn and relearn until they demonstrate their competence; and
2. provide enrichment objectives for students to go beyond initial mastery to expand, organize, apply, and teach their newly acquired knowledge and skills.

Of course, depending on curriculum and/or teachers' professional judgment, what is an enrichment objective for one course or grade level could be a mastery objective for another. As such, in the ideal educational world, instruction would be sequenced in a spiral curriculum (Bruner, 1960) and teachers would adapt instruction to the prior knowledge of each student. This would still not be easy, because each individual would remember different things from prior instruction, have somewhat different misconceptions to unlearn, and relearn at different rates.

As Black and Wiliam (1998) and Stiggins and Chappuis (2008) argued, we raise standards by focusing on formative assessment and providing timely feedback on students' progress in learning. Feedback, in this conception, is neither a grade nor a summative test score. Rather, it is specific information on what was correct, what was incorrect, and how to improve (Gentile, 1993; Hunter, 1982). This implies that an exercise, assignment, or test will be tried and tried again until it is adequate. Conceived of this way, there is no such thing as negative feedback; all feedback is positive in the sense that it points the way to improvements in knowledge, skill, and self-efficacy.

To provide formative assessment and timely feedback requires that assessment and grading be *criterion-referenced* (Glaser & Nitko,

1971; Popham, 1978), meaning that each student's performance is interpreted relative to established instructional goals and standards, independent of other students' performances. This is in contrast to more traditional *norm-referenced* assessment, in which a student's score or performance is compared with the norm or distribution of scores provided by other students. In Bloom's (1976) succinct analysis, norm-referenced assessment is useful for *selecting* talent, but criterion-referenced assessment has the goal of *developing* talent (see also Gentile, 2005). And developing talent is what teaching is all about.

Assessing and Grading to Ensure Mastery

When schools attempt to implement mastery learning—as in the recent movement toward achieving benchmarks—they usually make the following fatal errors: (a) demonstrating mastery is conceptualized as the endpoint rather than the initial phase of the learning/memory/application process, (b) mastery tests and activities are limited to the knowledge/comprehension end of the thinking continuum, (c) there is no requirement or grading incentive for going beyond initial mastery and (d) assessment of student achievement remains embedded in a competitive or norm-referenced grading system.

To avoid such implementation errors, we propose four ways to incorporate the defining features of a good mastery learning program (Block, Efthim, & Burns, 1989; Gentile & Lalley, 2003):

1. clearly stated and published objectives, sequenced to facilitate transfer of prior learning to current and future competencies;
2. a standard for passing mastery tests sufficiently high (e.g., 75% correct or better) to assure that initial learning, once forgotten (as is almost inevitable) can be relearned quickly;
3. multiple and parallel forms of criterion-referenced tests, with corrective exercises and retesting as needed to demonstrate initial mastery; and
4. grading incentives to encourage students to reach beyond initial mastery and strive for fluency in the material, to better organize, apply, and even teach it to others.

To facilitate the successful implementation of these ideas, we will elaborate these four defining features of a good mastery learning program.

Clearly Stated and Published Objectives

Every discipline has a set of objectives that are so basic that failure to master one or more of these fundamentals would elicit such comments as, "How can one of our graduates not understand that?" These fundamentals range from facts and principles to skills and research methods, from historical discoveries and personalities to current theories and controversies. Each course within a discipline is optimally designed to address a piece or stage of development on the journey toward such understanding. Either explicitly or implicitly, each course focuses on a portion of those essential objectives, in a context of assumed prior knowledge and promised future understandings and applications.

The purpose of this first defining feature of mastery learning is to be explicit about these fundamentals. We do this by identifying—and publishing for students, parents, and colleagues—those fundamental objectives and, moreover, by explicitly establishing mastery of those fundamentals as necessary for a passing grade in the course (e.g., *D* or *C*, or 60 or 70). If such fundamental objectives are not immediately obvious, two ways of establishing them are to identify competencies that (a) are considered prerequisites for the next unit or course in the discipline, or (b) have been common to standardized or instructor-made exams on this material in the recent past.

By definition, mastery of fundamentals is likely at lower levels of cognitive processing (e.g., Bloom's 1956 taxonomy), and every teacher strives for more than minimal competence. This is where all of the other course objectives—higher-order or analytical thinking, applications, inventions, etc.—enter into the course and grading scheme. For this to occur, teachers must analyze the curriculum to identify what content will be revisited, as well as why and how it will be revisited. This will assist them in identifying key fundamentals. For example, if students will be learning about the effects of pollution on the Great Lakes in the middle school grades, they will need to develop a solid understanding of pollution and fresh water during the primary grades. This will enable the middle school teacher to primarily focus on the complexities of pollution's impact (e.g., companies produce highly valued commodities while tainting fresh water supplies) and spend minimal time assisting students in relearning the basics of pollution and fresh water.

A Sufficiently High Standard for Demonstrating Mastery

As portrayed in Figure 1, initial learning must attain a relatively high standard or, after the nearly-inevitable forgetting that follows, there will be little or no residue in memory nor savings in relearning. How high is high enough for a standard is not easily empirically established, and may depend upon the discipline or level of the course. For example, 80% correct on times tables may be sufficient at first, but 90% correct within five seconds may be a reasonable requirement in a subsequent course.

For most fields, a minimum passing score of 75% or 80% correct on a multiple-choice test of knowledge or a commensurate high rating of initial competence in a skilled performance might be sufficient, but 60% or 65% is probably too low. A good model for this is the driving test on which, in most states, it is necessary to pass a written test at 80% correct on rules of the road and other essential facts, as well as to demonstrate competence in authentic skills of driving. The material to be tested and the passing standards for the driving test are published for all applicants, and passing both parts of the exam is necessary to receive a license to drive. Note also that a person who scores 80, one who scores 100, and one who needs three tries to attain at least an 80 are all treated the same: All are considered sufficiently competent to receive a license that allows them to begin their careers as drivers (with some restrictions in enlightened states).

Although the analogy to driving tests probably ends there, we teachers need to impress upon students as well as the general public that initial mastery is only that: the beginning. So we congratulate students by awarding them a pass in the course (a *D* or *C*, or 60 or 70) and encourage them as promising novices in the discipline to strive toward expert status. Therefore, even 100% correct on the initial mastery objective does not result in top level grades (an *A*). They can only be earned by completing additional assignments designed to reinforce the mastery objectives while expanding upon that learning. Conversely, if students are given top-level grades for high achievement of mastery objectives without revisiting those objectives, they are sure to forget a great deal of what was originally learned, and therefore short-circuit the cumulative effects of the learning process as we know it.

Multiple Forms of Criterion-Referenced Tests with Corrective Exercises and Retesting

Each mastery objective requires several test questions to be written and randomly assigned to several parallel forms of a test. For example, suppose you are teaching a beginning unit on division of fractions (for other illustrations in math, science, social studies, and language arts, see Gentile and Lalley, 2003). An initial mastery test might have the following objectives: that students (a) can correctly calculate such problems as 3/8 divided by 1/5 (the Knowledge level of Bloom's taxonomy); (b) can demonstrate why we have the rule "Invert, then multiply," showing all steps (the Comprehension level); and (c) can solve word problems in which they must decide whether division is the correct procedure, or invent word problems (Application level).

For each parallel form of the test, you will need, say, four items at each of those three levels of cognitive processing, which yields a 12-item mastery test. Because this is a beginning unit, a standard of 75% correct seems fair and would require that students solve 9 of the 12 items correctly to pass. Those who did not pass could now be diagnosed: Did they miss only the higher complexity items? Did they miss the computational items? Both?

Remedial exercises would now be necessary for those students, including reteaching, more examples, peer tutoring by those who did pass, for example. When they have shown sufficient progress in these exercises, they are then eligible to retake the second parallel form of the test. Meanwhile, other students can work on enrichment objectives for this unit.

Writing of parallel forms of a test must be done before the course begins, because it is virtually impossible to create parallel test items—that is, questions that cover the same content at the same level of difficulty—after students did not pass the initial test. Another advantage of creating the tests before the course begins is that it helps define your fundamental objectives: If you cannot write good test questions for a concept, it is likely to be better assessed by a performance assessment such as a presentation, paper or project, rather than a mastery objective.

The goal of all of this, of course, is to facilitate teaching and learning. Good teachers continue to expand their repertoires of methods, which include finding alternate ways of helping each student succeed in the course. Parallel forms of the test remind us that not all students get it the first time and need additional attempts, and perhaps other methods or examples, before they try and try again. In addition, one of the parallel forms of the test can be used to review and test for prior knowledge from previous units or courses, instead of merely assuming it, so that new learning can truly build on those prerequisites. Parallel forms also enable periodic review, much as coaches require athletes to continue to review and automatize fundamental skills. Moreover, as Roediger

and Karpicke (2006) concluded from their comprehensive review, testing is one of our most powerful tools for enhancing memory.

Grading Incentives to Encourage Reaching beyond Initial Mastery

Passing a mastery test is often conceived as a benchmark or end point for learning, and earns a spuriously high grade for that unit. Instead, initial mastery must be considered the beginning, and thus earn only the lowest passing grade for that unit. Higher grades are reserved for going beyond mastery to demonstrating fluency, ability to apply the material, analytical or creative skills, and the ability to teach the material to others.

Enter the enrichment objectives—those which are fundamental but not easily tested, or might be considered optional in that not all students need to know all of them, or that they require extended time frames to learn and be assessed. These should also be published as projects or exercises which, when judged OK, earn a higher grade or a specified number of points to add to the course grade (e.g., to move from a D to C with one satisfactory project, to B with two, etc.; or to add 10 points to the basic pass of 60 or 70 for this extended project, six points for a less difficult one, etc.). To earn an OK on the project may, of course, also require more than one attempt, with feedback and resubmissions, as necessary.

Enrichment projects include conducting an experiment, analyzing data, composing or creating a story or poem, doing critical reviews of literature, inventing problems or test items, and so forth. Such projects can be completed individually or, with appropriate procedures and supervision, as pairs or cooperative teams. And, in keeping with the emphasis on teaching to demonstrate learning, tutoring other students is an exemplary project: When the tutee passes the mastery test, the tutor earns an OK on an enrichment project.

The point of building enrichment exercises on top of mastered fundamentals is that we are encouraging students on the road toward expertise. Thus we must emphasize the cognitive growth that is accruing—fluency, application, creativity, memory, and coaching ability vis-à-vis the material. That a higher grade follows is simply a well-deserved recognition of that additional competence.

Conclusion

One of the questions that always seems to arise during discussions of mastery learning is "What happens to the faster students while the slower ones are still trying to pass the mastery test?" The question is moot when the above principles of mastery learning are followed. The faster students are doing enrichment projects, including helping the slower ones, because they would never be permitted to settle for the lowest passing grade in the course. Along the way, they are doing more than they needed to do under competitive norm-referenced grading systems in which they only had to beat out their slower compatriots to get the highest grades in the course. Meanwhile, the slower students can also be doing enrichment exercises, earning OKs that will increase their grade when they finally pass the mastery test. In this criterion-referenced grading scheme, everyone has incentive: (a) to certify they are competent on the fundamentals (because it is the only way to pass the course), and (b) to go beyond initial mastery because it is the only way to get above the minimum passing grade.

That said, mastery learning might not affect the extant competitiveness among students, particularly if the rest of their schooling emphasizes class ranks. The fastest learners in a discipline are likely to get higher scores on the test, to master more quickly, to do more enrichment projects, and thus to earn higher grades. Nevertheless, their higher grades will have been earned by more advanced achievements, not by simply besting slower or less motivated learners. The slower learners can also be empowered because they, too, can succeed. Thus, even if our norm-rcferenced and criterion-referenced measures of student achievement remain correlated, it is fundamentally different psychologically for both students and their teachers to conceive of passing a test as a certification of competence, rather than as a competition.

References

Bahrick, H. P. (1984a). Associations and organization in cognitive psychology: A reply to Neisser. *Journal of Experiment Psychology: General, 113*, 36–37.

Bahrick, H. P. (1984b). Semantic memory content in permastore: Fifty years of memory for Spanish learned in school. *Journal of Experiment Psychology: General, 113*, 1–29.

Black, P., & Wiliam, D. (1998). Inside the black box: Raising standards through classroom assessment. *Phi Delta Kappan, 80*, 139–148.

Block, J. H., Efthim, H. E., & Burns, R. B. (1989). *Building effective mastery learning schools.* New York: Longman.

Bloom, B. S. (Ed.). (1956). *Taxonomy of educational objectives: The classification of educational goals, handbook 1. Cognitive domain.* New York: McKay.

Bloom, B. S. (1976). *Human characteristics and school learning.* New York: McGraw-Hill.

Bruner, J. (1960). *The process of education.* New York: Vintage.

Chi, M. T. H., Glaser, R., & Rees, E. (1982). Expertise in problem solving. In R. J. Sternberg (Ed.), *Advances in the psychology of human intelligence, vol. 1.* (pp. 7–75). Hillside, NJ: Lawrence Erlbaum Associates.

deGroot, A. D. (1965). *Thought and choice in chess.* The Hague, The Netherlands: Mouton.

Ebbinghaus, H. (1964). *Memory: A contribution to experimental psychology* (H. A. Ruger & E. C. Bussenius, Trans.). New York Dover. (Original work published 1885).

Gentile, J. R. (1993). *Instructional improvement: A summary and analysis of Madeline Hunter's essential elements of instruction and supervision* (2nd ed.). Oxford, OH: National Staff Development Council.

Gentile, J. R. (2004). Assessing fundamentals in every course through mastery learning. In M. V. Achacoso & M. D. Svinicki (Eds.), *Alternative strategies for evaluating student learning* (pp. 15–20). San Francisco: Jossey Bass.

Gentile, J. R. (2005). Improving college teaching productivity via mastery learning. In J. E. Groccia & J, E, Miller (Eds.), *On becoming a productive university* (pp. 291–301). Boston: Anker.

Gentile, J. R., & Lalley, J. P. (2003). *Standards and mastery learning: Aligning teaching and assessment so all children can learn.* Thousand Oaks, CA: Corwin Press.

Gentile, J. R., & Monaco, N. M. (1986). Learned helplessness in mathematics: What educators should know. *Journal of Mathematical Behavior, 5*, 159–178.

Glaser, R., & Nitko, A. J. (1971). Measurement in learning and instruction. In R. L. Thorndike (Ed.), *Educational measurement* (2nd ed., pp. 625–670). Washington, DC: American Council on Education.

Halpern, A. R., & Bower, G. H. (1982). Musical expertise and melodic structure in memory for musical notation. *American Journal of Psychology, 95*, 31–50.

Hunter, M. (1982). *Mastery teaching.* El Segundo, CA: TIP Publications.

Peterson, E., Maier, S. F., & Seligman, M. E. P. (1993). *Learned helplessness: A theory for the age of personal control.* New York: Oxford University Press.

Popham, W. J. (1978). *Criterion-referenced measurement.* Englewood Cliffs, NJ: Prentice-Hall.

Roediger, H. L., III, & Karpicke, J. D. (2006). The power of testing memory: Basic research and implications for educational practice. *Perspectives on Psychological Science, 1*, 181–210.

Rumelhart, D. E., & Norman, D. A. (1981). Analogical processes in learning. In J. R. Anderson (Ed.), *Cognitive skills and their acquisition* (pp. 335–359). Hillsdale, NJ: Lawrence Erlbaum Associates.

Schneider, W., & Shiffrin, R. M. (1977). Controlled and automatic human information processing: 1. Detection, search, and attention. *Psychological Review, 84*, 1–66.

Stiggins, R., & Chappuis, J. (2008). Enhancing student learning. *District Administration, 44*(1), 42–44.

Critical Thinking

1. Explain how a mastery learning program differs from traditional instruction.

2. What are the four essential defining components of an effective mastery learning program?

3. Use the four essential components to develop a unit plan using mastery learning. Identify the fundamental objectives, enrichment objectives, and activities to extend students' learning, the types of assessments you would use, and the standard you would set/expect for students to demonstrate mastery of the objectives.

4. According to Lalley and Gentile, every discipline has a set of fundamental objectives that are necessary prerequisites for learning in a content area/subject, and failure to master them impedes all future learning. As you think about your content, can you identify some of these fundamental objectives?

5. Compare the fundamental objectives you identified with the learning objectives/content standards for your state. What similarities and differences do you find?

JAMES P. LALLEY is an associate professor of education at D'Youville College in Buffalo, NY; **J. RONALD GENTILE** is a SUNY Distinguished Teaching Professor, Emeritus, at the University at Buffalo.

Correspondence should be addressed to **JAMES P. LALLEY**, Associate Professor of Education, D'Youville College, 320 Porter Avenue, Buffalo, NY 14201. E-mail: lalleyj@dyc.edu.

Backward Design
Targeting Depth of Understanding for All Learners

Mrs. Kinney loves science—she just wishes that her students were as enthusiastic about the subject as she is. She covers all the information in the textbook with lectures and PowerPoint notes, and even includes an experiment at the end of most units. Even with all of this, her students at best memorize information for a test; they never retain it beyond the test. In the last unit she covered, her students kept complaining. "Why do we have to know this?" "This is not going to help me in life." How can she get her students excited about learning? How can she help them to truly understand the content and how it relates to their lives?

AMY CHILDRE, JENNIFER R. SANDS, AND SAUNDRA TANNER POPE

As teachers respond to the mandates of the No Child Left Behind Act of 2001 and contemplate the import of research documenting poor learning outcomes for students with disabilities, the key challenge is to design curriculum and instruction that facilitate understanding, retention, and generalization (Bulgren, Deshler, & Lenz, 2007). To meet this challenge and adequately prepare students to meet curricular standards, teachers must reach beyond past practices of teaching for curriculum exposure and utilizing books as curricular guides (Carnine, 1991; Gersten, Baker, Smith-Johnson, Dimino, & Peterson, 2006). This requires a paradigm shift in which textbooks are one of a variety of teaching tools rather than the sole basis for daily teaching.

The move away from textbook-driven curriculum, though, is not a novel approach. It is rooted in the constructivist approach currently finding favor in education through the work of educational theorists applying the approach in curriculum design models (Wiggins & McTighe, 2006). Past and current applications of *constructivism* focus on how students construct understanding. Students' prior knowledge and experiences are organized into schema, patterns, and connections for understanding and remembering. Key to all applications of constructivism is that children need opportunities to connect their prior knowledge and experiences with new information through their own thought processes and through interactions with others and the environment (Scruggs & Mastropieri, 1994). Such opportunities allow students to use their schema as a basis on which to build a framework for understanding

new ideas and information. Through this gradual building or *scaffolding* of knowledge and skills, students can be supported to move beyond rote knowledge and develop depth of understanding.

Curriculum design is at the center of developing student ability to construct understanding. Without appropriately designed curriculum, instruction can be ineffective at scaffolding understanding. Often students with disabilities need more explicit instruction or guidance in applying their schema to new information (Mastropieri, Scruggs, & Butcher, 1997). Thus, instruction must not only be carefully scaffolded; it must also address students' unique learning needs (see "What Does the Literature Say About Engaging Students and Responding to Special Learning Needs?").

Why do so many students fail to develop understanding of key concepts within content? The answer is that instruction is too often driven by textbooks, lectures, worksheets, and activities that fail to make learning relevant for students (Scruggs, Mastropieri, & McDuffie, 2007) and are not grounded in curricular standards. Designing curriculum and instruction that scaffolds learning is a vast paradigm shift for many teachers and may require retraining of teaching methods. One design approach that has been highly useful for retraining teachers to design curriculum for scaffolding learning is the *backward design* approach (Wiggins & McTighe, 2006), easily utilized with general education curriculum. This approach can be implemented in inclusive classrooms with students with disabilities and across content areas and grade levels.

What Does the Literature Say about Engaging Students and Responding to Special Learning Needs?

Scruggs, Mastropieri, Bakken, & Brigham (1993) found that students engaged in an inquiry-oriented and experiential science curriculum performed better on end-of-unit tests and follow-up tests as compared to students whose curriculum utilized a textbook approach. Further research has indicated fewer discipline problems (e.g., suspensions, behavioral conferences, vandalism) when students are engaged in a hands-on, experiential curriculum (Cawley, Hayden, Cade, & Baker-Kroczynski, 2002). Development of social and personal responsibility often accompanies decrease in negative behaviors.

Despite these benefits, students with disabilities may still need individualized support and accommodations to benefit from classrooms employing experiential or other active learning methods (Deshler, Schumaker, Lenz, et al., 2001). Research indicates that students with disabilities—especially students with mild intellectual disabilities—need to receive increased training in research-based learning strategies and increased guidance to direct their knowledge construction (Deshler, Schumaker, Lenz, et al.; Scruggs & Mastropieri, 1994). The level of support needed must be determined by ongoing formative assessment of student understanding and knowledge construction (Scruggs & Mastropieri). Such learning needs do not necessitate a restrictive learning environment; general education classrooms utilizing active learning, ongoing assessment, and appropriate support strategies are supportive learning environments that can optimize student learning and potential for students with disabilities (Schumaker et al., 2002).

Children need opportunities to connect their prior knowledge and experiences with new information through their own thought processes and through interactions with others and the environment.

The Backward Design Approach

Teacher understanding of the difference between student knowledge and student understanding is critical to implementing a backward design approach. Just because a student can memorize facts for a test does not mean he understands what they mean. For example, a student may know that the tilt of the earth's axis causes the earth's seasons because he memorized the fact. However, he may have no idea how the tilt actually causes the seasons; if asked to explain his answer, he would be unable to articulate an explanation.

Developing instruction that targets such level of understanding requires thoughtful planning and the backward design steps can serve as a guide. Authors Wiggins and McTighe (2006) argue that you cannot plan how you're going to teach until you know exactly what you want your students to learn: backward design planning focuses on learning outcomes, and standards and the assessments for accomplishing those standards. These assessments then guide the development of the learning activities (i.e., instruction and activities). With the learning outcomes clearly articulated as assessments, creating learning activities that scaffold understanding toward those outcomes is a more straightforward process. Applying this approach in classrooms with students with disabilities involves four key steps.

Step 1: Identify Learners

Knowing your learners is foundational to designing curriculum (Bulgren et al., 2007). Prior knowledge, experiences, and interests students bring to the classroom—as well as special learning or behavioral needs—influence student learning. Thus, learner needs should be considered throughout all steps of the design process.

For students with disabilities, accommodations are an integral component to scaffolding understanding.

Identify Classroom Needs

First, identify the class targeted with the curricular unit. Beyond general information such as grade and subject, it is important to consider the contextual variables that impact your students and shape their experiences outside of school. Consider such factors as community location, resources, socioeconomic level, extracurricular activities, and educational background, all of which have an immense impact on students and the prior knowledge and schemas they bring to the classroom.

Identify Individual Student Needs

Second, you must identify learners who have special needs and determine their individual learning needs. A teacher should be intimately aware of each individual student's strengths and weaknesses, how a student's disability impacts learning, and what techniques or accommodations are necessary to support the student's learning. Identification of these needs and supports must be in place before a teacher can design appropriate assessment and learning activities, because student needs must shape instructional design. Accommodations must be woven throughout the fabric of instruction; never should they be an afterthought, an add-on to a lesson. For students with disabilities, accommodations are an integral component to scaffolding understanding (Bulgren et al., 2007).

Step 2: Identify Curricular Priorities
Determine State and Local Standards

State and local standards will focus the unit. Some teachers have more freedom in this decision, wheareas others have strict parameters. For instance, some school systems publish pacing guides to outline curricular requirements; in some schools, teachers work in teams to determine content to target; in yet other schools, individual teachers determine how and when they will address specific standards. Regardless of how curricular priorities are chosen, the steps of the process work the same: The standards serve as the learning goals that will shape the instructional unit.

If you are determining your own standards, choose a key standard to drive the unit that targets deeper and broader understanding, a standard that encompasses or readily bridges to other standards. For instance, with social studies standards related to Africa, a standard on African civil war is a broad issue that could incorporate other standards (e.g., natural resources, geographic locations, the independence movement, political development). To further enhance your unit, consider timing. Design units around standards that address current news topics (e.g., teaching about the role of the judicial branch in government as the Supreme Court reviews a hotly debated issue) or target standards during times of the year when key teaching resources are available (e.g., a unit on ecosystems taught during spring would offer much more opportunity for experiential learning than if taught in inclement winter weather).

Create Essential Questions

Essential questions frame the standards of the unit in a way that hooks or engages learners, and serve to bridge the standards and the curriculum by guiding students in creating meaning around the standards (Bulgren et al., 2007). Well-written essential questions pique student curiosity and draw them into the subject, encouraging learning beyond rote memorization. Ideally an essential question is not answered after a single lesson, but is continually revisited throughout a unit. What should be most clear to students from the essential question is that their job is inquiry, not just a simple answer (Wiggins & McTighe, 2006). Revisiting the essential questions throughout a unit keeps students focused on the "big ideas" so that they continually consider how the various learning tasks and

content contribute to their understanding of the major goals or standards of the unit.

Identify Prerequisite Knowledge and Skills

Because scaffolding student learning is critical to the development of schema and student understanding (Carnine, 1991), examine your standards and consider if there are prerequisite knowledge and skills students need to successfully accomplish the identified learning standards. Failing to consider necessary prerequisite knowledge and skills is a frequent mistake of beginning teachers, but it also occurs with experienced teachers. For beginning teachers the mistake may involve failing to recognize prerequisite *content* knowledge or skills needed to accomplish a standard (such as a teacher creating a unit on budgeting without first ensuring students have prerequisite math knowledge and skills). For experienced teachers, the gap is more often in recognizing the *enabling* skills that students need to convey content in the manner requested. Students might perform poorly when expected to engage in debate, research, or group work, not because they fail to understand the content but because they do not have the skills for conveying knowledge in the manner requested.

If the class does not possess prerequisite skills, consider how to proceed. Are the prerequisites minimal such that they could be adequately addressed within the unit? Would the unit be more constructive later in the year after other prerequisite standards have been taught? Also, consider individual students. Are there individuals who do not possess prerequisite knowledge and skills (e.g., spelling skills for a writing unit) due to disability? If so, consider accommodations be made so they can successfully participate. As you move forward, you will find it useful to revisit this step to ensure students have prerequisite knowledge and skills for successful completion of all components of the unit.

Step 3: Design Assessment Framework

In this step, you develop the assessments used to determine if students have mastered the standards. The key question is "What evidence will demonstrate student understanding of the unit standards?" Evidence is never a single assessment product (Swanson & Deshler, 2003). Ongoing and frequent assessment is fundamental to scaffolding student understanding. Also key is a framework of assessments that gradually build student ability to use knowledge and skills at increasingly sophisticated levels. The aim is to move students beyond the recall of memorized facts to deeper understanding of the meaning of content in applied contexts and in relation to other concepts. The understanding targeted within each unit varies depending on the standards, but students can reach deeper understanding through assessments that require explanation, interpretation, application, analysis, synthesis, and self-evaluation. To target this depth of understanding, build an assessment framework including the following types of assessments (Wiggins & McTighe, 2006).

Performance Tasks or Projects

Create one or two tasks or projects that require students to demonstrate depth of understanding of major or overall unit concepts. This assessment will serve as the anchor to your unit. A performance task or project should challenge students to use the content in a flexible way to answer or solve problems that mirror real life. A detailed rubric should be developed to clarify expectations, guide student performance, and encourage student self-assessment.

Oral or Written Prompts

These are open-ended questions that move beyond memorized facts by requiring students to explain, analyze, and/ or evaluate. Prompts are similar to essay questions, but always require critical thinking to develop and justify a response. Prompts are most effective when used as a more formal assessment (i.e., typical test conditions).

Quiz or Test

Although teachers usually use tests at the end of a unit as a summative assessment, tests are best used as a formative assessment to gauge if students have gained the knowledge and skills needed for activities and assessments that target deeper understandings. Include tests or quizzes for vocabulary, knowledge, and skills students need to accomplish prompts and performance tasks or project assessments.

Informal Assessments

Informal assessments are the means for preparing students for all other assessments. Use a variety of informal assessments such as observations, class activities, discussions, and teacher questions throughout the unit to reveal student understanding or misunderstanding, and determine any need for additional instruction (Gersten et al., 2006).

Step 4: Create Learning Activities

This final step integrates information from all prior steps into a sequence of lessons that guides students toward accomplishing the desired understanding and assessments. In developing learning activities, consider the specific needs of students with disabilities so that any required accommodations are an integral part of the unit. Often it is supportive of classwide learning to provide accommodations to the group rather than to an individual (e.g., interactive group work, graphic organizer; Gersten

et al., 2006). As you move through building a sequence of lessons, continually refer to student learning needs (Step 1), standards (Step 2), and assessments (Step 3) to maintain your focus.

Design and Sequence Learning Activities

Keep in mind these key considerations as you plan your learning activities: How will you encourage immersion in and exploration of the essential questions? How will you use learning activities to build knowledge and skills, and promote deeper understanding? How will you prepare students for accomplishing the project and prompt assessments? To translate these questions into practice, consider utilizing the following components to facilitate the scaffolding process:

- Engage students with essential questions and unit vocabulary
- Break instruction and activities into manageable parts
- Weave assessment across the unit

Begin the unit by engaging students with the essential questions and key unit vocabulary. Engaging students with the standards and essential questions using techniques such as visuals, problems to solve, and controversial issues not only generates interest and excitement, but makes the learning meaningful (Wiggins & McTighe, 2006). Students need to know where they are going and what they are expected to accomplish (Swanson & Deshler, 2003). Provide instruction of key vocabulary prior to reading and learning activities so that when students encounter vocabulary within the learning activities they have a base understanding on which to build. This is particularly beneficial for students with disabilities (Vaughn & Bos, 2009). Beginning with the essential questions and vocabulary provides opportunities to connect with student prior knowledge and experiences to build new schema and to address misconceptions so that students are not building knowledge on faulty bases.

Break instructional parts of the unit into manageable elements; divide class time into mini-instruction, activity, and reflection/discussion sessions to actively immerse students in the content. Breaking up instruction in this way not only provides students an opportunity to develop schema by utilizing the new content, but also eliminates the risk of frontloading a unit with instruction that diminishes student engagement. In designing learning activities, avoid teacher-directed and textbook-driven instruction where students merely recite notes or readings (Scruggs, Mastropieri, Bakken, & Brigham, 1993). Instead, give students opportunities to make the content meaningful by connecting it to real life. Personalize the learning by creating opportunities to see how the information relates to what they know and to their lives—their past, present, or future (Deshler, Schumaker, Bulgren, et al., 2001). Learning activities should encourage students to apply information, make interpretive judgments, and/or synthesize information to generate knowledge and gain understanding of the larger issue (Bulgren et al., 2007; Scruggs & Mastropieri, 1994). Start small and build toward the higher levels of understanding expected in the assessment prompt and performance task or project. The learning should be driven by student efforts to answer essential questions and solve problems posed through unit activities and assessments. Through reflection and discussion continually revisit essential questions and central concepts so that students understand how new information applies to the larger understanding targeted (Gersten et al, 2006). This overall approach to learning activities moves students out of passive roles into active learning roles more supportive of learning for students with disabilities, because learning is hands-on and meaningful.

Give students opportunities to make the content meaningful by connecting it to real life.

Weave in assessments across the unit to enable continuous insight into the development of student understanding (Wiggins & McTighe, 2006). Assessments should gradually build toward depth of understanding; tests and quizzes should be applied early on as formative assessment of student understanding of base concepts, but project and performance assessments are most effective as summative, culminating assessments as they allow students to demonstrate an integrated understanding of unit concepts. Further, it should be completely transparent to students how the content relates to the assessments and what is expected from each assessment. This is accomplished by designing learning activities that provide the students with experience in making the types of transfer sought and by providing explicit assessment instruction through such means as detailed rubrics and clearly defined steps. When students fail to perform on assessments, it is often because teachers failed to prepare them to make the transfer of knowledge. Use learning activities to develop the understanding sought for assessment.

Check for Integration of Accommodations

Review learning activities to ensure all learners' needs identified in Step 1 are supported. Certain needs, accommodations, or individualized education program (IEP) goals (e.g., graphic organizers, group interaction, organization skills) work well and, when implemented classwide,

can enhance performance for all students (Gersten et al., 2006; McTighe & Lyman, 1988). For instance, if oral expression is targeted on one student's IEP, might not the entire class benefit from working on this skill? You could work oral expression into one of your assessments and then enhance a learning activity to provide the instruction, modeling, and guidance students need to develop the skill. Other student needs may require individual support (e.g., a student may need to talk through project instructions individually with a teacher or may need assistive technology for reading and writing activities).

The process is not completely linear. Once you have the general framework of the information generated from the steps, you may find that it is necessary to move back and forth within the steps as you further conceptualize your instructional unit. As you move into implementation, ongoing analysis of learning results and reflection on implementation will provide feedback for refining your use of the approach.

Applying Backward Design in the Classroom

Figure 1 outlines the use of the process with an inclusive second-grade classroom and Figure 2 outlines use with an inclusive high school biology class. Key applications of the process illustrate how to design instruction to support higher levels of understanding for all students.

Elementary-Level Example

Most of the students in this inclusive second grade class had not traveled outside their rural county, so they did not have travel experiences upon which to build schema for the new content (Step 1). In addition, a large number of the students had disabilities and needed interactive learning experiences with repetition and feedback. The general and special education teachers chose to address standards from two separate disciplines (i.e., social studies and language arts); the social studies unit would serve as an engaging framework for instruction in writing (Step 2). The teachers used essential questions to focus students on critical state content requirements and to link those requirements to the motivating topic of vacation plans. The brochure project linked the required writing and social studies understandings as well as anchored the assessments and subsequent learning activities (Step 3). Additional assessments helped build knowledge and skills for the completion of the brochure. Assessments guided students to use content to identify, then to compare and contrast, and finally to persuade readers about state regions and topographical features.

For Step 4, learning activities for developing understanding of the social studies content included interactive

Step 1: Identify Learners	Identify classroom needs	• Second-grade inclusive classroom • One third of students have disabilities • Low- to mid-income families • Limited travel and experiences outside of local rural area
	Identify Individual Student needs	• Mario, Vicky, Darius, Kayla: simplified instructions, visuals and graphic organizers to break down content and to increase recall, small group, repetition • Adam, Terrika: redirection, encouragement/positive feedback, small group, hands-on learning • Trey: extensive feedback and encouragement
Step 2: Identify Curricular Priorities	Determine state/local standards	• Social Studies: The student will locate major topographical features of the state and will describe how these features define the state's surface. • Language Arts: The student will write a paragraph that states and supports an opinion; use planning ideas to produce a rough draft; give and receive feedback; and make revisions based on feedback.
	Create essential questions	• What cities, landmarks, and attractions are in different regions? Why? • How would information about the regions guide your vacation plans? • Which region would you most/least like to visit and why?
	Identify prerequisite knowledge and skills	• Basic map reading skills • Write sentences to form simple paragraph
Step 3: Design Assess- ment Frame- work	Performance tasks or projects	• Create a brochure to persuade others to visit a chosen region of the state; use rubric to clarify requirements for brochure.
	Oral or written prompt	• Written reflection in booklet about each region: What makes this region unique?
	Quiz or test	• Vocabulary quiz (e.g., climate, topography, region, mountain, river) • Regions and rivers quiz
	Informal assessments	• Small group or class activities (e.g., Jeopardy activity, Velcro-create-a-map; website quiz games) addressing region information cumulatively • Small group map creation

Step 4:
Create
Learning
Activities
	Design and
	sequence
	learning
	activities
		• Present essential questions, vocabulary, map, and intriguing landmark photos
		• Vocabulary quiz
		• Present region information
		  – Encourage student sharing of prior knowledge, vocabulary use, and student contrasting/comparing regions
		  – Prompt student completion of graphic organizer during lesson
		  – Written reflection for booklet
		  – Include informal assessment activity (small group or whole class)
		• Small group clay map creation activity
		• Regions and rivers quiz
		• Trip to visit landmarks in our region
		• Introduce brochure project; model use of think sheet to guide writing process for brochure
		• Model use of peer editing checklist; guide peer assessment of writing and revision of writing
		• Complete writing and artwork for brochures; share brochures

	Check for integration of accom- modations	• Visuals (e.g., slides to show unique aspects of each region) • Mini-lessons and activities to increase engagement • Learning supports (e.g., graphic organizer for regions, think sheet for writing) • Center and small-group activities for individual support

Figure 1   Elementary level unit: second grade social studies and language arts.

instruction, a reflective writing prompt, and an activity to apply information. Interactive instruction used discussion and informational slide shows replete with photos, along with teacher modeling and student completion of graphic organizers. Activities ranged from small-group activities where students tracked and e-mailed a hiker as he traversed regions of the state to class activities in which students created clay map models while the teacher guided them with questions targeting basic knowledge (e.g., "What river empties into the Atlantic Ocean?" "What region is north of

Step 1: Identify Learners	Identify classroom needs	• Inclusive biology classroom • 20 students, Including 5 with disabilities • Several students in science club
	Identify individual student needs	• Ryan: provide visuals, verbal directions/explanations, processing time • Venicia: pair with peer for written class tasks, oral responses to quizzes and writing prompts • Latrell: pair with organized, even-tempered peers • Marcus: prompts to focus, hands-on activities • Tina: extra time, additional support with abstract ideas

Step 2:
Identify Curricular Priorities
	Determine state/local standards	• Students will analyze how biological traits are passed on to successive generations.
		  – Using Mendel's laws, explain the role of meiosis in reproductive variability.
		  – Explain how mutations occur and why genetic disorders result.
		  – Examine use of DNA technology in medicine and agriculture.
		• Students will demonstrate content area vocabulary knowledge through writing and speaking.

	Create essential questions	• What does probability have to do with genetics? • How are traits, including some you do not see, passed from one generation to the next? • How do meiosis and mitosis impact genetic information and cell production? • What happens to traits when meiosis fails? • Who has the right to access and make decisions about your genetic code?
	Identify prerequisite knowledge and skills	• Prior understanding: DNA
Step 3: Design Assess-ment Frame-work	Performance tasks or projects	• Predicting and designing offspring project: Given cases with mono and dihyrid crosses, and incomplete dominance and co-dominance, students will predict genotypic and phenotypic combinations of offspring. • Genetics defense project: Research and defend a controversial topic related to use of genetics in medicine or agriculture.
	Oral or written prompt	• Use Mendel's laws to explain the presence or absence of a link between a dog's hair color and tail length. • What different occurrences in mitosis and meiosis explain why human families look different from one another, whereas bacteria show no variation from parent to offspring?
	Quiz or test	• Vocabulary quiz • Vocabulary/content quiz
	Informal assessments	• Informal discussion • Create-a-face coin toss activity • Classroom trait survey • Mutations activity • Genetic mutations activity
Step 4: Create Learning Activities	Design and sequence learning activities	• Present essential questions, Mendel and his experiments; check for misconceptions about genetics • Introduce probability and Punnett squares Activity: determine facial phenotypes using coin-toss. • Vocabulary quiz. • Prompt: applications of Mendel's law. Introduce incomplete dominance and co-dominance. Activity: create and explain cartoon parents' offspring • Predicting and designing offspring. Performance task: Punnett squares • Introduce meiosis. Activity: survey of classroom traits. • Introduce mitosis. Class discussion: compare/contrast mitosis and meiosis; utilize graphic organizer • Vocabulary/content quiz. • Prompt: mitosis and meiosis. Introduce genetic mutations using videos that demonstrate traits of disorders caused by mutations to genetic code. Activity; use interactive whiteboard to create and explain different types of mutations. • Introduce genetic ethical issues with segment of movie *Gattaca* (Niccol, 1997) and discussion. Genetics defense project: choice of topic; rubric to clarify required components; pair sharing and graphic organizer to support reading and formulation of arguments. • Students present and defend research-informed position. Self- and peer assessment to identify strengths and weaknesses of argument and presentation.
	Check for integration of accommodations	• Break up lessons into instruction, activities, and discussion • Use small-group time to provide additional explanations • Instruct students how to teach one another in small group activities • Use classwide learning supports (e.g., graphic organizers, rubric) • Address individual needs (e.g., prompt sheet for Punnett squares, screen-reading software)

Figure 2 High school level unit: biology.

the region in which we live?") and higher-order thinking (e.g., "Why are so many man-made attractions centered in that region?" "How does the climate and geography of the Coastal Plains region differ from the Blue Ridge region?"). Most of the needed accommodations for this unit were implemented classwide as they constituted best practices for all students. Use of photos, website tours, and a field trip created visuals and experiences upon which students could develop their schema. Use of a graphic organizer for each region and a think sheet to guide the writing process supported the learning for all. Finally, there were opportunities for small-group learning with peer interaction for both social studies activities and writing feedback.

With this approach, performance increased for all students, with and without disabilities. The author implementing this instruction attributed the increase to (a) the use of essential questions which gave students the big picture and encouraged more in-depth thought; and (b) scaffolding and active learning that created a student-centered environment and encouraged students to develop understanding step by step. Due to the interactive nature of the learning activities, the teacher needed to redirect students and focus attention more often, but the learning outcomes far outweighed the increased classroom management needs. Students normally reticent to participate eagerly engaged, and, weeks after the instruction, students continued to discuss the activities.

High School Example

This class comprised a range of science-related experience and learning level. Although most students had limited interest, several were involved in Science Club and brought unique insight into the classroom (Step 1). With appropriate prompting, the Science Club students shared this interest with their classmates and served as a support for struggling students (needs ranging from learning disabilities to mild intellectual disabilities to attention deficit hyperactivity disorder). The curriculum sequence for this unit was determined by the school and was designed to build on prior understanding of DNA (Step 2). The challenging task in designing the unit was making the content real and connecting it to student lives so as to reduce abstraction and enhance understanding. Multiple essential questions guided students to see overall connections between genetics and their lives, and guided scaffolding by breaking down complex ideas. In Step 3, assessments continued to build these connections by making concepts applicable to student interests and "real life" (e.g., cartoon characters, pets, classmates, current news issues).

In Step 4, learning activities that involved instruction were divided into introductory lecture, application

activity, and discussion. Stopping activities midway to prompt students to verbalize connections between content and the activity facilitated scaffolding. Students put their ideas into their own words, which served multiple purposes: it helped solidify student understandings, gave insight into struggles with concepts, and allowed the teacher to use student understanding as a stepping stone for extending ideas. Students supported and guided one another when working in small groups or pairs. Teachers continually modeled for students how to teach one another through questioning rather than just by giving answers. Various supports ensured that all student learning needs were met: for example, a student who struggled with abstract and complex concepts used a prompt sheet for creating Punnett squares and was then able to progress to understanding how Punnett squares applied to genetic traits. In other instances, supports applied classwide enhanced learning for all students. The research project on ethical issues surrounding genetic research incorporated both individual and classwide supports:

- Screen-reading software helped students with disabilities access the articles.
- All students were paired with peers by topic to paraphrase articles and discuss how the information related to their stance.
- The teacher provided and modeled use of a graphic organizer to guide translation of article information into a persuasive argument.

This combination of supports enhanced learning for all students.

With use of this approach, students with disabilities maintained active engagement in learning activities and achieved the general curriculum objectives. The essential questions and differentiation of learning activities were key to learning success. The essential questions made the science concepts more concrete and created a focus for learning activities, especially helpful for students with disabilities. Prior to any discussion, students understood how the activity related to the question they were trying to answer; the questions served as a reference point upon which students created a framework to organize and understand the concepts. In addition, the small-group application activities and project enabled differentiation of instruction and addressed diverse learning styles. Grouping students based on individual needs and teaching questioning techniques within these activities allowed students with disabilities to actively participate in applying and explaining concepts. The backward design approach facilitated the equal participation of students with disabilities in all aspects of the classroom learning community.

Final Thoughts

Increasing numbers of students with disabilities are being educated in inclusive general education classrooms; the challenge is to provide appropriate instruction to support student success. Traditional instructional approaches too often fail to engage learners with disabilities, to address their individual needs, and to ultimately support academic success. Designing curriculum that both accommodates learning needs and targets deeper levels of understanding is possible. Through the use of the backward design approach, learning can become relevant and meaningful for all students, supporting their mastery of general curricular standards. When standards, assessment, and inquiry-oriented activities drive the curriculum, learning can be transformed.

References

Bulgren, J., Deshler, D. D., & Lenz, K. (2007). Engaging adolescents with LD in higher order thinking about history concepts using integrated content enhancement routines. *Journal of Learning Disabilities, 40,* 121–133.

Carnine, D. (1991). Curricular interventions for teaching higher order thinking to all students: Introduction to the special series. *Journal of Learning Disabilities, 24,* 261–269.

Cawley, J., Hayden, S., Cade, E., & Baker-Kroczynski, S. (2002). Including students with disabilities into the general education science classroom. *Exceptional Children, 68,* 423–435.

Deshler, D., Schumaker, J., Bulgren, J., Lenz, K., Jantzen, J., Adams, G., et al. (2001). Making learning easier: Connecting new knowledge to things students already know. *TEACHING Exceptional Children, 33*(4), 82–85.

Deshler, D. D., Schumaker, J. B., Lenz, B. K., Bulgren, J. A., Hock, M. F., Knight, J., et al. (2001). Ensuring content-area learning by secondary students with learning disabilities. *Learning Disabilities Research and Practice, 16,* 96–108.

Gersten, R., Baker, S. K., Smith-Johnson, J., Dimino, J., & Peterson, A. (2006). Eyes on the prize: Teaching complex historical content to middle school students with learning disabilities. *Exceptional Children, 72,* 264–280.

Mastropieri, M. A., Scruggs, T. E., & Butcher, K. (1997). How effective is inquiry learning for students with mild disabilities? *The Journal of Special Education, 31,* 199–211.

McTighe, J., & Lyman, F. T., Jr. (1988). Cueing thinking in the classroom: The promise of theory-based tools. *Educational Leadership, 45,* 18–24.

Niccol, A. (Writer/Director). (1997). *Gattaca* [Motion picture]. United States: Sony Pictures.

Schumaker, J. B., Deshler, D. D., Bulgren, J. A., Davis, B., Lenz, B. K., & Grossen, B. (2002). Access of adolescents with disabilities to general education curriculum: Myth or reality? *Focus on Exceptional Children, 35*(3), 1–16.

Scruggs, T. E., & Mastropieri, M. A. (1994). The construction of scientific knowledge by students with mild disabilities. *The Journal of Special Education, 28,* 307–321.

Scruggs, T. E., Mastropieri, M. A., Bakken, J. P., & Brigham, F. J. (1993). Reading versus doing: The relative effects of textbook-based and inquiry-oriented approaches to science learning in special education classrooms. *The Journal of Special Education, 27,* 1–15.

Scruggs, T. E., Mastropieri, M. A., & McDuffie, K. A. (2007). Co-teaching in inclusive classrooms: A metasynthesis of qualitative research. *Exceptional Children, 73,* 392–416.

Swanson, H. L., & Deshler, D. (2003). Instructing adolescents with learning disabilities: Converting a meta-analysis to practice. *Journal of Learning Disabilities, 36,* 124–135.

Vaughn, S., & Bos, C. S. (2009). *Teaching students with learning and behavior problems* (7th ed.). Upper Saddle River, NJ: Prentice Hall.

Wiggins, G., & McTighe, J. (2006). *Understanding by design* (2nd ed.). Upper Saddle River, NJ: Prentice Hall.

Critical Thinking

1. What are the essential features of constructivist learning?
2. Define scaffolding and describe how you would design learning activities to scaffold students' learning of a specific topic.
3. How are "essential questions" similar to "clearly stated objectives" in the previous article?
4. Review the state standards in your content area (most are available on the state's Department of Education website). Are they stated in such a way that it is easy to identify the essential questions and BIG ideas? Provide some examples you found.
5. What are the two different types of mistakes teachers often make while failing to identify prerequisite knowledge and skills critical to development of schema and understanding of content?

AMY CHILDRE (CEC GA Federation), Associate Professor, Department of Special Education and Educational Leadership, Georgia College & State University, Milledgeville. **JENNIFER R. SANDS** (CEC GA Federation). Teacher, Jones County Ninth Grade Academy, Gray, Georgia. **SAUNDRA TANNER POPE** (CEC GA Federation), Teacher, Putnam County Elementary School, Eatonton, Georgia.

Address correspondence to Amy Childre, Georgia College & State University, Department of Special Education and Educational Leadership, CBX 072, Milledgeville, GA 31061 (e-mail: amy.childre@gcsu.edu).

Learning-Style Responsive Approaches for Teaching Typically Performing and At-Risk Adolescents

ANDREA HONIGSFELD, EdD AND RITA DUNN

W e live in a decade of assessments. Since the No Child Left Behind (NCLB) Act was signed into law in 2002, standardized assessments have been a driving force behind educational decisions, program development, material selections, and daily lesson planning in most, if not all, middle schools and high schools across the United states. Standardized tests strongly favor analytic, sequential cognitive processors—that is, students who can concentrate on, internalize, and retain new and difficult information through traditional teaching. Chalk and talk, lectures with required note-taking, assigned readings, and end-of-chapter or end-of-text questions are still common teaching practices in secondary schools. But many at-risk students do not perform well on standardized tests when taught with these methods. Despite their efforts to succeed, many of these youth often struggle academically, lose interest, suffer reduced motivation, and find themselves embarrassed and even depressed by failure.

In response to the increase presence of high-stakes testing in our schools, Boudett et al. (2005) note that "much has been written about the possibility that school faculties will resort to "'drill and kill,' a response that will reduce the quality of children's education" (700: "drill and kill" refers to the potentially harmful overuse of repetitive, drill-based activities that leads to the destruction of student joy in learning and motivation). We share Boudett et al.'s concern and propose new strategies to better equip typically performing and at-risk students to reach high expectations.

Who Is at Risk of Academic Failure?

Students officially classified as *at risk* fall into several categories. These students

- are diagnosed or misdiagnosed as learning disabled;
- grow up in isolated communities and do not begin learning English until they enter school;
- do not speak English because they have recently arrived from another country;
- live in poverty and lack basic and educational resources in their homes;
- are the children of migrant workers or undocumented immigrants whose presence in our schools is transient; or
- are homeless and do not have their basic needs of safety and security met. (Dunn and Honigsfeld 2009)

However, many students are at risk but do not fit into any of these categories. Some students are *typically performing* adolescents, who strive to excel but invariably remain in the average or middle group in the eyes of their teachers and parents, as well as in their own eyes. Other students seem initially to perform well in school but then fall behind, become chronic underachieves, and read less well each year, or even fail to learn to read. Finally they become restless or hyperactive. Many of these youth

- process new and difficult information globally and find it difficult to follow analytic, step-by-step teaching;
- do not seem to try or take school seriously (e.g., draw or doodle while listening; appear bored, tired, or listless);
- are nonconforming or disobedient (e.g., refuse to remain in their seats);
- cannot sit still, concentrate, or pay attention to the teacher for more than a few minutes; or
- may read, but cannot remember and often do not understand what they read.

During the past two decades, Bauer (1987), Braio et al. (1997), Dunn and Dunn (1993), Favre (2007), Fine (2003), and Lister (2005) have established that students who do not respond to traditional teaching are likely to be engaged by hands-on, activity-oriented lessons. Each practitioner-researcher experimented with tactual-kinesthetic resources and implemented a series of nontraditional lesson strategies. They repeatedly found that at-risk students responded well to these lessons and revealed significantly increased achievement, as well as higher levels of engagement and motivation.

Characteristics of Students with Tactual and Kinesthetic Preferences

Many at-risk adolescents in middle schools and high schools tend to be highly tactual learners (i.e., need hands-on learning experiences and manipulatives), kinesthetic learners (i.e., need frequent mobility), or both. Because adolescents have not biologically developed strong auditory skills, at-risk adolescent students are particularly unlikely to remember at least 70 percent of what they hear or read and thus either do not read well or cannot maintain concentration when they are not interested in the required reading (Restak 1979). These youth often struggle and fall behind in traditional classes in which teachers rely on lectures, discussions, and readings. Even when teachers use advanced technology—such as PowerPoint presentations or video streaming—tactual and kinesthetic learners need more than the visual support these resources offer.

How Do Tactual and Kinesthetic Learners Learn?

The best strategies for engaging tactual and kinesthetic learners' minds are to engage their hands and bodies with manipulative instructional resources or to allow them to learn on their feet. These strategies help them form lasting connections between concepts and their applications. Tactual and kinesthetic learners are more likely to internalize comprehensive information while using small- or large-motor movements, rather than while remaining stationary and passively receiving input from the teacher.

Related Research

Researchers have conducted over 850 studies at more than 135 institutions of higher education using the Dunn and Dunn Learning Style Model (www.learningstyles.net). For documentation of the reversal of academic failure through learning-style responsive approaches throughout United States schools, see Dunn and DeBello (1999) and Dunn and Dunn (2008). At least thirty studies have compared the effectiveness of tactual and kinesthetic strategies and traditional teaching for at-risk, special education (SPED),

and English-language-learner (ELL) students at various levels.

For example, Fine (2003) gradually added soft classroom lighting and teacher-designed and student-created tactual and kinesthetic instructional resources and permitted his high school SPED students to work independently, in pairs, or in small groups, instead of relying on direct teaching and assigned readings. He reported higher achievement test scores with average to large effect sizes, as well as measurably improved behavior and attitudes toward school and reduced lateness.

Lister (2004, 2005) compared the effects of traditional social studies instruction with the effects of instruction using tactual and kinesthetic resources for the same content. The achievement of her Bermudian SPED middle school students increased statistically, and she found a large effect size favoring the tactual and kinesthetic resources.

Crossley (2007) examined the relative effectiveness of a Multisensory Instructional Package (MIP; Dunn and Dunn 1992) versus traditional teaching (TT) on science achievement and attitude test scores of middle school ELL and English-speaking students. Students in all three grades received both traditional and multisensory instruction in three subunits. The results revealed a significant impact on achievement and attitude scores when multisensory instruction was introduced.

Similar practice-oriented and classroom-based research studies have documented the rapidity with which learning-style instructional approaches—specifically tactual and kinesthetic resources—can enhance academic achievement among at-risk student populations.

What Do Tactual and Kinesthetic Learning Activities Look Like in the Secondary Classroom?

Both tactual and kinesthetic activities are designed to be self-corrective exercises in which students do not require teacher feedback on their work, because the resources themselves have the correct answers built in; these exercises can be used independently, in pairs, or in small groups of three or four. Corners and empty sections of the classroom can be used for these activities at designated times during the period. Such instructional resources are enjoyable because of their game-like nature; can be adapted to any content, grade, or ability level; and lead to increased student empowerment, responsibility, and success. Tactual and kinesthetic activities will meet with less resistance than other homework assignments and ensure long-term memory retention (Gremli 2001/2002; Mitchell et al. 2002; O'Connell, Dunn, and Denig 2001). Resources can be created by teachers, individual students, or pairs of students, either at home or in the classroom.

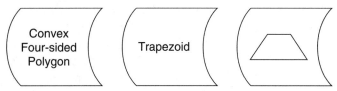

Figure 1 A sample of three trapezoid task cards, each of which offers different information about a trapezoid.

Tactual Resources

Task cards are pairs of cards that look like puzzle pieces. The two parts contain matching information that allows learners to connect definitions to key words or questions to responses (see Figure 1).

Pic-A-Holes are self-corrective tactual resources. Teachers can use an inexpensive, two-pocket folder to hold the Pic-A-Holes and 5 × 8 index cards for Question Cards. The hole for the correct answer on each card should be cut through. Then the Question Cards can be placed in the case and a golf tee given to each student. When he or she inserts the golf tee into the hole for the correct answer, the card can be removed from the case (see Figure 2).

Kinesthetic Activities

Floor, wall (in which the game board is placed on an available wall surface), or tabletop games; demonstrations; dramatizations; roleplays; and skits all activate students' large-motor skills and enhance their retention of complex content. A typical floor, wall or tabletop game can follow a board-game template or a tic-tac-toe outline. Students engage in the game by generating as many questions as possible about the target content alone, in a group, or with a teacher. The teacher then transfers the questions onto index cards and puts the correct answer on the back of each card. Once the props are ready, established rules for the game are set. For a more detailed description of tactual and kinesthetic resources and explicit directions for making them, see Dunn and Honigsfeld (2009).

Tactual and Kinesthetic Learning and Test Preparation: Oxymoron or Key to Success?

Even the most creative teachers who use multiple modalities, innovative techniques, advanced technology, and nontraditional teaching techniques are perplexed when preparing their students for standardized tests. High-stakes test preparation using tactual and kinesthetic resources and activities needs special attention. A few examples of successful practices in this area are provided:

- A seventh-grade social studies class practiced answering document-based questions (DBQs) in preparation for their annual standardized assessments.

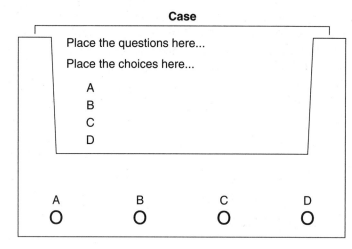

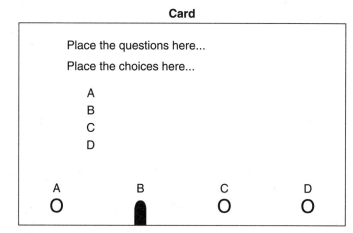

Figure 2 A template of a Pic-A-Hole case and card, showing how the correct answer on the card is cut out.

Instead of asking students to complete test preparation packets, however, the teacher recreated the DBQ exam as a gallery walk. He placed eight enlarged documents (e.g., cartoons, quotes, pictures, historical photographs, short paragraphs) around the classroom for students to examine and distributed a response sheet that required answers to any five questions from an itemized list. Students could work independently, in pairs, or in small groups as they chose.

- In preparation for an eighth-grade English and language arts exam, an English teacher designed a wall game using a tic-tac-toe template. Two teams competed to name literary elements exhibited in assigned excerpts. Once the literary elements were correctly identified, the team placed an X or O on an erasable tic-tac-toe board mounted on the wall.

- In a high school living-environment class, the teacher encouraged his students to think like test writers and assigned teams of three students the task of generating Pic A-Hole cards with sample test questions. The students wrote question stems using key concepts from the assigned chapter and generated three "distractor" answers that were not obviously incorrect for each question.

Why Do Tactual and Kinesthetic Resources Work When Other Strategies Do Not?

Tactual and kinesthetic instruction work because the learners' strongest perceptual modalities are in these areas. Auditory and verbal processing often lag behind tactual and kinesthetic learning, which are the first perceptual modalities to develop, even at the high school level. At the same time, at-risk learners often are attentive to visual elements. Therefore, all tactual and kinesthetic resources that teachers use, create, or ask their students to create should include colorful pictures, diagrams, or other eye-catching images that reflect the content students need to master.

How to Introduce Kinesthetic and Tactual Strategies to the Classroom

Normally lethargic, uninterested students will become engaged in participatory learning—particularly when they are not only permitted but required to move. The following strategies are useful for experimenting with tactual and kinesthetic teaching with your students:

- Use simple tactual resources as homework assignments first.
- Design lessons that include gallery walks and invite students to visit exhibits placed around the room on available wall space.
- Encourage adolescents to generate questions or answers to problems in small groups and then have a representative member of each team walk to an adjacent team and share ideas.
- Once you expose students to floor or wall games, encourage them to design their own.

A Word of Caution

Tactual and kinesthetic resources alone may not produce the increased achievement desired from at-risk youth. Reinforcing knowledge and skills through students' secondary and tertiary perceptual preferences ensures that they master the required skills and knowledge. A learning style comprises a complex set of individual characteristics that range from environmental, emotional, and psychological to physiological and sociological preferences. Research and best practices both validate that style-responsive instruction generates more engaged, motivated, and successful students—so keep thinking and teaching outside the box!

References

Bauer, E. 1987. Learning style and the learning disabled: Experimentation with ninth-graders. *The Clearing House* 60 (5): 206–8.

Boudett, K., R. J. Murnane, E. City, and L Moody. 2005. Teaching educators how to use student assessment data to improve instruction. *Phi Delta Kappan* 86 (9): 700–6.

Braio, A., T. M. Beasley, R. Dunn, P. Quinn, and K. Buchanan. 1997. Incremental implementation of learning style strategies among urban low achievers. *Journal of Educational Research* 91 (1): 15–25.

Crossley, H. 2007. Effects of traditional teaching versus a multi-sensory instructional package on the science achievement and attitudes of English-language learners versus other middle-school minority students. EdD diss., St. John's University.

Dunn, K. I., and R. Dunn. 2008. Teaching to at-risk students' learning styles: Solutions based on international research. *Insights on Learning Disabilities: From Prevailing Theories to Validated Practices* 5 (1): 89–101.

Dunn, R., and T. C. DeBello, eds. 1999. *Improved test scores, attitudes, and behaviors in America's schools: Supervisors' success stories.* Westport, CT: Bergin & Garvey.

Dunn, R., and K. Dunn. 1992. *Teaching elementary students through their individual learning styles: Practical approaches for grades 3–6.* Boston: Allyn & Bacon.

———. 1993. *Teaching secondary students through their individual learning styles: Practical approaches for grades 7–12.* Boston: Allyn & Bacon.

Dunn, R., and A. Honigsfeld. 2009. *Differentiated instruction for at-risk students: What to do and how to do it.* Lanham, MD; Rowman & Littlefield.

Favre, L. R. 2007. Analysis of the transformation of a low socioeconomic status African-American, New Orleans elementary facility into a demonstration Learning-Style School of Excellence. *Journal of Urban Education: Focus on Enrichment* 4 (1): 79–90.

Fine, D. 2003. A sense of learning style. *Principal Leadership* 4 (2): 55–59.

Gremli, J. 2001/2002. Learning sequenced instruction on the short- and long-term achievement of seventh- and eighth-grade general music students. *National Forum of Applied Educational Research Journal* 11 (2): 63–73.

Lister, D. 2004. Comparisons between the learning styles of underachieving and regular education sixth-grade Bermudian students and the effects of responsive instruction on the former's social studies achievement- and attitude-test scores. PhD diss., St. John's University.

———. 2005. Effects of traditional versus tactual and kinesthetic learning-style responsive instructional strategies on Bermudian learning-support sixth grade students' social studies achievement- and attitude-test scores. *Research for Educational Reform* 10 (2): 24–40.

Mitchell, D., R. Dunn, A. Klavas, V. Lynch, N. Montgomery, and J. Murray. 2002. Effects of traditional versus tactual/kinesthetic instruction on junior-high school learning-disabled students. *Academic Exchange Quarterly* 6 (3): 115–22.

O'Connell, D. M., R. Dunn, and S. Denig. 2001. Effects of traditional instruction versus instruction with teacher-constructed and self-teaching resources on the short- and long-term achievement and attitudes of tenth-grade science students. *American Biology Teacher* 65 (2): 93–102.

Restate, R. M. 1979. The other difference between boys and girls. In *Student learning styles: Diagnosing and prescribing programs,* ed. National Association of Secondary School Principals, 75–80. Reston, VA: National Association of Secondary School Principals.

Critical Thinking

1. Describe typical characteristics of students who are most often identified as being "at-risk." What does being "at-risk" mean?
2. Summarize the key findings from the section on related research.

3. Select one of the articles to read in depth and critique. What are some of the strengths and weaknesses of the study you selected?
4. Given what you know or read about human memory in the article in this unit, why do you think some of the tactual and kinesthetic activities might lead to information being more likely to be retained in long-term memory?
5. Look up definitions of tactual and kinesthetic online. Based on the definitions you found, how would you characterize the activity suggestions presented in the article?
6. Read the *Science Daily* news article and watch the video by Daniel Willingham (links are posted with the unit overview), how does knowing this information impact your perception of the claims made by the authors of this article?

ANDREA HONIGSFELD, EdD, is an associate dean of the Division of Education, Molloy College, Rockville Center, NY, and codirector of the Colorado Learning Styles Center. **RITA DUNN,** EdD, is a professor in the Department of Administrative and Instructional Leadership, coordinator of the Instructional Leadership Doctoral Program, and director of the Center for the Study of Learning and Teaching Styles, St. John's University, New York, NY.

"To Find Yourself, Think for Yourself"
Using Socratic Discussions in Inclusive Classrooms

BARBARA FINK CHORZEMPA AND LAURIE LAPIDUS

Students in Ms. Lapidus's inclusion class have just finished reading *Cinderella* and are preparing for their first Socratic seminar. To do so, the students begin the process of questioning the components of the story, including the author's style and the literary elements, specifically the theme. Ms. Lapidus reminds the students to generate questions that should be supported with evidence from the text (i.e., inferential questions) including those that can be open to interpretation. "For example," she says, "You can't ask any questions about the magic in the story because magic is an element of fairy tales. That is, we can't argue how the fairy godmother did the magic—just assume it's so." After all the students' questions have been recorded, the students collaboratively decide which 10 questions they would like to discuss during their seminar. Next, they independently search through the text to find support for their answer to each of the 10 questions, using sticky notes to mark the reference. The students are now ready for the Socratic seminar.

To facilitate a good discussion, the students move their desks to form a circle. As they do so, Ms. Lapidus reminds them of the rules for a Socratic discussion. Once the students are in place, she begins the discussion with one of the 10 inferential questions they identified (i.e., Was Cinderella able to find true happiness?). As the students are discussing this possibility, John, a student with a learning disability, responds with another question. "Why didn't the fairy godmother just change Cinderella's life?" "Wow, That's a good question. Can you repeat that?" says Ms. Lapidus. After the question is repeated, Ms. Lapidus paraphrases the question and poses it to the students, "Why if the fairy godmother was capable of magic, did she not just change Cinderella's life? Who'd like to share their thoughts?" After reflecting, another student says, "Cinderella had to go to the ball to experience self-worth before she believed in herself." Knowing the students had reached one of the implied themes, Ms. Lapidus encourages them to wrap up their discussion and move into their writing assignment.

Aristotle said, "To find yourself, think for yourself" (Quotationspage.com). As schools and teachers strive to align instruction with state and national standards, teachers often struggle with developing students' abilities to think for themselves. As a result, students may find analyzing a piece of literature and writing proficiently about it to be a daunting task. Ms. Lapidus found in her classroom that although elementary students might be able to critically analyze a text reading through discussion, they often have difficulty doing so in their own writing. She related this challenge to her own training in education: Teacher preparation programs place a greater emphasis on teaching students to read than on teaching them how to write. For some students, particularly those with disabilities, writing is intimidating, challenging, and labor intensive (Fink-Chorzempa, Graham, & Harris, 2005; Graham, 2006). Thus teaching students how to write, especially when teachers have been taught only a few strategies themselves, can be a very difficult undertaking. These observations and beliefs are also documented in the research about writing instruction (cf., Graham & Perin, 2007; National Commission on Writing, 2006).

Realizing the challenges many of her students encountered, Ms. Lapidus was determined to improve their writing and thought that before she could do so, she needed to first teach students how to think using supporting details. She recalled professional development she received as a middle school teacher, learning how Socratic seminars can be used as a way to teach students to think critically, and she decided to explore how she could adapt that method to make it work in her elementary inclusive classroom.

What are Socratic Seminars?

Socratic seminars, defined as "exploratory intellectual conversations centered on a text" (Lambright, 1995, p. 30), are a group-discussion model and are designed in such a way to resemble Socrates's instruction-through-questioning method (Chorzempa & Lapidus, 2006; Polite & Adams, 1997). They are held in a student-centered environment to foster authentic engagement and to prompt ideas to occur (Loan, 2003). Simply stated, this method involves students' reading a selection and then generating questions and exploring their ideas and questions in an open discussion (Queen, 2000). The open-discussion method not only allows students to support their own opinions with details but also strengthens their ability to exhibit a personal voice in their writing and improves the depth of their papers (Sorenson, 1993). Elder and Paul (1998) linked critical thinking, or establishing an "inner voice of reason," and Socratic discussion as the public forum that cultivates it.

The open-discussion method not only allows students to support their own opinions with details but also strengthens their ability to exhibit a personal voice in their writing.

The procedures and justifications for the use of Socratic seminars as a means of developing critical thinking skills are well documented in middle and high school classrooms (cf., Loan, 2003; Mawhinney, 2000; Metzger, 1998; Polite & Adams, 1997; Queen, 2000; Strong, 1997; Tanner & Casados, 1998; Tredway, 1995). However, its use is rarely documented in elementary inclusive classrooms. Therefore, in light of the potential benefits of the Socratic seminar and using the experiences of Ms. Lapidus and her third- and fifth-grade students, this article provides a model and guidelines for using the Socratic method to develop students' critical thinking and writing skills within elementary inclusive classrooms.

Establishing the Foundations

Prior to using the Socratic method, it is important to establish the foundations that help students engage in the Socratic method. Similar to other educators who use this approach, Ms. Lapidus realized the importance of developing in her classroom a sense of community that fosters mutual respect for one another. She encouraged her students to express their views and to disagree respectfully and appreciate the different perspectives held by their classmates while still holding on to their own perspectives without feeling insecure. She established this climate by employing trust-building activities in the beginning of the year, specifically during her morning meetings. Those meetings along with other group activities (e.g., academic games) always closed with students' reflection on the experience. That is, she asked students to consider such questions as what they did well and what they could do better. She also modeled how to provide constructive feedback to one another by giving specific praise to students for a response and offering a suggestion for next time.

Ms. Lapidus also ensured that all students had in-depth knowledge of the literary elements and devices (e.g., plot, setting, point of view, symbolism) before seminars were held, because these elements provide the basis for establishing literary connections among works and are needed to develop critical thinking skills, such as making inferences and identifying implicit themes. She frequently asked her students to engage in Reader's Theatre (see description under "Preparing for the Discussion") as a way to deepen their understanding of these elements.

Knowledge of the different types of questions that can be asked in response to a reading also needs to be established before students can engage in a Socratic seminar. Specifically, students need to know the difference between "in the book" and "in your head" questions, the two general types of questions used in the Question Answer Relationships (QAR) strategy (Raphael & Au, 2005). Ms. Lapidus referred to the literal questions as the "right there" questions to help her students under-

stand that the answers to such questions can be found explicitly in the text. The "in your head" questions she explained as either inferential questions (i.e., those for which answers are obtained by reading between the lines or putting information together) or evaluative questions (i.e., those for which the answers are not in the text but rather come from within). To help her students learn how to distinguish and generate the different types of questions, Ms. Lapidus first modeled the use of them for her students. This familiarity is important not only because students generate "in your head" questions when preparing for the Socratic seminars but also because 70% to 80% of the questions they face on high-stakes testing will be these types of questions (Raphael & Au, 2005).

Preparing for the Seminar

Before a Socratic seminar can be conducted, it is important for teachers to prepare for the seminar by selecting an appropriate story and becoming familiar with its elements. The selected text should be thought-provoking and at a level at which every reader in the class can successfully read. When selecting a piece of literature, Ms. Lapidus found the *Junior Great Books* (The Great Books Foundation, 2006) and *Touchpepples* (Touchstones Discussion Project, 1993) to be excellent resources, as these texts contain readings with identifiable themes or issues that were familiar and relevant to her students and their lives.

Before introducing the story to students, teachers read through the text carefully and identify the main themes. Teachers then consider a final discussion topic, one that the students will be asked to reflect on in their writing at the conclusion of the seminar. The final discussion topic should be one that encourages students to analyze the text critically and requires them to provide support for their statements with details from the text. Although a final discussion topic is prepared in advance, teachers should be flexible and willing to revise their topic on the basis of student questions and interpretations during the seminar, thus making it more powerful and meaningful.

Conducting the Seminar

Once the planning has been carefully considered, teachers serve as facilitators of the process by first introducing the text to the students and then engaging them in their preparations for the Socratic seminar. During the seminar, both the students and teachers accomplish a variety of tasks, which are outlined in the following paragraphs.

The Students' Role
Preparing for the Discussion

Before the Socratic discussion is held, students should be exposed to the text at least three times. Teachers read through the text first, encouraging students to listen aesthetically, and then ask students what questions they have. All students' questions are accepted, as long as they are "in your head" questions, with each question written down on chart paper for later examination. For the second reading, students read the text independently to answer two to three guided questions, ones that begin to focus on the themes of the text. After they read the story the third time, teachers ask students to respond to the guided questions orally and then allow students to add any questions to their list. Often these questions are more insightful than the ones constructed after the first reading, and teachers should point out to students that each time a text is read, more details to reflect on often become apparent. For example, on the first reading of *Cinderella,* one student in Ms. Lapidus's class asked, "Why were the stepsisters so mean?" After the third reading of the text, Alice, a student with emotional disturbance and reading difficulties, asked the following questions as students were discussing the story, "Why at midnight did everything change except for the glass slipper?"

Depending on the complexity of the text, students may use Reader's Theatre to present a scene or excerpt from the text. First, students work cooperatively in small groups to prepare what they consider an important scene from the text, one that focuses on a theme. Next, they perform the scene in front of the class, thereby experiencing another way to interact with the text. Having students engage in this strategy allows them to assume the role of a character and view the story from the character's perspective, thus possibly broadening their view of the events in the text.

As the last step before the discussion is held, teachers and students analyze each question generated after the first and third readings. Students are reminded that although these may all be good questions, only questions that can be supported from the text should be used in the discussion. The list of questions is then narrowed to a reasonable number (i.e., 10 to 15) that can be answered in one Socratic discussion. Students are then given sticky notes to mark where the evidence in the text is found, reinforcing their ability to provide supporting statements.

Holding the Socratic Discussion

Once the students are ready to begin the Socratic discussion, teachers outline and discuss several rules and procedures for teachers and students to follow (see Figure 1), allowing for a successful discussion by the students. These differ slightly from procedures used in secondary classrooms, modified specifically for use in an elementary classroom. For example, in Ms. Lapidus's class she has students raise their hands and wait to be called on to speak, whereas a Socratic discussion usually involves free expression of ideas and thoughts by participants. She also explains to the class that this rule is necessary to reduce the chance that one or more students monopolize the discussion and to give all students opportunities to speak. She also tells her students that one of her goals for the end of the year is for them to engage in a literary dialogue without raising their hands.

Teachers open the discussion by asking students to discuss the 15 or so questions they generated, one at a time. Not all students are required to participate in the discussion; however, Ms. Lapidus has experienced that many of her students want to share their ideas with their peers or respond to comments made by others. She does, however, subtly encourage all students to participate through posi-

tive reinforcement. The only time every student is required to participate is at the end of the seminar when Ms. Lapidus asks them to reflect on the discussion by responding to two questions: What did you learn from this discussion? and What could be done differently next time to improve the discussion?

During the discussion, students are asked to look at their classmates, another goal set at the beginning of the year. Often when students are first engaged in the Socratic seminar, they will look to teachers for a reaction or confirmation when they make a point. As the year progresses, though, students naturally begin talking with one another, sensing they are in an environment of mutual respect. The teacher continues as facilitator of the discussion, but students begin to refer to one another's comments and build on one another's ideas. As one fifth-grade student with Asperger's syndrome articulated, "The Socratic discussion is like building a brick wall: Each idea is a brick, and when someone says something, another person builds on top of it. Because of that, it is never-ending."

Applying the Writing Component

After the seminar is completed, students are asked to respond to a written prompt. Students also are expected to write about points made in the discussion and to support their statements with examples from the text. As mentioned before, one of the purposes for holding the seminar is to help students identify their own thoughts on a topic and articulate their point of view in writing.

The Teacher's Role
During the Seminar

The Socratic seminar requires teachers to assume a variety of roles as well. In the role of facilitator, teachers must refrain from sharing their thoughts throughout the discussion to allow the students to develop their own critical thinking skills. Also, sometimes during the seminar, students stray from the original question and teachers must decide whether they should allow the discussion to continue or bring it back to the original question. Teachers should facilitate the discussion by capitalizing on the strengths of students. Knowing each student's particular strengths helps teachers guide the discussion in such a way that the students are able to reach an intended outcome without teachers' having to share their own views. For example, Ms. Lapidus realized that one of her students with impulsivity, Cindy, surpassed her peers in the ability to clearly articulate her thoughts. Therefore Ms. Lapidus facilitated participation during the discussion so that Cindy was often one of the last to contribute, allowing her the opportunity to connect many of the points made in response to a question.

Teachers also may find it useful to paraphrase comments the students make. By doing so, teachers are able to highlight important points made, usually ones that focus on the themes or relate to the final discussion topic. Paraphrasing student comments also can help students with attention difficulties and second language learners pay attention to and understand the discussion. An example of how Ms. Lapidus used paraphrasing is provided in the opening vignette.

Procedures

1. Every time discussion is held, teachers review the procedures and rules with the students.

2. The students are to sit in a circle so that every student can see every other student as they speak.

3. Teachers sit in the circle as well but do not participate in the discussion except as the facilitators.

4. Teachers do not give an opinion until the reflection time and are the last to speak.

5. Preparing a final discussion topic before the seminar is held allows teachers to select particular students whose ideas allow the discussion to be guided toward the intended topic or theme.

6. Time must be left at the end of the discussion for reflection. This is the only time during the seminar that every student must contribute.

Rules for Students

1. Students must raise their hands during the discussion, waiting to be called on by a teacher before they share their idea or thoughts.

2. Students are to listen attentively to one another, respecting the rule that one person speaks at a time.

3. Mutual respect for one another must be shown.

Figure 1 Rules and procedures for the socratic discussion.

Addressing the Needs of All Learners

With a wide range of levels in her classroom, Ms. Lapidus has found several components of this method helpful for all levels of learners because although teachers serve as facilitators, the instruction is nonetheless structured with clear expectations.

Because most of the activities are done as a whole class and thoughts are articulated verbally, students are not asked to write their thoughts down. This approach allows students who have difficulty articulating themselves in writing to share their higher level thinking in an open-discussion format. Ms. Lapidus has observed that often these students become the leaders during the Socratic discussion and feel quite comfortable obtaining roles when engaged in the Reader's Theatre component of the seminar. Ms. Lapidus also uses the Socratic discussion to teach appropriate social and communication skills (e.g., making eye contact, waiting for your turn to speak, responding appropriately to another's comments) that are included in her students' individualized education program.

Ms. Lapidus makes instructional accommodations to support the participation of her students with disabilities in the Socratic seminar; she has found these accommodations beneficial for all her students. When the text is beyond the independent reading level of one or more students, she works with them in a small group to read the text orally a second time, stopping during the reading to monitor each student's comprehension. She also has provided "mini-

workshops" to students who need further instruction on necessary components. Mini-workshops also provide supplemental instruction on identifying the literary elements, as well as on generating in-your-head questions instead of right-there questions.

Ms. Lapidus also adapts the Socratic seminar's writing component to address her students' strengths and challenges. Although all students are encouraged to use the writing process, Ms. Lapidus holds conferences with the students who struggle with writing at all stages of the process. When necessary, she, a special education teacher, or a paraeducator serves as a scribe to assist students in noting their initial thoughts and then guides them as they use their prewriting to construct a draft.

Benefits and Outcomes for Using Socratic Seminars

Just as Ms. Lapidus had envisioned when she began using Socratic seminars in her inclusive classrooms, engaging students in literary dialogue encourages the complex thinking associated with the writing process. In her inclusive classroom, students learned to analyze a text through questioning, find evidence in the text, explore the elements of the story through discussion, and finally prepare a written response reflecting the main themes of the story. She noted that these skills helped prepare students to respond to a document-based question, a task required on many state assessments.

Engaging students in literary dialogue encourages the complex thinking associated with the writing process.

Ms. Lapidus also observed that the seminars helped develop responsibility and independence in her students and promote a sense of community, which are important goals for inclusive classrooms (Salend, 2008). After using Socratic seminars, Ms. Lapidus noticed that her students felt more comfortable sharing their ideas, encouraging one another to "think out of the box." One of the most enjoyable moments of holding the seminars for Ms. Lapidus has been watching the students eagerly respond to one another in a positive way, allowing themselves to be open to others' viewpoints and not criticizing others for points that are not concurrent with their own point of view. They often then follow through with their own opinions, or personal voice, in their writing, but sometimes because of others' comments during the discussion, they reverse their initial feelings and their writing as a response to, or validation of, another's viewpoint. For example, during the discussion of *Cinderella,* Ms. Lapidus watched her students move from a literal interpretation of the text (i.e., the fairy tale as presented by Disney) to a deeper understanding about a journey of self-worth.

For her students with special needs, Mrs. Lapidus has found that the seminars have helped the students focus their thoughts, resulting in a more organized written product. One of her former students, Adam, a student with processing difficulties, was very creative in his writing: however, it lacked organization. He often included what Mrs. Lapidus referred to as "gems" in his writing, profound or insightful statements but that seemed out of place in the larger piece. The Socratic seminars provided him the opportunity to retrieve statements made during the discussions and make use of them to support his thoughts. One example that illustrates this development was following a discussion on "The Enchanted Sticks" (Myers, 1979), a story in which the character used his mind to outwit others and in doing so, proved his strength through intellect. During the discussion of the text, Adam literally jumped out of his seat, screaming "I get it!" and became the leader of the Socratic discussion. This interaction between Adam and the text, which arose because of the discussion with his peers, led to a writing product that was not only insightful but well organized and full of supporting detail.

"True knowledge exists in knowing that you know nothing. And in knowing that you know nothing, that makes you the smartest of all. To find yourself, think for yourself" (Aristotle, Quotationspage.com). The third- and fifth-grade students in Ms. Lapidus's classes have shown in their discussions during the Socratic seminars and in their writing after the seminar that they think about the text not as how they think their teacher wants them to, but rather as what they perceive the story to be about. In Ms. Lapidus's class, the students often generate 70 or more questions after they listen to the story and read it themselves. They make Ms. Lapidus proud by truly thinking for themselves; she thinks Socrates and Aristotle would be proud, too.

References

Aristotle. Retrieved March 19, 2007, from http://www .quotationspage.com/quote/3079.html

Chorzempa, B. F., & Lapidus, L. (2006, November). *Using Socratic seminars with third graders to promote critical thinking.* Presentation at annual Council for Learning Disabilities (CLD) conference, November.

Elder, L., & Paul, R. (1998). The role of Socratic questioning in thinking, teaching, and learning. *Clearing House, 71,* 297–301.

Fink-Chorzempa, B., Graham, S., & Harris, K. R. (2005). What can I do to help young children who struggle with writing? *TEACHING Exceptional Children, 37*(5), 64–66.

Graham, S. (2006). Writing. In P. Alexander & P. Winne (Eds.), *Handbook of educational psychology* (2nd ed., pp. 457–478), Mahwah, NJ: Lawrence Erbaum.

Graham, S., & Perin, D. (2007). A meta-analysis of writing instruction for adolescent students. *Journal of Educational Psychology, 99,* 445–476.

The Great Books Foundation. (2006). *Junior great books.* Chicago, Author.

Lambright, L. L. (1995). Creating a dialogue: Socratic seminars and educational reform. *Community College Journal, 65*(4), 30–34.

Loan, B. (2003). A strong case for more talk in a Montessori classroom. *Montessori Life, 15*(3), 40–42.

Mawhinney, T. S. (2000). Finding the answer. *Principal Leadership, 4*(1), 44, 46–48.

Metzger, M. (1998). Teaching reading. *Phi Delta Kappan, 80,* 240–247.

Myers, S. J. (1979). *The enchanted sticks.* New York: Penguin Group (USA).

National Commission on Writing. (2006, May). *Writing and school reform.* Retrieved January 12, 2008, from http://www .writingcommission.org/

Polite, V. C., & Adams, A. H. (1997). Critical thinking and values clarification through Socratic seminars. *Urban Education, 32,* 256–278.

Queen, J. A. (2000). Block scheduling revisited. *Phi Delta Kappan, 82,* 214–222.

Raphael, T. E., & Au, K. E. (2005). QAR: Enhancing comprehension and test taking across grades and content areas. *The Reading Teacher, 59,* 206–221.

Salend, S. (2008). *Creating inclusive classrooms: Effective and reflective practices* (6th ed.). Upper Saddle River, NJ: Pearson Education.

Sorenson, M. (1993). Teach each other: Connecting talking and writing. *English Journal, 82,* 42–47.

Strong, M. (1997). *The habit of thought: From Socratic seminars to Socratic Practice.* Chapel Hill, NC: New View.

Tanner, M. L., & Casados, L. (1998). Promoting and studying discussions in math classes. *Journal of Adolescent and Adult Literacy, 41,* 342–350.

Tredway, L. (1995). Socratic seminars: Engaging students in intellectual discourse. *Educational Leadership, 53*(1), 26–20.

Touchstones Discussion Project, (1993). *Touchpepples.* Annapolis, MD. Author.

Critical Thinking

1. Describe how a Socratic seminar differs from a traditional whole-class discussion.
2. Explain the stages and essential components involved in preparing and conducting a Socratic discussion.
3. In the article, the focus is on the use of Socratic seminars with literature. How might this method be applied to other content areas? List three or four topics/subjects you think would be appropriate for this method.
4. This method might be more difficult to use with students in the early elementary grades. However, what modifications could you make to begin building prerequisite skills that would foster their development as critical thinkers?

Barbara Fink Chorzempa (CEC NY Federation), Assistant Professor, Department of Elementary Education, SUNY New Paltz, 1 Hawk Drive, New Paltz, NY 12561 (e-mail: chorzemb@newpaltz.edu) and **Laurie Lapidus**, Classroom Teacher, Monroe Woodbury Central School District, Monroe, New York.

Setting the Record Straight on "High-Yield" Strategies

Watching your work adopted by educators across the nation is flattering, but not if it's widely misinterpreted.

ROBERT J. MARZANO

Across the country there seems to be a great deal of discussion about "high-yield strategies"—classroom techniques that have research supporting their utility at enhancing student achievement.

I've seen this term in online courses, district documents, and even in state documents. It's probably safe to say that I and my colleagues have unwittingly fostered this phenomenon by our comments in at least three books: *Classroom Instruction That Works* (Marzano, Pickering, and Pollock 2001); *Classroom Management That Works* (Marzano, Marzano, and Pickering 2003), and *Classroom Assessment and Grading That Work* (Marzano 2006). In each book, we tried to explain that our findings and recommendations were general and there was still much to be learned about pedagogical expertise. For example, in *Classroom Instruction That Works,* we mentioned that a number of very important questions about the instructional strategies that we identified remained unanswered:

> Are some instructional strategies more effective in certain subject areas? Are some instructional strategies more effective at certain grade levels? Are some instructional strategies more effective with students from different backgrounds? Are some instructional strategies more effective with students of different aptitudes?

We also cautioned that research indicates that the instructional strategies we identified might have a positive effect on student achievement in some situations, but have a negligible or even negative effect on student achievement in other situations. Our conclusion was: "Until we find the answers to the preceding questions, teachers should rely on their knowledge of their students, their subject matter, and their situations to identify the most appropriate instructional strategies". Finally, we emphasized that our list was highly limited in perspective. Effective pedagogy involves a variety of interacting components. We tried to make the same points in all three books.

The instructional strategies we identified might have a positive effect on student achievement in some situations—or a negligible or even negative effect on student achievement in other situations.

Given the qualifiers we placed on our findings and our suggestions, we felt quite good about the initial reaction to the books. They appeared to encourage discussions about effective pedagogy in schools and districts across the country. While the positive effects of these books are gratifying, there are some negative outcomes that seem to be growing in scope and influence. Specifically, educators are making at least three mistakes when using the lists of strategies presented in our books (and other books like them). Left unchecked, these mistakes can impede the development of effective teaching in classrooms across the country.

Mistake 1: Focusing on a Narrow Range of Strategies

Perhaps the most pervasive mistake is focusing on a narrow range of strategies. We wrote the three aforementioned books (as well as other related books) to convey the message that effective teaching is a complex endeavor with many components. *Classroom Instruction That Works* identifies nine categories of instructional strategies. *Classroom Management*

That Works identifies five categories of management strategies. *Classroom Assessment and Grading That Work* identifies four categories of activities that go into developing and implementing effective formative assessments. Focusing on any single set of categories *exclusively* is a serious mistake. In each book, the message is the same: The entire constellation of strategies is necessary for a complete view of effective teaching. Unfortunately, in some schools and districts, this message was lost. This happens quite frequently with the strategies listed in *Classroom Instruction That Works*.

Focusing on any single set of categories *exclusively* is a serious mistake.

Classroom Instruction That Works listed nine categories of instructional strategies: 1) identifying similarities and differences, 2) summarizing and note taking, 3) reinforcing effort and providing recognition, 4) homework and practice, 5) nonlinguistic recommendations, 6) cooperative learning, 7) setting objectives and providing feedback, 8) generating and testing hypotheses, and 9) cues, questions, and advance organizers. These categories were quite broad. For example, by definition, the category cues, questions, and advance organizers combined at least three independent but related types of instructional strategies. We referred to these strategies as "high-probability" strategies as opposed to "high-yield" strategies. We explained our purpose in writing the book as follows: "to identify those instructional strategies that have a high probability of enhancing student achievement".

We explicitly warned that these categories of strategies are only part of a comprehensive view of teaching:

> We need to make one final comment on the limitations of the conclusions that educators can draw from reading this book. Although the title of this book speaks to instruction in a general sense, you should note that we have limited our focus to instructional strategies. There are certainly other aspects of classroom pedagogy that affect student achievement.

In spite of this warning, many teachers have told me that their school or district focuses solely on those nine categories. Principals provide teachers with feedback on using these strategies after doing instructional walkthroughs. In these schools and districts, the so-called nine high-yield strategies represent the totality of what's expected regarding effective teaching. This is poor practice, just as it is poor practice to focus solely on the strategies in *Classroom Management That Works* or *Classroom Assessment and Grading That Work*.

While beginning with a narrow focus is legitimate, a school or district must expand the breadth of its discussion of effective teaching. Where to begin is a matter of preference. Starting with the nine high-probability strategies

---

Article at a Glance

Many schools and districts are encouraging—and often requiring—teachers to use nine strategies identified in *Classroom Instruction That Works* by Robert Marzano, Deborah Pickering and Jane Pollock. But teaching is a complex endeavor with many components.

Marzano writes that schools and districts that overemphasize the nine strategies are making three mistakes. They are:

- Focusing on a narrow range of strategies;
- Assuming that high-yield strategies must be used in every class; and
- Assuming that high-yield strategies will always work.

He presents a broader set of strategies related to instruction, management, and assessment and demonstrates how those can be used to broaden and deepen instruction that leads to improved student learning.

---

in *Classroom Instruction That Works* makes good sense. Starting with strategies for classroom management also makes sense. Indeed, based on the research, one can make a case that classroom management strategies should be the initial focus if one is beginning with a narrow approach. To illustrate, as a result of their analysis of 228 variables identified in 86 chapters from annual research reviews, 44 handbook chapters, 20 government documents, and 11 journal articles, Wang, Haertel, and Walberg (1993) rated classroom management strategies first in terms of their impact on student achievement. Finally, given the impressive findings reported by Black and Wiliam (1998) in their analysis of 250 studies, one could make a case that classroom formative assessment strategies are the best place to start.

The important message here is that providing feedback to teachers regarding effective instruction necessitates articulating a broad array of strategies organized into a comprehensive framework. To adapt a well-worn cliché, *the whole is "more valid" than the sum of its parts*. In the book, *The Art and Science of Teaching* (Marzano 2007), I tried to provide a view of how a comprehensive framework of teaching might be organized. This is shown in Figure 1.

The chart lists 41 categories of strategies that represent the major areas of pedagogy identified in research as related to student achievement. In addition, over the years, I've been involved in hundreds of experimental/control studies on the effects of these strategies (see marzanoresearch.com).

While 41 categories of strategies may seem daunting at first, something as complex as teaching can't be reduced to nine categories of instructional strategies, or five categories of management strategies, or four categories of assessment strategies. These categories aren't random behaviors that might occur at any point during any class. Each is best employed in a particular context.

I. CONTENT

A. Lessons Involving New Content
STRATEGY
1. Identifying critical information (e.g., the teacher provides cues as to which information is important) **A&S**
2. Organizing students to interact with new knowledge (e.g., the teacher organizes students into dyads or triads to discuss small chunks of content) **CITW**
3. Previewing new content (e.g., the teacher uses strategies such as: K-W-L, advance organizers, preview questions) **CITW**
4. Chunking content into "digestible bites" (e.g., the teacher presents content in small portions that are tailored to students' level of understanding) **A&S**
5. Group processing of new information (e.g., after each chunk of information, the teacher asks students to summarize and clarify what they have experienced) **CITW**
6. Elaborating on new information (e.g., the teacher asks questions that require students to make and defend inferences) **CITW**
7. Recording and representing knowledge (e.g., the teacher ask students to summarize, take notes, or use nonlinguistic representations) **CITW**
8. Reflecting on learning (e.g., the teacher asks students to reflect on what they understand or what they are still confused about) **CAGTW**

B. Lessons Involving Practicing and Deepening Content That Has Been Previously Addressed
STRATEGY
9. Reviewing content (e.g., the teacher briefly reviews related content addressed previously) **CITW**
10. Organizing students to practice and deepen knowledge (e.g., the teacher organizes students into groups designed to review information or practice skills) **CITW**
11. Practicing skills, strategies, and processes (the teacher uses massed and distributed practice) **CITW**
12. Examining similarities and differences (e.g., the teacher engages students in comparing, classifying, creating analogies and metaphors) **CITW**
13. Examining errors in reasoning (e.g., the teacher asks students to examine informal fallacies, propaganda, bias) **A&S**
14. Using homework (e.g., the teacher uses homework for independent practice or to elaborate on information) **CITW**
15. Revising knowledge (e.g., the teacher asks students to revise entries in notebooks to clarify and add to previous information) **CITW**

C. Lessons Involving Cognitively Complex Tasks (Generating and Testing Hypotheses)
STRATEGY
16. Organizing students for cognitively complex tasks (e.g., the teacher organizes students into small groups to facilitate cognitively complex tasks) **CITW**
17. Engaging students in cognitively complex tasks (e.g., the teacher engages students in decision-making tasks, problem-solving tasks, experimental inquiry tasks, investigation tasks) **CITW**
18. Providing resources and guidance (e.g., the teacher makes resources available that are specific to cognitively complex tasks and helps students execute such tasks) **A&S**

II. ROUTINE ACTIVITIES

D. Communicating Learning Goals, Tracking Student Progress, and Celebrating Success
STRATEGY
19. Providing clear learning goals and scales to measure those goals (e.g., the teacher provides or reminds students about a specific learning goal) **CAGTW**
20. Tracking student progress (e.g., using formative assessment, the teacher helps students chart their individual and group progress on a learning goal) **CAGTW**
21. Celebrating student success (e.g., the teacher helps student acknowledge and celebrate current status on a learning goal as well as knowledge gain) **CAGTW, CITW**

E. Establishing and Maintaining Classroom Rules and Procedure
STRATEGY
22. Establishing classroom routines (e.g., the teacher reminds students of a rule or procedure or establishes a new rule or procedure) **CMTW**
23. Organizing the physical layout of the classroom for learning (e.g., the teacher organizes materials, traffic patterns, and displays to enhance learning) **CMTW**

III. BEHAVIORS THAT ARE ENACTED ON THE SPOT AS SITUATIONS OCCUR

F. Engaging Students
STRATEGY
24. Noticing and reacting when students are not engaged (e.g., the teacher scans the classroom to monitor students' level of engagement) **CMTW**
25. Using academic games (e.g., when students are not engaged, the teacher uses adaptations of popular games to reengage them and focus their attention on academic content) **A&S**
26. Managing response rates during questioning (e.g., the teacher uses strategies to ensure that multiple students respond to questions such as: response cards, response chaining, voting technologies) **A&S**
27. Using physical movement (e.g., the teacher uses strategies that require students to move physically such as: vote with your feet, physical reenactments of content) **CMTW**
28. Maintaining a lively pace (e.g., the teacher slows and quickens the pace of instruction in such a way as to enhance engagement) **CMTW**
29. Demonstrating intensity and enthusiasm (e.g., the teacher uses verbal and nonverbal signals that he or she is enthusiastic about the content) **CMTW**
30. Using friendly controversy (e.g., the teacher uses techniques that require students to take and defend a position about content) **A&S**
31. Providing opportunities for students to talk about themselves (e.g., the teacher uses techniques that allow students to relate content to their personal lives and interests) **CMTW**
32. Presenting unusual information (e.g., the teacher provides or encourages the identification of intriguing information about the content) **A&S**

G. Recognizing Adherence and Lack of Adherence to Classroom Rules and Procedures
STRATEGY
33. Demonstrating "withitness" (e.g., the teacher is aware of variations in student behavior that might indicate potential disruptions and attends to them immediately) **CMTW**
34. Applying consequences (e.g., the teacher applies consequences to lack of adherence to rules and procedures consistently and fairly) **CMTW**
35. Acknowledging adherence to rules and procedures (e.g., the teacher acknowledges adherence to rules and procedures consistently and fairly) **CMTW**

H. Maintaining Effective Relationships with Students
STRATEGY
36. Understanding students' interests and backgrounds (e.g., the teacher seeks out knowledge about students and uses that knowledge to engage in informal, friendly discussions with students) **CMTW**
37. Using behaviors that indicate affection for students (e.g., the teacher uses humor and friendly banter appropriately with students) **CMTW**
38. Displaying objectivity and control (e.g., the teacher behaves in ways that indicate he or she does not take infractions personally) **CMTW**

I. Communicating High Expectations
STRATEGY
39. Demonstrating value and respect for low-expectancy students (e.g., the teacher demonstrates the same positive affective tone with low-expectancy students as with high-expectancy students) **A&S**
40. Asking questions of low-expectancy students (e.g., the teacher asks questions of low-expectancy students with the same frequency and level of difficulty as with high-expectancy students) **A&S**
41. Probing incorrect answers with low-expectancy students (e.g., the teacher inquires into incorrect answers with low-expectancy students with the same depth and rigor as with high-expectancy students) **A&S**

© Robert J. Marzano (2009)

CITW: addressed in *Classroom Instruction That Works* (Marzano, Pickering, and Pollock 2001). **CMTW:** addressed in *Classroom Management That Works* (Marzano, Pickering, and Marzano 2003). **CAGTW:** addressed in *Classroom Assessment and Grading That Works* (Marzano 2006). **A&S:** addressed in *The Art and Science of Teaching* (Marzano 2007) but not addressed in CITW, CMTW, or CAGTW.

Figure 1   A comprehensive list of strategies that relate to effective teaching.

The three broad areas in the chart represent the most general types of what Leinhardt refers to as a "lesson segments:"

> This research-based information points to the fact that lessons are constructed with multiple parts, or lesson segments, each of which has important characteristics. Each segment contains different roles for teachers and students. Each segment has multiple goals, which can be more or less successfully met by a variety of actions. Further, these segments are supported by fluid, well-researched routines. (Leinhardt 1990, pp. 21–22)

To paraphrase Leinhardt, at any point a teacher is probably engaged in a unified set of actions—or segments—that have a common purpose. In the parlance of *The Art and Science of Teaching,* there are three general categories of segments signified by Roman numerals I, II, and III. These general categories are organized into more specific types of segments. Under content (I) are three different types of segments that manifest as three different types of lessons (A, B, and C). Each lesson type is associated with a specific purpose and specific strategies. Under routine activities (II) are two types of segments (D and E) that would most likely occur in every lesson regardless of the content being addressed. Under behaviors that are enacted on the spot (III) are four types of segments (F, G, H, and I).

These segments and their related behaviors can be used to obtain a more precise view of teaching. Defining teaching using a narrow set of instructional strategies, management strategies, or assessment strategies doesn't do justice to the complexity of the teaching-learning process.

Mistake 2: Assuming That High-Yield Strategies Must Be Used in Every Class

A school or district that uses a narrow list of instructional, management, or assessment strategies will fall into the trap of assuming that all strategies must be used in every classroom.

A school or district that uses a narrow list of instructional, management, or assessment strategies will fall into the trap of assuming that all strategies must be used in every classroom.

Let me illustrate using the nine categories of instructional strategies reported in *Classroom Instruction That Works.* If an administrator or instructional coach observes a classroom and doesn't see evidence of the nine instructional strategies, teachers tell me they are asked why they didn't use one or more strategies. This contradicts the implicit message in our chart: *A specific instructional strategy is effective only when used in the specific situation for which it was designed.* To illustrate, consider summarizing and note taking—two strategies from *Classroom Instruction That Works.* These strategies make perfect sense when a lesson focuses on new content (see A). However, they don't make as much sense when a lesson involves cognitively complex tasks that require students to generate and test hypotheses (see C). In those lessons, teachers want students to apply what they've learned in previous lessons. The two types of lessons, then, have very different purposes and therefore employ different sets of strategies. Consequently, if a teacher is engaging students in a lesson that involves cognitively complex tasks that require generating and testing hypotheses, summarizing and note taking probably wouldn't be the best instructional strategies. Instead, as indicated in C, the teacher should be organizing students in groups to process cognitively complex tasks; engaging students in cognitively complex tasks like decision making, problem solving, experimental inquiry, or investigation; and then acting as a resource provider and guide. Summarizing and note taking are probably non sequiturs in this context—these strategies don't fit well within this particular type of lesson. Even worse, requiring a teacher to use summarizing or note-taking strategies during a lesson that's geared toward complex tasks involving hypothesis generation and testing is probably recommending poor practice.

To provide effective feedback to teachers as the result of a walkthrough or an extended observation requires that the observer first ask himself or herself, "What am I observing right now?" If it's the beginning or ending of class, the observer might expect to see routine activities. Those routine behaviors might involve communicating learning goals, tracking student progress, or celebrating success (see D) or they might involve establishing and maintaining classroom routines or organizing the physical layout of the classroom for learning (see E). If content is being addressed, the observer must determine which of three types of lesson is occurring. The lesson might involve new content (see A), it might involve practicing and deepening content that was previously addressed (see B), or it might involve applying knowledge through complex tasks that require generating and testing hypotheses (see C). Other than content, an observer might note that something has occurred in class that must be addressed immediately. This could involve the teacher attending to engagement when it appears to be waning (see F). The teacher could be recognizing and acknowledging adherence to a classroom rule or procedure or recognizing and acknowledging lack of adherence to a rule or procedure (see G). Or the teacher could be doing something to establish or maintain an effective relationship with students (see H). Finally, the teacher could be communicating that all students are expected to achieve at high levels (see I).

Mistake 3: Assuming That High-Yield Strategies Will Always Work

The term "high yield" encourages educators to assume that strategies identified in the research are guaranteed to work. For the record, I've tried to avoid using this term over the last decade. As mentioned previously, we used the term "high probability" strategies in *Classroom Instruction That Works*. If you examine the research on classroom strategies (whether they relate to instruction, management, or assessment), you'll find that some have an average effect size that's larger than others. To illustrate, Hattie (2009) examined 146,142 effect sizes from studies on educational strategies, programs, and practice. From this, he identified 138 variables, many of which were instructional strategies and school- or district-level innovations. He even ordered them from highest to lowest in terms of effect sizes. Feedback was one of the highest ranked instructional strategies. This strategy is reflected in 19, 20, and 21 of the chart—setting clear goals, tracking student progress, and celebrating success, respectively. But, an examination of the research on feedback indicates that even this "very high-yield" strategy doesn't always work to enhance student achievement. For example, when Kluger and DeNisi (1996) examined the results of 607 experimental/control studies on the effect of feedback, they found that over 30% of them showed a negative effect on student achievement.

I've observed the same phenomenon with virtually every strategy and every innovation I've examined. I've come to the conclusion that you can expect anywhere from 20% to 40% of the studies in any given area to report negative results. While this might surprise or even discourage some, that's simply the nature of the social sciences, in which there are a wide variety of variables that determine whether a particular strategy is going to produce positive results in any given situation. The lesson to be learned is that educators must always look to whether a particular strategy is producing the desired results as opposed to simply assuming that if a strategy is being used, positive results will ensue. If a strategy doesn't appear to be working well, educators must adapt the strategy as needed or use other strategies. This is yet another reason why teachers shouldn't be required to use specific strategies. Since none are guaranteed to work, teachers must have the freedom and flexibility to adapt or try something different when student learning isn't forthcoming.

What's a School or District to Do?

Given my cautions, a reasonable question is what is a district or school to do? First, a district or school should have a common language of instruction—a way to talk about instruction that's shared by everyone in the district or school. But that common language of instruction should be comprehensive and robust. It should involve segments that address three broad areas: content lessons, routines, and things that occur in class that must be addressed on the spot—sections I, II, and III respectively. A district can begin developing a language of instruction by focusing on a list of instructional strategies, management strategies, or assessment strategies. But this is just a beginning.

Second, the common language of instruction should become part of discussion and feedback with teachers. Both discussion and feedback are critical to developing expertise (see Ericcson and Charness 1994). Walkthroughs are probably the most common way that teachers receive feedback on their use of strategies. As mentioned above, feedback generated from walkthroughs must not be limited to a narrow set of instructional strategies. Rather, feedback from walkthroughs must identify the type of segment that was observed (routines, specific types of lessons, or behaviors that must be enacted on the spot) and the use of specific strategies appropriate to that segment.

In addition, rather than being seen solely as a vehicle to provide teachers with feedback, walkthroughs should be viewed as a vehicle for the observers to learn how strategies manifest in the classroom. When this is the perspective, administrators and supervisors aren't the only ones who observe classrooms. Indeed, they aren't even the most important ones involved in making observations. Rather, teams of teachers should observe classes, using the district or school language of instruction as the framework for their observations. As a result of their observations, they may provide the observed teacher with comments summarizing what they saw. More important, members of the observing group gather to debrief on their experiences. Typically, this involves the observer teachers comparing how they saw other teachers using a particular strategy with how they use the same strategy in their classrooms. The emphasis is on the observer teachers using the information gleaned from their observations to reflect on their own practice.

This is at the heart of what City and her colleagues (2009) refer to as "instructional rounds." Briefly, instructional rounds are modeled on medical rounds. Although there are several versions of medical rounds, City and her colleagues explain that the most common manifestation is for groups of medical interns, residents, and supervising or attending physicians to visit patients and then discuss possible treatments. City and her colleagues explain how groups of teachers, instructional coaches, and administrators can do the same by visiting classrooms and then discussing what they observed. Although teachers who have been observed receive feedback regarding the group's observations, the discussions that follow are intended to enhance the expertise of the observers.

City and her colleagues emphasize that rounds are not to be used for evaluative purposes. Rather, they are to be used to increase the pedagogical skill of educators within a district or school through the reflective discussion that ensues. Unfortunately, in many schools and districts, walkthroughs have devolved into terse, formulaic feedback to teachers. As City and her colleagues note:

> Unfortunately, the practice of walkthroughs has become corrupted in many ways by confounding it with supervision and evaluation of teachers. The purpose of some walkthroughs has been to identify deficiencies in classroom practice and to "fix" teachers who manifest these deficiencies. In many instances, judgments about what needs fixing are made on the basis of simplistic checklists that have little or nothing to do with direct experience of teachers in their classrooms. Groups of administrators descend on classrooms with clipboards and checklists, caucus briefly in the hallway, and then deliver a set of simplistic messages about what needs fixing. This kind of practice is antithetical to the purposes of instructional rounds and profoundly antiprofessional. (2009, p. 4)

This quote captures perfectly the sentiment expressed to me by many K-12 teachers across the country. They typically see walkthroughs as unprofessional because they focus on a narrow list of instructional strategies and feedback is given from the perspective that these strategies must be exhibited in every classroom.

Third, using strategies effectively is a means to an end. The ultimate criterion for successful teaching should be student knowledge gain. Classroom strategies are tools to produce knowledge gain. Of course, this means someone must collect data on student learning. This has always been problematic because test data in the form of common assessments and benchmark assessments aren't easily collected regarding a specific observation that has been made with a specific teacher. Fortunately for the purposes of informing discussion about effective teaching, such data can be quite informal (see *District Leadership That Works* (2009) by myself and Tim Waters for more detail on this subject). Teachers can assess students' knowledge gain by developing and using pretests and posttests and computing a simple gain score for each student. More sophisticated mathematical calculations, such as residual scores, can easily be calculated if pretest and posttest data are available. A very efficient way to estimate students' knowledge gain is simply to ask students to rate how much they have learned in a given lesson or a set of lessons. In Hattie's analysis of the research on 138 variables that encompassed 146,142 effect sizes, students' rating of their own knowledge gain had the highest average effect size—over three times larger than the average effect size exhibited in the 138 variables. Hattie referred to this as "self-report

grades." Student self-reports on their learning is an easy and apparently legitimate way to obtain information in the course of walkthroughs or instructional rounds regarding student achievement within the context of a specific lesson or set off lessons.

Conclusion

Classroom strategies in books like *Classroom Instruction That Works, Classroom Management That Works,* and *Classroom Assessment and Grading That Work* are good places to start. But districts and schools must move beyond simple lists to a comprehensive framework or language of instruction that is the basis for professional dialogue. In terms of providing teachers with feedback, the focus must always be on student learning and the perspective must always be that instructional strategies are a means to an end. Checklist approaches to providing feedback to teachers probably don't enhance pedagogical expertise, particularly when they focus on a narrow list of instructional, management, or assessment strategies. In fact, such practice is antithetical to true reflective practice. As City and colleagues note, such behavior is profoundly anti-professional.

References

Black, Paul, and Dylan Wiliam. "Assessment and Classroom Learning." *Assessment in Education* 5, no. 1 (1998): 7–75.

City, Elizabeth A., Richard Elmore, Sarah E. Fiarman, and Lee Teitel. *Instructional Rounds in Education: A Network Approach to Improving Teaching and Learning.* Cambridge, Mass.: Harvard Education Press, 2009.

Ericcson, K. Anders, and Neil Charness. "Expert Performance: Its Structure and Acquisition." *American Psychologist* 49, no. 8 (1994): 725–747.

Hattie, John. *Visible Learning: A Synthesis of Over 800-Meta-Analyses Relating to Achievement.* New York: Routledge, 2009.

Kluger, Avraham N., and Angelo DeNisi. "The Effects of Feedback Interventions on Performance: A Historical Review, a Meta-Analysis and a Preliminary Intervention Theory." *Psychological Bulletin* 119, no. 2 (1996): 254–284.

Leinhardt, Gaea. "Capturing Craft Knowledge in Teaching." *Educational Researcher* 19, no. 2 (1990): 18–25.

Marzano, Robert J. *The Art and Science of Teaching: A Comprehensive Framework for Effective Instruction.* Alexandria, Va.: ASCD, 2007.

Marzano, Robert J. *Classroom Assessment and Grading That Work.* Alexandria, Va.: ASCD, 2006.

Marzano, Robert J., Jana Marzano, and Deborah Pickering. *Classroom Management That Works: Research-Based Strategies for Every Teacher.* Alexandria, Va.: ASCD, 2003.

Marzano, Robert J., Deborah Pickering, and Jane E. Pollock. *Classroom Instruction That Works: Research-Based Strategies for Increasing Student Achievement.* Alexandria, Va.: ASCD, 2001.

Marzano, Robert J., and Tim Waters. *District Leadership That Works: Striking the Right Balance.* Bloomington, Ind.: Solution Tree Press, 2009.

Wang, Margaret C., Geneva D. Haertel, and Herbert J. Walberg. "Toward a Knowledge Base for School Learning." *Review of Educational Research* 63, no. 3 (1993): 249–294.

Critical Thinking

1. Explain what is meant by "high-yield" strategies.
2. Describe the most common mistakes made by school administrators when attempting to implement the strategies discussed in the article.
3. Review Figure 1. Think about a lesson you recently observed (either in a K-12 classroom or one of your classes in your program). Can you analyze the lesson and identify segments that fall into the three broad categories identified in the figure? How would you characterize the effectiveness of the lesson?
4. Under mistake three, Marzano states that it is "not surprising that anywhere from 20% to 30% of educational research studies on a given topic will report negative results." Why might we expect this to be more typical for educational research in comparison to research in other core science fields?

ROBERT J. MARZANO is cofounder and CEO of Marzano Research Laboratory in Denver, Colorado, and author of more than 30 books and 150 articles on topics such as instruction, assessment, writing and implementing standards, cognition, effective leadership, and school intervention.

What Happens When Eighth Graders Become the Teachers?

STEPHANIE STECZ

"We're going to Japan today!"

"I'm so nervous I have butterflies in my stomach! I could hardly sleep last night!"

"Me either! I practiced my part in the shower this morning for so long that my momma had to yell at me to get out."

— A conversation heard between two eighth-grade students the morning of their first day teaching a third-grade class about Japan

In October 2005, I took time from my position as an eighth-grade teacher in a Chicago public school to spend 3 weeks in Japan as a participant in the Japan Fulbright Memorial Fund Teacher Program. Established by the Japanese government in 1995, the program brings American teachers to Japan to learn about the history, culture, and people of their nation with the hopes of strengthening the ties of understanding and cooperation between the two countries. While I was there, I visited beautiful temples, listened to government officials, sampled delicious cuisine, learned about the history, economy, and religious practices, and met many wonderful people. But what I enjoyed the most was spending time in their schools.

I visited three schools—an elementary school, a junior high school, and a senior high school. Although I was fascinated by each experience, it was my day in the elementary school, which consisted of Grades 1–6, that had the greatest impact on me. I was impressed by the older students' levels of responsibility and leadership. Students of all ages and grade levels worked together; they walked to school together in groups, they played games together on the playground, and they cleaned the school together every afternoon. In each case, the oldest student, typically a sixth grader, was responsible for the group. For instance, during morning recess, each group of children had a leader. All the children wore reversible hats. The leader's hat was black, and everyone else in the group wore white. At the conclusion of recess, each group of children crouched in a huddle around the leader, who recorded that day's play activities on a clipboard. It was evident that the students respected each other and were used to functioning as a team.

What I observed that day was not an anomaly in Japanese elementary schools. Contrary to my (and many other Americans') preconceptions about Japanese schools, the idea of community and teamwork is a central tenet of Japan's educational philosophy. In fact, Japanese elementary teachers believe that students' "personal growth, fulfillment, and self-understanding" and "human relations skills" are a higher priority than "academic excellence" and "specific occupational skills" (Lewis & Tsuchida, 1998, p. 1). As a result, Japanese elementary schools are structured to promote community and responsibility: "There is no ability-grouping or tracking; students stay together for two years (usually with the same teacher); and about 30 days of the school year are devoted to activities designed to build human connections within the school community" (Lewis & Tsuchida, p. 1). What I observed while I was there—multiage groups of students playing and working together—is merely one example of how Japanese elementary schools strive to educate "whole" individuals.

Throughout my visit to Japan, I thought a lot about this idea of multiage students working and playing together. It seemed to accomplish several things. First, it teaches the older students responsibility and leadership; second, it provides younger students with mentors and role models; and third, "clique-iness," and showing off, which undermine any team's effectiveness, are minimized because students are grouped together with children of various ages.

I believed this model could be particularly beneficial in a school like mine, which consists of kindergarten through eighth grade. It is often difficult of think of middle school students and primary school students as schoolmates because they are so different. This is further exaggerated because our school is housed in two separate buildings, one for kindergarten through Grade 3, and the other for Grades 4–8. Students are rarely given the opportunity to see each other, let alone work together.

My school is located on the Southwest side of Chicago. Approximately 700 students attend prekindergarten through eighth grade. Almost all of them are from low-income families and receive free lunch. The racial/ethnic breakdown is 96% African American and 4% Hispanic. According to 2006 Illinois State Achievement Test (ISAT) scores, about 40% of our students meet or exceed state standards in reading, and about 45% meet or exceed standards in math.

My homeroom class was unique in several ways. First of all, I "looped" with my class from sixth grade through eighth grade. At the beginning of this project, I had 27 students, 14 of whom I'd had for 3 years, 9 for 2 years, and 4 for 1 year. During the 10-week project, 2 of my students transferred out to new schools and 1 was expelled, and I received 1 new student who was moved from sixth grade to eighth grade because of his age (data from all students were included in the study). My class was also unique because my students' test scores were notably higher than the average for the rest of the school. According to 2006 ISAT scores, 80% of my students met or exceeded grade level in both reading and math. My students' high achievement levels and their familiarity with my classroom culture of teamwork and independent learning positioned them, I believe, for success with a long-term multiage teaching project.

So, as a follow-up to my experience in Japan, I decided to do an action research project and look at what might happen if my eighth-grade students became teachers in a primary-grade classroom. I wanted my students to work together in teams and assume high levels of daily responsibility for their younger peers. I wanted them to be mentors, role models, and school leaders. In doing so, I was interested in studying how these roles and relationships would affect my eighth graders and their "students."

Considering "Cross-Age" Teaching

To begin my data collection, I first surveyed my school's staff. I was surprised to find that 78% of the 23 teachers and other faculty members responded that they either "moderately" or "strongly" agreed that it was good that the older students and younger students were housed in separate buildings. Only 17% disagreed that this separation was beneficial.

What underlies this opinion that it is better for older and younger students to be separated? Certainly there are many explanations, including grade-level colleagues wanting proximity for purposes of collaboration, but I suspected that there was also an underlying belief that younger and older students needed to be separated to keep the "misbehaving" older students from being "bad role models" for the younger students. In the same staff survey, I found that only 21% of teachers responded that the junior high students were good role models, whereas 53% of teachers said they were not. As an eighth-grade teacher, I observe my students on a daily basis, and it was disturbing to me that our school staff did not see the kindness, intelligence, and maturity that most of my students exhibited within my classroom. Inappropriate behavior, including violence, bullying, profanity, disrespect, "fooling around," and dress code violations do indeed occur, but this behavior is given more attention within the school community as compared with positive behavior and achievement. Thus, assumptions about my students' capability as role models stem from observations of junior high students seen on the playground before

and after school and walking through the hallways, which is when and where problems most frequently occur. The "bad" students attract enormous attention, and the "good" ones are overlooked. To overcome the misconception that the typical junior high student sets a bad example, I thought that a cross-age teaching project would be an ideal way to showcase my students' hard work, intelligence, and responsibility. I believed that my students would exceed expectations if empowered with a mentoring/teaching role.

Further, I thought that cross-age teaching was a natural fit for my school's neighborhood and community because older children do in fact assume major responsibilities in their families, particularly regarding younger siblings. Many of my students prepare dinner, help siblings with homework, and get them ready for bed every evening while the house-hold adult(s) is/are at work. Of my 28 students, 26 have younger siblings, and when asked, all but one of them professed to have significant responsibilities for their siblings' care at home. For example, in response to the question, "What specific responsibilities do you have caring for younger siblings at home?" one student wrote, "I do everything. I get him ready for school, make sure he gets in the tub at night, make sure he brushes his teeth, make sure his hair is combed, make sure his shoes are clean, and make sure he goes to bed on time." A second student echoed, "I do everything," and a third wrote, "I have to do whatever my mother doesn't do." Thus, for some middle-school-age children, it is typical to have extensive responsibilities at home, and therefore, as educators, we can and should entrust them with relevant responsibilities at school. Older children-younger children relationships have a prominent place in many communities and therefore should be valued, nurtured, and guided through leadership and mentoring development opportunities at school.

I thought that providing opportunities for older students and younger students to work together would have many positive results not only for the students directly involved but also for the school as a whole. Inspired by the Japanese children I saw playing, cleaning, and walking together, I was interested in seeing what would happen when older students and younger students actively learned together in a classroom. I had been planning to teach my eighth graders a 10-week unit on Japan. However, in the spirit of Japan's educational mantra—to inspire a "zest for life" within its students—I decided to see what would happen when I provided these learning opportunities for my students and then gave them the opportunity to provide similar experiences for younger students.

Students Teaching Students

In researching cross-age and multiage teaching, I found relevant, though limited, studies that pertained to my action research project. Most studies cited the cognitive and/or academic outcomes of older-younger or peer-peer student relationships. My research focus was neither cognitive nor academic outcomes; rather, I was interested in looking at if and how my students' attitudes and motivations toward school were affected by participating in the Japan project. I was similarly interested in the younger students' attitudes toward their participation in the project and perceptions of the older students. Naturally it was important to me that all students meet the learning objectives stated for each lesson, but it was not my intention, nor within the scope of my project, to analyze any quantitative measure of student academic achievement or growth.

A second difference between my project and the studies I read about was that I wanted *every* student from my class to participate in teaching every student from three other classes during the regular school day. I did not find any other studies in which such inclusiveness was the case. In most projects, some students were specifically targeted to tutor or teach other targeted students based on preexisting criteria.

A third difference between my project and others is that I wanted my students to teach their students something that was new to everyone. Unlike teaching younger children how to add double-digit numbers or fill out a Venn diagram, the Japan unit required that my eighth-grade students learn new content and then adapt it in a developmentally appropriate way to teach their students. Although I did not know this at the time I initially began my research, one of the things that most distinguishes this action research is the active role that my students would take in planning and designing the actual lessons they taught.

Despite these differences, I found extensive research on a variety of multiage teaching relationships that showed how and why student-to-student teaching experiences seem to benefit children. Whether in a one-on-one setting or in a setting in which responsibility for teaching is shared among members of a collaborative group, well-planned, well-organized, and well-executed student-student interactions have repeatedly shown positive evidence of student progress and learning (Cohen, Kulik, & Kulik, 1982; Kalkowski, 1995).

But why? What is it about students teaching other students that seems to work so well? Several causal explanations have been suggested, including theories of cognitive restructuring that benefit the tutor by increasing his or her own understanding of the content (Bargh & Schul, 1980; Slavin, 1996). But for the purposes of my research, I was most interested in motivational and attitudinal explanations. For the tutor, assuming the role of "teacher" means taking on a teacher's characteristics, including status, authority, self-perceptions, and attitudes (Puchner, 2003). This responsibility prompts action rather than passivity, and often even reluctant learners are energized by the idea that others, "novices," are dependent on them for assistance. Additionally, both tutors and tutees are motivated by this more flexible, democratic environment that reduces anxiety and facilitates learning (Cohen, 1986).

As for the tutee, he or she benefits from having someone closer to his or her developmental level who may be able to explain concepts in a variety of ways and in language that may not be apparent to the adult teacher. Damon and Phelps (1989) explained this idea in the following way:

> Unlike adult-child instruction, [in] peer tutoring the expert party is not very far removed from the novice party in authority or knowledge; nor has the expert party any special claims to instructional competence. Such differences affect the nature of discourse between tutor and tutee, because they place the tutee in a less passive role than does the adult/child instructional relation. Being closer in knowledge and status, the tutee in peer relation feels freer to express opinions, ask questions, and risk untested solutions. The interaction between instructor and pupil is more balanced and more lively. (p. 138)

Thus, child-to-child interactions not only empower the designated tutor but also may equally empower the tutee. Knowledge may feel more accessible coming from someone relatively close in age, and the process may feel more collaborative; therefore, the tutee may feel more actively involved and thus participate more in the process of learning.

In addition to understanding how and why student-to-student teaching seems to have positive motivational and attitudinal outcomes, I was also very interested in reading about the criteria for a successful program. According to Topping, Campbell, Douglas, and Smith (2003), research evidence shows that it is not enough just to put children together and let them "get on with it"; training is required. Lee and Murdock's (2001) "Ten Essential Elements" emphasizes that a strong curriculum, initial training, ongoing training and support, attention to details, recognition and reward, teambuilding, setting the stage for success, and providing feedback and evaluation are crucial elements of any teaching/tutoring program. Perhaps for this reason, I found little research on, or evidence of, effective student-to-student teaching experiences that occurred during the normal school day. Most programs cited were either after-school or summer programs in which adult guidance for training and support was more accessible.

Although research on the effects of peer and cross-age tutoring is extensive, there are certainly areas that require additional study. There has been little research on students assuming larger scale teaching responsibilities aimed at larger pupil groups or classrooms. Further, many of the existing studies have focused primarily on academic outcomes of cross-age student relationships rather than on more social outcomes such as how a school community may be affected by developed and sustained positive relationships between older and younger students. Finally, I have found no research related to adult teachers' attitudes toward cross-age teaching/tutoring and how it requires collaboration among the adult teachers to facilitate these sustained learning relationships. Thus, there is a significant need for additional research in these areas.

Data, Data, and More Data

Over the course of the research I collected data in the following ways:

Pre- and postproject surveys completed by students and teachers. Prior to the start of my research, I distributed surveys to the school staff, my eighth-grade students, and the second-, third-, and fourth-grade students participating in the project. The staff survey asked questions about the prevailing behaviors exhibited by junior high students in the school. I wanted to see how the adults in the school felt about the eighth graders and their influence on the overall school community, particularly on the youngest students. The eighth graders' survey was similar. I wanted to gauge how they perceived their own behaviors and how they thought the teachers and younger students perceived them. The second-, third-, and fourth graders' survey was a simpler form intended to find out how the younger students viewed the eighth graders and how they felt about the upcoming project. At the project's completion, I resurveyed all participating students to see if and how their perceptions changed and how they enjoyed the project.

Teacher journal. Beginning with the 1st week of the project, I kept a detailed daily journal of my observations and reflections on my successes, questions, and frustrations. I usually wrote an email to myself at the end of the school day so that my memory and reflections were fresh. I later compiled the e-mails into a chronological journal.

Observations and notes. Over the course of the project, I kept a detailed notebook chronicling observations of my students preparing for and debriefing their lessons; comments from conversations I heard among my students about the project and their work; and feedback I received from teachers, administrators, and other faculty members.

Feedback from participating teachers. I received feedback from the participating teachers in several ways. Formally, we met as a group at the beginning and at the end of the project. Informally, I met with each of the teachers individually at least once a week to get their feedback on how the eighth graders handled both themselves and the lessons; how their students enjoyed (or not) and benefited (or not) from the lessons; problems, issues, or concerns that I needed to address; and other data they noted while observing my students teach. I took notes at each of these meetings to record their thoughts. In addition, the teachers responded via e-mail to specific questions I asked regarding the lessons, my students' behavior, and their students' reactions so that I would have the teachers' responses in their own words.

Off and Running . . .

In November 2005, I began planning the 10-week Japan unit, integrating language arts, social studies, visual arts, and mathematics. Each week focused on a different topic: geography, language, food, schools, haiku, theater, origami, and traditional folk tales. During our Monday, Tuesday, and Wednesday language arts periods, my eighth-grade students would learn that week's Japanese content, and then they would teach it to their designated classes on Thursdays and Fridays for 45 minutes each day. I planned to write a lesson plan for each topic, model the lesson for my class, give the students time to practice the lesson, and then have them teach it to their class of younger students.

I divided my 27 students into three groups and assigned each group to a second-, third-, or fourth-grade class. I chose

classrooms where I had a good relationship with the teacher, whom I felt would be easy to work with and who would in general support our curriculum. I thought that by working with three different grade levels, I would be able to compare the types and quality of interactions between them and my eighth graders. I also felt, and hoped, that the overall impact on the school community might be stronger and more visible if the project spanned three grade levels rather than three classrooms in one grade level.

My goals were twofold. First, I wanted my students and their younger counterparts to learn about Japan and be able to compare aspects of its culture to the United States. Second, I wanted all of my students to assume leadership and responsibility within the school. From an action research perspective, I would be looking at what was happening as a result of my students acting as teachers. It was very important to me that all my students participate in the project and that the scheduling remain consistent from week to week.

We officially began the project the week of January 25, 2006. Each participating teacher received a copy of the unit curriculum and was expecting my students in his/her classroom every Thursday and Friday for 45–60 minutes. We staggered teaching times throughout the day because the lessons required materials that the groups needed to share. A significant disadvantage of this scheduling was that I would not be able to observe my students teaching because I needed to be in my classroom with my other students. Thus, I would need to rely on my students and the participating teachers to give feedback on the lesson.

Following the teacher meeting, I had a kick-off meeting with my students. I passed out copies of the unit overview, detailed lesson plans, and a document outlining logistics. Each teaching team would have two lead teachers, two assistant teachers, two materials managers, and three student assistants. I clearly defined the responsibilities of each job and planned for students to switch positions every 2 weeks so that everyone would have the opportunity to participate in each role. I planned for all participating students to journal each week about what they had learned and how they felt about the lessons. In addition, each of the groups was to have a debrief conference with me immediately upon its return from teaching.

Expected and (Even More Exciting!) Unanticipated Outcomes

Looking back on how the Japan project evolved over 10 weeks has proved more interesting to me than any before-after comparisons. I anticipated that this project would increase my students' enthusiasm for school, teach them more patience and responsibility, and help establish more positive relationships with younger students in our school. Indeed, that was why I implemented the project in the first place. It was exciting to validate those assumptions with the data.

Overall, my students were highly motivated by this project, as evidenced by their language and enthusiasm, attendance, and adherence to the school's dress code policy. Unprompted by me, they referred to the project by saying things such as, "We're going to Japan today," and "When do we leave for Japan?" On the postproject survey, 100% of my students responded that they had enjoyed teaching younger students and wanted to do the project again. A total of 62% of my students responded that the project made them think about their behavior at school and "act better." When asked what they liked most about the project, typical positive responses included, "Helping the little kids learn something new," "Acting like a teacher," "Walking around the school without teacher supervision," "Thinking of games to play with the little kids," and "Being in charge." When asked what they didn't like or would change, typical responses included, "Being in the class with a substitute teacher," "Getting the kids to be quiet," and "Only going two times a week." When asked what lesson was their favorite to teach, the responses widely varied. Each week's theme received at least two "my favorite" votes, with "Comparing Japan's Schools to Our School" receiving the most votes overall. On a separate survey that I gave at the end of the school year, 22 out of 26 of my students responded that the Japan project was the most memorable part of school that year.

A second indicator of how the Japan project motivated my students was the improvement in daily attendance. Typically, eighth-grade attendance is lower in the months following winter break and in comparison with the other grade levels. In March, however, my class had a 97% attendance rate, which was the highest in the school and our class's highest for the school year. When I announced this to my class and asked why they thought our attendance was so improved, one student responded, "Probably because nobody wanted to miss school because we were helping the little kids practice for their [reader's theater] performances." Another student added, "Yeah, school was fun in March."

A third indicator was the improvement in dress code. At my school, students must wear blue pants and a white shirt. Students were not allowed to participate in their teaching assignment if they came to school out of dress code because it would set a bad example for the younger students. Over the 10 weeks, there were only four dress code violations, which was a drastic improvement and very atypical for eighth graders at my school.

Although such results validated my assumptions about the benefits of multiage teaching, I believe that the more interesting results of this project were the outcomes that I hadn't anticipated. Looking at my data, particularly my teacher journal and notes, I began to see three central themes emerging:

- *Student "ownership."* Student investment changed the project from *my* predesigned lessons and plans to *their* new, improved lessons and plans.
- *New leadership.* Whereas I had been thinking primarily about how the project would affect my class as a whole, the most striking results were seen in individual students.
- *Pedagogy.* My approach to teaching was significantly enlightened by watching and listening to my students plan and teach their lessons.

Student Ownership

When the project began, everything was very structured, and the 1st week proceeded just as I had planned. Within their teams, students chose the roles they wanted and planned their detailed agenda based on the lesson I modeled for them. They actually wrote down who would say what and practiced their parts. It felt scripted, but was helpful because the students were nervous, and it gave them confidence to know exactly what to say. That first Thursday, the energy level was high, and as each group left and returned, nerves were replaced with confidence. Everyone was talking at once, competing to tell stories about their new young students. Ms. Butler,[1] who was the third-grade participating teacher, offered this summative feedback at the end of the first day: "My students listened better to your students than they listen to me." Ms. Rockford, the second-grade teacher, told me that one of her students went to the school library and checked out the only book about Japan, which made another student angry because he wanted to read it first!

Thus, the project began better than I hoped. My students were invested, the younger students were engaged, and management within the classrooms was tight. Each team had taught and practiced a "quiet" signal that had worked. All three participating teachers reported that their students were intimidated by their new "teachers" and were excited to participate. I was relieved, but I was already exhausted! From my end, it had required a lot of extra work. I had set the objectives, planned the activities, written a meticulous lesson plan for each class, aligned them to the state standards for the four different grade levels involved, and gathered and organized all the necessary materials. And this was just the introductory lesson! Had I gotten myself in over my head?

The 2nd week was a crucial milestone for me. I had anticipated that each week would progress as the first, with me planning and modeling a lesson and the teams practicing and implementing it. But the second lesson I had designed was a failure. Even though I had spent several hours over the weekend finalizing the details, on Monday I still felt unprepared. The topic for the week was the geography of Japan and the United States; I wanted students to study a map to compare and contrast the countries using a Venn diagram. To make the lesson more interesting, I wanted students to make their own map by gluing continent puzzle pieces onto blue construction paper and then labeling the continents, oceans, and two countries. I wanted to model this activity on Monday morning but couldn't finish all the cutting and sorting in time and had to wait until the end of the day, after we had finished our departmental classes:

I wasted about 35 minutes of valuable instruction time passing out materials and getting organized (writing my objectives on the board, covering the class map, etc.) I feel like I modeled *really bad* organization. The kids were sitting there bored. By the time I got their attention it was 1:50 and two of my students had to leave at 2:00 for an extracurricular activity. Then one of my students who had been in detention arrived back to my room and of course that caused further disruption. I was really flustered before the lesson even began. I was exhausted from the long day and had no patience left. I was unclear about my directions and was yelling. The whole class was sharing 4 bottles of glue, most of which didn't work and had to be opened and poured onto the paper and spread with their fingers. Thus, kids wanted to wash their hands in the middle of the lesson. I kept getting more and more frustrated and finally just sat down at my desk. The kids were being too talkative but I knew it was mostly my fault because I was unprepared. After about 5 minutes I got up and continued the lesson, but then I never finished it. I was hanging up our work on the bulletin board and the kids were milling about the room. There was no sense of conclusion; no reflection; no debrief.

I assumed the whole week—the whole project—was ruined. If I couldn't model a good lesson, then they wouldn't teach a good lesson.

The next day, I talked to my class about the lesson and what I thought had gone wrong. They didn't seem to think it had gone as badly as I thought—"It wasn't *that* bad; it was just boring"—which made me feel both better and worse. I was glad that they hadn't realized how unprepared I was, but I felt guilty that they didn't recognize an ineffective lesson for what it was. This was a bad sign, considering I was trying to teach them to be teachers. It seemed worse to have them teach badly than not to teach at all! But I wasn't ready to give up. We talked as a whole group about how the lesson could be improved, and then I split them into their teams to work on their agendas. Circulating to help, I was amazed at how seriously two of the three groups took this responsibility:

The second grade team decided that the students would work together in small groups to create big, poster-size maps rather than individual ones. Why hadn't I thought of that? Group work is always more fun and what an excellent way to reduce the prep work of cutting out the puzzle pieces and the amount of glue needed. They also wanted to make the activity into a game and Karisha said she'd bring in candy for the winning team. The fourth grade team also did a good job. They decided to do the map activity individually but in a smaller group setting where a teacher could oversee each group. I thought that was a really good idea.

At this point, I thought back to my original research question— What happens when my eighth-grade students work in teams to teach younger students about Japan?—and I realized that by trying to do all the prep work myself, I was depriving my students of a fundamental aspect of teaching—designing and planning! Having my students simply deliver a lesson I had planned was the same as having a teacher deliver a scripted, direct instruction reading lesson. How many times had I heard teachers complain about that? I realized that I was underestimating my students; if I was giving them the responsibility of going into a classroom and teaching for an hour, I needed to entrust them with the responsibility of preparing the lesson they wanted to teach.

This project required two distinct levels of teaching from me—teaching the content and teaching *how to teach*. This made my job both easier and more difficult. I no longer needed to agonize over modifying a lesson to four different grade levels, but I did need to demonstrate how to develop, plan, and execute effective, appropriate lessons.

I quickly realized that my students didn't have a problem brainstorming activities to meet stated objectives; that was the fun part. The third week, they changed the "Compare and Contrast the Japanese Alphabets" lesson by stapling paper plates together to make a Venn diagram, then premaking fact cards taken from an informational article that could be glued to the correct area of the graphic organizer—much more interactive and fun than writing on a boring Venn diagram! The 4th week, they enhanced the "Compare and Contrast Our School to a Typical Japanese School" activity, which was to clean the classroom from top to bottom (wearing slippers, of course) just like Japanese students would and by blasting music on the radio while they worked. This transformed the task from a chore to a party. Other classes wanted to know if they could clean their classrooms, too!

And so the weeks progressed, with me relinquishing more and more creative control to my students. At times it was hard for me to sit back and watch when I suspected they were underestimating an activity's difficulty or overpromising candy rewards for winning teams, but I realized that this was all part of the learning process. There was no doubt that the project was theirs, not mine. The final 2 weeks, when my students worked with their students every day for an hour to prepare reader's theater performances of Japanese folk tales, probably best illustrates the extent to which my students owned this project. As each group performed, I watched in amazement as props, costumes, and painted backgrounds were brought in and set up. Everyone participated, and everyone had fun. To give just a sample of the many accolades I overheard my students give their students: "You guys did great!" "That was awesome!" "Our group was definitely the best!" I don't know who was prouder that day— me or my students.

Looking back, I'm glad that I decided not to micromanage the project. By giving up (or at least sharing) my control over the actual lesson being taught, I introduced a new layer of complexity to my research. Once I had decided to truly let them be the teachers, I was able to observe as the groups' strengths and weaknesses emerged. Nine students make a very large group when it comes to decision making, and their abilities to negotiate a cohesive plan, delegate tasks, and take personal and collective responsibility became critical components of their effectiveness as teachers.

Coping with Challenges.

The second-grade team worked particularly well together and was the most successful, which I defined in terms of consistently meeting the curriculum objectives, maintaining excellent classroom management, and exhibiting positive attitudes even in the most challenging situations. For example, at some point during the project, each group had to teach its class when the regular teacher was absent and a substitute was there instead. Ms. Rockford actually called me at home and told me that she would be absent the next day and wanted to be sure that my students would still go to her class to teach, "because it may be the only time of the day that they actually learn something." When my students returned from teaching the next day, they expressed some frustration about their students' behavior and remarked that they had to spend extra time "reviewing the rules and expectations." Even as they told me this, they handed me a pile of beautifully written and illustrated haiku poems completed by every student. I was impressed.

The other two groups fared less well when confronted by the teacher's absence. The third-grade team had such a miserable experience the first time this occurred that when they showed up 2 weeks later and she was absent again, they decided not to stay and even attempt the lesson. They simply walked into the room, saw the substitute, and left. Personally, I was very disappointed and upset. During our debrief session, there was a lot of arguing among the group members over whether this was a good decision: "Those kids were out of control," "That lady needed to control those kids," "They weren't listening to us anyway," "There was nothing we could do," "We should have at least tried to stay," "*Some* of the kids were being good." Of course I could understand their frustration with out-of-control students; however, I was trying to teach them the importance of dependability and consistency. I was asking a lot of 14-year-olds, but I wanted them to take their roles seriously. But because I had consciously stepped back and allowed them to make their own decisions, I had to support them. I withheld my judgment and listened as they ranted about the "lack of home-training" that the third graders had. Ironically, it reminded me of an actual teacher's lounge conversation. But like most good teachers, once the venting had passed, potential solutions were offered. Should they ask to stay an extra 30 minutes tomorrow to make up the lesson? How would they reestablish their authority because it "looked bad" that they had left? There wasn't a consensus, and there wasn't full participation, but it was an unusual conversation for eighth graders.

Over the 10 weeks, the project continued to evolve in such progressive and regressive strokes. It represented a huge learning curve for my students, but there was no question that they took ownership of the project.

New Leadership

When assigning students to their teams, I had consciously separated my natural leaders. These were the students I pictured at the front of the classroom, teaching. But over the course of the project I was surprised by how group dynamics had a profound impact on the leadership that actually emerged. Some of the students who I thought would exert tremendous leadership failed to take charge; some of my natural leaders exceeded my high expectations; and, most gratifying, many of the students who had never exhibited any leadership suddenly blossomed in their roles!

I believe that these new leaders weren't really new leaders at all; they had probably been that way all along, but no one had ever asked them to exhibit these qualities. Darian is an excellent example. He had been in my class for 3 years. He was extremely well liked by his peers, mainly for his quick sense of humor. He could invent amazingly creative raps on the spot. He had above average standardized test scores in both reading and math, but he had never applied himself in school and therefore typically earned Ds and Fs in most subject areas. I had always liked Darian, but I would not have chosen him for a leadership position because he never seemed to take things seriously. He was often out of dress code, and I was constantly telling him to go to his desk, sit down, and stop talking. During the 1st week of the project, Darian was fooling around—hanging out the window when he was supposed to be working with his team—and I kicked him out of the project. I wrote about the incident in my journal:

> I already kicked Darian off the project. I feel bad, but at this point I had no choice. If I can't trust someone to make the right decisions in the classroom, there's no way I can send them to another classroom when I won't be there. That's not fair to that teacher. So he'll have to serve as an example. I gave sufficient warning and I have to look at it from the bigger picture perspective. *It is about students serving as positive role models and that role, let's face it, does not suit everyone!*

Darian sat out that first Thursday, and then he came to me Friday morning: "Could I please have another chance? I promise I can be good." I was happy to comply because I really did want all my students to have this opportunity, but was afraid that I was setting a dangerous precedent by reinstating him.

Looking back, this turned out to be the right choice. Darian was an excellent teacher. The second graders thought he was funny, but they respected him, too, because he kept them on task. Ms. Rockford described her observations of Darian the 2nd week:

> Darian was working with a small group reading the article about the Japanese alphabets. He had them taking turns reading and turned to Johnny and said, "It is your turn." Johnny put his head down and said he didn't want to read because he had a headache. I was about to tell Darian that Johnny couldn't read, but I didn't want to embarrass him. Before I could decide what to do, Darian said, "Naw, it is not your turn to read, it is your turn to glue the stuff on." Johnny instantly sat up and grabbed the glue. I was so impressed that Darian had been so perceptive and handled the situation so kindly.

At the project's conclusion, I surveyed all my students and asked them if they behaved any differently while participating in the project, and like many of my students (38%), Darian responded that no, he had not acted differently. I was surprised, because to me he *had* acted differently. After thinking more about it, though, I think that he was right. He had been himself; it was just that I was observing him in a new context. I had never given him leadership responsibilities before, nor had anyone else, so he hadn't needed to act like a leader. I could not help but wonder, how many other students are waiting to be given responsibilities, given the chance to prove themselves?

Perhaps my early journal entry about positive leadership roles not suiting all students was wrong; I discovered that each of my students contributed to this project and that many of the students I expected the least of actually showed the most dramatic transformations. Besides Darian, many of my other "troublemakers" also proved to be excellent role models. Perhaps they have some special insight into why wayward students act the way they do, but it may have been more that they felt the importance of their responsibility and truly stepped into the role of teacher. When you think of troublemaking itself as an exhibition of leadership—in the sense that it grabs others' attention and persuades some to "do" something—acting as a teacher is simply a more constructive way to exercise the same skill. And isn't multiage teaching a much more affirming source of attention? It allows students like Darian a chance to feel valued, respected, and successful while still maintaining a sense of control.

This element of self-control, of choice, is extremely significant for all young teenagers, but perhaps particularly so for inner city children, who are often forced to confront complicated life situations from a very early age. They become accustomed to making decisions and assuming responsibilities at home, and that mentality doesn't just switch off when they enter school every morning. If we entrust them with responsibility at school, we are meeting their needs in a very different way because we are showing that we trust and respect them and expect them to do important things *in* school. The results, in terms of the Japan project, are multiple. First, both older and younger students are learning the content we want them to learn. Second, older students are learning important and relevant life skills, including how to work in peer groups, how to manage time and resources, how to teach younger children, how to meet and debrief with adults, and how to deal with problems and make on-the-spot decisions. Third, younger students are observing positive behaviors from older students who are serving as role models and mentors.

These outcomes validate my belief that a multiage teaching project is not only appropriate but also extremely beneficial when *every* student in a given classroom is involved. The literature I read indicated that most multiage teaching projects were geared toward specific populations, either honor students or "at-risk" students. Most of these projects involved one-on-one or small-group multiage learning situations in which the older student was designated as a reading buddy or math tutor. They proved successful; however, I believe that the experience is much richer when all students from the "teaching" class are involved and the content is something new to both the "teachers" and the "students." Including all students will showcase natural leaders, but it also affords the opportunity for new leadership to emerge. Darian is just one example of many students who surprised me with their enthusiasm and leadership. In little and big ways, all my students contributed to the

success of our Japan project because they were all able to relate to their students in unique ways.

Pedagogy: My "Enlightened" View of Teaching

One of the things that most surprised me about this project was how much I learned about teaching by watching my students teach. Children have an embedded image of what teaching is "supposed" to be. After all, it is the career they have been exposed to the most. Further, by eighth grade, students have witnessed many different teachers and their various teaching styles, and they have a clear idea of what (and who) is "good" versus what (and who) is "bad." Interestingly, my students' favorite teachers were not necessarily those they identified as the best teachers. When I initially surveyed my class prior to starting this project, I asked them to identify the characteristics of a good teacher. The most common responses were that good teachers must be "strict," "structured," and "organized." They must also "be really smart and know what [they're] talking about." I then engaged my students in a discussion about "good versus bad" and "easy versus hard" teachers; one student claimed (with the consensus of his peers), "I usually like the easy teachers better because I have to do less work, but if you really think about it, the easy teachers aren't really doing their job and in the long run I'll have to make up that work anyway."

I was interested in how my students would present themselves to their students. Initially, I was concerned that they would try to be too friendly or too casual. I know that many adult new teachers make the mistake of trying too hard to be liked instead of respected. It definitely was the case with 3 boys in the second-grade group who let the girls be the "enforcers" while they were the "clowns." When the whole group worked together it was fine, but it became a major problem the last week of the project, when the class split into two smaller groups to work on the reader's theater performances.

The boys wanted to work together and boasted that their group would have more fun, but they quickly realized that the second graders had become so accustomed to chasing them around and climbing on their backs that they now refused to comply with directions. The boys knew their group was in trouble and that they "couldn't handle it." They asked Whitney, a strong leader from the other group, to help them. Immediately, the same second graders who had literally been running around the room began rehearsing with diligence for Whitney. She had established herself as an authority figure the first day; she was well liked, but she had presented herself as someone who was focused on the task and expected them to take it seriously, too. After the reader's theater performances, I talked to the boys about how they could have handled the situation differently. Freddy said, "We shouldn't have tried so hard to be like them. After all, we were the old ones and should have acted like it. I think we were *too* fun." I followed up by asking how it felt to watch their group perform so well. Raymond replied, "It was cool." I then asked if they thought their students had more fun playing around with them or performing reader's theater. Freddy responded, "I think they probably had more fun doing reader's theater because it made them feel smart and good about themselves. Don't get me wrong, fooling around is fun, but it is probably better to do on the playground than in the classroom."

Where does "fun" fit in? This conversation, along with the observations I had made over the 10-week project, made me reflect on this idea of "fun" in the classroom. Was fun really that important to student learning, or was it just an extra bonus when a focused lesson was enjoyable? When planning their lessons, my students adamantly and consistently insisted that the lessons they taught be conducted in small groups and, whenever possible, structured as games or contests. They always wanted to have a "winner" because they knew from their own experience that competition is a strong motivator. I was amazed at how they could make anything into a game: a chopsticks tournament, geography hot potato, pick a haiku topic out of a bag, and so on.

Watching and listening to my students plan lessons was a fascinating way for me, as their teacher, to access what they believed was important in a lesson and how this was best learned. To my students, the lessons they planned were only successful if they were "fun." To me, lessons are only successful if I meet my curricular objective. By watching my students teach, I learned more about *how* they wanted to learn. They wanted to play games and do projects; to compete; to draw, color, cut, and glue; to listen to music; to act things out; to work in groups; to stand up and move. They wanted a product—something they'd made—and they wanted it displayed in the hallway where kids from other classes could see it. This is not earth-shattering, but it affirms what we, as teachers, must do if we want to achieve maximum results in our classroom. It would never have appealed to my students (as teachers) to stand at the front of their classrooms and read aloud from a sheet of paper or write things on the board; that was "too boring." But like my boys who taught the second grade realized, just being fun isn't enough either. In fact, as Freddy said, it is more fun when you're actually learning something.

Thus, I discovered what students really want—focused, purposeful, "fun" lessons. They want to learn new things. I was amazed by how curious my students were about Japan and how they especially craved learning to say things in Japanese. It made them feel intelligent to be able to converse about Japanese culture and compare it to the United States. When I first started planning this project, I wasn't sure if my students would be enthusiastic because Japan seems so irrelevant to their daily lives. But they found connections that never even occurred to me. *America's Next Top Model* went to Tokyo. Some famous singer's back-up dancers are Harajuku girls. And anime? The boys love it! The fact that my students knew very little about Japan made it *especially* relevant, and what could make an eighth grader feel more significant than teaching an entire class of "little kids" something totally new? As teachers, we must consciously consider both *what* and *how* we teach and not be afraid to share the responsibility of both with our students!

Conclusions

I believe this action research makes a valuable contribution to current thinking about multiage teaching and learning on a number of levels. First, it is unique in that it looked at what happened when *all* students from a classroom were involved in teaching *all* students from other classrooms, rather than selecting tutors and tutees based on predefined criteria. This allowed new leadership to evolve and latent skills to become apparent because students were not prejudged as to how they would perform in this new context. There are natural academic, social, and physical stratifications that exist amongst classmates; this type of equally inclusive leadership opportunity allows students to reshuffle themselves and perhaps distinguish themselves in completely new ways.

A second important distinction is that students taught an integrated unit of "new-to-them" content, which is a different experience from being a math tutor or reading buddy, which relies on previously acquired (and mastered) skills. This levels the playing field for older students; being good at reading or math is irrelevant to being able to teach younger children how to count to 10 in Japanese. This is a refreshing and healthy departure from the necessary practice of "differentiating instruction" because it positions *all* students first as new learners and then as experienced teachers. Last, not only are the older students teaching new content, but they are also helping to create and plan the lessons. This teacher-student collaboration, quite literally, is a teacher-teaches-students-how-to-teach *and* students-teach-teacher-how-to-teach-better situation.

This research certainly has limitations. It was not my intention to look at whether or how participation in this project affected academic achievement in any subject area, whether for my own students or the younger ones; the focus began as, and remained, behaviors and attitudes. I did not administer any formal assessments to measure new knowledge gained or retained. Although the participating teachers and I considered the activities as performance-based assessments, we did not assign grades. We felt that it was not appropriate for us to do so because technically we were not the "teachers" and because it was outside the scope of this project for me to teach my students how to assess student work. In implementing this project, I was fortunate to have support from administrators at my school who recognized students' participation as a valuable use of school time, despite the content (Japan) being outside the mandated scope and sequence of the various grade levels' curriculum. This may not be the case at other schools.

Policy and Practical Recommendations

Based on my research, my recommendations for teachers and administrators are as follows:

- Especially in K–8 elementary schools, we need to find ways to invest in and meaningfully develop older students as mentors, role models, and teachers for younger students. Beyond traditional tutors and book buddies, older students can learn and teach something brand new (like Japan!), monitor literacy and math centers in primary classrooms, facilitate literature circles, open a writing center where teachers can send students to get help revising and editing their work, and write and/or direct reader's theater performances for younger students, to name just a few examples.

- A wide variety of schoolwide leadership opportunities should be available to all students in schools, and all students should be encouraged to participate. In addition to traditional forums such as student council and team captains, we need to provide a wealth of activities before, during, and after school hours. These can include roles such as office, library, and teacher assistants; lunchroom, bathroom, and playground monitors; and special event committees (Open House, Field Day, assemblies, field trips, holiday parties, spirit week, fundraisers, toy/food drives, and so on). Schools should reflect on what they *need* and allow students to help make these changes happen.

- Teachers of different grade levels should collaborate to create multiage projects. This requires time for planning and flexibility in the scope and sequence of content areas so that teachers can find effective ways to partner with other grade levels. There need to be opportunities for teachers and students to choose new-to-everyone content. It seems that there is a trend toward every minute of the school day being consumed by predetermined content, which is important for school-to-school consistency but which has the unintended consequence of alienating teacher innovation and creativity. It is imperative that we integrate teachers' and students' interests and passions into our school curriculums.

- Teachers must have the flexibility in their teaching schedule to be able to implement lessons. If every minute of the school day is specifically designated for predetermined core subjects, it is impossible to find the time to teach cross-curricular units, especially when partnering with other classes. In my case, I often had to shift my schedule to accommodate the Japan project, which meant teaching reading/language arts and math at "unconventional" times. I was fortunate to have the flexibility, especially as a middle school teacher, to do so. For a multiage project to succeed, teachers need some control in their daily and/or weekly schedule to accommodate special projects.

In conclusion, I believe that this project achieved its two goals: First, all participating students learned about the country and culture of Japan, and second, my eighth-grade students assumed leadership roles and served as mentors and role models for younger children. On a larger scale, I also believe that this project had a positive effect on my entire school community. In the weeks following the Japan project's completion, a sixth-grade class and a fourth-grade class partnered to study a unit on Ancient Egypt; the school librarian "employed" middle school students to assist in the library and work at the school book fair; and several primary-grade teachers set up small-group tutoring sessions facilitated by middle school students. In addition, I was approached by countless teachers asking me if my students could come teach their students or, at least, if I could help them set up a similar partnership with another class. Students, too, have sought me out to ask when my students are coming to *their* class. Whether it was the music blaring from the classrooms while the students were cleaning "Japanese style," the vast amounts of multiage student work exhibited in the hallways, the laughter erupting from the auditorium during the reader's theater performances, or just the general excitement of the four participating classes, it seems that every member of our school community knew about the Japan project. My hope is that many more student-student and student-teacher relationships continue to develop over time and that schools like mine stop seeing the older students as behavior problems or poor role models and instead begin to see and utilize our older students as agents of positive change and transformation.

Note

1. All names of teachers and students have been changed.

References

Bargh, J. A., & Schul, Y. (1980). On the cognitive benefits of teaching. *Journal of Educational Psychology, 72,* 593–604.

Cohen, J. (1986). Theoretical considerations of peer tutoring. *Psychology in the Schools, 23,* 175–186.

Cohen, P. A., Kulik, J. A., & Kulik, C. C. (1982). Educational outcomes of tutoring: A meta-analysis of findings. *American Educational Research Journal, 19,* 237–248.

Damon, W., & Phelps, E. (1989). Critical distinctions among three approaches to peer education. *International Journal of Educational Research, 58*(2), 9–19.

Kalkowski, P. (1995, March). *Peer and cross-age tutoring* Retrieved November 25, 2005, from Northwest Regional Educational Laboratory Website: www.nwrel.org/scpd/sirs/9/c018.html

Lee, F. C. H., & Murdock, S. (2001). Teenagers as teachers programs: Ten essential elements. *Journal of Extension, 39*(1). Retrieved November 25, 2005, from http://joe.org/joe/2001february/rbl.html

Lewis, C., & Tsuchida, I. (1998). The basics in Japan: The three C's. Educational Leadership, 55(6), 32–37.

Puchner, L. D. (2003, April). Children teaching for learning: What happens when children teach others in the classroom? Paper prepared for the annual meeting of the American Educational Research Association, Chicago, IL.

Slavin, R. E. (1996). Research on cooperative learning and achievement: What we know, what wc need to know. Contemporary Educational Psychology, 21, 43–69.

Topping, K. J., Campbell, J., Douglas, W., & Smith, A. (2003). Cross-age peer tutoring in mathematics with seven- and 11-year-olds: Influence on mathematical vocabulary, strategic dialogue and self-concept. *Educational Research, 45,* 287–308.

Critical Thinking

1. What was the author's stated purpose for the study?
2. How does the author's study differ from other research on peer tutoring?
3. As you critically reflect on the author's findings, what are some noteworthy things/points she made that really stood out to you?
4. If you were able to interview the teacher and her students about their experiences with the project, what would be some things you would ask them to discuss?
5. Analyze the article from the perspective of one of the other articles in Unit 2 or 5. How can the author's design of the project and her findings be supported by specific points or concepts presented in the article you selected?

STEPHANIE STECZ currently teaches fifth grade in the Chicago Public Schools. Her research interests include multiage student learning opportunities and creating, using, and sharing meaningful assessments.

From *Teachers College Record*, August 2009, pp. 1930–1953. Copyright © 2009 by Columbia University Teachers College. Reprinted by permission via Copyright Clearance Center.

Designing Learning through Learning to Design

This paper represents a conversation between a high school science teacher and a university researcher as they found common ground in the theory and experiences of designing powerful learning experiences. The teacher describes an instructional unit in which students designed a complex, interactive display showing what life may have been like during the Mesozoic Era. The researcher offers analysis of that activity through the lens of design and design-based learning. Their voices intentionally co-mingle as they illuminate aspects of one another's work—the pedagogical work of the teacher, and the theoretical analysis of the researcher. The conversation provides useful insight for teachers wishing to employ design-based learning in their classrooms and an important analytic lens for researchers to view teaching and learning.

PUNYA MISHRA AND MARK GIROD

Introduction

Much is written today about design-based learning (Author, Zhao, & Tan, 1999; Author & Koehler, in press; Kafai & Resnick, 1996;). Design, as a pedagogical activity, has come to be perceived as forward-looking, reform-oriented, and progressive (Roth, 1998). Reformers and writers commonly support design-based learning for its authentic outcomes and activities, and collaborative and cross-curricular nature (Brown, 1992). These, however, are only surface-level characteristics of design-based learning that fail to capture three, much deeper, psychologically-based characteristics, that illuminate the efficacy and potential of design-based learning.

This paper provides one teacher's account of a unique design-based learning situation in which 40 high school students worked to represent life during the Mesozoic age. Students' design projects had to: a) communicate (teach) a particular element related to life during the Mesozoic period such as plant and animal life, climate, or physiographic features of the earth's surface; b) provide something for both children and adults to do to help them learn or understand the point being made by the representation, and; c) be scientifically accurate and artistically crafted to provide a unique experience to those viewing the representations. Projects were displayed in a community open-house referred to as the Mesozoic Resource Center (MRC). Woven throughout an extended pedagogical description of the MRC, as told by the teacher (in italics), is a parallel, theoretical analysis through the lens of design, as told by the university researcher (in plain text). The intent is to illuminate salient features of both the pedagogical description and the theoretical analysis in ways educative to both teachers and researchers.

The Case of the Mesozoic Resource Center[1]

As I looked around my classroom I saw Reuben, a known gang member, reading a story he had written and illustrated about a young Pachycephalosaurus to five first graders. Chris, an eighteen-year-old sophomore labeled severely emotionally disturbed, was smiling and enthusiastically debating the feasibility of the asteroid impact theory with our school superintendent. Linda and Becky, both of whom had failed other science classes, were surrounded by several parents as they described the nesting behavior of hadrosaurs.

This was the scene at the opening of my classes' Mesozoic Resource Center. Forty high school science students and I had been working diligently for ten weeks in preparation for this evening. We had set up displays on both floors of our unusual two-story classroom. Downstairs visitors browsed through student constructed displays ranging from the diversity of pterosaurs to a debate over whether dinosaurs were warm or cold-blooded. Students manned their displays clarifying ideas and offering additional information to visitors as they passed.

In one corner, elementary children were invited to excavate dinosaur toys from a simulated paleontological dig, pour resin over insects to simulate the famous mosquito stuck in amber from Jurassic Park, or use a rubber stamp kit to construct their own dinosaurs. Each group was closely supervised by my students.

Upstairs, another group was conducting tours of a lost age. Guides assigned to each period, Triassic, Jurassic, and Cretaceous, led visitors through their respective age describing the plants, animals, and climate of that time. Visitors stood stunned at the bleakness of the dry, sandy, desert-like surroundings in the Triassic, marveled at the 8 meter long Apatosaurus model being eyed by the head of a Parasaurolophus peering through ferns and lush greenery, and were amazed by the 3 meter tall Tyrannosaurus Rex model glaring down at them as the first flowering plants appeared in the Cretaceous Period. The sights and conversation were academic, enthusiastic, and engaging for everyone involved.

What started as a trial in self-directed learning exploded in both size and scope. Before I knew it, these students, most previously characterized as disinterested, unmotivated, and apathetic, were tearing down the walls of traditional learning. In its place they built a community of scholars each working toward understanding and communicating what life was like millions of years ago in the Mesozoic Era. As their teacher, I could barely keep up.

New to teaching about dinosaurs and the era in which they lived, I had few resources and even less personal knowledge about these topics. I chose to involve my students, as well as myself, with a book called Dinosaur! (Norman, 1991). It is filled with information about current thinking regarding dinosaurs and is richly illustrated. We supplemented our reading with the four-part A&E television series by the same name. In areas where these two sources were insufficient in providing enough information, students consulted our school library, the Internet, local experts, university libraries, and even college professors. Just learning how to gather information was a worthwhile experience for many of my students.

We soon realized that to get a complete picture of life in the Mesozoic Era we needed to split up and become experts in many different areas. With a little guidance, my students were able to focus their inquiry into very specific topics. With their topic in mind, they had one goal. Each student was to become an expert in a particular area. I challenged each student to develop their knowledge of the subject far beyond mine or anyone else's in our school. These were empowering words for largely disenfranchised students. They eagerly accepted the challenge! As students' knowledge grew it became clear that I had to find a way to showcase their work. Our simple dinosaur projects became the Mesozoic Resource Center described above.

Ready to show off their products, my students suggested that I call the local newspaper and television station. To our surprise, both agencies were eager to come and do short stories. Everyone was thrilled to be on television but the pressure to look and sound impressive was mounting. The television crew arrived a couple hours before the grand opening as my high school students were hosting groups of second and third graders from our local elementary school. One of the requirements for each student display was that it must have something for both child and adult visitors to do. In this case, the elementary teachers examined the computer-generated overlays describing dinosaur anatomy while children distinguished Ornithischians from Saurischians using very realistic plastic models.

By far, the biggest hit of the Mesozoic Resource Center was the walk-through-diorama showing how life might have been during the each of the three periods of the Mesozoic. Together with my students and our school janitors, we had built fake walls of black plastic to separate the ages. Across several days we hauled in 500 gallons of sand and rocks to spread across the floor. Students working on the diorama spent two Saturdays hauling brush, driftwood, and small shrubbery to "plant" in our 200-million-year-old setting. Our local florist donated several large boxes of ferns to add to the realism. With back lighting and sound effects piped in through a hidden stereo system, our diorama became very impressive.

The highlights of the diorama were two very large dinosaur models built and assembled by my students. We ordered balsa wood snap-together models from a supply house and traced each of the pieces. Using an opaque projector and very steady hands, six students made patterns of dinosaur bones approximately 1/4 normal scale. The students traced the patterns onto sheets of plywood, and using jigsaws, cut them out. After sanding and painting all the pieces and using a few bolts and clamps, we assembled these massive dinosaur models in their appropriate time periods.

Second only to the huge dinosaur models in impressiveness were two dinosaur heads painted in exquisite detail. A student who was an avid hunter found a taxidermy magazine that sold closed-cell styrofoam forms of dinosaur heads. Taxidermists buy and display them on their wall in jest like any other trophy animal. But this student imagined the heads mounted on the wall peering out of bushes that would be planted in front. After airbrushing the forms to amazing realism, the effect was quite startling. Imagine walking through a darkened classroom, marveling at the magnitude of the dinosaur models in front of you, listening intently as students explained the hunting habits of small, carnivorous dinosaurs, and then suddenly eyeing one, head sticking out of some bushes lit by a soft green glow. The effect was fantastic. In fact, one first grader wet his pants!

A Researcher's Conceptualization of "Design"

Design activities are one class of activities that fall under the broader rubric of project-based activities. In such activities, students design complex interactive artifacts to be used by other students for learning about a particular subject (Harel, 1991). Design-based projects have involved the development of presentations, instructional software, simulations, publications, journals, and games (Carver, 1991; Guzdial, 1993; Kafai, 1995, 1996; Lehrer, 1991; Vyas & Author, 2002). With such projects, students learn both about design—through the process of developing complex artifacts—and a variety of academic disciplines, such as programming, social studies, language arts, etc.

Research and theory suggest that design-based activities provide a rich context for learning (Willet 1992). Within the context of social constructivism (Cole, 1997; Vygotsky, 1978) or constructionism (Papert, 1991), design projects lend themselves to sustained inquiry and revision of ideas. Other scholars have emphasized the value of complex, self-directed, personally motivated and meaningful design projects for students (Blumenfeld, Soloway, Marx, Krajcik, Guzdial, & Palinscar, 1991; Collins, Brown & Newman, 1990, Harel & Papert, 1990, Kafai, 1996).

Such design-based, informal learning environments offer a sharp contrast to regular classroom instruction, the effectiveness of which has been questioned by many scholars (Papert, 1991, 1993; Pea, 1993; Lave & Wenger, 1991). As one might imagine, adapting such open-ended problem solving situations into the structure and organization of the conventional classroom is often difficult to manage logistically.

Design, broadly speaking, can be seen as "structure adapted to a purpose" (Perkins, 1986, p. 2). Perkins' definition captures elegantly an essential quality of design: it is a process of constructing artifacts that exhibit "goodness of fit." Design can be seen both in material artifacts, such as a hammer or a piece of software, as well as in non-material artifacts, such as a poem, a theory or a scientific experiment. This conceptualization of design can play itself out within multiple contexts. In the MRC project, for instance, students designed complex educational artifacts based on their understanding of important ideas in science and art. Further, they acted as social scientists designing usability studies and evaluation tools to test how their exhibits were used by exhibit visitors.

At another level, design applies to educational researchers attempting to better understand the pragmatic and theoretical aspects of developing design-based activities. In essence, our perspective sees design as being both "an object of study as well as context for a study of learning" (Author, Zhao, & Tan, 1999; Kafai 1996, pg. 72; Koehler, Author, Hershey & Peruski, under review). This view of design as adaptation generates several significant implications that can help us understand the pedagogical value of design-based learning activities. These implications are discussed in terms of the MRC.

Design in Analysis of the Mesozoic Resource Center

One of the most interesting aspects of the MRC project is the multiple levels of understanding that were required for completing the design task. Students surely gained a deep understanding of the core ideas of deep-time and evolutionary biology, and the manner in which they play out in different domains. Students also developed strategies and techniques to help others learn these concepts through their exhibit. This required them to think beyond the science concepts to consider ways in which others would generate their own understandings of these ideas. Further, students needed to develop technological skills in order to construct the artifacts that embodied their ideas. To understand this, we can apply the design experiment approach (Brown, 1992), focusing on the following social and cognitive aspects of the design activities to help interpret what was observed:

- The role of knowledge in design, technology, and subject matter content in learning to design, the patterns of interaction among knowledge in different domains
- The role of audience, mentors, leaders, collaborators, and peers in learning and design; patterns of interaction, both face-to-face and online and their effects on learning and design

- The role of artifacts and ideas as tools for construction, expression, communication and inquiry
- The nature of representation and manipulation of symbols in the process of design

As these aspects of the design experiment approach suggest, design works at multiple levels; thus, understanding what happened in this classroom requires analysis at multiple levels as well. The unit of analysis is not merely the individual, but rather the interaction of the learner, the practices, the resources being used, the community within which these practices are nested and the constraints of the situation—i.e. the intersection of individual, activity, and context (Lave & Wenger, 1991; Roth, 1998).

Three themes emerge from this juxtaposition of the pedagogical instantiation of the Mesozoic Resource Center and the psychological analysis via design. Each theme is illustrated by a brief vignette drawn from the teacher's account of experiences during production of the Mesozoic Resource Center. The vignettes are designed to be broadly representative of the experiences of students' learning in this design-based setting. They should not be considered atypical or unusual. Three different stories could have been easily selected to illustrate these same three design themes. As with the intertwining of voices used previously, these themes as offered by the researcher appear in plain text, and their corresponding illustrative stories, supplied by the teacher, appear in italics.

Theme I: Design as a Transformative Experience

Vygotsky (1978) and Dewey (1933) emphasize the role of dialogue or interplay in learning. As the individual acts on the environment, the environment also acts upon the individual. Inquiry and learning, like design, are not simply about understanding and assembling materials. They are fundamentally about ideas and transforming oneself and the world through the process of working with those ideas.

At the heart of design is an interplay between theory and practice, between constraints and trade-offs, between designer and materials, and between designer and user/learner. Through this dialogue, meanings and artifacts are defined and understood (Dewey, 1934). The interaction is bi-directional and open-ended.

Design also requires that learners discern the essential qualities of an idea and represent it in a compelling manner. To have new ideas is more than simply labeling or thinking about the world differently; rather, it is to have a new way of *being* in the world. To have an idea is to be more fully alive with thought, feeling, and action (Dewey, 1934; Jackson, 1998). It is to have an "energy-for-action" that is directed by thought and fueled by emotion. The having of a new idea is more than the acquisition or application of information. It is, therefore, critical to have students work with ideas that are inherently empowering and generative.

Story I: Seeing the World Differently

Oscar was particularly captivated by the debate over the warm or cold-bloodedness of dinosaurs. After much research on predator to prey ratios, body mass to energy expenditure ratios, and heat dissipation and conservation anatomy and strategies, Oscar literally began to see the world through the eyes of this debate. Oscar told a story about seeing a mouse in his mother's kitchen to illustrate his new-found worldview, "See how it moves in quick, darting motions. I bet it needs to eat all the time because it expends so much energy moving in that jerking way." At our open-house, I overheard him explain to his mother, "Scientists believe these fin-backed dinosaurs actually pumped blood up in this sail-like thing to help cool off or warm up." This uniquely energizing idea had transformed Oscar's world from static observations of nature to more alive and dynamic ways of seeing and experiencing the world. In fact, Oscar enrolled in zoology class the next semester because he said he found animals interesting for the first time in his life. Design put Oscar in contact with powerful, transformative ideas in ways that led him into further inquiry and further educative experiences.

Theme II: Design as Inquiry

Design activities create opportunities to learn about the nature of inquiry itself. First, design forces students to pay attention to the process and consequences of their actions. Second, students learn to appreciate the nonlinear, often messy nature of inquiry. Design tasks are often ill-structured and afford many viable solutions. This perspective on knowledge and inquiry is quite different from the epistemological illusion typically found in classrooms, where problems are well-defined with clear-cut solutions. Additionally, to design is to engage in a fundamentally social activity. Students learn the value of communicating effectively and of attending to the experience of others. The design process requires building and negotiating ideas in a community of practice, just as ideas are generated and validated among practicing scientists. Students become experts in specific domains and share their knowledge with one another. Data gathering, validation, and accurate representation of those data force students to move beyond the constraints of their classroom, and school.

Story II: Imagining the Past

The guiding task was to present life in the Mesozoic in as much reality and detail as possible. Rachel, Heather, and Desiree thought deeply about the climate and plant life of the Mesozoic as they were assigned the task of making scenery for the walk-through diorama. They assumed their task would be to examine, and try to reproduce, artwork that portrayed dinosaurs, plant and animal life, and climate in the Mesozoic. However, after some research, they discovered that flowering plants did not appear until the Cretaceous period—no where near the Triassic period in which so many flowers appeared in our textbook! After a few more discoveries of inconsistencies, the three girls embarked on an all-out study of flora, fauna, and climate in the

Mesozoic. They wanted their contribution to the MRC to be as scientifically accurate as possible to provide the most authentic experience to visitors. Gradually, their understanding of the period developed and the scenery they produced was stunning in its accuracy and attention to detail. The opportunity to design had forced them to investigate best and most accurate ways to represent their ideas.

Theme III: Design Is Expression

Design is the process of exploring new ways of being in the world, and hence a deeply personal and expressive act. Design is an inner idea expressed outwardly—it is a private possibility acted upon publicly. Design-based activities, therefore, give students opportunities to bring their own unique interpretations to subject matter ideas. We contend that this idea stands in significant contrast with conventional schooling, where ideas are impressed rather then expressed and where, too often, artistic activity is seen as separate from scientific activity. Too often learning in science is viewed as solely cognitive. We believe the power and beauty of ideas to move and inspire is often disregarded. By allowing students to construct artifacts that are personally meaningful and communicative we allow students to tap into the aesthetic aspects of learning ideas. It allows students to develop their artistic potential as well, all within the overarching goal of developing expressive and engaging artifacts that communicate to an audience.

Story III: The Art of Science

Ruben had an incredible talent for art. Typically pensive and brooding, he wasn't interested in the difficult and academic tasks with which the rest of the class was engaged. After a few days considering options, halfhearted attempts, and dead-ends, Ruben remembered one of our goals was to share our findings with the community—in particular K–3 students from our local elementary school. Ruben posed to me his plan to author and illustrate a scientifically accurate story about a dinosaur as it moved through a day in the Cretaceous period. Ruben was able to couch his academic learning in the personal expression of his developing story. The end result was a well-written, conceptually faithful, wildly personalized and expressive story about Packy—a young Pachycephalosaur living and learning 80 million years ago. He joyfully read his story several times to different groups of young, enthusiastic MRC visitors. Ruben, who had been in trouble with the law, drugs, and violence, was newly perceived as a teacher, explorer, and artist by these young children and their parents. Ruben was clearly proud of his accomplishment and through this design process changed both his perceptions of himself and the world in ways that possibly no other school related experience had before.

Discussion

It is clear that not all design (or project based) activities have equal educational value. Merely giving students "something to construct" may keep them busy but it is unclear as to what pedagogical value exists in doing so. Elucidation of the pedagogical and psychological elements of design offer educators a framework useful in developing project-based experiences for students that can motivate, challenge and teach as well as researchers a framework for thinking more clearly about powerful classroom teaching and learning.

In this vein, valuable design based projects will be centered on important subject matter ideas that are powerful, generative, and expansive; ideas that move students to see the world in different ways. Powerful ideas lie at heart of all disciplines, though too often obscured by terminology and shallow understandings. Design based activities allow students to engage with these powerful ideas in a serious manner, and, most importantly, to act on them in ways that move students into the world engaged, curious, and poised to learn more.

Design-based learning centers learning on this goal of "acting on" an idea, both intellectually and physically. Intellectually, the designer engages with the ideas and concepts and attempts to learn more. Physically the designer works with the artifact, modifying, manipulating objects to fit the desired ends. This is essentially a dialogue between ideas and world, between theory and its application, a concept and its realization, tools and goals. This dialogue is at the heart of inquiry, involving as it does the construction of meaning and the evolution of understanding through a dialogic, transactional process. Thus, sound design-based projects carefully incorporate opportunities for inquiry within them.

Finally, design based activities hold the artistic/aesthetic aspects of learning as of equal value to the cognitive. Notions of the aesthetic are fundamental to both the intellectual and physical aspects of the design process. Intellectually, students learn to appreciate the beauty of ideas; physically, they learn the beauty of constructing an aesthetically pleasing artifact. In this view, design based projects offer students opportunities to explore affective aspects of learning and should be rewarded for doing so successfully.

Pedagogy centered on design raises important issues that effectively "raise the bar" on what a powerful, constructivist education entails. As a psychological lens, design expands definitions of teaching and learning in ways that bring other outcomes to bear on educational problems. In this way, we hope design and design-based learning enrich the work of both teachers and researchers.

Note

1. Some of the text describing the Mesozoic Resource Center has appeared previously as Author (1998). Educational Leadership.

References

Author (1998). *Educational Leadership.*

Author, & Koehler, M. J. (in press). In Y. Zhao (Ed.). *What teachers should know about technology: Perspectives and practices.*

Author, Yong, Z., & Tan, S. (1999). *Journal of Research on Computing in Education.*

Blumenfeld, P. C., Soloway, E., Marx, R. W., Krajcik, J. S., Guzdial, M., & Palincsar, A. (1991). Motivating project-based learning: Sustaining the doing, supporting the learning. *Educational Psychologist, 26* (2 & 4), 369–398.

Brown, A. L. (1992). Design experiments: theoretical and methodological challenges in creating complex interventions in classroom settings. *The Journal of the Learning Sciences 2:* 141–178.

Carver, S. (1991). *Interdisciplinary problem solving.* Paper presented at the American Educational Research Association, Chicago, IL.

Cole, M. (1997). *Cultural psychology: A once and future discipline.* Cambridge: Harvard University Press.

Collins, A. S., Brown, J. S., & Newman, S. (1990). Cognitive apprenticeship: Teaching the craft of reading, writing, and mathematics. In L. B. Resnick (Ed.), *Cognition and instruction: Issues and agendas* (p. 453–434). Hillsdale, NJ: Lawrence Erlbaum Associates.

Dewey, J. (1933). *How we think: A restatement of the relation of reflective thinking to the educative process.* Boston, MA: Heath.

Dewey, J. (1934). *Art as experience.* New York: Perigree.

Guzdial, M. (1993). *Emile: Software-realized scaffolding for science learners programming in mixed media.* Unpublished doctoral dissertation, Ann Arbor, MI: University of Michigan.

Harel, I. (1991). *Children designers.* Norwood, NJ: Ablex.

Harel, I., & Papert, S. (1990). Software design as a learning environment. *Interactive Learning Environment, 1* (1), 1–32.

Jackson, P. W. (1998). *John Dewey and the lessons of art.* New Haven: Yale University Press.

Kafai, Y., & Resnick, M. (Eds.)(1996). *Constructionism in practice: Designing, thinking and learning in a digital world.* Mahwah, NJ: Lawrence Erlbaum Associates.

Kafai, Y. (1995). *Minds in play: Computer game design as a context for children's learning.* Hillsdale, NJ: Lawrence Erlbaum Associates.

Kafai, Y. (1996). Learning design by making games: Children's development of design strategies in the creation of a complex computational artifact. In Y. Kafai & M. Resnick, (Eds.), (pp. 71–96). *Constructionism in practice: Designing, thinking and learning in a digital world.* Mahwah, NJ: Lawrence Erlbaum Associates.

Koehler, M. J., Author, Hershey, K., & Peruski, L. (under review). With a little help from your students: A new model for faculty development and online course design. *Journal of Technology and Teacher Education.*

Lave, J. & Wenger, E. (1991). *Situated learning: Legitimate peripheral participation.* New York: Cambridge University Press.

Lehrer, R. (1991). *Knowledge as design.* Paper presented at the American Educational Research Association, Chicago, IL.

Norman, D. (1991). *Dinosaur!* Upper Saddle River, NJ: Prentice Hall.

Papert, S. (1991). Situating constructionism. In I. Harel & S. Papert. (Ed.) *Constructionism.* Norwood, NJ: Ablex.

Papert, S. (1993). *The children's machine: Rethinking school in the age of the computer.* New York: Basic Books.

Pea, R. (1993). Practices of distributed intelligence and designs for education. In G. Salomon (Ed.), *Distributed cognitions: Psychological and educational considerations.* (pp. 47–87). Cambridge, UK: Cambridge University Press.

Perkins, D. N. (1986). *Knowledge as design.* Hillsdale, NJ: Lawrence Erlbaum Associates.

Roth, W.-M. (1998). *Designing communities.* Dordrecht: Kluwer Academic Publishers.

Vyas, S., & Author (2002). Experiments with design in an after-school Asian literature club. In R. Garner, M. Gillingham, Y. Zhao (Eds.). *Hanging out: After-school community based programs for children.* Greenwood Publishing Group: CT. 75–92.

Vygotsky, L. S. (1978). *Mind in society: The development of higher psychological processes.* Cambridge: Harvard University Press.

Willett, L. V. (1992). *The efficacy of using the visual arts to teach math and reading concepts.* Paper presented at the annual meeting of the American Educational Research Association, San Francisco, CA.

What Is Technology Education? A Review of the "Official Curriculum"

RYAN A. BROWN AND JOSHUA W. BROWN

"What is technology education?" Technology educators have been asked this question for many years. The field of technology education is a distinct area with a particular value for middle schools, high schools, and postsecondary institutions. Inspired by *The Clearing House*'s recent special issue on technology in education (Vol. 82, no. 2) we developed an article to answer the question of "what is technology education?" This question is entirely different than, but equally as important, as the question, "what is educational technology?" The two concepts are often confused. Discussion about public misconceptions regarding terms such as *technology education, educational technology,* and *computer literacy* can be found in the technology education literature (Dugger and Naik 2001; McCade 2001; Weber 2005). Through an analysis of the "official curriculum," this article provides education professionals in middle schools, high schools, and postsecondary settings with a brief description of the technology education curriculum by describing its educational aims, classroom elements, and context.

Official Curriculum

Over the past several decades, the technology education field has attempted to solidify the content that is taught in technology education classrooms. This new vision of technology education is presented here as an "official curriculum." The official curriculum, which Eisner labeled as the *intended curriculum,* was identified as the "formal and public course of study for which students, teachers, and schools, in one way or another, are held accountable" (1990, 63). The technology education official curriculum in this article has been determined based on the analysis of several documents that include standards and technological literacy documents (International Technology Education Association (ITEA) 2000; ITEA 2003; Indiana Department of Education 2007; National Academy of Engineering and National Research Council 2006; National Academy of Engineering and National Research Council 2002), state course guides, textbooks, monographs (Maley 1995), and numerous journal articles. The documents were analyzed and organized by modifying a framework suggested by Madaus and Kellaghan (1992). The resulting categories include the curriculum's context, broad educational aims and outcomes, and classroom elements. The findings are presented here as three basic questions: (1) What are the goals of technology education? (broad educational aims and outcomes); (2) What should technology education look like in the classroom? (class-room elements); and (3) Why is technology education important? (context).

What Are the Goals of Technology Education?

The stated goal of technology education is to "produce students with a more conceptual understanding of technology and its place in society, who can thus grasp and evaluate new bits of technology that they might never have seen before" (ITEA 2000, 4). This understanding is called *technological literacy* and is seen as both an aim and a potential outcome of technology education. It is clear in the literature that technological literacy, divided into five distinct categories by the *Standards for Technological Literacy,* is at the heart of the purpose and goals of technology education and is essentially what should be taught in technology education classrooms (ITEA 2000).

Technological Literacy

The International Technology Education Association (ITEA) states that "technological literacy is what every person needs in order to be an informed and contributing citizen for the world of today and tomorrow" (2003, 10). Gagel, in an effort to better define technological literacy, conducted a study aimed at bringing "the profession closer to a shared and deeper understanding of technological literacy" (1997, 6). He studied over two hundred frequently cited works by authors and institutions from a number of disciplines including anthropology, education, history, industry, technology, and theology to establish a clear meaning of technological literacy and found that there was little agreement on the meaning of the terms *technology* or *literacy*. Gagel's work did not develop a concrete definition of *technological literacy,* but it did determine the nature of such a notion. He concluded that technological literacy was a fluid idea, and that its utility would be judged on its ability to change or mirror evolving cultural traditions. Gagel likened technological literacy to Hirsch's concept of cultural literacy because it is difficult to list all the essential elements of both, yet both are proposed for all citizens. In the absence of a definition, Gagel concluded that if an "identity kit" were created to detect technological literacy, it would include "both technological and praxiological knowledge, a holistic understanding of technology's ambience, and a technical adaptability engendered by inventive and resourceful thinking" (25).

The National Academy of Engineering (NAE) and the National Research Council (NRC) have also attempted to define technological literacy, which they state is "more of a capacity to understand the broader technical world rather than the ability to work with specific pieces of it" (National Academy of Engineering and National Research Council 2002, 22). These organizations have identified knowledge, critical thinking and decision making, and capabilities as the three dimensions of technological literacy. The knowledge dimension includes the basic nature and fundamental concepts of technology. The understanding of technological benefits, risks, and trade-offs, and participation in discussions and debates constitute the critical thinking and decision-making dimension. The capabilities dimension consists of being able to use the design process, troubleshoot a mechanical or technological problem, and effectively use technology (National Academy of Engineering and National Research Council 2002; National Academy of Engineering and National Research Council 2006). Lastly, ITEA defines technological literacy as the ability to use, manage, evaluate, and understand technology (ITEA 2006).

When technological literacy was initially introduced as a goal of technology education, the creation of a deeper and more meaningful definition of technological literacy was seen as "an unexpectedly complex and difficult task" (Gagel 1997, 6). Schultz claimed that developing technological literacy in students is a "noble, but darn-near-impossible-to-achieve goal" (1999, 83). The outcome of technological literacy is, in reality, very difficult to assess. The National Academy of Engineering and the National Research Council state that the "assessment of technological literacy in the United States is in its infancy" (National Academy of Engineering and National Research Council 2006, 7).

Technology Education Standards

A more tangible and visible outcome of technology education resides in the content identified in the Standards for Technological Literacy ITEA 2000). The official curricula of the technology education field are outlined largely in standards that, in essence, identify the knowledge that is needed for students to achieve the educational aims of the official curriculum. The Standards for Technological Literacy promote what students should know and be able to do to gain technological literacy and, in the process, they attempt to clear up confusion about the aims of technology education. The standards are organized into five major categories: nature of technology, technology and society, design, abilities for a technological world, and the designed world. Each category includes three to seven content standards, with a total of twenty standards for technological literacy overall. The standards are then broken down into a number of benchmarks for students in grades K–2, 3–5, 6–8, and 9–12.

The *nature of technology category* encompasses the understanding that technology extends potential human knowledge and includes knowledge, process, and artifacts. This category has similarities to the work of Carl Mitcham, a philosopher of technology, which stated that technology can be conceptualized using four main approaches: objects, knowledge, actions, and volition (de Vries 2005). This category also defines the main concepts of technology as systems, resources, requirements, optimization, processes, controls, and trade-offs. The linkage between technology and other subject areas, such as science, mathematics, and social studies, is also addressed by a standard in the nature of technology category (ITEA 2000).

The standards in the second category, *technology and society,* focus on the influence, role, and effects of technology. This category addresses the desirable and undesirable cultural, social, economic, and political effects of technology. Students also learn about the effects of technology on the environment and the values and beliefs that the use and development of technology reflect. Last, students are introduced to the history of the development of technology (ITEA 2000).

The third category relates to *design*. This group of standards focuses on the attributes of design, the engineering design process, and methods of problem solving. Design attributes include criteria, constraints, optimization, creativity, and the creation of possible solutions. Engineering design is presented as a process in which a designer identifies a problem, generates ideas, creates and tests prototypes, and then builds a final solution. In this category, students learn that problem solving involves processes such as research and development, invention and innovation, and experimentation (ITEA 2000). Design is an area that has been debated throughout the history of the field and is seen as "arguably the single most important content category set forth in the standards" (Lewis and Zuga 2005, 52).

The *abilities for a technical world* category continues the theme of design and includes other abilities that students should develop in technology education curricula. The first standard is the ability to apply the design process and solve technical problems. Skills in this standard include measuring, sketching, drawing, and computer skills. The second ability is to use and maintain technological products and systems, and it consists of using tools and processes to troubleshoot, test, diagnose, and use technological artifacts. The final ability required is the development of the capacity to assess the impact of products and systems. Forecasting, analyzing trends, and determining benefits and risks are all skills that are grouped under the ability to assess technology (ITEA 2000).

The *designed world* is the final and largest category of the Standards for Technological Literacy. The seven standards of this category each focus on one of the following areas: medicine, agriculture, energy and power, information and communication, transportation, manufacturing, and construction. Students that attain the benchmarks in this category will be able to select, use, and understand technologies from one of these seven areas. For example, regarding the transportation standard, students should understand transportation and vehicular systems, have experience designing and using transportation systems, and be able to discuss the positive and negative impacts of transportation technology (ITEA 2000). The areas represent the ways in which humankind uses technology and are sometimes referred to as the *contexts of technology*.

What Should Technology Education Look Like?

The official curriculum, as the question implies, includes the actions that take place inside the classroom, where teaching and learning occur. It comprises Madaus and Kellaghan's (1992) *objectives of specific curricula,*
curricular materials, and *transactions and processes* categories, as well as assessment. This article presents a discussion of instructional methods and strategies, and assessment techniques.

Instructional Methods and Strategies

The technology education literature includes a number of suggestions regarding what technology education should "look like" and how students should learn about technology. Many of the references to teaching technology education revolve around the idea of student engagement. The descriptors "hands-on, minds-on education" and "action-based" are often used to describe technology education courses. Students should be engaged in cognitive and psychomotor activities that foster critical thinking, decision making, and problem solving (ITEA 2003). Activity-based learning is the main approach of technology education.

Design and problem-solving activities are strongly encouraged in the technology education literature. Students should be given opportunities to solve practical, "real-world" problems, and they should be engaged in the design process. Students in technology education courses should also be given the opportunity to use and maintain technological products (ITEA 2005a). *Realizing Excellence* (ITEA 2005b) calls for students to examine ideas from several perspectives, and several of the standards include affective elements, but, as a whole, methods to teach those aspects are not easily found in the technology education curriculum. The importance of affective learning is aptly described by de Vries, who labels technology education as a "poor situation if a technology is taught without any kind of reflection, just as a collection of bits and pieces of knowledge and skill" (2005, 8).

Assessment

Student assessment is fairly well described in *Advancing Excellence in Technological Literacy* (ITEA 2003), in which it is divided into five assessment standards. The document states that both formative and summative assessment should be used in program enhancement and to gauge student learning and inform teachers of the effectiveness of instruction. Although the official curriculum lacks instructional methods for the affective domain, all three domains are covered in the assessment category.

According to the official curriculum, student assessment should be consistent with the Standards for Technological Literacy and should "include cognitive learning elements for solving technological problems. . . [and] psychomotor learning elements for applying technology. . . and [they should] guide student abilities to operate within the affective domain" (ITEA 2003, 21). Cognitive assessment is designed to allow students to describe and apply their knowledge. Assessment of psychomotor learning should be performance-based and should allow the students to use and apply their tactile knowledge and skills. Affective domain assessment should require students to demonstrate their knowledge of impacts and consequences of technology, as well as their understanding of critical perspectives (ITEA 2003).

The Standards for Technological Literacy (ITEA 2000) also lists potential assessment tools such as daily records of student work, quizzes, tests, portfolios, and standardized tests. Demonstrations, design briefs, prototyping, multiple-choice and true-false tests, projects, and self and peer assessments are also identified as possible assessment tools in technology education courses (ITEA 2004). The assessment tools should aid technology teachers in checking student understanding and ensuring that students are reaching the desired outcomes.

Why Is Technology Education Important?

The focus on technological literacy and the creation of the Standards for Technological Literacy comes at a time in history when technology and technological advancements have taken center stage in our society. Bybee, however, suggests that "in contrast to the dominant role of technology in society[,] one finds a citizenry with little knowledge and understanding of technology" (2003, 26). ITEA (2006) warns of a widening gap between people who use technology, the average citizen, and the inventors and designers that create technology. As technology continues to become more advanced, "society has become more specialized. As a result, all of us know more about fewer things" (National Academy of Engineering and National Research Council 2002, 49).

This lack of understanding of and connection with technology is evident in two Gallup polls conducted to determine the public's view of technology and technological literacy (Rose and Dugger 2002; Rose et al. 2004). The studies found that 98 percent of all Americans polled believed that it was either *somewhat* or *very important* to understand and use technology. Eighty-eight percent recognized the importance of knowing how various technologies work, and approximately 90 percent believed it is important to know whether it is better to repair or throw away products and to be able to develop solutions to practical technological problems (Rose et al. 2004).

These findings imply that society is interested in being able to understand and use technology. The respondents, however, generally felt uninformed and believed they had little influence in technological decisions. Nearly half

of those surveyed believed they were either *not very* or *not at all* informed about various technologies, and over 60 percent of respondents stated that they have little or no influence in regards to technological issues such as automobile efficiency, road construction in the community, and genetically modified foods. Finally, when asked specifically about technology education, respondents were nearly unanimous in stating that technology education, as defined by the ITEA, should be included in the school curriculum, and almost two-thirds believed that it should be required for high school graduation (Rose et al. 2004).

If this poll is representative of society as a whole, then it would be fair to say that there is general agreement that technology and technology education are important to society. That being the case, Zilbert and Mercer (1992) still found that technology has no well-defined place in the curriculum taught to most students. Understanding technology and becoming technologically literate are believed to help students achieve a better understanding of the technological society in which they live, not through vocational or specific job training, but by developing a holistic understanding of technology (Seemann 2003).

Gagel (1997) suggests that a technologically literate person is someone who can stay abreast of new technology, solve technical problems, use technology effectively, and assess its impacts. Being technologically literate and understanding technology is also believed to benefit students personally, socially, and academically. The personal values found in the literature include exploring interests, achieving a feeling of success, developing both problem-solving and interpersonal skills, and developing "a broad sense of career awareness" (Maley 1995, 7). In regard to personal development, ITEA states that "people benefit both at work and at home by being able to choose the best products for their purposes, to operate the products properly, and to troubleshoot them when something goes wrong" (2000, 2).

The societal values attributed to technology education are "those contributions that enhance and strengthen the individual's capabilities of functioning effectively as a citizen in a democratic, technological society" (Maley 1995, 3). These values include learning the skills required for proper selection and assessment of technology, developing informed citizens, heightening awareness of the social and environmental impacts of technology, and questioning the use, value, and abuse of technology. In support of the value of questioning technology, Gilberti says:

In a democracy, citizens and consumers are continually being asked to make evaluations of the applications and limitations of technology to human wants, desires, and problems. By providing students with the skills to evaluate the appropriateness of various technological devices and fixes, the curriculum area of technology education helps to promote a more just and sustainable future. (quoted in Maley 1995, 16)

The final area of values that can be attributed to technology education's official curriculum is academic values. These values "provide enrichment of the academic experience as well as its relevance—personal and social" (Maley 1995, 3). These values include the relevant integration of other subjects, the development of technological skills and understanding, the connection between theoretical and practical knowledge, the understanding of history and evolution of technology, and the development of inquiry, research, and problem-solving skills.

Conclusions

The personal, social, and academic values that have been attributed to technology, like technological literacy, are both very ambitious and difficult to quantify. They are, however, present in the "official curriculum," as are the answers to the questions posed throughout this article: what are our goals, how should we teach technology education, and why is it important. Teachers, administrators, and those interested in the difference between technology education and educational technology need only review the curricular documents to discover that there is an "official curriculum" of technology education. In doing so, they will find that the broad educational aims and outcomes of technology education focus on the goal of attaining technological literacy within the areas of the Standards for Technological Literacy. Instructional methods of the official curriculum focus mainly on student engagement with the subject of technology in activities, design problems, and problem-solving opportunities, while other methods discussed include presentations, debates, journals, and discussions. Teachers will also discover that student assessment should be designed to correspond with the aims of technology education and should measure students' understanding and abilities in the cognitive, psychomotor, and affective domains. Finally, it is clear that technology education can contribute to a range of personal, social, and academic values.

References

Bybee, R. 2003. Fulfilling a promise. *The Technology Teacher* 62(6): 23–26.

de Vries, M. J. 2005. *Teaching about technology.* Dordrecht, The Netherlands: Springer.

Dugger, W., and N. Naik. 2001. Clarifying misconceptions between technology education and educational technology. *The Technology Teacher* 61(1): 31–35.

Eisner, E. 1990. Creative curriculum development and practice. *Journal of Curriculum and Supervision* 6(1): 62–73.

Gagel, C. W. 1997. Literacy and technology: Reflections and insights for technological literacy. *Journal of Industrial Teacher Education* 34(3): 6–34.

Hirsch, Jr., E. D. 1998. *Cultural literacy: What every American needs to know.* New York: Vintage Books.

Indiana Department of Education. 2007. *Technology education content standards.* Indiana Department of Education 2004. www.doe.state.in.us/standards/docs-Technology/ 2006–08-15-TechEd-Stds.pdf (accessed March 13, 2007).

International Technology Education Association (ITEA). 2000. *Standards for technological literacy: Content for the study of technology.* Reston, VA: ITEA.

——. 2003. *Advancing excellence in technological literacy: Student assessment, professional development, and program standards.* Reston, VA: ITEA.

——. 2004. *Measuring progress: Assessing students for technological literacy.* Reston, VA: ITEA.

——. 2005a. *Planning learning: Developing technology curricula.* Reston, VA: ITEA.

——. 2005b. *Realizing excellence: Structuring technology programs.* Reston, VA: ITEA.

——. 2006. *Technological literacy for all: A rationale and structure for the study of technology.* Reston, VA: ITEA.

Lewis, T., and K. Zuga. 2005. A conceptual framework of ideas and issues in technology education: National Science Foundation. http://teched.vt.edu/ctte/ImagesPDFs/ ConceptualFramework2005.pdf (accessed December 28, 2009).

Madaus, G., and T. Kellaghan. 1992. Curriculum evaluation and assessment. In *Handbook of research on curriculum,* ed P. Jackson, 119–154. New York: Macmillan.

Maley, D., ed. 1995. *Quotations in support of technology education: A compendium of positive outcome that may be attributed to an effective program in the area of technology education.* Reston, VA: Council on Technology Teacher Education.

McCade, J. 2001. Technology education and computer literacy. *The Technology Teacher* 61(2): 9–13.

——. 2002. *Technically speaking: Why all Americans need to know more about technology.* Washington, DC: National Academy Press.

National Academy of Engineering and National Research Council. 2006. *Tech tally: Approaches to assessing technological literacy.* Washington, DC: National Academy Press.

Rose, L., and W. Dugger. 2002. ITEA/Gallup poll reveals what Americans think about technology. *The Technology Teacher* 61(6): 1–8.

Rose, L., A. Gallup, W. Dugger, and K. Starkweather. 2004. The second installment of the ITEA/Gallup poll and what it reveals as to how Americans think about technology. *The Technology Teacher* 61(8): 1–8.

Schultz, A. E. 1999. What we teach and why we teach it. *Journal of Industrial Teacher Education* (1), http://scholar.lib.vt.edu/ ejournals/JITE/v37n1/schultz.html (accessed March 14, 2008).

Seemann, K. 2003. Basic principles in holistic technology education. *Journal of Technology Education* 14(2): 28–39.

Weber, K. 2005. A proactive approach to technological literacy. *The Technology Teacher* 64(7): 28–30.

Zilbert, E., and J. Mercer. 1992. *Technology competence: Learner goals for all Minnesotans.* St. Paul, MN: Minnesota State Council on Vocational Technical Education.

Critical Thinking

1. What is meant by "technological literacy"? Multiple perspectives and definitions are presented in the article—what common themes do they share?

2. The authors present five categories of technology standards. Briefly describe each one.

3. Explain how you would integrate technology into a specific lesson/unit. Identify which of the five standards you are supporting and how the use of technology in the lesson is aligned with that standard.

4. Technology has often been touted as the great "panacea" that will level the educational playing field and eliminate gaps between higher achieving and lower achieving groups of students. Do you agree? Why or why not? What potential do you see in terms of the impact of technology in schools?

5. What social and ethical issues do you think need to be considered as schools seek new ways to integrate technology education?

RYAN A. BROWN is an assistant professor in the Department of Curriculum and Instruction, Illinois State University, Normal, IL. **JOSHUA W. BROWN** is an assistant professor in the Department of Technology, Illinois State University, Normal, IL.

Plagiarism in the Internet Age

Using sources with integrity is complex. The solution is teaching skills, not vilifying the Internet.

REBECCA MOORE HOWARD AND LAURA J. DAVIES

Many teachers see plagiarism as a simple, black-and-white issue. Teachers often bring up the topic at the beginning of a research paper unit, discuss it in one classroom period, and never say the word *plagiarism* again unless students are caught copying, when this term is dragged out once more to accuse and punish the guilty. Teachers warn students not to copy—or else—and present them with citation guides and the trinity of techniques to write using others' research without plagiarizing: quoting, paraphrasing, and summarizing. The onus then falls on the students, who are expected to use these techniques well, assuming that they know how to do so.

In an age when students gravitate to online sources for research—and when tremendous amounts of both reputable and questionable information are available online—many have come to regard the Internet itself as a culprit in students' plagiarism. Some teachers go so far as to forbid students from researching online, in the mistaken assumption that if students are working from hard-copy sources only, the problem will disappear.

We believe that an approach far different from either warnings and punishment or attempts to curtail online research is warranted. Teachers who wish to prevent plagiarism should devote extensive instruction to the component tasks of writing from sources. This instruction should focus on the supposedly simple technique of summarizing sources, which is in truth not simple. Many students are far from competent at summarizing an argument—and students who cannot summarize are the students most likely to plagiarize.

Our argument may seem innocuous, but it profoundly contradicts widely shared attitudes. Most approaches to confronting plagiarism start from the premise that it is something to prevent simply by imparting information and "getting tough." A didactic children's book and accompanying instructor's manual that we saw recently exemplified this premise. The book told the tale of a young student who unknowingly plagiarizes by copying information from an online source into her report on the American Revolution. The teacher in this tale uses the incident to teach students that using others' words without attribution is a serious crime. He then emphasizes to students the importance of citation and source integration techniques and enlists the school librarian to model how to cite outside works used in a piece of writing.

Instructional materials like these imply that teachers can stop inappropriate use of sources through three strategies: (1) teaching students from early grades the nuts and bolts of crediting all sources they use; (2) designing plagiarism-proof assignments that spell out how works should be cited and that include personal reflection and alternative final projects like creating a brochure; and (3) communicating to students that you're laying down the law on plagiarism ("I'll be on the lookout for this in your papers, you know").

However, good writing from sources involves more than competent citation of sources. It is a complicated activity, made even more complex by easy access to a seemingly limitless number of online sources. Any worthwhile guide to preventing plagiarism should

- Discuss intellectual property and what it means to "own" a text.
- Discuss how to evaluate both online and print-based sources (for example, comparing the quality and reliability of a website created by an amateur with the reliability of a peer-reviewed scholarly article).
- Guide students through the hard work of engaging with and understanding their sources, so students don't conclude that creating a technically perfect bibliography is enough.
- Acknowledge that teaching students how to write from sources involves more than telling students that copying is a crime and handing them a pile of source citation cards.

Students don't need threats; students need pedagogy. That pedagogy should both teach source-reading skills and take into consideration our increasingly wired world. And it should communicate that plagiarism is wrong in terms of what society values about schools and learning, not just in terms of arbitrary rules.

Students don't need threats; students need pedagogy.

The Blame-the-Internet Game

Many commentators point to easy accessibility of a plethora of information on the Web as a chief cause of student plagiarism. Researcher Sue Carter Simmons (1999) quickly dispels that myth: Students have been systematically plagiarizing since at least the 19th century Doris Dant's 1986 survey of high school students, conducted well before the Internet became a cultural phenomenon, confirms this finding: Eighty percent of the high school students Dant surveyed reported having "copied some to most of their reports," although 94 percent said they had received instruction in attribution of sources. The Internet is at most a complication in a long-standing dynamic.

The Internet is at most a complication in a long-standing dynamic.

However, certain features of online research may affect how plagiarism creeps into writing, and it's little wonder that educators are alarmed by the potential of the Internet to encourage unlawful copying. The Internet offers a host of downloadable text for nefarious cheaters and desperate procrastinators alike. And because text can be easily appropriated through cutting and pasting, it is easy for well-intentioned students to overlook the boundaries between what they themselves have produced and what they have slid from one screen (their Internet browser) to another (their word-processed document). As the writer leaps ahead, brainstorming creatively while reading various online sources, he or she may not pause to insert quotation marks and citations, fully intending to do that later. And "later" never comes.

Little wonder, too, that educators are turning to a combination of severe punishments for infractions and automated plagiarism-detecting services such as Turnitin.com to discourage inappropriate copying from online temptations. But trying to legislate the wired world simply won't work.

What *Will* Work
Start with Values

Teachers need to focus attention on the entire set of activities involved in using outside sources in writing. Review with students the values and precepts that are still valid in the era of literacy 2.0. One of these precepts is that through formal education, people learn skills they can apply elsewhere—but taking shortcuts lessens such learning.

Educators should also communicate why writing is important. Through writing, people learn, communicate with one another, and discover and establish their own authority and identity. Even students who feel comfortable with collaboration and uneasy with individual authorship need to realize that acknowledged collaboration—such as a coauthored article like this one—is very different from unacknowledged use of another person's work. The line between the two is not always bright, but it does exist.

These values and precepts are at risk when student writers plagiarize. A student who plagiarizes is undermining his or her community's ethics, jeopardizing his or her authority, and erasing his or her identity. That student is missing an opportunity to become a better researcher and writer and is probably not learning whatever the assignment was designed to teach.

Guide Students in Online Research

Many of us must first learn methods of online research ourselves. We know the principles of good research, but we may not be experienced in applying those principles to an online environment, and we can't assume that students are, either.

How much unattributed copying from online sources, for example, derives from poor source selection? If students don't know how to find good sources online, they will enter a search term in Google and look only at the first few sources that come up. Consulting only general sources, and therefore going no deeper than a general understanding of the topic, students "can't think of any other way to say it," so they copy.

Teachers should also address how to use Wikipedia as a source rather than banning it. Even if it's forbidden as a source, many students will consult Wikipedia because it provides a starting point for research on an unfamiliar topic. Students who don't know how to dig deeper have their hands tied because they can't cite a significant source of their research—and then they are busted for plagiarizing from Wikipedia. It may be more useful to assign a research project for which you tell students to begin with Wikipedia but then guide them in how to find more varied, deeper sources of information using library databases such as EBSCO, LexisNexis, or ProQuest to verify Wikipedia's claims. You can make this project entertaining by beginning with a Wikipedia entry you have chosen for its flaws or incorrect information. For example, according to the *New York Times,* actor/director Clint Eastwood, a happy omnivore, was shocked to discover that the Wikipedia entry on him said he followed a vegan diet (Headlam, 2008).

Teach Summarizing

K–16 teachers must spend more time teaching students how to read critically and how to write about their sources. Rodrigue, Serviss, and Howard (2007) studied papers written by 18 college sophomores in a required research writing course, reading not only the 18 papers but also all the sources cited in them. The researchers discovered that all the papers included some mishandling of sources—absence of citation, absence of quotation marks, paraphrases too close to the source language—and some mishandling was extensive. More significant, they found that none of the 18 papers contained any *summary* of the overall argument of a source. Many student writers paraphrased adequately, restating a passage in their own language in approximately the same number of words, but none of them used fresh language to condense, by at least

50 percent, a passage from a source text of a paragraph or more in length. When these student writers did use a longer passage, they did so by copying the entire paragraph, with or without citation.

These sophomores at a well-regarded college worked at the sentence level only, selecting and replicating isolated sentences and weaving them into their arguments. This puts the writer at great risk of inappropriate copying. A writer who works only at the sentence level must always quote or paraphrase. The paraphrase will sometimes veer too closely to the language of the source, and quotations may accumulate in such quantity that the writer feels the need to conceal some of them, for fear the paper will sound too much like a tissue of quotations (which indeed it is).

Teachers often forget how difficult summarizing another writer's argument is. Miguel Roig (2001) demonstrated that even professors who are expert writers have difficulty summarizing texts on unfamiliar topics. How great, then, is the task confronting our students, who regularly read texts on unfamiliar topics? We could assign only easy, familiar texts, but that would bring the educational project to an abrupt halt. Our task is instead to teach students strategies for entering and participating in the challenging topics and texts that we assign them.

Such instruction might begin with techniques of paraphrase. Sue Shirley (2004) has developed a series of steps through which she takes college students. She begins by explaining that inserting synonyms is not paraphrasing. She then guides students in studying a passage and identifying its key words and main ideas that must be retained to paraphrase the passage. Shirley shows her students poor paraphrases of the passage for them to critique. Finally, she has them write their own paraphrase of a 50- to 100-word source passage that they themselves choose.

With well-practiced paraphrasing skills, students are ready to work on summarizing. Similar pedagogy can be used for this exercise. How long and challenging the source text is will depend on the level of students' education, but students should be guided through identifying key terms and major ideas, with the goal of being able not just to restate an idea but to understand a text so well that they can compress it by at least 50 percent.

These practices are essential to successful researched writing and are also excellent techniques for critical reading. If we fail to teach these skills, our students will always be in peril of plagiarism, notwithstanding all the pricey plagiarism-detecting software we employ and all the threats we make.

References

Dant, D. (1986). Plagiarism in high school: A survey. *English Journal, 75*(2), 81–84.

Headlam, B. (2008, December 14). The Films Are For Him. Got That? *The New York Times,* p. AR1.

Rodrigue, T., Serviss, P., & Howard, R. (2007, November). *Plagiarism isn't the issue: Understanding students' source use.* Paper presented at the annual meeting of the National Council of Teachers of English, New York.

Roig, M. (2001). Plagiarism and paraphrasing criteria of college and university professors. *Ethics and Behavior, 11*(3), 307–324.

Shirley, S. (2004). The art of paraphrase. *Teaching English in the two-year college 22*(2), 186–189.

Simmons, S. (1999). Competing notions of authorship: A historical look at students and textbooks on plagiarism and cheating. In F. Buranen & A. Roy (Eds), *Perspectives on plagiarism and intellectual property in a postmodern world* (pp. 41–54). Albany, NY: SUNY Press.

Critical Thinking

1. Using the links provided in the Unit Overview, review the information on plagiarism and intellectual property presented by the Online Writing Lab (OWL) at Purdue University and the World Intellectual Property Organization (WIPO). Once you have finished reviewing the information, write a summary about intellectual property and plagiarism, being sure to use proper citations for the two sources when necessary. (Information on citing sources can also be found on the OWL website.)

2. Go to your institution's library page and look for links to resources about writing research papers, plagiarism, and citing sources. Write a brief critique summarizing what resources and information were provided, how easy they were to locate and access, and how clearly and thoroughly you think the information is presented.

3. Develop a 15-minute lesson to teach students in your age/grade level and or content area about intellectual property and plagiarism.

4. Read *The Art of Paraphrase,* by Sue Shirley (citation listed in the references) and use the framework she presents to design an activity for your students.

5. Reflect on how things like online blogs and wikis may have influenced or changed the perception of what constitutes "intellectual property."

Rebecca Moore Howard is Associate Professor in the Writing Program at Syracuse University, in Syracuse, New York; rehoward@syr.edu. **Laura J. Davies** is a doctoral student in composition and cultural rhetoric at Syracuse University; ljdavies@syr.edu.

R U Safe?

Who better to teach young adolescents about online dangers than other adolescents?

JOHANNA MUSTACCHI

I t's not just on the bus or during recess anymore. Bullying can happen the minute our students wake up, can creep in during class time, and can continue after the school day ends—and then follow them home, right into their bedrooms.

My generation was safe from the pressures of peer judgment and abuse once we arrived home from school (the class bully would never actually call your house back then). But cyberspace has no boundaries, and students today have only their wits to protect them from teasing, harassment, and threats that can reach them online anytime.

What I call *cyberabuse* is rampant at school, adding to the old-fashioned face-to-face taunting and power plays that take place among students. (I use the term *cyber* rather than *Internet* to include all mobile communication devices.) Such abuse even goes on as we teach. I once confiscated cell phones from two students who were texting each other during another teacher's class. They showed me the conversation, which was full of insults and vulgar language.

According to a series of studies conducted by the *Journal of Adolescent Health,* more than 80 percent of adolescents own at least one form of new media technology, which they use to communicate with one another, present information about themselves, and share new media creations. The studies examined the relationships among bullying, harassment, and aggression among youth and how these issues translated to electronic media. According to one of these studies (Kowalski & Limber, 2007), which surveyed almost 4,000 middle school students, 11 percent had been electronically bullied at least once in the two months preceding the questionnaire, and 7 percent admitted to being both a bully and a victim. Another study (Williams & Guerra, 2007) showed that electronic bullying peaks in middle school and is inflicted most often through instant messaging, although bullying occurs frequently through text messaging, e-mails, chat rooms, and content on websites.

The *Journal of Adolescent Health* research revealed that some state education departments—in Florida, South Carolina, Utah, Oregon, and Washington—have created policies to combat online harassment (David-Ferdon & Hertz, 2007). But many of the authors agreed that stopping adolescents'

use of electronic media in school or installing blocking and filtering software does not adequately address this pervasive problem.

Ideally, we should convince all students to abstain from bullying, and we certainly must try to do so. But it is equally crucial to arm students with the tools they need to protect themselves from bullying, particularly now that bullies take advantage of far-reaching online tools. As a middle school teacher, I've found that a powerful way to arm students against cyberbullying is to have them research some aspect of this phenomenon and then teach others what they have learned—or directly experienced—as they navigate the online world.

Getting Students Talking . . .

During my first year teaching media literacy at the Pierre Van Cortlandt Middle School in Croton-on-Hudson, New York, I developed a unit on social networking sites and cyberbullying. For the culminating project, 8th grade students wrote and performed skits portraying a cyberbullying incident, including the motivation for the incident, the consequences, and any resolution the players came to. "Can we curse?" students asked, amazed that I wanted them to show the real deal. My response: Make it realistic.

On the day students presented their skits to their classmates, I called in some reserves: the school psychologist, guidance counselor, student assistance counselor, and our school's drug abuse resistance education officer (a member of our local law enforcement department). The skits raised important issues that captured every student's interest: body image, "stealing" boyfriends and girlfriends, and threats of violence. They also raised anxious questions. My professional colleagues provided advice for students, and the police officer explained legal consequences and how extensively the police will get involved.

Many parents thanked the school for exposing their children to these issues as part of their education. And when school personnel saw how much students had to say—and ask—about online bullying, the seeds were sown for more comprehensive teaching about cybercitizenship. Principal Barbara Ulm had already received numerous requests for help from parents of students in 5th and 6th grades who had been targeted in cyberspace by other students. She asked me to develop a full-blown Internet safety curriculum for the school's 6th, 7th, and 8th graders.

. . . and Getting Them Teaching

When I began implementing this curriculum the next fall, I noticed how much the 8th graders knew and were eager to impart to one another—with almost desperate urgency. As if riding a rollercoaster, students relayed stories and advice to one another, hitting highs and lows at breakneck speed. They were experts in some aspects of online interaction and risks but complete novices in others. I realized that their knowledge and thirst to exchange information provided a rare opportunity. So I charged my 8th grade students with the job of teaching my 6th graders.

As any middle school teacher knows, there is a vast difference in development between a 6th grader and an 8th grader. The first is a child; the second a young adult. The first wants to emulate the second; 6th graders literally and figuratively look up to their older schoolmates. Most 8th graders realize this and feel a tangible sense of responsibility as role models. These are perfect conditions for motivating older students to present information on a public safety issue—and getting younger students to take it seriously.

One research study showed that electronic bullying peaks in middle school.

Eighth graders first learn *netiquette*—appropriate, courteous online behavior and communication. Students discuss their own definitions of appropriate online behavior. My 8th graders have identified a number of rules, including (1) If you wouldn't say it to the person's face, don't say it online; (2) Be careful with sarcasm—it can be misread; and (3) Be extra careful about what you say online because your audience can't hear tone or see facial expressions.

I then describe certain deviations from appropriate behavior and how to recognize these deviations and safeguard against becoming a victim or perpetrator. I divide 8th graders into groups and make each group responsible for researching one subtopic and creating an engaging 15-minute lesson to deliver to a 6th grade class.[1]

The first year we tried this, students wrote lessons on flaming, phishing, cyberbullying, cyberharassment, cyberbullying or harassment by proxy, and online grooming. They created a list of definitions of these terms followed by succinct advice for coping with each one, which they handed out to 6th graders (see "The Student Guide to Stamping Out Cyberabuse"). Students created PowerPoint presentations, SmartBoard drawings, diagrams, and graphics. They incorporated into their presentations online media they found about cyberbullying, such as videos from TeacherTube.com and the group Netsmartz.org. (One

powerful resource they found is a British-made public service announcement video available on YouTube called "Think U Know" that shows a young girl reporting a predatory online groomer.) They shared surveys, bookmarks, and a list of Internet safety tips with their peers.

I also infused the unit with instruction in public speaking, and on the day of the presentations, I assessed each student on his or her presentation, including organization, content knowledge, mechanics, delivery, and the quality of visual aids.

As you might expect, every 8th grade student rose to the occasion, even the most traditionally reluctant participants. Their talks, materials, and activities kept the younger students fully engaged. They asked questions and got their peers to think and reflect, sometimes with creative tactics.

For example, one group burst into the classroom in a friendly manner. They handed out lollipops and asked 6th graders to fill out a questionnaire providing their e-mail passwords, addresses, phone numbers, and parents' and siblings' names, explaining that they needed this information for their presentation. The older students handily made their point about how online groomers befriend victims first to gain their trust.

The "teachers" alerted their students to how seemingly innocuous messages can be precursors to harassment and abuse. In addition to showing realistic examples of bullying and aggressive communiqués, they also informed their younger counterparts about protective tools, like procedures that block certain messages or senders, privacy settings, and logistics for reporting incidents to an Internet service provider. In a clever twist, one group included in their PowerPoint presentation the kinds of questions a groomer might send, leaving the victim's answers blank. They asked 6th graders to write how they would respond to the messages.

Some 8th graders later told me they had been very nervous during their presentations, but it wasn't evident at the time. Students displayed a mature understanding of the seriousness of their responsibility. As Dylan noted in his final reflection,

> Presenting to the 6th graders helped me realize how easily kids will give out their information for a small prize. . . . It's important to always educate kids on Internet safety.

Emily reflected:

> I found it really interesting to hear the 6th graders' responses to our questions and to see their faces as they slowly realized the truth with some parts of the Internet. I was glad to see that they took this seriously, and not as a joke. . . . We wanted to scare them, and we did just that. We wanted to show them that this does happen to people all over, and it could very easily happen to them if they are not careful.

6th Graders Reflect and Respond

Following the 8th graders' cybersafety lessons, I asked my 6th grade students to write an article about the experience for our upcoming class newspaper. This fit in well with my 6th grade

The Student Guide to Stamping out Cyberabuse

The 150 8th grade students at Pierre Van Cortlandt Middle School collaboratively wrote these definitions of aggressive communication practices in cyberspace, as well as tips for handling each one.

Flaming

When someone insults someone else, usually by e-mail, instant message, or text message. To prevent flaming, do not respond, save the messages so you can show a trusted adult, and don't worry if the message is from someone you don't know or recognize; there are ways to track the person down.

Phishing

An attempt to get your personal information by pretending to be a site you are familiar with or trust. Always be sure you know where your e-mails come from. Don't give information over the Internet to sites that don't look valid.

Cyberbullying

A child bullying another child on the Internet. Bullying involves repeated put-downs, insults, and threats, with the emphasis on *repeated.* If you get bullied, tell an adult that you trust. To avoid this situation, do NOT talk to people on the Internet whom you don't know.

Cyberharassment

Harassment through the Internet that involves an adult. An adult can harass a child, a child can harass an adult, and an adult can harass another adult.

Cyberbullying or Harassment by Proxy

(1) When cyberbullies get someone else (or several people) to do their dirty work, or (2) When a bully intentionally provokes a victim to lash back to get the victim in trouble. If this happens to you, don't lash back. Contact your Internet service provider, talk to an adult, or talk to your friends about it.

Online Grooming

When a predator builds an online relationship with a child by giving compliments or a "shoulder to lean on" or sending gifts until the child trusts the predator. Typical "grooming" lines include

- Where is the computer in the house?
- Are your parents around much?
- You can always talk to me.
- I'm always here for you.
- You don't deserve how they treat you.
- You have a great personality.
- You're beautiful. You should be a model.

To protect yourself from a groomer, (1) always know whom you are talking to online, (2) don't give out personal information, (3) don't post seductive or inappropriate pictures of yourself or others online, (4) never meet up in person with anyone you meet online, and (5) talk with your parents if you feel suspicious about something online.

8th Graders' Top Ten Internet Safety Tips

1. Don't give out personal information.
2. Don't talk to anybody you don't know.
3. Use a secure password.
4. Don't give your password to anybody.
5. Be careful about what you post online.
6. Don't put pictures of yourself online.
7. Tell someone if you get cyberbullied.
8. Be honest.
9. Don't click on pop-ups.
10. Only go to sites you know are safe.

media literacy curriculum that year, which focused on print media. It was a perfect opportunity to teach "angle" in journalistic writing. I encouraged students to come at the experience from any vantage point that felt relevant to them and to experiment with different types of articles. They had ample material to draw from because they all took notes during the presentations and received handouts from the 8th grade "teachers."

Students rose to the challenge of choosing varied angles and formats: straight news about the fact that students were teaching students, reviews of the lessons and the 8th graders' teaching skills, an Internet safety advice column, editorials on different subtopics, and informational features on how to protect yourself from online dangers. The pieces they created—such as this excerpt from Rita's article "Staying Safe Online"—show that they took in what their older peers imparted to them:

> The most serious of the online dangers is grooming. Grooming usually happens over instant messaging and e-mail. The 8th graders taught the 6th graders that grooming is when someone tries to create an emotional relationship with another person who is usually younger than them. The reason grooming is so dangerous is because the "groomer" potentially wants to meet the victim in person and abuse or kidnap them.

Another 6th grade student, Sean, wrote,

> With the computer age booming, PCs everywhere are catching fire. But it's not because of unsafe wiring; it's the work of one of the most basic forms of cyberbullying: flaming. Flaming is like an emotional bacteria—small, short

sentences, sometimes casual, sometimes accidental—that make feelings of anger or depression (sometimes both) spread all through the victim's body.

The 6th graders were unanimously grateful for learning about this issue in the safety of the classroom, where all their questions and concerns could be aired. One student wrote, "I am now so much safer and more aware of the Internet and all the dangers. They pop out at me."

> **The 6th graders were unanimously grateful for learning about this issue in the safety of the classroom.**

Another acknowledged the positive effect of being taught by the 8th grade students using digital media:

With all the PowerPoints [on] Internet safety from the 8th graders, I learned more than I normally would. The pictures and everything really got my attention.

Arming Students to Help One Another

As difficult as it may be for us to accept, our students are potentially threatened with bullying and even predation any time they are online or communicating electronically. In a commentary connected to the *Journal of Adolescent Health*'s study, Maria Worthen (2007) writes that educators owe their students education in media literacy—including training that makes them aware of the dangers of cybercommunication.

> **We must guide students in how to inform and arm one another.**

We must help our students acquire the new literacy skills of recognizing and avoiding aggression in cyberspace. But because this territory is probably more alien to teachers than to students, increasingly students will find *themselves* acting as peer counselors for their friends or fellow students encountering this kind of abuse. We must guide students in how to inform and arm one another. My experience turning 8th graders into peer teachers shows that adolescents are not just up to this task—they will relish it. This new 2.0 world will belong to today's youth. It's our job to help them shape and protect it with courage and wisdom.

Note

1. Many Internet safety organizations offer lesson plans, videos, role-playing games, advice, and even school visits. These include Netsmartz Teens (www.netsmartz.org/netteens .htm), SafeTeens.com (www.safeteens.com), Teen Angels (www.teenangels.org), and Web Wise Kids (www .webwisekids.org).

References

David-Ferdon, C., & Hertz, M. F. (2007). Electronic media, violence, and adolescents: An emerging public health problem. *Journal of Adolescent Health, 41*(6), 1–5.

Kowalski, R., & Limber, S. (2007). Electronic bullying among middle school students. *Journal of Adolescent Health, 41*(6), 22–30.

Williams, K., & Guerra, N. (2007). Prevalence and predictors of Internet bullying. *Journal of Adolescent Health, 41*(6), 14–21.

Worthen, M. (2007). Commentary: Education policy implications from the expert panel on electronic media and youth violence. *Journal of Adolescent Health, 41*(6), 61–63.

Critical Thinking

1. Interview a school psychologist or school counselor at a local middle or high school about issues related to student use of Internet/social media. What do they say about how frequently there are problems among students related to interactions that take place via social networking? What is the school's policy regarding the use of social media and how are situations handled when problems arise beyond the boundaries of the school environment? What are some things the school has implemented to educate students and minimize the risk of incidents related to Internet safety?

2. What were some of the benefits of the activity identified by the sixth- and eighth-grade students?

3. How could this serve as a model for your classroom?

4. Interview three students of different ages (elementary, middle, high school) about Internet and social media use and behaviors. How much similarity was there between the kinds of things your interviewees discussed and the items on the questionnaire used in the study?

JOHANNA MUSTACCHI teaches media literacy at Pierre Van Cortlandt Middle School in Croton-on-Hudson, New York; jmustacchi@croton-harmonschools.org.

Assessing Middle School Students' Knowledge of Conduct and Consequences and Their Behaviors Regarding the Use of Social Networking Sites

STACEY L. KITE, ROBERT GABLE, AND LAWRENCE FILIPPELLI

At a young age, children are taught consequences for their actions. The Internet has introduced consequences of which we never dreamed. Cyberbullying and threats of Internet predators, not to mention the enduring consequences of postings, may lead to dangerous, unspeakable outcomes. Cyberbullying and threats of predation through social networking sites and instant messaging programs have created numerous problems for parents, school administrators, and law enforcement on a national level (McKenna 2007, 60). Students today have access to cell phones, personal digital assistants, and computers to access the Internet and communicate with peers almost instantly, leaving them less time to contemplate the words with which they communicate. Jenkins and Boyd (2006) identify one important aspect of the problem to be the permanence and accessibility of online activity:

> Indeed, one of the biggest risks of these digital technologies is not the ways that they allow teens to escape adult control, but rather the permanent traces left behind of their transgressive conduct. Teens used to worry about what teachers and administrators might put on their permanent records since this would impact how they were treated in the future. Yet, we are increasingly discovering that everything we do online becomes part of our public and permanent record, easily recoverable by anyone who knows how to Google, and that there is no longer any statute of limitation on our youthful indiscretions. (Jenkins and Boyd 2006)

The purpose of this study was to access the knowledge of middle school students with regard to appropriate use of social networking sites. Specifically, we examined their conduct and its consequences when online using a self-administered survey.

Cyberbullying

Franek defines a cyberbully as "anyone who repeatedly misuses technology to harass, intimidate, bully, or terrorize another person" (2005/2006, 36). The typical schoolyard bully, whose torment of students would stop when the final bell rang, now has new forums to carry out this behavior. The cyberbully has almost limitless time to harass, degrade, and assert control over his or her victims. When students leave school and log on at home, the cyberbully pops up on their instant messenger and engages them in the same hurtful conversations and torment as they did earlier in the day.

Engaging the digital age bully poses many problems. One such problem is the removal of social cues. With the schoolyard bully, both the bully and the victim can read each other's social cues, such as body posture, speaking volume, facial expressions, and level of engagement. Cyberbullying removes all of the social cues that are learned through face-to-face interactions, and the bully and victim are left with caustic words being exchanged without any other interactions.

Franek (2005/2006, 41) suggests that students who have been bullied online are more likely to turn into cyberbullies themselves. This possibility is of great concern, considering the two national studies cited by Erb (2006) that indicate that between 20 percent and 33 percent of adolescents have reported being victims of cyberbullying (Southern Poverty and Law Center 2006; Patchin and Hinduja 2006). As Erb (2006) stated in his *Middle School Journal* editorial, bullies can establish power over their victims with little responsibility for their actions. This should be of great concern to school administrators.

Social Networking Sites

Social networking sites are not new ideas. Similar sites were created shortly after the Internet boom of the mid 1990s. America Online and Yahoo offered Web sites where people could connect with old friends, post pictures, and write descriptions of recent activities. At that time, posting an e-mail or instant messenger screen name on such sites was not popular, because people (even teenage students) thought that it was not a good idea to post that type of information online. Less than a decade later, students of all ages are posting personal information, conversation threads, blogs, and inappropriate pictures, which sometimes include illegal activity such as alcohol and narcotics use. In some areas of the country, gangs use social networking sites to recruit members, post messages in code, and conduct other gang-related activity. "There is no doubt that these online teen hangouts have a huge influence on how adolescents today think and behave. The challenge for school administrators is to keep pace with how students are using these tools in positive ways and consider how they might incorporate this technology into the school setting" (Bryant 2007).

Access to the Internet does not always mean trouble for students. The Internet is a vast resource for many uses. Proper education and supervision allows school administrators to work in conjunction with parents and the school community to teach their students about the dangers of social networking sites, cyberbullying, and instant messaging. To assist in the development of educational programs, schools should assess students' knowledge of their conduct and its consequences regarding the use of social networking sites. The research reported in this article can contribute to these efforts.

Methodology
Sample

A total of 588 male and female students in grades 7 and 8 from an urban ($n = 185$) and a suburban ($n = 403$) school responded to the our Survey of Internet Risk and Behavior during a regularly scheduled school activity period.

The urban school population was 9 percent Asian American, 7 percent African American, 11 percent Hispanic, and 73 percent Caucasian. The district where the school was located scored 40 percent in reading proficiency, 33 percent in math proficiency, and 27 percent in writing proficiency on a state standardized test.

The suburban school district achieved a higher level of proficiency, reaching 74 percent in reading, 67 percent in

math, and 57 percent in reading on the state standardized test. The school population was less than 1 percent American Indian, less than 1 percent Asian American, 1 percent African American, 1 percent Hispanic, and 97 percent Caucasian.

Instrumentation

The Survey of Internet Risk and Behavior was developed for this study to assess student knowledge and behavior at two schools in a northeast state. The instrument was developed using the literature and expert opinions from two current middle school leaders (not from the schools under investigation). The details of the content, format, validity, and reliability are presented in the following sections.

Dimension/item Content

The Survey of Internet Risk and Behavior contained thirty-three items. Following the item analysis and data reliability assessment, the findings reported in this article are based on twenty-eight of the original thirty-three items. The first seven investigate the views and experiences of the students with regard to social networking. The remaining items assess two global dimensions: Knowledge and Behavior. The Knowledge dimension is composed of sixteen items describing the students' knowledge of appropriate behavior on social networks and potential risk of Internet predators. The Behavior items are categorized into two subdimensions: Bullying Behavior and Internet Use. Bullying Behavior encompasses two items that directly query the students on their bullying behaviors on both MySpace and instant messenger sites. Finally, Internet Use is composed of three items that assess whether the respondents use the Internet for instant messaging, e-mail, or social networking on a daily basis.

Response Format

Students responded to each item by selecting *agree, disagree,* or *don't know.* Using a "correct" response grid, each statement received 1 point for the "appropriate" or "correct" response and 0 points for the "incorrect" or "don't know" response.

Validity and Reliability

Content validity of the survey items was supported through the literature (Franek 2005/2006; McKenna 2007; Weaver 2007) and a judgmental review by five middle school teachers. Cronbach's alpha for the respective dimensions was as follows: Knowledge = .84; Bullying Behavior = .72; Internet Usage = .78.

Data Analysis

Response percentages for the agree, disagree, and don't know options are presented for all items. For the Knowledge, Bullying Behaviors, and Internet Use dimensions, the overall percent "correct" for the set of items defining the respective dimension is also presented. Items were also ranked within each category based on the percentage of "correct" responses to identify the high and low knowledge or behavior areas.

Results and Discussion
Social Networking Experiences and Opinions

Table 1 contains the response percentages for the students' ratings of their social networking experiences and opinions. Inspection of the data for some key items indicates that only 10 percent of the students had been bullied by another student at home while online (item 1). Although the majority (53%) of students were not sure if their friends' parents were aware of what they were doing online, 70 percent of the students felt that their parents knew about their social networking sites (item 7). According to 74 percent of the students, their friends used social networking sites like MySpace or Facebook. Although roughly half (51%) of the students disagreed that adding friends to their Instant Messaging account would make them more popular, only 17 percent agreed, and 32 percent did not know if this was the case.

Knowledge

Table 2 contains the ranked response percentages for students' knowledge of appropriate behaviors and risk of Internet predators. The "correct" or "appropriate" response percentages are boxed in the table. The behaviors associated with the boxed "disagree" percentages exceeding 60 percentage indicate positive results, since appropriate student behaviors are indicated. Of particular concern are the five items (24, 17, 20, 21, and 32) with boxed bold "agree" percentages at the top of the table. The behaviors described by these items reflect two areas of concern: knowing how easily predators can contact students and willingness to inform a parent or adult about possibly inappropriate Internet contact. Regarding contact, only 29 percent of the students

felt that a predator would make contact with them based on the information they had posted online (item 24), and only 37 percent felt that it would be easy for a predator to contact them based on the contact information they put on their MySpace or Facebook page (item 17). Likewise, only 43 percent felt that it would be possible for an Internet predator to locate their home or school using Google Earth or MSN live (item 21). One would hope that students think this is the case because they have not listed specific contact information on their site.

The potential to inform an adult of inappropriate contact on a site such as MySpace or Facebook is an issue of great concern. Only 40 percent of the students indicated that they would tell an adult if they were contacted on instant messenger by someone they did not know (item 20). Furthermore, only 44 percent indicated that they would tell a teacher, parent, or another adult if mean or threatening things were said about them on a site such as MySpace or Facebook (item 32).

Overall, for the set of sixteen items defining the Knowledge dimension, only 59 percent of the students indicated what most educators would consider a "correct" or "appropriate" response. If we are applying any version of our usual educators' concept of mastery in the realm of knowledge, it appears that school officials and teachers have some serious areas that require discussion with our students.

Behavior

Table 3 contains the ranked response percentages for students' bullying behavior and Internet use. A somewhat positive finding is that 78 percent of the students indicate that they have not threatened or bullied another student using an instant messenger program (item 18); additionally, 83 percent indicate that they have not threatened or bullied a friend (item 22). We note that 10 percent of the students did agree that they have engaged in these behaviors. While 10 percent may seem low, it raises a valid concern, since it represents 59 of the students in this study. Overall, 81 percent of the

Table 1 Social Networking Experiences and Opinions: Response Percentages (N = 588)

Item	Agree	Disagree	Don't Know
1. I have been bullied by another student at home while online.	10	83	7
3. My friends' parents don't know what they do online.	18	29	53
7. My parents do not know about my social networking sites.	10	70	20
11. Most of my friends have social networking sites like myspace or facebook.	74	9	17
15. I am much better with computers and the internet than my parents.	62	21	17
23. The more "friends" you add to your Instant Messenging account, the more popular you are.	17	51	32
31. I log onto an instant messenging program at least three times per week.	52	37	11

Table 2 Knowledge of Appropriate Behaviors and Risk of Internet Predators: Ranked Response Percentages [a] (N = 588)

Item	Agree	Disagree	Don't Know
24. An internet predator will make contact with me based on the information I have posted online.	29	32	39
17. With the contact information I put on myspace or facebook, it would be easy for an internet predator to contact me.	37	38	25
20. If I were contacted by some I didn't know on Instant Messenger, I would tell an adult.	40	31	29
21. An internet predator can easily use sites such as google earth, MSN live or other programs to locate my school and house.	43	18	39
32. If I had mean or threatening things said about me on a site like myspace or facebook, I would tell a teacher, parent or another adult.	44	28	28
25. Threats online that I carry out at school can get me into trouble.	54	21	25
6. I have told a parent or another adult that I have been bullied online.	55	24	21
29. If I were being harassed by another student, I would tell a teacher, parent, or another adult.	57	23	20
2. Making threats online can get me in trouble with the police.	60	17	23
13. A predator would never contact me from a social networking site even if I posted my personal information on it.	7	62	31
5. Putting personal contact information on a social networking site is no big deal.	12	69	19
12. If I were contacted by someone on myspace that I did not know, it would be OK to add them as a friend.	14	70	16
14. I would create a "hatespace" about another student on a site like myspace or facebook.	5	77	18
9. Giving my personal information away to an IM buddy I am unfamiliar with is no big deal.	8	79	13
10. I would post mean or threatening statements about another student a site such as myspace or facebook.	6	79	15
16. If I were contacted by someone on myspace that I did not know, it would be OK to share my information with them.	4	85	11
Overall "Appropriate" Response for Knowledge 59%			

[a]Boxed percents indicate "appropriate" response.

Table 3 Student Behavior—Bullying and Internet Use: Ranked Response Percentages [a] (N = 588)

Dimension/Item	Agree	Disagree	Don't Know
Bullying			
18. I have threatened or bullied another student online using an instant messenger.	10	78	12
22. I have threatened or bullied one of my friends online.	6	83	11
Overall "Appropriate" Response for Bullying 81% Internet Use for Instant Messaging and Social Networks			
27. I log onto an instant messenging program daily.	49	40	11
30. I access social networking sites more than three times per week.	41	42	17
33. I access social networking sites at least once a day.	39	44	17
Overall "Appropriate" Response for Internet Use 43%			

[a] Boxed percents indicate "appropriate" response.

students indicated an "appropriate" response for the set of two Bullying items.

Table 3 also lists the findings for three items describing the frequency of Internet use for instant messaging and accessing social networks. Less than half of the students indicated that they frequently engage in these behaviors, and overall, 43 percent responded with what many educators would consider to be an "appropriate" response.

Summary, Conclusions, and Implications for Educators

Internet predator threats and cyberbullying through the use of social networking sites are major issues. Although the media presents concerns of social networking sites (usually Internet predator risks), we rarely hear of cyberbullying through these sites. While the threat of predators is a serious concern, a child is far more likely to be bullied online. Educating students on the risks they may encounter through social networking sites is paramount. As can be seen from the findings outlined in the following sections, many students do not fully understand the risks they are taking. Some of the key findings from this survey of middle school students were as follows:

Internet Predators

Most students (71%) do not think that an Internet predator will contact them based on postings online. Furthermore, 63 percent do not fully understand the potential risk of Internet predators (i.e., their ability to track students on the Internet). It is clear that more education on the risk of cyber behaviors is needed. Additionally, the education about students' online behaviors needs to extend to more than just the educational community. Parents and law enforcement groups are crucial players in keeping students safe from online predators.

Only 40 percent of the students indicated that they would tell an adult if they were contacted by someone they did not know. The fear is, perhaps, that they would not be allowed to continue using the Internet if this were to happen. Parents need to keep a closer eye on their children's behaviors and discuss Internet dangers with them, as they would discuss any important topic. This low percentage will be shocking to anyone who is familiar with this type of research. The National Association of Secondary School Principals' publication *News Leader* (National Association of Secondary School Principals 2006, 9) has indicated that only 16 percent of teens and preteens affected by online bullying or predatory behavior would tell someone. The finding of 40 percent for this sample of students is more positive but still much too low and therefore quite significant.

Cyberbullying

Similar to the finding for the Internet predation item, only 44 percent indicated that they would tell an adult if they were the victim of cyberbullying. When asked if they had been bullied while online, 10 percent indicated yes. The 2006 NASSP publication *News Leader* indicated that 33 percent of all teens aged 12 to 17 years have had mean, threatening, or embarrassing things said about them online. While our findings of 10 percent may appear low in light of the national average, there is still a need for concern for this behavior. For our sample of 588 students, this percentage indicates that approximately fifty-nine of the students have been bullied by another student at home while online. Some would conclude that *one* is too many in this case.

Shariff (2008) reports that an extreme but real consequence of this behavior could be suicidal thoughts or action. It is clear that parents need to take a more active role in the development of their child's behaviors, particularly in the digital world. Shariff states:

> As human beings, we teach our children how to eat, clean themselves, and communicate, and we protect and nurture them, until they are old enough to go to school. Once they are at school, we suddenly place more emphasis on supervision, discipline, authority, subordination, punishment, and consequences, with less attention to the social survival skills they will need in the contemporary world. (2008, 113)

We anticipate that the findings presented in this article will facilitate further understanding of students' awareness and behaviors regarding these issues and their consequences; and support school administrators' and teachers' increased attention to them.

References

Bryant, A. L. 2007. Keeping pace with online networking. (What they're saying). *Communication Curriculum Review* 47. www.marcprensky.com/blog/archives/000050.html.

Erb, T. 2006. Cyberbullying; A growing threat to young adolescent well-being. *Middle School Journal* 38 (2): 2.

Franek, M. 2005/2006. Foiling cyberbullies in the new wild west. *Educational Leadership* 63 (4): 39–43.

Jenkins, H., and D. Boyd. 2006. Discussion: MySpace and Deleting Online Predators Act (DOPA). *Digital Divide Network*, May 30. http://myspacesafetytips.com/entry_28.php.

McKenna, P. 2007. The rise of cyberbullying. *New Scientist* 195 (2613): 26–27.

National Association of Secondary School Principals. 2006. Millions are victims of cyberbullying. *NewsLeader* 54 (2): 9.

Patchin, J., and S. Hinduja. 2006. Bullies move beyond the schoolyard: A preliminary look at cyberbullying. *Youth Violence and Juvenile Justice* 4: 148–69.

Shariff, S. 2008. *Cyberbullying: Issues and solutions for the school, the classroom, and the home.* New York: Routledge.

Southern Poverty and Law Center. 2006. Parent turns to center when child gets hate e-mail. *Southern Poverty and Law Center Report* 36 (2): 5.

Weaver, R. 2007. What they're saying. *Curriculum Review* 47: 2.

Critical Thinking

1. What was the overall purpose of the study?

2. How did the authors go about collecting information from students? Describe the different types of things they asked students about and how they were asked to respond.

3. What is your opinion of the items in Table 3? How likely do you think students would be to respond truthfully to these items? Why might they choose NOT to answer honestly?

4. What do you think about the diversity of the students who participated in the study? Do you think this might have influenced students experiences and therefore how they responded on the questionnaire? Why or why not?

5. Interview three students of different ages (elementary, middle, high school) about internet and social media use and behaviors. How much similarity was there between the kinds of things your interviewees discussed and the items on the questionnaire used in the study?

STACEY KITE, DBA, is a professor of research in the School of Education at Johnson & Wales University, Providence, RI. **ROBERT GABLE**, EdD, is a professor of research the School of Education at Johnson & Wales University, Providence, RI. **LAWRENCE FILIPPELLI**, EdD, is the assistant superintendent at Scituate Schools, Scituate, RI

From *Educational Leadership*, February 2010, pp. 50–55. Copyright © 2010 by Kathleen Cushman. Reprinted by permission of the author.

UNIT 5

Motivation, Engagement, and Classroom Management

Unit Selections

Learning Outcomes

After reading this unit, you will be able to:

- Identify the potential positive and negative impact of "praise" on student motivation and engagement, describe appropriate ways to praise students, and explain what it means to have a "growth mind-set."

- Discuss the main arguments against the use of rewards and provide suggestions for how rewards can be effectively implemented in the classroom.

- Define "intellectual engagement" and provide examples of strategies for keeping students intellectually engaged in your classroom.

- Describe what is meant by "assertive communication." Explain the benefits of developing assertive communication skills with students.

- Identify common habits and behaviors of experts, regardless of their field of expertise and the implications for learning in school.

- Explain how person-centered classroom management differs from more traditional teacher-centered classrooms.

- Examine your beliefs about the nature of the relationship between yourself as a teacher and your students.

- Reflect on your assumptions and attitudes about students from different backgrounds and how they might impact your communication and behavior management styles.

Student Website

www.mhhe.com/cls

Internet References

Brainology
www.Brainology.us

Consistency Management and Cooperative Discipline
www2.ed.gov/pubs/ToolsforSchools/cmcd.html

Curriculum Based Measurement (CBM)
www.studentprogress.org/families.asp

Effect Sizes Explained
www.psychology.wikia.com/wiki/Effect_size

I Love Teaching
www.iloveteaching.com

The Jigsaw Classroom
www.jigsaw.org

Mihaly Csikszentmihalyi on Flow
www.ted.com/speakers/mihaly_csikszentmihalyi.html

North Central Educational Regional Laboratory
www.ncrel.org/sdrs

Teaching Helping Teachers
www.pacificnet.net/ mandel

What Kids Can Do
www.whatkidscando.org

Several theories of motivation, each highlighting different reasons for sustained goal-oriented behavior, have been proposed. We will discuss three of them: behavioral, humanistic, and cognitive. The behavioral theory of motivation suggests that an important reason for engaging in behavior is that reinforcement follows the action. Motivation is said to be extrinsic when reinforcement is controlled by someone else and is arbitrarily related to the behavior (such as money, a token, or a smile). In contrast, behavior may also be initiated and sustained for intrinsic reasons, such as curiosity or mastery.

Humanistic approaches to motivation are concerned with the social and psychological needs of individuals. Humans are motivated to engage in behavior to meet these needs. Abraham Maslow, a founder of humanistic psychology, proposes that there is a hierarchy of needs that directs behavior, beginning with physiological and safety needs and progressing to self-actualization. Some other important needs that influence motivation are affiliation and belonging with others, love, self-esteem, influence with others, recognition, status, competence, achievement, and autonomy.

The dominant view of motivation in the educational psychology literature is the cognitive approach. This set of theories proposes that our beliefs about our successes and failures affect our expectations and goals concerning future performance. Students who believe that their success is due to their abilities and efforts are motivated toward mastery of skills. Students who blame their failures on inadequate abilities have low self-efficacy and tend to set ability and performance goals that protect their self-image.

As a form of verbal reinforcement, praise can have powerful positive and negative effects on students' effort and motivation. In the first article about motivation, Carol Dweck discusses the potential impact of praise on students and advocates that teachers help students develop a "growth mind-set" instead of a fixed-ability mind-set. In Should "Learning Be Its Own Reward," Daniel Willingham highlights the debate about using external rewards for learning using examples of states that have implemented initiatives that involve paying students for performance on standardized tests. The next two articles on motivation focus on increasing student engagement in learning through instructional practices that foster self-efficacy, self-regulation, and self-determination. In the final article for this section of the unit, Kathleen Cushman discusses the importance of practice to developing expertise, regardless of the profession, content, or skill.

Regardless of how motivated students are to learn, or the teacher's attempts to create lessons that will engage and motivate students, teachers also need to be effective managers of their classrooms. Classroom management is more than

© Corbis

controlling the behavior of students or disciplining them following misbehavior. In addition, teachers need to initiate and maintain a classroom environment that supports successful teaching and learning. The skills that effective teachers use include preplanning, deliberate introduction of rules and procedures, assertiveness, continual monitoring, consistent feedback to students, and specific consequences.

The next four articles cover a range of topics from addressing specific behavior or classroom management issues to more general discussions about how to create positive learning environments. As students grow and develop, they become less easily influenced by adults and more influenced by peers, which creates unique classroom management issues for secondary teachers. The first three articles in this section provide a unique look at the social world of adolescents in middle school, a description of classroom management that is person- or student-centered and how it differs from teacher-centered classrooms, and the importance of relationships to not just the overall classroom environment, but to the academic, social, and emotional well-being of students. Each of these articles takes a more social-emotional perspective that focuses on developing students' feelings of connectedness to school. In the final article, Matthew Kraft makes the important distinction between classroom management and behavior management. He suggests a number of specific strategies that fall under each category that can benefit both the students and the teacher by fostering a classroom environment that is more like a "symphony of learners."

The Perils and Promises of Praise

**The wrong kind of praise creates self-defeating behavior.
The right kind motivates students to learn.**

CAROL S. DWECK

We often hear these days that we've produced a generation of young people who can't get through the day without an award. They expect success because they're special, not because they've worked hard.

Is this true? Have we inadvertently done something to hold back our students?

I think educators commonly hold two beliefs that do just that. Many believe that (1) praising students' intelligence builds their confidence and motivation to learn, and (2) students' inherent intelligence is the major cause of their achievement in school. Our research has shown that the first belief is false and that the second can be harmful—even for the most competent students.

As a psychologist, I have studied student motivation for more than 35 years. My graduate students and I have looked at thousands of children, asking why some enjoy learning, even when it's hard, and why they are resilient in the face of obstacles. We have learned a great deal. Research shows us how to praise students in ways that yield motivation and resilience. In addition, specific interventions can reverse a student's slide into failure during the vulnerable period of adolescence.

Fixed or Malleable?

Praise is intricately connected to how students view their intelligence. Some students believe that their intellectual ability is a fixed trait. They have a certain amount of intelligence, and that's that. Students with this fixed mind-set become excessively concerned with how smart they are, seeking tasks that will prove their intelligence and avoiding ones that might not (Dweck, 1999, 2006). The desire to learn takes a backseat.

Other students believe that their intellectual ability is something they can develop through effort and education. They don't necessarily believe that anyone can become an Einstein or a Mozart, but they do understand that even Einstein and Mozart had to put in years of effort to become who they were. When students believe that they can develop their intelligence, they focus on doing just that. Not worrying about how smart they will appear, they take on challenges and stick to them (Dweck, 1999, 2006).

More and more research in psychology and neuroscience supports the growth mind-set. We are discovering that the brain has more plasticity over time than we ever imagined (Doidge, 2007); that fundamental aspects of intelligence can be enhanced through learning (Sternberg, 2005); and that dedication and persistence in the face of obstacles are key ingredients in outstanding achievement (Ericsson, Charness, Feltovich, & Hoffman, 2006).

Alfred Binet (1909/1973), the inventor of the IQ test, had a strong growth mind-set. He believed that education could transform the basic capacity to learn. Far from intending to measure fixed intelligence, he meant his test to be a tool for identifying students who were not profiting from the public school curriculum so that other courses of study could be devised to foster their intellectual growth.

The Two Faces of Effort

The fixed and growth mind-sets create two different psychological worlds. In the fixed mind-set, students care first and foremost about how they'll be judged: smart or not smart. Repeatedly, students with this mind-set reject opportunities to learn if they might make mistakes (Hong, Chiu, Dweck, Lin, & Wan, 1999; Mueller & Dweck, 1998). When they do make mistakes or reveal deficiencies, rather than correct them, they try to hide them (Nussbaum & Dweck, 2007).

They are also afraid of effort because effort makes them feel dumb. They believe that if you have the ability, you shouldn't need effort (Blackwell, Trzesniewski, & Dweck, 2007), that ability should bring success all by itself. This is one of the worst beliefs that students can hold. It can cause many bright students to stop working in school when the curriculum becomes challenging.

Finally, students in the fixed mind-set don't recover well from setbacks. When they hit a setback in school, they *decrease* their efforts and consider cheating (Blackwell et al., 2007). The idea of fixed intelligence does not offer them viable ways to improve.

Let's get inside the head of a student with a fixed mind-set as he sits in his classroom, confronted with algebra for the first time. Up until then, he has breezed through math. Even when he barely paid attention in class and skimped on his homework, he always got As. But this is different. It's hard. The student feels anxious and thinks, "What if I'm not as good at math as I thought? What if other kids understand it and I don't?" At some level, he realizes that he has two choices: try hard, or turn off. His interest in math begins to wane, and his attention wanders. He tells himself, "Who cares about this stuff? It's for nerds. I could do it if I wanted to, but it's so boring. You don't see CEOs and sports stars solving for *x* and *y*."

By contrast, in the growth mind-set, students care about learning. When they make a mistake or exhibit a deficiency, they correct it (Blackwell et al., 2007; Nussbaum & Dweck, 2007). For them, effort is a *positive* thing: It ignites their intelligence and causes it to grow. In the face of failure, these students escalate their efforts and look for new learning strategies.

Let's look at another student—one who has a growth mind-set—having her first encounter with algebra. She finds it new, hard, and confusing, unlike anything else she has ever learned. But she's determined to understand it. She listens to everything the teacher says, asks the teacher questions after class, and takes her textbook home and reads the chapter over twice. As she begins to get it, she feels exhilarated. A new world of math opens up for her.

It is not surprising, then, that when we have followed students over challenging school transitions or courses, we find that those with growth mind-sets outperform their classmates with fixed mind-sets—even when they entered with equal skills and knowledge. A growth mind-set fosters the growth of ability over time (Blackwell et al., 2007; Mangels, Butterfield, Lamb, Good, & Dweck, 2006; see also Grant & Dweck, 2003).

The Effects of Praise

Many educators have hoped to maximize students' confidence in their abilities, their enjoyment of learning, and their ability to thrive in school by praising their intelligence. We've studied the effects of this kind of praise in children as young as 4 years old and as old as adolescence, in students in inner-city and rural settings, and in students of different ethnicities—and we've consistently found the same thing (Cimpian, Arce, Markman, & Dweck, 2007; Kamins & Dweck, 1999; Mueller & Dweck, 1998): Praising students' intelligence gives them a short burst of pride, followed by a long string of negative consequences.

In many of our studies (see Mueller & Dweck, 1998), 5th grade students worked on a task, and after the first set of problems, the teacher praised some of them for their intelligence ("You must be smart at these problems") and others for their effort ("You must have worked hard at these problems"). We then assessed the students' mind-sets. In one study, we asked students to agree or disagree with mind-set statements, such as, "Your intelligence is something basic about you that you can't really change." Students praised for intelligence agreed with statements like these more than students praised for effort did. In another study, we asked students to define intelligence. Students praised for intelligence made significantly more references to innate, fixed capacity, whereas the students praised for effort made more references to skills, knowledge, and areas they could change through effort and learning. Thus, we found that praise for intelligence tended to put students in a fixed mind-set (intelligence is fixed, and you have it), whereas praise for effort tended to put them in a growth mind-set (you're developing these skills because you're working hard).

We then offered students a chance to work on either a challenging task that they could learn from or an easy one that ensured error-free performance. Most of those praised for intelligence wanted the easy task, whereas most of those praised for effort wanted the challenging task and the opportunity to learn.

Next, the students worked on some challenging problems. As a group, students who had been praised for their intelligence *lost* their confidence in their ability and their enjoyment of the task as soon as they began to struggle with the problem. If success meant they were smart, then struggling meant they were not. The whole point of intelligence praise is to boost confidence and motivation, but both were gone in a flash. Only the effort-praised kids remained, on the whole, confident and eager.

When the problems were made somewhat easier again, students praised for intelligence did poorly, having lost their confidence and motivation. As a group, they did worse than they had done initially on these same types of problems. The students praised for effort showed excellent performance and continued to improve.

Finally, when asked to report their scores (anonymously), almost 40 percent of the intelligence-praised students lied. Apparently, their egos were so wrapped up in their performance that they couldn't admit mistakes. Only about 10 percent of the effort-praised students saw fit to falsify their results.

Praising students for their intelligence, then, hands them not motivation and resilience but a fixed mind-set with all its vulnerability. In contrast, effort or "process" praise (praise for engagement, perseverance, strategies, improvement, and the like) fosters hardy motivation. It tells students what they've done to be successful and what they need to do to be successful again in the future. Process praise sounds like this:

- You really studied for your English test, and your improvement shows it. You read the material over several times, outlined it, and tested yourself on it. That really worked!
- I like the way you tried all kinds of strategies on that math problem until you finally got it.
- It was a long, hard assignment, but you stuck to it and got it done. You stayed at your desk, kept up your concentration, and kept working. That's great!
- I like that you took on that challenging project for your science class. It will take a lot of work—doing the research, designing the machine, buying the parts, and building it. You're going to learn a lot of great things.

What about a student who gets an *A* without trying? I would say, "All right, that was too easy for you. Let's do something more challenging that you can learn from." We don't want to make something done quickly and easily the basis for our admiration.

What about a student who works hard and *doesn't* do well? I would say, "I liked the effort you put in. Let's work together some more and figure out what you don't understand." Process praise keeps students focused, not on something called ability that they may or may not have and that magically creates success or failure, but on processes they can all engage in to learn.

Motivated to Learn

Finding that a growth mind-set creates motivation and resilience—and leads to higher achievement—we sought to develop an intervention that would teach this mind-set to students. We decided to aim our intervention at students who were making the transition to 7th grade because this is a time of great vulnerability. School often gets more difficult in 7th grade, grading becomes more stringent, and the environment becomes more impersonal. Many students take stock of themselves and their intellectual abilities at this time and decide whether they want to be involved with school. Not surprisingly, it is often a time of disengagement and plunging achievement.

We performed our intervention in a New York City junior high school in which many students were struggling with the transition and were showing plummeting grades. If students learned a growth mind-set, we reasoned, they might be able to meet this challenge with increased, rather than decreased, effort. We therefore developed an eight-session workshop in which both the control group and the growth-mind-set group learned study skills, time management techniques, and memory strategies (Blackwell et al., 2007). However, in the growth-mind-set intervention, students also learned about their brains and what they could do to make their intelligence grow.

They learned that the brain is like a muscle—the more they exercise it, the stronger it becomes. They learned that every time they try hard and learn something new, their brain forms new connections that, over time, make them smarter. They learned that intellectual development is not the natural unfolding of intelligence, but rather the formation of new connections brought about through effort and learning.

Students were riveted by this information. The idea that their intellectual growth was largely in their hands fascinated them. In fact, even the most disruptive students suddenly sat still and took notice, with the most unruly boy of the lot looking up at us and saying, "You mean I don't have to be dumb?"

Indeed, the growth-mind-set message appeared to unleash students' motivation. Although both groups had experienced a steep decline in their math grades during their first months of junior high, those receiving the growth-mind-set intervention showed a significant rebound. Their math grades improved. Those in the control group, despite their excellent study skills intervention, continued their decline.

What's more, the teachers—who were unaware that the intervention workshops differed—singled out three times as many students in the growth-mindset intervention as showing marked changes in motivation. These students had a heightened desire to work hard and learn. One striking example was the boy who thought he was dumb. Before this experience, he had never put in any extra effort and often didn't turn his homework in on time. As a result of the training, he worked for hours one evening to finish an assignment early so that his teacher could review it and give him a chance to revise it. He earned a *B+* on the assignment (he had been getting *C*s and lower previously).

Other researchers have obtained similar findings with a growth-mind-set intervention. Working with junior high school students, Good, Aronson, and Inzlicht (2003) found an increase in math and English achievement test scores; working with college students, Aronson, Fried, and Good (2002) found an increase in students' valuing of academics, their enjoyment of schoolwork, and their grade point averages.

To facilitate delivery of the growth-mind-set workshop to students, we developed an interactive computer-based version of the intervention called *Brainology*. Students work through six modules, learning about the brain, visiting virtual brain labs, doing virtual brain experiments, seeing how the brain changes with learning, and learning how they can make their brains work better and grow smarter.

When students believe that they can develop their intelligence, they focus on doing just that.

We tested our initial version in 20 New York City schools, with encouraging results. Almost all students (anonymously polled) reported changes in their study habits and motivation to learn resulting directly from their learning of the growth mind-set. One student noted that as a result of the animation she had seen about the brain, she could actually "picture the neurons growing bigger as they make more connections." One student referred to the value of effort: "If you do not give up and you keep studying, you can find your way through."

Adolescents often see school as a place where they perform for teachers who then judge them. The growth mind-set changes that perspective and makes school a place where students vigorously engage in learning for their own benefit.

Going Forward

Our research shows that educators cannot hand students confidence on a silver platter by praising their intelligence. Instead, we can help them gain the tools they need to maintain their confidence in learning by keeping them focused on the *process* of achievement.

Maybe we have produced a generation of students who are more dependent, fragile, and entitled than previous generations. If so, it's time for us to adopt a growth mind-set and learn from our mistakes. It's time to deliver interventions that will truly boost students' motivation, resilience, and learning.

References

Aronson, J., Fried, C., & Good, C. (2002). Reducing the effects of stereotype threat on African American college students by shaping theories of intelligence. *Journal of Experimental Social Psychology, 38:* 113–125.

Binet, A. (1909/1973). *Les idées modernes sur les enfants* [Modern ideas on children]. Paris: Flamarion. (Original work published 1909).

Blackwell, L., Trzesniewski, K., & Dweck, C. S. (2007). Implicit theories of intelligence predict achievement across an adolescent transition: A longitudinal study and an intervention. *Child Development, 78,* 246–263.

Cimpian, A., Arce, H., Markman, E. M., & Dweck, C. S. (2007). Subtle linguistic cues impact children's motivation. *Psychological Science, 18,* 314–316.

Doidge, N. (2007). *The brain that changes itself: Stories of personal triumph from the frontiers of brain science.* New York: Viking.

Dweck, C. S. (1999). *Self-theories: Their role in motivation, personality and development.* Philadelphia: Taylor and Francis/Psychology Press.

Dweck, C. S. (2006). *Mindset: The new psychology of success.* New York: Random House.

Ericsson, K. A., Charness, N., Feltovich, P. J., & Hoffman, R. R. (Eds.). (2006). *The Cambridge handbook of expertise and expert performance.* New York: Cambridge University Press.

Good, C., Aronson, J., & Inzlicht, M. (2003). Improving adolescents' standardized test performance: An intervention to reduce the effects of stereotype threat. *Journal of Applied Developmental Psychology, 24,* 645–662.

Grant, H., & Dweck, C. S. (2003). Clarifying achievement goals and their impact. *Journal of Personality and Social Psychology, 85,* 541–553.

Hong, Y. Y., Chiu, C., Dweck, C. S., Lin, D., & Wan, W. (1999). Implicit theories, attributions, and coping: A meaning system approach. *Journal of Personality and Social Psychology, 77,* 588–599.

Kamins, M., & Dweck, C. S. (1999). Person vs. process praise and criticism: Implications for contingent self-worth and coping. *Developmental Psychology, 35,* 835–847.

Mangels, J. A., Butterfield, B., Lamb, J., Good, C. D., & Dweck, C. S. (2006). Why do beliefs about intelligence influence learning success? A social-cognitive-neuroscience model. *Social, Cognitive, and Affective Neuroscience, 1,* 75–86.

Mueller, C. M., & Dweck, C. S. (1998). Intelligence praise can undermine motivation and performance. *Journal of Personality and Social Psychology, 75,* 33–52.

Nussbaum, A. D., & Dweck, C. S. (2007). Defensiveness vs. remediation: Self-theories and modes of self-esteem maintenance. *Personality and Social Psychology Bulletin.*

Sternberg, R. (2005). Intelligence, competence, and expertise. In A. Elliot & C. S. Dweck (Eds.), *The handbook of competence and motivation* (pp. 15–30). New York: Guilford Press.

Critical Thinking

1. Compare and contrast students with a fixed mind-set versus a growth mind-set in terms of their approaches to learning. What are some typical responses of each when faced with challenge or difficult content to master?

2. Read the article, "The Strive of It" by Kathleen Cushman presented later in this unit. Which mind-set would you expect these students to have? Review the quotes/comments of students presented in the article and identify words or phrases consistent with a growth mind-set.

3. What would be some things you could ask students or look for in their behaviors to help you identify whether they have a growth or fixed mind-set?

4. Suppose you have a student with a fixed mind-set in your classroom. What would be some examples feedback or comments you could give him or her to help foster a growth mind-set?

CAROL S. DWECK is the Lewis and Virginia Eaton Professor of Psychology at Stanford University and the author of *Mindset: The New Psychology of Success* (Random House, 2006).

Should Learning Be Its Own Reward?

DANIEL T. WILLINGHAM

How does the mind work—and especially how does it learn? Teachers' instructional decisions are based on a mix of theories learned in teacher education, trial and error, craft knowledge, and gut instinct. Such gut knowledge often serves us well, but is there anything sturdier to rely on?

Cognitive science is an interdisciplinary field of researchers from psychology, neuroscience, linguistics, philosophy, computer science, and anthropology who seek to understand the mind. In this regular American Educator column, we consider findings from this field that are strong and clear enough to merit classroom application.

Question: In recent months, there's been a big uproar about students being paid to take standardized tests—and being paid even more if they do well. Can cognitive science shed any light on this debate? Is it harmful to students to reward them like this? What about more typical rewards like a piece of candy or five extra minutes of recess?

There has been much debate recently about boosting standardized test scores by paying students. Here are a few examples that I read about in the news. In Coshocton, Ohio, third- and sixth-graders are being paid up to $20 for earning high scores on standardized tests. In New York City, fourth-grade students will receive $5 for each standardized test they take throughout the year, and up to $25 for each perfect score. Seventh-graders will get twice those amounts. In Tucson, Ariz., high school juniors selected from low-income areas will be paid up to $25 each week for attendance. These and similar programs affect just a tiny fraction of students nationwide. But rewarding students with things like small gifts, extra recess time, stickers, certificates, class parties and the like is actually pretty common. Most teachers have the option of distributing rewards in the classroom, and many do. For example, in a recent survey of young adults, 70 percent said that their elementary school teachers had used candy as a reward (Davis, Winsler, and Middleton, 2006).

So whether or not your district offers cash rewards for standardized test scores or attendance, you've probably wondered if rewarding your students for their classwork is a good idea. Some authors promise doom if a teacher rewards students, with the predicted negative effects ranging from unmotivated pupils to a teacher's moral bankruptcy (e.g., Kohn, 1993). Others counter that rewards are harmless or even helpful (e.g., Cameron, Banko, and Pierce, 2001; Chance, 1993). Where does the truth lie? In the middle. There is some merit to the arguments on both sides. Concrete rewards can motivate students to attend class, to behave well, or to produce better work. But if you are not careful in choosing what you reward, they can prompt students to produce shoddy work—and worse, they can cause students to actually like school subjects less. The important guidelines are these: Don't use rewards unless you have to, use rewards for a specific reason, and use them for a limited time. Let's take a look at the research behind these guidelines.

> **Concrete rewards can motivate students to attend class, to behave well, or to produce better work. But if you are not careful in choosing what you reward, they can prompt students to produce shoddy work—and worse, they can cause students to actually like school subjects less.**

Do Rewards Work?

Rewarding students is, from one perspective, an obvious idea. People do things because they find them rewarding, the reasoning goes, so if students don't find school naturally rewarding (that is, interesting and fun), make it rewarding by offering them something they do like, be it cash or candy.

In this simple sense, rewards usually work. If you offer students an appealing reward, the targeted behavior will generally increase (for reviews, see O'Leary and Drabman, 1971; Deci, Koestner, and Ryan, 1999). Teachers typically use rewards like candy, stickers, small prizes, or extra recess time. They use them to encourage student behaviors such as completing assignments, producing good work, and so on. In one example

(Hendy, Williams, and Camise, 2005) first-, second-, and fourth-graders were observed in the school cafeteria to see how often they ate fruits and vegetables. Once this baseline measure was taken, they were rewarded for eating one or the other. Students received a token for each day that they ate the assigned food, and tokens could be redeemed for small prizes at the end of the week. Not surprisingly, students ate more of what they were rewarded for eating.

But things don't always go so smoothly. If you mistakenly offer a reward that students don't care for, you'll see little result. Or, if you reward the wrong behavior, you'll see a result you don't care for. When I was in fourth grade, my class was offered a small prize for each book we read. Many of us quickly developed a love for short books with large print, certainly not the teacher's intent. In the same way, if you reward people to come up with ideas, but don't stipulate that they must be good ideas, people will generate lots of ideas in order to gain lots of rewards, but the ideas may not be especially good (Ward, Kogan, and Pankove, 1972). It's often possible to correct mistakes such as these. Unappealing rewards can be replaced by valued rewards. The target behavior can be changed. My fourth-grade teacher stipulated that books had to be grade-appropriate and of some minimum length.

Because rewards are generally effective, people's objection to them in the classroom is seldom that they won't work. The op-ed newspaper articles I have seen about the student payment plans described above don't claim that you can't get students to go to school by paying them (e.g., Carlton, 2007; Schwartz, 2007). They raise other objections.

The common arguments against rewards fall into three categories. Let me state each one in rather extreme terms to give you the idea, and then I'll consider the merits of each in more detail. The first objection is that using rewards is immoral. You might toss your dog a treat when he shakes hands, but that is no way to treat children. Classrooms should be a caring community in which students help one another, not a circus in which the teacher serves as ringmaster. The second objection is that offering rewards is unrealistic. Rewards can't last forever, so what happens when they stop? Those who make this argument think it's better to help students appreciate the subtle, but real rewards that the world offers for things like hard work and politeness. After all, adults don't expect that someone will toss them a candy bar every time they listen politely, push their chair under a table, or complete a report on time. The third objection is that offering rewards can actually decrease motivation. Cognitive science has found that this is true, but only under certain conditions. For example, if you initially enjoy reading and I reward you for each book you finish, the rewards will make you like reading less. Below, I'll explain how and why that happens. Let's consider each of these arguments in turn.

Are Rewards Immoral?

Don't rewards control students? Aren't rewards dehumanizing? Wouldn't it be better to create a classroom atmosphere in which students wanted to learn, rather than one in which they

reluctantly slogged through assignments, doing the minimal work they thought would still earn the promised reward? Cognitive science cannot answer moral questions. They are outside its purview. But cognitive science can provide some factual background that may help teachers as they consider these questions.

It is absolutely the case that trying to control students is destructive to their motivation and their performance. People like autonomy, and using rewards to control people definitely reduces motivation. Even if the task is one students generally like, if they sense that you're trying to coerce them, they will be less likely to do it (e.g., Ryan, Mims, and Koestner, 1983). It is worth pointing out, however, that rewards themselves are not inherently controlling. If students are truly offered a choice—do this and get a reward, don't do it and get no reward—then the student maintains control. Within behavioral science, it is accepted that rewards themselves are coercive if they are excessive (e.g., National Commission for the Protection of Human Subjects of Biomedical and Behavioral Research, 1978). In other words, if I offer you $200 to take a brief survey, it's hard to know that you're freely choosing to take the survey.

Rewards in classrooms are typically not excessive, and so are not, themselves, controlling. Rather, rewards might be an occasion for control if the teacher makes it quite clear that the student is expected to do the required work and collect his or her reward. That is, the teacher uses social coercion. So too, we've all known people we would call "manipulative," and those people seldom manipulate us via rewards. They use social means. In sum, the caution against controlling students is well-founded, but rewards are not inherently controlling.

Are rewards dehumanizing? Again, it seems to me that the answer depends on how the student construes the reward. If a teacher dangles stickers before students like fish before a seal, most observers will likely wince. But if a teacher emphasizes that rewards are a gesture of appreciation for a job well done, that probably would not appear dehumanizing to most observers.[1] Even so, rather than offer rewards, shouldn't teachers create classrooms in which students love learning? It is difficult not to respond to this objection by saying "Well, duh." I can't imagine there are many teachers who would rather give out candy than have a classroom full of students who are naturally interested and eager to learn. The question to ask is not "Why would you use rewards instead of making the material interesting?" Rather, it is "After you've wracked your brain for a way to make the material interesting for students and you still can't do it, then what?" Sanctimonious advice on the evils of rewards won't get chronically failing students to have one more go at learning to read. I think it unwise to discourage teachers from using any techniques in the absolute; rather, teachers need to know what research says about the benefits and drawbacks of the techniques, so that they can draw their own conclusions about whether and when to use them. Considering the merits of the two other objections will get us further into that research.

Sanctimonious advice on the evils of rewards won't get chronically failing students to have one more go at learning to read. I think it unwise to discourage teachers from using any techniques in the absolute; rather, teachers need to know what research says about the benefits and drawbacks of the techniques.

What Happens When Rewards Stop?

This objection is easy to appreciate. If I'm working math problems because you're paying me, what's going to happen once you stop paying me? Your intuition probably tells you that I will stop doing problems, and you're right. In the fruits and vegetables study described earlier, students stopped eating fruits and vegetables soon after the reward program stopped.

Although it might seem obvious that this would happen, psychologists initially thought that there was a way around this problem. Many studies were conducted during the 1960s using token economies. A token economy is a system by which rewards are administered in an effort to change behavior. There are many variants but the basic idea is that every time the student exhibits a targeted behavior (e.g., gets ready to work quickly in the morning), he or she gets a token (e.g., a plastic chip). Students accumulate tokens and later trade them for rewards (e.g., small prizes). Token economies have some positive effects, and have been used not only in classrooms, but in clinical settings (e.g., Dickerson, Tenhula, and Green-Paden, 2005).

When the idea of a token economy was developed, the plan was that the rewards would be phased out. Once the desired behavior was occurring frequently, you would not give the reward every time, but give it randomly, averaging 75 percent of the time, then 50 percent of the time, and so on. Thus, the student would slowly learn to do the behavior without the external reward. That works with animals, but normally not with humans. Once the rewards stop, people go back to behaving as they did before (Kazdin, 1982; O'Leary and Drabman, 1971).[2]

Well, one might counter, it may be true that students won't spontaneously work math problems once we stop rewarding them, but at least they will have worked more than they otherwise would have! Unfortunately, there is another, more insidious consequence of rewards that we need to consider: Under certain circumstances, they can actually decrease motivation.

How Can Rewards Decrease Motivation?

The previous section made it sound like rewards boost desired behavior so long as they are present, and when they are removed behavior falls back to where it started. That's true sometimes, but not always. If the task is one that students like, rewards will, as usual, make it more likely they'll do the task. But after the rewards stop, students will actually perform the previously likable task *less* than they did when rewards were first offered.

A classic study on this phenomenon (Lepper, Greene, and Nisbett, 1973) provides a good illustration. Children (aged 3 to 5 years old) were surreptitiously observed in a classroom with lots of different activities available. The experimenters noted how much time each child spent drawing with markers. The markers were then unavailable to students for two weeks. At the end of the two weeks, students were broken into three groups. Each student in the first group was taken to a separate room and was told that he or she could win an attractive "Good Player" certificate by drawing a picture with the markers. Each was eager to get the certificate and drew a picture. One-by-one, students in a second group were also brought to a separate room, encouraged to draw, and then given a certificate, but the certificate came as a surprise; when they started drawing, they didn't know that they would get the certificate. A third group of students served as a control group. They had been observed in the first session, but didn't draw or get a certificate in this second session. After another delay of about two weeks, the markers again appeared in the classroom, and experimenters observed how much children used them. The students in the first group—those who were promised the certificate for drawing—used the markers about half as much as students in the other two groups. Promising and then giving a reward made children like the markers less. But giving the reward as a surprise (as with the second group of students) had no effect.

This has been replicated scores of times with students of different ages, using different types of rewards, and in realistic classroom situations (see Deci et al., 1999 for a review). What is going on? How can getting a reward reduce your motivation to do something? The answer lies in the students' interpretation of why they chose to use the markers. For students who either didn't get a reward or who didn't expect a reward, it's obvious that they weren't drawing for the sake of the reward; they drew pictures because they liked drawing. But for the children who were promised a reward, the reason is less clear. A student might not remember that he drew because he wanted to draw, but rather he remembered really wanting the certificate. So when the markers were available again but no certificate was promised, the student may well have thought "I drew because I wanted that certificate; why should I draw now for nothing?"

The analogy to the classroom is clear. Teachers seek to create lifelong learners. We don't just want children to read, we want children to learn to love reading. So if, in an effort to get children to read more, we promise to reward them for doing so, we might actually make them like reading less! They will read more in order to get the pizza party or the stickers, but once the teacher is no longer there to give out the rewards, the student will say "Why should I read? I'm not getting anything for it."

The key factor to keep in mind is that rewards only decrease motivation for tasks that students initially like. If the task is dull, motivation might drop back down to its original level once the rewards stop, but it will not drop below its original level. Why does the appeal of the task make a difference? As I mentioned, rewards hurt motivation because of the way students construe the situation: "I drew with markers in order to get a certificate," instead of "I drew with markers because I like to draw with markers." But if the task is dull, students won't make that mistaken interpretation. They never liked the task in the first place. That hypothesis has been confirmed in a number of studies showing that once the reward is no longer being offered, having received a reward in the past harms the motivation for an interesting task, but not for a dull task (e.g., Daniel and Esser, 1980; Loveland and Olley, 1979; Newman and Layton, 1984).

The key factor to keep in mind is that rewards only decrease motivation for tasks that students initially like. If the task is dull, motivation might drop back down to its original level once the rewards stop, but it will not drop below its original level.

This finding might make one wonder whether rewards, in the form of grades, are behind students' lack of interest in schoolwork; by issuing grades, we're making students like school less (Kohn, 1993). It is true that students like school less and less as they get older. But it is wise to remember that motivation is a product of many factors. Researchers often distinguish between extrinsic motivators (e.g., concrete rewards or grades that are external to you) and intrinsic motivators (things that are internal to you such as your interest in a task). The effect described above can be succinctly summarized: Extrinsic rewards can decrease intrinsic motivation. We would thus expect that intrinsic and extrinsic motivation would be negatively correlated. That is, if you work mostly for the sake of getting good grades and other rewards, then you aren't very intrinsically motivated, and if you are highly intrinsically motivated, that must mean you don't care much about rewards. That's true to some extent, but the relationship is far from perfect. College students whose intrinsic and extrinsic motivation have been measured usually show a modest negative correlation, around -.25[3] (Lepper, Corpus, and Iyengar, 2005). This seems reasonable since motivation is actually pretty complex—we rarely do things for just one reason.

What Makes Rewards More or Less Effective?

If you decide to use rewards in the classroom, how can you maximize the chances that they will work? Three principles are especially important. Rewards should be desirable, certain, and prompt.

The importance of desirability is obvious. People will work for rewards that appeal to them, and will work less hard or not at all for rewards that are not appealing.[4] That is self-evident, and teachers likely know which rewards would appeal to their students and which would mean little to them.

If you decide to use rewards in the classroom, how can you maximize the chances that they will work? Three principles are especially important. Rewards should be desirable, certain, and prompt.

Less obvious is the importance of the certainty of a reward, by which I mean the probability that a student will get a reward if he or she attempts to do the target behavior. What if you've set a target that seems too difficult to the student, and he won't even try? Or what if the target seems achievable to the student, he makes an attempt and does his best, but still fails? Either reduces the likelihood that the student will try again. Both problems can be avoided if the reward is contingent on the student trying his best, and not on what he achieves. But that has its drawbacks, as well. It means that you must make a judgment call as to whether he tried his best. (And you must make that judgment separately for each student.) It is all too likely that some students will have an inflated view of their efforts, and your differing assessment will lead to mistrust. Ideally, the teacher will select specific behaviors for each student as targets, with the target titrated to each student's current level of ability.

A corollary of rewards being desirable is that they be prompt. A reward that is delayed has less appeal than the same reward delivered immediately. For example, suppose I gave you this choice: "You can have $10 tomorrow, or $10 a week from tomorrow." You'd take the $10 tomorrow, right? Rewards have more "oomph"—that is, more power to motivate—when you are going to get them soon. That's why, when my wife calls me from the grocery store, it's easy for me to say "Don't buy ice cream. I'm trying to lose weight." But when I'm at home it's difficult for me to resist ice cream that's in the freezer. In the first situation, I'm denying myself ice cream sometime in the distant future, but in the second I would be denying myself ice cream right at that moment. The promise of ice cream two minutes from now has higher value for me than the promise of ice cream hours from now.

It is possible to measure how much more desirable a reward is when given sooner rather than later. In one type of experiment, subjects participate in an auction and offer sealed bids for money that will be delivered to them later. Thus, each subject might be asked "What is the maximum you would pay right now for a reward of $10, to be delivered tomorrow?"[5] Subjects are asked to make bids for a variety of rewards to be delivered at delays varying from one to 30 days. Then, researchers use subjects' bids to derive a relationship between the amount of time that the reward is delayed and how much people value the delayed reward. Subjects typically show a steep drop off in how much they value the reward—with a one-day delay, $20 is worth about $18 to most subjects, and with a one-week delay, the value is more like $15 (e.g., Kirby, 1997). In other words, there is a significant cost to the reward value for even a brief delay. Other studies show that the cost

What is the Difference between Rewards and Praise?

You may have noticed that I have limited my discussion to the effects of concrete rewards—candy, cash, and so on. Isn't praise a reward as well? It can be, but praise as it's usually administered has some important differences. The most important is that praise is usually given unpredictably. The student doesn't think to himself, "If I get 90 percent or better on this spelling test, the teacher will say 'Good job, Dan!'" Rewards are different. There is usually an explicit bargain in the classroom, with the understanding that a particular behavior (e.g., 90 percent or better on a spelling test) merits a reward. As described in the main article, the decrease in motivation for a task only occurs if the reward was expected (and if the students enjoy the task). Since praise is not expected, it does not lead to an immediate decrement to motivation.

Another important difference between praise and concrete rewards is that the former is often taken as a more personal comment on one's abilities. Rewards typically don't impart information to the student. But praise can carry quite a bit of meaning. For starters, it tells the student that she did something noteworthy enough to merit praise. Then too, the student learns what the teacher considers important by listening to what she praises. A student may be told that she's smart, or that she tried hard, or that she's improving. In the short run, sincere praise will provide a boost to motivation (Deci et al., 1999), but in the long run, the content of praise can have quite different effects on the students' self-concept and on future efforts (e.g., Henderlong and Lepper, 2002; Mueller and Dweck, 1998). The key is in what type of praise is given. When faced with a difficult task, a child who has been praised in the past for her *effort* is likely to believe that intelligence increases as knowledge increases and, therefore, will work harder and seek more experiences from which she can learn. In contrast, a student who has been praised for her *ability* will likely believe that intelligence is fixed (e.g., is genetically determined) and will seek to maintain the "intelligent" label by trying to look good, even if that means sticking to easy tasks rather than more challenging tasks from which more can be learned.

A final difference between praise and rewards lies in students' expectations of encountering either in school. At least in the U.S., praise is part of everyday social interaction. If someone displays unusual skill or determination or kindness, or any other attribute that we esteem, it is not unusual to offer praise. In fact, a teacher who never praised her students might strike them as cold, or uncaring. No such expectation exists for rewards, however. It is hard to imagine teaching students without ever praising them. It is easy to imagine teaching students without ever offering them a concrete reward.

For more on praise and its effects, see "Ask the Cognitive Scientist," *American Educator,* Winter 2005–2006, available at www.aft.org/pubs-reports/american_educator/issues/winter05-06/cogsci.htm.

—D.W.

is greater for elementary school students than college students (e.g., Green, Fry and Myerson, 1994). That finding probably matches your intuition: As we get older, we get better at delaying gratification. Distant rewards become more similar to immediate rewards.

In this section I've summarized data showing that rewards should be desirable, certain, and prompt if they are to be effective. These three factors provide some insight into the extrinsic (but non-tangible) rewards that almost all schools offer: grades and graduation. Grades are not as rewarding as we might guess because they are seldom administered right after the required behavior (studying), and the reward of a diploma is, of course, even more distant. Then too, low-achieving students likely perceive these rewards as highly uncertain. That is, hard work does not guarantee that they will receive the reward.

Putting It All Together: Are Rewards Worth It?

When all is said and done, are rewards worth it? I liken using rewards to taking out a loan. You get an immediate benefit, but you know that you will eventually have to pay up, with interest. As with loans, I suggest three guidelines to the use of rewards: 1) try to find an alternative; 2) use them for a specific reason, not as a general strategy; and 3) plan for the ending.

Try to Find an Alternative

It is very difficult to implement rewards without incurring some cost. If the reward system is the same for all class members, it won't work as well as an individualized approach and you will likely reward some students for tasks they already like. If you tailor the rewards to individual students, you vastly increase your workload, and you increase the risk of students perceiving the program as unfair.

The size of the costs to motivation, although real, should not be overstated. As mentioned earlier, there are many contributors to motivation, and putting a smiley sticker on a spelling test will probably not rank high among them. Still, why incur the cost at all, if an alternative is available? The obvious alternative is to make the material intrinsically interesting. Indeed, if you follow that precept, you will never offer an extrinsic reward for an intrinsically interesting task, which is when the trouble with motivation really starts.

It is also worth considering whether student motivation is the real reason you use rewards. Do you put stickers on test papers in the hopes that students will work harder to earn them, or just for a bit of fun, a colorful diversion? Do you throw a class pizza party to motivate students, or to increase the class's sense of community? You might still distribute stickers and throw the party, but not make them explicitly contingent on performance beforehand. Announce to the class that they have done such a good job on the most recent unit that a party seems in order. Thus, the party is still an acknowledgement of good work and still might contribute to a positive class atmosphere, but it is not offered as a reward contingent on performance.

Use Rewards for a Specific Reason

A wise investor understands that taking out a loan, although it incurs a cost, might be strategic in the long run. So too, although a rewards program may incur some cost to motivation, there are times when the cost might be worth it. One example is when students must learn or practice a task that is rather dull, but that, once mastered, leads to opportunities for greater interest and motivation. For example, learning the times tables might be dull, but if students can get over that hump of boredom, they are ready to take on more interesting work. Rewards might also be useful when a student has lost confidence in himself to the point that he is no longer willing to try. If he'll attempt academic work to gain a desirable extrinsic reward and succeeds, his perception of himself and his abilities may change from self-doubt to recognition that he is capable of academic work (Greene and Lepper, 1974). Thereafter, the student may be motivated by his sense of accomplishment and his expectation that he will continue to do well.

> **Although a rewards program may incur some cost to motivation, there are times that the cost might be worth it. For example, learning the times tables might be dull, but if students can get over that hump of boredom, they are ready to take on more interesting work.**

Use Rewards for a Limited Time

No one wants to live with chronic debt, and no one should make rewards a long-term habit. Although the cost of using rewards may not be large, that cost likely increases as rewards are used for a longer time. In addition, there would seem to be an advantage to the program having a natural ending point. For example, students are rewarded for learning their times tables, and once they are learned, the rewards end. The advantage is that any decrease in motivation might stick to the task. In other words, students will think "times tables are boring, and we need to be rewarded to learn them" rather than "math is boring, and we need to be rewarded to learn it." In addition, if students are told at the start of the program when it will end, there may be fewer complaints when the goodies are no longer available.

Notes

1. Such positive framing of rewards does not reverse the negative impact of rewards on motivation, but telling students that rewards signal acknowledgement of good work, rather than the closing of a bargain, seems more in keeping with the spirit of education.
2. Readers who are familiar with interventions to reduce students' aggressive or antiscoial behavior may be surprised at this finding. Such interventions do often use rewards and then phase them out. But keep in mind that the rewards are just one part of a complex intervention and that in order to be effective, such interventions must be implemented in full. To learn more about the use of rewards in such an intervention, see "Heading Off Disruption: How Early Intervention Can Reduce Defiant Behavior—and Win Back Teaching Time," *American Educator,* Winter 2003–2004, available at www.aft.org/pubs-reports/american_educator/winter03-04/index.html.
3. A correlation of zero would indicate that they were unrelated, and a correlation of -1.0 would indicate that they were perfectly related.
4. There are exceptions to this generalization, notably in the social realm. People will work hard without reward as part of a social transaction. In such situations a small reward will actually make people less likely to work (e.g., Heyman and Ariely, 2004). For example, if an acquaintance asks you to help her move a sofa, you would assume that she's asking a favor as a friend, and you might well help. But if she offers you $5 to move the sofa you think of the request as a business transaction, and $5 may not seem like enough money. These social concerns could apply to the classroom; some students might work to please the teacher. But such social transactions rest on reciprocity. If your friend with the poorly placed sofa never helps you out, you will get tired of her requests. It would be difficult to set up a classroom relationship that used social reciprocity between teachers and students.
5. The procedure is actually what researchers call a second-bid auction; the highest bidder wins the auction, but pays the price of the second highest bid. This procedure is meant to ensure that people bid exactly what the item is worth to them. The workings of the auction are explained in detail to subjects.

Critical Thinking

1. What do you think about the evidence presented about the effectiveness of rewards? What about the moral arguments for/against their use?
2. Describe a situation where you think it would be appropriate to implement an individual reward system with a student. What are some key considerations mentioned in the article to ensure the reward has the impact you intend?
3. Think back to a situation when you were in school and your class was promised a reward (e.g., pizza party, movie day) for meeting a goal. Was the goal something you already were motivated to work toward or something you did not find engaging/interesting? How did students react when the class earned or failed to earn the reward? Describe your perception of how the class was impacted by the idea of the reward, specifically were the relationships among students impacted.

DANIEL T. WILLINGHAM is professor of cognitive psychology at the University of Virginia and author of *Cognition: The Thinking Animal.* His research focuses on the role of consciousness in learning. Readers can pose specific questions to "Ask the Cognitive Scientist," American Educator, 555 New Jersey Ave. N.W., Washington, DC 20001, or to amered@aft.org. Future columns will try to address readers' questions.

Beyond Content: How Teachers Manage Classrooms to Facilitate Intellectual Engagement for Disengaged Students

DEBORAH L. SCHUSSLER

This article explores how teachers manage classrooms to facilitate the intellectual engagement of disengaged students. The author proposes that teachers create an environment conducive to intellectual engagement when students perceive: (a) that there are opportunities for them to succeed, (b) that flexible avenues exist through which learning can occur, and (c) that they are respected as learners because teachers convey the belief that students are capable of learning. When teachers purposefully manage classrooms so that these elements intersect optimally, students perceive that they are known and valued. Furthermore, opportunities for success, flexibility, and respect generally are present when teachers challenge their students at appropriate levels, provide academic support, use instructional techniques that convey excitement for the content, and make learning relevant. To illuminate how teachers succeed in managing classrooms for intellectual engagement, the author provides numerous quotes from students attending an alternative high school designed for disengaged students who possess academic potential.

> [Here] I'm more, I guess, a free thinker or something. . . . [The teachers] don't rush us, they don't force us. But they don't make it easy and they don't give us forever. . . . At my other school I just kind of felt like they're giving all this stuff to me because I had to do it, and they didn't care. . . . Here it's just different. I care about what I'm doing. (Peter,[1] 10th grade)

Peter was once at risk of dropping out of school. Despite attending a middle-class, suburban, comprehensive high school where the average SAT score was 1126 and the percent of students on free or reduced lunch was 8%, Peter almost decided to quit. Although most of his grades were passing, Peter had disengaged from school on all levels—behavioral, emotional, and cognitive (Fredricks, Blumenfeld, & Paris, 2004). Osterman (1998) summarized Peter's situation quite well: "Even for those students who succeed in school on standard achievement criteria, lack of engagement with learning is a serious problem" (p. 41). Fortunately, Peter had the option to attend a small, alternative school that followed the Middle College concept. Middle Colleges are public high schools collaborating with local colleges. They seek to prevent capable students from dropping out of school by creating academically enriched environments that also support students' social and personal development.[2] For Peter, who is not unlike many high school students, the issue was not whether he was capable of challenging intellectual work; he was capable. The issue involved whether Peter was in an environment conducive to his engagement in learning.

What was it about the alternative school that kept Peter, and others like him, from dropping out? Even more importantly, what was it that captured his interest and helped him care about what he was doing academically? The brief quote from Peter provides powerful clues into ways teachers can engage disengaged students in intellectual work. Contrary to the beliefs of legislators myopically focused on accountability, it has little to do with helping students meet proficiency requirements on standardized tests, though accountability and proficiency are important. Contrary to the beliefs of those preoccupied with particular instructional strategies, it extends beyond the actual content of what teachers teach (Ritchhart, 2002) and the mere elimination of student misbehavior (McCaslin & Good, 1992). Teachers can create an environment conducive to intellectual engagement when students perceive three pervasive elements are a part of all classroom discourse:

1. There are opportunities for students to succeed.
2. Flexible avenues exist through which learning can occur.
3. Students are respected as learners because teachers convey the belief that students are capable of achieving academic success.

It seems so basic. Yet disengaged students perceive opportunities for success, flexibility, and respect as pervasively lacking in schools (Altenbaugh, 1998; Liaupsin, Umbreit, Ferro, Urso, & Upreti, 2006; Pressley, Gaskins, Solic, & Collins, 2006). In this article, I explain how teachers can manage classrooms to facilitate these three pervasive elements that are crucial to engaging students intellectually. To augment the explanations,

I provide quotes from students—primarily Peter's classmates at a Middle College in a suburban district in the southeastern United States. I use these students' voices for two reasons. First, students are frequently ignored in conversations of educational policy and practice (Cook-Sather, 2002; Yazzie-Mintz, 2006), yet students decide their engagement or disengagement in school. Second, Middle College students provide a unique glimpse into aspects of engagement. These 126 students possessed academic potential, but for any number of reasons—from academic to social—disengaged from their previous schools only to re-engage at Middle College. Their insights suggest that effective classroom management and pedagogy that supports intellectual engagement are inextricably linked, as they involve knowing the students well and finding where opportunities for success, flexibility, and respect intersect optimally.

Before proceeding, I should explain what I mean by intellectual *engagement*. Although some define engagement in learning as the tangible behaviors that students exhibit in the classroom (Greenwood, Horton, & Utley, 2002) or outside the classroom related to homework and study habits (Yazzie-Mintz, 2006), I take a more comprehensive view. Engagement in learning involves formulating a deeper connection between the student and the material whereby a student develops an interest in the topic or retains the learning beyond the short term. There are no precise formulas for managing a classroom for intellectual engagement. However, opportunities for success, flexibility, and respect generally are present when teachers challenge their students at appropriate levels, provide academic support, use instructional techniques that convey excitement for the content, and make learning relevant. I describe these in greater detail in the next sections.

Academic Challenge

> They'll make you seep in as much as you can right up to the point that you'd turn it off . . . and then it's pulled back a little bit. (James, 11th grade)

Lack of academic challenge has often been attributed to the "bargains" (Sedlak, Wheeler, Pullin, & Cusick, 1986) or "compromises" (Sizer, 1984) teachers establish with students, whereby students tacitly agree to maintain order and teachers tacitly agree to hold expectations to a minimum. However, substantial evidence exists that students across school contexts want teachers to challenge them academically (Sizer & Sizer, 1999; Yazzie-Mintz, 2006). The desire for a challenge is especially true when classroom discourse mirrors authentic conversations, as opposed to typical classroom talk, and includes issues students perceive are relevant (Alpert, 1991; Sizer & Sizer, 1999). Furthermore, it is imperative that teachers couple academic challenge with academic support.

It becomes more obvious why academic challenge must operate in tandem with academic support when one considers how the three pervasive elements intersect to portray a *sweet spot* for achieving engagement. Students feel appropriately challenged when teachers combine flexibility with opportunities to succeed, which results in the students feeling respected as students and

having a positive attitude toward their academics (Turner & Meyer, 2004). When students perceive academic work as too difficult or too easy, which usually means there is either no flexibility or too much flexibility in how students achieve academic success, they feel a lack of respect. Lack of respect generally manifests in a negative attitude toward their academics. Compare James's words to those of a student in Pittsburgh who eventually decided to drop out of school, a decision he attributed to his reaction toward the "cynical and calloused teachers" who did little more than pass students along: " 'they sort of had an 'I don't care' attitude. Get you in and get you out. Just so long as you get that D' " (Altenbaugh, 1998, p. 60). This student perceived a lack of respect because teachers did not care enough to challenge him. In contrast, James described the sweet spot of where the optimal academic challenge exists. Students have to feel pushed. When they do not feel pushed, students disengage. When they are asked to "seep in" more than they can handle, students disengage.

The challenge for teachers, then, is to determine how much to push students. Where is the sweet spot? As the Pittsburgh student's quote indicates, it stems from teachers' attitudes. A combination of care and high expectations is essential for students to reach their highest capacity as evidenced in academic achievement and motivation (Gay, 2000; Turner & Meyer, 2004; Wentzel, 1997), positive social outcomes (Wentzel, 1997), and increased ownership (Stefanou, Perencevich, DiCintio, & Turner, 2004). This is true for students across school contexts. Teachers create a synergy of care and high expectations when they provide opportunities for students to succeed, both for the present-oriented purpose of achieving good grades and for the future-oriented purpose of living a good life. Kathleen, a 10th grader, highlighted how care and high expectations operated synergistically for present and future purposes when she said, "They care about your grades and they want you to succeed and it just made me feel like there's somebody that wants me to graduate; there's somebody that wants me to do something with my life."

Teachers foster opportunities to succeed and provide flexibility through a curriculum that is student-driven, rather than curriculum-driven. Curricular flexibility means demonstrating both acute awareness of ways students understand the material and responsiveness to student needs. The idea of responsiveness is prevalent in research on at-risk students (Catterall, 1998), culturally relevant pedagogy (Gay, 2000), and special education (Fuchs, Mock, Morgan, & Young, 2003). Across these bodies of literature, the most compelling commonality that applies to all teachers, regardless of context, is the importance of knowing and responding to students' needs, as individuals. This means meeting students where they are, which seems obvious, but for a variety of reasons often does not occur in high schools. When describing her teachers at Middle College, Stephanie, an 11th grader, said, "They'll actually help you with what you don't know. . . . When I came here I didn't have like really any study skills . . . because I had been moving around so much. . . . In Geometry she's taught different ways that you can study for tests and how to prepare for certain things." When James says teachers "make you seep in as much as you can right up to the point that you'd turn it off," this implies that teachers know how much each student can seep in and also know the point where each student would turn it off. In other words, for each individual student, teachers provide just the right amount of challenge, along with just the right amount of support.

Academic Support

Teachers should teach so everybody can understand, not just so a few elite kids can know what's going on. (Peter, 10th grade)

Students who disengage academically from school often feel as though success is meant only for certain elite students, or those who have experienced success in the past, or those who are just lucky (Altenbaugh, 1998). To complicate matters, intellectual disengagement frequently occurs as a result of students' emotional and behavioral disengagement (Fredricks et al., 2004). In other words, students who do not feel that they belong on the football field or in the student council also feel that they do not belong in the classroom. To engage students, teachers must make them feel like they not only belong in the classroom, but also that they are capable of doing challenging intellectual work. This means not just pushing them to achieve, but also providing the support through which achievement is possible.

Academic support is possible when teachers convey an attitude that students can succeed. This attitude should mirror those of high-reliability organizations, such as air traffic control towers; those working in such organizations view success as the expectation, not a chance occurrence, and they do everything possible to create conditions that facilitate success (Irmsher, 1997). At her alternative school, Leah describes her teachers as having exactly this attitude toward student success: "They'll do anything they can because they know we can do it. . . . They all know us, and they're going to keep pushing us to do it." Leah's perception that her teachers possessed a steadfast belief in her ability to achieve led her to adopt this same belief.

As Leah also indicates, teachers must know students individually in order to translate their beliefs into actions. Because each student varies in terms of learning style, interests, background knowledge, culture, and cognitive scaffolding, teachers must make efforts to know students within these various dimensions and to respond accordingly. Only through such knowing can teachers provide the appropriate type and amount of academic support.

My teacher actually sat there and watched me do some math problems. I didn't know she was watching me and she was like, "You're a very verbal learner.". . . I'd never thought about it. . . . She had observed how I learned and she had noticed that when I was doing really well on a problem, I was talking my way through it. (James, 11th grade)

Not only did his teacher become aware of James's learning style, the teacher also helped James become aware of his own learning style. This was accomplished through a very simple technique: observation. James's teacher simply observed him as he engaged in the learning process. Obviously, this takes time. However, when the goal is curriculum coverage, a likely

end result is teachers covering more and students engaging less (Ritchhart, 2002).

The three pervasive elements—opportunities to succeed, flexibility, and respect—are readily apparent in the specific ways teachers provide academic support to facilitate students' engagement. These include conducting diagnostic assessments as a way of knowing students' strengths and needs. These assessments may include formal instruments, like a learning styles inventory, but most are the result of simply observing students. The informal assessment James's teacher conducted provided valuable information to both James and the teacher about how he worked through math problems. To help James engage, and therefore succeed, the teacher can be flexible in allowing James to talk his way through his work. James will feel respected because not only will he know a strategy he needs to function successfully in math class, but he will also be encouraged to use it.

Formative assessment and differentiated instruction are other specific ways teachers provide academic support to facilitate students' engagement. Bob, an 11th grader in a challenging math class, highlighted the importance of formative assessment when he noted, "She makes sure that we know how to do it before we take a test, before we leave that classroom." When teachers frequently check on students' understanding, through low-risk assessments, students know that teachers want them to succeed academically. When teachers use differentiated instruction, modifying the content, process, or products of learning, students know there is flexibility in how they can develop and demonstrate their understanding (King-Shaver & Hunter, 2003). A classroom that accommodates this level of academic support must be very organized. Teachers must be purposeful about determining students' strengths and needs and about ensuring the availability of appropriate resources, described next.

Instruction

High school isn't all about necessarily learning facts. . . . [Teachers] are so concerned with "Am I going to meet my deadline? Are my standarized tests going to be up to par?" that they don't have time to stop and think about it. (James, 11th grade)

When monotony and task completion characterize a majority of classroom instruction, students are less likely to engage intellectually. In contrast, when students perceive they have opportunities to succeed on authentic tasks through the flexible instruction of their teachers, they are more likely to engage. Teachers manage classrooms to facilitate student engagement when they demonstrate enthusiasm for authentic content and purposefully use instructional strategies to capture students' interest.

As James and Peter noted, students equate learning disparate facts from the book with rigidity and lack of instructional creativity on the part of the teacher. In the mind of the students, when a teacher teaches straight from the book, it is the teacher being lazy; students then have little motivation to complete academic work, much less become excited about it. They may demonstrate overt misbehavior or quietly subversive resistance through nonparticipation in classroom discourse (Alpert, 1991). In contrast, a number of students at Middle College mentioned the infectious enthusiasm of the ecology teacher who had worked in the private sector before teaching at the college level then teaching at Middle College. Caesar, a 12th grader, said, "The teachers here cover more, like the ecology teacher. She gets really into it because she's a big environmentalist. . . . She just talks from personal experience and incorporates things. She's a very good teacher." Caesar wanted to engage in the content because the teacher combined knowledge with a desire to share her passions with her students.

No single instructional technique operates as a panacea for increasing student interest in course content. In fact, when Bryk, Lee, and Holland (1993) investigated the educational processes of Catholic high schools, they were surprised to find "students' positive reactions to rather ordinary teaching" (p. 99). Despite ubiquitously traditional pedagogy, the researchers observed "high levels of engagement with classroom activities" (p. 99). They found that the "quality of human relations" (p. 99) was more important than specific instructional techniques. My own work exploring care in educational contexts supports the conclusion that how students perceive teachers' attitudes is one of the most important factors in determining the extent of their intellectual engagement (Schussler, 2006). When teachers structure instruction in ways that demonstrate their desire to interest students in the content, students notice. It is not that the instructional techniques are unimportant; rather, it is that the attitude with which the teacher employs the techniques is more important. Knowing how to structure instruction entails knowing the students, specifically, knowing how to challenge and support students, as well as how to tap into their interests and demonstrate the relevance of the content.

Relevance

I can tell that I'm learning in his class because outside of his class I'll be flipping through the channels and something on history will come on and I'll be like, "Let's watch this." It's an interest. (Trixie, 11th grade)

In a study of over 80,000 students at 110 high schools, researchers found that when asked why they were bored in class, 75% of students said because the material was not interesting and 39% said the material was not relevant to them (Yazzie-Mintz, 2006). Teachers help increase students' interest in academic content, and their engagement, by giving students authentic tasks. Authentic tasks include opportunities to problem solve situations that mirror the kind of ambiguity students face in real life (Alpert, 1991; Ritchhart, 2002). In describing how to help students put intelligence into action, Ritchhart advocated "conditional instruction" (p. 140). In conditional instruction, teachers present facts open-endedly. For example, students are told, "This may be the cause of the evolution of city neighborhoods," instead of "The cause of [the] evolution of city neighborhoods is . . ." (p. 140). Studies on conditional instruction found that students in both conditions retained the

information equally well, but students who received the information via conditional language demonstrated more creativity and flexibility in being able to solve problems. They also shifted from being passive to being more active learners, developing "a sense of their own agency," (p. 141) as they attempted to make sense of ambiguous situations.

Thinking about the curriculum outside of traditional, academic content is also crucial to helping students see the relevance in what they are learning. Noddings (2006) emphasized the importance of being purposeful about teaching personal and social skills that students will use throughout their lives. "Possibly no goal of education is more important—or more neglected—than self-understanding" (p. 10). These goals should not exist as separate from, but rather as integrated with, the academic curriculum. Notice that David, a 12th grader, does not view the academic and personal curricula as mutually exclusive, but rather as infinitely relevant: "I'm learning about me and who I want to be. . . . Basically with what I'm concentrating on—writing or trying to figure out some economic equation—I'm trying to figure out what I want to do, where I want to be five, ten years down the road." Similarly, Kathleen, a 10th grader, notes how the social skills were important for her life-long learning: "I'm not only learning the actual curriculum stuff, but here you're also learning . . . adult skills. . . . You learn how to communicate with people. . . . They're preparing you for life here."

Clearly, academic content is not unimportant. However, it becomes more relevant when it is purposefully integrated with the development of social and personal skills. As adults, we do not choose to engage in tasks in which we see no relevance. We should not expect students to be any different.

Concluding Comments

Middle College does not represent the traditional high school, yet all schools can learn something about classroom management and intellectual engagement from a school that succeeds in engaging previously disengaged students. Opportunities to succeed, flexibility, and respect undergird students' experiences at Middle College. More specifically, teachers purposefully balance offering an academic challenge with support, use instructional techniques that convey excitement for the content, and make learning relevant. Managing a classroom within these pedagogical parameters means moving beyond thinking primarily about content and into thinking about knowing students as individuals. Certainly, many teachers pursue this goal. Small alternative schools do not hold sole proprietorship on holding the students central. It may be that alternative schools are more purposeful about creating an environment that enables teachers to know students well. Maybe this is where future reform efforts should focus.

Notes

1. All proper names have been changed.
2. For more information about the Middle College concept, see Weschler (2001).
3. All students are from Middle College unless otherwise noted.

References

Alpert, B. (1991). Students' resistance in the classroom. *Anthropology and Education Quarterly, 22*(4), 350–366.

Altenbaugh, R. J. (1998). "Some teachers are ignorant": Teachers and teaching through urban school leavers' eyes. In B. M. Franklin (Ed.), *When children don't learn: Student failure and the culture of teaching* (pp. 52–71). New York: Teachers College Press.

Bryk, A. S., Lee, V. E., & Holland, P. B. (1993). *Catholic schools and the common good.* Cambridge, MA: Harvard University Press.

Catterall, J. S. (1998). Risk and resilience in student transitions to high school. *American Journal of Education, 106*(2), 302–333.

Cook-Sather, A. (2002). Authorizing students' perspectives: Toward trust, dialogue, and change in education. *Educational Researcher, 31*(4), 3–14.

Fredricks, J. A., Blumenfeld, P. C., & Paris, A. H. (2004). School engagement: Potential of the concept, state of the evidence. *Review of Educational Research, 74*(1), 59–109.

Fuchs, D., Mock, D., Morgan, P. L., & Young, C. L. (2003). Responsiveness-to-intervention: Definitions, evidence, and implications for the learning disabilities construct. *Learning Disabilities Research & Practice, 18*(3), 157–171.

Gay, G. (2000). *Culturally responsive teaching: Theory, research, and practice.* New York: Teachers College Press.

Greenwood, C. R., Horton, B. T., & Utley, C. A. (2002). Academic engagement: Current perspectives on research and practice. *School Psychology Review, 31*(3), 328–349.

Irmsher, K. (1997). *Education reform and students at risk: ERIC Digest, Number 112* (No. ERIC Document Reproduction Service ED 405 642). Eugene, OR: ERIC Clearinghouse on Educational Management.

King-Shaver, B., & Hunter, A. (2003). *Differentiated instruction in the English classroom.* Portsmouth, NH: Heinemann.

Liaupsin, C. J., Umbreit, J., Ferro, J. B., Urso, A., & Upreti, G. (2006). Improving academic engagement through systematic, function-based intervention. *Education and Treatment of Children, 29*(4), 572–589.

McCaslin, M., & Good, T. L. (1992). Compliant cognition: The misalliance of management and instructional goals in current school reform. *Educational Researcher, 21*(3), 4–17.

Noddings, N. (2006). *Critical lessons: What our schools should teach.* Cambridge, MA: Cambridge University Press.

Osterman, K. F. (1998, April). *Student community within the school context: A research synthesis.* Paper presented at the Annual Meeting of the American Educational Research Association.

Pressley, M., Gaskins, I. W., Solic, K., & Collins, S. (2006). A portrait of Benchmark School: How a school produces high achievement in students who previously failed. *Journal of Educational Psychology, 98*(2), 282–306.

Ritchhart, R. (2002). *Intellectual character: What it is, why it matters, and how to get it.* San Francisco: Jossey-Bass.

Schussler, D. L. (2006). An empirical exploration of the who? what? and how? of school care. *Teachers College Record, 108*(7), 1460–1495.

Sedlak, M., Wheeler, C. W., Pullin, D. C., & Cusick, P. A. (1986). *Selling students short: Classroom bargains and academic reform in the American high school.* New York: Teachers College Press.

Sizer, T. R. (1984). *Horace's compromise: The dilemma of the American high school.* Boston: Houghton Mifflin Company.

Sizer, T. R., & Sizer, N. F. (1999). *The students are watching: Schools and the moral contract.* Boston: Beacon Press.

Stefanou, C. R., Perencevich, K. C., DiCintio, M., & Turner, J. C. (2004). Supporting autonomy in the classroom: Ways teachers encourage student decision making and ownership. *Educational Psychologist, 39*(2), 97–110.

Turner, J. C., & Meyer, D. K. (2004). A classroom perspective on the principle of moderate challenge in mathematics. *Journal of Educational Research, 97*(6), 311–318.

Wechsler, H. S. (2001). *Access to success in the urban high school: The Middle College movement.* New York: Teachers College Press.

Wentzel, K. R. (1997). Student motivation in middle school: The role of perceived pedagogical caring. *Journal of Educational Psychology, 89*(3), 411–419.

Yazzie-Mintz, E. (2006). *Voices of students on engagement: A report on the 2006 high school survey of student engagement.* Bloomington, IN: Center for Evaluation and Education Policy.

Critical Thinking

1. Describe some specific ways you can provide support while academically challenging students from across a range of different academic, social, and behavioral strengths and weaknesses?

2. Explain how you would monitor and evaluate students' intellectual engagement in your class.

DEBORAH L. SCHUSSLER is an associate professor of education and human services at Villanova University.

Correspondence should be addressed to: **DEBORAH L. SCHUSSLER**, Department of Education and Human Services, Villanova University, 800 Lancaster Ave., Villanova, PA 19085. E-mail: deborah.schussler@villanova.edu.

"The Strive of It"

What conditions inspire teens to practice toward perfection?

KATHLEEN CUSHMAN

In a high school on the west side of Chicago, a 9th grade boy named Joshua is describing the thing he does best in life. I am in Joshua's classroom, and 28 students are sitting in a circle with me. "I'm real good at architecture," Joshua says matter-of-factly.

I am startled, even skeptical. Architecture in 9th grade?

Joshua goes on. His interest started, he says, when he was 11 as he watched his uncle, a building contractor, draw up plans on a computer.

> I was, like, "Can I do it?" Once I tried it, I liked it. I can draw the layout of a building, make electrical wires in the layout, stuff like that. It was hard learning how to use the software, because it was something I'd never used before. It took me a couple months—it was real frustrating. I remember trying to find out how to make a wall longer, and my uncle wasn't there to help me. I had to go to "Help" to read how to do it. I don't like reading, but I was determined to learn how to use this software.

All of us in the room believe him now, because Joshua is talking about something most of us know well: trying to master something hard. We recognize his frustration as he goes after something just beyond his reach. We hear how his resolve and confidence increase as he pushes past obstacles. And when Joshua tells us the result, we hear his pride. Last summer, one of his neighbors was putting up a small strip mall. The neighbor knew Joshua had expertise in this area, so he asked Joshua to help draw up the plans.

The Practice Project

What does it take, I asked the students listening to Joshua that day, to get really good at something? It's a simple question that matters equally to youth and adults, rich and poor, professional, artist, and tradesperson—and its answer could transform schools and communities. To learn more, I brought together the perspectives of young people and cognitive researchers in the Practice Project, a yearlong inquiry sponsored by the nonprofit What Kids Can Do.

Exciting evidence has emerged in recent decades showing that opportunity and practice have far more influence on performance than does innate talent. The people we call experts have typically spent 10,000 hours in deliberate practice getting to that point—the equivalent of 10 years of practicing three hours a day, six days a week (Eriksson, 1996).

To understand what these findings meant for everyday teaching and learning, I started asking adolescents themselves. Reaching out to schools and youth organizations, I looked not for prodigies, but for 160 ordinary teenagers willing to talk with me about their lives and learning. They came from diverse backgrounds around the United States, ranging from cities to rural communities. Together, we explored how young people acquire the knowledge, skills, and habits that help them rise to mastery in a field.

To my surprise, every one of these youth could name something they were already good at. Many of them—not just the unusually talented—were even growing expert at it. The examples kept coming: music, dance, drawing, drama, chess, video games, soccer, building robots, writing poems, skateboarding, cooking. So much sustained work in the pursuit of mastery—and so much of it happening outside school!

In days of discussion, we picked apart how the teenagers got started at these activities, why they kept going, and what setbacks and satisfactions they experienced as they put in the necessary practice. We discovered a great deal about why young people engage deeply in work that challenges them. And as we analyzed their experiences, the kids and I also began to think differently about what goes on in schools. Could what these young people already understood about practice also apply to their academic learning? Could teachers build on kids' strengths and affinities, coaching them in the habits of experts?

Getting Started, Keeping Going

These teenagers' stories brought into vivid relief research on how expertise develops. Few of them started their chosen activity because they had "natural talent." Largely, they gravitated to something because it looked like fun, because they wanted to be with others who were doing it, and because someone gave them a chance and encouraged them.

Joey, a nationally ranked archer at age 16, first picked up a bow and arrow at 6, because he wanted to "hang out with my dad in the backyard and shoot bales." Ninoshka learned to knit from her grandmother, who "would not be mad at me, no matter what came out wrong, because she was trying to make me better at it." Kellie tried double-dutch jump rope only when her big sister counted her down to the first scary move.

Kids have to want something before they risk trying it, said Ariel, a young skateboarder:

> If something's very fun-looking to you, you just get right into it. That inspiration from watching other people do new things, it gives you confidence.

Not far into their learning, all those I interviewed faced significant frustration. What happened next made a crucial difference as they realized that to succeed, they had to persist. As Darrius, a student bent on becoming an artist, said,

> It's not like one day you can just get up and say, "I'm going to do something." You got to practice at it. You might be good at it when you first start off, but you still got to practice at it so you can get better, because no one's perfect. Like me: I can draw real good. But certain things that I want to learn how to do in drawing, I can't do right now. So I just keep working at it.

When they hit discouraging points, most students said they only continued if they had a strong relationship with someone who supported them through the rough spots. As Janiy, who studied piano, observed,

> The people who sit next to you have a big part in how you get better. Without [someone encouraging you] you can start getting lazy, and you may want to give up if you don't get it right the first time. [If] I give up on the inside, she tells me, "[Try] again. Come on."

In school, too, these youth persisted with challenging material only when their practice was supported. Erika described one teacher who made her feel her tentative ideas were valid:

> I was afraid of sounding stupid. But she would never let you just sit and observe. She always wanted you in the conversation. She would make you talk, but . . . in a really encouraging way, like, "Hey Erika, what do you think about this?" And if I said a quick answer, "Can you elaborate on that?"

Through their outside activities, these teenagers had gained a healthy respect for the base of knowledge they needed before they could do something well. They had experience taking their practice step by step, continuing to reach for the next thing they could realistically manage. As Iona said, "When people are only faced with their failures, they tend to want to give up."

The students were describing, we realized, what cognitive researchers like K. Anders Eriksson call *deliberate practice.* Their learning tasks were set at a challenge level just right for them. They repeated a task in a focused, attentive way, at intervals that helped them recall the task's key elements. All along, they received and adjusted to feedback. And when they kept at it, they were rewarded by what Mihaly Csikszentmihalyi (1990) calls *flow:* the energized, full involvement of going after a challenge within their reach. As Aaron, a basketball player, described it:

> Running down the court, it's like a lion hunting for its prey. There's nothing else on its mind but that prey. And that's what makes it so beautiful, just the strive of it.

Their best schoolwork, these students said, got them to practice the habits we had seen experts using.

Learning from Experts

Watching accomplished people do something well often made these teenagers want to practice even more. Talking to experts directly was even better. "If I meet a musician I look up to, everything he says is like it was bolded out," said Mike. So I sent students out to interview people from their communities whom the students considered masters in their fields—plumbers, farmers, church organists, psychologists, engineers, and so on.

The kids saw many similarities to their own learning journeys. Every expert's story started with a spark of interest that somebody noticed and fanned. All had the opportunity to explore that interest further, with someone nearby to encourage and critique them. Small successes along the way rewarded hours of practice—and with each challenge met, the experts wanted to go further.

Whether the person interviewed was a surgeon, a tattoo artist, or a detective, each of these experts had developed certain habits along the way (see "The Habits of Experts"). Some were ways of thinking, and others were ways of approaching work. The students and I made a list and returned to it often, checking whether students were developing these habits.

The Habits of Experts

From fabric art to medicine, experts practice common habits:

- Ask good questions.
- Break problems into parts.
- Look for patterns.
- Rely on evidence.
- Consider other perspectives.
- Use familiar ideas in new ways.
- Collaborate with others.
- Welcome critique.
- Revise repeatedly.
- Persist.
- Seek new challenges.
- Know yourself.

We also questioned what drove these experts through their years of practice—competition or collaboration, public performance or private satisfaction? In all the different answers students gathered, they recognized the quality of flow. Energized by that discovery, the kids explored what brought that same feeling into schoolwork.

Taking Practice to School

Nothing compared to "the strive of it," these young people agreed. Yet they felt this sense of flow most fully outside the classroom. Was there something teachers could do to transfer the excitement of learning from one realm to the other? The kids I interviewed did not suggest making direct links between their interests and school subjects. Instead, they reminded teachers of the meaning and value they found in commitments outside school and asked teachers to look for such meaning in school subjects, too.

Aaron failed science two years in a row at his Long Beach high school before a teacher helped him make this kind of connection:

> I never understood why we have a moon, or why we orbit around the sun. And now, my teacher really breaks down why certain things happen. We have a moon because there was a large asteroid that ran into earth and broke off and orbited around the earth. I love that type of science. It makes me want to learn more and more about it, to understand the concept.

Some teachers, Nick said, brought boring material to life, connecting it to a story, conflict, or question that gave it more meaning:

> Any field has something interesting about it, so tell us! You can start by saying, "Look how interesting this is," and ask us to think about "Why is this? Where does this come from?"

Their best schoolwork, these students said, got them to practice the habits we had seen experts using. Although these activities focused on deep questions and concepts, teachers also adapted them to fit each learner's needs. Like good coaches, they tailored homework to what individual students needed to practice and followed up when kids had trouble.

To a striking degree, the successful curriculums kids described involved interdisciplinary projects that had students work in teams toward an outcome that mattered to them. Because they valued the projects goal, they went after the knowledge and skills required to reach it, putting what they were learning into use along the way. When they ran into trouble, a good teacher gave them encouragement and help. As they engaged in the practice necessary to succeed, very different kinds of students began to act like members of an expert team.

For example, on a class trip to Washington, D.C., student teams arranged interviews with embassies and nongovernmental organizations about one of 10 crucial world issues and then held a symposium to share their learning after they returned. In another project, an economics teacher challenged students to analyze their city's traffic congestion, research ideas for improvement, and present their proposals to the local transportation authority.

The motivating assignments students mentioned shared these characteristics:

- They started with a question, problem, or challenge that required extending the understanding of the group.
- Team members not only had individual parts to play, but also traded tasks as they worked toward a common goal. They cooperated to fill in gaps in their knowledge and to build new competence.
- As conditions shifted during the project, participants adapted to changes and made new discoveries.
- The shared challenge forged bonds within the group and created deeper investment in the work itself.
- A culminating product, performance, or presentation provided recognition and the opportunity to evaluate both the process and the outcome of the project.
- Most interesting, students who worked on such projects reported a level of absorbed involvement that matched their experiences of flow outside school.

The Practice Project yielded many insights about how the right conditions can motivate youth to practice until they reach mastery. We learned that many kids are already building habits that experts use. On the basketball court, they are honing their ability to look ahead, adapt to new information, and contribute to an interdependent system. Ripping out stitches in a knitted scarf, they are working toward the precision and persistence that make a result just right. As they grow to be experts, they connect new information with what they already know, predict what might happen if something changes, and communicate powerfully.

If educators were to recognize such practice as key to all learning, couldn't we coach students' developing habits in equally compelling ways at school? Ten thousand hours roughly corresponds to the in-class time spent in four years of high school and four years of college. What are we asking our youth to practice in that precious time?

References

Eriksson, K. A. (Ed.). (1990). *The road to expert performance: Empirical evidence from the arts and sciences, sports, and games.* Mahwah, NJ: Erlbaum.

Csikszentmihalyi, M. (1990). *Flow: The psychology of optimal experience.* New York: Harper and Row.

Critical Thinking

1. One of the key concepts of the article is the importance of practice to developing expertise. How is this related to the ideas in the article on "mastery learning" in Unit 4?

2. How can you make tasks more meaningful and provide greater opportunities to engage in activities that allow students to positively impact their environment/community both within and outside of school?

3. Identify an area/skill in which you excel. Based on the behaviors and habits listed in the table in the article, would you consider yourself an expert? Why or why not? What additional practice would you need to engage in to raise your level of expertise beyond where it is currently?

4. How can you transfer the things you identified in the previous question to the classroom environment? How can you help your students make a similar shift?

KATHLEEN CUSHMAN is author of *Fires in the Bathroom* (New Press, 2003). In her new book to be published in spring 2010, adolescents investigate questions of motivation and mastery; kathleencushman@mac.com.

Author's note—The MetLife Foundation provided support for this project.

Middle School Students Talk about Social Forces in the Classroom

Kathleen Cushman and Laura Rogers

The social world of young adolescents comes into the classroom with them. It can cause kids to sit with blank or glum faces while you present your most fascinating assignments. It can drive them to make inappropriate comments at moments that should elicit serious thought. Although we tend to think of middle schoolers as risk-takers, they do not take risks in classrooms. Instead, they are worrying about where they stand in relation to others.

Adolescence brings with it this new power: One can consider how others think about oneself. This development not only allows for more mature social interactions, but may also produce the intense self-consciousness sometimes referred to as "adolescent egocentrism" (Elkind, 1967). Suddenly, what a child imagines that everyone else is thinking infuses each choice he or she makes in the classroom. At the same time, as Elkind noted, young adolescents do not yet accurately distinguish between their internal imaginary audience and the actual perceptions of their friends. They may swing rapidly from an intense desire for privacy to an equally audacious desire for attention. This tension is just one of many that young adolescents experience, and act out, during this period of rapid physical, cognitive, and psychological change.

The new cognitive competencies of adolescence influence social relationships in myriad ways. Students' motivation to succeed academically may become overshadowed by their desire to succeed socially. They become more alert to their standing—both in relation to other students and in the eyes of their teachers—and they begin to doubt themselves and the whole enterprise of schooling (Kagan, 1972). Adolescents are now increasingly aware of the evaluative attributes that influence their social standing (intelligence, athletic prowess, courage, musical talent, personal flair, and so on). As they become more socially aware, Kagan speculated in his characteristically understated way, those who are not at the top of the class find that their "motivation for geometry may descend in the hierarchy" of motives (p. 100). He urged schools to consider how their practices may undermine young adolescents just as they are ready to meet new challenges.

Studies consistently prove Kagan right. Adolescents tend to lose confidence in their academic abilities in the transition to middle school and find social activities more interesting and more important than academic endeavors, as Wigfield and Eccles (1994) have shown. Because of the way schools are organized, these authors noted, middle grades teachers are also less likely to know their students well and to trust them. Consequently, they expect less of students and are less

likely to create opportunities to listen to them or to offer them choices and opportunities for decision making and social interaction.

Teachers in the middle grades could spend all their time trying to resist these social forces. However, if they can figure out just what concerns their students are dealing with, they might put these currents in their classrooms to good use, rather than working against them. In a single classroom, students in the middle grades will express many points of view reflecting their developmental accomplishments and differences (Kegan, 1982). They tend to be passionate about matters of justice and fairness, and they are acutely sensitive to how their teachers express care for them. They may think about issues of fairness according to a concrete, reciprocal exchange schema, or they may be beginning to shift toward shared social norms and expectations in their assessment of "the right thing to do" (Kohlberg, 1984). In their social relationships, they are learning new strategies for negotiating conflict and agreement. They are becoming adept at reciprocal interaction and cooperation, and they are just learning to collaborate to achieve mutually defined goals (Selman, 1980, 2003). They are seeking opportunities to practice social interactions. In fact, research has consistently shown that when students have the opportunity to collaborate, they are more likely to focus on learning, are more interested in the subject matter, and feel less anxious (Pintrich, Roeser, & DeGroot, 1994; Willis, 2007).

As teachers help students navigate their uncertainties, learners will become more engaged, adventurous, and willing to take risks in their academic experiences. As teachers tune in to the issues of fairness that loom large for students, they are better able to resolve some of the conflicts that keep them from learning. Any subject in the middle grades will be enlivened when you deliberately weave social learning into the curriculum and support students' engagement with each other (Schnuit, 2006).

At the request of the MetLife Foundation, over several months in 2005 we asked students from around the country to describe what might stand in the way of their enthusiastic response to the academic opportunities their teachers set forth for them. After consulting with approximately 20 middle grades teachers working in urban schools who had gathered at a conference on learning in the middle grades, Kathleen Cushman framed 65 questions. The questions centered on academic, social, physical, and emotional matters, probing for issues that young adolescents saw as interfering with a positive school experience and for ways that students thought teachers could help them with such issues.

By calling on the extensive network of the nonprofit organization What Kids Can Do (WKCD), Cushman identified 42 middle grades students in five urban areas, including schools configured as grades K–8, 6–8, and 7–8. Of these students, 38 attended public schools, one went to a parochial school, and three attended independent schools. None came from backgrounds of economic privilege, and 35 were students of color. Most came not via their schools but through youth development settings: a New York City neighborhood organization (two students); a "bridge" program, preparing students for high school (eight Providence students and nine San Francisco students); and an after-school community arts center in Middletown, Connecticut (eight students). Of the 42 students, 15 were new ninth graders from two Indianapolis high schools, interviewed specifically about their recent transition from middle school. Seven were interviewed in the summer after they completed sixth grade, six after they completed seventh grade, seven in the early fall of seventh grade, and three in the early fall of eighth grade.

Interviews took place in small groups of two to eight students, with two or three sessions, each lasting two to three hours. Cushman facilitated these tape-recorded discussions, which were later transcribed in their entirety. As with most collaborators on What Kids Can Do books, students were paid for their time (in this case, $7 per hour). Parents or guardians granted permission for the students to participate and for WKCD to publish their actual first names and photographs in published work resulting from their interviews.

As we pored over their eloquent and sometimes poignant answers to questions about life in the classroom, we heard them making six crucial requests of their teachers:

- Help us find common ground with each other.
- Teach us how to work together in safe, collaborative groups.
- Let us practice working out issues that affect the class.
- Treat us all with the same respect.
- Let us tackle problems that help develop our ideas about what is fair.
- Watch closely what is really going on with us, inside and outside the classroom.

In the following pages, we present the responses of 21 of these students, as they describe what they notice, what they care about, and what their teachers do and do not do that affects how it feels to learn, work, and be in school.

What's Going on with Us?

Many middle school students are aware of the competing expectations of their teachers and their peers in the classroom. They may feel pulled in different directions at different times.

We Don't Want to Act Too Good

Middle school kids do recognize what a good student looks like to the teacher:

> The typical good kids stay in a line when the teacher's walking [with them]. When the teacher's out of the room, they continue doing their work. They're full of ideas, they're always raising their hand instead of just sitting there and waiting for someone to have their hand up. They do pretty good on their work, and they hand in their homework all the time.
>
> —Genesis

But their social norms may make it hard for them to want to adopt that image as their own.

> They don't want to be embarrassed by being goody-goodies in school, and so they try to act up just to get approval from the other kids at school. Sometimes, some kids will go through physical torture, like getting in fights at school, just to fit in with the other kids. It makes no sense at all.
>
> —Daquan

When you ask boys and girls to work with each other in class or help each other out, they may be uncomfortably aware that other kids will start pairing them up romantically.

> In my fourth period class, this girl was sitting a couple of seats behind me. She was in my third period pre-algebra class too, and she came up and started asking me did I remember what we had for homework. So, she sat down, and I started telling her so she could write it down. Her friends, they were calling her, and she was like, "Wait a minute, wait a minute." After, they started yelling things: "Oh, you like him." And she was like, "No, I don't! I'm just asking him what the homework was." And they said, "You don't have to hide it," and all this other stuff. It made me feel, like, nervous and embarrassed.
>
> —Denue

They are often very confused, themselves, about their motives when they interact with the opposite sex.

> I think it's different with girls and boys. Girls sometimes get, like, harassed, or people make judgments about them. Because, I don't know, boys just can't control their hormones or something. So, they make fun of girls, and they start saying inappropriate stuff. Maybe it's because they like the girl. They just like picking on people. And the girls might not like what they hear, but they might not want to go to anyone, because they might not feel safe.
>
> —Kenson

They are counting on teachers to know—even if *they* do not know—when they need help. The way a teacher reacts can send a clear message about what is considered sexual harassment and what is simply exploring how to interact socially.

> The girls, they're always bothering the boys, and the boys are always bothering the girls, and the teacher knows that it's just for fun. But one kid, he was bothering this girl. I saw the teacher knew that she didn't like it, so he told the boy to stop it.
>
> —Jason

Being Different Hurts

In the middle school years, students' appearances and capabilities vary even more widely than at other ages. Young adolescents are painfully aware of this.

> There's this girl at my school, and nobody likes her because she smells like she takes a shower once upon a Christmas. The teachers can't make you be friends with her or any other person. You choose who you want to be friends with. You wouldn't want to be caught hanging around that person, because they would think you took a shower once upon a Christmas.
>
> —Daquan

I'm not saying I'm perfect or anything, but sometimes kids like to hate on people, and I'm one person to hate on—I stutter.

—Eric Q.

Students with limited English or students with disabilities face additional hurdles to being included.

There's this girl at my school, she speaks French. So it's like, people actually think she's stupid in a way—the students use her as a clown. They go, "What? Can you say that again?" The teachers, I think they notice it, but they feel they can't control the kids.

—Amelia

I can't read, and that's not my fault. God made me the way he wanted to make me. Did I ask God to do that? I don't think people should pick on me just 'cause I can't read. They come up to me, and they be like, "Read this word for me, I can't read it." I'll be like, "You know I can't read, can you get out of my face please?" They'll be like, "Too bad. I forgot you stupid, and you in that retarded class." And I be getting mad, and I want to punch them and stuff.

—Amanda

It is all too easy for students to maintain a connection to their friends by ostracizing someone who is different. Still, kids do not necessarily want to be heartless. Even when they do not speak out about someone's exclusion, they often sympathize.

I don't think it matters, just the way somebody smells or something. The way they smell doesn't mean the kind of person they are. Maybe you [could] just tell them, in a respectful way, "Maybe you should try showering more." Maybe you should try to be their friend.

—Javier

People think about themselves that they're too fat, too thin, too stupid, and they think that people are going to notice whatever they're insecure about. I think that it's just in their mind. I think people should just think positive about themselves, not think in a negative way, and that might help them a little.

—Daniel

Help Us Find Common Ground

Over the course of a year, a teacher will have plenty of opportunities to help middle grades students grow in confidence and reach out to others in positive ways. Students want to know how to find common ground, without sacrificing their own individuality and emerging style. School provides a context in which they can learn about themselves and their classmates, accepting and respecting their strengths and differences.

Faced with the disparities among students, teachers can offer them ways to bridge their differences and discover what each has to offer.

Teachers can try to find out what the kids have in common, [and have them] discuss what they have in common, [so they can] use that to get closer to each other as friends.

—Daquan

It's good to see how you have something in common with a lot of other kids. Maybe, you all tell about an embarrassing

moment, and then you're recognizing that everybody has gone through an embarrassing moment. Or a fear most kids might have. And afterwards, you're, "Oh, that happened to me once."

—Genesis

At the beginning of this year, the teachers made all of us act silly in front of each other. When we're playing games, we're all acting silly and everyone is laughing at each other. You can see other people doing it—not just one person. We played the game "Zip, Zap." One person stands in the middle and says, "zip." The person he says "zip" to has to duck, and the two people shoot each other and say "zap." And we all start laughing if we duck, or if we miss it and get in the middle.

—Javier

Having broken the ice, kids will keep up the process on their own.

This year, I met this kid, and we were talking about baseball, about the Yankees and the Red Sox, and another kid jumped in and started saying how the Red Sox were going to win. And then we started arguing and playing and from that moment on, we always hanged out.

—Denue

In organizing academic work for your class, you can also encourage these connections to develop.

Instead of just having kids do individual work, do more group activities. Because in my room, there's only some people who talk to some people. There are, like, groups. Everybody grew up together, but still, we don't talk to each other as much as you would think, [even though] we've known each other for years.

—Kenson

There's only a small amount a teacher can do, because it's really up to the kids. But if there's a project, she could try to pair up people who really don't talk to each other, don't respect each other. And they could actually learn to become friends and respect each other, knowing they're both being their selves in a way they both can relate to.

—Javier

As teachers get a clearer picture of what is going on among students socially, they will find opportunities to help their students safely connect to each other.

As teachers get a clearer picture of what is going on among students socially, they will find opportunities to help their students safely connect to each other in new and important ways. Just as students are sorting out the ways they want to behave, teachers will be sorting what kind of responses to make to them.

We Care That You're Fair

In matters of their behavior, middle school students often hold a different perspective about what is fair than their teacher does. You can show students that they have an important part in working things out fairly. As a start, you might ask for their thoughts on what is desirable in the classroom, perhaps with questions like these:

- What does it look like when a student shows respect for another student?
- What does it look like when a teacher shows respect for a student?
- What does it look like when a student shows respect for a teacher?
- What can other people do to make it feel safe to speak up when you disagree with another student in class?
- What makes it feel safe to say you don't know the answer?
- What can other people do to make it safe to speak up when you do know the answer?

Make Us Part of the Conversation

Many teachers of the middle grades start the year by establishing norms of behavior on which everyone agrees. Having students collaborate in setting the expectations can be a powerful process.

> The third week, our teacher decided to let the kids make up their own rules that we would follow by ourselves. It's the whole seventh-grade contract, we did it together as a community, because we didn't want the same old school rules that we had last year. Right now, it's working good. We each get a contract with the rules, to make sure we're following them. We judge ourselves every day, and we are honest; if we really know that we didn't do well, we put a "no." If we do something bad, it comes back on the person who messed up. If we are following it, we put down a "yes" or a check. On Friday, at advisory, they check it.
>
> —Jessica

But not all kids will be ready at once to start putting the group's needs before their individual desires. Simply creating classroom norms, as Jessica notes, does not guarantee compliance. As behavior issues come up, you will need to keep referring back to the classroom norms.

> My history teacher this year in eighth grade, she said some kids were eating in her class. She was like, "Oh, every time somebody breaks the rule, I'm going to refer back to the rules that's on the wall." She kept running down the list, the rules, and then kids stopped.
>
> —Kenson

Even when kids want to cooperate in meeting the needs of the class, they may find it difficult to do so. Their attention naturally goes to other things going on around them, and when the teacher is talking to the whole group, they may not hear you.

> Our teacher tells everybody but me and my friend when our class has to leave from lunch for upstairs. So, we get in trouble when we get back to class, and then we have to walk upstairs every day with her. I try to say, "How come you don't tell us?"
>
> —Katelin

Students want to work with you to find solutions to recurring problems, and they often have ideas that are worth considering. When you agree to try out the things they suggest, you also set the stage for future collaborative problem solving.

> When one person goes to the bathroom, then more people will want to go. After a while, when you ask the teacher,

she's going to say "no," 'cause she thinks that you're going to be playing around. And then it will happen to someone who really needs to go to the bathroom. They should just say, "Everyone go at once and come back."
>
> —Edward

Fairness issues also show up in the academic context. For example, if you ignore what students have to say in class, they feel dismissed.

> My teacher will get us interested in a topic, and we'll all be raising our hands and wanting to say something about it. But he only picks on two people to say something, and then he goes into a different thing. I usually call out, because I'm dying to get this comment out, and then the teacher's like, "You're supposed to raise your hand." How am I supposed to raise my hand, if you're not picking me at all? I feel like he doesn't really care what we have to say. He just wants to get over with the day.
>
> —Genesis

Setting norms together for classroom discourse creates a process that kids can trust when they want their voices heard (See Figure 1 for an exercise that can help a teacher better understand students' ideas of fairness).

> They could write names on the board and go in that order. I was in English class, and I had my hand up for 30 minutes, after the teacher told me I was next. She was picking other kids, and then she looked straight at me and just picked somebody else.
>
> —Javier

> For class discussions, we have a ball you throw to someone, and nobody talks if they don't have the ball. It keeps everybody quiet, because you don't want anybody talking when *you* have the ball.
>
> —Amelia

Treat Us All with the Same Respect

Students are more likely to trust a teacher to be fair if he or she knows who individual students are and what matters most to them.

> Many times, the kids who behave good in school, teachers don't know them that much. You have to do something bad so the teachers will know your name—so the teachers will think you're somebody.
>
> —Amelia

On the other hand, nobody likes it when the teacher picks someone out for special treatment.

> Teachers let that favored student do more, even if it's just like a little thing like moving up in the room, or leaving when you want to. As much as students say, "I don't care," they know deep inside that they care.
>
> —Heather

> The band teacher favored this really good clarinet player. It made me feel angry, like I wasn't important to the band, or they don't need me, and I should just quit. Instead of bringing up one person and leaving behind 61, she could have treated everyone the same.
>
> —Daniel

Students in the middle grades vary widely in their ideas about fairness and social responsibility. Some kids still see a dilemma solely from their own point of view. Others have begun to balance competing claims and perspectives. Still others have reached the point where they appeal to a social norm to decide what's fair to all.

At any point in the school year, you can gain insight into the spectrum of how students in your class think about fairness by presenting a dilemma for them to discuss, then noticing what kinds of answers students give and how they share their ideas about working out agreements.

You can use dilemmas that emerge directly from your class experiences, like this one on eating in the classroom:

—*Should we allow eating in the classroom?*

—*If we do, and some students do not clean up after themselves, what should we do:*

- *Suspend the privilege of eating?*
- *Ask the whole class to clean up their mess?*

—*Who is responsible for keeping the class clean—students, teacher, or janitors?*

You might also use dilemmas from your curriculum. For example, you could present choices made by historical or scientific figures, or by fictional characters, in order to achieve a goal or outcome that had negative consequences for someone else. Ask students:

—*What decision was made?*

—*Was it fair? To whom was it fair?*

—*Who might have thought it wasn't fair? What other decision could that person have made? Would it have been more fair? To whom? Why?*

For every action students suggest, make sure to ask them to explain clearly why it seems fair to them. Make clear to them that no one right answer exists, and encourage them to share their opinions, even when they disagree with others.

At the end of the discussion, ask students to help you summarize the discussion:

What things does the class agree about?

_____

_____

_____

What things does the class disagree about?

_____

_____

_____

After such a discussion, a teacher might reflect on what it reveals about how individual students think about fairness. Answering the questions below could help you later, when other issues of fairness come up in class.

Which students took an individual point of view and had trouble thinking about fairness from multiple perspectives?

_____

_____

_____

Which students thought of fairness in terms of a tit-for-tat reciprocity of benefits and injuries?

_____

_____

_____

Which students appealed to social norms of leadership, generosity, responsibility, promises made or broken, group loyalties?

_____

_____

_____

Now think about the students as a group. Which reasons seemed to sway the class more than others?

_____

_____

_____

Figure 1 What's fair from a student's standpoint? An exercise for teachers.

Students may easily—and sometimes accurately—conclude that teachers discriminate against kids based on their race and ethnicity.

> I had this person in my honors classes, he was the only African-American in our class, and he was really funny, he was a nice person to be around. But he jumped around a lot, I guess, and you could kind of tell that these two teachers hated him. When he raised his hand, they would ignore him. I would say that they were disrespecting him because of his race. I think it was a factor.
> —Daniel

> I think my teacher was racist of black people. The whole year she was mean to me, wasn't letting me go to the bathroom. When everybody else asked, she would give them a pass: "Be right back." But if I asked: "No! You can't go!" How's that sound?
> —Katelin

> Today at lunch, a white boy was sitting at a table where he wasn't supposed to, "cause we are supposed to sit with our class. And, he said that black people are ignorant. We told the vice principal, and he came over and said, 'Just leave it alone.' If it was us, he would have said what he says to everybody: 'Pick up your tray and come to the office.' "
> —Thea

Itai's teacher made it clear to the class that all students mattered to her equally, even though her reactions to them might vary from time to time.

> She cared about everyone. And she didn't stereotype; she always said that she wouldn't be biased towards anyone. When she was grading a test, she would always cover up the names and just mark what they didn't get, because she felt that if she wasn't proud of that student that day, maybe she would give them a lower mark.
> —Itai

Guard Our Right to a Fair Decision

Whether students are acting within the limits or outside them, everyone is closely watching how teachers respond. Students will draw their own conclusions as to how fair a teacher is.

> My math teacher, it's like he's trying to please the kids that are bad. There's this girl, she doesn't do any of her work, but he lets her get out of the class at any time. He's afraid of getting cussed. But the good kids, he doesn't let them. It's like he's punishing them for being good.
> —Amelia

Middle school students also have a sharp eye for teachers who respond to students on the basis of race, ethnicity, or socioeconomic status.

> Teachers should treat all students the same, no matter what color they are or how they do in school. But some teachers treat black students different. At my school, they say a whole bunch of bad stuff about us. And, when a student goes to tell the principal, the principal believes the teacher over the student, if it's someone who doesn't do that well in school.
> —Tatzi

Listening well to any such complaints and talking openly with the group about issues of bias and privilege can help us unearth and address entrenched attitudes that hold back students from the conviction that they can learn and taking advantage of the opportunity to do so.

Hold Us to the Norms We Agreed On

When a teacher needs to make the call about what is fair, it helps to refer back to the behavior norms the class earlier helped to shape. If students also have had input into the consequences when someone departs from those agreements, teacher decisions are less likely to seem arbitrary or unfair to them.

Students appreciate it when teachers find humor in their breaches of good conduct, even as they correct them.

> When people swear, I've heard my gym teacher say, "Do you kiss your mother with that mouth?" People laugh, but it makes people understand how they're acting.
> —Kenson

Many issues of fairness require balancing the rights of the individual with the rights of the group. Students pointed out certain key areas in which this particularly matters to them.

Punishing everybody for what one person does. Most middle school kids hate it when the whole class gets blamed for what only some of them have done—no matter how clearly you may try to justify such an approach.

> They're trying to say, "The whole class has to take the punishment, because we're all in this together." Well, for me, it's not fair.
> —Genesis

On the other hand, they may not know exactly what's fair when a teacher does not know who is responsible for the unacceptable behavior.

> I guess, obviously, then we all gonna have detention or something like that. But they should ask, or people should tell them, or something. Don't punish the whole class. But if you have to, I guess you're gonna have to do what you gotta do.
> —Thea

Cleaning up after other people. In the world of young children, people only have to clean up their own messes. Many middle schoolers may not yet see a shared responsibility to maintain the space their group uses for learning.

> If we made the mess, or we didn't, my Spanish teacher makes us pick up papers before we leave his class. He makes you clean the spot that you are sitting at. So, if someone threw a paper next to your desk, or if anyone threw a paper at your desk, you'll end up cleaning up. I don't think that's fair. We didn't put it there.
> —Amelia

> I think that the teacher should make kids clean after every period. It's their mess that they made. Nobody else should be responsible for cleaning it up. If you come into that classroom, and you share that seat, the teacher might think that you made the mess.
> —Denue

As teachers create opportunities for students to collaborate in the classroom, they will learn the value of teamwork. With time and practice, their role in the group will start to matter more to them, and this will extend to how they see themselves in the larger school community.

Coming to class on time. Tardiness also challenges teachers to help kids see themselves as members of a group in which their presence matters. Conventional consequences like detention can have some effect, but they reinforce students' perceptions that being late is a personal issue, not a group one.

> I'm not saying you have to threaten kids for them to show up on time for school. But my teacher gave me a detention because I was late three times. And that showed me. I didn't want another detention. I just showed up on time every day.
>
> —Javier

> I think they should give us more time to get to class. Sometimes kids have to use the bathroom, and they don't get out by the time they're supposed to be there. And most teachers don't take excuses. You're trying to explain to them, and they're like: "I don't care. You're late for my class, you get a detention."
>
> —Genesis

Motivating students to show up on time for what is going to happen in class tends to work much better in preventing tardiness.

> Teachers should do something good at the beginning of class to make kids want to come early. My teacher does the boring stuff first, and then he gives kids time to relax. So, most kids don't really care when they come late, and when you give them detention, they don't really care either. [In another class], at the beginning of class, we did this game to warm us up, like, if you answer some question, you get a prize. So, kids came, because you wouldn't want to miss the beginning of class.
>
> —Amelia

Here again, many teachers find that humor works well. Javier and Amelia describe an effective song-and-dance ritual, used at their summer program whenever someone arrives late to the morning meeting.

> They just stop the whole lesson and start singing: "Pop, pop, fizz, fizz, pop, pop, fizz, fizz. Check him out, check-check him out. Check him out, Check-check him out." And then—say I was late—I would have to say, "My name is Alex." And then they would say, "And that's no lie, check." And I would go, "Pop, pop, fizz, fizz," and they say, "Mm-mmm, how sweet it is." It works—you don't want to show up late, because people are going to make you do that dance. Because it is a little embarrassing to shake your booty or something. It doesn't feel *really* bad, it's better than that, but it's something that you don't want to get. And it's good, because the teachers get it too, if they're late. It happens a lot.
>
> —Javier

> It's like they're laughing with you, but they're laughing at you, too. And some people don't want to do it, so they just come early so they don't have to do the dance.
>
> —Amelia

Amelia and Javier's teachers have established this playful embarrassment as a norm of classroom life, which helps students consciously experience a kind of physical metaphor for the disruption they cause to the group when they show up late. Other activities might bring them along to a point where they identify even more with the group's needs and priorities.

> We were separated into groups of, like, sixteen, called "families." We didn't do things individually, we did it together as a family, and the families got into competition, like chair-building. When we get into stuff together and we compete, even if you don't like a person, you have to cheer them on, because they're in the family. And if they lose, that means your family loses.
>
> —Amelia

As more students develop attitudes like this, teachers can eventually turn problems like tardiness into something that the whole class can discuss and work on together.

> I think [talking about the problem] is better with the whole class. It can get chaotic, but if you really want this to happen, then it will work out. Because we realized how bad we've been, and we found the problem, and so we really try to work to become a better class.
>
> —Carmela

Reward Our Efforts with Things We Really Want

The gold stars and stickers of elementary school no longer will motivate middle schoolers. Instead, they want gestures and items that fit with their new, more social sense of self. That might mean actual activities, but it also could come across in little signals that the teacher regards students with increased respect.

> I don't think we should get candy. Candy kind of makes the situation worse, 'cause you end up getting hyper. [A good reward is] that the teacher will ease up on you, give you more chances, or respect you more.
>
> Gabe

> A better reward is giving us funner activities, like playing games or academic activities that are fun.
>
> —Carmela

Giving students a choice can feel like a reward, as they feel they are earning a teacher's respect.

> I think they should take a survey first, to see what would be a good reward if we finished all our work on time. Maybe some people don't want to do something that other people do, so teachers could switch off, and change it after a certain time. I really like reading, so sometimes I wish we could take a break from school, and we would have time at school where we could just read. Or, if you didn't like reading, you could do something else.
>
> —Itai

Help Us Learn As You Correct Our Behavior

Students do not want to change their behavior when teachers humiliate them in front of others. If they feel a teacher's disappointment too keenly, they are likely to withdraw or retaliate.

My science/math teacher always embarrasses kids, in a way. Like, if you forgot your math book, or if your homework is overdue for this amount of time, she'll announce it to the whole class, instead of just telling you privately. I don't think they should do that. It kind of makes me feel embarrassed, I just want to go away and crawl into a hole or something.

—Gabe

Teachers should know, like, when somebody's having a bad day. They sit there and yell at us, and we're going to flip out on them. [One teacher] kept telling me to do this, do that, 'cause I was behind in work. And I was trying to do my work as fast as I can, but I don't write that fast. So, I kept going "Whooo! Hufff!" and sucking my teeth and stuff, just to get on her nerves. She was sitting there saying, like, "Amanda, be quiet, Amanda, stop." I got mad, and I just got up and left. [It would have helped me if she would] talk to me about it—like, just let me sit there for a little bit, in the classroom, and be me.

—Amanda

If teachers let them save face by addressing the matter in a private conversation, students are much more likely to shift toward a more positive action.

The way in which teachers impose consequences can make the difference in whether or not students learn from their mistakes. They need both adult insight and adult firmness.

A lot of times teachers are, like, "Don't make these mistakes." But the reason why I am how I am right now is because I learned from my own mistakes. We're going to learn from the consequences, whether it's a time out for a five-year-old or, like, suspension for a 13-year-old. I think it's necessary for kids, especially our age—not too much, but a little bit, so we know not to do them.

—Alma

And when teachers call home, students still want them to be on their side, even when the call is about a problem with their behavior.

I've noticed that the only reason teachers ever call parents are to tell them their kids are in trouble. And how does that help? I'm sick of it. It's horrible. Yeah, well, "Your child, I found out that he or she stole from my classroom," or something. But it doesn't help. They should say, "I think maybe your kid might be experiencing some issues and that's why maybe they're failing their work. Is there anything . . . ?" And they should recommend things to help. Like, maybe recommend a tutor, you know. Actually, like, involve yourself in the child's life, not just in the child's education.

—Alma

Know Everything, See Everything

As middle schoolers experience the confusing pushes and pulls of their daily social interactions, they want and need a teacher's presence and watchful eyes. Students are continually exploring the boundary between what adults see and hear and what they do not.

When the teacher's not watching, then the kids curse at each other or throw things. And then the teacher finds out about it, but she don't know who to blame, so she just blame everybody. So, then everybody get in trouble. The people who did not do it should not get in trouble, but that's how people are. But I tell on people, 'cause I'm not getting in trouble for what I did not do.

—Thea

The teacher should know that, like, when her back is turned, kids are making faces about her or talking about her, or stuff like that. And then when they turn back around, we start acting like we wasn't doin' nothin'. I've done it myself sometimes. And I got caught, but then I said I didn't do it, but the teacher knew I did it, cause she seen me.

—Tatzi

School is a complicated social world for kids, and they want you to recognize its different aspects.

[My friend] found this wallet in the gym and stole it, kind of. And, I guess my teacher loves her still, but she found out how bad my friend really acts. She doesn't see the masks anymore. She's more aware. I'm thankful that there's a teacher like that. But not a lot of teachers are like that.

—Carmela

Teachers think that some people are star students, they're the best, they're really smart, they're just great. They don't know that outside of their classroom, they're swearing, doing other stuff that the teachers think are inappropriate. In my class, there was this one kid who was always smart, well behaved, and then outside the classroom, he was always swearing and doing bad stuff. I think they should know more about that.

—Daniel

They need you to help them sort out the many pressures that may interfere with their focus in the classroom.

In my class we've been going through so much trouble 'cause of peer pressure. We started to have class discussions about problems and about things we see each other doing that we don't like to see each other doing. Even if it takes time off math, this is really important, because teachers are the people who teach the students how to be when they grow up. The children are the future. We don't want our leaders in the future to be hypocrites. We don't want them to be confused. And, if we do have leaders like that, think about how the followers will be!

—Carmela

Students know that a teacher's presence in informal moments is just as important as his or her classroom role. If a teacher knows them already, students count on him to understand and perhaps to help them through some difficult moments in the halls or on the playground.

I just wish that there was a teacher during passing period that would stand outside and watch the hallway, 'cause at my school there's a lot of fights.

—Edward

Kids ask to use the bathroom, and they don't really go to the bathroom, they wander around the hallway.

—Katelin

The teachers should try to interact a little bit with the students, like during recess, even though the students may not like it. Teachers should really observe. Because it really helps. People are getting really touchy at my school, and sometimes people cover up for people so they can make out. And a lot of the boys are really also, like, perverts there. They touch girls, and the girls, well, they're so used to it that they don't do anything about it. And everyone swears now. It's like a habit. After every single frickin' word, they swear. And it's very annoying.

—Carmela

As teachers notice the dynamics among kids outside the classroom, they will not only be keeping students safe from harm, they will also be responding to students' need to have adults see what is really going on with them in their groups.

Bullies don't pick on people bigger than them, they just pick on shrimpy little kids. You can see that they can't do anything back to the bullies. I feel like I should try to stand up for them, but then, if I do, then the bullies might beat me up. There could be, like, a line of bullies, and they try to chase you or beat you up, and you have to try to run away from them. I just walk away, and if I see a teacher or something, tell them.

—Edward

Sometimes it's good for the teachers to step in, sometimes it's not. If a kid gets scared of something—if he's, like, down, and you see him getting bullied—and then he walks over to, like, a group or a teacher, then the teacher might know that he's getting bullied. Most of the kids that get picked on just ignore it. But I don't think it's fun.

—Jason

All too often, the problems students experience outside the classroom will also surface, in little ways, inside the classroom.

When you got a problem with a student [in class], teachers don't want to listen to it. They just be like, "Ignore it, ignore it." But you can't really ignore the problem that you having, and then you [go to] settle the problem, and you all end up fighting.

—Thea

The time teachers take to work out such issues lets students see that the benefits of conflict resolution can carry over into the classroom, too.

On Thursdays, [seventh-grade classes] have this little extra section called "goal time," and we talk about little goals we want to accomplish in the class. And, then my class has time for, like, issues. Like, kids can say, "Oh, I have an issue with this person," and then they try to solve it right there. Everybody else in the class will listen and try to help, instead of just listening to the argument and gossiping or something.

—Genesis

I had a problem with my best friend. She was getting jealous of me hanging out with her other best friend. And so we had a fight, and [the teacher] talked to us, and how he settled it was kind of weird for me. We had to change our shoes and act like we were the other person, and that's how we settled our problems. She put on my shoes. Then we had to pretend like we were the other person and talk about why we might be mad at each other, and why were we sad, and what were we thinking. I was shy at first, I've never settled something before like that. Then we kind of started being friends again, and I want to be thankful for that.

—Jessica

Jessica is not alone in feeling relieved and grateful. Teachers who hear what students say about the social obstacles that keep them from learning will find a world of effective ideas to address those issues. Along the way, they are likely to see students relax and blossom in the classroom, developing the social habits that support their academic skills and understanding.

References

Elkind, D. (1967). Egocentrism in adolescence. *Child Development, 38,* 1025–1034.

Kagan, J. (1972). A conception of early adolescence. In J. Kagan and R. Coles (Eds.), *Twelve to sixteen: Early adolescence* (pp. 90–105). New York: Norton.

Kegan, R. (1982). *The evolving self: Problem and process in human development.* Cambridge, MA: Harvard University Press.

Kohlberg, L. (1984). *Essays on moral development: The psychology of moral development* (vol. 2). San Francisco: Harper & Row.

Pintrich, P. R., Roeser, R. W., & DeGroot, E. A. M. (1994). Classroom and individual differences in early adolescents' motivation and self-regulated learning. *Journal of Early Adolescence, 14*(2), 139–161.

Schnuit, L. (2006). Using curricular cultures to engage middle school thinkers. *Middle School Journal, 38*(1), 4–12.

Selman, R. (1980). *The growth of interpersonal understanding: Developmental and clinical analyses.* New York: Academic Press.

Selman, R. (2003). *The promotion of social awareness: Powerful lessons from the partnership of developmental theory and classroom practice.* New York: Russell Sage Foundation.

Wigfield, A., & Eccles, J. S. (1994). Children's competence beliefs, achievement values, and general self-esteem: Change across elementary and middle school. *Journal of Early Adolescence, 14*(2), 107–138.

Willis, J. (2007). Cooperative learning is a brain turn-on. *Middle School Journal, 38*(4), 4–13.

Critical Thinking

1. Identify a quote from a student that was really meaningful/powerful for you. Explain why it had such an impact and discuss what you would do as a teacher to respond to what the student expressed.

2. The article presents a brief summary of some of the key developmental changes children undergo in early adolescence. How can you help students negotiate their often conflicting and competing needs and goals, especially as they related to maturing as learners? If you are preparing to be an elementary teacher, what kinds of things can you do to better prepare students for these developmental changes?

KATHLEEN CUSHMAN, author of *Fires in the Bathroom: Advice for Teachers from High School Students* (New Press, 2003) and *First in the Family: Advice about College from First-Generation Students* (Next Generation Press, 2005, 2006), is a co-founder of What Kids Can Do, Inc. E-mail: kathleencushman@mac.com. LAURA ROGERS, who with Theodore R. Sizer and others founded the Francis W. Parker Charter Essential School in Massachusetts, teaches at Tufts University, Medford, Massachusetts. E-mail: laura.rogers@tufts.edu.

Author note—This article is adapted from the forthcoming book *Fires in the Middle School Bathroom: Advice for Teachers From Middle Schoolers* (New Press, April 2008). Its research and writing was supported by MetLife Foundation.

Cushman, K., & Rogers, L. (2008). Middle School Students Talk About Social Forces in the Classroom. *Middle School Journal,* 39(3), pp. 14–24. Reprinted with permission from National Middle School Association.

Classroom Management Strategies for Difficult Students: Promoting Change through Relationships

MARY ELLEN BEATY-O'FERRALL, ALAN GREEN, AND FRED HANNA

Teachers in middle level schools face overwhelming demands and challenges in their classrooms. They are expected to know content and pedagogy, develop engaging lessons that meet the needs of diverse learners, and use a variety of instructional strategies that will boost student achievement while they simultaneously develop positive relationships with, on average, 125 students each day who are experiencing the personal, social, and cognitive challenges and opportunities of early adolescence (Carnegie Council on Adolescent Development, 1995; Schmakel, 2008).

Teaching is complex and cannot be reduced to discrete tasks that can be mastered one at a time. Teachers must "win their students' hearts while getting inside their students' heads" (Wolk, 2003, p. 14). As Haberman (1995) suggested, this winning of the hearts occurs through very personal interactions, one student at a time. This perspective is supported by research suggesting that teachers who develop such relationships experience fewer classroom behavior problems and better academic performance (Decker, Dona, & Christenson, 2007; Marzano, Marzano, & Pickering, 2003).

How can teachers engage students through enhanced personal interactions while simultaneously managing classroom climate and instruction? The purpose of this article is to suggest specific strategies that integrate knowledge and skills from education, counseling, and psychotherapy to help teachers develop a strong management system based on the development of personal relationships with students. These techniques are specifically adapted for use by teachers and more clearly delineate the nature of developing relationships and deepening them for the purpose of making education more effective.

Classroom management and relationship building

Research indicates that teachers' actions in their classrooms have twice as much impact on student achievement as assessment policies, community involvement, or staff collegiality; and a large part of teachers' actions involves the management of the classroom (Marzano, 2003; Marzano & Marzano, 2003). Classroom management is critically important in the middle grades years when students are more likely to experience declines in academic motivation and self-esteem (Anderman, Maehr, & Midgley, 1999). Research indicates that these declines can be linked to the classroom, and particularly to teacher-student relationships (Furrer & Skinner, 2003). When surveyed about their goals, adolescents have claimed that academics and the completion of their education are important to them. However, repeated studies of sixth through ninth graders have shown interest in academics, motivation for academics, and academic achievement levels decline dramatically during early adolescence, and especially during seventh grade (Carnegie Council on Adolescent Development, 1995).

One of the keys to effective classroom management is the development of a quality relationship between the teacher and the students in the classroom. Marzano, Marzano, and Pickering (2003), in a meta-analysis of more than 100 studies, reported that teachers who had high-quality relationships with students had 31% fewer discipline problems, rule violations, and other related problems over a year's time than did teachers who did not. This significant statistic justifies further investigation into developing relationships.

A critical component of developing relationships is knowing and understanding the learner. Teachers must take steps to learn and understand the unique qualities of middle grades students, who are at a crucial time in their development. Although they are good at disguising their feelings, they have been described as actually craving positive social interaction with peers and adults; limits on behavior and attitudes; meaningful participation in families, school, and community; and opportunities for self-definition (Wormeli, 2003). Teaching middle grades students is unique in its demand for unconventional thinking; therefore, middle grades teachers must be willing to break the rules and transcend convention. The strategies that will be described for dealing with the most difficult of students are in many ways just that—unconventional.

Teachers who adopt a relationship-building approach to classroom management by focusing on developing the whole person are more likely to help students develop positive, socially-appropriate behaviors. The characteristics of effective teacher-student relationships are not related to the teacher's personality or whether the teacher is well liked by the students. Instead, the relationships are characterized by specific behaviors, strategies, and fundamental attitudes demonstrated by the teacher (Bender, 2003) This approach involves taking personal interest in students; establishing clear learning goals; and modeling assertive, equitable, and positive behaviors (Hall & Hall, 2003; Rogers & Renard, 1999).

Research indicates that the most effective classroom managers do not treat all students the same. Effective managers employed different strategies with different types of students (Brophy, 1996; Brophy & McCaslin, 1992). Teachers with effective classroom management skills are aware of high needs students and have a repertoire of specific techniques for meeting some of their needs (Marzano & Marzano, 2003).

Adelman and Taylor (2002) reported that 12% to 22% of all students in schools suffer from mental, emotional, and behavioral disorders, and relatively few receive mental health services. The Association of School Counselors noted that close to one in five students has special needs and requires extraordinary interventions and treatments beyond the typical resources available to classroom teachers (Dunn & Baker, 2002). It is often these very students who create the most daunting challenges for teachers.

Strategies for building relationships

According to Wolk (2003), "Teacher-student relationships permeate the classroom, with relationships both helping and hindering learning and affecting everything from curriculum to choice of teaching methods." Wolk asserted that for most teachers, "their relationships are their teaching" (p. 14). Current literature on building relationships as a means to manage classrooms includes recommendations such as using gentle interventions, finding time for bonding, avoiding punishments, and building activities that ensure success for all students (Hall & Hall, 2003).

These strategies, though helpful, may still leave teachers struggling with the most difficult students. Ideas from the fields of counseling and psychotherapy can be applied to these classroom struggles. Rogers and Renard (1999) asserted that we need to understand the needs and beliefs of our students as they are—not as we think they ought to be" (p. 34). What follows are specific strategies from the fields of counseling and psychology that teachers can apply in classroom settings when dealing with difficult students. The strategies of empathy, admiring negative attitudes, leaving the ego at the door, and multicultural connections will be explored.

Building empathy

Probably the most important aspect of a positive helping relationship is empathy on the part of the helper (Garfield, 1994; Goldfried, Greenberg, & Marmar, 1990; Luborsky, Crits-Christoph, Mintz, & Auerbach, 1988; Orlinsky, Grawe, & Parks, 1994; Sexton & Whiston, 1994). In actual practice, empathy on the part of the teacher results in the student feeling understood. Empathetic relationships are especially important for difficult adolescents (Bernstein, 1996; Mordock, 1991). Unfortunately in education, empathy is a concept largely misunderstood and even trivialized as a form of affection or caring. To the contrary, caring and empathy are not at all the same. Adler (1956) defined empathy as "seeing with the eyes of another, hearing with the ears of another, and feeling with heart of another" (p. 135). The end result of having been shown empathy is that the person "feels understood." This is crucial to reaching and relating to young adolescents (Hanna, Hanna, & Keys, 1999).

Many teachers simply assume they understand the student's problems and dilemmas, and mistakenly try to communicate their understanding in ways that only distance the student. For example, a female middle grades student once told a disappointed teacher that things were really hard at home and studying was difficult. The teacher responded by saying, "Well, you have to get past it and study anyway. I have been teaching for a long time, and there isn't any excuse I haven't heard." The student, of course, had no indication that the teacher understood at all and was actually discouraged by the teacher's unempathetic response. If this teacher had taken the time to show that she understood the student's dilemma, she would have learned that the parents of the student were verbally fighting with each other every day, threatening each other with divorce, and arguing over custody of the children. They also fought about the father's drinking.

The teacher could have easily encouraged the student with an empathetic response such as, "It must be really difficult trying to study while listening to your parents fighting and wondering what is going to happen with your family." Such a response would have communicated understanding to the student that she would have found valuable and that would have enhanced the level of respect she had for the teacher. Such a response also would have encouraged the student to communicate with the teacher so that the teacher and student could brainstorm ways to keep the student on task with her various assignments.

Admiring negative attitudes and behaviors

At first glance, this approach would seem to violate all that we know about behavior modification, but it is based on a well established area of research called "positive psychology" (Seligman, 1999). This approach looks upon negative student behavior as a skill he or she has been practicing and refining for many years. Most of these skills have their beginning in the student's family life. In the case of a manipulative female teen, for example, being manipulative might have been the only or best way of getting her needs met in her family. It is to be entirely expected that she would bring these same skills to school in an effort to meet her needs there as well.

Rather than engage in a power struggle with such a student, a teacher should acknowledge the skill that the student has worked so hard to develop—and then redirect it. Give her credit for all of the years she has practiced the skill. This will also lead to an increase in the student's perceived empathy from the teacher. After acknowledging the skill, reframe the skill and then redirect it. It is important that this skill be applied with sincerity. Any hint of sarcasm could lead to further alienation between the student and the teacher.

Let us extend the example of a manipulative, young adolescent girl. She is engaged in a behavior that, in all likelihood, annoys both adults and her peers. However, there is a skill that may be present in the girl that can be reframed as the "ability to influence people." Rather than address the girl's manipulations as such, mention to her, "I have noticed that you have the ability to influence people, is that true?" She will probably reply with something like, "What do you mean?" The teacher can respond by saying, "Well, I have noticed that you can get people to do what you want them to do. Am I wrong?" It would help if the teacher used specific examples. At this point, the student will likely look at the teacher somewhat suspiciously and smile, saying, "Well that's true sometimes, I guess." The teacher can then respond, saying, "You have a valuable skill there. If you used it in other ways, you may find more successful ways of getting your needs met. This skill could be valuable in certain careers, such as corporate management, sales, or even counseling." The young adolescent is usually quite surprised to hear something that she has previously been criticized for now being admired and looked upon as something potentially valuable.

Another example of the application of this approach would be the case of a young adolescent who consistently displays the infamous "bad attitude." Quite at variance with the usual characterization of the bad attitude, we look at it as a skill that is often practiced and has a particular goal. The goal is to display and announce defiance and, to a certain degree, independence. Instead of fighting the attitude, punishing it, or even ridiculing it, try admiring it, putting aside any disgust or exasperation. "Wow," the teacher might say, "You sure do have an impressive attitude. It is very well constructed, and I can tell you have been working on it for years." One's first thought on reading this might be to conclude that such an approach is simply crazy. However, a large percentage of young adolescents respond to this tactic with a smile and a greater willingness to continue the discussion. Admiration is extremely rare in the lives of young adolescents, and we dare say, much rarer than love. To receive it from an adult is precious indeed, and it often inspires immediate loyalty and respect toward a teacher. When communicated genuinely and honestly, it also increases the level of perceived empathy from an adult.

Disruptive behaviors, when displayed by a student who takes charge in his or her own way, can sometimes be reframed as great leadership skills. The teacher can ask the student to use those abilities to help lead the class. In the case of the disruptive class clown, the reframe would be along the lines of admiring the student, then reframing the clown act as natural comedic skill. A possible redirect could consist of a challenge to the student to use that skill in a creative way and in an appropriate setting that can be set up by the teacher according to the personality of the student.

Disruptive behaviors, when displayed by a student who takes charge in his or her own way, can sometimes be reframed as great leadership skills.

Leaving the ego at the door

It is readily apparent that to follow this relationship approach, a teacher or school administrator must have the capacity to suspend the flaring up of his or her own impulses, issues, and negative reactions. Young adolescents are highly skilled at reading teachers and identifying the things that make them impatient, rigid, angry, and upset. Young adolescents often share insights with each other about what annoys teachers and school administrators. The ability to manage one's own issues as they arise is one of the counselor's most demanding skills. It also marks the difference between the effective and the ineffective counselor (Van Wagoner, Gelso, Hayes, & Diemer, 1991). It is also an assessment of truly effective relationship-based teaching. Once a professional gives in to emotions such as anger, exasperation, or displeasure, his or her ability to function becomes impaired to a degree. It seems no one knows this better than some young adolescents, who may be quite aware of the effects they have on adults.

When a teacher takes the comments and manipulations of students personally, interpersonal chaos is likely to follow. Thus, it is a good idea for a teacher to learn to suspend his or her own issues as they arise—to "place them on the shelf," so to speak, to be addressed later. One of the hidden advantages of working with young adolescents is that they have much to teach us about our own reactions and habitual ways of interacting. All too often, the student becomes the teacher of lessons that may not be learned in any other context (Hanna, 2002). Suspending one's own reactions is a skill, to be sure, and it is a skill that can be improved with practice.

Leaving the ego at the door of the classroom is perhaps the most valuable suggestion we have to offer, along with showing empathy. Without this, however, empathy may never get a chance to emerge. Young adolescents closely watch the reactions of adults to see if they practice what they preach. For example, if Tom, a seventh grade student, erupts in class one day because he is being teased for being a "suck-up," a very typical teacher response is, "Just try to ignore what the other kids are saying." However, if a teacher or counselor tells a student to "ignore" the taunts or insults of another and then reacts angrily to being disrespected, the student, like most of us, will have little respect for what amounts to hypocrisy. Demanding respect is not as effective as earning it, and how the teacher comports himself or herself has much to do with how he or she is viewed and respected by students. To successfully build relationships and apply the skills mentioned in this article, leaving the ego at the door can be viewed as a prerequisite. At various times, leaving the ego at the door can be connected to issues of culture as well.

When a disruptive young adolescent routinely pushes a teacher's buttons, that teacher has an ideal opportunity to apply the practice of leaving the ego at the door. It is human nature for teachers, or anyone for that matter, to get upset when an adolescent pokes fun at a personally sensitive topic or issue. This is especially true when it comes to the topic of authority. Many teachers believe that they must have absolute authority in the classroom. They also believe that this authority comes automatically with their status as the teacher and does not necessarily have to be earned. When students question this authority by being non-compliant or engaging in disruptive behaviors, they may easily trigger an emotional reaction from the teacher. For example, Sammy, an eighth grade student, might say, "Why should I listen to you? You're just a middle school teacher. Why don't you have a good job?" The unexamined response that a teacher might give is this: "You have no right speaking to me like this. I know a lot more than you do, and I know you have detention today. See me after school." Because teachers do have authority and certain privileges afforded to them by their position, anger and frustration often lead to the abuse of power in punitive ways. This usually happens when the adult does not take the opportunity to examine his or her own vulnerabilities on a regular basis. When the disruptive adolescent repeatedly insults or disobeys the teacher, the teacher's ego takes over, demanding respect.

If the teacher had taken the time to examine his or her own vulnerabilities, he or she might have said, "You sound like my mother. She didn't think I should become a teacher either. She wanted me to wear a starched shirt and tie every day and work in a big law firm. But I tell her I get to be a part of the lives of more than 120 seventh graders—including yours, Sammy. What more power do I need?" Then the teacher can turn the topic around to question the student by saying, "What does your family say to you about what you hope to do someday?"

When a teacher is self-aware of vulnerabilities, such as the need for power, he or she is more likely to respond strategically rather than emotionally. For example, a teacher who knows he is sensitive to students questioning his authority can anticipate that middle grades students will, in fact, question his authority. Such awareness can lead to the use of empathy or the admiration of negative behaviors, as previously discussed. In essence, the key to leaving one's ego at the door is awareness.

Multicultural Connections

Developing relationships with students who come from culturally different backgrounds can be challenging and requires specific skills from new and experienced teachers alike (Nieto, 1999a, 1999b, 2008). The recommendations for forming relationships made earlier in this article are essential when cultural differences are present. That is, having empathy, admiring negative behaviors, and leaving one's ego at the door can go a long way toward bridging the gap between culturally or linguistically different (CLD) learners and the teacher.

The challenges within the cross-cultural encounter lie in overcoming the additional barriers that prevent teachers from letting down their guard to empathize and develop stronger relationships with students. These barriers exist due to a fear of the culturally different, a lack of knowledge about the differences and similarities between cultures, persistent negative stereotyping, and general intolerance. To overcome these barriers and develop multicultural competence, a teacher must overcome his or her fears and unresolved issues regarding cultural difference. This can be achieved by gaining deeper knowledge about himself or herself and the culturally different student (Bradfield-Kreider, 2001).

Practices from the field of counseling have great promise for enhancing relationships in the culturally diverse classroom. In counseling, multicultural competence consists of being acutely aware of cultural attitudes, beliefs, knowledge, and skills of both the counselor and the client (Arredondo, 2003). Training new counselors involves an examination of how the new counselors feel about themselves and culturally different clients. Such competencies can easily be used as a guide for classroom teachers who want to enhance their relationships with CLD students.

It is important to help teachers become aware of how their racial and cultural heritages may impact their classroom climates. This awareness helps prepare teachers to identify and work through any existing intolerance they may have for students who come from different ethnic, racial, class, or religious backgrounds. It is equally important for teachers to be aware of their negative and positive emotional reactions to CLD students. For example, if the disruptive adolescent described in the previous scenario happens to come from a racial or ethnic background that is different from that of the teacher, checking one's ego becomes more complicated. It is, therefore, vital for the teacher to be aware of his or her cultural and personal biases and the connections between the two. Then, when challenges to authority occur, the teacher who is aware of his or her "stuff" is better equipped to respond in more strategic ways. Such self-examination helps teachers leave their egos at the door and ultimately develop empathy for those they teach.

For teachers to engage in successful intercultural interactions, they must maintain an astute approach to learning relationships and be aware of the ways schooling helps to reinforce social class differences (Hipolito-Delgado & Lee, 2007). Marginalization refers to the historic and systemic ways in which people are adversely affected by racism, poverty, and other forms of oppression (Green, Conley, & Barnett, 2005). Teachers who are vested in educating students who come from such backgrounds should develop relationships by making meaning of the curriculum as it relates to their lived experiences outside the school. Taking this approach allows teachers to share their own personal experiences about hardship, triumph, and failure, regardless of the similarities or differences with the student's life.

Programs such as *Facing History and Ourselves* (www .facinghistory.org) and *Rethinking Schools* (www .rethinkingschools.com) provide curricular materials that are designed to provide these kinds of shared self-examination experiences in the classroom. *Facing History and Ourselves* engages students from diverse backgrounds in an examination of racism and prejudice to promote a more informed and tolerant citizenship. Through study and discussions of current and past historical events, students are encouraged to analyze their own thinking, see the world from more than one perspective, and place themselves in someone else's shoes as they examine events from history around the world. Together, students and teachers struggle to form judgments about human behaviors. Curricular materials expose students to such topics as violence in Northern Ireland, genocide in Cambodia, AIDS victims in Africa, anti-Semitism in London, or Mexican immigration struggles in California. Even though many of these events may occur miles away in different states and different countries, many of the core issues are still the same. When teachers use curriculum and content that hold personal meaning to them and their students, barriers are more likely to break down for everyone, and relationship building has a better chance.

One strategy from *Teaching History and Ourselves* is called the Life Road Map (www.facinghistory.org), which allows teachers and students to develop a map of their lives

by creating sequences of events, including important decisions and inspirations. This strategy would be useful to a teacher with students who have recently immigrated to the United States. It would promote an appreciation for one's own culture and for the cultures of others that are represented in the classroom. It also would provide a forum for sharing difficulties that teachers and students have faced, some of which will be a result of culture and race.

A similar strategy, developed by *Rethinking Schools,* provides a template for teachers and students to write a poem called "Where I'm From" that reveals information about their lives outside school (Christensen, 2002). Students are encouraged to include information in the poem by studying items found in their homes, in their yards, and in their neighborhoods and the names of relatives, foods, and places they keep in their childhood memories. For a teacher with students from a variety of cultures in one classroom, these poems could be read aloud and posted to provide a powerful way of building relationships and community in the classroom. For both of these strategies, it is critical that the teacher participate by completing the assignments and sharing them as well.

Conclusion

Efforts to improve education must focus on the single most important component: the classroom teacher (Ingwalson & Thompson, 2007). Teachers in middle level schools must be well prepared to face the challenges of working with young adolescents; and critical components of teacher preparation are the knowledge and skills from education and related fields that will enable them to develop effective, and often unconventional, management systems in their classrooms. This effort must begin with a new paradigm in which teachers view classroom management as an ongoing exercise in building relationships.

When teachers use curriculum and content that hold personal meaning to them and their students, barriers are more likely to break down for everyone, and relationship building has a better chance.

For dealing with the most challenging of students, teachers can learn and apply strategies used in the field of counseling and psychotherapy, such as building empathy, admiring negative attitudes and behaviors, and leaving one's ego at the door. It seems particularly important to provide specific strategies for dealing with what can often be the problems that prevent us from persevering in the important work of helping students learn. In the area of classroom management, it is critical that teachers find ways of building relationships with *all* students, from the most motivated to the most difficult.

To borrow the words of Rogers and Renard (1999), when we enter into understanding human needs and relationship-driven teaching, "amazing things can happen" (p. 34).

Extensions

Identify three obstacles that interfere with your ability to make meaningful connections with your students.

Think of an educator from your past with whom you did not connect. What would you say to that educator about building relationships with students?

References

Adelman, H. S., & Taylor, L. (2002). School counselors and school reform: New directions. *Professional School Counseling, 5,* 235–248.

Adler, A. (1956). *The individual psychology of Alfred Adler: A systematic presentation in selections from his writings.* New York: Harper & Row.

Anderman, E. M., Maehr, M., & Midgley, C. (1999). Declining motivation after the transition to middle school: Schools can make a difference. *Journal of Research and Development in Education, 32*(3), 131–147.

Arredondo, P. (2003). *Applying multicultural competencies in white institutions of higher education.* In G. Roysircar, D. S. Sandhu, & V. B. Bibbins (Eds.), *A guidebook: Practices of multicultural competencies* (pp. 229–242). Alexandria, VA: ACA Press.

Bender, W. L. (2003). *Relational discipline: Strategies for in-your-face students.* Boston: Pearson.

Bernstein, N. (1996). *Treating the unmanageable adolescent: A guide to oppositional defiant and conduct disorders.* Northvale, NJ: Jason Aronson.

Bradfield-Kreider, P. (2001). Personal transformations from the inside out: Nurturing monoculture teachers' growth toward multicultural competence. *Multicultural Education, 8*(4), 31–34.

Brophy, J. E. (1996). *Teaching problem students.* New York: Guilford.

Brophy, J. E., & McCaslin, N. (1992). Teachers' reports of how they perceive and cope with problem students. *Elementary School Journal, 93*(1), 63–68.

Carnegie Council on Adolescent Development. (1995). *Great transitions: Preparing adolescents for a new century.* Waldorf, MD: Carnegie Corporation of New York.

Christensen, L. (2002). Where I'm from: Inviting student lives into the classroom. In B. Bigelow (Ed.), *Rethinking our classrooms volume 2: Teaching for equity and justice,* (p. 6). Milwaukee, WI: Rethinking Schools.

Decker, D. M., Dona, D. P., & Christenson, S. L. (2007). Behaviorally at-risk African-American students: The importance of student-teacher relationships for student outcomes. *Journal of School Psychology, 45*(1), 83–109.

Dunn, N. A., & Baker, S. B. (2002). Readiness to serve students with disabilities: A survey of elementary school counselors. *Professional School Counseling, 5,* 277–284.

Furrer, C., & Skinner, E. (2003). Sense of relatedness as a factor in children's academic engagement and performance. *Journal of Educational Psychology, 95,* 148–162.

Garfield, S. L. (1994). Research on client variables in psychotherapy. In A. E. Bergin & S. L. Garfield (Eds.), *Handbook of psychotherapy and behavior change* (4th ed.) (pp. 190–228). New York: John Wiley.

Goldfried, M. R., Greenberg, L. S., & Marmar, C. (1990). Individual psychotherapy: Process and outcome. *Annual Review of Psychology, 41,* 659–688.

Green, A., Conley, J. A., & Barnett, K. (2005). Urban school counseling: Implications for practice and training. *Professional School Counseling, 8,* 189–195.

Haberman, M. (1995). *STAR teachers of poverty.* Bloomington, IN: Kappa Delta Pi.

Hall, P. S., & Hall, N. D. (2003). Building relationships with challenging children. *Educational Leadership, 61*(1), 60–63.

Hanna, F. J. (2002). *Therapy with difficult clients: Using the precursors model to awaken change.* Washington, DC: American Psychological Association.

Hanna, F. J., Hanna, C. A., & Keys, S. G. (1999). Fifty strategies for counseling defiant and aggressive adolescents: Reaching, accepting, and relating. *Journal of Counseling and Development, 77,* 395–404.

Hipolito-Delgado, C. P., & Lee, C. C. (2007). Empowerment theory for the professional school counselor: A manifesto for what really matters. *Professional School Counseling, 10,* 327–332.

Ingwalson, G., & Thompson, J., Jr. (2007). A tale of two first-year teachers: One likely to continue, one likely to drop out. *Middle School Journal, 39*(2), 43–49.

Luborsky, L., Crits-Christoph, P., Mintz, J., & Auerbach, A. (1988). *Who will benefit from psychotherapy: Predicting therapeutic outcomes.* New York: Basic Books.

Marzano, R. J. (2003). *What works in schools.* Alexandria, VA: Association for Supervision and Curriculum Development.

Marzano, R. J., & Marzano, J. S. (2003). The key to classroom management. *Educational Leadership, 61*(1), 6–13.

Marzano, R. J., Marzano, J. S., & Pickering, D. J. (2003). *Classroom management that works.* Alexandria, VA: Association for Supervision and Curriculum Development.

Mordock, J. B. (1991). *Counseling the defiant child.* New York: Crossroad Publishing.

Nieto, S. (1999a). *Affirming diversity: The sociopolitical context of multicultural education.* Boston: Pearson/Allyn & Bacon.

Nieto, S. (1999b). *The light in their eyes: Creating a multicultural learning community.* New York: Teachers College Press.

Nieto, S. (2008). *Affirming diversity: The sociopolitical context of multicultural education* (5th ed.). New York: Allyn & Bacon.

Orlinsky, D. E., Grawe, K., & Parks, B. K. (1994). Process and outcome in psychotherapy. In A. E. Bergin & S. L. Garfield (Eds.), *Handbook of psychotherapy and behavior change* (4th ed.) (pp. 270–376). New York: Wiley.

Rogers, S., & Renard, L. (1999). Relationship-driven teaching. *Educational Leadership, 57*(1), 34–37.

Schmakel, P. O. (2008). Early adolescents' perspectives on motivation and achievement. *Urban Education, 43,* 723–749.

Seligman, M. E. (1999). The president's address. *American Psychologist, 54,* 599–567.

Sexton, T. L., & Whiston, S. C. (1994). The status of the counseling relationship: An empirical review, theoretical implications, and research directions. *The Counseling Psychologist, 22*(1), 6–78.

Van Wagoner, S. L., Gelso, C. J., Hayes, J. A., & Diemer, R. A. (1991). Countertransference and the reputedly excellent therapist. *Psychotherapy, 28,* 411–421.

Wang, M. C., Haertel, G. D., & Walberg, H. J. (1993). Toward a knowledge base for school learning. *Review of Educational Research, 63*(3), 249–294.

Wolk, S. (2003). Hearts and minds. *Educational Leadership, 61*(1), 14–18.

Wormeli, R. (2003). *Day one and beyond: Practical matters for middle-level teachers.* Portland, ME: Stenhouse.Extensions

Critical Thinking

1. What was your reaction to the section of the article entitled, *Admiring Negative Attitudes and Behaviors?* How could this potentially benefit or create a barrier to your relationship-building with students?

2. What are some attitudes and behaviors of students that are very likely to "get under your skin" and lead to potential power struggles? What are some things you can do to recognize this when it is happening or ways you can strive to "check those things at the door"?

3. Read the article, *Examining Student Engagement and Authority: Developing Learning Relationships in the Middle Grades* by Anne-Marie Dooner and her colleagues (*Middle School Journal,* March 2010). Compare and contrast two vignettes in terms of what the communicate about concepts such as building empathy, admiring negative attitudes, leaving ego at the door, and making multicultural connections.

Mary Ellen Beaty-O'Ferrall is associate professor of education at the Johns Hopkins University School of Education in Baltimore, MD. E-mail: mebo@jhu.edu. **Alan Green** is an associate professor of clinical education and school counseling program lead at the Rossier School of Education, University of Southern California, Los Angeles, CA. E-mail: alangree@usc.edu. **Fred Hanna** is professor and director of the School of Applied Psychology and Counselor Education at the University of Northern Colorado, Greeley. E-mail: fred.hanna@unco.edu

From Ringmaster to Conductor

10 Simple Techniques Can Turn an Unruly Class into a Productive One

Students deserve teachers who are encouraging conductors of learning rather than domineering ringmasters focused on maintaining order.

MATTHEW A. KRAFT

We teach because we love working with students. We're dedicated to helping students gain knowledge and develop their intelligence. However, our efforts to consistently deliver high-quality instruction are undercut when we can't maintain a productive learning environment. Lack of training, anxiety, and inexperience cause many new teachers to feel overwhelmed when a group of rambunctious students doesn't cooperate. Even high-quality instruction by veteran teachers is rendered ineffective when students are disrupted, distracted, or feel threatened by their peers.

When the classroom feels like a three-ring circus, many of us, including myself, instinctually revert to draconian classroom management tactics. We become ringmasters, monopolizing the spotlight in front of the classroom while forcing students to repeatedly perform some routine or face our disciplinary whip. We sacrifice interactive learning and student collaboration in favor of the pacifying effects of worksheets and teacher-centered instruction. Unfortunately, this ringmaster approach undercuts student engagement and exacerbates power struggles between students and teachers. Students eventually identify defiant behavior and apathy toward academics as a means of student empowerment.

Effective teaching and learning can take place only in a harmonious learning environment. Instead of a three-ring circus, imagine a classroom that resembles a symphony of learners rehearsing for a show. This teacher-as-conductor approach replaces the coercion and chaos of the circus-like classroom with the coordination and collaboration of a symphony orchestra. The teacher composes engaging lessons and uses a baton to conduct students with different strengths to work together. Students are personally motivated because they see explicit connections between the knowledge and skills they're learning and their future goals.

Educators who find themselves reverting to ringmaster techniques need new strategies. At Life Academy, a small academy for at-risk 9th-graders at Berkeley High School in California, we developed a comprehensive approach to engineering academic success, engendering personal motivation, promoting positive student interactions, and modifying inappropriate classroom behavior. We identified five classroom management techniques and five behavior management techniques that can be adopted across K-12 classrooms.

Classroom Management Techniques

Well-established classroom procedures are the foundation of any comprehensive management system. The following five practices, used together, can help teachers develop harmonious classroom environments by reducing the causes and frequency of inappropriate student behavior.

#1. What You Teach

Without question, the most essential classroom management tool is a rigorous and relevant curriculum. Walk the halls of any school, and you'll find that it's not the strictest teacher with the most rules, but the personable teacher with the most interesting and challenging lesson plan who has the best behaved students. There's no substitute for teaching a rigorous curriculum that's relevant to students' lives and actively engages students in their own learning. However, high expectations are effective only when there are multiple entry points to assignments and differentiated levels of support so that all students can access the challenging curriculum. When teachers fall short in this difficult duty, classroom management issues arise.

Despite common assumptions about the immature and impulsive nature of students, more often than not, they're making very calculated, rational choices to act inappropriately. Students are off-task when they don't perceive any benefit from on-task behavior. This occurs when students believe that no amount of effort will allow them to access the curriculum, when they feel there's nothing new they can learn, and when they don't perceive any connection between their goals and the learning objectives. I've found Wiggins and McTighe's *Understanding by Design* (ASCD, 2005), the Buck Institute for Education's *Project Based Learning Handbook* (Winsted and Taylor, 2003), and Expeditionary Learning Outward Bound's *Core Practice Benchmarks* (www.elschools.org/publications/CorePracticeBenchmarks.pdf) to be excellent resources for designing rigorous and relevant curriculum. These guides have helped me develop my most successful units in which students are engaged in project-based learning centered on core essential questions and supported by differentiated instruction.

> **Instead of a three-ring circus, imagine a classroom that resembles a symphony of learners rehearsing for a show.**

#2. *Nonnegotiable Rules*

Teachers often face behavior management problems because they choose too many rules to enforce and they don't clearly differentiate between classroom values and nonnegotiable rules. Unlike normative classroom values that are best created as a community, nonnegotiable rules are clear and specific rules that should be chosen unilaterally by the teacher. While teachers should work daily to uphold such positive community values as mutual respect, in difficult times pointing to a few simple and unambiguous rules is helpful. Prioritize the two or three most essential rules for maintaining an acceptable classroom environment and ensure that they're specific and clear. For example, I have two fundamental classroom rules: Don't interrupt the speaker and don't use inappropriate language. Establishing, practicing, and enforcing a few, focused, nonnegotiable rules helps to engineer a classroom environment that's conducive to learning.

#3. *Clear Expectations*

By the time students begin middle school, they're expected to successfully navigate diverse and sometimes conflicting expectations of five or more classes. Students might be rewarded for interjecting ideas during history class while they're reprimanded in math for speaking without being called on. They may be encouraged to get out of their seats in art class while they're prohibited from leaving their seats in English. Effectively communicating classroom procedures for each activity can greatly reduce the number of disruptions that arise from appropriate classroom behavior that occurs at inappropriate times.

Almost every type of classroom activity falls within three categories: direct instruction, working time, and individual silent time. Before beginning any lesson, I direct students' attention to the wheel depicted in Figure 1 and place the arrow on the type of classroom expectations that the next activity requires.

Figure 1 Classroom Wheel Directing Students to Type of Activity

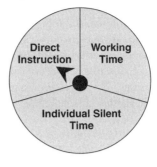

Direct Instruction
Students stay at their desks.
Students direct attention to the teacher.
Students raise hands before speaking.
Students speak one at a time.

Working Time
Students can get out of their seats.
Students direct attention to their collective work.
Students can speak freely.
Students can work with each other.

Individual Silent Time
Students remain in seats.
Students direct attention to their own work.
Students should not speak out.
Students should work individually.

This helps students clearly understand where they should be, where to direct their attention, how to participate, and with whom they can work.

#4. *Managing Transitions*

Disruptive behavior and conflicts frequently occur during the transitional moments in a classroom when time is unstructured and the teacher's attention shifts to setting up the next activity. The common practice of beginning class with a timed warm-up question helps keep students on task during the first few minutes of class. A simple warm-up that requires students to demonstrate understanding of the previous day's material works well. In my class, I ask students to write an original sentence using the vocabulary word from the previous day.

Assigning student jobs also makes transitions smoother and reduces down time. Student volunteers should do all of the classroom tasks, such as collecting work, passing out materials, moving desks, and erasing the board. This not only makes teaching less stressful, it also allows teachers to better monitor the class, it gives physical tasks to active students, and it fosters students' sense of ownership over the classroom. Finally, a daily closing procedure is fundamental to maintaining student discipline. Begin cleaning up with at least five minutes left in the period to allow time to address the class before the bell. After all students are quietly seated, I use a closing statement in which I briefly reflect on how the day went and preview what's to come. Once this routine is well established, which might require several days of keeping students late, students will begin to monitor each other because they're always eager to be dismissed.

#5. *Getting Attention*

One of the simplest but most commonly cited frustrations among teachers is that they can't get their classes to quiet down. Being able to quickly get attention and quiet a class is an essential part of good classroom management. I've found three techniques to be effective. The first is to ask for students' attention and then wait. All too often, teachers pressed for time shout above the classroom noise for students' attention until they finally get it. By repeatedly shouting over students, teachers undermine their own expectation that students will quiet down when first asked. Instead, wait while students realize that fewer people are talking and begin to quiet each other down. If it continues to take an inappropriate amount of time, keep the class for as long as it took them to quiet down. Another effective method is to use a zero-noise device such as a rain stick or chimes, which provide both a visual and auditory signal to students. Last, if things get out of control, don't be afraid to raise your voice and shout with a serious tone. If you rarely shout, this is extremely effective because it startles students. But be careful not to abuse it, or it loses its impact.

Effective curriculum design, clear classroom rules and expectations, and smooth transitions will create a more manageable classroom environment. With these structures and procedures in place, teachers will face fewer disruptions and be better prepared to deal with inappropriate student behavior.

Behavior Management Techniques

Clear, consistent, and individualized behavior management techniques are an essential element for creating a positive and safe classroom learning environment. When disruptions occur, the teacher must diffuse the situation, discern the root cause behind the disruption, and enforce consequences while working to eliminate the factors that caused the inappropriate behavior. Fundamentally, all behavior is a form of communication. Students are often unable to communicate or are uncomfortable expressing their feelings, so they act out. Five techniques will aid teachers in addressing, interpreting, and preventing individual student behavior problems.

#1. Behavior Modification Systems

The cornerstone of any classroom management system is an established behavior modification system. This system, no matter what form it takes, should clearly communicate to students when their behavior is inappropriate.

I use a citizenship grade system. If a student uses profanity, socializes during individual silent time, or talks over someone, I will lower his or her citizenship grade according to the severity of the instance. This avoids lengthy arguments and heated confrontations because it quickly and clearly communicates the inappropriateness of the student's behavior. Each day, the grades are reset to A's, and students begin with a clean slate. I then factor the students' average citizenship grade into their overall grades. Formalized behavior management systems provide an equitable structure to address most types of individual student discipline problems while being flexible enough to allow for teacher discretion.

#2. Avoiding Public Confrontations

Students will go to great lengths to avoid being embarrassed in front of their peers. When students are publicly reprimanded, they often feel disrespected and respond by drawing teachers into arguments to bolster their image.

The best way to avoid being drawn into dead-end arguments is to reprimand students in ways that aren't public affronts to their image. Hand motions and facial expressions are subtle ways to communicate to an off-task student. Rephrasing such statements as "Get back to work" as sincere offers of help—"Do you need anything to get started?"—will be less embarrassing to students while communicating the same message. Sometimes, simply walking by students' desks or sitting down next to them is enough to refocus their attention. Short notes or quiet comments during transitional moments also keep issues private. If none of these methods are effective, then turn to the behavior modification system to communicate with students without engaging in public arguments.

#3. Private Conversations

Inevitably, some students will challenge teachers. When this happens, always tell the student that you're willing to discuss the issue privately. Students looking to argue for argument's sake will often drop the issue. If a student continues to press the issue, then send him or her to the back of the room or outside the class. Give the student a few minutes to calm down, then start the class on the next activity before having the private conversation.

Once in private, first listen to the student. A short lecture to start the conversation will stifle any chance of a productive two-way dialogue aimed at identifying the cause of the behavior. Make sure the student understands why he or she was reprimanded, and then discuss ways to avoid the incident from happening in the future. In more serious situations, require the student to sign a contract or write a letter before they can enter the classroom again.

> Even high-quality instruction by veteran teachers is rendered ineffective when students are disrupted, distracted, or feel threatened by their peers.

#4. Overcome the Discipline Myth

Creating a positive classroom environment means dispelling the common student perception that teachers love to get students in trouble. Classes become unmanageable when students and teachers become engaged in a power struggle. In this paradigm, the unrulier the class is, the more power the students have. Convince students that you hate disciplining and are willing to ignore the behavior modification system if they're able to check their own behavior and work productively. Remind students daily that you're a teacher because you want to help them achieve their goals, not because you want to police them in the classroom. In my classroom, I use the saying, "check yourselves so I don't have to."

#5. Communicating About Moods

Open communication between students and teachers about how we're feeling can prevent easily avoidable conflicts from arising. Teachers should set an example by telling students when we're tired or frustrated. Encourage students to give a heads-up when they're feeling sad, angry, or noncommunicative. When students learn to communicate about their moods, they're offering precious information that teachers can use to prevent conflicts. Allowing an irritated student to work individually instead of in a group or to skip a turn at reading aloud is far better than forcing them into a situation that will likely cause them to act out.

A well-structured classroom learning environment with a clear and equitable behavior management system is a fundamental prerequisite for supporting the academic success of at-risk youth. No amount of dedication, lesson planning, or content knowledge is sufficient to compensate for ineffective classroom and behavior management techniques that result in discordant learning environments.

Students deserve teachers who are encouraging conductors of learning rather than domineering ringmasters focused on maintaining order. The classroom and behavior management strategies outlined here will help teachers with challenging classrooms to have the confidence and skills to put down whips and pick up batons.

Critical Thinking

1. Explain the difference between classroom management and behavior management.

2. Come up with a personal metaphor that describes how you envision your classroom environment. Explain how it reflects your personal beliefs about the roles of the teacher and students in the classroom.

3. What is the difference between "rules" and "classroom values"? Identify three rules and classroom values you believe are essential to a productive learning environment.

4. Develop a list of three to five behaviors you would find particularly disruptive or difficult to manage. Brainstorm ways you could turn some aspects of those behaviors into positive qualities/skills that you can build on with the student.

5. One thing we often forget about as teachers is the degree to which our students' (as well as our own) ability to focus and engage productively in a task is shaped and influenced by their mood on any given day. How can you communicate to students that you understand are "having a bad day" without undermining your expectations for them in your classroom?

MATTHEW A. KRAFT is a doctoral candidate in the Quantitative Policy Analysis in Education Program at the Harvard Graduate School of Education, Cambridge, Mass. He is founder and former lead teacher of Life Academy at Berkeley High School, Berkeley, Calif.

UNIT 6
Assessment

Unit Selections

Learning Outcomes

After reading this unit, you will be able to:

• Identify some of the common criticisms of No Child Left Behind (NCLB) and evaluate their merit from the perspective of existing educational research.

• Explain why a single measure of achievement should not be used as the sole indicator of a student's mastery of content, particularly if it will be used to make high-stakes decisions.

• Discuss the usefulness of high school exit exams and whether they are related to other school and post-graduation outcomes.

• Define "multiple measures," explain their importance to validity, and identify different ways multiple measures can be used effectively within the classroom also for broader school or policy-level decisions.

• Describe reliability and validity as they relate to both classroom and large-scale assessments.

• Provide a rationale to support the use of self-assessment to foster the development of metacognitive skills.

• Reflect on the relationships among formative assessment, teacher feedback, and self-assessment.

• Describe some of the benefits and potential pitfalls when using peer assessment.

• Discuss how both classroom and district/state level assessments can be used to inform instruction in meaningful ways.

• Identify the benefits, as well as the cautions with regard to implementing a "no failure" grading policy.

Student Website

www.mhhe.com/cls

Internet References

Awesome Library for Teachers
www.neat-schoolhouse.org/teacher.html

FairTest
www.fairtest.org

Kathy Schrocks's Guide for Educators: Assessment
www.school.discovery.com/schrockguide/assess.html

National Assessment of Educational Progress (NAEP)
www.nces.ed.gov/nationsreportcard/

National Council on Measurement in Education
www.ncme.org

Phi Delta Kappa International
www.pdkintl.org

Washington (State) Center for the Improvement of Student Learning
www.k12.wa.us

In which reading group does Jon belong? How do I construct tests? How do I know when my students have mastered the course objectives? How can I explain test results to Mary's parents? Teachers answer these questions, and many more, by applying principles of assessment. Assessment refers to procedures for measuring and recording student performance and constructing grades that communicate to others levels of proficiency or relative standing. Assessment principles constitute a set of concepts that are integral to the teaching–learning process. Indeed, a significant amount of teacher time is spent in assessment activities.

Assessment provides a foundation for making sound evaluative judgments about students' learning and achievement. Teachers need to use fair and unbiased criteria in order to assess student learning objectively and accurately and make appropriate decisions about student placement. For example, in assigning Jon to a reading group, the teacher will use his test scores as an indication of his skill level. Are the inferences from the test results valid for the school's reading program? Are his test scores consistent over several months or years? Are they consistent with his performance in class? The teacher should ask and then answer these questions so that he or she can make intelligent decisions about Jon. On the other hand, will knowledge of the test scores affect the teacher's perception of classroom performance and create a self-fulfilling prophesy? Teachers also evaluate students in order to assign grades, and the challenge is to balance "objective" test scores with more subjective, informally gathered information. Both kinds of evaluative information are necessary, but both can be inaccurate and are frequently misused.

In addition to making appropriate decisions regarding an individual child's learning in the classroom, schools must also ensure they are monitoring and evaluating student progress in ways that are consistent with accountability mandates included in No Child Left Behind. Meeting standards and high-stakes testing have become a routine focus of educators' daily practice. Since No Child Left Behind was signed into law in 2002, the educational community has struggled to develop methods of assessment that effectively measure student achievement, leading to the current climate of high-stakes testing. The ongoing debate is not only about how to fairly, equitably, reliably, and effectively evaluate whether students and schools are meeting established accountability benchmarks, but also whether the standards of accountability set forth by No Child Left Behind are appropriate and attainable.

The articles in this section focus on two contemporary issues in assessment—standards and the use of high-stakes standardized tests and classroom assessment that is integrated with teaching. The first three articles in this unit provide an overview of some of the key issues in the education community related to accountability, standards, measuring achievement, and the use of assessment results for high-stakes decisions. The authors of

© Royalty Free/CORBIS

"Grading Education" provide a critique of NCLB and suggest the foundation of an alternate model of accountability based at the state, rather than the federal level. The next two articles focus on the appropriate use of student achievement data and the impact of high school exit exams on graduation rates. In the final article in this section, Ms. Brookhart explains exactly what is meant by "multiple measures" using definitions from a number of professional educational organizations. As we continue to examine the effectiveness of No Child Left Behind and prepare for the possibility of new performance mandates, understanding both the importance of measuring performance using a complement of assessments and how to use multiple measures for classroom-, school-, or policy-level decisions is crucial.

The second group of articles focus on issues related to classroom assessment, more specifically, the benefits of using self- and peer-assessment in a variety of contexts. In the final article, Mr. Corbett and Mr. Wilson describe how a "no-failure" policy for assignments in a low-income middle school impacted students' perceptions, and as a result, teacher practice.

Grading Education

Test-based accountability can't work, but testing plus careful school inspections can.

RICHARD ROTHSTEIN, REBECCA JACOBSEN, AND TAMARA WILDER

Noble though its intent may be, the No Child Left Behind Act—the federal law that requires virtually all students to be proficient in reading and math by 2014—is an utter failure. Many critics have denounced it, as well as similar state accountability policies based exclusively on quantitative measures of a narrow set of school outcomes. Critics have described how accountability for math and reading scores has inaccurately identified good and bad schools, narrowed the curriculum (by creating perverse incentives for schools to ignore many important purposes of schools beyond improving math and reading test scores), caused teachers to focus on some students at the expense of others, and tempted educators to substitute gamesmanship for quality instruction.

Despite widespread dissatisfaction with No Child Left Behind (NCLB), Congress has been unable to devise a reasonable alternative and so, for now, NCLB remains on the books. There have been many proposals for tinkering with the law's provisions—extending the deadline for reaching proficiency, measuring progress by the change in scores of the same group of students from one year to the next (instead of comparing scores of this year's students with scores of those in the same grade in the previous year), adding a few other requirements (like graduation rates or parent satisfaction) to the accountability regime, or standardizing the definitions of proficiency among the states. Yet none of these proposals commands sufficient support because none addresses NCLB's most fundamental problem: although tests, properly interpreted, can contribute some important information about school quality, testing alone is a poor way to measure whether schools, or their students, perform adequately.

Perhaps the most important reason why NCLB, and similar testing systems in the states, got accountability so wrong is that we've wanted to do accountability on the cheap. Standardized tests that assess only low-level skills and that can be scored electronically cost very little to administer—although their hidden costs are enormous in the lost opportunities to develop young people's broader knowledge, traits, and skills.

The fact is, schools have an important but not exclusive influence on student achievement; the gap in performance between schools with advantaged children and schools with disadvantaged children is due in large part to differences in the social and economic conditions from which the children come.[1] For this reason, schools can best improve youth outcomes if they are part of an integrated system of youth development and family support services that also includes, at a minimum, high-quality early childhood care, health services, and after-school and summer programs. An accountability system should be designed to ensure that *all* public institutions make appropriate contributions to youth development. When schools are integrated with supporting services, they can substantially narrow the achievement gap between disadvantaged and middle-class children.

A successful accountability system, such as the one we will propose in this article (and which we more fully explain in our book, *Grading Education: Getting Accountability Right*), will initially be more expensive. Our proposal calls for both a sophisticated national assessment of a broad range of outcomes and a corps of professional inspectors in each state who devote the time necessary to determine if schools and other institutions of youth development—early childhood programs, and health and social services clinics, for example—are following practices likely to lead to adult success. But while such accountability will be expensive, it is not prohibitively so. Our rough estimate indicates that such accountability could cost up to 1 percent of what we now spend on elementary and secondary education. If we want to do accountability right, and we should, this level of spending is worthwhile.

In the long run, trustworthy accountability is cost effective. Because narrow test-based accountability can neither accurately identify nor guide schools that need to improve, we now waste billions of dollars by continuing to operate low-quality schools. And we waste billions by forcing good schools to abandon high-quality programs to comply with the government's test obsession. We cannot know how much money could be saved by more intelligent accountability, but it is probably considerable.

Of course, no accountability system can be successful without first defining the outcomes that schools and other institutions of youth development should achieve. Before we put forth our vision for a new approach to accountability, let's take a moment to compare the goals that Americans have long valued with the goals that we are currently pursuing.

First Things First: Accountability for What?

From our nation's beginnings, Americans have mostly embraced a balanced curriculum to fulfill public education's mission. Looking back over 250 years, we reviewed a small sample of the many statements produced by policymakers and educators to define the range of knowledge, skills, and character traits that schools ought to develop in our youth. We were struck by how similar the goals of public education have remained during America's history. Although some differences of emphasis have emerged during different eras, our national leaders—from Benjamin Franklin to Horace Mann to various university presidents and school superintendents—seem consistently to have wanted public education to produce satisfactory outcomes in the following eight broad categories:

1. *Basic academic knowledge and skills:* basic skills in reading, writing, and math, and knowledge of science and history.
2. *Critical thinking and problem solving:* the ability to analyze information, apply ideas to new situations, and (more recently) develop knowledge using computers.
3. *Appreciation of the arts and literature:* participation in and appreciation of musical, visual, and performing arts as well as a love of literature.
4. *Preparation for skilled employment:* workplace qualifications for students not pursuing college education.
5. *Social skills and work ethic:* communication skills, personal responsibility, and the ability to get along with others from varied backgrounds.
6. *Citizenship and community responsibility:* public ethics; knowledge of how government works; and participation by voting, volunteering, and becoming active in community life.
7. *Physical health:* good habits of exercise and nutrition.
8. *Emotional health:* self-confidence, respect for others, and the ability to resist peer pressure to engage in irresponsible personal behavior.

Having examined recent surveys of the public's goals for education and having conducted our own poll (in 2005) of the general public, school board members, and state legislators, we are fairly confident that these are, indeed, the outcomes that Americans still want from our schools and other youth institutions.

Unfortunately, today's obsession with reading and math scores means that almost all of these eight goals are ignored. Several surveys of school and district officials, principals, and teachers confirm that the public school curriculum has been dangerously narrowed. But the narrowing did not begin with No Child Left Behind; there was evidence of it throughout the last couple of decades as math and reading tests steadily gained importance. In a 1994–95 survey of Maryland teachers, two-thirds said that they had reduced the amount of time they spent on instruction in nontested subjects, especially art, music, and physical education.[2] In the 1990s, similar curricular shifts were also common in Texas (which, being George W. Bush's home state, provided the model for NCLB). In that state, and especially in schools serving disadvantaged minority students, teachers of art, history, and science were required to put their curricula aside to drill students in the basic math and reading skills that were tested by the state exam.[3]

A survey of school principals in North Carolina, after the state implemented a test-based accountability system in 1999, found that over 70 percent had redirected instruction from other subjects and from character development to reading, math, and writing, and that this response was greatest in the lowest-scoring schools.[4] A 2003 survey of school principals in Illinois, Maryland, New Mexico, and New York found that those in high-minority schools were more likely to have reduced time for history, civics, geography, the arts, and foreign languages to devote more time to math and reading.[5]

The most comprehensive investigations of test-driven curricular shifts have been conducted by the Center on Education Policy, which surveyed 349 representative school districts during the 2006–07 school year. It found that accountability does work: 62 percent of these districts had increased time devoted to reading and math. The increases were greatest in urban districts sanctioned under NCLB because their test scores were too low; in such districts, the increase in reading and math instruction totaled an average of over four hours a week.[6]

This is just what test-based accountability systems intend to accomplish. Students whose reading and math performance was lowest were getting a lot more instruction in these subjects. But increased time for test preparation in reading and math comes at the expense of time for something else. These districts cut an average of an hour or more per week from instruction in social studies, science, art and music, physical education, and recess. Most districts facing sanctions cut time from several of these subject areas to make room for more reading and math test preparation.

To make matters worse, even such drastic measures are unlikely to bring all students to proficiency in reading and mathematics. Inadequate schools are only one reason disadvantaged children perform poorly. They come to school under stress from high-crime neighborhoods and economically insecure households. Their low-cost daycare tends to park them before televisions, rather than provide opportunities for developmentally appropriate play. They switch schools more often because of inadequate housing and rents rising faster than parents' wages. They have greater health problems, some (like lead poisoning or iron-deficiency anemia) directly depressing cognitive ability, and some (like asthma and vision difficulties) causing more absenteeism or inattentiveness. Their households include fewer college-educated adults to provide more sophisticated intellectual environments, and their parents are less likely to expect academic success.[7] Nearly 15 percent of the black-white test-score gap can be traced to differences in housing mobility, and 25 percent to differences in child and maternal health.[8]

Yet contemporary test-based accountability policies expect that school improvement alone will raise all children to high levels of achievement, poised for college and professional success. Teachers are expected to repeat the mantra "all children can learn," a truth carrying the false implication that the level to which children learn has nothing to do with their starting points or with the out-of-school supports they receive. Policymakers and school administrators warn teachers that any mention of children's socioeconomic disadvantages only "makes excuses" for teachers' own poor performance.

Of course, there are better and worse schools, and better and worse teachers. And of course, some disadvantaged children excel more than others. But our current federal and state test-based accountability policies have turned these obvious truths into the fantasy that teachers can wipe out socioeconomic differences among children simply by trying harder.

It is surprising that so many education policymakers have been seduced into thinking that simple quantitative measures like test scores can be used to hold schools accountable for achieving complex educational outcomes. After all, similar accountability systems have been attempted, and have been found lacking, in other sectors, both private and public, many times before. The corruptions and distortions resulting from test-based accountability are no different from those that have been widely reported in the business world, as well as in fields like health care, welfare, job training, law enforcement, and other government services.

Teachers are expected to repeat the mantra "all children can learn," a truth carrying the *false implication* that the level to which children learn has nothing to do with the out-of-school supports they receive.

The solution, as we briefly stated in the introduction, is not to abandon testing, but to supplement it with periodic inspections of both schools and other organizations that support our youth. Appreciating the arts, developing a strong work ethic, accepting responsibility as a citizen—these goals are as important as our academic goals, and our accountability system should treat them as such. Simply put, we must devise ways of holding schools and other youth development institutions accountable for achieving all eight of the goals that Americans have long valued. And, instead of setting fanciful targets that set up our institutions to fail, we must devise realistic targets that inspire continuous improvement.

Test Prep or True Learning: What's behind Those Test Scores?

Other nations have also struggled with accountability for public education. Yet while Americans have relied upon test scores alone—and even worse, proficiency cut scores—to judge school quality, others have supplemented standardized testing with school inspection systems that attempt to assess whether students are developing a balanced set of cognitive and noncognitive knowledge and skills. While England, Scotland, Wales, Northern Ireland, the Netherlands, the Czech Republic, Belgium, Portugal, France, and New Zealand[9] all have some form of inspection system, Her Majesty's Inspectors in England offer us a particularly intriguing model because they hold schools and other social welfare institutions accountable for education and youth development.

Because the English inspection system continually undergoes revision, the following describes the English inspectorate as it existed until 2005, when a major revision commenced.

Accountability is overseen by an independent government department, the Office for Standards in Education (Ofsted). In the early part of this decade it had a corps of about 6,000 inspectors who visited schools and wrote reports on their quality. Most inspectors, usually retired school principals or teachers, were directly employed by a dozen or so firms with which Ofsted contracted to conduct the inspections. An elite group, about 200 of "Her Majesty's Inspectors" (HMIs), were employed directly by Ofsted and oversaw the entire process. Ofsted trained the contracted inspectors, required them to attend annual retrainings, and certified them prior to employment. Ofsted also assured the reliability of inspectors' judgments by having several inspectors judge the same educational activity and then comparing their ratings. Ofsted monitored the inspectors' work and removed those whose quality was inadequate—for example, those who never found lessons to be unsatisfactory.[10]

To ensure quality, the leader of each school inspection team underwent a higher level of training than the other team members, and an HMI sometimes also participated in each larger team of contracted inspectors. Ofsted also required each team to include one lay inspector, often a retiree from another profession, to give the inspections greater credibility with the public. Each inspection resulted in a report published on the Internet within three weeks; the report was mailed to every parent, with photocopies also made available to the public.[11] In the case of schools that persistently failed to pass inspection, local governments assumed control and, in the most serious cases, closed them.[12]

Until 2005, a typical full-time English inspector may have visited from 15 to 30 schools each year, and part-time inspectors (usually retired principals) may have visited seven or eight.[13] Because of this experience and their training, English inspectors were highly respected by teachers and principals, who were thus more likely to take inspectors' advice seriously and consider inspectors' evaluations legitimate. Ofsted inspectors were required to spend most of their time observing classroom teaching, interviewing students about their understanding, and examining random samples of student work.[14] Ofsted inspectors decided which students to interview and which classrooms to visit at any particular time.[15] Although they spent relatively little time meeting with administrators, Ofsted inspectors did require principals to accompany them on some classroom observations, after which the inspectors asked the principals for their own evaluations of the lessons. In this way, the inspectors were able to make judgments (which became part of their reports) about the competence with which the principals supervised instruction.[16]

Ofsted's contracted inspectors observed every teacher in each school, evaluating pupil achievement in all academic as well as in noncognitive areas.[17] Ofsted inspectors rated everything they observed, including teaching skill, student participation, achievement, and academic progress, on a seven-point scale, with supporting paragraphs justifying the ratings. They also wrote reports on student assemblies, playground practice, school cafeteria quality, student behavior in hallways, the range of extracurricular activities, and the quality of physical facilities.[18]

Ofsted reports also evaluated how well schools teach not only academic knowledge and skills but personal development: "the extent to which learners enjoy their work, the acquisition of workplace skills, the development of skills which contribute to the social and economic well-being of the learner, the emotional development of learners, the behaviour of learners, the attendance of learners, the extent to which learners adopt safe practices and a healthy lifestyle, learners' spiritual, moral, social, and cultural development, [and] whether learners make a positive contribution to the community."[19]

Inspections used to be every six years, but then Ofsted changed them to every three years[20] and became more flexible about the frequency of inspections. As the system developed, schools with a history of very high ratings were visited less frequently, with smaller teams, and without every classroom and teacher visited. Schools with a history of poor ratings were visited more often and more intensively.[21]

In recent years, Ofsted added on inspections of early childhood care providers and vocational education programs, and evaluations of how well schools coordinate their own programs with such services. When possible, Ofsted conducts inspections of schools and other child and welfare services in the same community simultaneously.[22]

Ofsted has made no effort to produce fine rankings of schools by which the public could judge each school in comparison with all others. Rather, Ofsted has reported which of three categories schools fall into: those that pass inspection, those in need of fairly modest improvements, and those requiring serious intervention to correct deficiencies.

In addition to regular school inspections, the English system has also included special inspections to evaluate particular problems or curricular areas—for example, music instruction, physical education, the underachievement of minority students, or disparate punishments meted out to them.[23] For these, HMIs visited only a representative group of schools. There were enough of these special inspections, however, that schools were likely to have experienced an inspection for some purpose more frequently than was required by the regular schedule.[24]

England's inspection system may not be perfect—and even if it were, we could not simply adopt it in this country. But it does offer a compelling alternative to our test-based accountability. In the United States, there have been attempts to create a similar inspection system. In the late 1990s, a student of the English inspection system designed a school visit system for the state of Rhode Island.[25] But with the advent of NCLB, it lost importance as schools came to be judged solely on progress toward universal proficiency levels in math and reading. The Chicago school system hired a former English HMI to design a school review system for the district.[26] New York City hired an Ofsted contractor to visit and evaluate all New York City schools; the evaluations resulting from these visits apparently have credibility with both district administrators and teachers.[27] But these efforts are in conflict with contemporary state and federal accountability standards, which make schools almost exclusively accountable for math and reading test scores.

Such attempts to create better accountability systems shouldn't be allowed to collapse under the weight of our obsession with reading and math scores. To fulfill our desire to hold American schools and their supporting public institutions accountable, it makes sense to design a system that draws upon the best elements of standardized testing and inspection systems.

A Better Model: What Would It Look Like?

It is not our intent to present a fully developed accountability proposal; that is a task for policymakers, public officials, and citizens. We only hope to provoke discussion that will help move American policy beyond an exclusive reliance on standardized testing of basic skills.[28]

To begin, we assume that accountability should be a state, not federal, responsibility. Not only do we have a constitutional tradition of state control of education, but the failure of No Child Left Behind has made it apparent that in this large country, the U.S. Congress and U.S. Department of Education are too distant to micromanage school performance.

There are, however, two important tasks for the federal government: (1) to ensure that each state has the fiscal capacity to provide adequate education and other youth services, and (2) to expand the National Assessment of Educational Progress (NAEP) to provide state policymakers with information on the achievement of their states' young adults and 17-, 13-, and 9-year-olds in the eight broad areas we presented earlier. These two tasks are prerequisite to an accountability system that ensures we, as a nation, are raising the performance of disadvantaged children—and of middle-class children as well. We'll briefly discuss each.

For the last 30 years, reformers concerned with the inadequate resources devoted to the education of disadvantaged children have directed attention almost entirely to intrastate equalization—trying to see that districts serving poor students have as much if not more money to spend as districts serving middle-class children in the same state. These reformers have largely ignored the vast resource inequalities that exist between states. Yet about two-thirds of nationwide spending inequality is between states and only one-third is within them.[29] Efforts to redistribute education funds within states cannot address the most serious fiscal inequalities. Consider one of the most extreme cases,

Mississippi: no matter how deep the commitment of its leaders may be to improving achievement, its tax base is too small to raise revenues in the way that wealthier states can, while its challenges—the number of its low-income minority children relative to the size of its population—are much greater than those of many states that are considered more progressive. In general, fewer dollars are spent on the education of the wealthiest children in Mississippi than on the poorest children in New York or New Jersey.

> **In general, fewer dollars are spent on the education of the wealthiest children in Mississippi than on the poorest children in New York. Yet *federal aid exacerbates inequality* in states' fiscal capacities.**

Yet federal aid exacerbates inequality in states' fiscal capacities. Federal school aid—to districts serving poor children—is proportional to states' own spending.[30] New Jersey, which needs less aid, gets more aid per poor pupil than Mississippi, which needs more.

It is politically tough to fix this, because sensible redistribution, with aid given to states in proportion to need and in inverse proportion to capacity, must take tax revenues from states like New Jersey (whose representatives tend to favor federal spending) and direct them to states like Mississippi (whose representatives tend to oppose it).[31] Nonetheless, it is unreasonable to expect states that lack sufficient resources to hold their schools and other institutions of youth development accountable for adequate and equitable performance in each of the eight goal areas.

The second critical task for the federal government should be gathering valid and reliable information on the relative performance of students in the different states. One helpful aspect of No Child Left Behind was the requirement that every state participate in NAEP reading and math assessments for the fourth and eighth grades every two years. Because these are the only assessments administered in common to representative samples of students in all states, they provide a way to compare how each state ensures that its elementary school children gain these two academic skills. To spur effective state-level accountability, the NAEP state-level assessment should:

- *Assess representative samples of students at the state level and on a regular schedule, not only in math and reading, but in other academic subject areas*—science, history, other social studies, writing, foreign language—as well as in the arts, citizenship, social skills, and health behavior. These assessments should include paper-and-pencil test items, survey questions, and performance observations.
- *Gather better demographic data.* NAEP has collected systematic demographic data from its samples of test takers only for race, Hispanic ethnicity, and free or reduced-price lunch eligibility. The range of characteristics within these categories is wide. For example, first- and second-generation Hispanic immigrant children are in different circumstances from those who are third generation and beyond, and students eligible for free meals come from families that may be considerably poorer than those in the reduced-price program. Since 2000, NAEP has collected data on maternal educational attainment, and it would be relatively easy to collect a few other critical characteristics—most notably family structure (e.g., single parent) and the mother's country of birth. Such data could be collected by schools upon a child's initial

enrollment and become part of a student's permanent record. Adding these demographic characteristics to state-level NAEP may require minimal expansion of sample sizes, but the payoff to this relatively modest expansion would be substantial, and it would facilitate the ability of state leaders to draw valid conclusions about their policy needs.

- *Report NAEP scores on scales, not achievement levels.* Reports of average scale scores at different points in the distribution, such as quartiles, could be published in language easily understood by the public. State policymakers should then be interested in how the average scale scores of students in each quartile of each relevant demographic subgroup compare with scores of similar students in other states. Successful progress should then be judged by whether such average scores in each achievement quartile make progress toward the scores of comparable students in better-performing states. Note that this approach does away with today's ill-considered achievement levels (which are based on fanciful definitions of "proficiency" that vary wildly from state to state). Since there would be no all-or-nothing cut score, there would then be no "bubble" of students just below the cut score, and teachers and schools would have no incentive to concentrate instruction only on these students. All students would be expected to make progress.

- *Use age-level, not grade-level, sampling.* Age-level assessment is the only way to get an accurate reading of the relative effectiveness of state education and youth policies. With the current grade-level assessment, one state's eighth-grade scores may be higher than another's only because more low-performing seventh graders were held back, not because its ultimate outcomes are superior. If 13-year-olds were assessed regardless of grade, this distortion would be avoided. With age-level sampling, results from states with different promotion and school-age policies could be compared accurately.*

- *Supplement in-school samples with out-of-school samples.* The best evidence of the quality of our education and youth development policies is the performance of 17-year-olds, for whom states are completing their normal institutional responsibility, and of young adults, to see whether knowledge and skills developed earlier are being retained. To get representative samples of 17-year-olds and young adults, assessments should include an out-of-school household survey that covers each of the eight broad goals.

A *full accountability system* requires judgment about whether schools, along with other institutions of youth development, are likely to generate *balanced outcomes* across the eight goals.

Dramatic expansion of NAEP in this fashion need not have the harmful effects that standardized testing under contemporary state and federal accountability policies has produced. Incentives for teachers to "teach to the test" are avoided because NAEP is a sampled assessment, with any one particular school rarely chosen, only a few students in the selected schools assessed, and those students given only portions of a complete exam. There are no consequences for students or schools who do well or poorly, because results are generated only at the state level; nobody knows how particular students or schools performed. Because an expanded NAEP should assess the full range of cognitive and noncognitive knowledge and skills encompassed by the eight broad goals of education, NAEP can give state policymakers and educators no incentives to ignore untested curricular areas.

With this federal support, states can design accountability systems that include academic testing in core subject areas and in those nonacademic fields where standardization is possible, such as health awareness and physical fitness. State accountability systems can supplement such testing and provide detailed school-level data by use of inspection procedures that ensure that adequate performance in each of the eight goal areas is achieved, and that schools and other institutions of youth development implement strategies likely to improve that performance.

State-Level Accountability That Encourages School Improvement

An expanded NAEP can tell governors, legislators, and citizens the extent to which their states are doing an adequate job of generating student success in each of the eight goal areas. Then, citizens and state policymakers can use this information to guide the refinement of state policy. They will want to ensure that particular schools and school districts, children's health care institutions, early childhood and preschool programs, parental support and education programs, after-school and summer programs, and community redevelopment agencies are contributing to, not impeding, the achievement of such success. This requires ways for state government to hold these school districts, schools, and other supporting institutions accountable.

The following proposals sound like a great deal of testing, but keep in mind that it is not necessary to test each subject in each grade level each year. Decisions about what to test, in which grade, and how often should be made at the state level, but a great deal of useful information can be gathered without more tests than students currently take. With that in mind, we propose that states:

- *Cover all eight goals of public education* to avoid the goal distortion that results from accountability for only a few basic skills. Many standardized tests in subjects other than math and reading now exist, but few include constructed-response items, in which students are not given multiple choices but must work out factual or prose answers on their own. Certainly, higher-quality academic tests in history, writing, the sciences, and other academic areas should be

---

*Age-level sampling in NAEP need not mean that states' own tests used for school-level accountability must be standardized for age instead of grade level. Because states, if they choose, can standardize school entry ages and social promotion policies, grade-level test results are less subject to misinterpretation if confined to particular states. States have an interest in using tests to determine if mandated grade-level curricula are being implemented successfully. Provided that NAEP assesses samples of students of the same age, not grade, we will have the data we need to understand if the combination of age-to-grade policies in some states are more effective than they are elsewhere.

deployed, as should standardized assessment instruments, where possible, in nonacademic areas. For example, instruments exist that can assess a student's upper-body strength and, combined with data on the student's weight and height, inform the evaluation of a school's physical education program.[32]

- *Use standardized test scores very cautiously to judge schools, and only in combination with other data.* If states' tests are improved, as they should be, to include higher-quality items that cannot be machine scored, the precision with which the tests can be scored will decline. Many schools are too small to generate reliable results for particular age groups even on existing low-level tests of basic skills. With more complex items included, reliability will decline further.

- *Supplement information from standardized tests with expert evaluation of student work.* Even the most sophisticated test questions are not fully adequate to reveal students' abilities. NAEP exams include a large number of constructed-response items. But even these questions are no substitute for expert examination of drafts and redrafts of student essays for evidence of how students respond to critiques of their initial efforts and how they develop themes that are longer than those of a brief constructed response on an exam.

- *Collect richer background information on students to make test score comparisons meaningful.* As more states develop good student data systems, with unique student identification numbers and maintenance of cumulative records for each student in secure school databases for the student's entire school career, it will become easier to attach richer background information to student assessment results for purposes of analysis. As one example, schools already know which students are eligible for free meals and which are eligible only for reduced-price meals. Yet in their school "report cards," many (but not all) states and school districts combine these categories, rendering them less useful for understanding and comparing student performance. It would be a simple matter for elementary schools to record, upon a student's initial enrollment, not only the student's subsidized lunch eligibility but also the educational attainment of the mother (or primary caretaker), whether the mother was born in the U.S., and the number of parents or other responsible adults in the student's household.

- *Use NAEP to set realistic goals that inspire continuous improvement.* Goals are valuable, but they should always be feasible, not fanciful. Once NAEP has been expanded, states can establish goals based on the performance of students with similar characteristics in other states. Such goals should be established not only for average performance but also for NAEP performance at the higher and lower ends of the student achievement distribution. If all states regularly established and revised such realistic goals, it would result in a permanent process of continuous improvement.

B ut test scores and evaluations of student work, even for larger schools, and even when connected to more nuanced student background characteristics, are of only partial value. A full accountability system requires evaluation of student performance in areas more difficult to standardize (for example, cooperative behavior), and judgment about whether a school's curriculum and instruction, along with a community's other institutions of youth development, are likely to generate balanced and adequate outcomes across the eight goals.

To supplement test scores and evaluations of students' written work, states wanting to hold school districts, schools, and supporting institutions accountable require an inspection system. Each state should:

- *Conduct mandatory inspections in each school and in each related community institution* (children's health care services, early childhood and preschool programs, parental support and education programs, after-school and summer programs, and community development agencies) approximately once every three years. Where feasible, accreditation of all these institutions in a particular community should be coordinated. Once the system is firmly established, inspections might be conducted less frequently in communities and schools with satisfactory youth outcomes, and more frequently in communities and schools where outcomes are not satisfactory.

- *Design school inspections to determine primarily whether students are achieving adequate outcomes in all eight goals,* not whether schools are meeting the idiosyncratic goals of their faculties and administrations. Inspection teams should compare schools' performance to higher-performing schools with similar demographic characteristics. Such a standard necessarily will lead to continual improvement by all schools.

- *Make most inspectors professional evaluators,* not volunteers, trained to ensure consistency of judgment, and certified as competent by state (or regional) inspection agencies.

- *Include members of the public, representatives of the business community, or designees of elected officials on inspection teams.* Not only would such participation give inspection greater public credibility, but these members, with their varied backgrounds and perspectives, may detect aspects of school quality requiring improvement that may not be apparent to professional educators.

- *Conduct inspections with little or no advance notice, and give inspectors access to all classrooms for random observation.* Likewise, inspectors should choose random students to invite to interview, and whose work to review.

- *Have teams include in their reports an evaluation and interpretation of schools' standardized test scores, but supplement this* by examining student work, listening to student performances, observing student behavior, and interviewing students to gain insight into their knowledge and skills.

- *Require inspectors to make clear recommendations* about how curriculum, instruction, or other school practices should be improved if they find a school's performance to be inadequate in one or more goal areas. Although schools may choose not to follow the specific advice of inspectors, subsequent inspections (more frequent than once every three years in cases where performance is inadequate) should determine whether performance has improved and, if not, why schools did not follow recommendations for improvement. Inspections of other community institutions should employ similar procedures.

- *Make inspection reports public,* and in a timely fashion. Reports should include responses by administrators or teachers to inspectors' criticisms.

- *Establish consequences.* States should assume direct control of schools and other public institutions of youth development when improvement does not follow repeated inspection reports that indicate severe problems.

The *total cost* of the accountability system we have outlined here would be no more than *1 percent* of total elementary and secondary public school spending in the U.S.

The accountability system outlined here would not be cheap. But neither would it be so expensive that this proposal is unrealistic, as the following "back-of-the-envelope" estimate shows. At present, the federal government spends about $40 million annually to administer a state-level NAEP exam in math or reading in grades 4, 8, and 12. Assessing 9-, 13-, and 17-year-olds instead could add a little, but not much, to the cost (because, for example, a few 13-year-olds might be found in high schools, not middle schools). Design costs (including substituting new items as old items are rotated out) also add relatively little cost. Expanding samples so that state-level information can be disaggregated into finer demographic subgroups also adds relatively little cost. Adding additional academic and nonacademic subjects (writing, history, other social studies, science, foreign language, health knowledge, physical fitness, and understanding of the arts and vocations) at the state level need not duplicate the full cost for each subject if only paper-and-pencil items are used, because NAEP could use many of the same schools that it samples for math and reading. There would, however, be additional costs for preparing test booklets that included sophisticated multicolor maps or art reproductions. Adding performance and other nontraditional items that can easily be standardized (for example, tests of upper-body strength or identification of musical themes) would incur substantial additional expense. As a very rough estimate, expanding regular state-level NAEP into all eight goals and into all subject areas within the academic categories, and administering such assessments every three years, with appropriate subgroup reporting, might cost a total of $500 million annually.

Supplementing these in-school assessments with a NAEP for out-of-school 17-year-olds and young adults, requiring a house-hold survey conducted once every three years, might cost as much as an additional $20 million annually.

In England, when inspections in each school took place approximately every six years, the school inspection system cost about one-quarter of 1 percent of total elementary and secondary school spending. If we assume a similar ratio for a system in the U.S., with teams visiting schools approximately every three years, the annual cost would be about $2.5 billion, or one-half of 1 percent of current federal, state, and local spending on elementary and secondary education. Additional costs would be incurred for inspecting other institutions of youth development.

Even with the additional costs of an expanded in-school state NAEP, and of a young adult and 17-year-old out-of-school state NAEP, the total cost of the accountability system we have outlined here would still be no more than 1 percent of total elementary and secondary public school spending in the U.S. This is not an unreasonable price for an accountability system that measures whether schools in every state, in coordination with other institutions of youth development, are preparing young adults to have adequate academic knowledge and skills, appreciation of the arts and literature, preparation for skilled work, social skills and work ethic, citizenship and community responsibility, physical health, and emotional health. If this system succeeded in correcting even some of the unproductive practices in schools and other institutions, the gains in efficiency would more than justify this expenditure. When accountability funds are spent correctly, they eliminate waste and save funds.

But saving money, probable though that might be in the long run, is not the primary purpose of an accountability system. If we truly want to hold institutions accountable for fulfilling the missions to which they have been assigned by the nation, and if we are determined to reverse the corruptions we have visited on schools by narrow test-based accountability policies, we should willingly entertain a system of accountability that might require higher expenditures in the short run.

No Child Left Behind has given accountability a bad name. An alternative program along the lines suggested here could redeem accountability's reputation. And it could give the citizens of this nation a better means to fulfill our responsibilities to provide for our youth and the nation's future.

Notes
What's Wrong with Accountability by the Numbers?

1. Herbert A. Simon, "Rational Decision-Making in Business Organizations" (Nobel Memorial Lecture, December 8, 1978), 352, 366.

2. Donald T. Campbell, "Assessing the Impact of Planned Social Change," *Evaluation and Program Planning* 2 (1979): 67–90 (reprinted, with minor revisions and additions, from *Social Research and Public Policies*, ed. Gene M. Lyons (Hanover, NH: University Press of New England, 1975), 85.

3. Michael Murray, "Why Arrest Quotas Are Wrong," *PBA Magazine*, Spring 2005.

4. Scott Jaschik, "Should U.S. News Make Presidents Rich?" *Inside Higher Ed*, March 19, 2007.

5. Alan Finder, "College Ratings Race Roars on Despite Concerns," *New York Times*, August 17, 2007.

6. David Seidman and Michael Couzens,"Getting the Crime Rate Down: Political Pressure and Crime Reporting," *Law & Society Review* 8, no. 3 (1974): 457–494.

7. Seidman and Couzens, "Getting the Crime Rate Down," 462.

8. Lisa I. Iezzoni, "Risk and Outcomes," in *Risk Adjustment for Measuring Health Care Outcomes*, ed. Lisa I. Iezzoni (Ann Arbor, MI: Health Administration Press, 1994), 4.

9. Allen Schick, "Getting Performance Measures to Measure Up," in *Quicker, Better, Cheaper?: Managing Performance in American Government*, ed. Dall W. Forsythe (Albany: Rockefeller Institute Press, 2001), 41.

10. Lawrence P. Casalino et al., "General Internists' Views on Pay-for-Performance and Public Reporting of Quality Scores: A National Survey," *Health Affairs* 26, no. 2 (2007): 492–499, 495.

11. Marc Santora, "Cardiologists Say Rankings Sway Choices on Surgery," *New York Times*, January 11, 2005; and Casalino et al., "General Internists' Views," 496.

12. Lawrence K. Altman, "Heart-Surgery Death Rates Decline in New York," *New York Times*, December 5, 1990.

13. This article is not the first, or only, discussion of the applicability of Campbell's law to contemporary test-based educational accountability policies. The following have made similar observations: Sharon L. Nichols and David C. Berliner, *Collateral Damage: How High-Stakes Testing Corrupts America's Schools* (Cambridge, MA: Harvard

Education Press, 2007); Daniel Koretz, "Inflation of Scores in Educational Accountability Systems: Empirical Findings and a Psychometric Framework" (powerpoint prepared for the Eric M. Mindich Conference on Experimental Social Science, in *Biases from Behavioral Responses to Measurement: Perspectives From Theoretical Economics, Health Care, Education, and Social Services,* Cambridge, MA, May 4, 2007); and Daniel Koretz, *Measuring Up: What Educational Testing Really Tells Us* (Cambridge, MA: Harvard University Press, 2008).

14. Martin West, "Testing, Learning, and Teaching: The Effects of Test-Based Accountability on Student Achievement and Instructional Time in Core Academic Subjects," in *Beyond the Basics: Achieving a Liberal Education for All Children,* eds. Chester E. Finn Jr. and Diane Ravitch (Washington, DC: Thomas B. Fordham Institute, 2007), 45–62, 57.

15. Steven Kerr, "On the Folly of Rewarding A While Hoping for B," *Academy of Management Journal* 18, no. 4 (1975): 769–783.

What Really Happens in the Private Sector?

1. Elissa Gootman, "Teachers Agree to Bonus Pay Tied to Scores," *New York Times,* October 18, 2007.

2. Michael Bloomberg, "Mayor Bloomberg, Chancellor Klein and UFT President Weingarten Announce Schoolwide Bonus Plan to Reward Teachers at Schools that Raise Student Acheivement," Mayor's Press Release No. 375, October 17, 2007.

3. Scott J. Adams and John S. Heywood, "Performance Pay in the U.S.: Concepts, Measurement and Trends" (2nd Draft, Economic Policy Institute, November 19, 2007), Tables 2 and 7.

4. Robert S. Kaplan and Anthony A. Atkinson, *Advanced Management Accounting,* 3rd ed. (Englewood Cliffs, NJ: Prentice Hall, 1998), 692–693.

5. Christopher D. Ittner, David F. Larcker, and Marshall W. Meyer, "Performance, Compensation, and the Balanced Scorecard" (Philadelphia: Wharton School, University of Pennsylvania, November 1, 1997), 9. That labor market success seems to be correlated with employees' physical attractiveness confirms that supervisory evaluations are flawed tools for objective evaluations of performance. See Daniel S. Hamermesh and Jeff E. Biddle, "Beauty and the Labor Market," *American Economic Review* 84, no. 5 (1994): 1174–1194.

6. William H. Bommer et al., "On the Interchangeability of Objective and Subjective Measures of Employee Performance: A Meta-Analysis," *Personnel Psychology* 48, no. 3 (1995): 587–605, 602.

Grading Education

1. The conclusions of many researchers and policy experts on this point are summarized in Richard Rothstein, *Class and Schools: Using Social, Economic, and Educational Reform to Close the Black-White Achievement Gap* (New York: Teachers College Press, 2004).

2. Daniel Koretz, Karen Mitchell, Sheila Barron, and Sarah Keith, *Final Report: The Perceived Effects of the Maryland School Performance Assessment Program,* CSE Technical Report

No. 409 (Los Angeles: National Center for Research on Evaluation, Standards, and Student Testing, University of California, 1996), Table 6.

3. Linda M. McNeil, *Contradictions of School Reform: Educational Costs of Standardized Testing* (New York: Routledge, 2000), 242–243 and passim.

4. Helen F. Ladd and Arnaldo Zelli, "School-Based Accountability in North Carolina: The Responses of School Principals," *Educational Administration Quarterly* 38, no. 4 (2002): 494–529, Figures 5 and 11.

5. Claus Von Zastrow, with Helen Janc, *Academic Atrophy: The Condition of the Liberal Arts in America's Public Schools* (Washington, DC: Council for Basic Education, 2004), Figure 17.

6. Jennifer McMurrer, *Choices, Changes, and Challenges: Curriculum and Instruction in the NCLB Era* (Washington, DC: Center on Education Policy, July [revised December] 2007), Table 3; and Jennifer McMurrer, *Instructional Time in Elementary Schools: A Closer Look at Changes in Specific Subjects* (Washington, DC: Center on Education Policy, February 2008).

7. These problems are discussed at length in Rothstein, *Class and Schools,* chapter 1. More recent and eloquent treatments of these issues are in Susan B. Neuman, *Changing the Odds for Children at Risk: Seven Essential Principles of Education Programs that Break the Cycle of Poverty* (Westport, CT: Praeger, 2008); and Susan B. Neuman, "Education Should Lift All Children," *Detroit Free Press,* July 31, 2008.

8. For estimate of effect of mobility: Eric A. Hanushek, John F. Kain, and Steven G. Rivkin, "Disruption Versus Tiebout Improvement: The Costs and Benefits of Switching Schools," *Journal of Public Economics* 88, nos. 9–10 (2004): 1721–1746; for estimate of effect of child and maternal health: Janet Currie, "Health Disparities and Gaps in School Readiness," *The Future of Children* 15, no. 1 (2005): 117–138.

9. Melanie C. M. Ehren and A. J. Visscher, "The Relationships Between School Inspections, School Characteristics, and School Improvement," *British Journal of Educational Studies* 56, no. 2 (2008): 205–227.

10. Peter Matthews and Pam Sammons, *Improvement Through Inspection: An Evaluation of the Impact of Ofsted's Work* (London: Institute of Education, University of London, and Office for Standards in Education [Ofsted], July 2004), 83–84.

11. Matthews and Sammons, *Improvement Through Inspection,* 9; Thomas A. Wilson, *Reaching for a Better Standard: English School Inspection and the Dilemma of Accountability for American Public Schools* (New York: Teachers College Press, 1996), 134; and Office for Standards in Education (Ofsted), *Every Child Matters: Framework for the Inspection of Schools in England from September 2005* (London: Ofsted, April 2008).

12. W. Norton Grubb, "Opening Classrooms and Improving Teaching: Lessons from School Inspections in England," *Teachers College Record* 102, no. 4 (2000): 696–723, 709.

13. Tim Brighouse (visiting professor of education at the Institute of Education, London University, former chief adviser to London Schools and former chief education officer for Birmingham), personal correspondence and telephone interview with author (various dates, and May 8, 2008).

14. Grubb, "Opening Classrooms and Improving Teaching," 701, 703; and Wilson, *Reaching for a Better Standard,* 127.

15. Grubb, "Opening Classrooms and Improving Teaching," 703; and Wilson, *Reaching for a Better Standard,* 71.

16. Brighouse, personal correspondence and telephone interview with author.

17. Matthews and Sammons, *Improvement Through Inspection,* 14, 34; and Grubb, "Opening Classrooms and Improving Teaching," 701.

18. Grubb, "Opening Classrooms and Improving Teaching," 701; and Brighouse, personal correspondence and telephone interview with author.

19. Ofsted, *Every Child Matters,* 22.

20. Ofsted, *Every Child Matters.*

21. Brighouse, personal correspondence and telephone interview with author.

22. Ofsted, *Every Child Matters,* 9.

23. Matthews and Sammons, *Improvement Through Inspection,* 112, 108; and Rebecca Smithers, "Punishment for Black Pupils Appears Harsher: Watchdog's Report Points to Inconsistency Over Exclusions," *Guardian,* March 1, 2001.

24. Matthews and Sammons, *Improvement Through Inspection,* 150; Smithers, "Punishment for Black Pupils"; and Ofsted, *Every Child Matters.*

25. The system was designed, and then implemented, by Thomas A. Wilson, whose study (Wilson, *Reaching for a Better Standard*) of the English system prior to the 1993 reforms made it familiar to American education experts. See Rhode Island Department of Elementary and Secondary Education, "School Accountability for Learning and Teaching (SALT)" (Providence, RI: RIDE, 2008).

26. Grubb, "Opening Classrooms and Improving Teaching," 718.

27. Randi Weingarten, Keynote Address (33rd Annual Conference of the American Education Finance Association, Denver, CO, April 10, 2008).

28. Others are also helping to provoke this discussion. The proposal set forth here joins a conversation in which Ladd (Helen F. Ladd, "Holding Schools Accountable Revisited" [Spencer Foundation Lecture in Education Policy and Management, Association for Public Policy Analysis and Management, 2007]), Nichols and Berliner (Sharon L. Nichols and David C. Berliner, *Collateral Damage: How High-Stakes Testing Corrupts America's Schools* [Cambridge, MA: Harvard Education Press, 2007]), and Dorn (Sherman Dorn, *Accountability Frankenstein: Understanding and Taming the Monster* [Charlotte, NC: Information Age Publishing, 2007]) have engaged. Jones (Ken Jones, "Thinking Ahead," in *Democratic School Accountability,* ed. Ken Jones [Lanham, MD: Rowman and Littlefield Education, 2006]), and Fruchter and Mediratta (Norm Fruchter and Kavitha Mediratta, "Bottom-Up Accountability: An Urban Perspective," in *Democratic*

School Accountability, ed. Ken Jones [Lanham, MD: Rowman and Littlefield Education, 2006]) envision an accountability system with elements similar to those proposed here, but where accountability is primarily to local governing bodies (school boards or parent councils), not state government.

29. Sheila E. Murray, William N. Evans, and Robert M. Schwab, "Education-Finance Reform and the Distribution of Education Resources," *American Economic Review* 88, no. 4 (1998): 789–812, 808.

30. Goodwin Liu, "Improving Title I Funding Equity Across States, Districts, and Schools," *Iowa Law Review* 93 (2008): 973–1013.

31. Rothstein (Richard Rothstein, "Equalizing Education Resources on Behalf of Disadvantaged Children," in *A Notion at Risk: Preserving Public Education as an Engine of Social Mobility,* ed. Richard D. Kahlenberg [New York: Century Foundation Press, 2000]) and Liu (Goodwin Liu, "Interstate Inequality in Educational Opportunity," *New York University Law Review* 81, no. 6 [2006]: 2044–2128) offer proposals for interstate finance equalization. They differ in that Liu proposes an adjustment for state tax effort, and Rothstein does not.

32. Cooper Institute, *Fitnessgram/Activitygram* (Dallas: Cooper Institute, 2008).

Critical Thinking

1. Identify three things mentioned by the authors as frequent characteristics of disadvantaged students attending poor performing schools.

2. If you were developing/revising the educational system in your hometown, what agencies, organizations, and services would you include as essential partners to ensure an "integrated system of youth development and family support"?

3. Under the section of the article, "What Would It Look Like"? summarize one of the points made by the authors about assessment.

4. Reread the nine bullet points presented about holding institutions accountable. What do you see as two strengths or advantages of these ideas? What about two barriers to implementing the strategies proposed?

RICHARD ROTHSTEIN is a research associate at the Economic Policy Institute, former national education columnist with the *New York Times,* and author of several books, including *Class and Schools: Using Social, Economic, and Educational Reform to Close the Black-White Achievement Gap.* **REBECCA JACOBSEN** is an assistant professor of teacher education and education policy at Michigan State University. Tamara Wilder is a postdoctoral fellow at the University of Michigan's Ford School of Public Policy. Adapted with permission from a book by Rothstein, Jacobsen, and Wilder, *Grading Education: Getting Accountability Right* (www.epi.org/publications/entry/books_grading_education), published in 2008 by the Economic Policy Institute and Teachers College Press.

From *American Educator* by Richard Rothstein, Rebecca Jacobsen, and Tamara Wilder, Spring 2009, pp. 24–33. Copyright © 2009 by Richard Rothstein, Rebecca Jacobsen, and Tamara Wilder. Reprinted with permission of the American Educator, the quarterly journal of the American Federation of Teachers AFL-CIO, and Richard Rothstein, Rebecca Jacobsen, and Tamara Wilder.

Measuring the Achievement Elephant

You can't get a comprehensive picture of student achievement by looking at isolated chunks of data.

PAUL E. BARTON AND RICHARD J. COLEY

It's an old story. A group of blind people want to know what an elephant looks like. One feels the elephant's trunk, another a leg, and another the tail. The first concludes that the elephant is like a snake, the second like a tree, and the third like a rope. It's impossible to get an accurate image of the whole elephant by examining only a few of its parts.

The story illustrates the problem of getting a fix on student achievement. Like the elephant, the subject of student achievement is big. A few pieces of data can give an incomplete picture—or worse, a misleading one.

To illustrate this point, let's look at a few examples that represent starting places for thinking about some little-recognized aspects of student achievement data. With a better understanding of the whole elephant, school leaders can not only make better use of test score data but also convey the meaning of these data more effectively to school personnel, students, and parents.

The Problem with Cut Points

A common approach in this era of test-based accountability is to measure student achievement in terms of how many students score at or above some predetermined "proficiency" level, which statisticians call a *cut point*. State and federal accountability systems, with a few exceptions, are nearly always set up this way.

Focusing on the cut point has at least one major drawback: It provides no information about changes in the achievement of students who remain above or below this point. Further, in a high-stakes environment, the use of a single cut point can have negative consequences, encouraging teachers to focus most of their attention on those students who are just below the cut point in an effort to boost them over the line so the school can show "improvement." Meanwhile, what's happening to students who are well above this cut point? What's happening to students who are so far below the cut point that there seems to be only a remote possibility of getting them above it before the next round of testing?

We need to consider measures that yield a broader understanding of student achievement. These measures could result in a better approach to accountability and a more equitable and effective distribution of precious instructional resources.

We need to consider measures that yield a broader understanding of student achievement.

Looking at the Whole Distribution

One way of moving beyond the cut point approach is to examine the whole distribution of scores by percentiles. Figure 1 taken from the long-term trend series of the National Assessment of Educational Progress (NAEP), illustrates some of the insights that we can gain from this approach.

This figure shows average NAEP reading scores at selected percentiles for 1990 and 2004. We can see that 9-year-old students at the 50th, 25th, and 10th percentiles improved significantly, and students at the 90th and 75th percentiles decreased or did not improve significantly. When we look at different racial/ethnic groups, we see that black students showed significant gains at all percentiles and Hispanic students made significant gains at all but the 90th percentile during this period.

Now look at older students' reading scores. The contrast is striking. The total group of 13-year-old students showed no significant improvement at any percentile. Seventeen-year-old white, black, and Hispanic students showed declines at every level; and when all three racial/ethnic groups are added together, the sample is large enough to disclose that these declines were statistically significant at the 75th, 25th, and 10th percentiles.

The news was better in mathematics, where gains were made throughout most of the score distribution for 9- and 13-year-olds. But the mystery of the disappearing achievement gains has been evident during the last few decades. The student achievement gains we've seen at ages 9 and 13 typically disappear at age 17. Looking at achievement trends at different percentiles and at different ages can inform policymakers about where changes may or may not be occurring—where students are being helped and where they may be falling behind.

Looking at Quartiles

We can tell a more concise story by examining quartiles, calculating average scores for each quartile, and tracking changes. Ever since NAEP made such comparisons possible, the public has widely recognized that achievement gaps by race and ethnicity exist. But it may come as a surprise that the largest and *only* reduction in the minority achievement gap for 17-year-olds in reading, looking at black and Hispanic students combined, occurred from 1975 to 1990. From 1990 through 2004 (the most recent data available from the long-term NAEP), there has been no reduction in the gap. The reduction from

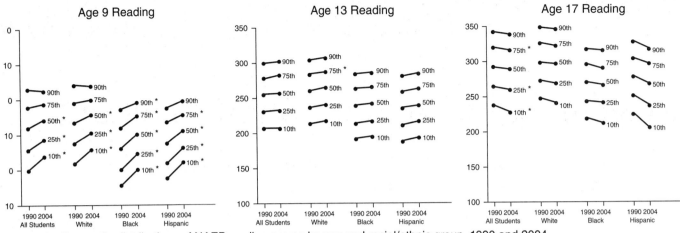

Figure 1 Percentile distributions of NAEP reading scores by age and racial/ethnic group, 1990 and 2004.

*Indicates a statistically significant difference from 1990 to 2004.

Source: Data from the National Assessment of Educational Progress analyzed by Educational Testing Service.

1975 to 1990 was large—the gap was nearly halved—and it happened across the board in all four quartiles (Barton & Coley, 2008).

Many people consider the period of the 1990s and early 2000s to be the time of the flowering of education reform, including the implementation of standards-based reform and test-based accountability. Why the reduction in the minority achievement gap for older students stopped during this period—and why the large gap reduction between 1975 and 1990 occurred in the first place—is unknown. We should seek the answer as policymakers craft new programs to raise overall levels of student achievement and to close the achievement gap.

End-of-Year Comparisons vs. Gains

There has been considerable debate in the United States, particularly since the passage of No Child Left Behind (NCLB), about how to use test scores to set standards for accountability. NCLB uses end-of-year test scores to determine how many students meet a set level of proficiency, thus comparing different cohorts of students each year. We have been among those arguing that we would get more useful information by measuring how much students *gain* in knowledge during the school year. A considerable number of studies have shown that schools found to be "failing" on one measure are not "failing" on the other. That is, there is a low correlation between the results obtained by the two different measures (Barton, 2008).

Data from the National Assessment of Educational Progress illustrate this discrepancy. NAEP reports results in terms of end-of-year scores: for example, by comparing 8th graders in 1996 with 8th graders in 2000. In contrast, to obtain a view of "growth," we would calculate how much the scores of students who were 4th graders in 1996 grew by the time they were in 8th grade in 2000. (For a discussion of the statistical and measurement challenges inherent in this latter approach and a comparison of how the various states did on each of the two measures, see Coley 2003).

The differences in state rankings in student achievement on NAEP using these two measures are large. For example, at the end of grade 8, Maine ranked number one in "level of knowledge," with an average score of 273 on the 0–500 scale. However, it placed fourth from the bottom in terms of the gain in scale points from 4th to 8th grade (Barton & Coley 2008).

These two methods will produce similar disparities in the rankings of individual schools. A school that does not make adequate yearly progress as measured by end-of-year comparisons may actually be doing well in terms of student gains during the year, whereas a school showing high end-of-year test scores may be doing poorly if we look at how much its students are gaining during the year.

A Panoramic View of Achievement Inequality

The purpose of disaggregating achievement test scores is to gain insight about inequality and achievement gaps. The most informative view of these gaps is seen by looking at the full distribution of achievement scores from top to bottom, as well as looking at scores of students of different ages and grades side by side. NAEP long-term trend data permit such analysis on an age basis, as we saw in Figure 1. The degree of overlap in the score distributions of 9-year-old students, 13-year-old students, and 17-year-old students is substantial. When we display such a chart during speeches, the gasp from audiences is sometimes audible.

The bottom line: In reading, about the bottom one-fourth of 17-year-olds score at about the same level as do the top one-tenth of 9-year-olds. This wide range of achievement levels occurs within each racial/ethnic group to varying degrees. However, overlaps also shed light on the differences between racial/ethnic groups. For example, the distribution of scores for 17-year-old black and Hispanic students looks similar to that for 13-year-old white students.

When we see such huge disparities in achievement among students of the same age and grade, it is hard to understand what the frequently used phrase *being on grade level* means. Across the United States, students in every grade fall at different points in an achievement range that starts very high and ends very low; there is nothing "level" about it.

Achievement Gap Misunderstandings

No Child Left Behind requires states to "close the achievement gap" and bring all racial and ethnic subgroups to the same level—or so it has been widely declared. However, the law is precise in what it says, and although its successful operation might well narrow achievement gaps, it does not require that they be closed.

NCLB requires only that all defined population subgroups reach the "proficient" level a state has established. But even if all the subgroups increase their scores to above the cut point, the gaps between average scores of different groups may remain. In addition to tracking the gap in the percentage of subgroups reaching a particular cut point, we need to measure and compare the average scores in each subgroup to identify whether gaps are being reduced or closed (Holland, 2002).

The difference between using a cut point standard and an average score is seen in the 2007 NAEP mathematics data for 8th graders. The gap between white and black students varies depending on whether we compare the difference in average scores or the percentage reaching the basic or proficient level. West Virginia, for example, has a 21-point gap in average scores, a 32-point gap in the percentage of students reaching the basic level, and only a 15-point gap in the percentage of students reaching the proficient level. Massachusetts, on the other hand, has a 40-point gap in average scores, a 37-point gap in the percentage of students reaching the basic level, and a 45-point gap in the percentage of students reaching the proficient level (Barton & Coley, 2008).

If ever the circumstance arose, some states might be shocked to find they have met the required proficiency levels for each subgroup while maintaining exactly the same gaps in average scores that they had before.

Giving More Meaning to Test Scores

When the results of standardized tests are reported in terms of average scores or the percentage reaching a particular cut point or level, students, parents, and even teachers are left pretty much in the dark about what, specifically, a student is able to do at any particular score level. As in many areas of testing, NAEP has led the way in communicating in understandable ways what test results mean. For reading and mathematics at both grades 4 and 8, NAEP provides examples of tasks that students who reach a specific scale score are likely to be able to perform successfully. NAEP calls this "item mapping." In the case of 8th grade mathematics, NAEP arrays 30 different task items on the scale. For example,

- A student with a scale score of 259 would probably be able to recognize misrepresented data.
- A student with a score of 305 could probably identify fractions listed in ascending order.
- A student with a score of 355 would most likely be able to estimate the side length of a square, given the area.

From the standpoint of the student, the parent, the public, and the teacher, a "scale score" on a standardized test can be abstract and uninformative. Item mapping provides better information about what students can and cannot do. And reviewing this information for subgroups of students can help policymakers better comprehend the meaning of the achievement gap.

The Goal: Better Understanding

Test score data are abstract—and important. Here, we have described different methods for clarifying the meaning of test scores, using data available from the National Assessment of Educational Progress. When education leaders apply similar methods to clarify meaning of test scores at the state and local level, they are rewarded by a better understanding of student achievement, greater public acceptance of important decisions that affect students, and greater success in using tests to improve teaching and learning.

References

Barton, P. (2008). The right way to measure growth. *Educational Leadership, 65*(4), 70–73.

Barton, P. E., & Coley, R. J. (2008). *Windows on achievement and inequality.* Princeton, NJ: Educational Testing Service Policy Information Center.

Coley, R. J. (2003). *Growth in school revisited: achievement gains from the fourth to the eighth grade.* Princeton, NJ: Educational Testing Service Policy Information Center.

Holland, P. W. (2002). Two measures of change in gaps between the CDFs of test score distribution. *Journal of Educational and Behavioral Statistics, 27*(1), 3–17.

Critical Thinking

1. Explore your state's department of education website for information about the standardized tests used to fulfill NCLB requirements. Locate information about the cut points (performance standards) for your grade level and subject area (elementary majors may want to focus on reading or mathematics in grade 4). Summarize the information available explaining how cut-points were identified and what they are for different levels of achievement proficiency. Is the information readily available and easily understood?

2. According to the authors, what is one of the major drawbacks of using set cut-points as the only measure of learning?

3. Use the information in Figure 1 in reference to the following quote: "In reading, about the bottom one-fourth of 17-year-olds score at about the same level as do the top one-tenth of 9-year-olds." Describe how you can verify this based on the information provided in the figure.

4. What do the authors identify as problematic about using end-of-year comparisons instead of gain scores and the NCLB requirement that all subgroups of the population reach "proficiency"?

PAUL E. BARTON (paulebarton@aol.com) is a Senior Associate and **RICHARD J. COLEY** (rcoley@ets.org) is Director of the ETS Policy Information Center, Princeton, New Jersey.

Author's note—For a more detailed presentation of the data discussed in this article, see Barton, P. E., & Coley, R. J. (2008). *Windows on achievement and inequality.* Princeton, NJ: Educational Testing Service Policy Information Center.

The Many Meanings of "Multiple Measures"

To use multiple measures appropriately, start by understanding their purposes.

Susan M. Brookhart

W e wouldn't think of making most of our important life decisions on the basis of one measure alone. For example, people who are considering buying a house look at the house's age, condition, location, style, features, and construction, as well as the price of nearby homes. Doctors diagnosing an illness use multiple assessments: the patient's medical history, lab tests, answers to questions about how the patient feels, and so on. The question is, Why do education policymakers and practitioners sometimes opt to make important decisions based on only one indicator?

What Do We Mean by *Multiple Measures?*

Many people think of *multiple measures,* in the plain English sense of the term, to mean using more than one score to make judgments about groups (such as classes, schools, and school districts) as well as individual students. The principle seems simple enough. As the National Council on Measurement in Education (1995) states in its *Code of Professional Responsibilities in Educational Measurement* (Section 6.7),

> Persons who interpret, use, and communicate assessment results have a professional responsibility to use multiple sources and types of relevant information about persons or programs whenever possible in making educational decisions.

The Standards for Educational and Psychological Testing (American Educational Research Association, American Psychological Association, & National Council on Measurement in Education, 1999, Standard 13.7) confirms,

> In educational settings, a decision or characterization that will have major impact on a student should not be made on the basis of a single test score. Other relevant information should be taken into account if it will enhance the overall validity of the decision.

In fact, Title I of the 1994 Improving America's Schools Act required the use of multiple measures to judge the performance of schools, and that language carried over unchanged, in 2001, to No Child Left Behind (NCLB):

> Such assessments shall involve multiple up-to-date measures of student academic achievement, including measures that assess higher-order thinking skills and understanding.

Seems clear, but consider this. The 2004 NCLB guidelines count anything that measures higher-order thinking as "multiple measures." Some states count more than one opportunity to pass the same graduation test as "multiple measures." Are these interpretations what you had in mind when you read the three standards just listed?

To make good decisions about how to use multiple measures, both policymakers and practitioners need a clear understanding of what they mean by the term. Such an understanding begins with knowing what these measures are supposed to accomplish.

The Rationale for Multiple Measures

There are two important reasons to use multiple measures, for decisions about education. The first is that multiple measures enhance *construct validity*. A *construct* is the attribute you are trying to measure. (In education, this is often achievement in a specific domain, but constructs also can be psychological traits, attitudes, and so on.) Construct validity is the degree to which any score conveys meaningful information about the attribute it measures.

We can't really get a full picture of Johnny's reading comprehension from one test score. The set of items or tasks on any one measure can't adequately represent the depth and breadth of complex concepts like reading comprehension or math problem-solving. Several measures, taken together, are likely to more adequately sample the things students should know and be able to do in the achievement domain being measured. Using more than one measure also helps us recognize performance variations caused by format, timing, and other logistical aspects of testing.

We can't get a full picture of Johnny's reading comprehension from one test score.

The second reason for using multiple measures is that they enhance *decision validity*. For any particular decision, there are usually several relevant types of information, each of which could have one or more measures. Johnny's reading comprehension is not the only important thing to know before we decide whether to place him in special education. We might also consider his achievement

in other school subjects; his history with other interventions (for example, a reading support program); his affective responses to school; and his parents' observations of his work at home.

Another example: To decide whether a school is doing a good job, we need to consider several different achievement measures (reading, mathematics, and so on); as well as information about resources (personnel, financial, policy); processes (curriculum, instruction, school climate); and other school outcomes (safety, graduation rate, student and parent satisfaction).

In practice, there are many ways to define and apply the concept of multiple measures. Two questions are at issue. First, what counts as a "measure"? Second, how are the multiple measures combined? Here we'll discuss three different ways of counting what a measure is and three different ways of combining measures to make instructional decisions. If put these together, we end up with the nine different combinations shown in Figure 1.

Figure 1   Using Multiple Measures for Education Decisions

Three Ways to Define Multiple Measures	Three Ways to Combine Multiple Measures		
	Conjunctive Student or school must pass all measures.	**Compensatory** Higher performance on one measure can compensate for lower performance on another.	**Complementary** Passing any one of several multiple measures suffices.
Measures of different constructs	In Virginia, school accreditation ratings are based on students meeting achievement standards on tests in English, history/social science, mathematics, and science (with possible adjustments for ELL and transfer students and for preparing students for retakes of the state tests).	*U.S. News and World Report* compiles a list of "America's Best High Schools." One of its criteria involves computing a college-readiness index as a weighted average of advanced placement/international Baccalaureate participation rates and AP/IB performance quality	The NCLB "safe harbor" provision means a school can meet its adequate yearly progress target if all subgroups meet the target percentage scoring proficient (achievement) or if the percentage of students who score below the proficient level in a subgroup decreases by 10 percent from the previous year (improvement)
Different measures of the same contruct	An elementary school reading teacher requires a student to pass a reading comprehension test on at least two stories at the same reading level before allowing the student to read stories at the next higher reading level.	For a student's standards based report card grade, under "Measures length to the nearest inch and/or centimeter," a teacher averages results from two quizzes and two performance assessments	A teacher allows students to choose whether they will write a term paper or do a class presentation to show their understanding of Roosevelt's New Deal.
Multiple opportunities to pass the same test	In Louisiana, students who have met all gradution requirements except passing the graduate exit exam may continue to retake it—even after completing grade 12—until they pass.	A science teacher allows a student to retake a test that he or she failed after a unit on ecosystems and uses the average of the two test scores in the student's grade.	In Washington State, students in the class of 2013 will have to pass a mathematics test to graduate from high school. They may choose either the math portion of the state test or an Algebra I or Geometry end-of-course exam.

What Counts as a "Measure"?

"Multiple measures" describes at least three different ways of using more than one score: (1) measures of different constructs, (2) different measures of the same construct, and (3) multiple opportunities to pass the same test.

Measuring different constructs is helpful when we should base a decision on a combination of factors. For example, in the 1990s, as the standards movement was gaining momentum but before NCLB prescribed what sorts of measures states must report, states began experimenting with different indicator systems for school accountability. These systems included measures of school context (resources, student background variables, and so on); processes (curriculum coherence, leadership and teaching, and so on); and outcomes (student achievement, graduation rate, school safety, and so on). Indicator systems were designed because decisions about school effectiveness should be based on many different factors. Meaningful evaluations of outcomes, and especially decisions about what to change to bring about improvement, require that we also consider the context and process factors that work together to determine those outcomes.

Different measures of the same construct are especially helpful if the construct is some aspect of student achievement. To measure the construct thoroughly and to make sure all students have a chance to show what they know, several measures are better than one. If a student can't read and scores poorly on one assessment, additional measures of reading should confirm that fact; but if the student *can* read and performed poorly on one assessment for some other reason (perhaps an inability to connect with the stories or items on one particular test, or spatial difficulties that make it difficult to fill in bubble sheets efficiently), then additional measures will probably pick up his or her true capability.

Multiple opportunities to pass the same test may seem like an odd definition to include in the list. Nevertheless, in practice, this is sometimes called "multiple measures." For example, most states with graduation tests build in multiple opportunities for students to take the test.

How Are the Multiple Measures Combined?

Methods of combining information from multiple measures include (1) conjunctive, in which the student or group must pass all measures; (2) compensatory, in which higher performance on one measure can compensate for lower performance on another; and (3) complementary, in which the student or group must achieve the standard on just one of the multiple measures (Chester, 2005).

Most teachers' classroom grading policies are compensatory: They summarize students' scores on several achievement measures, usually either by calculating an average or by reviewing the whole set of measures with a rubric. Good performance on one measure can make up for poor performance on another. Typically, these classroom grades don't all measure the same construct—performance on a test and performance on a project tap different sets of knowledge and skills—but they are treated as though they do and summarized into a grade with one name ("Mathematics").

We can use multiple measures in a compensatory way at the school level, too. For example, Maryland's School Performance Index (SPI), which was used for state accountability before NCLB, judged a school's performance by combining 13 factors: percent satisfactory or better on each of six tested content areas for 3rd grade and for 5th grade, plus the school's overall attendance rate divided by the criterion of 94 (giving a school with 94 percent attendance a "perfect" score). Decisions about the schools' overall effectiveness were based on the total School Performance Index score. Other decisions—for example, those related to school improvement plans or curriculum—were based on the results of particular tests and subtests. Thus, the performance index not only provided an average measure of school quality, but also provided more fine-grained results to guide improvement (Schafer, 2003).

The current NCLB accountability system, at least as regards achievement, uses multiple measures in a conjunctive way. Districts must show adequate yearly progress overall, but also for every subgroup. Good results for one subgroup don't compensate for poor results for another subgroup. NCLB's safe harbor provision, however, uses complementary logic: A subgroup that does not achieve its annual performance goal can still "pass" if the percentage of students scoring below proficient in that subgroup decreases by 10 percent or more.

Multiple Measures Linked to Purpose

In many cases, individual educators don't have a choice about the application of multiple measures—for example, in their school's reporting of adequate yearly progress under NCLB. Even in these cases, though, it's important to have a clear understanding of what's going on. Knowing the nature of the measures and the combination method in any particular application of multiple measures helps us understand the results and the value of decisions or consequences based on those results.

Sometimes, however, educators do have a choice. The guiding principle for decisions about what measures to use and how to combine them should be *purpose:* What do you need to know, and why do you need to know it (Chester, 2005)? Here are some examples.

Classroom-Level Decisions

First, the bad example. Classroom rubrics sometimes mass multiple measures together in ways that distort the purpose of accurately reporting how well students have achieved learning goals. To evaluate student-created posters about different U.S. states, an elementary social studies teacher used a rubric consisting of four different measures: directions followed (5 points); information conveyed (10 points); creativity (10 points); and design/color/neatness (5 points). These are, arguably, measures of at least two different constructs: knowledge about states and poster-making skills. To arrive at the grade, the teacher added the points together (a compensatory method); only one-third of the resultant decision about achievement (10 points out of 30) was based on content. Thus, a grade intended to reflect achievement of a social studies objective actually largely reflected achievement of design and construction skills.

Now, a good example. A high school English teacher's class showed a wide range of ability to communicate in standard written English. The teacher wanted to assess the students' understanding of the plot of a novel the class had read. She used several different measures of the same construct (understanding of the plot) in a compensatory manner.

One measure was a test that had two parts: a written essay, which demonstrated students' ability to apply their understanding but was also, of course, affected by students' writing ability; and a multiple-choice section that didn't require writing but couldn't measure extended thinking about the novel. Another measure was an assignment in which students wrote open-ended questions at the end of each chapter; this task revealed students' thinking about the plot without requiring much formal writing. The teacher combined grades from all three measures to give a richer picture of plot understanding for all students in the class.

School-Level and Policy Decisions

If our main concern is to know for certain whether a school has reached a goal on a particular achievement construct (for example, a certain level of reading or mathematics performance), then we might want to use a compensatory approach combining multiple measures of that construct. If false negatives are a major concern—for example, if severe consequences are in place for failing to meet a standard—then we might want to use complementary multiple measures so that a school can pass by meeting the standard on any one measure. But if we are convinced that each of several measures is vital to quality we'll probably want to use a conjunctive approach in which a school must pass all measures.

When states design high school graduation policies, a multiple-measures policy can help them avoid defining achievement narrowly as performance on one test. Darling-Hammond, Rustique-Forrester, and Pecheone (2005) reported that graduation rates stayed the same or declined slightly from 1998 to 2001 in five states that required students to pass an exit exam (Indiana, North Carolina, New York, Florida, and South Carolina). Four states that used a multiple-measures approach to graduation during that time (New Jersey, Wisconsin, Pennsylvania, and Connecticut) fared better: Rates stayed the same in three states and rose in one. In addition, the graduation rates for these four states were higher overall in 2001 (73–86 percent) than those for the five exam-only states (51–67 percent).

Evaluations of school programs are also best accomplished by using multiple measures of different constructs. For example, suppose a district wanted to evaluate its K–12 science curriculum. One obvious measure would be performance on state exams mapped to district science standards—both absolute levels of achievement (status) and the amount of change in achievement (growth).

To make wise decisions about the science curriculum, however, the district would probably want to include other measures—for example, the number of graduates who go on to major in science or work in a scientific field, how students perceive the importance of science or how confident they feel as science learners, student participation in science-related clubs and activities, and so on. These are all different constructs, but they all have a bearing on making decisions about the science program.

Multiple Measures for Meaningful Decisions

The term *multiple measures* can mean many things. What's important is that multiple measures result in meaningful, useful decisions. A clear understanding of the many faces of multiple measures helps us think about the logic used in each case. Wise actions can only result if the measures and logic are right for their intended purposes.

References

American Educational Research Association, American Psychological Association, & National Council on Measurement in Education. (1999). *Standards for educational and psychological testing.* Washington, DC: Authors.

Chester, M. D. (2005). Making valid and consistent inferences about school effectiveness from multiple measures. *Educational Measurement: Issues and Practice, 24*(4), 40–52.

Darling-Hammond, L., Rustique-Forrester, E., & Pecheone, R. L. (2005). *Multiple measures approaches to high school graduation.* Stanford, CA: Stanford University School Redesign Network. Available: www.srnleads.org/data/pdfs/multiple _measures.pdf

National Council on Measurement in Education. (1995). *Code of professional responsibilities in educational measurement.* [Online]. Available: www.natd.org/Code_of_Professional _Responsibilities.html

No Child Left Behind Act of 2001, Pub. L. No. 107–110, Sec. 1111(b)
(3)(C)(vi). Available: www.ed.gov/policy/elsec/Ieg/esea02/pg2
.html

Schafer, W. D. (2003). A state perspective on multiple measures and
school accountability. *Educational Measurement: Issues and
Practice, 22*(3), 27–31.

Critical Thinking

1. Define what a construct is and explain why construct validity is important in assessing learning.

2. Explain what is meant by the term "multiple measures"
and describe the different ways in which measures can be
combined and for what purposes they are used.

3. Use the table in Figure 1 to describe three different ways
multiple measures could be used in your classroom or school.

SUSAN M. BROOKHART is Senior Research Associate at the Center for
Advancing the Study of Teaching and Learning (CASTL), Duquesne
University, Pittsburgh, Pennsylvania. She is the author of *Exploring
Formative Assessment* (ASCD, 2009) and *How to Give Effective Feed-
back to Your Students* (ASCD 2008); susanbrookhart@bresnan.net.

Using Self-Assessment to Chart Students' Paths

MARGARET HERITAGE

Emergent economies of the last several decades have created a global market in which international competition is a reality. At the same time, knowledge and information are growing exponentially, and it is almost certain that the skills of today will not be the skills of tomorrow. Learning how to learn (LtL) is, thus, a critical life and career skill that students must develop long before they exit the formal education system.

New developments in the science of learning emphasize the importance of learners taking control of their own learning. These metacognitive approaches to learning increase the degree to which students transfer learning to new settings and include sense-making, self-assessment, and reflection on learning strategies—in other words, learning how to learn (Bransford, Brown, & Cocking, 2000).

While schools have traditionally concerned themselves with what students are to learn, less attention has been paid to these metacognitive dimensions of learning. This is, perhaps, especially evident in the field of assessment. Large-scale assessments, such as annual state tests, evaluate how well students meet state standards. Interim or quarterly assessments determine whether students are on the way to meeting state standards, and classroom assessments are typically used to decide whether students have learned what they are supposed to learn for a given period of instruction. What is missing in contemporary assessment practices is any involvement of students in evaluating their own learning and making decisions about how they can improve. However, U.S. educators are increasingly recognizing the need to alter the balance away from assessment in which students are passive recipients toward assessment that involves them as active participants. This student-involved approach to assessment is not intended to replace accountability measures. After all, for a total outlay of approximately $500 billion for public education in fiscal year 2005 (National Center for Education Statistics, 2008), schools should be accountable for the effectiveness of this expenditure. Rather, involving students in assessment is an educational approach in its own right: it is a means of helping them develop the skills of learning how to learn.

Ripe for Learning How to Learn

Middle school students are beginning the developmental transition from childhood dependency to adult independence and, ultimately, to the world of work. As they develop independence, they are still reliant on guidance and help from adults. They are becoming increasingly self-aware, more able to reflect on themselves, and conscious of their strengths and weaknesses. Consequently, this period of schooling is a time when students are ripe for developing an increased awareness of themselves as learners. Developmentally, middle school students have the capacity to become effective in monitoring and evaluating their own learning, and to build a repertoire of learning strategies they can employ strategically during the course of learning. Schools must take advantage of this developmental capacity and ensure that learning how to learn is an integral part of middle school education. Indeed, if middle school students are not on track with LtL skills by this stage of their education, they could well find the train leaving the station in high school. Worse, by the time they reach higher education and the workplace, the train definitely will have left with many students remaining on the platform. Fortunately, teachers can adopt assessment practices that will foster students' abilities to learn how to learn through student self-assessment.

Formative Assessment

Due, in part, to literature suggesting that formative assessment can have a powerful effect on student learning (e.g., Black & William, 1998; Black, Harrison, Lee, Marshall, & Wiliam, 2003; Brookhart, 2007), it has attracted the attention of educators across the U.S. in recent years. Formative assessment is assessment that is carried out during instruction for the purpose of improving teaching or learning (Shepard et al., 2005). It is important to recognize that, according to these and other scholars, the purpose of formative assessment is not just to improve teaching but also to improve *learning*. Improving learning must involve students, because, in the end, no one else can learn for them.

Formative assessment requires teachers to gather evidence of how student learning is progressing toward desired goals during instruction and partner with students in a process of reciprocal feedback to improve learning: teacher feedback resulting from interpretation of evidence gathered and student feedback as a result of self-assessment. In their landmark review of formative assessment research, Black and Wiliam (1998) concluded that student self-assessment is an essential part of formative assessment, noting that when people are trying to learn, they need information about the goal, evidence about where they are in relation to the goal, and an understanding of what they must do to close the gap between the two. Self-assessment, as a means to improve learning, includes two components: monitoring learning and managing learning. When students are involved in self-assessment, they monitor how well their learning is developing toward specific goals, and in self-management, they select from a repertoire of learning strategies to make adjustments to how they are learning to keep their learning on course. The students' actions in formative assessment very much mirror the teachers'; teachers monitor the effectiveness of their teaching in moving students toward the learning goal and select from a repertoire of pedagogical strategies when they want to make adjustments to teaching.

The Educational Environment

Self-assessment requires an educational environment in which students are able to take responsibility for their own learning. To take responsibility, students must be clear about learning goals—what it is they are going to learn and why. They must have the opportunity to develop and exercise the skills of monitoring their learning toward the goal and be able to use internal feedback to make adjustments to their learning when they are not moving successfully toward the goal. However, this is far from the school experience of many middle school students. Their experience is still very much as Mary Alice White observed in 1971 when she likened students at school to being on a ship sailing across an unknown sea to an unknown destination. The students know they are going to the school, but the compass and chart are neither available nor intelligible to the students. Instead of the voyage and its destination being all-important, the daily life aboard ship, the chores, the demands, and the inspections are all that count (White, 1971). What can be done to change students' experience of school, to involve them in learning, and enable them to become self-directed and responsible for their own learning?

Teaching and Learning as a Partnership

Watkins (2003) argued that learning is constituted of three elements: being taught, individual sense making, and building knowledge as part of interactions with others. The dominant conception of learning in the U.S. has focused almost exclusively on the first of these: that learning is being taught. To be taught, students are provided with activities, often without a real grasp or understanding of their purpose, leading to the common response of "the teacher told me to" when asked what they are doing and why they are doing it—hardly a response from students who are taking responsibility for learning and learning how to learn!

If we are serious about middle school students learning how to learn, we must address the other constituents of learning: individual sense making and building knowledge by doing things with others. Individual sense making requires students to be reflective about what they are learning and to have the strategies to take action if things are not making sense. For example, students who are reflecting on their learning in science or math might choose from a range of learning strategies such as reorganizing the information, doing a drawing, making a table, or finding more information that will fill gaps in knowledge. Doing things with others means working with and learning from peers, but it also means partnering with teachers. A partner relationship with teachers capitalizes on the developmental characteristics of middle school students; they are seeking independence from adults, yet still need adult support and guidance.

Imagine a classroom in which students are clear about learning goals and the criteria for success in meeting those learning goals. Through exemplars and discussions with the teacher, the students have a conception of what success means in the context of their own work. The students know what they are learning and why, and they have been taught the skills of self-assessment and reflection. They have also developed a repertoire of strategies to adjust their learning when their self-assessment against the success criteria indicates to them that they

are not moving forward. They use this internal feedback, together with the external feedback provided by their teachers, to discuss how their learning is progressing and what needs to be done to move forward. Teachers make adjustments to teaching and students to learning. In this scenario, teachers and students are partners who share responsibility for learning. And most important, the students are developing the lifelong skills of learning how to learn.

Teacher Practices

Making student self-assessment a widespread reality in middle school classrooms will necessitate some changes in teacher knowledge, skills, attitudes, and practices. For many teachers and students, this may involve a fundamental shift in the ecology of classroom environments that is both new and motivating. Teachers must first understand how to use formative assessment and have the skills to implement formative assessment in their classrooms. They must understand what student self-assessment entails and be able to teach students the skills of self-monitoring and self-management. They can begin by asking the students to reflect on their performance on the assessment relative to the criteria for success using questions like "Do you think that your response demonstrated understanding of . . .? If yes, why do you think this? If not, why do you think you did not demonstrate understanding?" From this basis, students can learn to be more independent and recognize when they do not understand and when they need to do something about it.

By giving students feedback about strategies that they can use to improve learning, rather than telling them what the solutions are, teachers can help students develop awareness of how to make adaptations to learning. Consider this example. In a science class, the students were focusing on designing a fair test. The criteria for success were that the students would be specific about what they wanted to measure, identify the key variable and which factors remain constant, and then show a plan to conduct the test. One student wrote in his design that he was going to measure the time it takes a parachute to fall to the ground. He noted that he would change the size of the parachute, but keep the weight and shape of the parachute the same and the length and thickness of the parachute strings the same.

The feedback the teacher gave to this student was,

> Your design shows that you are clear about what you want to measure and that you have listed four factors that should remain constant in your test and one that will change. For your test to be fair, there is one other factor that must remain constant. You are planning to measure the time parachutes of different sizes take to fall to the ground. With this in mind, can you review your plan and think about what else needs to be constant? I will be back in a few moments to see what you have come up with.

The student reviewed his plan and realized that the height from which the parachute is dropped needs to be constant. The next round of feedback for this student from the teacher was,

> You have planned your fair test in general terms. Now think about how you would conduct your test in a systematic way so that you can draw conclusions from your test. Go back to some of the examples of fair tests we looked at from last year's students and consider how you will conduct your measurements and record your data in systematic ways so that you can compare your results.

Through the use of strategic feedback, the teacher successfully assisted the student in moving forward and understanding how to conduct a fair test.

Teachers must also have the skills to create a classroom culture that is conducive to self-assessment. Middle school students are very self-conscious and sensitive to the opinions of their peers. For self-assessment, they need a classroom culture in which they feel it is acceptable to admit they do not understand something or are having difficulties and need to work on solutions. It is essential that the classroom culture is characterized by respect, trust, and individual self-worth so that students can be reflective about learning without any threats to their self-esteem.

Finally, teachers must have the attitude that self-assessment is beneficial and will make a difference in students' abilities to learn in the near-and long-term. They must also see the value of partnering with students and be willing, in many cases, to change the classroom contract from one in which learning is a product of teaching, to one in which learning is a shared responsibility between teachers and students.

Charting the Course

Rather than experiencing school as a journey on a unknown sea to an unknown destination, it is possible for students to use formative self-assessment as a navigational chart and compass—to know where they are going, how they are going to get there, and whether they need to make learning adjustments along the way. In short, to chart the course of their learning. At a time when lifelong learning is an expectation for personal and societal success, it is incumbent upon middle school educators to take advantage of their students' stage of development and make self-assessment, as a means of learning how to learn, an essential part of teaching and assessment practices. Without it, we risk limiting the potential and prospects of our students, which is something we must not do.

References

Black, P., Harrison, C., Lee, C., Marshall, B., & Wiliam, D. (2003). *Assessment for learning: Putting it into practice.* Berkshire, England: Open University Press.

Black, P., & Wiliam, D. (1998). Assessment and classroom learning. *Assessment in Education: Principles, Policy and Practice, 5*(1), 7–73.

Bransford, J. D., Brown, A. L., & Cocking, R. R. (Eds.). (2000). *How people learn: Brain, mind, experience, and school.* (Committee on Developments in the Science and Learning, Commission on Behavioral and Social Sciences and Education, National Research Council). Washington, DC: National Academy Press.

Brookhart, S. M. (2007). Expanding views about formative classroom assessment: A review of the literature. In J. H. McMillan (Ed.), *Formative classroom assessment: Research, theory and practice* (pp. 43–62). New York: Teachers College Press.

National Center for Education Statistics. (2008). *Digest of Education Statistics, 2007* (NCES 2008-022). Washington, DC: U.S. Department of Education.

Shepard, L. A., Hammerness, K., Darling-Hammond, L., Rust, F., Snowden, J. B., Gordon, E., et al. (2005). Assessment. In L. Darling-Hammond & J. Bransford (Eds.), *Preparing teachers for a changing world: What teachers should learn and be able to do* (pp. 275–326). San Francisco: Jossey-Bass.

Watkins, C. (2003). *Learning: a sense-maker's guide.* London: Association of Teachers and Lecturers.

White, M. A. (1971). The view from the pupil's desk. In M. Silberman (Ed.), *The experience of schooling* (pp. 337–345). New York: Rinehart and Winston.

Critical Thinking

1. What is formative assessment? How is the purpose of formative assessment different from the assessment you typically do at the end of a unit (usually referred to as summative assessment)?

2. Using developmentally appropriate practice, describe some general/global strategies you can implement in your classroom to help students develop their ability to self-assess. (Although the current article is focused on middle school students, even early elementary students can begin to develop skills to help them monitor and manage their own learning.)

3. One mistake we often make as teachers is assuming students "know how" to monitor and manage their learning. How will you monitor and provide feedback to students as they practice the skills you identified in the previous question?

4. Describe an experience you had in school when a teacher asked you to engage in self-assessment. How did it (or would it have if you did not have this experience) improve/enhance your learning?

5. Reflect on the classes in your program and the types of evidence you need to present that you have mastered important knowledge and skills (e.g., final teaching portfolio, video teaching lesson), what opportunities for self-assessment have your been provided?

6. The authors make a specific point that "a classroom culture characterized by respect, trust, and individual self-worth [are essential] to student reflection." Describe three practices focused on assessing students, grading, and providing feedback that you would use to help foster such a culture.

MARGARET HERITAGE is assistant director for professional development at the National Center for Research on Evaluation, Standards, and Student Testing and an expert on formative assessment at the University of California at Los Angeles. E-mail: mheritag@ucla.edu.

Heritage, M. (2009). Using Self-Assessment to Chart Students' Paths. *Middle School Journal, 40*(5), pp. 27–30. Reprinted with permission from National Middle School Association.

Peer Assessment

KEITH J. TOPPING

Peer assessment is an arrangement for learners to consider and specify the level, value, or quality of a product or performance of other equal-status learners. Products to be assessed can include writing, oral presentations, portfolios, test performance, or other skilled behaviors. Peer assessment can be summative or formative. A formative view is presented here, in which the intent is to help students help each other plan their learning, identify their strengths and weaknesses, target areas for remedial action, and develop metacognitive and other personal and professional skills. Peer feedback is available in greater volume and with greater immediacy than teacher feedback. A peer assessor with less skill at assessment but more time in which to do it can produce an assessment of equal reliability and validity to that of a teacher. This article describes effective approaches to peer assessment and encourages teachers to incorporate it into their practice.

P eer assessment appears to be a new form of assessment but in fact has been deployed for centuries. George Jardine, a professor at the University of Glasgow from 1774 to 1826, described the methods and advantages of peer assessment of writing (Gaillet, 1992). In recent years, there has been much renewed interest in peer assessment, especially in terms of formative assessment. Why should teachers, teacher educators, and researchers be interested in these developments? Can peer assessment enhance quality and/or reduce costs? Does it work, and under what conditions? This article explores the reliability, validity, and effects of peer assessment in schools, and describes effective approaches to putting it into practice.

Definition and Typology

Peer assessment is an arrangement for learners to consider and specify the level, value, or quality of a product or performance of other equal-status learners. *Equal-status* can be interpreted exactly or with flexibility; in the latter case, a peer can be anyone within a few years of schooling. Peer assessment takes the form of feedback, face-to-face or otherwise, often reciprocally among the assessors and assessed.

Peer assessment activities can vary in a number of ways, operating in different curriculum areas or subjects. A wide variety of products or outputs can be peer assessed, including writing, portfolios, oral presentations, test performance, and other skilled behaviors. The participant constellation can vary: The assessors and the assessed may be pairs or groups. Directionality can vary as well: Peer assessment can be one-way or reciprocal. Even the objectives of peer assessment may vary: The teacher may target cognitive or metacognitive gains, time saving, or other goals. Methods for computerizing peer assessment are now appearing (e.g., Tseng & Tsai, 2007), with generally positive results. Finally, it can occur in or out of class: Peer assessment happens not just in school but throughout our lives. All of us may expect to be peer assessor and assessee at different times and in different contexts. Consequently, involvement in peer assessment at school can develop transferable skills for life.

An Example of Peer Assessment in Action

A secondary school teacher in an English department wants to explore peer assessment of written analyses of a piece of Shakespeare. The hope is that this will engage the students more in what could otherwise become a mechanical exercise—writing only for the teacher. She is looking for more interactivity, better thinking, and greater generation of novel ideas. She discusses peer assessment with a colleague in her department, who is happy for her to take the initiative and will try it later in her own class if it works.

Knowing the students might balk at this new process, especially if it involves appearing unpleasant to their friends, the teacher takes care to introduce the idea gradually over a period of a few weeks. She divides the whole class into small groups to discuss the upcoming written task about Shakespeare. What might be the assessment criteria for this task? At first, the students are slow to respond, but they warm up and generate a wide range of ideas about what a good essay would look like and what should be sought in the writing. The teacher works with them on synthesizing the criteria. Eventually, they have a reasonably short list of clear criteria. With one or two exceptions, the list is pretty much the same as the one the teacher herself would have used for assessing these papers, but the students do not know that.

The students are told that they will use these criteria to give feedback on each others' essays. They are divided into teams of three students of roughly similar ability in writing. This means that quite a few of the more able groups are all female and several of the less able groups are all male, but many in the middle are of mixed gender. The teacher takes care that each group contains no close friends (or enemies). Some students try to arrange to work with their friends, but the teacher tells them that would not be effective and is not part of the system.

The teacher then takes some time for training. She uses a similar, anonymous piece of writing done in the previous year. Displaying the piece together with the assessment criteria, she talks and shows by annotation how her mind is working as she makes assessment decisions about the manuscript, addressing each of the criteria. Then she invites the students to assess another previous year's paper in their groups, while discussing the task. They do this quite quickly. As she circulates, she can see that some groups manage very well, yet others need some encouragement or coaching, which she gives.

The teacher sets them to work on the new task. Each student completes their essay, knowing that it will be peer assessed by both of the other members of the group. This sharpens their motivation to make a good job of it. They also know that they will need to peer assess two papers themselves. The groups convene and students complete their peer assessments without discussion in the group, referring to the written assessment criteria and a short list of useful tips about peer assessment. They know that they have forty minutes to complete the task of assessing two essays. As they work, the teacher goes round to look at what is being written and have a quiet word if anyone seems to be stuck. Most have finished within 30 minutes, and the teacher encourages them to make sure their assessments are all written down. She then lets them discuss the exercise until the end of the lesson, but not change their assessments. At the end of the lesson, each group hands in their written peer assessments to the teacher—six from each group of three people.

The teacher compares the two peer assessments for each essay. Where the two assessments are similar, she is content, and will pass both of these to the student who produced the work. Where they are very different, she notes that she will have to talk to this group next time they meet, and maybe even assess that essay herself before passing the assessments back to the student. Although there has been a tendency for students' comments to verge towards the average (common with a first experience of peer assessment), she is aware that the next time the students will be more courageous. She is relieved that there is little sign of anyone giving a bad or good peer assessment just on the basis of personal preference.

At the next lesson, she gives the peer assessments back to the groups. An animated discussion ensues, not only about the nature of the comments on their analyses of Shakespeare but also about the merits and disadvantages of peer assessment. The students are a little dismayed that the teacher has not assessed the work herself but, on reflection, can see that their peer assessments are, by and large, just as useful in guiding revision. The class talks about how they might improve peer assessment the next time they do it. Somebody suggests that they apply it to another upcoming task, giving group presentations. The teacher agrees, noting that she has expended time on the training and peer assessment sessions but saved considerable time in not having to provide feedback on all these pieces of work herself overnight.

Benefits of Peer Assessment

Peer assessment has been successfully deployed in elementary, middle, and high schools, including with very young students and those with special educational needs or learning disabilities (Scruggs & Mastropieri, 1998). There is substantial evidence that peer assessment can result in improvements in the effectiveness and quality of learning, which is at least as good as gains from teacher assessment, especially in relation to writing. Importantly, there are gains from functioning as either assessor or assessee.

Feedback

The overriding goal of peer assessment is to provide feedback to learners. Peer feedback can be confirmatory, suggestive, or corrective. Feedback can reduce errors and have positive effects on learning when it is received thoughtfully and positively. It is also essential to the development and execution of self-regulatory skills. Butler and Winne (1995) argued that feedback serves several functions: to confirm existing information, add new information, identify errors, correct errors, improve conditional application of information, and aid the wider restructuring of theoretical schemata.

Perhaps the most significant quality of peer assessment is that it is plentiful. Because there are more students than teachers in most classrooms, feedback from peers can be more immediate and individualized than can teacher feedback. Students react differently to feedback from adults and peers; the former is perceived as authoritative but ill-explained, yet the latter gives richer feedback that is open to negotiation (Cole, 1991).

Cognitive Gains

Peer assessment is associated with gains for assessors, assessees, or both (Topping, 2005; Topping & Ehly, 1998). These gains can include increased levels of time on task and practice, coupled with a greater sense of accountability. Formative peer assessment is likely to involve intelligent questioning, coupled with increased self-disclosure and, thereby, assessment of understanding. In addition, peer assessment can enable earlier error and misconception identification and analysis, which can lead to the identification of knowledge gaps and engineering their closure. Peer assessment can also increase reflection and generalization to new situations, promoting self-assessment and greater metacognitive self-awareness. Cognitive and metacognitive benefits can accrue before, during, or after the peer assessment. That is, sleeper effects are possible.

Improvements in Writing

Evidence of the effectiveness of peer assessment in writing is substantial, particularly in the context of peer editing (O'Donnell & Topping, 1998). Here, peer assessment seems to be at least as effective in formative terms as teacher assessment, and sometimes more effective. Peer assessment of writing can involve giving either general feedback or very specific feedback about possible improvements. Peer assessment can focus on the whole written product, or components of the writing process, such as planning, drafting, or editing.

Peer response groups are a group medium for peer assessment that involves different social demands than assessment between paired individuals. They have been shown to be effective. For example, the effects of revision instruction and peer response groups on the writing of 93 sixth grade students were compared by Olson (1990). Students who were engaged in peer assessment wrote rough and final drafts that were significantly superior to those of students who received teacher instruction on revision only.

Although teachers often value the feedback provided by peer response groups, students sometimes need to be educated about its benefits. Weaver (1995) surveyed over 500 teachers about peer response groups in writing. Regardless of the stage in the writing process (early vs. late), teachers generally found peer responses to be more effective than their own. In contrast, students stated that they found the teacher's responses to be more helpful in all stages of writing. There are implications here for how students are introduced to peer assessment; with more resistant students, introduction should be gradual and include much concrete activity before any labeling of the process.

Improvements in Group Work

Peer assessment can complement other approaches, such as cooperative learning. Salend, Whittakcr, and Reeder (1993) examined the efficacy of a consensus-based group evaluation system with students with disabilities. The system involved: (a) dividing the groups into teams; (b) having each team agree on a common rating for the group's behavior during a specified time period; (c) comparing each team's rating to the teacher's rating; and (d) delivering reinforcement to each team based on the group's behavior and the team's accuracy in rating the group's behavior. Results indicated that the system was an effective strategy for modifying behavior. Similarly, Ross (1995) had grade seven students assess audiotape recordings of their own math cooperative learning groups at work. The results included increases in the frequency and quality of help seeking and help giving, and improvements in students' attitudes about asking for help.

Possible Savings of Teachers' Time

It has been suggested that peer assessment is not costly in terms of teachers' time. However, other authors (Falchikov, 2001) have cautioned that there could be no saving of time in the short to medium term, because establishing good quality peer assessment requires time for organization, training, and monitoring. If peer assessment is to be supplementary to teacher feedback, rather than substitutional, then no time saving is likely, and extra teacher time will need to be devoted to training students how to provide constructive feedback. However, there are likely to be benefits for teachers, as well as learners. Peer assessment can lead teachers to scrutinize and clarify assessment objectives and purposes, criteria, and grading scales.

Common Concerns about Implementation

Many teachers successfully involve learners collaboratively in learning, and thereby relinquish some control of classroom content and management. However, some teachers could be anxious about going so far as to include peer assessments as part of summative assessment, where consequences follow from terminal judgments of accomplishments. This is a reasonable concern. By contrast, the conception of peer assessment presented here is formative; peer feedback is given while the learning is actually happening, helping students plan their own learning, identify their own strengths and weaknesses, target areas for remedial action, and develop metacognitive and other skills. It does not involve students in assigning final grades.

Any group can suffer from negative social processes, such as social loafing (failing to participate), free rider effects (having the work of others accepted as one's own), diffusion of responsibility, and interaction disabilities (Salomon & Globerson, 1989). Social processes can influence and contaminate the reliability and validity of peer assessments. Peer assessments can be partly determined by friendship bonds, enmity, or other power processes, the popularity of individuals, perception of criticism as socially uncomfortable, or even collusion to submit average scores, leading to lack of differentiation.

Both assessors and assessees can experience initial anxiety about the peer assessment process. Giving positive feedback first will reduce assessee anxiety and improve subsequent acceptance of negative feedback. In addition, students should be told that peer assessment involves students directly in learning, and should promote a sense of ownership, personal responsibility, and motivation. Teachers can also point out that peer assessment can increase variety and interest, activity and interactivity, identification and bonding, self-confidence, and empathy with others.

Social factors require consideration by the teacher. When carefully organized, potentially negative social issues can be ameliorated and students can develop social and communication skills, negotiation and diplomacy, and teamwork skills. Learning how to give and accept criticism, justify one's own position, and reject suggestions are all useful, transferable social skills.

Reliability and Validity

This section considers the degree of correspondence between student peer assessments and the assessments made of student work by external experts such as professional teachers. This could be termed *accuracy* of peer assessment, if one assumes that expert assessments are, themselves, highly reliable and valid. As this is a doubtful assumption in some contexts, it is debatable whether studies of such correspondence should be considered to be studies of reliability or validity or both or neither. Many purported studies of *reliability* could be considered studies of accuracy or validity, comparing peer assessments with assessments made by professionals, rather than with those of other peers, or the same peers over time. Additionally, some studies compare marks, scores, and grades awarded by peers and staff, rather than upon more open-ended formative feedback (Magin & Helmore, 2001).

Research findings on the reliability and validity of peer assessment mostly emanate from studies in higher education (Falchikov, 2001). In a wide variety of subject areas, the products and performances assessed have included essays, hypermedia creations, oral presentations, multiple choice test questions, practical reports, and individual contributions to a group project. Over 70% of the studies find reliability and validity adequate (Sadler & Good, 2006); a minority find them variable (Falchikov & Goldfinch, 2000; Topping, 1998). A tendency for peer marks to bunch around the median is sometimes noted. Student acceptance (or belief in reliability) varies from high to low, quite independently of actual reliability.

Contradictory findings can be explained in part by differences in contexts, the level of the course, the product or performance being evaluated, the contingencies associated with those outcomes, clarity of judgment criteria, and the training and support provided. Reliability tends to be higher in advanced courses; lower for assessment of practice than for academic products. Discussion, negotiation, and joint construction of assessment criteria with learners is likely to deepen understanding, give a greater sense of ownership, and increase reliability (Karegianes, Pascarella, & Pflaum, 1980; MacArthur, Schwartz, & Graham, 1991). Peer assessments are generally more reliable when supported by training, checklists, exemplification, teacher assistance, and monitoring.

In summary, peer assessment offers triangulation, and thus seems likely to improve the overall reliability and validity of assessment. A peer assessor with less skill at assessment but more time in which to do it could produce an equally reliable and valid assessment. Peer feedback should be available in greater volume and with greater immediacy than teacher feedback, which compensates for a quality disadvantage.

How to Organize Peer Assessment

Providing effective feedback is a cognitively complex task requiring understanding of the goals of the task and the criteria for success, and the ability to make judgments about the relationship of the product or performance to these goals. Good organization is perhaps the most important quality of implementation integrity, leading to consistent and productive outcomes. Important planning issues evident in the literature (Topping, 2003; Webb & Farivar, 1994) are outlined below.

1. Seek to work with colleagues rather than developing the initiative alone.
2. Clarify purpose, rationale, expectations, and acceptability with all stakeholders. Are you aiming for cognitive, attitudinal, social, or emotional gains? Specify the nature of the products of learning to be assessed. Broach the idea with the students very early and, over time, seek their advice on and approval of the scheme.

3. Involve participants in developing and clarifying assessment criteria. Students need to be involved in developing the criteria for assessment in order to feel a sense of ownership and decrease any anxiety, even if they come up with something similar to what the teacher would have given them anyway. Small group discussion of teacher-proposed draft criteria should lead to a modest amount of suggested change.

4. Match participants and arrange contact. Generally aim for same-ability peer matching. If the peer partners are from the same class, roughly list them in order of ability in the subject of assessment, and pair the first two, the second two, and so on down the list (or the first three or four for peer response groups). Pairs or groups of students at the bottom of the list may be operating at the lowest level, but with some teacher support they may gain more than expected, as they will be involved in the same processes but at a simpler level.

5. Provide training, examples, and practice. Quality training will make a great deal of difference. Talk to students about what is expected of them, including the roles and behaviors expected of assessor and assessee. Then show them how to do it, perhaps by using a role play between two adults. Have the students practice peer assessment on a very short task selected for the purpose. While they practice, circulate to monitor their performance. Give feedback and coaching where needed.

6. Provide guidelines, checklists, or other tangible scaffolding. Some kind of written and/or pictorial reminders or clues to the process to be followed will help, e.g., a simple sheet with not more than eight reminders of what to do and how to do it.

7. Specify activities and timescale. Make clear what needs to be done, within what timescale, and what records (if any) need to be kept. What of those who finish early—should extra peer assessment work be available or can they switch to some other kind of work? What of those who finish late—how can they be given timescales and reminders to keep them up to speed?

8. Monitor and coach. Whenever students are involved in peer assessment, keep a low profile and circulate among them, giving feedback and coaching as necessary.

9. Examine the quality of peer feedback. Particularly in the early days, check at least a portion of the peer assessments against your own assessments of the work. Choose a high, middle, and low ability student for this. Do not be surprised if the feedback is different from your own. The more feedback there is, the more chance it will be diverse. If it is very different, discuss this with the partners involved.

10. Moderate reliability and validity of feedback. Over time, keep consistent checks on the match between peer assessments (if more than one peer assesses the same piece of work), and on the relationship between peer and teacher assessments. Do not assume the teacher's are any more reliable than the peers'! You might want to match yours against the average of several peer assessments.

11. Evaluate and give feedback. Give the students information about your observations of their performance as peer assessors and your check on the reliability of their assessments. Unless they have this information, their ability to provide useful feedback will not change for the better.

Summary and Conclusions

Peer assessment has been shown to be effective in a variety of contexts and with students of a wide range of ages and abilities. The reliability and validity of peer assessments tend to be at least as high, and often higher, than teacher assessments (Topping, 1998). Peer assessment requires training and practice, arguably on neutral products or performances before full implementation, which should feature monitoring and moderation. Given careful attention, a developmental process may be started that leads toward more sophisticated peer assessment, and the delivery of plentiful feedback that can help learners identify their strengths and weaknesses, target areas for remedial action, and develop metacognitive and other personal and professional skills.

References

Butler, D. L., & Winne, P. H. (1995). Feedback and self-regulated learning: A theoretical synthesis. *Review of Educational Research, 65,* 245–281.

Cole, D. A. (1991). Change in self-perceived competence as a function of peer and teacher evaluation. *Developmental Psychology, 27,* 682–688.

Falchikov, N. (2001). *Learning together: Peer tutoring in higher education.* London: RoutledgeFalmer.

Falchikov, N., & Goldfinch, J. (2000). Student peer assessment in higher education: A meta-analysis comparing peer and teacher marks. *Review of Educational Research, 70,* 287–322.

Gaillet, L. I. (1992, March). *A foreshadowing of modern theories and practices of collaborative learning: The work of the Scottish rhetorician George Jardine.* Paper presented at the 43rd Annual Meeting of the Conference on College Composition and Communication, Cincinnati, OH.

Karegianes, M. L., Pascarella, E. T., & Pflaum, S. W. (1980). The effects of peer editing on the writing proficiency of low-achieving tenth grade students. *Journal of Educational Research, 73,* 203–207.

MacArthur, C. A., Schwartz, S. S., & Graham, S. (1991). Effects of a reciprocal peer revision strategy in special education classrooms. *Learning Disabilities Research and Practice, 6,* 201–210

Magin, D., & Helmore, P. (2001). Peer and teacher assessments of oral presentation skills: How reliable are they? *Studies In Higher Education, 26,* 287–298.

O'Donnell, A. M., & Topping, K. J. (1998). Peers assessing peers: Possibilities and problems. In K. J. Topping & S. Ehly (Eds.), *Peer-assisted learning* (pp. 255–278). Mahwah, NJ: Lawrence Erlbaum Associates.

Olson, V. L. B. (1990). The revising processes of sixth-grade writers with and without peer feedback. *Journal of Educational Research, 84,* 22–29.

Ross, J. A. (1995). Effects of feedback on student behavior in cooperative learning groups in a grade-7 math class. *Elementary School Journal, 96,* 125–143.

Sadler, P. M., & Good, E. (2006). The impact of self- and peer-grading on student learning. *Educational Assessment, 11,* 1–31.

Salend, S. J., Whittaker, C. R., & Reeder, E. (1993). Group evaluation—A collaborative, peer-mediated behavior management system. *Exceptional Children, 59,* 203–209.

Salomon, G., & Globerson, T. (1989). When teams do not function the way they ought to. *International Journal of Educational Research, 13,* 89–99.

Scruggs, T. E., & Mastropieri, M. A. (1998). Tutoring and students with special needs. In K. J. Topping & S. Ehly (Eds.), *Peer-assisted learning* (pp. 165–182) Mahwah, NJ: Lawrence Erlbaum Associates.

Topping, K. J. (1998). Peer assessment between students in college and university. *Review of Educational Research, 68,* 249–276.

Topping, K. J. (2003). Self and peer assessment in school and university: Reliability, validity and utility. In M. S. R. Segers, F. J. R. C. Dochy, & E. C. Cascallar (Eds.), *Optimizing new modes of assessment: In search of qualities and standards* (pp. 55–87). Dordrecht, The Netherlands: Kluwer Academic.

Topping, K. J. (2005). Trends in peer learning. *Educational Psychology, 25,* 631–645.

Topping, K. J., & Ehly, S. (Eds.). (1998). *Peer-assisted learning.* Mahwah, NJ: Lawrence Erlbaum Associates.

Tseng, S. C., & Tsai, C. C. (2007). Online peer assessment and the role of the peer feedback: A study of high school computer course. *Computers and Education, 49,* 1161–1174.

Weaver, M. E. (1995). Using peer response in the classroom: Students' perspectives. *Research and Teaching in Developmental Education, 12,* 31–37.

Webb, N. M., & Farivar, S. (1994). Promoting helping behavior in cooperative small groups in middle school mathematics. *American Educational Research Journal, 31,* 369–395.

Critical Thinking

1. How do peer assessment and self-assessment complement one other?

2. Based on the example described in the article, what are some considerations/cautions you might suggest about using peer assessment successfully?

3. When might it NOT be a good idea to incorporate the use of peer assessment?

4. Similar to engaging in self-assessment, students must be provided direct instruction and modeling in order for them to successfully engage in peer assessment. Describe how you would go about formally teaching these skills.

5. Review the list of 11 planning issues associated with peer assessment. Focusing on items 2, 4–7, 10, and 11, describe how you would revise an existing lesson or unit plan to incorporate peer assessment.

KEITH J. TOPPING is a professor in the School of Education at the University of Dundee, Scotland.

Correspondence should be addressed to **KEITH J. TOPPING**, Professor of Educational & Social Research, School of Education, University of Dundee, Nethergate, Dundee DD1 4HN, Scotland, E-mail: k.j.topping@dundee.ac.uk.

From *Theory Into Practice*, January 2009, pp. 20–27. Copyright © 2009 by Taylor & Francis–Philadelphia. Reprinted by permission via Rightslink.

Assessment-Driven Improvements in Middle School Students' Writing

Heidi Andrade et al.

One lesson I've learned is that this is a process; it does not change students' writing overnight. But if you make it a continuous effort and incorporate it in all the writing you complete, the students will slowly develop their writing skills and their writing will improve. The most valuable lesson I learned is that students really do want to be successful and can rise to a challenge. (Mrs. Buff, eighth grade ELA teacher)

In the fall of 2005 the principal and teachers at Knickerbacker Middle School (KMS) were worried. KMS was a "School in Good Standing" but had not hit federal or state benchmarks because of low subgroup scores on the English Language Arts (ELA) test—especially scores received by economically disadvantaged students, about half of this urban school's student population. KMS would be identified as a "School in Need of Improvement" in 2006 if the ELA scores did not improve. This article chronicles a successful attempt by the authors and their colleagues to teach writing by making improvements in the assessment of writing in the classroom.

Our Goals: What We Attempted and Why

Our work together began in the fall of 2005, when Shaun Paolino, the principal, invited Heidi Andrade to help improve students' writing skills and scores. To meet the overarching goal of improving the assessment of writing at KMS, Prof. Andrade collaborated with the sixth, seventh, and eighth grade teachers of English and social studies. We set three goals:

1. Make assessment processes, criteria, and standards crystal clear to students.
2. Provide frequent, useful feedback to students about the quality of their work via teacher, peer, and self-assessment.
3. Use the assessments to analyze the strengths and weaknesses in students' work and to plan instruction.

These three goals are grounded in the literature on formative assessment. Most people think of assessment as the test at the end of a unit that tells teachers whether or not students "got it." That is a summative view of assessment, and tells only part of the story. Formative assessments happen before and while students work on assignments. A significant element of effective classroom assessment is formative—the kind of ongoing, regular feedback about student work that leads to adjustment and revision by both the teacher and the students (Centre for Educational Research & Innovation, 2005).

A formative conception of assessment honors the crucial role of feedback in the development of understanding and skill building. This perspective on assessment is common in sports and in the arts, where students expect and receive frequent comments from coaches and directors about their performance (White, 1998). However, in spite of research that shows that feedback promotes learning and achievement (Black & Wiliam, 1998; Butler & Winne, 1995; Chappuis, 2005), many students get little informative feedback about their work. Often, this is because few teachers have the luxury of regularly responding to each student's work and learning. Fortunately, research shows that students themselves can be useful sources of feedback via peer and self-assessment (Andrade & Boulay, 2003; Andrade, Du, & Wang, 2008; O'Donnell & Topping, 1998).

Peer and self-assessment are key elements in formative assessment, because they involve students in thinking about the quality of their own and each others' work, rather than relying on their teachers as the sole source of evaluative judgment. There are many ways to scaffold effective peer and self-assessment. Self-assessment can be as simple as students circling the text on a rubric that best describes their work and attaching the marked-up rubric to the assignment before handing it in (Andrade & Boulay, 2003). Peer assessment is often done by giving rubric-referenced verbal feedback in class (O'Donnell & Topping, 1998). Regardless of how it is done, neither the peer nor the self-assessments count toward final grades, because this is formative, not summative, assessment.

Our work at KMS taught us that formative assessment can play a key role in helping students learn to write. Predictably, however, assessment was not a silver bullet: We had to define and address other important issues before students could not only learn but also demonstrate what they had learned on the ELA test.

The Process: What We Did and How

The collaboration between a university consultant and Knickerbacker Middle School teachers began after a brief workshop in October of 2005 that introduced the notion of assessment as a moment of learning, research on the ways in which feedback can promote learning and achievement, and rubric-referenced assessment techniques, including peer and self-assessment. Monthly meetings started in November. The meetings were attended by the co-authors of this article and six other teachers, including one special education teacher. Held after school from 2:15 to 3:30, the meetings initially focused on finding or developing rubrics for writing and using them with students.

Designing a Common Rubric for Writing

In February of 2006 the team decided to create consistency across classes and grade levels by designing a common writing rubric. Drawing on the New York State standards for English/Language Arts and the 6 + 1 Traits of Writing (Northwest Regional Educational Laboratory, 2008; see Figure 1), we developed two rubrics (Figures 2 & 3). The rubrics are nearly identical except for slightly more sophisticated standards for sentence fluency and word choice on the eighth grade version. The sixth grade rubric is used in grade six and in the first half of the seventh grade year. The eighth grade rubric is used in the second half of the seventh grade year as well as in eighth grade. Joe Terry, one of the sixth grade teachers, describes how he began using the rubric with his students:

> I realized that it would not be that difficult to adapt my teaching to the rubrics. I was using a 4, 3, 2, 1 method, which I had been trained to use to evaluate social studies essays, and I had already adapted that method to my ELA instruction. The new rubric had more categories than I had used before. As I began experimenting with it, I only used some of the categories. I left off voice and word choice and decided to concentrate on the organization of the essay. After a couple of tries, I added voice and word choice.

Teaching Peer and Self-Assessment

Knowing that simply handing out rubrics would not magically produce good writers and high test scores, we concerned ourselves with the matter of engaging students in carefully considering the strengths and weaknesses of their works in progress, according to the standards set in the rubrics. During the monthly meetings we shared approaches to peer and self-assessment. Meghan D'Adamo, a sixth grade teacher, videotaped her students doing a "fishbowl," in which two students gave and received feedback while Mrs. D'Adamo coached, and the rest of the class observed. The videotape was shared with other interested teachers. Prof. Andrade was also videotaped doing a demonstration of her favorite approach to self-assessment in a seventh grade classroom, during which she guided students in using colored pencils to determine which criteria

Ideas: The ideas are the heart of the message, the content of the piece, the main theme, together with all the details that enrich and develop that theme.

Organization: Organization is the internal structure of a piece of writing, the thread of central meaning, the pattern, so long as it fits the central idea.

Voice: Voice is the writer coming through the words, the sense that a real person is speaking to us and cares about the message. It is the heart and soul of the writing, the magic, the wit, the feeling, the life and breath.

Word Choice: Word choice is the use of rich, colorful, precise language that communicates not just in a functional way, but in a way that moves and enlightens the reader.

Sentence Fluency: Sentence fluency is the rhythm and flow of the language, the sound of word patterns, the way in which the writing plays to the ear, not just to the eye.

Conventions: Conventions are the mechanical correctness of the piece—spelling, grammar and usage, paragraphing (indenting at the appropriate spots), use of capitals, and punctuation.

Figure 1 The 6 + 1 Traits of Writing®, excerpted from the NWREL website (http://www.nwrel.org).

on a rubric their drafts had and had not yet met (see Andrade & Boulay, 2003, for details).

All of the teachers agreed to implement some form of peer and/or self-assessment in their own classrooms, according to their judgments about what would work best with their students. Colleen Buff, one of the eighth grade teachers, took the following approach:

> I began the school year by introducing the rubric to my eighth grade students and using it on every writing assignment we completed. At the beginning of each assignment, we would review each criterion and the specific aspects of the assignment to be thinking about when writing. After students wrote rough drafts, we came back together as a class and began the process of self-assessment. The process had to be scaffolded, but students began to develop the skills necessary to really look at their writing and determine its strengths and weaknesses.
>
> I began the self-assessment process with students receiving model essay papers. Together we used the rubric and walked through each model essay. Students color coded their rubric using colored pencils, and then the class color coded the model essays. After working through model essays several times, the students did the same color coding to their *own* essays. This technique allowed students to visualize which criteria they were strong on and the areas that could be improved. Not only were students looking at their own writing, determining strengths and weaknesses, but they were also enjoying it.
>
> For the first three writing assignments, we walked through this process together, and then slowly I gave up control and let the students work through the process on their own. After each new writing assignment, the writing I was receiving from students was better than the previous one.

	4	3	2	1
Ideas and Content	The topic and main ideas are clear. Details and examples (e.g., facts, similes, metaphors, or comparisons) support the ideas.	The topic and ideas are clear, but there is not enough detail.The writing stays on topic but doesn't address minor parts of the assignment.	There is a very general topic, but the writing strays off topic or doesn't address major parts of the assignment.	The topic and ideas are unclear. It's hard to tell which information is most important. May be repetitious or disconnected thoughts with no main point.
Organization	The writing has a catchy beginning to grab the reader's attention, a developed middle, and meaningful ending. The order of ideas makes sense. Transitions show how ideas connect.	The paper has a beginning. middle, and end. The order makes sense. Transitions are used, but some don't work well.	The paper has an attempt at an intro and conclusion. Some ideas seem out of order. Transitions need a lot of work.	There is no real introduction or conclusion. The ideas seem strung together in a loose fashion.
Paragraphs	Paragraphs are properly indented and begin in the right spots. Each has one topic and has topic, supporting, and closing sentences.	Paragraphs are indented; some begin in the right spots and have topic, supporting, and closing sentences.	Paragraphs often begin in the wrong places; may not have topic sentences.	There is either one long paragraph or random paragraph breaks.
Voice	The writing has personality. The writer cares about the topic and speaks right to the reader.	The writing seems sincere. but the author's personality fades in and out.	The paper could have been written by anyone. The writing hides the writer.	The writing is bland or sounds like the writer is annoyed or doesn't like the topic.
Word Choice	Uses vivid words and phrases that help make the meaning clear. May include 5 senses words.	Words are ordinary, with a few attempts at descriptive words.	Words used are ordinary but generally correct.	The same words are used over and over, some incorrectly.
Sentences	Sentences are clear and complete. Some are longer than others. They begin in different ways.	Sentences are usually complete. Some variety in beginnings and length.	Many poorly constructed sentences. Little variety in beginnings or length.	The paper is hard to read because of incomplete, run-on, and awkward sentences.
Conventions	Few, if any, errors in spelling, punctuation, capitalization, grammar.	Spelling, punctuation, and caps usually correct. Some grammar problems.	Errors are frequent enough to make the writing hard to understand.	Errors are so frequent they are distracting. The paper is almost impossible to read.

Figure 2 Generic grade six writing rubric.

Marilyn Erano, another eighth grade teacher, incorporated the writing rubric into a peer editing technique she had been using for years.

> Working in pairs or groups of three, students switched papers and edited each other's work. They use the COACH process in addition to the rubric. COACH is an acronym for Commend (offer praise), Observe (note ways in which their writing is similar to the writing they are editing), Ask (ask the writer questions about what he or she meant or intended), Consider (always be considerate of the writer's feelings), and Help (offer help in a useful way).

Students responded well to the feedback generated with this process. I have found that it works especially well with the rubric. To no one's surprise, students seem more interested in each other's comments than in mine. They were surprisingly willing to revise. In the past, they would rather have their teeth pulled with a pair of rusty pliers than revise a paper. I now sense that the idea of revision may not have been planted firmly enough in the writing process. Without the rubric and the COACH process, they may not have fully understood what specific changes to make as they revised, or how to make them.

At each monthly meeting the team discussed the teachers' experiments with the rubrics and with peer and self-assessment, talked about what did and did not work, and planned next steps.

Checking Validity and Reliability

In April of 2006 the team turned its attention to the validity and reliability of the assessments. We already knew that our rubrics reflected the New York State standards, so they passed one test of validity. Another important quality to test was the rubrics' accessibility to students. We informally polled the students for their

	4	3	2	1
Ideas and Content	The topic is focused. Main ideas are clear. Numerous relevant and accurate details or examples support the ideas (e.g., facts, similes, metaphors, or comparisons).	The topic and ideas are clear, but there is not enough detail. The writing stays on topic but does not address minor parts of the assignment.	There is a very general topic, but the writing strays off topic or does not address major parts of the assignment.	The topic and ideas are unclear. It's hard to see which information is most important. May be repetitious or disconnected thoughts with no main point.
Organization	The writing has a catchy beginning to grab the reader's attention, a developed middle, and meaningful ending. The order of ideas makes sense. Transitions show how ideas connect. Pacing is well-controlled.	The paper has a beginning, middle, and end. The order makes sense. Transitions are used, but some do not work well. Pacing is reasonable.	The paper has an attempt at an Introduction and conclusion. Some ideas seem out of order. Transitions need a lot of work. Writing may lunge ahead or hover over details.	There is no real introduction or conclusion. Ideas seem strung together in a loose fashion. Pacing is uncontrolled.
Paragraphs	Paragraphs are properly indented and begin in the right spots. Each has one topic, and has topic, supporting, and closing sentences.	Paragraphs are indented; some begin in the right spots and have topic, supporting, and closing sentences.	Paragraphs tend to begin in the wrong places. May not have topic sentences.	There are either one or two long paragraphs or random paragraph breaks.
Voice	The writing has personality. The writer cares about the topic and speaks right to the intended audience.	The writing seems sincere, but the author's personality fades in and out.	The writer seems to be aware of an audience but does not attempt to engage it.	The style is mismatched with the purpose or audience. The tone is bland.
Word Choice	Vivid, precise words and phrases help make the meaning clear (e.g., 5 senses words). Avoids cliches and jargon.	Words used are adequate and correct, with a few attempts at colorful language.	Words used are ordinary. Some language may seem forced or full of clichés.	Limited, repetitive vocabulary. Words are sometimes used incorrectly.
Sentence Fluency	Sentences are well-constructed and have different beginnings and lengths. Fragments, if used, add style. Dialogue, if used, sounds natural.	Sentences are usually constructed correctly. Some variety in beginnings and lengths.	Many incorrect sentences. Little variety in beginnings or lengths. Dialogue, if used, sounds unnatural.	Incomplete or run-on sentences make the paper hard to read. Little or no variety in beginnings or lengths.
Conventions	Few, if any, errors in spelling, punctuation, capitalization, and grammar. Misspellings are of sophisticated vocabulary.	Spelling, punctuation, caps, and grammar are usually correct.	Errors are frequent enough to make the writing hard to understand.	Errors are so frequent that they are distracting and make the paper almost impossible to read.

Figure 3   Generic grade eight writing rubric.

reactions to the rubrics. Students had a few questions about the meanings of some words, which their teachers addressed. Other than that, students told us that they understood and valued the rubrics. The teachers' classroom observations of peer and self-assessment sessions confirmed the students' claims.

To examine the reliability of our assessments, we examined the similarities and differences in grading with the rubrics. Was everyone using the rubrics in ways that produced similar grades, or were we grading idiosyncratically and, perhaps, unfairly? Lisa Puckey, a seventh grade teacher, volunteered to bring copies of two students' biographical essays on Malcolm X to a meeting. We each scored an essay independently and then compared scores. We were surprised to discover that our scores tended to be close. Though we did not strive for perfect inter-rater reliability, given the nature of writing, minor changes to the wording and organization of the rubric resulted in an even better assessment tool.

Using Assessment Results to Plan Instruction

In the fall of 2006 we turned to our third goal, which was to use the information provided by the rubrics to evaluate trends in students' performances and guide instructional decisions. Mr. Terry proposed an approach that was elegant in its simplicity:

> I have always evaluated essays by looking for trends. With previous experience in item analysis, I devised a way to chart the class trends using our generic rubric. I simply charted the number of 4s, 3s, 2s, and 1s received by my students for each criterion on the rubric. The first essay I looked at this way showed a weakness in paragraphing for that particular class. Seeing this trend helped me to design a group lesson based on the common weakness. That way, no student needed to feel singled out.

The other teachers adopted or adapted Mr. Terry's approach to pinpointing weaknesses in student writing. Mrs. Erano, for example, used peer assessment data to make on-the-spot decisions about targeted, short lessons, which motivated her classes to write better.

> I would ask students to raise their hands if they got a 1, 2, 3, or 4 for a certain criterion on the rubric. If the hands showed that a third or a quarter of the students needed improvement in paragraphing or organization, I demonstrated the way I would edit if I were peer editing. Students would give me additional suggestions to improve the example on the overhead, and I incorporated their suggestions in front of their eyes.

> An unexpected rivalry soon sprang up between two of my classes, and scores on the rubric became a way for them to win a contest. When I told one class that the other class did exceptionally well on paragraphing—"only three kids got threes and the rest all got fours!"—the news would not sit well with them. One class would work harder to "catch" the other class. Of course, I had to tell the winning class that they "owned" organization on that day, but they would have to keep working to stay on top. Being able to tally the scores quickly made the competition manageable.

As a result of the teachers' experiments with rubric-referenced peer and self-assessment, our subsequent meetings focused on discussing weaknesses in students' writing and sharing resources designed to address them.

Solving the Transfer Problem

In November of 2006 Mrs. Buff made a distressing discovery: Although her eighth graders were writing more effectively when she scaffolded rubric-referenced formative assessment in the classroom, the quality of what they wrote under practice test conditions was very disappointing. This discovery was especially distressing because the state ELA test was coming up in January. The team devoted a meeting to this problem and identified it as one of transfer: Though students could use the rubric to write well, they did not transfer their new skills to rubricless contexts. Because writing, in general, and the ELA test, in particular, happens in rubricless contexts, we were worried.

We decided to address the transfer problem by teaching students to jog their memories by writing an acronym at the top of their papers before they began writing. With the students' help, we developed the following acronym for the criteria on the writing rubrics: Ideas, Organization, Paragraphs, Voice, Word choice, Sentences, and Conventions became IOPVWSC, which stood for I Only Play Videogames While Snacking Chips. To reinforce the acronym,

Mrs. Buff had her students snack on chips as they wrote. She also spoke with them about the transfer problem:

> The students and I had several discussions about scenarios in which they might be asked to write and how the rubric could be beneficial in each of those situations. Our discussion included students looking at all the writing they had completed up to this point and filling out worksheets that outlined their strengths and weaknesses. This led to an in-depth discussion about why students were struggling with writing and what I could do to help them improve. Students responded honestly to my questions:

1. What is so difficult about writing essays?
   - Finding information to include
   - Too much writing
   - Distractions in the room (people talking, it's too hot in the room)
   - Organizing my thoughts
   - Why do we have to write essays anyway?

2. Why don't you include everything we go over, including the criteria from the rubric?
   - My hand hurts when I write too much.
   - I don't feel like it.
   - I just want to get it done.
   - There is too much information to remember.
   - I think about what I want to write and not how to write it.
   - We're lazy.

3. How can I help you?
   - Have us write essays once a week.
   - More quizzes on the different criteria areas
   - Five minutes to let our brains rest before we write
   - A quick review before each essay
   - Have us review what we read.
   - Give us rewards for improvement.

4. What would help you remember all the criteria?
   - studying; review classes
   - the IOPVWSC acronym
   - more free writing time

The best response was this:

> "I don't think there is much more you can do for us. I think it is us. If we are lazy, we have to just do it. I guess it all really depends on us." I loved that comment because it made me feel like the students noticed how much work had been done to help them, and now it was time for them to step up and make it work. But I wondered how quickly they could shift gears. I truly believed each one of them could write amazing essays, but I still questioned how to get them to do it.

Mrs. Buff decided to take her students' advice and give them rewards for making improvements in their writing. We all knew that extrinsic rewards could undermine the intrinsic reward of writing well, yet it was clear from the students' comments that they wanted and needed more motivation so the risk seemed small. Mrs. Buff set them a challenge: All students in the class had to receive a score of three (out of four) or higher on every criterion on the writing rubric. If they were successful they would receive one free Friday class, including snacks, board games, and video games. In addition, the grade they received on the writing assignment would count as a test grade. Mrs. Buff describes the challenge as a roller-coaster ride of emotions:

> The challenge began. The class was given two days to work on the writing assignment. On the first day they completed their outlines and rough drafts. Most students seemed positive and receptive to the challenge. One student, however, was struggling and very negative about the task before him. When I noticed his frustration, I pulled him into the hallway for a quick chat. He communicated to me that he was too nervous to complete the task: He knew he was going to ruin it for the rest of the class. He stated, "There is no way I can get a 3 on every criterion, yeah right, that will never happen, even if I really try."

> I made a deal with him and told him it could be our little secret. Since this student struggled academically and had had difficulties with writing in the past, I thought it would be fair that, if he received a two for every criterion, the whole class could still receive the reward. He was relieved and felt confident that he could perform at a level two. As we entered the classroom, he sat down and started feverishly writing his essay. This was the most I had seen him write the whole year.

> I collected everyone's rough drafts to preview before the following day's final draft session. That evening I went through the rough drafts and almost had a meltdown. I could not believe how much the students had forgotten to include. I kept questioning whether I had been clear in my expectations. I could not figure out what I was doing wrong. I calmed myself down by remembering that students would be self-assessing the next day. Hopefully, they would find and fix their mistakes at that time.

> The following day I briefly reviewed the acronym we were using to remind of us the rubric and asked students to give examples for each criterion. The students then got to work and worked hard and quietly the entire class period. When I graded their final essays I was shocked, elated, and over-whelmed. The students had risen to the challenge. Every single student in the class had scored a three or higher on every criterion on the rubric—including the boy with whom I had made the deal.

Without tools such as the rubric and the COACH process, peer editing and self-direction would be almost impossible for most students.

> What was even more amazing was that the students were just as excited as I was. When I announced the results the next day, I could see the pride they had in their accomplishment. They high fived each other and said, "We did it. We actually did it. Way to go!"

> This was the best experience of my teaching career thus far. Never before had I felt that I had reached the students

in a way that let them understand their own wonderful accomplishments. I also felt reassured that it is OK to set high expectations for students, because they really will rise to the challenge. Above all, the best lesson learned was to never give up on students. I always have to keep pushing them forward, because it will pay off.

The Payoff
Improvements in In-Class Writing

Mrs. Buff and the other teachers noticed consistent improvements in the processes and products of students' writing. Mr. Terry, for example, observed the ways in which knowing what counts and engaging in self-assessment tended to lead students to work harder at writing well:

> It is not uncommon to see more students looking for the thesaurus to find that enchanting word that they can't seem to put their finger on. For instance, one of my students was writing about horses in a parade. Instead of saying, "The horse looked magnificent," she wrote, "The Lipizzaner stallions were the most magnificent horses in the parade." It was gratifying to see the extra effort.

Mrs. Erano made similar observations about her eighth grade students' skills and attitudes toward writing:

> I believe the rubric helped lessen student resistance to writing and revising. As students grow more familiar with the rubric, they seem to better understand how to evaluate themselves and each other, as well as how to complete the writing process. The rubric is their tool to use whenever they need it. Working with it allows them to focus on details that help them to develop, extend, and clarify their ideas.

> A self-disciplined attitude is one by-product. At the risk of sounding cliché, I believe true learning became their own. As students take responsibility for helping themselves and each other, they become more self-directed. Without tools such as the rubric and the COACH process, peer editing and self-direction would be almost impossible for most of them. The rubric allows students to monitor their own progress and achieve to the best of their ability.

Mrs. Buff reported that, by the end of the school year, students' writing and their ability to self-assess had dramatically improved:

> Students are aware of what makes good writing, and they use it in all their ELA writing assignments. Most of the students are continuously scoring a level three or four on all criteria on the rubric. Students are also able to self-assess independently. They are aware of their strengths and weaknesses and make noticeable efforts to focus on their weaknesses on each new writing assignment. Now that they understand the process of self-assessment, they enjoy it and are ready to begin even before I am. The self-assessment gives them a sense of independence and helps them take ownership of their writing.

Improvements in Test Scores

Fortunately, the students' new skills appear to have transferred to the extended response portion of the ELA test as well. Figure 4 contains the passing ELA scores (level three or four) for 2006 and 2007. In grades six and eight, the scores for all students, taken together,

Grade Level Subgroup	2006 ELA scores of 3 or 4	2007 ELA scores of 3 or 4	Difference
Sixth Grade			
All students	50%	57%	+7
African American	30%	46%	+16
Special needs	5%	20%	+15
Economically disadvantaged	28%	48%	+20
Seventh Grade			
All students	47%	47%	0
African American	35%	34%	−1
Special needs	0%	5%	+5
Economically disadvantaged	31%	33%	+2
Eighth Grade			
All students	37%	52%	+15
African American	23%	45%	+22
Special needs	3%	15%	+12
Economically disadvantaged	20%	40%	+20

Figure 4 Scores on the English Language Arts test for 2006 and 2007 by grade level and subgroup, and between-year differences.

increased by seven and 15%, respectively. Subgroup scores also went up. Most impressive are the improvements in scores received by economically disadvantaged students, which were 20% higher in both grades.

The scores for seventh grade were essentially unchanged, probably because the seventh grade test does not require students to actually write. In seventh grade, students are asked to answer multiple choice questions, write short responses, and edit a passage. Their new skills in writing extended responses were not measured.

Although we were very pleased with the results of the ELA test for the sixth and eighth grades, it is important to note that the increased scores cannot be attributed solely to our work. Different students were tested each year, so some variation was to be expected, regardless of what we did. The ELA test scores had been relatively stagnant in previous years, however. The percentages of passing scores at eighth grade, for example, were 44%, 35%, 39%, and 37% for the years 2003 through 2006, respectively. By 2007, 52% of the eighth graders passed the ELA test. Given that trend and the improvements in the writing students did in class, we have reason to believe that our work had an impact. Our original goals—making assessments clear to students; providing frequent feedback about the quality of their work via teacher, peer, and self-assessment; and using classroom assessment results to plan instruction—appear to have served student learning and school progress.

References

Andrade, H., & Boulay, B. (2003). The role of self-assessment in learning to write. *The Journal of Educational Research, 97*(1), 21–34.

Andrade, H., Du, Y., & Wang, X. (2008). Putting rubrics to the test: The effect of a model, criteria generation, and rubric-referenced self-assessment on elementary school students' writing. *Educational Measurement: Issues and Practices, 27*(2), 3–13.

Black, P., & Wiliam, D. (1998). Inside the black box: Raising standards through classroom assessment. *Phi Delta Kappan, 80,* 139–148.

Butler, D., & Winne, P. (1995). Feedback and self-regulated learning: A theoretical synthesis. *Review of Educational Research, 65,* 245–281.

Centre for Educational Research and Innovation. (2005). *Formative assessment: Improving learning in secondary classrooms.* Paris: Organisation for Economic Co-operation and Development.

Chappuis, J. (2005). Helping students understand assessment. *Educational Leadership, 63*(3), 39–43.

Northwest Regional Educational Laboratory. (2008). *6 + 1 trait writing®: Trait definitions.* Retrieved April 4, 2008, from www.nwrel.org/assessment/definitions.php?odelay=0&d=1

O'Donnell, A., & Topping, K. (1998). Peers assessing peers: Possibilities and problems. In K. Topping & S. Ehly (Eds.), *Peer-assisted learning* (pp. 255–278). Mahwah, NJ: Lawrence Erlbaum Associates.

White, E. (1998). *Teaching and assessing writing: Recent advances in understanding, evaluating, and improving student performance* (2nd ed.). Portland, ME: Calendar Islands Publishers.

Critical Thinking

1. In the article, the authors discuss a technique they used to assist student in transferring the criteria for writing from the rubric to other writing situations. Refer to Article 25 by Daniel Willingham and identify the type of mnemonic device represented in the example.

2. Review one of the two rubrics presented in this article. If you were a student, what questions would you have about things in the rubric or how it was supposed to be used? What would be unclear or would you want clarified?

3. How could you use a similar approach to help students develop their writing skills in other content areas? What aspects of the rubric would you change?

4. A common concern of teachers in terms of using rubrics for writing is worrying whether they are giving "too much"

information to students, essentially giving them a "script" or checklist to follow. Based your knowledge of rubrics, how might you use evidence from research to respond to a colleague who shares this concern with you?

5. Look up a rubric online for a lesson on a topic of your choice what is good/bad about the rubric. How clearly is information presented? Does it focus on the important learning objectives of the lesson or get "cluttered" with things that don't specifically relate to students' understanding of essential content? Does it provide for grading and feedback for different levels of understanding or proficiency, or is it essentially an itemized checklist of things that must be included? How does it help students understand what strengths and skills they have mastered versus those that still require additional practice?

HEIDI ANDRADE is an assistant professor of education at The State University of New York at Albany. E-mail: handrade@uamail.albany.edu. **COLLEEN BUFF** is an eighth grade English/language arts teacher at Knickerbacker Middle School, Troy, New York. **JOE TERRY** is a retired sixth grade social studies and English/language arts teacher at Knickerbacker Middle School, Troy, New York. **MARILYN ERANO** is an eighth grade English/language arts teacher at Knickerbacker Middle School, Troy, New York. **SHAUN PAOLINO** is the principal of Knickerbacker Middle School, Troy, New York.

Acknowledgements—We are grateful to the teachers with whom we worked, including Camille Amodeo, Patrick Amyot, Meghan D'Adamo, Lisa Puckey, Karen LaPierre, Chris Jura, and Trish Bronson, and to the Lansingburgh superintendents, Lee Bordick and George Goodwin, and the students of Knickerbacker Middle School.

Andrade, A., Buff, C., Terry, J., Erano, M., & Paolino, S. (2009) Assessment-Driven Improvements in Middle School Students' Writing. *Middle School Journal*, 40(4), pp. 4–12. Reprinted with permission from National Middle School Association.

Students' Reactions to a "No Failure" Grading System and How They Informed Teacher Practice

DICK CORBETT AND BRUCE WILSON

Students are clear about what they want to see in their teachers. They want teachers who are willing to help—whenever and however help is needed, who explain material and assignments clearly and repeat those explanations as often as requested, who can control their classes, who make sure all students do their work, who vary their activities from time to time, and who establish relationships with their students (Wilson & Corbett, 2001). And students have a single word under which they bundle these six qualities of a good teacher: caring. For students, caring is all about teachers not giving up on them, as these urban middle school youth explain:

S: A good teacher is someone who stays on top of you and gives you homework. Someone who prepares you for the next grade. A good teacher cares about you.

I: What do you mean by cares?

S: If you don't do it, she doesn't just say "it's on you" to get the work in.

S: I like the ones that don't allow excuses. It's my turn to get an education. I need to have someone to tell me when I'm tired and don't feel like doing the work that I should do it anyway.

Caring, then, is often hard-nosed, in students' opinion, as one marveled about her teacher: "My teacher is mean, out of the kindness of her heart."

We have visited nearly 500 low achieving schools, K–12, around the country over the last 30 years. They all have some teachers who behave in the student-preferred ways, but it is rare to find an entire faculty that adopts, with a single mind, the perspective that it is solely their responsibility to insure students' success (Corbett, Wilson, & Williams, 2005). Thus, most students tend to get a *luck-based* education. That is, they have to be fortunate enough to be placed in classrooms where their teachers refuse to let them fail. The unlucky ones are left to endure the "I already told you that," "I'm not going to keep repeating myself," and "You'll have to catch yourself up"

statements that signal to students that their teachers are not very concerned whether they learn. Indeed, an all-too-prevalent pattern in schools is for teachers to settle for using good instructional practices and leaving it up to students to decide if they want to do their part. Tragically, in urban schools especially, many students—when given the choice to fail—do.

Imagine, however, a school environment where every teacher insists that every student must complete every assignment well—in other words, a school where teachers simply do not let students shrug off their work. We have come across a handful of such schools. These buildings took part in the Academy for Educational Development's Middle Start program (www.middlestart.org/) and adopted a specific strand of the overall initiative known as Achievement by Continual Improvement (ABCI; www.middlestart.org/what/abci.cfm). As independent, third-party evaluators of the program since 1999, we conducted yearly in-depth interviews with educators and students to document their perceptions of and reactions to ABCI. The educators said that they were less concerned with heightening student motivation and increasing parental involvement than with altering their own beliefs and actions. Put simply, they decided that they had to assume responsibility for student success and not worry with success factors out of their control. Otherwise, they argued, learning would be left to the vagaries of youthful whim and to the taxed energy of multitasking adults. To that end, the schools adopted ABCI, the core principle of which, according to participants, was failure is not an option.

This article briefly describes the central tenets of the program and then details students' reactions to it. It draws on the 5 years of interviews with nearly every teacher and more than 50 students across all performance levels in several low-income, urban middle schools in Michigan. These schools were typical of many of the nation's urban schools, with high concentrations of students of color and achievement levels well below state averages. At first blush, one might predict that students would have enthusiastically welcomed seeing all of their teachers begin to act in ways that communicated to students that the adults cared about their learning. However, the students spoke not with a voice but with voices, and so the faculties discovered that ABCI's effectiveness improved as they paid attention to, and gave credibility to, young people's varied reactions. The article concludes with an oft-repeated, but not yet widely adhered to call, to allow students to actually participate in reform efforts rather than just be the beneficiaries of them (Fullan & Steigelbauer, 1991).

The Program's Features

Educators participating in ABCI attempted to create four essential conditions in their buildings:

1. Educators assumed responsibility for student success.
2. Schools instituted a no-failure grading system.
3. Staff established numerous interventions.
4. Teachers reassessed the definition of assignments.

The first condition involves educators assuming responsibility for student success. Students, parents, and teachers are joined at the hip in the search for ways to enable all students to enjoy academic excellence and healthy development. Conventional wisdom says that none can succeed at this task without the full cooperation of the others. However, ABCI argued that the responsibility for producing desired outcomes resided with educators. Educators recognized that motivated students and actively engaged parents make life a lot easier, but understood that they only had control over what happened at school. Thus, "It's on us," they concluded, because once they relinquished the responsibility for success to students or parents, the game was lost. Many exasperated teachers have thrown up their hands and said, "I've done all I can do; you've had your opportunity to do this and so you'll get a zero." But the educators in these schools decided that they would never again say this.

The second condition involves the development of a no failure grading system. All the *D*s, *E*s, or *F*s were removed from the grade books. And the zeroes disappeared, too. Instead, teachers graded only work that had been done to an acceptable level of quality—an *A* or *B* or *C*. They used placeholders for work that had not yet met the desired standard—an *I* for incomplete, an *NY* for not yet quality, or an *NQ* for not quality. The philosophy underlying this idea is not new. After all, *mastery learning* has been around a long time (Bloom, 1971). The novel part was that an entire school's operation became organized around the principle that every student could and would do quality work. Some students might take longer than others, but no teacher would ever signal the end of an assignment with an *F* or zero. Furthermore, every student was expected to do every assignment. No grade was forthcoming until every piece of work was completed to an acceptable level of quality.

One of the complications with doing this was that there were always at least two possible reasons why someone did not do an assignment to the desired level of quality—either the student did not understand what he or she was doing or the student just did not want to do it. The former obviously should set in motion some form of reteaching; the latter warranted

further prodding. Teachers could not say "You've had enough time" or "You've passed up your last chance." Students could not settle for responding "So, just give me a zero" or "Whatever." Thus, the schools had to put in place *interventions* to help the students who needed more time and to motivate or, more accurately, annoy the students who were persistent procrastinators. These included Saturday School, before and after school tutoring, lunch time makeup sessions, various tangible incentives, reteaching and enrichment periods during the day, and, ultimately, summer school, as well as the teachers themselves doing professional development that would help them develop engaging, thought-provoking, and rigorous lessons.

Consequently, teachers began to reassess the quality and quantity of their graded assignments. They realized that if students were going to have to go to summer school to finish certain tasks, then the assignment had better be pretty worthwhile to begin with. In other words, having a bunch of kids completing word search puzzles in June was not an appealing image of an improved education. Teachers said that, as a result, they had numerous conversations among themselves about what a good assignment should look like and what criteria they should use for judging whether to include an assignment in their array of requirements. A parallel benefit was that teachers discovered having deeper and richer collegial discussions than they had ever had before.

Students' Reflections on the Program

Given students' near universal desire to see signs of caring from their teachers, one might have suspected a ready acceptance of putting the ideas discussed above into practice. And, in fact, many students did embrace the major changes they saw in their instructors, especially the unwavering insistence that all students must do all the assigned work. For instance: "The program is good because it makes us get our work done. We have to pay attention." Or "You learn more because you have to do all the work, not some of it."

Students especially seemed to like the idea of getting second chances. A common complaint among students was that they often did not understand a concept the first time or the first way a teacher explained it. The program acknowledged explicitly that students might need extra chances to get the work done to an acceptable level and students embraced that idea: "If we get lower than a C, we have to do the assignment over again. It's good because it gives us a chance to pass."

S: If I fall behind, I can make it up and I won't just flunk because I didn't get it the first time.

I: Are you a better student now?

S: Yes, now when I get an *NQ* it better prepares me to make up the work. I would rather do the work again than take a *D* or *F*. That way I will be better prepared for the next grade.

Students also pointed out the value of an increased sense of accountability brought on by the new practices. Instead of the old system where students accepted whatever grade they were issued, what students have previously referred to as "It is what it is," students were now always striving to do better, and there were important implications associated with the kind of progress they were making: "We didn't have this program last year and people didn't care about their grades. There were no real consequences. This year it affects everything."

I: Are you learning more here? [Compared to the student's other middle school]

S: Yes. Here they challenge you more.

I: What do you mean?

S: There is no way you can fail and get away with it.

Or, as a teacher phrased the same idea, "We've made the invisible students visible." In fact, the tone of the schools had changed enough that one eighth grade student was prompted to advise her younger sibling:

> My sister is in sixth grade here. I tell her that she's not focused enough on her schoolwork. She's got to be more responsible for her assignments and for asking for help when she needs it. That's what the teachers here expect.

However, it seemed students liked for their teachers to push them and give chances to them, in particular, but were not so generous with their underperforming peers. Like many adults, some students clearly felt that it was the responsibility of students to do the work and if they chose not to do it, then the consequence would be straightforward and simple—lower grades, less comprehension, and a higher risk of failure. Accurately reflecting a concern of many teachers, a student pointed out that "I don't like that kids can wait all year to make up their work because they can just mess around until the end."

For some students, *D*s, *E*s, *F*s, and zeroes had been solutions, not problems. For example, a student explained that he would rather have the choice of getting an *E* because, (a) he knew what he would get if he did not do his work—"I know if I don't do my work, I'll get an *E*"—instead of facing a continuous barrage of reminders and work sessions to make it up and, (b) by actually receiving a grade, even if it were an *E,* the student could still average it in with better grades and pass the class: "This is my opinion. I'd rather get an *E*. If you do get an *E,* at least you get a grade. And if you pass, you pass with whatever you get." Complaints surfaced about being penalized for having just one missing assignment: "I like the chance to make up work, but I hate that with all *A*s and *B*s an *I* can still make you fail." To be accurate, the student would not fail with an *I,* but would have to keep the *I* until the assignment was completed, but students regarded summer school as having failed.

Students with generally good grades sometimes chafed at teachers' insistence on completing all of their assignments. For example, a couple of *A* middle schoolers did poorly on a specific assignment, well below a *C*. However, averaging the lower grade in with their other results would not have affected their overall *A,* so they did not want to retake the test until they got a *C*. The teacher explained:

> I had two very good students in my class. They got 60s on an assignment. Even with the 60s, they were still carrying

an *A*. I returned the assignment to them and told them they still had to get at least 70. "We have an *A* and you're making us do it again?" I said that everything has to be quality.

The students' parents stepped in and argued that there was no reason for them to go back and restudy the now past material. The teacher did not give in, much to the students' and parents' dismay, and said that since the tested content was deemed necessary to learn, it had to be learned at an acceptable level—by everyone.

Teachers realized, then, that if they were going to be instructionally stubborn and enforce the completion of all assignments, they needed to take a very careful look at what they were asking students to do and make sure that the work was worth doing in the first place.

> We try to keep assessments at the level of higher order thinking. We've actually raised the bar because every kid is accountable for the benchmarks. What is the purpose of an assignment after all? To show that they attained the benchmarks.

Students picked up on the consequences: "The program makes teachers give better assignments because they don't want to fight with us about stupid things."

But being able to make up the work was not without its challenges for struggling students. As one student observed, teachers did not just put new work completely on hold, unless the whole class was struggling. Instead, some students had to juggle making up work while also trying to keep up with new work: "They give us lots of chances to make up work, but teachers still give new assignments, which makes it hard to catch up."

However, the dissenters often ended up realizing that what they said actually made the case for the program. For instance, one student grimaced somewhat shyly after saying: "Ms. M—is so mean. She expects us to do all the assignments and then to do them over if they're not good enough!" Likewise, another student recognized the potential good embedded in his criticism: "I don't like it because I am not that good in school and if I don't do well, I get an *I*. I have to redo my work and pass. . . . I guess it gives me a chance to do my work better."

It was unclear, to the interviewer at least, whether the following student saw the irony of her comment: "It works for some students, but not me because I do my work. It may not always be *C* quality but I'm fine with that and sometimes I just want to move on."

Ultimately, for every "I hate it" there was an "It makes you buckle down and finish things." Sometimes students made the point-counterpoint in the same answer: "I used to be a *C* student but now I am *A* and *B*. It helped me a lot. I try harder now. I try not to get *I*'s cause it's annoying and it's just better to do it right the first time." Taken together, the positive and negative reactions of students still underscored the central premise of ABCI: If allowed to fail, some students would. And that was the condition that prompted the schools to be so keen on using work completion as the primary academic lever.

Educators' Responses to Students' Reactions

The principles behind this idea and the appealing simplicity of not permitting failure made the program particularly attractive to adults, at least on an intellectual level. But students' less than wholehearted acceptance and their specific reactions prompted educators to make a host of adjustments that they did not anticipate having to make ahead of time.

For example, legitimate absences and procrastination together conspired to generate a plethora of *I*s. Students worried that they would never catch up and teachers became overwhelmed with all the attendant record keeping. Moreover, students were apparently going to resist *busy work* no matter how hard their teachers urged them to do it. Teachers obviously had to get a handle on which assignments were worth being graded.

This topic became the subject of much faculty discussion. As part of Middle Start, teachers had worked hard to form effectively functioning grade-level teams. During their common planning times, they kept each other informed about the number of *I*s that students were accumulating and discussed which interventions might work best. Noting the statistics prompted them to consider the relationship between assigned tasks and the emergence of *I*s. They discovered that one problem was the quantity of graded assignments, and that many of these mostly reinforced desired skills, instead of instigating new learning or demonstrating proficiency. Only the latter two tasks, they reasoned, really needed to be graded. Reinforcement was tantamount to practice and whether a student had engaged in enough practice would be patently clear by their efforts on culminating tasks. This caused them to reclassify homework and much of the students' daily work as non-graded activities. An easy out? Teachers worried about this but, as several maintained, the change also put the burden on teachers to come up with meaningful ways of making sure that students could actually demonstrate skill mastery. At the time this article was written, teachers acknowledged that they still had a lot of work to do in this respect, but they felt that their foray into considering the quality of assignments—precipitated by students' reactions to their initial efforts—had put them on the path to improving instruction in significant ways.

Teachers also realized that they needed to put two types of interventions into place: extra time and alternative tasks for students who were struggling with comprehension, and annoyances like lunch study for students who did not need extra time but chose to put off doing something they were perfectly capable of completing on time. Giving good students the freedom to procrastinate—and watching them take advantage of it—was probably the most surprising and frustrating development, according to teachers.

Educators had to work even harder than the kids just to get students to do their work. This caused them to constantly question whether the results were worth the effort. Five years into the ABCI reform, however, teachers continued to answer in the affirmative and stridently reaffirmed that going back to blaming students and parents for poor performance and to failing scores of students each year was not what they wanted to do.

Ultimately, the program was, at its core, a way of thinking about schooling more than it was a set of practices to put into place, and it was an arduous task to manifest those thoughts in daily school life. Teachers did not go into ABCI imagining that doing so would force them to match wits with students. But it did. In hindsight, the educators realized that the program might work best if all participants, younger and older, started out as mutual advocates for change, rather than potential adversaries.

The nuanced comments of students showed that doing something for them will not succeed without also inviting them to be partners alongside the reformers. For example, some students readily blamed peers for their failure and thought it fair that they did so, just as many adults would. The teachers had spent a long time examining this issue and determined that they were not willing to accept the status quo. Students might well have benefited from having opportunities to foreshadow what was to come and to reconcile their beliefs ahead of time with those the program espoused. Indeed, had they been involved in early reform conversations, they might also have begun to take some ownership for its implementation. And, instead of having a good number of them trying to *game the system,* students might have done their part to see that things worked more smoothly.

Therein lies the real value of learning about students' perspectives on schooling. Fullan and Steigelbauer (1991) offered the stark assessment that "Unless they [students] have some meaningful role in the enterprise, most educational change, indeed most education, will fail" (p. 170). In light of what we have learned from students' reactions to a reform based on principles they valued in the first place (i.e., teachers who did not give up on them), just having adults work harder at putting a program into place will not be sufficient. Students need to be participants and not just beneficiaries of the reform. A critical piece of that involves listening carefully to their opinions and inviting them to be part of the process of modifying the reform in ways that take their perspectives seriously.

References

Bloom, B. S. (1971). Mastery learning. In J. H. Block (Ed.), *Mastery learning: Theory and practice* (pp. 47–63). New York: Holt, Rinehart, & Winston.

Corbett, D., Wilson, B., & Williams, B. (2005). No choice but success. *Educational Leadership,* 62(6), 8–13.

Fullan, M., & Steigelbauer, S. (1991). *The new meaning of educational change* (2nd ed.). New York: Teachers College Press.

Wilson, B. L., & Corbett, H. D. (2001). *Listening to urban kids: School reform and the teachers they want.* Albany, NY: SUNY Press.

Critical Thinking

1. What did you find most interesting or surprising from the quotes by students and their reactions to the policy change?

2. What are your personal reactions/response to the "no failure" policy and the additional interventions the school put into place?

3. Identify evidence and concepts from two different articles that support a rationale for why this approach to grading assignments reflects sound educational practice.

4. Review information about the ABCI program online and identify two things you could adopt for your classroom.

Dick Corbett and **Bruce Wilson** are independent educational researchers.

Correspondence should be addressed to Bruce Wilson, 11 Linden Avenue, Merchantville, NJ 08109. E-mail: bruce.wilson8@verizon.net

Test-Your-Knowledge Form

We encourage you to photocopy and use this page as a tool to assess how the articles in *Annual Editions* expand on the information in your textbook. By reflecting on the articles you will gain enhanced text information. You can also access this useful form on a product's book support website at *www.mhhe.com/cls*.

NAME: DATE:

_____

TITLE AND NUMBER OF ARTICLE:

_____

BRIEFLY STATE THE MAIN IDEA OF THIS ARTICLE:

_____

LIST THREE IMPORTANT FACTS THAT THE AUTHOR USES TO SUPPORT THE MAIN IDEA:

_____

WHAT INFORMATION OR IDEAS DISCUSSED IN THIS ARTICLE ARE ALSO DISCUSSED IN YOUR TEXTBOOK OR OTHER READINGS THAT YOU HAVE DONE? LIST THE TEXTBOOK CHAPTERS AND PAGE NUMBERS:

_____

LIST ANY EXAMPLES OF BIAS OR FAULTY REASONING THAT YOU FOUND IN THE ARTICLE:

_____

LIST ANY NEW TERMS/CONCEPTS THAT WERE DISCUSSED IN THE ARTICLE, AND WRITE A SHORT DEFINITION:

We Want Your Advice

ANNUAL EDITIONS revisions depend on two major opinion sources: one is our Advisory Board, listed in the front of this volume, which works with us in scanning the thousands of articles published in the public press each year; the other is you—the person actually using the book. Please help us and the users of the next edition by completing the prepaid article rating form on this page and returning it to us. Thank you for your help!

ANNUAL EDITIONS: Educational Psychology 11/12

ARTICLE RATING FORM

Here is an opportunity for you to have direct input into the next revision of this volume.
We would like you to rate each of the articles listed below, using the following scale:

1. **Excellent: should definitely be retained**
2. **Above average: should probably be retained**
3. **Below average: should probably be deleted**
4. **Poor: should definitely be deleted**

Your ratings will play a vital part in the next revision.
Please mail this prepaid form to us as soon as possible.
Thanks for your help!

RATING	ARTICLE	RATING	ARTICLE
	1. What Makes a Great Teacher? PDK Summit Offers Many Ideas		26. Classroom Assessment and Grading to Assure Mastery
	2. Reform: To What End?		27. Backward Design: Targeting Depth of Understanding for All Learners
	3. Embarking on Action Research		28. Learning-Style Responsiveness Approaches for Teaching Typically Performing and At-Risk Adolescents
	4. Teaching with Awareness: The Hidden Effects of Trauma on Learning		29. "To Find Yourself, Think for Yourself": Using Socratic Discussions in Inclusive Classrooms
	5. Supporting Adolescents Exposed to Disasters		30. Setting the Record Straight on "High-Yield" Strategies
	6. Play and Social Interaction in Middle Childhood		31. What Happens When Eighth Graders Become the Teachers?
	7. Childhood Obesity in the Testing Era: What Teachers and Schools Can Do!		32. Designing Learning through Learning to Design
	8. Why We Should Not Cut P. E.		33. What Is Technology Education? A Review of the "Official Curriculum"
	9. Adolescent Decision Making: An Overview		34. Plagiarism in the Internet Age
	10. Safe at School: An Interview with Kevin Jennings		35. R U Safe?
	11. What Educators Need to Know about Bullying Behaviors		36. Assessing Middle School Students' Knowledge of Conduct and Consequences and Their Behaviors Regarding the Use of Social Networking Sites
	12. The Bridge to Character		37. The Perils and Promises of Praise
	13. Academic Instructors or Moral Guides? Moral Education in America and the Teacher's Dilemma		38. Should Learning Be Its Own Reward?
	14. Improving the Way We Think about Students with Emotional and/or Behavioral Disorders		39. Beyond Content: How Teachers Manage Classrooms to Facilitate Intellectual Engagement for Disengaged Students
	15. Sam Comes to School: Including Students with Autism in Your Classroom		40. "The Strive of It"
	16. Universal Design in Elementary and Middle School: Designing Classrooms and Instructional Practices to Ensure Access to Learning for All Students		41. Middle School Students Talk about Social Forces in the Classroom
	17. How Can Such a Smart Kid Not Get It?: Finding the Right Fit for Twice-Exceptional Students in Our Schools		42. Classroom Management Strategies for Difficult Students: Promoting Change through Relationships
	18. The Relationship of Perfectionism to Affective Variables in Gifted and Highly Able Children		43. From Ringmaster to Conductor: 10 Simple Techniques That Can Turn an Unruly Class into a Productive One
	19. Social and Emotional Development of Gifted Children: Straight Talk		44. Grading Education
	20. Understanding Unconscious Bias and Unintentional Racism		45. Measuring the Achievement Elephant
	21. Improving Schooling for Cultural Minorities: The Right Teaching Styles Can Make a Big Difference		46. The Many Meanings of "Multiple Measures"
	22. Becoming Adept at Code-Switching		47. Using Self-Assessment to Chart Students' Paths
	23. Gender Matters in Elementary Education: Research-Based Strategies to Meet the Distinctive Learning Needs of Boys and Girls		48. Peer Assessment
	24. A Fresh Look at Brain-Based Education		49. Assessment-Driven Improvements in Middle School Students' Writing
	25. What Will Improve a Student's Memory?		50. Students' Reactions to a "No Failure" Grading Policy and How They Informed Teacher Practice

BUSINESS REPLY MAIL
FIRST CLASS MAIL PERMIT NO. 551 DUBUQUE IA

POSTAGE WILL BE PAID BY ADDRESSEE

McGraw-Hill Contemporary Learning Series
501 BELL STREET
DUBUQUE, IA 52001

NO POSTAGE
NECESSARY
IF MAILED
IN THE
UNITED STATES

ABOUT YOU

Name   Date
_____   _____

Are you a teacher? ☐ A student? ☐
Your school's name
_____

Department
_____

Address   City   State   Zip
_____

School telephone #
_____

YOUR COMMENTS ARE IMPORTANT TO US!

Please fill in the following information:
For which course did you use this book?
_____

Did you use a text with this ANNUAL EDITION? ☐ yes ☐ no
What was the title of the text?
_____

What are your general reactions to the Annual Editions concept?
_____

Have you read any pertinent articles recently that you think should be included in the next edition? Explain.
_____

Are there any articles that you feel should be replaced in the next edition? Why?
_____

Are there any World Wide Websites that you feel should be included in the next edition? Please annotate.
_____

May we contact you for editorial input? ☐ yes ☐ no
May we quote your comments? ☐ yes ☐ no

NOTES

NOTES